CASE STUDIES ON HUMAN RIGHTS AND FUNDAMENTAL FREEDOMS

CASE STUDIES ON HUMAN RIGHTS AND FUNDAMENTAL FREEDOMS

A World Survey

VOLUME FOUR

WILLEM A. VEENHOVEN

editor-in-chief

WINIFRED CRUM EWING

assistant to the editor-in-chief

CLEMENS AMELUNXEN   JAN PRINS
KURT GLASER   NIC RHOODIE
STEFAN POSSONY   JIRO SUZUKI
L. P. VIDYARTHI

associate editors

PUBLISHED FOR THE FOUNDATION FOR THE STUDY OF
PLURAL SOCIETIES

BY

MARTINUS NIJHOFF / THE HAGUE
1976

ISBN 90 247 1779 5
90 247 1956 9 (vol. IV)

PRINTED IN THE NETHERLANDS

Table of Contents

Justus M. van der Kroef

Arye Oded

Mozambique under Frelimo Rule

JACQUES LEGUÈBE

JACQUES LEGUÈBE became a specialist in German affairs in the French War Ministry after attending the prestigious French military academy of St.-Cyr from 1930–1932. During World War II he undertook numerous missions in the Balkan and the Levant, serving under General Weygand.

In 1944 the author joined the French Foreign Service and occupied various diplomatic posts in Mexico, Stettin, Port of Spain, Rabat, Djakarta, Helsinki, Kinshasa and Kampala.

He closely followed the war in Algeria since its beginning in the middle fifties and became particularly interested in the consequences of this conflict to minority groups such as the *Harkis*.

Jacques Leguèbe is the author of several works of factual and of fictional nature. One of his novels, "La Vallée Enchantée," received the award of the *Académie Française*.

Mozambique under Frelimo Rule

JACQUES LEGUÈBE

Armed insurrection against Portuguese rule in Mozambique, the huge (770,826 km²) strategically situated African country along the southern seaboard of the Indian Ocean, was launched on September 25, 1964. Nearly ten years later, on April 24, 1974, came the coup d'état in Lisbon that was to lead to rapid withdrawal by the Portuguese from Mozambique and other Portuguese territories in Africa. On June 25, 1975 full independence was granted to Mozambique under the government of the *Frente de Liberaçao de Moçambique* (Frelimo), the organization that had waged the terrorist war against the Portuguese.

The initial period of independence was to be characterized by extreme measures of suppression against the peoples of Mozambique as the Frelimo leadership imposed what can only be described as the severest socialist dictatorship in Africa and one closely resembling a Communist totalitarian oligarchy. The post-independence period was one of bitter disillusionment for the peoples of Mozambique, who had expected a new life under independent rule but found themselves confronted with a regime and daily way of life that superseded in its suppression and severity anything that the former Portuguese colonialists had practised in Mozambique.

I. FRELIMO's POLITICAL OUTLOOK

A. *Machel's Condemnation of Colonialism and Undertaking to Serve the People*

Portuguese colonial rule – the subject of the ten year terrorist war waged by Frelimo – was bitterly condemned immediately prior to the assumption of independence by all Frelimo leaders, including Samora

Machel, first President of independent Mozambique, who stated:

The brutality of repression and the terror it sustained, the systematic and deliberate cultural obscurantism, which aimed at uprooting the person from his environment, the coldly planned spread of alcoholism and other vices, the prostitution, the implantation of racism and its inherent complexes, the programmed division of the people on the basis of religion, ethnic and regional origin, the systemization of passivity and submission to colonialism with the active support of the churches, were among many other means used by foreign domination to asphyxiate the spirit of resistance and the creative capacity of the masses and to maintain them divided and impotent.[1]

This vitriolic attack on the former regime would prompt one to believe that a priority of the new Frelimo Government would be to destroy all vestiges of repression and terrorism and in the process establish a truly democratic society in which the people are served, human freedoms would be guaranteed and human dignity respected. Mozambicans who had been led to believe in these ideals, and those who had fought for and made sacrifices for these ideals, were however immediately and bitterly disappointed on independence. The Frelimo Government under President Machel moved swiftly on taking over power in Mozambique to gain total control, physically and mentally, of the peoples of the country. This was to be achieved through the imposition of a process of deprivation of human rights that was to be more brutal in its application than had been the case even under the Caetano administration. And this despite the solemn oath taken by Machel on becoming President of Mozambique:

I vow by my honour as FRELIMO militant to dedicate all my energies to the defence, promotion and consolidation of the conquests of Revolution, to the welfare of the Mozambican People, to see that the Constitution is respected and to do justice to all the citizens.[2]

Earlier, on the Investiture of the Transitional Government of Mozambique, Machel had solemnly declared: "For the first time the Mozambican people have a Government of their own, a Government of their representatives, a Government to serve them." Later, in the same speech, he declared: "Power belongs to the people. It has been won by the People and it must be exercised and defended by the People."

The Constitution of independent Mozambique likewise declares:

Personal liberties are guaranteed by the State to all citizens of the People's Republic of Mozambique. These liberties include the inviolability of homes and the secrecy of correspondence, and are not subject to limitations except in cases specially envisaged by law.[3]

B. *The Move towards Totalitarianism and the Rejection of Democracy*

Despite these solemn pledges, the factual position in Mozambique after independence was a far cry from the assurances given by Frelimo. Frelimo itself assumed power without having submitted to a democratic test of strength through a general election or referendum. Furthermore, no political opposition was allowed or tolerated. The degree of totalitarian rule in Mozambique under the Frelimo Independence government exceeded that of the Caetano administration. In the years preceding independence, the Portuguese authorities had moved to relax their severely autocratic control of Angola and Mozambique through a process where they would no longer be provinces strictly integrated with the Motherland but autonomous states, albeit under the ultimate control of Lisbon in perpetuity. In 1970, Mozambique was given its own elected government with legislative powers, the right to negotiate contracts independently and to levy taxes and control the budget. Foreign affairs, defence and commerce remained the responsibility of the Portuguese Government.

In 1973 the Legislative Assembly was an elected one and almost half the representatives were Black. For the first time in many years an opposition party was permitted to participate in the election. Although these provisions fell short of sovereign independence, as demanded by the Frelimo movement, even this advance towards a more democratic system was reversed by the Frelimo Government after independence. No political parties other than Frelimo were permitted and there were no popularly elected representatives on the major executive and legislative organs of Mozambique. Autonomous rule was replaced by independence but in the process a modicum of democracy was destroyed and in its place totalitarian oligarchy and suppression of human rights were instituted. This oligarchy was based on the dehumanizing precepts of Marxism.

C. *The New One-Party Regime*

The government of Mozambique resembles a totalitarian oligarchy in several respects. It is a one-party system in which the party – FRELIMO – was declared supreme. The party leaders are an exclusive elite not accountable to the people whose political roles are extremely passive. All opposition is suppressed in the names of the ideology and the party which had been formulated by the rulers themselves. This is typical of any Marxist-Leninist state anywhere in the world.

The governmental structure of the one-party system is as follows: At the apex of the system is the president. He is Samora Moises Machel who was born in the Limpopo Valley of the Gaza Province in southern Mozambique in 1933. His family was Protestant, but he went to a Catholic school which he attended for six years only. Thereafter he trained for a while as a medical assistant, but he did not complete his studies. Meanwhile political stirrings grabbed his imagination and subsequently he left Mozambique and arrived in Dar es Salaam in 1963 where he joined Frelimo. He is therefore not a founder member of Frelimo which had already been founded in 1962. Thereafter, with a few others, he went to Algeria for military training and after his return to Tanzania he was put in charge of Frelimo's first military training camp. On September 25, 1964, the armed struggle was launched in Mozambique and Samora Machel was among the 250 guerillas who formed the Frelimo armed forces in those early days of combat.[4]

After the death of Frelimo's first Defence Secretary, Filipe Magaia, Samora was appointed to take over this key post, which effectively made him commander of the Frelimo army. At the Second Congress of Frelimo in July, 1968, he was elected to the Central Committee.

In February, 1969, the movement's first President, Dr. Mondlane, was murdered. Soon the movement was in a state of crisis. Vice-President Uriah Simango, a Protestant pastor from Beira, decided that the leadership ought properly to be passed to him, but his power base within Frelimo was too weak to permit this transfer to be engineered smoothly. He evidently thought it necessary to destroy the credibility of the two key men in the leadership: Samora Machel, leader of the army, and Marcelino dos Santos, a poet and intellectual, highly respected within Frelimo and one of the sharpest ideological brains in the movement.

Simango, using ultra-revolutionary language, accused Samora and dos Santos of murdering Frelimo militants at the behest of imperialism and described Mondlane's White American wife as "the source of massive corruption in Frelimo." At any rate, Simango was removed from his post by the Executive Committee and left Tanzania.

After the rout of Simango and his supporters Frelimo's Central Committee met in May, 1969, and elected Samora President and dos Santos

Vice-President. Dos Santos is currently the Minister of Development and Economic Planning in Mozambique.

The President of Frelimo, Samora Machel, is the President of the country and he appoints not only Ministers but the President and Vice-President of "the People's Supreme Court," the Governor and Vice-Governor of the central bank, the heads of the security services, and even the Rector of the university. And so predominant is the party that the constitution provides that the President can declare war or conclude peace only after a decision by FRELIMO's central committee which is very powerful and dominates all the other institutions of government.

The highest legislative organ in the new Republic is the People's Assembly with a maximum membership of 210. It is composed of the Central Committee of Frelimo, the Executive Committee, ministers and vice-ministers, provincial governors, members of the army, two representatives from each of Mozambique's eleven provinces and ten other citizens. Below the People's Assembly is a Permanent Commission of 15 members which takes up the responsibilities of the Assembly while it is in recess. Then there is a Council of Ministers who are collectively responsible for the administration of the country. At present, the People's Assembly does not exist, it will be elected at the third Congress of Frelimo.[5]

To ensure "participation" of the ordinary people and facilitate a two-way process of communication between them and the higher organs of the state, the country is also administratively and politically organized on provincial, regional and district levels. However, these structures, Frelimo insists, are not eternal and immutable; they can be altered if the needs of the people demand it.

But this is not deemed likely. The explicit military character and overt security-consciousness of the regime do not permit this kind of participation, not as long as the party reigns supreme. Machel himself made this abundantly clear at an early stage:

Therefore it is FRELIMO's political line, forged in the intransigent struggle to defend the interests of the masses, that must guide Government action, it is FRELIMO that must guide Government action, FRELIMO that must orientate the Government and the masses.

In every factory, every department, every service, every commercial establishment, in every agricultural enterprise, Party Committees must be formed to implement the watchwords of FRELIMO and the Transitional Government, thus releasing the people's initiative and setting in motion the masses' creative ability.[6]

On independence, Machel reaffirmed this basic outlook of his government:

On all levels the primacy of the decisions of the Party over those of the Government will be affirmed.[7]

The Constitution of an independent Mozambique confirmed this position:

The People's Republic of Mozambique is oriented by the political line defined by FRELIMO, which is the directive force of the State and Society. FRELIMO outlines the basic policy of the State and guides and supervises the action of State organs so as to ensure that State policies conform to the interests of the people.[8]

Furthermore:

The President of the People's Republic of Mozambique is the President of FRELIMO.
The President of the People's Republic of Mozambique is the Head of State. He symbolizes national unity and represents the Nation in the internal and international fields.[9]

The Constitution also stipulates that during his Investiture the President of the Republic should take an oath of office towards the people of Mozambique in which his position as a "FRELIMO militant" is stressed.

D. *The Socialistic and Communistic Outlook*

A special correspondent of *Africa*[10] reported as follows on the socialist goals of FRELIMO:

Since independence the Mozambican people and government have progressed steadily towards the socialist goals outlined in Frelimo policy, both internally and in foreign relations. Announcing sweeping socialist measures to take effect immediately, President Machel told the largest public meeting ever held in Mozambique: "Our comrades sacrificed themselves, the people were bombed and burned by napalm to be able to free the land – which now continues to be controlled by a handful of people here in our country ... Where is Freedom? ... We did not fight a war to feed the exploiters here in Mozambique."

The President told the crowd that the land belonged to the people to be controlled by the state. All private and church schools were nationalised. Schools and the universities are continuing to be reorganised to replace the colonial education system with a Mozambican one. During their summer vacation 1,600 students and teachers from the University of Lourenço Marques were sent to work in the countryside or in factories in an attempt to 'wash off' the old elitist ideas of the colonial system.

Private medical practice was prohibited and private clinics and mission hospitals nationalised. There are less than a hundred doctors in Mozambique for a population of nine million, and a priority is the establishment of facilities in the rural areas. Starting with the closing down of private law firms, the judicial system is being reorganised."

However, the ideological orientation is not only socialistic, but explicitly communistic as well. Communist influence in the ideological outlook of Frelimo is evidenced, for instance, in its slogans and propaganda. Examples include the following:

In the process of the material construction of the new society, having agriculture as the base and industry as the dynamizing factor, counting on its own forces and supported by its natural allies, the People's Republic of Mozambique will build an advanced, prosperous and independent economy, will secure the control of its natural resources for the benefit of the popular masses and progressively will apply the *just principle to each according to their work and from each according to their capacities.* (Italics added.)
The People's Republic of Mozambique will endow itself with political and administrative structures aimed at applying the principle of People's Democratic Power in which the representatives of the working masses chosen democratically will exercise power at all levels.[11]

In accordance with orthodox Communist principles, the President of the sole political party in Mozambique – and hence the head of state – is as mentioned before declared officially to be the sole ruler of the country. The independence Constitution states, inter alia, that it is incumbent on the President to nominate and dismiss the President and Vice-President of the People's Supreme Court as well as the Attorney General; nominate and dismiss the Commandant General and Vice-Commandant of the Security Police Corps as well as the Governor and Vice-Governor of the Bank of Mozambique; nominate and dismiss the Rector of the University; promulgate and order the publication of laws and decrees. This is in addition to his prerogative of nominating and dismissing members of the Council of Ministers and of creating ministries and defining their functions. Furthermore, the President has the power to quash resolutions approved by provincial assemblies.[12]

The Communist orientated attitude of the rulers of Mozambique is also to be seen in their international affiliations. Samora Machel declared in his Message of Proclamation on the Independence of Mozambique (italics added):

The People's Republic of Mozambique has as *natural allies the socialist countries which constitute a liberated zone of humanity,* the young African states engaged with the movement of national liberation is one of the principal fronts of anti-imperialist combat, *the democratic and progressive forces,* the working masses of all humanity.

Significantly, the national flag of Mozambique has a red star which, according to the Constitution, symbolizes "the internationalist spirit of the People of Mozambique." The emblem of the Republic of Mozambique similarly contains a red star which again, according to the Constitution, symbolizes the internationalist "spirit" of the Mozambique "revolution."[13]

The relationship between Frelimo and the Red Chinese and later the Soviet Union is well-publicized and will not be repeated. Suffice to state that the Soviet Union gained tremendous influence since independence, especially at the expense of Western powers and the Red Chinese. And this probably explains the close relationship between the South African Communist Party (which is Moscow-directed) and the Frelimo-regime. In a recent issue of the *African Communist,* the SACP congratulated Frelimo on its assumption of power and hailed it as:

The finest tribute our people can pay to your magnificent achievements is to intensify their own struggles against colonialism and racism....

II. Suppression of Human Freedoms

Control of the people of Mozambique was attained by the new rulers after independence through traditional totalitarian means of coercion. A major vehicle in this regard was the political committees, also known as "dynamization committees," which were instituted in places of work (sometimes referred to as "rehabilitation centres" or "co-operative villages") as well as in residential suburbs to keep a strict control over the actions of individuals. These committees have been described as "a replica of the Russian 1917 street Soviets."[14]

The ominous nature of these political dynamization committees was foreshadowed by Samora Machel himself when he declared:

The political must never be subordinated to the technical. In practice this means that in each productive unit, in each Ministry, in each public service throughout the whole of our nation, our main effort must be to develop People's consciousness of their destiny, their awareness that to build Mozambique, to build freedom, means work, doing away with laziness and poverty.[15]

In addition to the political committees, strict control of individual movement in Mozambique was ensured by the People's National Security Service which was formed in order to assist Frelimo in the fight against "reactionaries." The Security Service was given powers of house search, arrest and confiscation of property, and was empowered to arrest people and hand them over to police or send them to "rehabilitation centres" where they have to perform hard manual work. It was also given the power to decide how long arrested individuals would be detained and to confiscate the property and other assets of individuals whom the service decided were working "against independence or national unity." Even before independence, the political committees and the armed forces of Frelimo were being used to instill a reign of terror against the people of Mozambique. This reign of terror was intensified after independence. In addition to the security police, the army was used as a terror force to intimidate individuals and compel unswerving allegiance to Frelimo on the part of all in Mozambique.

Much of the suppression of human rights and especially human dignity, was directed against the White population of Mozambique. This was in spite of assurances given to them that there would be no discrimination on the basis of race or colour. Samora Machel personally gave an assurance to the White population:

Finally we wish to address ourselves to Mozambique's white population, whether Portuguese or foreign nationals in general. The first words we wish to convey to them are words of calm and trust. FRELIMO has never fought against the Portuguese people or against the white race. FRELIMO is an organisation for all Mozambicans without distinction as to race, colour, ethnic group or religion.[16]

The Constitution of Mozambique gives similar assurances in this regard:

All citizens of the People's Republic enjoy the same rights and are subject to the same obligations whatever their colour, race, sex, ethnic origin, place of birth, religion, degree of education, social position or profession.

All actions aimed at disturbing social harmony, creating divisions or positions of privilege based on colour, race, sex, ethnic origin, place of birth, religion, degree of education, social position or profession are punishable by law.[17]

Despite these assurances, Frelimo instituted a campaign of racial discrimination aimed at terrorizing the White population, both Portuguese and foreign. After independence Frelimo troops and police began a deliberate campaign of harassment against foreigners living in Mozambique. The victims of the campaign were almost always Whites, and tension and fear were mounting in the cities of Maputo (at the time still known as Lourenço Marques) and Beira. Armed troops and members of the all-powerful Judiciary Police had been raiding private homes, hotels, restaurants and cinemas and arresting people not carrying foreigners' identity cards – including women and children.

Among the many similar reports that have been published since before, and after the independence of Mozambique, is one in the Lisbon newspaper *Tempo* in February 1976. According to this report the Frelimo Government in Mozambique is forcing White women to strip to the waist and clear land in prison camps, whose inmates include South Africans. The newspaper said that Frelimo had filled the prisons of Mozambique with Whites in overcrowded cells and had created a slave labour camp at a former game reserve.

Women are being crammed into cells with men without room for anyone to lie down and a daily diet based on a single spoonful of cooked flour. In prison camps, white women are forced to strip to the waist like the Blacks and work in the fields and are subjected to all kinds of abuses.

The newspaper said it based its story on a letter in its possession which was smuggled out by Portuguese held in the central prison in Maputo. It said the prisoners there included South Africans, Britons, Americans, Europeans, and Black and White Africans.

Mozambicans, Tanzanians, Zambians, Angolans, Nigerians, Somalis, Rhodesians, Swazis, South Africans, Portuguese, Italians, English, Germans, Americans, and Brazilians are all equally exposed to insult and suffering and all are unanimously accused of being reationary and CIA spies.

These reports were confirmed by the underground publication *Magaia's Voice*:

White women stripped to the waist, work in the fields from dawn, dreading their return to the prison compound at sunset. In the compound they are sexually assaulted by the guards and hired to outsiders for sex at 50 escudos.

Despite the suppression and attacks on Whites and other foreigners, the attention of Frelimo's police and troops is not confined solely to Whites. Black Mozambicans are also terrorized. As early as February

1975, a document known as the "Mocuba Plan" was drawn up in which a purge of "reactionary elements" within Frelimo was proposed. In implementation of the purge, 500 opponents or former members of Frelimo were denounced in May as traitors. The Frelimo leadership also launched a purge of the dynamic committees. In April and May, a number of Mozambicans were also reportedly expelled for "inability to integrate themselves in the existing social atmosphere and harming the ... decolonisation process." One overseas correspondent confirmed that suppression of human rights was widespread in Mozambique:

But not only the whites are kept under constant harassment. Still the people most vulnerable to prosecution and always in fear of "re-education" at the mental decolonising camps are the members of the Soviet-type dynamisation committees. Expected to be paragons of virtue, immune to the evils of alcoholism, prostitution and corruption, they find themselves easy prey to police informers, most of whom see themselves as candidates for vacancies in the influence-yielding committees. Hardly a day goes by without announcements of further purges in these committees.

It is also known that the National Popular Security Service (SNASP, formed on 14 October, 1975) was now as much dreaded as had been Pide, the Portuguese secret police. The jails are full and thousands have already been arrested and sent to collective labour farms for 'political re-education'. In Beira, Mozambique's second biggest city, Sebastiao Marcos Mabote, Chief of the Armed Forces High Command, warned recently that the campaign would be pursued to the bitter end. "We are going to persecute, persecute, search, persecute, search and annihilate", he declared. This determination to cleanse the country and the movement of 'internal reactionaries' and 'active representatives of colonialism' has led to fears of a new exodus among the remaining 30,000 Portuguese Whites. Already, arrests of Whites, especially those in management jobs or suspected of a capitalist background, are commonplace, and even though they are usually only held for a few days or sometimes deported, it has induced what a recent visitor described as 'a kind of paranoia'.

Some observers also spoke of an "undercurrent of fear that makes both White and Black tread carefully" in Mozambique. It stems, according to local residents quoted by newspaper reports from the new order, from daily incidents, arrests and Frelimo purges. Almost every White interviewed in Maputo, and many Blacks as well, told stories of confrontation with FRELIMO soldiers. Residents maintain it is a regular sight to see the army trucks, despairing Whites on the back, heading out of the city to take the detainees to work in the fields for 're-education'.

So serious has been the suppression, that even the authorities in Mozambique have admitted to the reign of terror. The Governor of Mozambique's Inhambane district disclosed in November 1975 that many people were fleeing from Frelimo purges in his area where tension and fear were "especially noticeable." The Governor, Mr. Joao Pelembe, claimed that "only people with guilty consciences live in fear." Admitting to the tension and fear in his area, Mr. Pelembe stated: "Prompt action is taken whenever there are signs of trouble."

No one, it appeared, was immune from the reign of terror instituted by the Frelimo elite leadership. In August 1975, shortly after independence, a major purge of the Frelimo army was ordered after allegations of unbecoming behaviour, constant violation of Frelimo's political line and a refusal to abandon vices on the part of senior officers. In this purge, eight high ranking members of the armed forces and 19 political commissars were expelled. Ominously, it was announced by Frelimo that they had been expelled despite many "fraternal warnings, public confession sessions and even periods of re-education." Another purge came in January 1976. This purge, described as a "massive" purge of the army and police, followed a police and troop mutiny in Mozambique the previous month. Allegations of widespread indiscipline, corruption and crime in Frelimo armed ranks were made at this time. In March 1976 five members of the Frelimo Central Committee were dismissed, as were a number of lower-ranking Party members. The five Central Committee members were accused of deviating from the party line and of leading corrupt lives that included "moral, material and sexual corruption." They were accused of creating a favourable climate for "enemy" subversive activities.

Political opponents of Frelimo are known to support the Movement for Free Mozambique (MFM), the political wing of the "Dragons of Death."[18]

III. INDOCTRINATION PROGRAMME

The Frelimo leadership also moved quickly to seize control of all information and mass media in Mozambique. The Mocuba Plan, referred to above, recommended improved communications with the masses through "indoctrination of journalists" as early as February 1975 – four months before independence. After independence, a Frelimo school of journalism was established with the aim of giving training to journalists on the psychological handling of the news. After completion of their training, journalists are required to join the Frelimo-controlled news-papers on broadcasting stations and to take a pledge to serve the party and the revolution. This is one vehicle by which Frelimo has sought control of the news media. Another has been the nationalization of all three broadcasting stations, namely, Radio Clube de Mozambique, Emissora do Aeroclube da Beira and Radio Pax. It was announced on September 23, 1975 that in the place of these three stations, a single in-stitution, to be called Radio Mozambique, would be established and have a monopoly of the production and the broadcasting of radio programmes.

One harrowing experience in revolutionary Mozambique is the round-the-clock brainwashing carried out with unrelentless zeal by the Frelimo-controlled news media. Mostly run by former staunch supporters of the Portuguese regime, Radio Mozambique, with its powerful network of transmitters, floods the country with an unceasing flow of propaganda.

The aim of the Frelimo leadership in respect of the "re-orientation" of the information services in Mozambique, has been described as an attempt to "popularise Frelimo's policies, serve national unity and spread national culture."[19]

FRELIMO, on assuming power, was particularly critical of the Portuguese judicial system, Samora Machel having said:

The judiciary must be reorganised so as to make justice accessible and comprehensible to the ordinary citizen of our land. The bourgeois system surrounded the administration of justice with unnecessary complexity, with legalism which made it inaccessible to the masses, with deliberately con-fusing and misleading jargon, and with such slow proceedings and high costs as to create a barrier between the people and justice.[20]

The Frelimo recipe for replacing the Portuguese judicial system with one more akin to its own views, amounted to a substitution of Portugue-se justice with summary justice meted out by armed troops and police.

The oppressive and authoritarian mien of the Frelimo leadership was particularly noticeable in its treatment of women. Much emphasis was placed in its propaganda on the rôle of the woman. Machel himself, for instance, declared on a number of occasions that his movement placed great store on the dignity of womanhood. "Even a woman's dignity had exchange value for obtaining employment," he said in reference to the despised colonial era. "Mozambican women are still weighed down by two burdens: on the one hand reactionary traditions which deprive them of initiative in society and reduce them to mere instruments of

men and, on the other, the colonial-capitalist system which regards
them as objects of exploitation and a means of production. We must
wage a close struggle for the emancipation of women and the restoration of their dignity," he said in the same speech.[21]

On the independence of Mozambique, Machel returned to this
theme:

The People's Republic of Mozambique, following the line of FRELIMO,
will engage itself in the struggle for the emancipation of women....[22]

The Constitution of an independent Mozambique likewise declared:

The emancipation of women is one of the essential tasks of the State. In the
People's Republic of Mozambique women enjoy equal rights and have the
same obligations as men, and this equality embraces political, economic and
cultural fields.[23]

Despite these noble sentiments, the reality of the situation in post-
independence Mozambique is that women have no rights unless they
give unswerving allegiance to the political dogma of Frelimo; any
deviation from this subjects them to the same humiliation and suppression as any other individual in Mozambique. The women slave
labourers referred to in the report above bear testimony to the slim
regard that Frelimo leaders have in reality for women, despite their
protestations to the contrary. In addition, in the attempts to exorcise all
forms of prostitution (regarded by Frelimo as an evil relic of the colonial
era), the position of women in every day life has become intolerable.
For example, a new law promulgated in 1976 stipulated that any woman living on her own was regarded officially as a prostitute, even
though she might be a spinster, divorcee or widow. The result of this
law is that all women in Mozambique must now be married, live with
their families, or obtain a six-months permit allowing them and their
boy-friends to be seen together in public. After expiry of the six-month
period, they have to marry or face imprisonment. Women dare not be
seen on the streets alone or with boy-friends, day or night.

IV. EXTREME ECONOMIC AND SOCIAL MEASURES

A. *Constitutional Guidelines*

The economic guidelines for the new Mozambique are laid down in
the constitution:

Article 6: "The People's Republic of Mozambique, taking farming as a basis and industry as a dynamising and decisive factor, will direct its political economy in the sense of eradicating underdevelopment and creating conditions for the improvement of the standard of living of the working people."

Article 8: "The land and natural resources to be found in the soil and in the subsoil, in territorial waters and on the continental platform of Mozambique will be the property of the State."

Article 11: "The State will encourage peasants and individual workers to organise themselves in collective forms of production, the development of which it will support and guide."

Article 14: "Foreign capital may be authorised to operate within the framework of the economic policy of the State."

The potential for agricultural development is immense. The land is fertile: cashew nuts, cotton, sisal, coconuts and sugar cane are grown as cash crops, and maize, cassava and rice as staple products. Other sources of income are transit traffic from Rhodesia and South Africa through the harbours of Beira and Maputo, the selling of hydro-electric power generated at Cabora Bassa to South Africa, the migrant labour agreement between South Africa and Mozambique which enables more than a hundred thousand Mozambicans to work in South African mines annually, and finally tourism from Rhodesia and South Africa. Yet, the government's socialistic policies and commitment to overthrow the Smith regime in Rhodesia have had negative effects on the utilization of most of these potential sources of income.

B. *Nationalization*

The Frelimo leadership lost little time on independence in implementing nationalization measures and sweeping socialist measures in general. All land was nationalized in 1975, although individual farmers continued to utilize it. When Machel nationalized the land he made the following statement already mentioned:

Our comrades sacrificed themselves, the people were bombed and burned by napalm to be able to free the land – which now continues to be controlled by a handful of people here in our country ... Where is Freedom? ... We did not fight a war to feed the exploiters here in Mozambique.[24]

He also emphasised that all the land of Mozambique belonged to the people and should be controlled by the State.

Frelimo also announced on independence that all church and private schools were to be nationalized and that the Government would take over direct control of the entire educational system. The nationalization directive said that special and private schools had all been nationalized "to ensure the political orientation of Frelimo in this vital sector." Schools and the universities, the latter being taken over completely by Frelimo, were reorganized in terms of Frelimo policy in order to replace the colonial system with what Frelimo regarded as a Mozambican system.

On the same day that schools were nationalized, namely July 24, 1975, it was announced that all private clinics were to be nationalized and all licences for private medical practices were to be withdrawn. In terms of a Frelimo directive, any doctor who saw a patient privately now faced a fine of $287 (R250) for a first offence and jail without the option of a fine for subsequent offences. The Ministry of Health would in future decide which privately owned clinics and hospitals would be kept open under State control and which were to be closed altogether. Stiff penalties were decreed, not only for doctors who engaged in private work, but also for any individuals or groups acting as "collaborators."

In announcing these moves in Maputo on July 24, 1975, Machel described teachers, doctors and lawyers as "social parasites"; doctors, he said, were "traitors" whose surgeries were places where medicines were dispensed like beer in a bar.

The sweeping ban on all private activities in medicine, coupled by the total nationalization of the educational sphere, caused a further exodus of White residents from Mozambique. In 1974, there were 366 doctors in Mozambique; by the end of 1975, following the nationalization measures, less than 60 were left. Frelimo concluded aid agreements with Communist countries under which Communist specialists moved in to take over skilled positions vacated by Portuguese and other Whites. A large number of Bulgarian doctors entered Mozambique. At about the same time, Frelimo announced that all private law firms were to be closed down, in accordance with the Government's decision to reorganize the judicial system in such a way that it would be placed under total government control.

In addition to the nationalization of information media such as broadcasting, Frelimo also moved into economic spheres such as the fishing industry where two of the country's largest crayfish and prawn fishing companies, Impescal and Copesca, were nationalized on October 29, 1975. Administrative boards were appointed to run the two companies. The Government also announced that the whole of Mozambique's fishing industry, including the organization for small scale Black fishermen, was to be reorganized into co-operatives. Russia was reportedly called in to assist with the restructuring of the entire fishing industry.

All funeral parlours were also nationalized by Frelimo in 1975. The manufacture of coffins was declared a punishable offence and the Government announced that it was to set up a national funeral service "which will be responsible for all funeral activities."

Even the International Red Cross in Mozambique came under the Frelimo nationalization hammer, with the government announcing that all the organization's assets and equipment had been seized by the State. The organization was ordered to surrender its ambulances, and senior officials were told to submit reports to Frelimo.

In February 1976, President Machel moved more firmly into the economic sphere, announcing the nationalization of all privately owned buildings in Mozambique. In terms of this decree, announced on February 3, 1976, all buildings, or parts of them, which were leased became State property. These are defined as buildings for housing or other purposes, such as commerce, industry or agriculture, which are not occupied by the owners. People owning more than one building were ordered to choose which building they wished to retain and live in permanently. Tenants already in buildings would have to leave within 90 days and in future all rents collected would have to be paid over to the Frelimo Government. Furthermore, it was decreed that no building could be sold or transferred without the approval of the State.

In March 1976 Machel's Government imposed a sweeping ban on private owned social and welfare clubs. In all 47 clubs and associations were banned and all their property and assets confiscated. To prevent a repetition of the recent widespread destruction of nationalized buildings carried out by the dispossessed owners, Frelimo held the committee members of the banned clubs responsible for the confiscated assets. Other clubs and associations in Mozambique not included in the banned list will be kept under close scrutiny and were ordered to submit their rules to the government within 90 days. Black, Coloured, Portuguese, Indian and Chinese clubs were on the list. Many of the clubs and associations banned by Frelimo were humanitarian organizations which before the nationalization of private medicine and education, ran clinics and schools for Blacks.

C. *Other Socialistic Measures*

The Council of Ministers published a blue-print for the future, including a programme of austerity and economy in many fields, the development of rural collective farms, a fight against favouritism and corruption, and the creation of new industries.

The emphasis had clearly been on rural development – a possible emulation of the Maoist model – despite the harsh criticism by Frelimo of the aldeamentos system of communal villages introduced by the Portuguese – emphasis was placed by Frelimo on communal farming and the aldeamentos were retained. Problems arose, however, because as in other African countries such as Tanzania, where the Ujamaa village system is experiencing similar problems, Black farmers began revolting against the idea of communal farming. So serious did the situation become, that the Government-controlled Radio Mozambique was compelled to make an unusually strong criticism of Black farmers who refused to accept the idea of communal farming. On October 12, the radio claimed that "large numbers" of the Black population were refusing to live in the communal villages and work on communal farms, adding:

Many continue to throw away their hoes and to live a life of vice, corruption and immorality, which only serves the purpose of the reactionary forces still active in our ranks.

However, the uncertainty and confusion caused by Frelimo's extreme policies possibly arise from the fact that an avowedly capitalistic bureaucracy and middle class which emerged during colonial times cannot reconcile themselves with the new dispensation.

Agricultural production in Mozambique dropped by 75% in some provinces in the period of transitional and independence rule. In Manica and Sofala, for example, potato production fell from 15,000 tons in 1974 to 3,000 tons in 1975, onion production from 41,000 tons to 7,000 over the same period, and citrus production from 265,000 boxes to 11,000 boxes. The maize crop in these provinces declined over the same period from 20,000 to 8,000 tons. Agricultural department estimates say that the production of maize and other local foodstuffs in Mozambique as a whole will be down by 60% in the 1974/75 season, compared with the 1973/74 season. The same sources estimate that export crops will be down by at least 30%.

Mozambique has been compelled to import foodstuffs from countries including South Africa and Rhodesia. By the end of 1975, long food queues were commonplace in Maputo, as residents queued for potatoes, bread and rice. Machel maintained these were queues of "freedom."

The public service also showed signs of running down after Frelimo took over the reigns of government. One journalist reported that it took an hour to clear formalities when arriving from Johannesburg by air at Maputo, even though there were few people on the flight from Johannesburg.[25] Another report, in February 1976, spoke of labour problems on the vital Trans-Zambesi line causing slow-downs in rail traffic. Frelimo party officials blamed the slow-down on "workers' indiscipline and low productivity" and said that the main problems were absenteeism, inefficiency and time lost on interminable political meetings, held almost daily. Most of the railway operation was localized after the exodus of White railwaymen in 1974. Untrained men were appointed to key positions in the railways' head office and along the lines as the complex operation was handed over to members of Frelimo's dynamization committees.

As in Communist Russia, after the Bolshevik revolution, the implementation of widespread socialist measures has caused considerable upheaval and disruption in the life of the peoples of Mozambique. Again, as in the case of Russia, the long food queues, the inefficiency in Government departments and the general inconvenience, and even spirit of terror, caused amongst the ordinary population by these socialization measures, have not been felt by the elite leadership of the new Mozambique. On taking over the country, the Frelimo leadership pledged itself, in accordance with true Marxist dogma, to align and relate itself to the people:

To maintain the austerity required for our life as militants and thus preserve the meaning of the sacrifices of our People, all FRELIMO militants with government tasks must now, as in the past, shun material preoccupations, particularly regarding salaries. What is more, we cannot tolerate one of our representatives owning means of production or exploiting the labour of others.

For ten years we fought without any concern of an individual financial nature, involved only in devoting all our energies to serving the People. This is the characteristic of FRELIMO's militants, cadres and leaders.[26]

These noble sentiments, as in the case of other solemn pledges given by Frelimo, were to prove not worth the paper on which they were written. Although Machel denied Frelimo soldiers a salary for some

time after independence, one of his first decisions on becoming President
of Mozambique was that he himself should receive a salary of $1725
(R1500) a month and his cabinet ministers (one of whom he married) a
salary of $920 (R800) month – both exorbitant figures, given the im-
poverished state of the Mozambican economy; yet only weeks before
announcing these salaries, Machel had solemnly declared that he and
the rest of the Government would do without salaries and that an equivalent amount would be paid into the national treasury. In addition to
reneging on this pledge, Machel also approved the purchase by his
cabinet of brand new motor cars, specially imported from South Africa.
He himself rides around Maputo in an expensive black car donated by
Communist China. The presidential, bullet-proof car is always accompanied by four other vehicles full of armed soldiers. Machel lives in the
former Portuguese Governor's residence and on taking occupation he
ordered that all buildings within a radius of one kilometre be evacuated
for security reasons.

V. Vendetta against the Churches

The churches in Mozambique were amongst the first to feel the effect
of Marxist rule after Frelimo took over power. Several solemn pledges
on religious freedom were given by Frelimo, but were soon torn up by
the Frelimo Government itself. Machel himself declared on independence:

The People's Republic of Mozambique will be a lay state in which there
will exist complete separation of State and Church.[27]

The Constitution of an independent Mozambique likewise declared:

In the People's Republic of Mozambique the State guarantees to citizens
the freedom to practise, or not, any religion.[28]

As is often the case with Communist documents, however, this Constitution gave guarantees on basic human rights while in the same
breath providing for them to be taken away legally:

The People's Republic of Mozambique is a secular State in which there is
complete separation between the State and religious institutions. *In the
People's Republic of Mozambique the activities of religious institutions must conform
to the laws of the State.*[29] (Italics added.)

On less formal occasions Machel made his intentions towards the churches of Mozambique abundantly clear. Speaking at Cuambo, on June 1, 1975, Machel declared that Frelimo regarded the body as more important than the spirit and therefore churches and chapels would be converted into maternity homes. "Catholics were allies of the Portuguese colonialism. In each Portuguese military company there was a chaplain to baptise the soldiers who were sent to kill the people of Mozambique. Every soldier used to sleep in the churches or chapels where they planned their crimes." News reports said that Machel was addressing a roaring crowd of 10,000 as he declared:

For that reason, in churches and chapels we shall install maternity hospitals. Where there were crimes, we shall see the birth of the new man.

In the same speech Machel defined freedom of religion as follows:

Each shall be free to choose if he wants to be a Catholic or a Muslim or Protestant, or if he does not want to be religious at all.

About two months later Machel returned to his attack on the churches in another major speech, this time in Maputo. He accused the churches of trying to divide the peoples of Mozambique, of being dominated by the capitalist system, and of using religion to slow down the development of Mozambique. Some of the Black priests in the country, he claimed, were actually imperialist agents.

The Catholics have their head in the Vatican, the Presbyterians in Switzerland, and the Methodists in America.

The state of tension already existing at this stage between church and state – even prior to Mozambique's independence – was summarized by Archbishop Alexandre of Lourenço Marques, head of the Catholic Church in Mozambique. In an exclusive interview with a Johannesburg newspaper, the *Rand Daily Mail*, Archbishop Alexandre said he was convinced that his growing confrontation with Frelimo would send him eventually to jail. He said that Frelimo was forcing him into a crisis of conscience where he must choose between his God and the principles of Marxism.

President Machel has called my church an instrument of colonial oppression. He has said we forced the people to co-operate with the Portuguese. Now he has told Mozambicans not to bring up their children in Christ. He has said a man must wait until he is 21 before choosing whether to join the church or not.

As Archbishop Alexandre pointed out:

How can a man, brought up through his school years to believe in Marxism, turn to Christ at such an age?[30]

On October 16, Armando Gubuza, Minister of the Interior in Mozambique, issued a statement in which he declared, inter alia:

Today, we need to remember more than ever before that the enemy, the agents of imperialism, are attempting to enter all our ranks in the midst of religious sects, through the intervention of national and foreign missionaries. To manipulate the followers of these sects to better serve the interests of the exploiters, the enemy is using a false and a suspect concept of religion, preaches as being inevitable the existence of a world divided between some rich and millions of exploited, and blinds the people into an unscientific understanding of the world. They are trying to enslave us into believing that the oppression and the misery in which we lived were immutable, which only the religious sects with their Gods would remedy, by creating a reign of love.

The statement went on to attack the Catholic Church for its involvement with the Portuguese Government in the war against those who were seeking to "liberate" Mozambique from oppression. The Church was condemned because, said the statement, whenever the soldiers went out into battle and when they came back from having violated Mozambique's women, the chaplains were there to bless them when they went and to absolve them when they returned.[31]

The immediate post-independence period in Mozambique was marked by the detention and expulsion of a number of clergymen. In addition to persecution of the Roman Catholic church by the Frelimo Government, a number of other religious groups also felt the wrath of atheistic Marxist dogma. The Jehova's Witnesses were singled out for particular attack, being described as known agents of imperialists. The Jehova's Witnesses have refused to give allegiance to Frelimo, the national anthem and national flag, following the same arguments that led to Jehova's Witnesses coming into conflict with governments in countries such as Malawi in earlier years. On October 12, at a rally in Chibuto, Fernando Matavelas, the provincial governor of Gaza, warned the Jehovah's Witnesses that they would be sent to rehabilitation centres if they refused to "take part in the tasks of nation-building." Four days later the governor of Zambezia province, Bonifacio Gruverta, threatened that he would send Jehova's Witnesses in his province to Zambia, which he described as their country of origin, unless they complied in full with the rules and directives of Frelimo. "We cannot tolerate the presence of people who deviate from the ideological lines of Frelimo and do not obey the party strictures," said Gruverta.[32]

Also to incur the wrath of Frelimo were the Nazarenes, a fundamentalist religious group, and the Assemblies of God. Another nine religious groups have been named by Frelimo as counter-revolutionaries and an official communique in November 1975 hinted that other churches might find themselves similarly named.

These mentioned were the Church of the Apostles in Mozambique, the South African Church, the United Apostolic Church of Zion, the Ethiopian Church of Portuguese Africa, Complete Church of God, the Ned. Geref. Kerk Mission, the Church of Christ the Saviour, the Seventh Day Adventists and Church of the Good Father in Mozambique. On October 28, Frelimo accused the USA of giving financial and material support to the Church of the Nazarene to foster anti-revolutionary forces in the country. Five Catholic missionaries were expelled in November 1975 because they were declared "anti-revolutionaries." The five included Portuguese Abbot José-Luzia Gonçalves, secretary to the Bishop of Nampula, and Manuel Vieira Pinto, who had himself been expelled from Mozambique by the former Portuguese colonial regime for "defending Africans." The other expelled priests were Julio-Andreu Gamboa and Manuel Ramos, of the Portuguese Cucujaes Missionary Society, and two Italians of the Comboniani Missionary Order.

Latest statistics show there are about 559 priests in Mozambique of various denominations. In addition, there are 215 missionaries and 1,323 nuns working in the country.[33]

VI. Youth Indoctrination

In addition to its barely concealed objective of destroying freedom of worship in order to strengthen the control of individuals by the State, the Frelimo Government of Mozambique has made it abundantly clear that it intends using the educational system to indoctrinate the youth towards total acceptance of Marxist ideology as interpreted by Frelimo. Samora Machel made this perfectly clear on the Investiture of the Transitional Government:

We are engaged in a Revolution whose advance depends on the creation of the new man, with a new mentality. We are engaged in a Revolution aimed at the establishment of People's Democratic Power. Therefore at school level we must be able to introduce collective work and create an open climate of criticism and self-criticism. Teachers and pupils muts learn from one another in a climate of mutual trust and harmonious comradely relations in which it will be possible to release the initiative of each and develop the talents of all, so that all grow together in the great task of national reconstruction.

Our schools must truly be centres for the propagation of national culture and political, technical and scientific knowledge. The propaganda of knowledge must be aimed at mobilising nature and human potentialities for development and progress of society.

It is therefore necessary to democratize teaching methods. Pupils and trainees must play a responsible part in creating a school of a new type in which manual labour is accorded its due value as one of the sources of knowledge, closely related to practice, drawing inspiration from it and serving the people.[34]

On independence, Machel was even more forthright in his plans for indoctrination of children:

The People's Republic of Mozambique has as its objective the cultural welfare of all citizens. It will promote the diffusion of education to all levels, through democratization directed by the State; it will promote the liquidation of elitism and of educational discrimination on the basis of wealth; and it will promote the formation of a new mentality, a people's morality, a revolutionary mentality in the heart of the new generations.

The youth, sap of the nation, will be protected, the State ensuring its education in constant linkage with life and the interests of the masses.

The State will promote the knowledge, the renewal and the national and international diffusion of Mozambican culture, as an element of consolidation of national unity and essential part of the Mozambican personality.[35]

Among the ways in which indoctrination is being achieved in Mozambique became clear immediately after independence when 1,600 students and teachers from the University of Lourenço Marques were ordered into the countryside or factories in an attempt to "wash off" the old elitist ideas of the colonial system.

The Frelimo Government's attitude towards university students was also defined by Machel when he spoke in Maputo on August 24, 1975:

Learning is only for the rich, and university graduates, once they get their degrees have only one thought in mind, to obtain capitalist positions in order to exploit the people.

Indoctrination of the youth of Mozambique was also to be achieved, in terms of Frelimo planning, through compulsory politico-military instruction. It was announced soon after independence that thousands of young Mozambicans, boys and girls, would be required to undergo compulsory training for two years in the armed forces; those not called up would be required to undergo politico-military training in order to "participate in national tasks." This politico-military training is to be undertaken by the National Defence Reconstruction Service, which covers military training, political indoctrination and communal work in the fields.

VII. CONCLUSION

The uncertainty, confusion and fear that has permeated Mozambique since before and immediately after independence, resulting from the Frelimo Marxist takeover of the country, is perhaps best exemplified by the notice at Maputo airport on independence that read: "Dial 74-2081 the moment you hear reactionary talk." The repressive climate is also reflected in many newspaper reports and comment. For example, the *Financial Times* of London has stated:

But the new Government is more uncompromisingly socialist than any black Africa has yet seen, in intention at least, and quite probably soon in practice. This fact is gradually coming home to Black and White Mozambicans alike, but in these immediate post-independence days there is an air of unreality, confusion and, just under the surface, tension.[36]

NOTES

1. Machel, Samora, "Message of Proclamation of Independence for Mozambique," in *Africa Today*, July-September 1975.
2. Constitution of *The People's Republic of Mozambique*, Art. 50.
3. *Ibid.*, Art. 33.
4. Christie, I., "Portrait of President Machel," in *Africa Report* (New York), May-June 1975, p. 15-17.
5. *Cf.* "The People's Republic of Mozambique" in *African Development* (London), August 1975, p. 34.
6. Machel, Samora, "Message from the President of Frelimo on the occasion of the Investiture of the Transitional Government of Mozambique."
7. Machel, "Message of Proclamation...," *op. cit.*
8. *Cf. Constitution* ..., *op. cit.*, Art. 3.
9. *Ibid.*, Art. 47.
10. *Cf.* "Mozambique takes shape," *Africa* (London), December 1975, p. 71.
11. Machel, "Message of Proclamation ...," *op. cit.*
12. *Constitution* ..., *op. cit.*, Art. 48-49.
13. *Ibid.*, Art. 68-69.
14. *Cf. Rand Daily Mail* (Johannesburg), 23.12.1975.
15. Machel, "Message of Proclamation...," *op. cit.*
16. *Ibid.*
17. *Constitution*..., *op. cit.*, Art. 26.
18. *Quarterly Economic Review* (London), No. 1, 1975, p. 11-13.
19. *Cf. Africa* (London), No. 52, December 1975.

20. Machel, "Message of Proclamation...," *op. cit.*
21. *Ibid.*
22. *Ibid.*
23. *Constitution...*, *op. cit.*, Art. 17.
24. *Cf. Africa* (London), No. 52, *op. cit.*
25. *The Star* (Johannesburg), 5.12.1975.
26. Machel, "Message of the President...," *op. cit.*
27. Machel, "Message of Proclamation...," *op. cit.*
28. *Constitution...*, *op. cit.*, Art. 33.
29. *Ibid.*
30. *Cf. Rand Daily Mail* (Johannesburg), 14.7.1975.
31. Quoted by the Rev. E. K. Smith, Superintendent of the Methodist Missionary Work in Mozambique at the Annual Conference of the Methodist Church of Southern Africa on 21.10.1975.
32. *Quarterly Economic Review* (London), No. 4, 1975.
33. *Africa Research Bulletin* (Exeter, England), November 1975, p. 3830.
34. Machel, "Message from the President...," *op. cit.*
35. Machel, "Message of Proclamation...," *op. cit.*
36. *Financial Times* (London), 3.11.1975.

The Lapps of Sweden

ERIC BRODIN

ERIC BRODIN was born in Sweden and became a citizen of the United States in 1955. He obtained his B.A. from San Francisco State College, his M.A. from the University of California, Berkeley, and his Ph.D. Studies were completed at the Graduate Institute of International Studies, University of Geneva, Switzerland, in the field of political science and international relations. He has received travel/study grants from the Relm Foundation, Michigan, the Ford Foundation and the Rockefeller Foundation, New York. He is an Earhart Fellow for doctoral studies (Relm Foundation), and Visiting Scholar, Hoover Institution on War, Revolution and Peace (Stanford). He is a member of the Mont Pelerin Society, the Philadelphia Society and the Academie Européenne de Science Politique. He has published numerous articles in journals and magazines in the United States, Europe and South Africa.

The Lapps of Sweden

ERIC BRODIN

The Lapps constitute the only resident ethnic minority in Scandinavia today, and it is therefore particularly interesting to study this minority in an area remarkable for linguistic, cultural and ethnic homogeneity.[1] The area of Lapp settlement extends nowadays over the entire Scandinavian arctic region and stretches along the mountain districts on both sides of the Norwegian-Swedish border down to the northern-most part of the province of Dalarne in Sweden. Russian Lapps live as far east as the Kola Peninsula.[2] Of the estimated total of 35,000, the majority live in Norway (20,000). There are about 3,000 in Finland, and between 2,500 and 3,000 in the USSR. In Sweden the number has been estimated at 10,000 of which less than a third 3,000 are characterised as reindeer-keeping. This study will be concerned with the Lapp minority in Sweden, which has been the subject of the most scholarly analyses, but parallels can also be drawn to the plight and problems of the Lapps of northern Norway.[3]

I. Origins

It is generally agreed that the Lapps were the earliest inhabitants of the area of the Scandinavian North which later became known as Finland, Sweden and Norway. The ultimate provenance of the Lappish tribes is lost in the midst of antiquity, but it is clear that they had arrived in the area already before the commencement of the Christian era. Some students believe that the Lapps were already in the Scandinavian North at the time of the second glacial period. Linguistically the Lapps belong to the Finno-Ugric language group, a non Indo-European language group. A modern philologist says:

The Lappish language belongs to the western main part of the Finno-Ugric branch of the Ural language family. This language family also includes the

Samoyed language spoken in the northernmost parts of European Russia
and western Siberia. To the West Finno-Ugric group besides Lappish and
Finnish are the related languages (Cerelian, Vepsish, Votish, Estonian,
Livonian).... To the East Finno-Ugric languages belong Hungarian and
languages related to it.[4]

II. HISTORY

The first mention of the Lapps in historic sources was in the historic
work *Germania* written by Tacitus in 98 A.D. He there mentions the
existence of a tribe he calls the *fenni*, believed to live somewhere east
of the Baltic Sea. That this is the Lapps, and not the Finns is evident
from the cultural descriptions. Both the Swedes and the Norwegians
have in the past called the Lapps "finns," and the Norwegians do so
even today. It is evident that the knowledge of the Lapps by Tacitus
was scant, and that the information was based on vague reports and
myths. By 555 A.D., Procopius, when writing about the history of the
Goths then invading the Italian peninsula, mentions a people living in
Europe's unknown north (which he called Thule) called the "*scritfinni*."
It is a nomadic people described as living in miserable mud-huts and
deriving its livelihood from fishing and hunting. The next historic
mention of these tribes is found in the works of the Langobard monk
Paulus Diaconus. In his history of the Langobards written in 780 he
talks about a people which he in Latin calls *Scritobini* "living in the other
parts of Germania which is beyond the Baltic in a land white with snow
even in the summer months." Paulus Diaconus also mentions, for the
first time, the existence of "an animal which recalls the deer."[5]

At the end of the 9th century comes a more complete account of the
Lapps. Ottar, a wealthy Norwegian farmer in the employ of Alfred the
Great of England, describes for the king his journeys in the arctic north,
an account which King Alfred ordered to be recorded. Ottar describes
how during his travels in the Norwegian north, and to the coast of the
Arctic Sea in the Kola peninsula, he encountered both the tribe known
as *biarni* (Finns), and what he calls the *ter-finns*, or the Lapps of the Kola
Peninsula. Ottar in his account also mentions that he has a herd of 600
reindeer, and it is evident that by this time the domestication of the
reindeer was already highly developed.[6]

Not long after this account it is evident that the representatives of
non-Lapps made contacts with the reindeer-keeping and hunting
nomads. Ottar already describes how the richest of the Lapps had to

pay "a tax" of 15 valuable skins and pelts. During the Middle Ages a
lively trade for furs and skins developed. These traders became known
as *Birkarlar*, as they originated from a place called Birkala near Tam-
merfors in Finland. These traders divided up northern Sweden between
them based on the territories between the vast rivers which originated
in the mountains and flowed into the Gulf of Bothnia. These territorial
divisions, called *Lappmarks*, were named after the river and called Kemi,
Torne, Lule and Pite. The trade led to the settlement of Birkarlar in the
isthmus of the rivers and this constituted the earliest known settlement
of non-Lapps in the area.

As there were no definite agreements as to what really constituted
borders between the developing, neighbouring states, the Lapps had to,
on occasions, pay taxes to more than one ruler or local lord. Not until
1323 was the first border delineation agreed on between Russia on one
hand and Sweden-Finland on the other. Subsequently similar agreements were drawn up between Sweden-Finland on one hand and
Denmark-Norway on the other.[7]

The modern Swedish state came into being with the ascent of Gustav
Wasa to an independent Swedish throne in 1523. Gustav Wasa was a
monarch with a definitely economic bent and one of his many fiscal
reforms was to eliminate the Birkarlar as middle men. He appointed
Lapp sheriffs who were responsible directly to the Crown. They had
among their royal instructions the charge to assure that the Lapps were
left alone by settlers, and that they faithfully paid their taxes, and took
good care of the reindeer which belonged to the crown. (By 1550 one
account says that the Crown owned 126 reindeer in Torne Lappmark
alone). During the fratricidal struggle which ensued among the king's
sons on the monarch's death many of these reindeer were lost. As Guardian of the Realm, Duke Charles concluded a peace treaty with Tsarist
Russia in 1595 during which he emphasised Swedish controls of the
Lapplands of Sweden and Finland. He built forts in strategic northern
places and appointed Lapp sheriffs. The Danes, controlling Norway,
did not like these developments and made their presence felt in the
north, and after the war of 1611–1613, the Swedes lost their previous
access to the Arctic Sea.[8]

III. Laws Governing Lapp Settlements

The first laws that had been passed in Sweden regulating ownership of the land in the northern Wastes of Sweden were passed by King Magnus Eriksson at the beginning of the 14th century, and confirmed by him after gaining his majority in 1340. Access to these areas was to "be open to all." These provisions for open settlement were confirmed in 1544 by Gustav Wasa when he warned the Birkarlar not to prevent anyone from settling there as "the forests and waste-lands are quite sufficient for all in that part of the land." In a later decree he warns that the areas which had not been settled "belong to God, Us and the Swedish Crown and none other." The decree found further confirmation in 1683 by Charles XI when he stated that all land which was not settled and fenced in belonged to the Crown, and he decreed that clear demarcations should be made between settled and open lands.

The insistence by the Swedish Kings and governments for the control by the Crown of the land in Lappland was as much in order to protect the Lapps from encroachment by the settlers, as to assert Crown ownership of the land. The first legislation regarding borders between the areas of the settlers and the open areas for the nomadic Lapps was passed in 1584, subsequent legislation in 1665 confirmed the division of land, limiting the area where the settlers might organise themselves, and strictly affirming the traditional rights of the remaining areas to the reindeer-keeping Lapps.

IV. Immemorial Usage

The claims by the Lapps to these areas as domains provided by prescriptive rights, is based on the ancient concept of Immemorial Usage (*urminnes hävd* in Swedish, *praescriptio immemorialis* in Latin). "Land shall by Law be Governed" is an ancient concept and institution in Sweden. The first provincial laws were written down in 1200, and by 1350 the various provincial laws had been codified and unified into a national law. In this law of Magnus Eriksson's, and in some of its predecessors, the principle of immemorial usage had been recognised. The concept was confirmed in the national Law of King Kristopher 1442, a law whose effect was reconfirmed in 1608 by Charles IX. Three years later the same monarch instructed a Lapp Sheriff, Reinhold Steger, that he "should keep the Lapps fully after the printed law, to which we have consented, and keep them from experiencing any injustice or violence." A number of Swedish academicians within jurisprudence have through the subsequent centuries defined the implications of the concept of Immemorial Usage within Swedish laws. One of the origins of ownership was in terms of occupation. The occupation of the land implied a right to usufructuary rights benefits, and when the borders between Denmark-Norway and Sweden-Finland were drawn 1740, the Danish judicial expert Henrik Stampe, citing Hugo Grotius and Samuel Pudendorf, judged the Lapps entitled to ownership of the land based on the system of initial occupation and subsequent use.[9]

John III in a letter dated 10 July 1584 stated about the rights of the Lapps:

As the Lapps have requested that their lands, which are theirs by immemorial usage, they may without hinder and free for all enjoy, use and keep, so have We, for the sake of justice, indulged them and none other to enjoy, use, and benefit from those lands which lie within the stated areas of the Lappmark.

The present state of litigation by the Lapps against Sweden's central government centres around the problem whether the concept of Immemorial Usage can also be applied against the Crown's claims to ownership of the land. On this issue there is strongly divergent interpretations among legal advocates in Sweden. It is true that from the 17th century on attempts were made to weaken the Lapps' ancient prescriptive rights. By 1673 settlers were given rights to settle in areas previously defined as Lapp areas, and the system of burn-beaten land clearing (*svedjeland*) soon began to have negative effects on the reindeers' grazing which required large areas.

The system of Lapp-taxation-lands (*Lappskatteland*) was variously emphasized in different areas and in different ages. It was strongest in the middle of the 17th century and in the Pite *lappmark*. The land for which the Lapps paid a taxation, could be inherited, and the right to that land could also be sold or bought. The new purchaser of the right (leaser?) had to confirm his ownership of the right in a Lapp court of Law, however. Among the first measures to weaken the Lapp rights in courts of law, was the provision that these rights should no longer be determined by a Lapp court, but by a representative of the Crown, a provincial governor or his representative. The *raison d'être* of a number of the new decisions was that the land was in actual ownership of the Crown. The new interpretations of the rights of eminent domain was restricting prescriptive right to the usufructuary "right to graze, to fish and to hunt." The Lapp had the right to these lands as long as they were needed for grazing, furthermore he could not prevent any settlement on it, unless he could prove that these evidently interfered with his reindeers' grazing.

V. Modern Developments

The 1880s came to have important effects on the Lapps, due to the legislation passed which affected the Lapps' traditional rights severely. The Reindeer-keeping Legislation of 1886, which was to protect a threatened form of traditional livelihood, had in some ways a reversed effect. New detailed regulations made it difficult for the reindeer-keeping Lapps to adjust to the new economic requirements of a modern society. In addition it began a division of the Swedish Lapps into the reindeer-keeping and all the others – the majority. The legislation was intended only for the nomadic and reindeer-keeping Lapps, they alone were to be enabled to continue exercising usufructuary rights – all other Lapps were excluded from these. With the growing industrialization additional legislation was enacted which was further to erode traditional rights as the expansion of the lumber industry required further inroads on the forested sections of traditional grazing areas. When the mineral ore excavations and explorations began at the turn of the century, and later expanded to become Sweden's largest export item (iron-ore), it was evident that the expansionistic modern industrial state, could no longer be hampered by the traditional protection of a mere 3,000 Lapps engaged in the quaint, but uneconomic venture of reindeer-keeping. The need for a network of transport, and the expansion of cities and towns, together with the requisite development of hydro-electric power sources, cut into the traditional Lapp way of life in a number of ways.[10]

The relationship between a native minority and the encroachment of a more dominant majority of later arrivals has often been pointed out. The plight of the Swedish Lapps has been compared to that of the Indian in North and South America for example. One of the Lapps' most able defendants, Professor Edmund Dahlström has said in this regard:

The Peoples of the Scandinavian North have, in the same way as the colonisers of Africa, taken over vast areas of land which previously belonged to the native inhabitants, they have appropriated to themselves the major part of the area's riches, and banished the natives to more isolated and less economically rewarding areas....[11]

Some of the defenders of the Lapps' cause, notably Tomas Cramér, Tom G. Svensson and Ronny Ambjörnsson, have assigned as the cause of the erosion of the Lapps' position, what they call "vulgar Darwinism" which entered into the Swedish ideological debate during the last two decades of the past century. The younger and more radical of the Lapps' defenders, Ronny Ambjörnssen, calls the development an "argument related to the ideas of imperialism."[12] As typical of the "vulgar Darwinism" Lapp advocates quote the statement in 1965 by the provincial governor of Lappland, Ragnar Lassinanti:

It is in the very nature of things that when two cultural circles approach one another, the stronger and more dominant will always expand at the cost of the smaller and weaker. Nor do I believe that the Lapps will be able to escape defeat in this struggle.[21]

The present court case which was decided against the Lapps in a court of first instance in 1973, involves the right to three "taxation mountains" and 10,000 square kilometers in the county of Jämtland. The judgement, 600 pages long in a printed version, is now on appeal in the circuit court of appeal of lower Norrland. The "White books" published by the National Association of the Lapps, and by the Lapp *ombudsman*, Tomas Cramér provide numerous incidents of the encroachment of both private, but especially state-owned industries and enterprises on the Lapps' life and livelihood. Ambjörnsson, in his article refers to the effect of the largest of Sweden's state enterprises, the iron ore mining company of LKAB. He says:

The present plant area of LKAB in Kiruna is 15 square kilometers, almost all of which is in a traditional reindeer calving area of Laevas Lapp Village (*lappby*). Now an additional area of similar size is being prepared. If the Kalix river is enlarged as planned two major water reserves will develop, which will cause alien reindeer to encroach on the Laevas village grazing lands, at the same time as a serious reduction of the best grazing lands is taking place, lands which are already reduced due to the anti-grazing effect of large-scale forestry undertakings.[14]

In the "White Book" volume 3 issued in 1975, the authors give additional evidence of negative effects within the Laevas Lapp village area. It points out, *inter alia*, that the expanding tourism also has adverse effects. Snow scooters, when misused, have become a real environmental problem. In Allesjaure the tourists' cottages have been placed right in the traditional path of the migrating reindeer-herds. The Lapps had not been consulted when the Tourists Association of Sweden placed them there. Critics of government decision also point out that when the railway Kiruna-Svappavaara was built 1965 the state promised to provide a fence for the protection of the reindeer, a promise not yet fulfilled.[15]

The Department of Public Domain have also, on a number of occasions, been accused of callous attitudes toward the Lapp minority and their undertakings. In the county of Norrbotten, for example, licences were granted to industries which proceeded in polluting the waters through industrial wastes resulting in the poisoning of all the fish. The fish in the lake, pike and perch, had been an important source of food for the Lapps, which they had caught with nets. The Department restocked the lake with salmon intended to be caught with hook, for the benefit of the sports fishermen whose licence fees provide the Department and the county with an important income. When the Lapps requested funds from the Lapp Fund to employ judicial counsel for their side in the pleading of their case, their request was denied.[16]

Mention has been made of the Lapp Fund and an explanation is in order. All money which is paid for the rights to exploit any natural resource in the grazing areas of the mountains (generally above the line of cultivation), or fines due to damage on Lapp ground, is placed in a special Lapp Fund. But the allocation of these Funds is not reserved for the Lapp Village representatives or the Lapp organisation, or the Lapp ombudsman. Such allocations are determined solely by the government representatives. In some instances therefore, the government might be guilty and required to pay a fine, while the allocation of such funds go to another governmental appointee.

The Swedish government has assumed exclusive right as to who is going to represent the reindeer-keeping Lapps in any judicial case, the so called Kammarcollegiet (Chamber Collegial Body). The Lapps have since 1950 organised themselves into a representative interest organisation, National Association of Lapps. Since 1962 they have employed a legally trained, full time *ombudsman*. Yet Kammarcollegiet refused the Lapps the right to determine who is going to speak on their behalf. As a result in some court cases, both the attorney for the defence and for the accused may be government appointees.[17] The National Meeting of the Lapps in 1965 stated:

In the opinion of the National meeting the real meaning of the present system must be considered. In lawsuits the crown is both plaintiff (exploiter) and defendant (for the Lapps) at the same time in the same case. The Crown as the exploiter appears in forestry, mining, water regulation and railways. An extensive settlement of claims take place, not in the full publicity of courts of law, but inside the closed doors of a government department, where the Lapps' representative has to wage an uneven fight against an adversary, the crown, with gigantic resources of power and money. This takes place with the support of clause 5 of the reindeer pasturage law, which gives the Lapps' rights a defencelessness, otherwise quite unknown in Swedish judicial life, through expropriation without the decision of a court of law.[21]

The parliamentary commissioner for the Lapps, (or *ombudsman*) Tomas Cramér, further exemplified the dangerous effect of clause 5 of the reindeer pasturage law in eroding the judicial position of the Lapps:

Our country supports, rightly, efforts to guarantee without regard to race and other circumstances, a legally secure existence for population groups in foreign countries. It is therefore a self-evident duty that we ourselves should protect the small minority which the Lapps comprise, and see that legislation gives this population group, which, in the course of time has been encroached on more and more, and whose sources of livelihood is threatened by social development, the means to safeguard the rights belonging to the Lapps since time immemorial, rights that have been acknowledged by law.[19]

One of the Lapps, Tore Lampinen, has expressed similar sentiments with more acerbic quality:

Stop treating us as grown children. That is a reasonable request. It is difficult to understand how any popularly elected government can, at length, continue to ignore such a request. The Lapps have altogether too long permitted themselves to be cowed by a power-mad /*maktfullkomlig*/ authority. There has to be an end to it. If this does not happen there remains no other alternative than to initiate a case of prosecution against the Swedish government at the Court of Europe in Strasbourg.[20]

The Swedish Lapps and their advocates, and indeed all those in Sweden concerned with human rights generally, recalls the Council of Europe's Convention on Human Rights, which in clause 6 provides:

Everyone shall, when it concerns his civil rights and obligations, or accusations against him for crimes, be entitled to an impartial and public trial within a reasonable period of time, before an independent and impartial judge or jury as determined by law.[21]

Of the many problems facing the small minority of Lapps in Sweden today, being in effect deprived of proper representation in a court of law is of the most fundamental character. The ethnic needs for self-expression by way of encouragement of the retention of the language, through schools, radio and television programmes and other cultural institutions, are vitally needed if the Swedish Lapps are to be able to withstand the approaching threats of ethnic genocide. The recognition by the Swedish government of the Lapps judicial "coming of age" would be an important element in the retention of the human dignity needed for the survival of any small, and economically vulnerable minority. A seat as a member (or even an observer status) on the Nordic council for the 32,000 Lapps of Sweden, Norway and Finland would be another step in the right direction, but this too has also been denied (although the Faroe Island and Åland populations have full and separate membership on the Nordic Council.)

The struggle is not yet over. The outcome of the present case in the Circuit Court of Appeals in Östersund is still unknown. And if the decision is against the Lapps, there is no doubt but that the case will be carried to the Swedish Supreme Court.

One of the Lapps' most consistent defenders, Professor Tom G. Svensson, in a memorable article in one of Sweden's leading newspapers, wrote:

The Lapps are today struggling for their right to their territory. A similar strategy of action has been applied by similar minorities such as Indians, Inhuits etc. The present case about the *skattefjällen* must therefore be seen as a part of an ongoing international process, to which also the United Nations has paid attention. This is a fact that can no longer be hidden either by the Swedish government or our courts. The Lapps are in the right when they refer to such moral support in their own struggle.[22]

The Swedish government has been one of the most active advocates in international fora of human and civil rights around the world. But many within Sweden now point out that there is still "unfinished business" at home. The Lapps in Sweden have a unique quality as a minority. As an official report puts it:

A fundamental basis for the Commission on Lapps has been that the Lapps are an aboriginal population, which would appear to be of as long – or longer – standing in Sweden as the majority population ... The Lapps are in their own country, but comprise an ethnic minority within the total population. This gives them a clear, special status in relation to other minorities, and there is reason to apply, to some extent, different judgement in relation to the Lapps.[23]

NOTES

1. The term Lapp (from Finnish *lappalainen*) is being replaced in Sweden by the term 'same' (from Lappish *samit*). Lapp in Swedish today carries a negative connotation.
2. The Swedish Institute, "The Lapps in Sweden," Stockholm, 1975.
3. The Lapp ombudsman Tomas Cramér claims that there may be as many as 25,000 Lapps in Sweden; he criticises the government for refusing to determine the exact number by means of a census.
4. Collinder, Björn, *Lapparna* [The Lapps], Forum, Stockholm, 1953, p. 53.
5. Quoted in Bosi, Roberto, *The Lapps*, Thames and Hudson, London, 1960, p. 44 ff.
6. Ruong, Israel, *Samerna* [The Lapps], Aldus/Bonniers, Stockholm, 1969, p. 52.
7. Sweden-Finland existed from ca. 1100 to 1809; Denmark-Norway from ca. 1380 to 1814; Sweden-Norway from 1814 to 1905 (personal union).
8. Collinder, *op. cit.*, 1953, p. 38.
9. The most complete account of "Immemorial Usage" in Sweden is found in: *Samernas Vita Bok III:2* [The Lapps' White Book], vol. 2, Stockholm, the essay by Hafström, Gerhard, "Urminnes Hävd till skattefjällen i Jämtland och Härjedalen" [Immemorial Usage to the 'taxation-mountains' in Jämtland and Härjedalen] 1975, pp. 1–48.
10. Cramér, Tomas, & Prawitz, Gunnar, *Studier i renbetslagstiftning* [Studies in Reindeer pasturage legislation], P. A. Norstedt & Söner, Stockholm, 1970.
11. Svonni, Lars, ed., *Samerna-ett folki fyra länder* [The Lapps a people in four countries], the essay by Dahlström, Edmund, "Den Samiska minoriteten i Sverige" [The Lapp minority in Sweden] Prisma, Stockholm, 1974, p. 102.
12. Ambjörnsson, Ronny, "Vem skall äga samernas fjäll?" [Who shall own the Lapps' mountains?], *Dagens Nyheter*, Stockholm, 14 March 1976, p. 4.
13. Quoted in: *Samernas Vita Bok III:1*, vol. 1, Svenska Samernas Riksförbund [National Union of Swedish Lapps], Stockholm, 1975, p. 4.
14. Ambjörnsson, *op. cit.*
15. *Samernas Vita Bok III:1, op. cit.*, vol. 1, 1975, pp. 1–2.
16. Svonni, Lars, "Samerna i samhället: Ett perfekt kolonialistiskt system" [The Lapps in the Society: A perfect Colonialistic System], *Dagens Nyheter*, Stockholm, 2 May 1970, p. 5.
17. Svensson, Tom G., "De Renskötande samernas ställning i Sverige" [The position of the reindeer-keeping Lapps in Sweden], in Schwarz, David ed., *Svenska minoriteter* [Swedish minorities], Aldus/Bonniers, Stockholm, 1966, pp. 223–244.
18. Ruong, Israel, *The Lapps in Sweden*, Swedish Institute Forum, Stockholm, 1967, pp. 108–109.
19. *Ibid.*, pp. 107–108.
20. Lampinen, Tore, "Samernas Rättslöshet" [The Lapps' lack of judicial rights], *Dagens Nyheter*, Stockholm, 12 May 1969.
21. Quoted and discussed in: Kung, Andres, & Tandberg, Olof G., *Jordens Fätryckta: etniska minoriteter i världen* [The World's Oppressed: ethnic minorities in the world], 1960, p. 214 ff.
22. Svennson, Tom G., "Samekulturens framtid skall avgöras" [The future of the Lapp Culture must be decided], *Svenska Dagbladet*, Stockholm, 27 April 1976, p. 2.
23. Statens Offentliga Utredningar [government report] *Samerna i Sverige* [The Lapps in Sweden], Liber, Stockholm, 1975, p. 27.

Group Discrimination in Orissa

L. K. MAHAPATRA

Dr. Lakshman Kumar Mahapatra, at present Professor and Head of the Department of Anthropology, Utkal University, Bhubaneswar, was born in Orissa in 1929. With a B.A. (Hons) and M.A. in Anthropology 1st class from Calcutta University, he studied at Hamburg University as a Nehru Scholar and was awarded Dr.Phil. in Social Anthropology, Sociology and Comparative Education, Magna cum Laude in 1960. He was Visiting Professor in Social Anthropology, Sociology and Indology at Hamburg University, 1968, and delivered special lectures at Cologne, Heidelberg and Amsterdam Universities in 1969. He had also taught at Lucknow, Merut, Gauhati and Karnatak Universities in India.

He attended the International Congresses of Anthropological and Ethnological Sciences at Paris in 1960 and at Tokyo-Kyoto in 1968. He was selected by the University Grants Commission to deliver National Lectures at Delhi, Ravishankar and Gujarat Vidyapith Universities. He has undertaken field research in Orissa, Bihar, U.P., Assam, N.E.F.A. and Mysore and has directed several research projects. He is President of the Anthropological Society of Orissa, a Vice-President of the Anthropological Association of India and had been a member of the Central Advisory Board of Tribal Welfare, Govt. of India, and Member, Tribes Advisory Council, Government of Orissa.

His paper on "Gods, Kings and the Caste System in India" is being published by Mouton & Co in 2 volumes of the World Anthropology series. He is the author of two books. *The Contours of Social Welfare*, published by Karmatak University, and *Folklore of Orissa*, being published by the National Book Trust of India.

Group Discrimination in Orissa

L. K. MAHAPATRA

Differences in status, language, race, ethnic group or religion may not logically produce discrimination against a group. But, economic power and/or political authority, when distributed unequally, have usually led to discrimination against those who have less of them. Group discrimination may be conceptualized as consisting not merely in the awareness and recognition of differences in culture, race, language, religion etc. A group may be indifferent to the existence of such differences even when negatively evaluating such differences. This has been the inter-ethnic recognition of differences between human groups since their primordial beginnings. The negative evaluation of such differences is at this stage natural. But when the negative evaluation of others leads one group to deprive the other group or groups of enjoyment of certain opportunities or resources including that of status symbols to the advantage of one's own group, then this former group may be said to be discriminating against other groups. Such discrimination may be observed in manifest behaviour or perceived in attitudes.

In India ritual status, unaccompanied by economic and political power, has enjoyed authority and sanctioned discrimination in various fields. This is a unique feature of the social structure of India. Orissa, in its traditional social structure, is no exception to this general and basic feature of the Indian society. Even then, Orissa has its own distinctive characteristics as a cultural and geographical region of India. Its language and script, its temple architecture and village layout, its dress and ornaments, its musical and dancing traditions, its festivals and food habits, its kinship structure and marriage patterns, and religious systems, etc., show to what great extent there have been certain influences from the south with Dravidian civilization, from the west with its rich heritage of the hill tribes and Central Indian centres of civilization and from the north with the still migrating hordes of tribal groups and the glorious centres of north Indian Aryan civilization. The co-mingling of diverse civilizations, religions, languages, races and ethnic groups is, however, not the unique situation in Orissa. But the fact that the overwhelming importance and imprint of tribal heritage in the culture, physical constitution, religion, and social structure of the people of Orissa is not a thing of the past, but is in the process of becoming. Not merely the fact that there are continuities on several fronts between the tribal and non-tribal worlds, the continuities themselves are evolving. In this background it is easy to visualize a not-too-rigid caste structure as in South India, and a rather flexible or even aberrant caste structure as in the Punjab or in Assam. Here the tribal chiefs are found lording it over their principalities, or when engulfed by a larger political entity, maintaining their political importance and cultural and moral autonomy until the threshold of Independence was reached in 1947. The princes had to court and count upon the support and loyalty of the important tribal groups in order to remain in power. As the population pressure was not heavy, compared with the densely populated open plains in North and West India, a family or a sub-caste group could often migrate from one principality to settle down in another. In pre-British Orissa, it was often possible to wrest a new opportunity and reap a social reward for advancing one's caste and ritual status. In this process many tribal groups and cultivating and other castes became assimilated into the aristocratic status of Kshatriya rulers, and apparently to the highest ritual status of Brahmin (cf. Kulke, Mahapatra 1970). Under these pre-disposing circumstances, discrimination on basis of racial and ethnic distinctions, linguistic and even religious differences may be reasonably inferred not to lie beyond a tolerable degree of exploitation of the group discriminated against.

While discussing discrimination in Orissa it is neither theoretically possible nor pragmatically desirable to limit observation by the political boundary of the federating state of Orissa. As structural systems and cultural patterns, easily and invariably spill over the political boundaries, it is possible to take into consideration, without any distorting effect, the cases reported in some detail from the neighbouring states, viz. Andhra in the South, Madhya Pradesh in the West and Bihar and West Bengal to the North and North-east respectively.

Apart from drawing into our purview the cases occurring in the neighbouring states to provide an adequate empirical base of our study, we may consider the general all-India phenomenon as revealed in authoritative documents and also significant cases reported from other parts of India in 1974–75.

I. Ethnic Discrimination

If each caste or sub-caste and each tribal group are taken as separate ethnic groups, we may hazard a guess about the number of these ethnic groups in Orissa. There are 62 "Scheduled Tribes" in Orissa, declared as such by the President of India under the Constitution. In cultural and racial terms, there are at least four or five other tribal groups, who are either not included in the list of "scheduled tribes" or subsumed under some other scheduled tribes in the existing list. Besides these "scheduled tribes," we have 93 "scheduled castes" declared under the Constitution. Only 91 scheduled castes have been located and enumerated by the Census authorities in 1971. Besides the "scheduled castes," there are about one thousand other castes and sub-castes in Orissa. For example, the Brahmin caste in Orissa has at least seven sub-castes, who for all purposes are functioning as separate ethnic groups. Traditionally no marriage was allowed between the sub-castes.

It is difficult to chart the pattern of discrimination between the Brahmin, the highest caste and the other non-Brahmin castes and sub-castes who are so many. This aspect of discrimination will be taken care of when we deal with discrimination in the caste system.

Though racially Orissa contains, according to B. S. Guha, at least three racial groups, mainly the Mediterranean, the Alpinoid and the Proto-Australoid, it is most probably the Proto-Australoid racial element which is overwhelmingly manifest in the population of Orissa. Almost all the tribal peoples have been identified as the proto-Australoids and the other two racial elements are present more often among the non-tribal population than in the tribal. But because the tribal people usually live in the mountainous and forested tracts and are most often of Proto-Australoid racial stock, and because of their cultural, social and physical estrangement, they can be easily distinguished from the general population. At present people of tribal origin are referred to as *Adibasi* or autochthones, whether included in the lists of scheduled tribe or not. The *Adibasi* as a whole are slightly looked down upon as a lower breed of people by the general population, but not despised as the scheduled castes are. However, those tribes who take beef, buffalo meat, monkey's flesh, carrion, pork and other forbidden and polluting

food are no less despised than the scheduled castes by the general population. No Hindu caste serves them on ritual occasions. On the other
hand, there are some tribes like the Gond, the Bhuiyan, the Bathudi,
the Bhumiya, the Bhottada and a few Hinduized sections of some important tribes like the Khond and the Saora, who are considered equivalent to some 'clean' caste, being served by other Hindu castes on
important ritual occasions like birth, marriage and funeral ceremonies.
That is why the word *Adibasi* is a blanket term covering a wide variation
of ritual and social status of tribal groups. Another similar blanket term
is *Harijan* or the children of 'Hari', the God. Almost all the scheduled
castes are considered untouchables in the sense that a higher caste man
will have to purify himself if he comes in actual physical contact with
an untouchable person. The *Harijan* castes and sub-castes largely followed a defiling occupation and are hierarchically graded according to
ritual status of the occupation they follow, and food they eat (beef,
buffalo meat, pork etc.). The lowest in the hierarchy is despised rather
strongly by the highest in the *Harijan* hierarchy.

Just because another ethnic group, be it caste or tribe, follows its own
culture, traditions and social norms and is different from one's own
ethnic group in a particular area, this may be sufficient basis for restrictions on equality and interactions. But such restrictions are mutual
among these ethnic groups. In cases of reciprocal restrictions on intercourse between and sharing of resources among, ethnic groups, it will
be difficult to call the situation discriminatory. But when some tribal
groups consider other neighbouring ethnic groups, whether of caste or
tribal origin, as despisable or untouchable and such valuation is to the
advantage of the higher ethnic group, such situation can be an instance
of ethnic discrimination.

There is another facet of ethnic discrimination in some parts of Orissa
as between the tribal and the non-tribal sections of the population. In
tribal-dominated areas of north Orissa, where the tribal groups have
migrated from Bihar state and have not developed a strong sense of
belonging to the soil and a strong attachment, based on generations of
interaction and inter-dependence, with the local non-tribal population,
they designate the non-tribal people as *Diku* or foreigners or outsiders in
Mundari languages or as 'Hatua' or people of the market relationships,
where Oriya language is used. The estrangement between the *Diku* or
Hatua non-tribal and the tribal residents can go too far. They may
result in violent clashes as happened in Bihar and other states during
British regime. Just at the time of transfer of power from the British to

the Indian chiefs in the former princely states, some princes played upon this estrangement and fanned it into violent uprisings by some tribal people against the non-tribals in order to thwart the Nationalist movement organised mostly by the non-tribal people for merger of the princely states in the Indian Republic (cf. Mahatab).

II. Discrimination in the Caste System

It is often said that the caste system is based upon institutionalized inequality. There is a hierarchy of social and ritual statuses from the Brahmin castes at the top downwards to the untouchable castes at the bottom. Economic and political power usually got concentrated among the higher castes, so much so that the higher castes usually dominated villages and regions while the lower castes were tied to them in subservience service relationships, patron-client relationships, landlord tenant or creditor-debtor relationships. This subservience often took the shape of certain interference by the higher castes in the matter of purely intra-caste or inter-caste disputes not involving the higher castes. This is not to say that there were no rich men among the lower castes or to say that a potter or a drummer could not gain political sway or economic power. But such cases were rather exceptional. The lower castes had to serve the higher castes on ritual and social occasions in a system of patron-client relationships called "Jajmani System." That the Brahmin priest at the top of the ritual and social ladder had to serve the landowning and other high castes on ritual occasions, rather reinforced the basic features of the dominant-dependent relationship in the "Jajmani System." This is evidenced by a newly established village of peasants and other landowning groups including the high grade Brahmin landlords, sponsoring the settlement of barber, washerman, or even Brahmin temple priests, etc. to render necessary services. The untouchable castes who usually did not own any land for house sites or for cultivation were abjectly dependent on the landowning higher castes. As these landless labourers and servants formed a sizeable population in a village, and their subservience to their masters or landlords was not based on a free market situation of demand and supply, the rewards, the wages, and other forms of remuneration were to a large extent determined by the traditional ties rather than by the amount of labour or service rendered. At any rate, the lower castes rendering services to the higher one could not have received more than a mere subsistence allowance, which did not leave any thing to be accumulated over generations to produce a wealthy barber, washerman or carpenter. But wealthier Brahmin priests are no exception, even when they were largely dependent on ritual services to the clean castes. There is a controversy whether the "Jajmani" relationship was a relationship of exploitation of the dependent castes by the dominent ones. It can only be said that whatever exploitation was there, it could not have been galling or total. For, each of the service castes had its own caste-cum-guild association to safeguard the economic and status interests of the caste or sub-caste concerned. This has continued to exert strong pressure on the master castes till today (cf. Mahapatra, 1970a). This relative economic security as well as the religious tenets of *Dharma* and *Karma* binding the individual to his caste occupation and to his present status as a reward for his past deeds in a former life, susceptible of infinite improvements in future lives, must have produced a world view of acceptance of the given conditions in life without organized protest or revolt.

In another sense there was discrimination to the disadvantage of the lower castes. If rendering of manual and menial services would have been reciprocal, if lowly occupations of polluting nature were distributed more or less evenly among all the castes, there would be no discrimination on this ground in the caste system. This was not so; the lower and the lowest castes had to bear the brunt of all the heavy, dirty, polluting and degrading services. Apart from the abject poverty and hovels in which they lived the untouchable castes were segregated in a hamlet or hamlets of their own away from the main village or township.

We can look at discrimination in the caste system from still another angle. The appropriation of some status symbols like a turban on the head or shoes on the feet, or umbrella for protection or transport by palanquin on social occasions etc. by the higher castes to the exclusion of the lower castes, even if the latter could afford such things, constitutes a case of clear discrimination against the lower castes. In Brahmin-dominated villages in Puri District even men of the high caste of Kshatriya were debarred from walking along the village street wearing shoes or other footwear or using an open umbrella as late as 1930's. There have been clashes between the service castes and higher castes in recent years after Independence, mainly because the former wanted to assert their independence from their traditional degrading bindings to the higher and dominant castes and to disown their 'Jajmani' service relations, as these were economically unprofitable and did not afford them opportunity for economic mobility. There have been still more serious clashes in the villages in recent years for the simple reason that traditional status symbols reserved for the higher castes were suddenly devalued as the lower castes and even the untouchables took the liberty to use them for gaining higher, secular, social status.

Apart from these discriminations, there were the well known social discriminations, which continue till today in the villages, such as restrictive interaction with regard to food, drink and social intercourse. The Brahmin being at the top of the caste ladder can play the host to all the castes down the ladder, whereas a caste may not offer him any food or water or even may not touch him. Similarly lower caste men are not admitted to the house of the Brahmin, more so in the case of the untouchable castes. Such restrictive social relationships are not exclusive to the interaction between the Brahmin and the untouchable castes. Such restrictive and unequal relationships pervade the whole caste hierarchy. But all the disadvantages, restrictions, and deprivations get accumulated at the level of the untouchable castes. It is hardly any consolation to them that there are higher and lower status groups among the untouchable castes and the lowest among them is avoided by the other untouchables much in the manner of the upper castes avoiding the untouchables.

Under the aegis of a democratic constitution of India with a reservation of electoral constituencies and seats in favour of the hitherto deprived and backward castes, such discriminations have in most cases either disappeared or lost their teeth. The law courts do not recognise the caste privileges and the exclusive prerogatives like status symbols. Untouchability has been abolished by the constitution and severe punitive legal measures have been in operation since Independence and especially since 1974–75. Even then the caste distinctions and discriminations do still continue to plague the village social structure.

III. Case Studies of Discrimination against the Weaker Section

While considering case studies of discrimination against the weaker section comprising the scheduled castes and scheduled tribes, it is not necessary to restrict consideration to Orissa State only. On the one hand, it is profitable and quite appropriate to present a succinct account of such discrimination on an all-India plane, and on the other

hand, one can report some already published cases of discrimination in
Orissa and neighbouring states, as well as a few cases exposed in their
representations to the Government of India for redress during the
years from 1970 to 1975.

After the new constitution of India was adopted in 1950, untouchability was abolished as an act of discrimination under the article 17 of
the constitution of the Government of India. The Government of India
made a practice of untouchability in public places a serious crime with
effect from June 1955. Special provisions were made for uplift of the
scheduled castes and scheduled tribes. A senior authority, Commissioner for Scheduled Castes and Scheduled Tribes, was appointed by
the President of India immediately after the constitution was effective,
to act something like a watch dog for guarding the interests of these
weaker sections, and to report to the President and the Parliament on
the progress of measures for the uplift of these sections, and for suggesting ways of removing barriers to their advancement. The annual
reports of the Commissioner is a valuable source not only for gaining
an all-India perspective of discrimination in this field but also for
throwing some lurid light on the problems involved through the few
cases presented in these annual reports.

In the very first annual report of the Commissioner in 1951, it was
reported that in certain parts of Madhya Pradesh the scheduled castes
were not allowed to wear the *Dhoti* (untailored cloth garment) below
the knee nor a scheduled caste bridgeroom to put on a turban with a
turra. Band music was not allowed to be played at their marriages nor
could their women folk wear bangles and other ornaments made of
silver. They were also prohibited from riding a horse or on a bullock cart
(referred to by Sachchidananda, p. 282.)

From the annual reports of the Commissioner available to this author from the year 1957–58 to the year 1972–73, an attempt will be
made to present some statistics, based on complaints and representations received by the Government of India from members of the weaker
sections from time to time (see Table 1).

From a cursory glance at the number and variety of complaints and
representations received from scheduled castes and tribes from 1957–58
to 1960–61, from 1964–65 to 1965–66 and again from 1967–68 to 1972–
73, in all in 11 reports in 12 years, a few important observations can be
made. Under each item in Table 1 the number of complaints etc. is
highly variable from year to year and categories included in an item
for which specific figures are available are also variable. Even then, if

TABLE I

						Years							
Items	1957–58	1958–59	1959–60	1960–61	1964–65	1965–66	1967–68	1968–69	1969–70	1970–71	1971–72	1972–73	
1. Practice of untouchability	53	117	—	27	82	116	120	355	380	246	639	629	S.C.
											1	7	S.T.
2. Harassment	347	136	107	188	284	434							S.C.
													S.T.
3. Land and Agriculture and Housing problem	118	322	242	314	583	784	265	323	365	390	293	357	S.C.
											5	6	S.T.
4. Relating to service and appointments	89	222	485	630	685	765	801	995	1486	1341	1379	2078	S.C.
											177	115	S.T.
5. Miscellaneous including matters relating to education and drinking water	9	145	467	190	519	952	243	235	351	217	313	392	S.C.
											6	6	S.T.
Total complaints dealt with separately by Assistant Commissioners or Zonal Directors for 1957–58	Not given	800	805	551	2**	2**	Not given	Not given	Not given	Not given			S.C.*
					0	0					189	134	S.T.
TOTAL	616	1742	2106	1900	2153	3051	1429	1908	2582	2194	3002	3724	

* Assam, Manipur, Kerala and Tripura are not included.
** Includes complaints registered in the States.

all the items are taken together, it shows a more or less consistent trend of increasing frequency from 1957–58 to 1972–73. One item, relating to service and appointment, has shown a very consistent increase in frequency. Other items, like practice of untouchability and harassment show an inexplicable fall in number in 1959–60 (when only harassment is included) and 120 in 1967–68 (including both practice of untouchability and harassment), breaking away from the usual pattern of growth of these complaints. Two peaks are found in 1965–66 with 550 complaints in these items and in 1971–72, 640 and 1972–73, 636. Under the last item there is special mention of complaints regarding sharing of sources of drinking water till 1964–65. If this shows that harassment regarding drinking water has ceased to be a subject of complaints and if this is not included under item 2, then this is a very important improvement in the discriminatory situation. Very interestingly, regarding land and housing problems, the frequencies of complaints are almost uniformly high barring 1957–58 (numbering 118) and with a peak in 1965–66 (numbering 784) having a rising base in 1964–65 (numbering 583). Unfortunately, there is no break up available between land and agriculture problems and housing problems from 1964–65 to 1965–66. Assuming that the housing problems have attracted complaints more or less at a uniform level, the land and agriculture problems most probably have been severe during 1964–66, presumably due to land redistribution among the weaker sections, consequent upon land reforms in most of the states of India. It is also highly probable that representations regarding financial assistance and educational and scholarship matters are not in the nature of complaints but of requests for help and assistance.

That sometimes such complaints are exaggerated or even may lack any substance has been known at least since 1957–58. In the report for that year it is stated that the complaint regarding the death of a scheduled caste worker of a non-official agency under suspicious circumstances in a village temple in Orissa State was found by the district authorities to be merely a case of natural death. But discrimination against the scheduled castes in temple entry was very much in the air in the first decade after Independence and the 1957–58 report of the Commissioner refers to the denial of temple entry in Madras State. The State Government had warned the Board of Trustees and other persons responsible for the same and had taken steps to ensure that such incidents were not repeated.

In the neighbouring state of Madhya Pradesh in the year 1958–59 the very protectors under law of the scheduled castes committed the cognizable offence of practising untouchability and went scot free. It was reported that the wives of the policemen of high castes did not allow the family of a scheduled caste policemen to draw water from the common water tap. The complaint was duly lodged at the police station but with no result. On the contrary, some high caste women beat up the luckless scheduled caste woman by entering into her quarters. Interestingly, the higher authorities reported on the quarrelsome nature of the scheduled caste woman and took the only action of alloting another quarters away from the high caste women. It may be pointed out that the Government of India Act of 1955 making practice of untouchability a cognizable offence was barely introduced at that time. But, it is also a fact that till 1973–74 in Orissa State no offender had been punished under this Act, although a large number of complaints were registered and investigated.

Two cases from Orissa reported in 1958–59 deserve mention. The scheduled castes living in a village in Koraput District were beaten up and their houses set on fire by higher caste people, as the scheduled castes had insisted on using a public well and also wanted to partake of *prasad* (food offering) of a local goddess. There is no mention of any punishment in this case, though the State Government had resettled the scheduled castes to ensure a peaceful life. In the other case from a village in Puri District scheduled castes and high caste students were taking an active part in celebrating together the worship of *Saraswati* (Goddess of learning). The local leaders belonging to high castes forced their way into the premises of the public school and insulted one of the teachers who was a scheduled caste member. On the complaint lodged in this case the authorities reported that the matter was settled amicably.

The annual report of 1960–61 of the Commissioner goes somewhat systematically into the prevalence of discrimination against scheduled castes in eight villages of Puri, Cuttack, Keonjhar and Koraput districts of the State. Though these villages were not selected on any scientific principle of sampling, the results, however, were symptomatic and gave a lot of insight into the conditions generally prevailing at that time. (i) In all the 6 villages having temples there was restriction on entrance of scheduled caste people into the temples on ordinary days. In 2 temples, however, they were allowed to enter during certain festivals. In one village temple there was no restriction on temple entry, but then, there were no high caste Hindus in that village to share the temple. (ii) In 6 villages there was discrimination against one or more of the scheduled castes recognized in Orissa State in sharing services at tea stalls and hotels etc. The Scavenger caste, being one of the lowest in status among the scheduled castes, was not served tea in the common tumblers at the tea stalls. Separate tumblers were kept outside the Tea stalls for them. Otherwise the Scavengers were required to bring their own tumblers into which tea was poured from a distance. Obviously, meals of rice and other eatables were not served to them. (iii) Barbers and washermen did not serve most of the scheduled castes. (iv) In one village, however, the washerman caste was being served by a Brahmin priest of lower status exclusively meant for the washermen of the region. In the other villages the Brahmin priests did not serve the washerman.

There were also some specific cases reported in 1960–61. In a village in Singhbhum district in the former princely State of Kharsuan, the Dom Scheduled caste members complained that they were prevented from participating in the public singing of God's names and their own worship of the God was disturbed by the high caste people. The reason was that such action would pollute the deities whom the high castes traditionally worshipped to the exclusion of the untouchable castes. The complaint of the harassment before three police officials had brought no result. The Government considered the matter serious and ordered a judicial enquiry. Another complaint regarding service matters, especially on recruitment and promotion is a very typical one. Under the constitutional provisions the scheduled castes and scheduled tribes were given privileges and special consideration in recruitment and promotion. The very fact that they enjoyed the special privileges and consideration produced a lot of rancour, tension and violence between the employees of the scheduled categories and of the non-scheduled ones. A high railway official, a railway guard, belonging to a scheduled caste, had complained of harassment and difficulties at the hand of high caste employees throughout the five years of service. His name was contemptuously twisted to a term of abuse as SALA CHAMAR (low breed, Chamar scheduled caste brother-in-law). He was abused and assaulted by another high official of high caste, who was found guilty and was removed from service. As, however, the guard had returned the provoking assault, he was also penalized.

A complaint from a scheduled caste student residing in a hostel in Bihar, alleged that he was a victim of discrimination as an untouchable. Some high caste students had beaten him up several times because of caste prejudices. The 1965–66 report mentioned that the authorities had taken up the matter. Such cases of harassment, disparagement and abuse of the scheduled caste students at the hand of the higher caste students are not isolated phenomena. This is a direct result of the breaking up of the segregation of the scheduled castes in their own wards or quarters in a village and of the granting of special privileges in educational opportunities and financial assistance, not available to high caste students.

A ghastly case of beating up and burning, resulting in the death of a scheduled caste boy, caught red-handed while committing theft of some brass vessels, is an extreme instance of discrimination. Had he belonged to a higher caste, perhaps the villagers would not have taken this extremely severe step against a thief. According to the report of the Commissioner in 1967–68 this case from a village in Krishna district of Andhra Pradesh received wide publicity in the press and elicited a lot of sympathy and anxiety in Parliament and the accused were punished. In another case reported in 1968 from a village in Bilaspur district of Madhya Pradesh, five scheduled caste persons were killed by the higher caste Hindus as a sequal to an exchange of hot, abusive words between a *Satnami* scheduled caste creditor and an upper caste debtor. The State Government had ordered a judicial enquiry by a High Court Judge.

Such cases have their echoes also in Orissa. In the same report it was alleged that in a village of Dhenkanal district two scheduled persons were murdered and houses of the scheduled caste people set on fire. The Commissioner himself had visited the village and ascertained the facts, which occurred in November 1966. The immediate alleged cause of the extreme flare up was land and agricultural disputes including alleged theft of the standing paddy crop by the scheduled caste members. The case had come up before the courts and it was reported that the high caste Hindus were found guilty. A similar episode was reported from another village in Dhenkanal district according to the news item in the Samaj dated 1/2-12-1973. Nineteen huts of the scheduled castes were burnt, properties looted and presumably one woman was assaulted by the higher castes over a dispute regarding land and stealing of paddy crops from the fields of non-scheduled castes. It is interesting that the headman of the village council had also been arrested along with others in this arson case.

How the mere fetching of drinking water from the village tank had resulted in three deaths of scheduled caste persons including a scheduled caste head (*Sarpanch*) of the village council (*Panchayat*) in Guntur district, Andhra Pradesh, has been reported by the Commissioner in 1968–69. This happened allegedly when marriages were being celebrated in 8 houses of the scheduled castes in their segregated ward in the village and the scheduled caste ladies had gone to fetch drinking water. The high caste Hindu villagers opposed this and there was a violent clash when no attention was paid to the scheduled caste head of the council. High caste Hindus of neighbouring villages had taken up the cause of their caste men in the village and had raided the scheduled caste ward. This was the culmination of a phase of scheduled caste/ high caste conflicts and tensions, which had already resulted in the social and economic boycott of the scheduled caste people of the ward.

Even though scheduled castes have been permitted under law in various states to enter Hindu temples, two scheduled caste persons of a village in Krishna district, Andhra Pradesh, were beaten with leather slippers on 3.4.1969 by members of the Kamma high caste. The offenders were entering a village temple to offer coconut to the deity on the occasion of a marriage. The Commissioner's report of 1969–70 mentions that the accused were acquitted of the offences under the untouchability Act of 1955, though they were fined under another law of the Indian Penal Code.

An interesting case has been reported from the village of district Ujjain of Madhya Pradesh, which would not have assumed serious proportions under normal circumstances, had there been no involvement of the scheduled caste persons. A married girl, apparently not wanted at her husband's place and not actually sent back by her parents to her in-laws for the previous four years, had developed intimacy with a scheduled caste man working in her parental house. The police authority had found out that the girl had eloped with her scheduled caste paramour of her own free will. But this was enough to trigger a bloody attack on the local scheduled caste people, resulting in the cutting of noses of two men and one woman belonging to the scheduled caste. The Commissioner's report of 1969–70 mentioned the date of occurrence as 28.1.1969 and the fact that the accused were tried in a court.

Attention was drawn to a typical situation in recruitment for Government Service in the 1969–70 report. A post of Librarian reserved for a scheduled caste candidate was filled by promoting a non-scheduled caste person. The Government of India took prompt action and the post was ordered to be filled by a scheduled caste candidate.

In the 1970–71 report the Commissioner refers to the harrowing tale of the killing of 14 *Santal* scheduled tribesmen and the burning of 45 households in the *Santal Tola* or ward of Rupaspus village in Purnia district of Bihar state on 22.11.1971. The trouble was caused by the harvesting of a plot of land presumably belonging to the high caste, wealthy people. The mob of about 150 attackers were armed with guns, bows, arrows and other weapons and they had used tractors, trailers and station wagons for their transport. What is more, they had locked the houses from outside before setting fire to them. Those who tried to escape were shot. Some persons, including women and children, were roasted alive. The incident of this brutality leaked out after a week. This shook the entire nation and made the people roar with protests from all corners. The incident was condemned by everybody including the Prime Minister of India. The Chief Minister of Bihar and other ministers, and high officials and leaders of political parties visited the village and brought succour. The offenders were tried by the court, while the Government took all necessary steps to rehabilitate the families and to assure them of their safety.

The Commissioner in his 21st report for the years 1971–72 and 72–73 makes a wry comment on atrocities on, and harassment of the scheduled castes. Many of the atrocities, according to him, were committed by landlords, Government employees, including police and *Panchayat* (village council) members etc. It could be stopped if all persons realised their social obligation towards these under- privileged sections of the society.

How the apathetic villagers may tolerate atrocities on the scheduled caste people has been described by the Commissioner in this report. In Madhuban village of Saharsa district in Bihar State a boy of about 12 years belonging to a backward community of a status higher than that of the scheduled castes, had died of a snake bite. However, the bereaved family members and the superstitious villagers were made to believe that the boy died due to the sorcery of an aged scheduled caste woman, allegedly capable of such evils. Four scheduled caste women were accused of the murder and were asked to bring back life to the boy by chanting magic spells. When they pleaded their ignorance of such magic craft and their inability to resuscitate the boy, they were stripped naked and tortured with kicks, slaps and lastly with branding of their feet, arms and delicate parts. The most shameful part of the incident, according to the Commissioner, was that it went on for hours and was watched by hundreds of villagers including the elected village leaders and not a single person came forward to stop the inhuman act. The police also did not act very promptly on receipt of the news and the medical doctor at the local hospital was callous in the treatment given to the victims. This sad incident aroused the shocked conscience of Parliament, State legislature and the people in the country.

Even after conversion to Buddhism, the scheduled caste persons were treated in the same manner as before. It is reported that two neo-Buddhist women were stripped naked, after they were accused of collecting firewood from an agricultural field presumably belonging to some higher caste man. The authorities took prompt action and the offenders were sentenced to imprisonment.

A new twist in the discriminatory situation has been given in the wake of the ultra-leftist, so-called Naxalite movement of the landless oppressed against the landlords in districts of Bihar and West Bengal. The said report referred to numerous incidents of fighting and murder between the sharecroppers and landowners because of the increase of the share of the sharecropper from 50% of the harvest to 70% of the harvest. In a particular incident in village Chauri, district Bhojpur in Bihar State, 4 scheduled caste persons died as a result of police firing and 21 others were injured when a police party visited the village to arrest some alleged criminals. The Commissioner who has seen through the game has recommended that cases involving scheduled castes and scheduled tribes in the matter of land disputes be reviewed with sympathy and fairness to secure full justice to them.

Their cause has been taken up by the *Amrit Bazar Patrika*, a daily newspaper supporting the ruling party, in their issue of May 25/26, 1975.

The men folk — all branded as Naxalites — have fled away after the police and the upper caste people had unleashed a reign of terror. Their only fault was (that) they wanted justice and rights — the right to keep themselves alive, to safeguard the modesty of their women and the right to plough their fields .... The story relates to Madhuban village where, during the last week, at least 5 persons were killed in attack and counter attacks between the upper caste people and the politically indoctrinated Harijans (scheduled castes) who now believe in terrorist ideology. During the last seven months at least 4 Harijan young men were killed, five upper caste people were butchered and two police men assassinated in true medieval style. The genesis of the trouble has been traced by the newspaper report to land as the guiding factor. Soon after independence the Bihar Government took a decision to distribute land to the landless. The priority was to be given to the landless Harijans followed by scheduled caste tribe and upper caste communities. But in practice the decision was never implemented in earnest. The upper caste people in the near-by areas started grabbing lands and forced the *Harijans* to work as labourers. This is exactly what happened in Madhuban .... In 1968 the *Harijans* came to Madhuban where once jackals used to move freely in daylight. They started ploughing the lands. But the upper caste people from the near-by villages came, terrorised them and took away the land by force .... The inept government handling of this situation and the terror of the upper caste people mainly the Yadavas and the Kurmis, added to the frustration of the *Harijans* who were forced to join hands with the extremists.

It is not surprising that in Bihar things have taken this most serious turn, for the Chairman of the Parliamentary Committee for scheduled castes and scheduled tribes Mr. R. D. Basumatary, had stated in a press conference that prejudice against scheduled castes and scheduled tribes was more rampant in Uttar Pradesh and Bihar states than in other states (*The Statesman*, October 6/7, 1974.)

Although the situation has not drifted to the extreme in Orissa, unlike in Bihar, land continues to be the bone of contention. In the district of Sambalpur in the village Charmunda, the landlords are known to be evicting the scheduled caste tenants by instituting civil and even criminal cases against them. Similarly, the scheduled castes of Kaitapalli and Aainlapalli villages in the same district were being forcibly dispossessed of their validly held lands by the higher caste Hindu people. (*The Dharitri*, 23.8.1975.) It is inconceivable yet true that even in 1975 the scheduled caste villagers in West Bengal, an advanced state of India, would be attacked, their houses burnt and the women folk beaten up for a mere protest against the grazing on their paddy field of a cow owned by some non-scheduled caste people. It is alleged that the police arrested rather whimsically even some scheduled caste members who were themselves the complainants! (*The Statesman*, May 18/19.)

Because the members of the scheduled castes are poor, usually landless, and lead a hand to mouth existence, people in general suspect them of criminal habits. In the village Jandabhala of district Dhenkanal in Orissa State, some scheduled caste persons had complained to the authorities in 1970 that their higher caste co-villagers had accused some of them of stealing a radio set. They had also reported this to the police, whose officers found the accusation baseless. The villagers were angry about this decision. They thereupon closed the roads and denied the use of shops and other public utilities in order to force them to leave the village. The other villagers also decided to harass them in all possible ways. One scheduled caste man was murdered when he was coming out of the law court in connection with a case initiated by the police. Three others were also seriously injured. The murderers were sent to jail. But the scheduled caste members do not feel safe as their lives had been threatened. (Complaints registered with the Deputy Director, Backward Classes, Government of India.)

IV. Linguistic and Religious Discrimination

If by linguistic discrimination is meant an active, deliberate and aggressive denial of minimum opportunities to develop one's own language, literature and script, this is not in evidence in Orissa. There are languages like Oriya, spoken by the majority (84%), Telugu (2%), Bengali (1.5%), and Hindi (0.88%) etc. which are the vehicles of the ancient civilization of India. There are other languages spoken among the scheduled tribes. The most important of them are Kui and Kuvi (2.49%) spoken by the Kondh scheduled tribe, Oraon, Kissan and Koya spoken by the scheduled tribes belonging to the Dravidian family. The Saora (0.72%) Gadaba, Santali (1.69%), Munda, Ho (0.97%), Khadia, Mundari (0.53%), Juang and Parji languages belong to the Mundari group of Austric languages and are found only among the scheduled tribes in Orissa. While all the languages affiliated to the Indian civilization had scripts of their own, their classical and folk literature, the tribal languages did not have any script nor any written published literature till recently, when the Santal developed their own ol script and the Saora created a script of their own. These two tribal languages with newly emergent scripts and especially Santali have quite an impressive corpus of published literature in their languages and, a few in their scripts as well.

While there is tension, leading to alleged manipulation of Census figures along the borders of Orissa and Andhra Pradesh between the Oriya speakers and substantial Telugu speakers, there is no such tension in other parts of the state on linguistic grounds. But there is a feeling on the part of the tribal leaders representing those tribes which speak either a Mundari or a Dravidian language, that the young children would have fared better and the drop-outs would have been much less, if instruction were imparted through the medium of tribal languages. The State Government has been considering this question on the advice of the anthropologists, linguists and educationists during the last decade. The prevailing opinion endorsed the desirability of providing text books in tribal languages with tribal cultural contents as illustrative materials and for solving problems encountered in tribal day-to-day life for the young children in the first two years at the primary school. However, the script has, of necessity, to be Oriya as further education in high school and also college education is carried on in the regional language of Oriya. The Government, however, gives grants to the tribal institutions for propagating tribal literature printed in any script they like.

So far as the linguistic communities are concerned, they have no difficulty in running their own schools using their mother tongue as media of instruction. There are Bengali medium schools. Telugu medium schools, Hindi and Gujarati medium schools to cater for their needs. At the University level, a student can appear for his M.A. Degree in many of the Modern Indian languages represented in Orissa.

Among the religions of Orissa, Hinduism is professed by 96.25% of the total population, Islam by 1.49%, Christianity by 1.73%, Sikhism by 0.04%, Buddhism by 0.04%, and Jainism by 0.03%. Other religions and persuasions in which tribal religions are also included claim 0.42% of the total population. It is plausible that the tribal people have returned themselves overwhelmingly as either Hindu or Christian, but not necessarily sticking to their own tribal religions. This may be clearly inferred from a comparison of the population strength as ethnic groups with the number of adherents under other religions and persuasions. The population of the scheduled tribes in the whole state constitutes 23.11% of the total population, whereas adherents of other religions and persuasions constitute only 0.42% of the total population.

Though there is no direct interference in the pursuit of one's religion, cults, sects, or rituals, the general population by habit regard the Hindu Gods, Hindu festivals or Hindu rituals as something natural or normal for Orissa. Orissa was the last important Hindu State to hold out against the Islamic domination from the North. As the Muslims of Orissa were overwhelmingly of local ethnic stock, they had their local cultural moorings rather deep and co-operated with their Hindu neighbours on all occasions. There was a very cordial relationship between the two religious communities even during the worst days of communal passions at the time of the division of the country into India and Pakistan. Even some of the Moslem devotees had accepted Lord Jagannath, the supreme deity of Orissa as their saviour, and are revered by the people of Orissa as His great devotees. The Hindus and Muslims in Orissa had established ritual relationships enduring over generations (Mahapatra, 1968a).

In spite of this mutual tolerance extending over centuries of co-existence, there had been disturbing influences from inside or outside the country and violent communal rioting erupted in the year 1969 to widen the natural cleavage that always existed between the two religious groups. But so far as filling posts in the Government or positions in the professions or occupations are concerned, the Muslim people have gained a nice slice of the opportunities available to all on the basis of merit. Because they have filled many niches in the economic sphere, especially in trade and business, the general population not so adept in business acumen, cannot challenge or outdo them.

The Christian converts from the local population, especially from the lower castes and classes, had long enjoyed the patronage of the British regime and the foreign missionaries had done a lot to uplift the downtrodden in an exemplary manner. Those of them who are in the towns and have got themselves educated and have entered the administration, professions or business, have been a model to be emulated by the general educated public. The foreign Christian missionaries are held in even greater admiration, because of their selfless service and devotion to the cause of the suffering and the depressed sections of the population. The workers in villages and tribal areas, teachers and administrators are exhorted to exhibit "Missionary spirit" and to emulate the Missionaries. But there is one aspect of the work of the foreign as well as Indian missionaries which aroused bitterness in the minds of men who should ensure the freedom to preach Christianity or any other religion. It was found that the missionaries did not always convert the tribals, the scheduled castes, the destitute and other members of the vulnerably weak sections in the population after getting their consent to change religion as a matter of conviction and deep faith. Many times it was found to be cases of constraint or financial and other considerations. In order to ensure that the conversions to Christianity were genuine cases of conviction and not of constraint or considerations the Orissa Legislature passed an act to that effect in recent years.

So far as the Buddhists, the Jains and their places of worship are concerned, the Hindu always revered their Gods and have great respect for these religions especially in Orissa. Because, the first most famous conqueror King of Orissa was a Jain, the king Kharabela, and the supreme deity of Orissa, Lord Jagannath, who embodies the ninth incarnation of Lord Vishnu, is widely believed to have the sacred tooth of Lord Buddha enshrined inside the image. While in 1953 this author was a personal witness to the discriminatory ban on the entry of the Chinese Buddhists into the temple of Lord Jagannath, by 1960, however, the Chinese and Japanese Buddhists were allowed entrance to the innermost sanctum.

By nature, Hinduism has been greatly tolerant of other religious faiths and practices. As Hinduism has many levels of continuities with the regional tribal religions, from which it must have drawn a lot of its contents in Orissa, there was no occasion for religious discrimination against the tribal peoples of Orissa. The tribal village Goddesses and animal sacrifices, beliefs in sorcery and witchcraft, deities of the forests, mountains, rivers and groves, votive offerings – these and others – were shared by the tribal religions with Hinduism in Orissa. There are many deities of regional or of national importance derived from the originally tribal cults. The most famous of these is the Jagannath cult of Orissa, centering on the deity of the alleged '*Savara*' Lord Lingaraj at Bhubaneswar, and Lord Nrusingha (man-lion incarnation of Lord Vishnu) at Simbachalam in the former Orissa territory (now lying in Andhra Pradesh), are similarly alleged to be tribal deities of the '*Savara*.' No wonder, then, that many of the tribal groups are more or less Hinduized or have shown great inclination to be the votaries of Hinduism. Not a little has been contributed by those members of the higher castes, who had taken their abode in the interior tribal areas, by integrating themselves in the religious faith, lore, and rituals of the dominant tribals, like the Kondh and the Saora, amongst whom they have lived for generations.

V. Protective Discrimination and Compensatory Privileges

> The state shall promote with special care the educational and economic interests of the weaker sections of the people and, in particular of the Scheduled Castes and the Scheduled Tribes, and shall protect them from social injustice and all forms of exploitation. (Article 46 of the Constitution of India)

The welfare state in India as shaped by the independent constitution, was used by those who had struggled to gain freedom for India, as a very powerful instrument to bring a backward state like India into the forefront of the modern world by virtue of its moral stature in the true

Gandhian spirit. The state policy, designed after the constitution, was to bring the tribal groups and the former untouchable castes into the main stream of national life by securing some special privileges, economic, administrative and parliamentary, in about 10 years ending in 1960. This date has been shifted to 1980.

Considering the poverty and scarce means in the country a lot of funds were placed in the hands of the Federal and State Governments for what has been obliquely referred to as "protective discrimination." This was merely to counter discrimination inherent in the centuries-old oppression, exploitation or deprivation of the weaker sections. The protective discrimination more or less the unhindered progress of the neglected or dispossessed scheduled castes and scheduled tribes in particular. In a physical sense protection from the exploiters and oppressors from the plains in the tribal belts was a great boon. But the scheduled castes living dispersed mostly amongst the general population, cannot be insulated so physically. Even then, many of the protective laws and compensatory privileges have benefitted them immensely.

It has been found even during British days that education was a great catalytic agent for injecting a sense of self-respect, self-confidence and for opening some access to opportunities for increasing one's secular status via new occupations. Moreover, educational institutions were one of the first fields in which the children of the privileged and the deprived classes studied together and interacted more or less as equals. Untouchability was greatly challenged and subdued by such attendance of common classes and residence in common hostels. Moreover, education equipped the weaker sections to check the rapacity or oppression by the higher castes in authority or with an economic stranglehold. That is why, the Government after Independence considered provision of facilities for education as the most important instrument for the wellbeing of these weaker sections. Besides, there are scholarships available to all students from scheduled castes and scheduled tribes categories in both pre-matriculation and University stages of education, there have been book-grants, mid-day meals and uniforms in the school years, exemption from payment of tuition fees and examination fees in all stages, reservation of seats in schools, colleges, universities and technical institutions, provision of separate hostels and reservation of seats in general hostels, special coaching for competitive administrative examinations and provision of adult education in the interior tribal areas. During the 5th five year plan (1974–79) the Government of Orissa has chalked out a subplan for intensive development of tribal areas in Orissa. That progress in education has not been uniform or increasing from year to year is clear from the following facts about the scheduled castes in Orissa and India as a whole. The percentages of enrolment of scheduled castes students to total enrolment of students were 13.0 in 1967–68 and 12.8 in 1968–69 in Orissa, whereas in India as a whole the same percentages were 10.8 for 1967–68 and 10.3 for 1968–69. Therefore, there was a decrease of 0.2% in Orissa and a decrease of 0.5% in India as a whole, and in all this Orissa fared better than the Indian average. The rate of literacy in Orissa has, however, increased from 11.6% in 1961 to 15.6% 1971 among the scheduled castes and from 7.4% in 1961 to 9.5% in 1971 among the scheduled tribes. Thrown into a larger perspective in space as well as in time, we find the literacy rate of the scheduled castes in 1931 to be 1.9% as against the general literacy of 9.5% of India as a whole. This rose to 14.71% for the scheduled castes in 1971 against the general literacy of 29% in India.

In the sphere of economic development which is a sure antidote to exploitation and oppression, scheduled castes and tribes are encouraged by the Government to take to improved methods of agriculture through the programmes of demonstration farms, distribution of improved agricultural implements, and agricultural loans etc. etc. Similarly, institutional arrangements have been made to develop their cottage industry, marketing and credit, to grant industrial licenses and import and export licenses, to award contracts in various Government Departments and for establishment of other financial and industrial agencies for their economic development, housing etc. Their age-old debts extending over the past few generations have been recently cancelled by a Government decree and they are now, under another Act, free from any form of bonded labour or a sort of serfdom to the higher castes or those who were economically powerful. The lands released by stricter land reforms, during the 1970's are being distributed among the landless and nominal peasants. Special provisions have similarly been made for the development of health services in tribal areas and among the scheduled caste population. In Orissa as in many other States a Cell has been created in the Police Department to deal with cases of untouchability, harassment and atrocities against the scheduled castes, with all seriousness and alacrity. Again a special Cell is being set up under the direct supervision of the Governor of Orissa State to look into the grievances of the scheduled castes, scheduled tribes and other minorities. Under the Constitution, the Governor of a State has been charged with special responsibilities to safeguard the interests of scheduled tribes and scheduled castes.

It is to be noted that the protection and the privileges granted under the Constitution by the Government, Government managed institutions, and under Government directives, by private enterprise and institutions, have been accepted but not without a lot of resentment, jealousy, tension and even organized agitation by the general population. In a competitive world where population pressure is high and opportunities and means are very limited, there is very little room for magnanimity, compassion or even regret. When India's enlightened leadership exhorts the general population to extend to these weaker sections the privileges in compensation for the past neglect, discrimination, deprivation or exploitation, the general population cannot but view these privileges and protective measures as discrimination against themselves, against merit and against the very principles of a modern achieving society. Therefore, it is not at all strange to find the non-scheduled population of the Punjab State organizing an Association for safeguarding their own interests against the protective discrimination by the Government in favour of the scheduled castes and scheduled tribes.

In fact, this Association harks back to the famous parallel organization of the Self-Respect Movement and the Justice Party of the disinherited lower and lowest castes in self defence against the high castes, especially the Brahmin in the 1920's in the former Madras Presidency.

Orissa has the unique position as the pioneer in legislating against filling of posts by non-scheduled persons, when posts are reserved for scheduled tribes and scheduled castes. This legislation of 1975 has been hailed as a turning point in protective discrimination in favour of the scheduled castes and the scheduled tribes.

VI. Prospects of Integration

Hindsight is not always a safe guide for reliable prognosis. Yet, that is almost always the only means with which the social sciences may claim to discern the sustained trends of future development. Therefore, it is useful to go back to 1929 when the Indian Statutory Commission, commonly known as the Simon Commission had appointed the Auxiliary Committee, whose reports speak a lot about the prevailing conditions in those days.

When the British Government started publicly financed schools for all classes of the Indian population, when they abolished the caste privileges and the right of the caste council to ostracise its members, when they secured equality of all men before the law, abolishing the concessions in punishment for the Brahmin and others under Hindu Law, and when they created institutional mechanisms to protect the interests of the oppressed classes and of the primitive tribes, decisive steps were then taken for the cause of integration of the deprived sections with the general population in India. This is not to say that there were no forces of integration of these primitive tribes and Depressed Classes in the traditional structure of Indian society (cf. Bose, Ghurye). Under the traditional processes and mechanisms has the large majority of tribes become positively oriented towards Hindu Society, culture and religious since time immemorial. During the British regime a new, expanding, capitalistic economy could absorb the spurt in population, de-anchoring of castes from their traditional occupations and migration of thousands of surplus manpower of under-privileged classes to plantations and industries inside and outside the country. Even then, for the large majority of the masses of the depressed classes the life chances did not improve very much in the villages. In 1929 according to the report of the Auxiliary Committee.

In certain areas, an untouchable still causes pollution by presence as well as by contact and many of the public roads and wells cannot be used in daylight by the Depressed Classes. Publicly managed schools are not infrequently located on sites which are entirely inaccessible to Depressed Classes, and even in those areas in which their children are admitted to the ordinary schools it often happens that the Depressed Class pupils are made to sit separately in the class room or even outside the school building.

By the late 1920's there were two types of schools: the ordinary school and the schools for the backward or Depressed Classes. Quite a large number of the Depressed Classes or "Exterior Castes" were reading in the ordinary schools and a large number of general students were also studying in those schools maintained for the Depressed Classes. As a result of encouragement by the Government to the pupils of the Depressed Classes education spread rather fast and caste prejudices were reported to be gradually disappearing. Two trends have been noted very early in this report,

In the Central Provinces progress has been very slow but two tendencies have become increasingly manifest during the quinquennium. First, the Depressed Classes have a growing consciousness of their educational and social disabilities and a growing assertion of claims to social and political recognition. The second tendency has been the growing recognition on the part of the more advanced classes of the claims of the Depressed Classes.

The second tendency was to a large extent engendered through the herculean efforts made by Mahatma Gandhi, whose non-violence movement was also directed at the inside violence within the Hindu society as expressed through discrimination against the untouchable castes.

The institution of popularly elected Government in the provinces and at the Centre under the 1935 Constitution of India gave further evidence of the aroused conscience of the general public for the welfare and integration of the primitive tribes and Exterior Castes in the general Indian body politic. Although in other parts of India, the Nationalist Movement, especially of the Indian National Congress, was alleged to be dominated by the Brahmin and other high castes, in Orissa, however, many members of the Depressed Castes and Tribes jumped into the Nationalist resistance movement. They are given today the national honour of being the martyrs or the freedom fighters. After Independence, members of the scheduled castes and scheduled tribes were given a lot more facilities and special privileges in new spheres, and were given much more than their population strength warrants. As the five year plans progress and as the financial outlay increases from one plan to the next, the special opportunities, privileges and protective prohibitions increase in variety, quantum and impact. All this points to the heightening of the desire and the resolve of the general population to make good the loss in time and opportunities for bringing the backward brethren into the main stream of national life as fast as possible.

Even with the best intentions and the firmest resolve of the post-independence leaders of India, the discrimination in public life of being a tribal or a scheduled caste has not yet vanished. Some social scientists assert that it has been always very difficult for an untouchable caste to gain entry to the higher status in Hindu society, at which level his physical contact will not defile a high caste Hindu in ritual terms. That is, there is an impassable barrier in their upward status mobility. It is, however, not so difficult for an untouchable caste of the lowest grade or a lower grade to secure a higher status among the untouchable castes in a region. They may have their own priests, temples and rituals, and they have them now in plenty; but so far as the masses in villages are concerned, there is, according to them, no indication that they have ever crossed the Rubicon. For an educated member of the scheduled castes or scheduled tribes, when occupying an important position in the political, administrative or economic spheres, social acceptability has increased, even commensality on public occasions has been accepted, but the sphere of incommunicability including untouchability has not been eliminated. If it has been eliminated completely, at least in most parts of India as in Orissa, it is with regard to distance pollution, and untouchability in educational and other public institutions and places of work, in public transport and in places of public recreation. In the last mentioned sphere, the least expected may turn up as the long shadow of vanishing history. A scheduled caste boy in a village in Gulbarga District of Karnatak State was harassed and assaulted with leather slippers by some caste Hindus merely for the indiscretion of handing over a gift to the manager of a drama troupe in appreciation of a play it had staged (*The Statesman*, June 12/13, 1974). However, when 296 scheduled caste students of Uttar Pradesh were asked by social scientists (Chauhan *et al.*, p. 81) only 13 mentioned that either they themselves or members of their families had experienced ill-treatment because of their belonging to scheduled castes. The same study also refers to 12% of scheduled caste students having non-scheduled caste boys as their first best friends, 19% of them as their second best friends, and 24% as their third best friends, even though there was a concentration of homophily (*ibid*).

But it is yet too early or too much to expect a social revolution of an erstwhile untouchable caste being considered a commensal or conjugal associate by the high castes. If in the land of Mahatma Gandhi, Gujarat State cash rewards for a marriage between a scheduled caste and caste Hindu go unclaimed year after year, if in that state right in those villages which had received awards for the complete eradication of untouchability within their bounderies untouchability continues to exist (Sachchidananda, p. 297), it is not to be wondered at. Inter-caste marriage as well as untouchability are hard nuts to crack in the caste system. Even a recent case of inter-caste marriage in a village in Balasore district of Orissa State between an educated Warrior caste bridgegroom and a lower Weaver caste (non-scheduled) educated bride, resulted in the ostracization of the bridegroom's family and the eventual ritual incorporation of the bride into the warrior caste by way of expiation of the 'sin' of inter-marriage (*The Samaj*, 24/25-2-1975).

But it is also not true, much against the recent pronouncements of some social scientists, that it is not at all possible for erstwhile untouchable castes to succeed in securing higher status by marrying or dining with higher castes. The *Pulaya* untouchables of Kerala State are a case in point. They were formerly slaves, later on became bond serfs of the higher castes. At present literacy among *Pulaya* children is almost one hundred percent.

A large number of *Pulayas* said that high caste people accept food from their houses. There have been cases of marriage between *Pulayas* and high castes. (Sachchidananda, p. 289, based on Alexander.)

Another Kerala untouchable caste, the *Irava*, began their agitation back in 1911 to abolish distance pollution, and a decade later, they started an agitation for temple entry. Nowadays the *Irava* are looked upon as an advanced caste in Kerala. (Sachchidananda, pp. 287–88 based on Aiyappan). The *Ezhava* caste of toddy tappers (originally untouchable) gained higher caste status through a reform movement under a spiritualist, Narayan Guru's leadership (Sachchidananda, p. 280). Orenstein (1965) refers to the change towards higher status of untouchables after the famous 1942 struggle of Mahatma Gandhi to make the British 'quit India,' and "all people permitted the *Harijans* to enter their houses" in his area of study in Maharashtra State (Sachchidananda, p. 288). In a similar vein, Silversten (1963) gives importance to the vigorous campaign carried out by the workers of various political parties, wooing the scheduled caste electorate for their political support, backed by the welfare activities of the administration, and he discerns radical changes in the status of the untouchables. They have joined a union of cultivators to fight for their right against the landlords. Other castes in the union have conceded their claim to equal status (Sachchidananda, pp. 288–89). The *Vannan* washermen of Tamil Nadu have similarly changed their status after starting cooperatives and laundries and are no longer untouchable. (Sachchidananda, p. 291; Census, 1968.)

All these cases barring the exceptional *Ezhava* show that secular achievements (education, new occupations, affluences or secular alignments for higher economic gains) have contributed a lot towards changing the status of the untouchables and integrating them with the larger society. It is also not uncommon to change the name of one's caste or even surname from one connoting the low status of an untouch-

able caste to one signifying high caste status. The social mobility movements by adopting higher caste norms and eschewing the despised or
low grade customs or institutions have similarly benefitted many
scheduled castes (Census 1970).

Only one section of the Scheduled Castes, the *Mahar* of Maharashtra
State, had disavowed their affiliation to the Hindu society and had set
out to form a new society of Neo-Buddhists under the leadership of Dr.
Ambedkar. But that has not spread to other groups, though it has
presumably encouraged the emergence of militant youth and pressure
groups on the models of the "Black Panther" Movement of U.S.A.

There is not much room for doubt that as at present and in the foreseeable future, most of the former untouchables are rather positively
oriented towards integration with the Hindu society despite the horrid
atrocities by the higher caste Hindus here and there.

The scheduled tribes present a much clearer picture, although they
are more marginal to the general population. Those tribes who inhabited South India or Central and Eastern India, and have had centuries of intimate interaction with their Hindu neighbours and share
even the Hindu values of untouchability towards other castes and
tribes, are too much Hinduized to think of any other orientation. The
Gond and the *Bhuiyan* of Orissa are the cases in point. Large sections of
other tribes in Orissa, Bihar and Madhya Pradesh gravitate also in the
same direction, despite the protective discrimination and compensatory privileges awarded to them *qua* scheduled tribes. Even their change
of religion to Christianity does not take them away from their identification with and sense of participation in, the Indian condition and fate.
These may form at best some sub-nationalist aspirations to form a
tribal-dominated state in Orissa and Bihar or in Gujarat. They already
shared so much with the ordinary peasants in these areas that they cannot just turn back and run away from the rest of the country, whether
they are Christianized or Hinduized (cf. Mahapatra, 1968). The numerous *Santal*, spread in the States of Bihar, Orissa, West Bengal and
Assam in the industries or plantations, rather advanced in educational
and economic status, with a rich history of resistance to exploitation
and oppression in the past, may have changed perceptibly from emulation of the Hindu high castes to forge solidarity among themselves and
with other cognate tribes to spearhead the movement for a separate
tribal state. But this is evidently an exception. In the north-eastern
borders of India, the *Naga* tribes, *Mizo* and *Kuki* tribes, communicating
freely with their compatriots on the other side of the borders within

Burma, have been inspired by the fluid frontiers and some doses of foreign help, to turn to insurgency for creating one or more homelands. The ecological setting allowing little or no intimate interactions with the plains people of Assam and Tripura, has been the real basis for their clamour for an independent homeland. But as of 1975, the insurgents have come to realize the utility of their participation in the Indian Republic and the futility of their prolonged insurgency. Hence, there are political parleys going on to bring about reconciliation.

The Government of Indian Union and the States are aware and ashamed of the long-standing neglect and delay in integrating the scheduled castes and scheduled tribes. In the five year plan determined efforts are being made in this direction, so much so that in comparison with 680 million Rupees spent on the welfare of the scheduled castes during the 4th five year plan, 2250 million are slated to be used in this sphere during the 5th five year plan. Greater emphasis is being placed on the improvement of the living conditions and securing their emotional attachment by good behaviour towards them, rather than on the penal sections. The Home Minister of India has spoken out with a sense of urgency.

Members of the scheduled Castes and Scheduled Tribes should be completely integrated with the rest of (the) society. Nothing should happen which could create tension among people of different castes. (*The Statesman*, October 14/15, 1975.)

If this measures the strength of the official winds in favour of integration, and knowledge of the efforts of the scheduled castes and tribes point towards the same end, integration in the foreseeable future does not appear to be a figment of imagination.

Acknowledgements

The author is grateful to his former Research Assistant, Miss Ranjana Roy, P. K. Mishra, Lecturer in Anthropology, Khallikote College, Berhampur (Ganjam), P. K. Nayak, at present Research Assistant, Department of Anthropology, Utkal University, the Deputy Director, Backward Classes Welfare, Government of India and the Deputy Director, Tribal and Harijan Research-cum-Training Institute, Government of Orissa, for their unstinted help in preparation of this paper.

REFERENCES

Aiyappan, A., *Social Revolution in a Kerala Village*, Asia Publishing House, Bombay, 1966.

Alexander, K. C., "Changing Status of Pulaya Harijans of Kerala," *Economic and Political Weekly*, July, 1968, Special Number, pp. 1071–1075.

Bose, N. K., *Culture and Society in India*, Asia Publishing House, Calcutta, 1967.

Census of India, Vannan-Scheduled Caste of Madras, Part V–B (IV), Registrar General of India, New Delhi, 1968.

—, Social Mobility Movements among scheduled Castes and Scheduled Tribes of India, New Delhi, 1970.

—, A Portrait of Population: Orissa, Series 16, Controller of Publications, Delhi, 1971.

Chauhan, B. R., G. Narayana, & T. N. Singh, *Scheduled Castes and Education*, Anu Prakashan, Meerut, 1975.

Commissioner of Scheduled Castes and Tribes, Annual Reports, Government of India, New Delhi, 1951, 1957–73.

Ghurye, G. S., *The Aborigines So-called and Their Future*, Gokhale Institute of Politics and Economics, Bombay, 1943.

Government of India, Progress of Welfare and Development of Scheduled Castes, Ministry of Home Affairs, New Delhi, 1975.

Government of Orissa 1975, Sub-plan for Tribal Regions of Orissa 1974–79, (Draft), Department of Tribal and Rural Welfare, Bhubaneswar.

Kulke, H., "'Kshatriyaization' and Social Change in Post-Medieval Orissa," *Changing India*, ed. D. S. Pillai, Popular Prakashau, Bombay, 1974.

Mahapatra, L. K., "Social Movements among tribes of Eastern India with special reference to Orissa," *Sociologus*, Vol. XVIII, No. 1, 1968.

—, "Ritual Kinship in Orissa," Papers of 8th International Congress of Anthropological and Ethnological Sciences, Tokyo-Kyoto, 1968a.

—, "Role of the Hindu Princes in the Caste System," National Lectures Sponsored by University Grants Commission, unpublished, 1970.

—, "Patron-Client Relations," National Lectures Sponsored by University Grants Commission, unpublished, 1970a.

Mahatab, H. K., Beginning of the End, Students' Store, Cuttack, 1954.

Orenstein, H., *Gaon: Conflict and Cohesion in an Indian Village*, Princeton University Press, Princeton, 1965.

Sachchidananda, "Research on Scheduled Castes with special reference to Change — A Trend Report," in A Survey of Research in Sociology and Social Anthropology, Vol. I, Indian Council of Social Science Research, New Delhi, Popular Prakashan, Bombay, 1974.

Silversten, D., *When Caste Barriers Fall — A Study of Social and Economic Change in a South Indian Village*, Allen & Unwin, London, 1963.

A Christian Minority: The Copts in Egypt

Y. MASRIYA

Y. MASRIYA is the pseudonym of an Egyptian woman writer who was obliged to leave her native country in the fifties. She knows the problems discussed in this article from personal observation and from scholarly research.

A Christian Minority: The Copts in Egypt

Y. MASRIYA

The clashes which broke out in 1972 between Christian Copts and Muslims in Egypt prompted the Egyptian government to set up a parliamentary commission of enquiry to investigate the causes of these disturbances which had begun in 1971.

According to the official report, they "were the result of tensions aroused by a strong religious undercurrent, tinged by fanaticism."[1] According to the same report, one of the causes of the unrest was a law, passed in 1934, which permitted churches to be built only if ten conditions were fulfilled, one of which was the absence of any mosque in the vicinity. In practice, however, no sooner was any plot of land set aside for the building of a church than a mosque was immediately erected nearby, thereby dashing the hopes of the Christian community.

The Coptic population numbers about six million today out of a total Egyptian population of approximatively forty million.

I. THE PAST

The Copts descend from the early Egyptian Christians. Before the Arab invasion, Egypt was a province of the Byzantine Empire. Egypt's inhabitants were primarily Christians and the land was covered with numerous churches and monasteries.

At the end of the second century, the famous Catechetical School of theology and exegesis of early Christianity was founded in Alexandria, then the centre of Hellenistic culture. It was renowned due to the writings and teachings of Pantaenus, Clement of Alexandria and

This article was originally published, the 19th January 1973, by the Centre d'Information et de Documentation sur le Moyen-Orient (Geneva, Switzerland). This is an enlarged, revised and corrected English translation of that text.

Origen who opposed Hellenistic paganism. After Alexandria became the spiritual capital of Christianity, cœnobitic life extended into the desert along the valley of the Nile and deep into the oases. Communities of anchorites and monks were founded under the leadership of Paul, Anthony and Pachomius. The latter (292–346) established the monastic rules and vows that were to serve as a model for the religious orders of Europe in the Middle-Ages. In 323 Constantin the Great declared Christianity the state religion of the Byzantine Empire. Religious strife broke out throughout the Empire between pagans, Christians and heretics. The national struggle of Egypt against the Byzantine yoke took a religious form. The Church of Alexandria, orthodox at first, later adopted the monophysite heresy (one nature of Christ) and fought against the Byzantine orthodox church. At the time of the Arab conquest, Egypt was the scene of bloody religious battles between the Melchites, followers of Byzantium, and the more numerous Jacobites, adherents of the monophysite doctrine.

In 640, the Egyptians welcomed the Arab conquerors as liberators come to deliver them from Greek tyranny. The Arab army of occupation made no changes in the administration of the conquered territories and the Copts retained their posts. But this tolerance was due to the particular circumstances of the conquest – the necessity for the Arab army to control a large Christian population – and was short-lived. In fact, the relations between the Arab army and the subjected indigenous population changed as the Arab domination grew firmer and became an irreversible phenomenon of history as a result of the elaboration of a system of colonisation: the *dhimma*.

Originally, the dhimma was the treaty concluded between Muhammed and those he subdued. The tolerant character of these pacts, defining the obligations and duties which bound the indigenous populations to the conquering Arab Muslims, determined the sedentary populations of the towns and villages to capitulate before the advancing Bedouin armies. In theory, the lives and property – as well as religious liberty – were guaranteed to those who accepted this pact, on the condition that they did not transgress any of its stipulations; but very soon the interpretation and the application of its conditions transformed the dhimma into a codified system of legal tyranny, spiritual in theory, but which in practice often led to physical genocide and was at the base of the arabization and islamization of the Christian Orient. Its evolution, in the course of centuries, was governed throughout by the irrefutable belief in the superiority of Islam and in its universal supremacy. The following words are attributed to the Caliph Mu'Awia:

I found that the people of Egypt were of three sorts, one-third men, one-third like men, and one-third not men, i.e. Arabs, converted foreigners, and those who pretend to be Muslims, the Copts.[2]

II. The Pact of 'Umar

The *Pact of 'Umar*, generally attributed to 'Umar II (717-740), regulated the discriminatory status imposed upon the *dhimmis*, i.e. the non-Muslim native population living under the domination of Islam. They had to pay the *jizya*, a poll tax, symbolizing their subjection to Islam and also higher commercial taxes than were paid by the Muslims. The ownership of their land passed to the Muslim community and in order to have the right to cultivate it they had to pay a special land tax, the *kharāj*. Very often, whole communities were burdened with arbitrary impositions. At the beginning of the conquest, the Muslim occupants paid no taxes and therefore the Arab State and army were subsidized by the non-Muslim peasants and town dwellers.

The construction of new churches or the restoration of old ones, as well as the use of bells, banners, sacred books, crosses on churches or borne in procession, and any other non-Muslim cult-object were prohibited. So as not to disturb Muslims, the dhimmis had to hold their services in silence and abstain from lamentation at funerals. The social discrimination of the dhimmis and their exigency for security compelled them to live in separate areas. Their inferior and humble dwellings and tombs had to differ from those of the Muslims in size and decay. Marriage, sexual intercourse with a Muslim woman, blasphemy against Islam, were punishable by death. Relations between dhimmis and Muslims were forbidden, but as this proved impracticable, relations were strongly discouraged. The dhimmis were not allowed to exercise any authority over a Muslim and could not testify in a legal tribunal against him. Their movements were restricted and they had to go unarmed.

As the dhimmis were inferior to the Muslim, so they had to differ from him in their outward appearance – for instance in early Islam Christians had to shave their brows. They were denied the use of certain colours – e.g. green, which was the colour of the Prophet – and were forbidden to wear the clothes, belts, shoes and turbans worn by Muslims. Numerous decrees regulated in detail the colours, shape of

clothes, ill-fitting and ridiculous head-dress, belts and shoes that the
dhimmis and their slaves were obliged to wear so as to be easily recognized and humiliated in the streets. A little bell around the neck, or a
similar distinctive sign, made them recognizable at the public baths.
Noble mounts such as horses and camels were reserved for Muslims,
the dhimmis being only allowed to ride donkeys and use pack-saddles.
In some periods they were forbidden to ride their donkeys within the
towns, in other periods the Christians were humiliated by being forced
to ride their donkeys facing the tail.

Other vexatory measures also governed their every-day life, such as
the obligation to stand up and remain standing in the presence of
Muslims, to address them in low and humble tones and give them right
of way on the pavement by walking along the narrowest section of the
street, on their left side – the impure side for a Muslim. The dhimmis
could not relieve themselves naturally in the streets, nor assemble in
groups to converse. For a more detailed study of the life of the dhimmi
(Jews and Christians in Muslim lands the reader should consult the
authoritative monographs on this subject.[3]

The jizya was paid in the course of a ceremony during which the
dhimmi was publicly humiliated by receiving a slap in the face or a
blow on the back of the neck. The dhimmi was then issued with a
receipt which allowed him to travel; however, should he lose it, he
could be put to death. When a census was taken of monks in Egypt
(715–717) they were obliged to wear a metal bracelet bearing their
name and the date and name of their monastery. Any monk found
without his bracelet was liable to have his hand cut off or be executed.

The kharāj, the tax on non-Muslim land, reduced the Copts to
destitution: they abandoned their fields and mass conversions occured,
but they were forcibly brought back by the army and obliged to pay
the taxes (694–714). To prevent the Copts from abandoning their villages, the Arab army conducted a census and branded them on the
hand and brow (705–717). No Christian could travel without a passport. Boats on the Nile which carried a Christian without a passport
were set on fire. In 724, 24,000 Copts converted to Islam to escape
ruinous taxes. The conversions impoverished the State and to discourage them, the jizya was also imposed on new converts. Furthermore, they were forbidden to sell their lands to Muslims, as these lands
would then have been exempt from the kharāj; later a fixed sum was
levied on the Coptic community which covered any lost revenues from
new converts. At the beginning of the 8th century, Usame Ben Zaid,

Governor of Egypt, wrote to Caliph Abdel Malik (715–717): "I draw milk; if it stops, I draw blood; if it clots, I press the skin." The same caliph used to say: "Draw milk until it ceases to flow, draw blood until it is exhausted."

In Tinnis, taxes reduced the Copts to such destitution that they abandoned their children in slavery to the Arabs.[4] Those who did not pay were thrown into jail or tortured. Under the Abbasids, the dhimmis who could not pay their taxes were put into cages with wild animals. The church leaders were often held responsible for the sums levied on the community. Unable to pay, they were thrown into jail and tortured. Around 718, Abdel Malik ben Rifa'a, Governor of Egypt, had the Patriarch Michael thrown into a windowless cell dug into the rock, a block of wood attached to his feet and a heavy collar put around his neck. He remained in this position for 31 days until the required sum was paid. The exorbitant taxes and the tortures used to extort them provoked numerous revolts which were brutally crushed. Thousands of Copts were killed, women and children enslaved, their property expropriated by the Arabs who thus became more numerous in towns and villages.[5]

As the Pact of 'Umar forbade the dhimmis to exert any authority over a Muslim, they could not become civil servants nor join the army. In every period, numerous decrees resulted in the dismissal of Christians from the posts they held unless they converted to Islam. However, the Copts were indispensable as all the Egyptian bureaucracy was in their hands. The Muslims accused them of purposely trying to complicate the administration in order to retain their posts. These deviations from the dhimma provoked riots: the mob would then plunder the Christian quarter, massacre the Copts and destroy their churches.

In every period, monasteries and churches were despoiled, burned and destroyed. The Caliph Al Hakim (996–1020) renewed the clauses of the Pact of 'Umar. All the churches and synagogues in his Empire (Egypt, Syria, Palestine) were then looted and demolished – or converted into Mosques. The mob pillaged the Christian and Jewish quarters and the caliph forced the dhimmis to convert or leave his dominions. At the end of his reign, he allowed them to return to their religion and to rebuild their places of worship. In 1058, all churches were closed, the patriarch and the bishops thrown into jail and the Copts ransomed for 70,000 dirams. The slightest incident could provoke a massacre. In 1377, the mob was incensed at the sight of a Christian maltreating a Muslim and immediately clamoured for the

dismissal of Christian and Jewish public servants in the service of the
Emirs and then for their conversion or death. The Christians went into
hiding, but the mob ransacked their quarter, massacred them and forced
the women into slavery. Some Christians were grouped in a horse-
market; a pit was dug into which they were to be thrown and it was set
alight: all converted to Islam.[6] A Christian was riding by the Al-
Azhar Mosque, his spurs and handsome saddle angered the Muslims
who pursued him with the intention of killing him. Riots broke out,
forcing the Sultan to summon the leaders of the Jewish and Christian
communities and remind them that they were subject to the shame and
humiliation of the dhimma. When they left the Sultan, they were attacked by the mob which tore their clothes and beat them until they
agreed to apostasy. Stakes were set alight for the Jews and for the
Christians. The churches and the houses of dhimmis that rose higher
than those of the Muslims were destroyed. The dhimmis even feared to
go out into the streets. In 1343, Christians were accused of starting fires
in Cairo; in spite of the Sultan's efforts to protect them, they were
seized in the street, burned or slaughtered by the mob as it left the
mosques. Anti-Christian violence raged in the main towns. To enable
the Christians to go out into the streets, Jews would sometimes lend
them their distinctive yellow turban.

The history of the Copts is a lengthy tale of persecutions, massacres,
forced conversions, of devastated and burned churches. Thousands of
Copts fled to Abyssinia, but the greater part found refuge by accepting
Islam.

III. The Present

The founder of modern Egypt, Muhammed Ali (1801–1846), undertook the cultural and industrial revolution of his country with the help
of a team of French scientists. Tolerant and politically-minded, he
tried to mitigate religious discrimination in the face of the opposition of
a traditionalist population. The Copts made use of that period to build
schools and acquire modern skills and when the British occupied the
country (1882) the Christians were prepared to act as civil servants in
a modern administration. The British occupation brought stability and
economic development to Egypt. Schools were founded and new opportunities were created in the developing commerce, industry and
agriculture. The Copts perfected their skills and distinguished themselves in the liberal professions and in government service.

In spite of the liberal, albeit limited, trend which favoured the secu-
larisation of the State and the equality of its citizens, the rise of the
erstwhile dhimmis did not occur without shocking, even traumatising,
Muslim susceptibilities – as their former abject status had been the
basis of Islam's superiority and domination. To make matters worse,
the abolition of the discriminatory laws against non-Muslims in 1856
did not stem from an evolution *sui generis* in the Arab mentality, but
was imposed by the West.[7] In retaliation, thousands of Christians were
slaughtered in the Syrian provinces in 1860. This massacre prompted
France's brief intervention – in agreement with the other European
powers – and the establishment of an autonomous Christian region in
Lebanon, which remained nonetheless under Ottoman suzerainty.

Having thus been emancipated by Europe, the Christians – remnants of pre-Islamic cultures – in a cynical paradox of history, were
automatically associated with imperialism. Their hard-won equality
was considered by the Arabs as an additional humiliation imposed on
them by the Western powers. This was the reason why the struggle for
national independence, with its rejection of the West and its return to
Islam, has also manifested itself in the persecution of minorities. In
fact, justified as it may have been, the anti-colonial struggle was never
conceived of as a national war in the European sense. It was a *djihad* – a
holy war of Islam against Christianity. Inevitably then, religious fanaticism linked Eastern Christians to the West, which had not only liberated them, but, furthermore, by protecting them, had delivered them
from a traditional humiliation, thus violating the tenets of Islam established since the 8th century.

Worse: the situation of the minorities became more complicated by
the fact that in any litigation between Muslims and non-Muslims,
Islamic law was applicable, and then, as neither the testimony nor the
oath of a non-Muslim was admissible due to the infidel's congenital
depravity, the Muslim was automatically acquitted. In order to protect
their lives and property, the minorities tried to obtain consular protection or a foreign citizenship, thus benefiting from the system of Capitu-
lations. If by this device, they could escape from the discriminatory
Islamic courts, on the other hand this link with the West compromised
them even more. Thus, in the short or long run, no matter what they
did, the political situation of the religious minorities was foredoomed.

Under the British protectorate, the fact that a few Copts and Jews
became high government officials created the illusion of a liberalisation,
despite a violently xenophobic pan-islamic current which was the

manifestation of the revolt of Islam against the political and cultural supremacy of the West. Professor W. C. Smith has written:

Most Westerners have simply no inkling of how deep and fierce is the hate, especially of the West, that has gripped the modernizing Arab.[8]

This same hatred has accused the minorities of collusion with Western imperialism.

C. Issawi[9] attributes these anti-Coptic feelings to the high intellectual level of the Copts, but primarily to Islamizing tendencies, which resulted in economic discrimination against the Christians in the early thirties. During this period the Egyptian monarchy led an active panislamic campaign in the Arab countries. The progressive Islamization of national life inspired the rector of Al Azhar, the renowned Islamic University of Cairo, to declare in 1928 that nationality is religion.[10]

Already in 1927, Muslim political and religious associations proliferated, such as the Society of Young Muslims, the Society for the Benevolence of Islamic Morals, the Good Islamic Way, the Society for the preaching of Islamic virtues, the Society for the revival of religious law, the Salfiya Society, the Muslim Brotherhood and Young Egypt. Cairo became the centre of a religious nationalism from which missionaries went forth to the Sudan, Japan and India.[11] This proselytism carried with it a current of xenophobia, which manifested itself also against European orientalists, accused of undermining the faith of Islam. In March and April 1928, the activities of Christian missionaries were violently criticised. They were accused of utilising dangerous drugs and hypnosis to make new converts.[12] In 1933, in Kafr el Zayat, the Franciscan Sisters of Mercy were forced by a menacing crowd to release the pupils in their care.[13] The nationalist element in this religious current is best illustrated by the words of the Christian author, Salama Moussa, who stated in 1930: "Islam is the religion of my country, my duty is to defend it."[14]

In 1936, Makram Ebeid, the Coptic Finance Minister, declared: "I am a Christian, it is true, by religion, but through my country I am a Muslim."[15] From which it follows that to be an Egyptian it was necessary to act as a Muslim.

In 1937, Farouk with the help of his former tutor, Mustapha el Maraghi, rector of Al Azhar, attempted to abolish the constitutional government and transform Egypt into a theocratic State. The Wafd, the nationalist party which was very popular, became the main obstacle to the royal ambition. In order to discredit the Wafd, Maraghi resorted to religious xenophobia, accusing the Wafd of being controlled by the Copts, whom he described as "foxes" in a radio broadcast in February 1938. Friendship between Copts and Muslims is contrary to divine law, he declared.[16] In pursuit of his anti-Copt campaign, the rector of Al Azhar stated that Egyptian policy must only draw its inspiration from Islamic principles, which, as far as the relations with Christians were concerned, meant the re-introduction of the dhimma. Anti-Coptic and anti-missionary feelings were aroused and the reputation of the Wafd was ruined.

At the same time, the Muslim Brotherhood considerably increased the number of its members as well as its hold on the economic and political sectors of the country. The Brotherhood attempted to turn Egypt into an essentially religious State, governed according to the strictest interpretations of Islamic law. It condemned democratic parliamentarism, which, in its eyes, was a corrupt institution imported from the West. Divided into cells, the Brotherhood owned printing presses, clinics, schools, book-shops, recreation-centres as well as possessing its own secret terrorist organisation and para-military "army."

The part played by the Brotherhood is still a determining factor in Egypt. Remarkably well organised, it became the most powerful party in the country. Thanks to the support of the King and army, it had ramifications throughout the country – as well as in the Sudan, in Yemen and particularly in Palestine, where from 1948 to 1956 it provided the fedayeen with arms and money. After World War II, the Brotherhood became the most powerful party in Egypt and was at the zenith of its glory. Its fanaticism, the wave of murders and bloody riots instigated by its terrorist organisations, maintained xenophobia at fever pitch and created an atmosphere of terror and discrimination against non-Muslims. Possessing arms and training grounds, it set up military organisations and units of shock troops, which applied unbearable pressure on the Egyptian government and plunged the country, with the King's consent, into the 1948 war against Israel. After the defeat of the Arab forces, it started a regime of terror in Egyptian cities. The government, not having the means to control them, could only re-establish a comparative stability by imposing martial law. Nasser needed the help of the Brotherhood to seize power and Sadat collaborated with Hassah El Banna, the Brotherhood's Supreme Guide.[17] Yasir Arafat, born in Cairo in 1929, learnt from members of the Brotherhood how to make bombs and other explosives.[18] When the party was outlawed by Nasser, thousands of its members were imprisoned, others found refuge in Syria and especially in Jordan, where they joined the ranks of the Palestinian fedayeen organisations.

Though it never had a definite programme for social reform, the activity of the Muslim Brotherhood was varied and affected every sphere of life, whether social, economic, political, educational or cultural. In its pursuit to create an essentially Muslim society governed by the most rigorous precepts of Koranic law, it established, within the framework of the State, its own banks, industries, schools and army. If it can be said that the Muslim Brotherhood introduced reforms for the protection of wage-earners, it is no less true to say that, by religious intransigence, it contributed to the spread of a destructive hatred of the West, the foreigner and the non-believer, using, for this end, numerous publications and inflammatory sermons pronounced from mosques.

To understand Islamic pan-arabism, which in Western disguise ("Secular and Democratic Palestine," "Progressive-Muslim Lebanon") stirs the Arab world today, it is necessary to trace the steps of its evolution.

After the 1860 Syrian massacres, the Christians had tried to promote an Arab nationalism based on cultural identity. But this Arab nationalism, inspired by European conceptions, irritated the Muslims who looked upon it as an attempt by the West to divide and weaken them. The majority therefore rallied to the pan-islamic movement which advocated a return to traditional Islam. Thanks to the theologians of Al Azhar, the two movements, antagonistic at first, fused into Islamic pan-arabism. Today it is clear that Islam and Arabism are inseparable terms and that, in fact, pan-arabism is synonymous with the cultural, social and political rebirth of Islam. To be more precise, it is possible to be a Muslim and not an Arab, but the reverse is impossible: a true Arab must be a Muslim. As long as modern Egypt will proclaim itself to be "essentially an Arab and Muslim land," uncertainty will continue to weigh on the Copts, the only remaining native religious minority after the forced departure of eighty thousand Jews.

When Nasser came to power, Egypt resolutely turned its face towards Arabism and became its staunchest champion. Cairo proclaimed Islamic unity and pursued an active policy of pan-arabism which identified Islam with Arabism.

The precarious situation of the minorities became even more acute. Was it possible to be a Christian and an Arab? The problem was obsessively debated in literature and in the press and the solution was invariable: since Muhammed was an Arab and the sacred Koran was revealed in Arabic, only a Muslim could identify fully with Arabism.

In addition, Islam gave the Arab civilisation strength and grandeur. These beliefs were formulated by the Christian founder of the Ba'th party, Michel Aflak, who urged his co-religionists to convert, for as he maintained: "Islam is Arab nationalism."[19]

It was quite clear that in the context of this essentially religious nationalism, no religious minority could ever participate in the political life of the country. The islamization of the country led inevitably to discrimination against the Copts at all levels. Edward Watkin's book on this subject is particularly enlightening.[20] A recent article published by the late Georges Henein, a Coptic writer, gave valuable information on the economic discrimination imposed on the Copts during Nasser's rule.[21]

In August 1957, the Copts protested against persecutions which revived, in modern Egypt, a familiar thirteen-centuries-old tradition: restrictions in building churches, new laws affecting the personal status of Christians, discrimination against Christians in public office, in the distribution of land, in housing and for posts in the mass media.[22] These recent events must be examined in the context of the dhimma – churches destroyed by villagers, houses and shops burned down, bishops and Coptic congregants stoned.[23] The campaign of intimidation, inspired by the *Protocols of the Elders of Zion* as described by G. Henein in the above-mentioned article is not unlike that instigated against the Jews in the fifties which resulted in their total expulsion. Is the rebirth of religious fervour in Egypt a consequence of the islamization of governmental institutions, with President Sadat's tacit approval, or is it the work of the resurgent Muslim Brotherhood, organised into semi-clandestine cells?

The remarks made by the orientalist W. C. Smith on the Muslim Brotherhood of the fifties could well apply to certain trends now prevalent in the Arab world:

The reaffirmation of Islam endeavours to counter the failure of modern life but may not succeed in transcending it. Unfortunately, for some of the members of the Ikhwan (Muslim Brotherhood) and even more for many of their sympathizers and fellow-travellers the reaffirmation is not a constructive programme based on cogent plans and known objectives, or even felt ideas; but is rather an outlet for emotion. It is the expression of the hatred, frustration, vanity, and destructive frenzy of a people who for long have been the prey of poverty, impotence, and fear. All the discontent of men who find the modern world too much for them can in movements such as the Ikhwan

find action and satisfaction. It is the Muslim Arab's aggressive reaction to
the attack on his world which we have already found to be almost overwhelming — the reaction of those who, tired of being overwhelmed, have leapt
with frantic sadistic joy to burn and kill. The burning of Cairo (26th January
1952), the assassination of Prime Ministers, the intimidating of Christians,
the vehemence and hatred in their literature — all this is to be understood in
terms of a people who have lost their way, whose heritage has proven unequal
to modernity, whose leaders have been dishonest, whose ideals have failed.
In this aspect, the new Islamic upsurge is a force not to solve problems but to
intoxicate those who cannot longer abide the failure to solve them.[24]

The lessons of the past and the present isolation of the Copts does not
augur well for the future. When Nasser seized power and forbade all
political parties, no one dared question or criticize the dictatorial government of the military oligarchy. This was particularly distressing in
view of the fact that, at the beginning of the century, Egyptian intellectuals were the first from the Arab world to focus on the problems
created by the clash with the modern Western world.

Although the present, more liberal, regime of President Sadat has
loosened the totalitarian control in the political and intellectual spheres
of the State's institutions, it has hardly diminished anti-Christian discrimination in the political, economic and educational fields.[25] The
actual resurgence of Islam,[26] the massacre and flight of Lebanese
Christians as a result of the union of Islamo-Palestinian forces, Syrian
President Assad's military intervention in Lebanon, allegedly to protect
Christians, can only favour a general traditional policy of Arab-Islamic
domination.

As a confirmation of this tendency, at a recent manifestation of the
Muslim Brotherhood in Cairo, some Egyptian members of parliament
demanded that Koranic law should henceforth be the only source of
the country's legislation.[27]

The moment has come for Arab Muslim intellectuals to recognize,
courageously, that if the Arabs can condemn Western imperialism,
so have the Eastern Christian communities the right to demand equality of rights in the lands successfully colonized by Arab imperialism.

IV. Annex

Telegram (Summer 1972) addressed to President
Anwar el Sadat

by

The Assembly of Christian Churches in Egypt

The National Assembly of the heads of the Copt-Orthodox, Copt-Catholic, and Copt-Evangelical churches met at the Orthodox-Coptic Patriarchate in Alexandria. The delegates were shocked by recent provocations and the planned persecutions publicly announced by the Ministry of WAKFS (Muslim Ministry of Religion) and its various sections. These projects are intended to inflame the populace to hatred and to discrimination which can only lead to our annihilation. In spite of all this, no responsible department of the administration has done anything to stop these perfidious intrigues against national unity. Those intriguing knew very well that their action would lead to clashes between the two groups of the nation — the Muslims and the Copts — and this at a time when there is a great need to preserve our unity in order to create a united front against the enemy. All this has happened, even though on several occasions we have complained to those in authority.

We, members of this Assembly, subjected to considerable pressure engendered by all these injustices which are occurring throughout the country, conscious also that the Constitution guaranties liberty to all citizens, we request, Sir, that:

1) Sectarian and mischievous projects of the Ministry of WAKFS and other departments of this Ministry cease.

2) Restrictions imposed by the officials of the Administration concerning the construction of new churches be abolished. The argument used according to which this prohibition is based on an old Ottoman decree is invalid as this law was abrogated by the new Constitution.

3) Entrance to the Universities must be based solely on the final examination results at secondary school and not on a private interview. Furthermore, it should be forbidden for University courses to be held in mosques and Islamic Institutions.

4) Studies of our religion from a negative viewpoint, such as "Israel and Universal Zionism" and "Conference on Christianity," should not be published.

5) All discrimination regarding employment in certain departments of the Universities and the Institutes of Advanced Studies should be abolished, as well as the QUOTA system applicable to Christian students in specialized schools and similar institutions.

6) It should be forbidden to publish books or articles attacking our faith and our Holy Scriptures, in particular the Old Testament.

7) It is essential to apply the (National) COVENANT and protect the Christian family against the dangers which menace it through the pretext of grant-

ing legal protection. Divorce must be made more difficult in that part of the law relating to the personal status of non-Muslims.

8) The projects which are aimed at preventing Christians from acceding to high (government) posts should be abolished.

Sir, we await your reply, as soon as possible, to our just requests. We do not accept to be humiliated in this country which is ours. The delegates have called a further assembly in Cairo for TUESDAY 29 AUGUST 1972. There is thus sufficient time for our just requests to be accepted. If this will not be the case, martyrdom is preferable to a life of servitude.

We are sure of your wisdom, as we are sure that you will overcome this dangerous situation. May God protect you and through your efforts grant victory to our nation.

(signed)

For the Copt-Orthodox Patriarchate: The Reverend MENA, Patriarchal Vicar

For the Copt-Catholic Church: The Reverend GIBRAEL GHATTAAS, Patriarchal Vicar

For the Copt-Evangelical Church: Pasteur LABIB QALDAS

NOTES

1. *Le Monde*, 2nd December 1972. See Annex.
2. A. S. Tritton: *The Caliphs and their non-Muslim Subjects*, London, 1970, p. 1.
3. A. S. Tritton, *op. cit.*; Antoine Fattal, *Le Statut légal des non-Musulmans en pays d'Islam*, Beyrouth, 1958; E. Strauss (Ashtor), *The social Isolation of Ahl-Adh Dhimma*, in P. Hirschler Memorial book, Budapest, 1949.
4. A. S. Tritton, *op. cit.*, p. 145.
5. A. S. Tritton, *op. cit.*, p. 144.
6. *Ibid.*, p. 33.
7. Moshe Ma'oz: *Ottoman Reform in Syria and Palestine (1840–61)*, Oxford 1968, p. 27. By the *Hatt'i Hümayun* (1858) Europe forced the Ottoman Sultan, who was still the nominal suzerain of Egypt, to proclaim equality between Muslims, Christians and other minorities throughout his Empire.
8. W. C. Smith, *Islam in Modern History*, Princeton, 1957, p. 164.
9. C. Issawi, *Egypt, an economical and social analysis*, Oxford, University Press, 1947, pp. 161–62.
10. M. Colombe, *L'évolution de l'Egypte 1924–1950*, Paris 1951, p. 171.
11. *Ibid.*, p. 144.
12. *Ibid.*, p. 143.
13. *Ibid.*, p. 143.
14. *Ibid.*, p. 146.
15. *Ibid.*, p. 146.
16. Elie Kadourie, *The Chatham House Version*, London 1969, pp. 199–200. Maraghi no doubt alludes to the verses in the Koran (Sura 5, 51) and to the habits (acts and words attributed to Muhammed) that forbid or strongly discourage relations between Christians and Muslims. The segregation of the dhimmis was at the root of their social and political ostracism by the Islamic community (*Umma*).
17. Anouar Sadat, *Revolt on the Nile*, London 1957, p. 30.
18. Thomas Kiernan, *Yasir Arafat*, London 1976.

19. Silvia Haim, *Arab Nationalism*, University of California, 1962, p. 64.
20. Edward Watkin, *A Lonely Minority, The Modern History of Egypt's Copts*, New York, 1963.
21. *L'Express*, 20–26 November 1972.
22. P. Rondot, *Man, State and Society in the Contemporary Middle-East*, London, 1972, p. 276.
23. *Le Monde*, 16 novembre 1972.
24. W. C. Smith, *op. cit.*, pp. 163–164.
25. Josette Alia, *Les Chrétiens d'Orient*, Le Nouvel Observateur, No. 581, 29 décembre 1975–4 janvier 1976.
26. Bernard Lewis, *The Return of Islam*. Commentary, Vol. 61, No. 1. January 1976.
27. *Le Monde*, 26 mars 1976.

Ethnic Discrimination in Rwanda and Burundi

JEREMY GREENLAND

JEREMY GREENLAND, a native of Great Britain, born 1944, won the Educational Development Award from the Ministry of Overseas Development in 1974 to write his Ph.D. thesis at Oxford University, Department of Educational Studies, on "Curriculum Development in Burundi". He obtained his M.A. degree in Modern Languages after studying at Brasenose College Oxford and the Institut Maxilianeum, Munich University, and a Postgraduate Certificate in Education, London University Institute of Education, Education in Developing Countries Department. He also has a Diploma in Social Anthropology from Oxford University.

In 1966 he went to Burundi under the auspices of Voluntary Service Overseas to teach at the Ecole Secondaire de Matana, a former mission school. He became temporary headmaster and subsequently teacher of languages. After a three year period in Britain during which he taught English language to foreign students at the Centre of Economic and Political Studies, he returned to Burundi to take up the appointment of Director of Studies at Ecole Normale de Kibimba. He taught French and helped to run the teacher-training department. He also visited schools and colleges in neighbouring African countries.

Jeremy Greenland has contributed many articles to leading journals including *New Blackfriars*, *Comparative Education*, *African Affairs* and *Revue Française d'Etudes Politiques Africaines*.

Ethnic Discrimination in Rwanda and Burundi

JEREMY GREENLAND

The killing of tens of thousands of Tutsi in Rwanda between 1959 and 1964 and of more than one hundred thousand Hutu in Burundi in 1972[1] – not to mention the vast number of refugees to have fled both countries, well over 300,000 in total, – are events of such appalling magnitude that the 'blood' of the victims literally 'calls from the ground' for inclusion in any world-wide survey of discriminatory practices. Regrettably it is important to give representative and fully authenticated examples of the atrocities, partly because they have received such little attention in the forum of world politics, but also because some in authority, particularly in Burundi, have attempted to give a completely false picture of the situation.[2] Those interested primarily in the gruesome details of the violence and the practical forms which discrimination has taken since then will find them in Sections V, VI and VII. However, there is the danger that such 'reportage', read on its own, merely serves to reinforce an already stereotyped view of what western mass media like to refer to as 'tribesmen' and their one main problem which is said to be 'tribalism.' The attempt must therefore be made to put these events in a perspective which takes account both of ethnographic information and the historical evidence of the colonial experience.

I wish to thank Professor René Lemarchand for permission to consult his valuable collection of documents. I have also drawn extensively on his *Rwanda and Burundi* (Pall Mall Press, 1970), the standard work on the political development of the two countries, but he is in no way responsible for the use I have made of his facts.

I. Contested Definitions of
'Discrimination' and 'Ethnic'

First, however, both elements of the deceptively simple title, 'ethnic' and 'discrimination' require comment. 'Discrimination' in the basic sense of 'being able to make distinctions' is considered a desirable human quality. Less desirable is "the act ... of discriminating *categorically* rather than *individually*," the fourth definition in Webster's *Third New International Dictionary*. Western assumptions that the value of the individual surpasses that of the group or category suffuse the original United Nations Declaration of Human Rights and the subsequent International Conventions adopted in 1966. Paradoxically it is the countries of the Third World – whose own cultures in general approve discrimination on a group rather than individual basis – who have succeeded at the United Nations, in making human rights a world-wide political issue, to the point where the violation of such rights has even become 'justiciable' and not merely a topic for debate. This is because the Human Rights Declarations were invoked primarily as a stick with which to belabour the white supremacist régimes of southern Africa, and although 'self-determination' is claimed for all peoples under colonial rule, as Rupert Emerson[3] points out, it is far from clear who defines the 'self.'

The original concern for civil and political rights has been supplemented by a concern for what are termed economic, social and cultural rights, and this conjunction leads to a further paradox: whereas the protection of the individual's civil and political rights usually has the effect of restraining the powers of a central government, the implementation of economic, social and cultural rights demands that governments be released from their restrictive commitment to individuals to take the often drastic action which is needed. What appears to have happened in most Third World countries is that the elites who claimed and won independence now define themselves as the 'self' entitled to decide what form 'self-government' should take; they argue in addition that it is the more tangible economic, social and cultural needs of their peoples which demand priority treatment. In the familiar scenario which results, the violation of civil and political rights is almost universally attested but is removed from international agendas as being 'an internal matter.' Hence the sharp and lonely contrast which Nyerere has consistently provided, for example in 1973 when he urged the OAU not to let the principle of non-intervention block mediation in what he called 'Burundi's racial conflict.'[4]

The fact is therefore that the term 'discrimination' with its basically western, individualistic connotations, has not achieved full recognition as a politically potent concept, valid the whole world over. This half-baked state of affairs is reflected in the clumsy and still evolving United Nations procedures for dealing with allegations of violation of human rights. When the Commission on Human Rights and the Sub-Commission on the Prevention of Discrimination and the Protection of Minorities were first set up in 1946 by the Economic and Social Council of the UN, they explicitly disclaimed "power to take any action in regard to complaints concerning human rights."[5] The significant change occurred in 1966 as a result of pressure from Third World delegations that the régimes of southern Africa be arraigned for their white supremacist policies. Under ECOSOC Resolution 1235 the Commission on Human Rights and its Sub-Commission were authorised to undertake a "thorough study and investigation of situations that reveal a 'consistent pattern' of violations of human rights, and to report with accompanying recommendations concerning them." The fact that the African delegations have only accepted public debate on southern Africa, the Israeli-occupied territories, and latterly on Chile, lays them open to the charge of maintaining double standards. The OAU's explicit commitment to the Universal Declaration of Human Rights, noted in the Charter and reiterated on the OAU's 10th anniversary, and the commitment to set up an African Commission on Human Rights have largely remained empty rhetoric. Despite this and despite the fact that the procedures established for reviewing allegations of violation of human rights are cumbersome and those testifying are pledged to secrecy unless the Commission decides otherwise, there is hope in some quarters[6] that the double standard will gradually be resolved.

The massacre of Hutus in Burundi was reportedly discussed by the Sub-Commission but has now disappeared from the agenda without the Burundi régime receiving any public censure. Violation of human rights by at least two other African governments is thought to be under discussion at present. The crucial paragraph which the lawyers must pick over is:

In time of public emergency which threatens the life of the nation and the existence of which is officially proclaimed, the States Parties to the present Convention may take measures derogating from their obligations under the present Covenant to the extent strictly required by the exigencies of the situation, provided that such measures are not inconsistent with their other obligations under international law and do not involve discrimination solely on the ground of race, colour, sex, language, religion or social origin.[7]

Although those African governments arraigned so far have evaded conviction, the recent successful prosecution of the Chilean junta may later prove to have been a most significant step forward.

This apparent trend towards the 'universalisation' of terms such as discrimination is now being vehemently resisted by what might be called the 'authenticity' campaigns of some African régimes. Certain concepts implanted by the colonialists are said to be inapplicable to a given culture and should be replaced by truly authentic ones. The revival of traditional literature, art and music, which are patently unique to an individual or group of African cultures, serves as a cover for far less defensible assertions about pre-colonial judicial, economic and social structures. President Micombero may legitimately claim that "International Women's Year does not mean the same thing for the American woman, the European woman, and the Murundi woman .... In French you can say that 'such a girl married such a boy' ... in Kirundi that is not possible since it is the boy who asks for the girl in marriage and marries her."[8] On the other hand, the spokesman dealing with Belgian journalists anxious to discover the roots of the Hutu revolt in 1972 concealed the real issues by laying the following smokescreen: "Burundi has its own mentality and structures which are peculiar to itself .... The concept of democracy or at least the application of this notion must be understood differently, depending on whether one is in Africa or Europe."[9] He was really saying that the Burundi régime rejects the concept of democracy because it fears what J. S. Mill called 'the tyranny of the majority.'

When in 1972 foreign journalists took up the Belgian Foreign Minister's use of the word 'genocide' in interviews with Micombero, the President was quick to reply that whereas the initial Hutu attack clearly qualified as genocide – the leaflets found on the rebels urging them to kill every Tutsi man, woman and child, being conclusive evidence – the government action against the Hutu was certainly not genocide, merely the punishment of the guilty.[10] When ex-Foreign Minister Simbananiye informed the diplomatic corps in Bujumbura that peace had been fully restored, he contemptuously added that as foreigners they could not begin to appreciate the depth of meaning conveyed by the Kirundi word *amahoro*, crudely translated as 'peace.' But when in reality the restoration of peace signifies the prevention of aid from reaching orphans and widows, and discrimination against Hutu in the courts, in employment and in access to education, the term 'authenticity' has surely been corrupted to excess. The setting up of a Ministry of National Orientation in Burundi (12 November 1974) combining the former Ministries of Information and the Party, and the leading rank given to the Minister concerned, suggest that the present régime is determined to resist the inroads made by such foreign concepts as 'discrimination' which, if they once gained currency among the population at large, would threaten the legitimacy of their own position.

Since *ethnic* discrimination in Rwanda and Burundi has been selected as the most salient form of discrimination, and not, say, discrimination against women, or against protestants during the colonial era, it is essential to try and define 'ethnic.' The first fundamental is to reject utterly the definition of ethnicity made on the basis of genetic or biological characteristics alone. Kenneth Kirkwood notes that Huxley, Haddon and Carr-Saunders take this view and trace its honourable pedigree back as far as Herodotus who "comes to the sensible conclusion that a group such as the Greeks is marked off from other groups by complex factors of which kinship is one, but that at least as important are language, religion culture or tradition."[11] Kirkwood further quotes Ashley Montagu's *Man's most dangerous myth: the fallacy of race* as support for his contention that "the term 'race' ... can best be restricted to denote genetically transmitted characteristics alone."[12] This then clears the ground for the fundamental contention that ethnicity is 'in the eye of the beholder.' According to Edmund Leach, "there is no class of material 'thing' in the world-out-there to which it can readily be attached as a means of identification."[13] Recent studies emphasise that even such entities as populations, at first sight supremely fitted for statistical, 'objectifiable' analysis, are in fact "recognised according to some particular component which is of interest"[14] Edwin Ardener writes that "the population ... is not merely subject to a statistical determination on the part of the observer, it is dependent on the subjective definition of that population by the human beings concerned."[15] Thus we are not concerned with the analysis of the population of Burundi and Rwanda on genetic criteria, and its division into the three categories of Tutsi, Hutu, and Twa (Pygmies), despite the existence of eminent scientific monographs on the subject.[16] What is of concern is first the fact that Barundi and Banyarwanda *themselves* categorise the population of both countries as Tutsi, Hutu and Twa, and secondly that this particular mode of categorisation has superceded other modes, for example on a clanic basis, and has done so at certain times rather than others in the history of the two countries. This approach must be stressed since the Burundi regime appears to have an answer to the 'geneticists': the Barundi are no longer ethnically divided, if ever they were, says Térence Nsanze,[17] former Burundi ambassador to the UN, because there has been so much intermarriage between Tutsi and Hutu. Romain Forscher deals succinctly with this argument:

Certainly morphology does not permit certain distinction between a Tutsi and a Hutu, but that does not prevent every Murundi from knowing in practice to which ethnic group he belongs and it is at this level, that of ethnic *consciousness* that the problem lies .... Tribalism is therefore not the result of a racial fatality, it is a more or less conscious political choice. (His italics.)[18]

The fact that descent is traced patrilineally in both Burundi and Rwanda leads logically-minded outsiders to the mistaken assumption that in a mixed marriage the children's ethnic identity is determined by that of the father. A record of the Hutu killed in 1972 shows how little difference such subtle distinctions made. When the army and gendarmerie were purged in 1972 it is reliably alleged that those with even one Hutu grandparent were eliminated.

If the major part of this study deals with discrimination opposing Tutsi and Hutu in both Burundi and Rwanda, this is because of the extent of the atrocities and because the whole population of both countries was 'conscientised.' However, 'ethnic' as here defined allows for the description of discrimination by the Hutu and Tutsi together against the Twa, and also of discrimination practised between groups of Hutu in Rwanda and between groups of Tutsi in Burundi since independence, etc.

If the definition of an individual as Tutsi, Hutu or Twa is essentially a question of categorisation, a 'more or less conscious political choice,' it is all the more important to ask how this situation has arisen. Our investigation deals first with traditional concepts of ethnicity, as far as these are ascertainable; secondly with the impact on Burundi and Rwanda society of European concepts of ethnicity; and thirdly with the interaction between these two strands through the era of Belgian rule up to the present day.

II. Linguistic and Anthropological Contributions

There is abundant linguistic evidence (Kirundi and Kinyarwanda being considered variations of the same basic language) that a primary distinction was made between Tutsi, Hutu and Twa. The Kirundi word commonly used for 'sort' or 'kind' as is *amoko y'udukokogori ni menshi,* or 'there are lots of kinds of basket-work' is used in the context *'ubwoko bw'Abahutu,'* 'the kind/sort/caste of the Hutu,' and F. M. Rodegem[19] cites this sentence from an informant: *Abakora ico gikorwa bwari ubwoko bumwe bw'Abarundi muri ya moko atatu y'abantu,* 'those who did that sort of work only belonged to one caste of Rundi among the three castes of people.' The identification of 'separateness' with specialised occupations will be referred to again later. It is true that the *unity* between the three groups is stressed in certain contexts: the public buildings used by native administrators in Rwanda in the Belgian era bore the traditional motto *Imbaga 'Inyabutatu ijya mbera'*[20] or 'a triple alliance makes progress.' The weight of the linguistic evidence, however, is on the unequal status of these three groups and on the animosity existing between them. Legend speaks of the three sons of the original inhabitant of Rwanda (or Burundi), who were left to guard a bowl of milk overnight. Gatwa the pygmy could not restrain his greed and drank the milk; Gahutu clumsily knocked it over; Gatutsi diligently kept watch all night and was therefore rewarded with the right to exercise authority over his brothers. Well-known proverbs attest the Tutsi's disdain for the Hutu: 'the back grows but can never rise beyond the neck', and the Hutu's wry recognition of the Tutsi's trickery: 'the Tutsi to whom you give lodging in your corridor will finish by removing you from your bed.[21] Rodegem cites a similar pair of proverbs: *Wiza Umuhutu kurasa agakurasa ku nda,* 'Teach a Hutu to use a bow and without fail he will fire an arrow into your stomach,' and *Umututsi umuvura amenyo ejo akayakurisha,* 'if you cure a Tutsi's teeth for him, as soon as he is better he will bite you'! Significantly Rodegem goes on to cite a proverb showing that the present manifestation of acute rivalry between two broad groups of Tutsi in Burundi, Tutsi-Hima and Tutsi-Nyaruguru, has its origins far in the past: *Umuhima umuvura amaso bwaca akayagukanurira,* 'if you cure a Hima's eyes for him, as soon as he is cured, he will look down on you'![22] The Twa, or pygmies, are not even classed as *abantu,* 'people': when I once asked who lived in a particular group of houses I was told, 'They are not people (*abantu*), they are pygmies (*batwa*)!

Anthropological descriptions of 'traditional' Burundi and Rwanda society[23] commonly highlight four features: the occupational specialisation of the Tutsi (herdsmen), the Hutu (agriculturalists), and the Twa (hunters and potters); their overwhelming preference for endogamy; their relative positions in a hierarchy under a monarch; and their distinctive physical appearance and associated personality stereotypes. The cohesion of these 'caste' societies, according to the 'classic' anthropological texts, was assured by the institution of clientship, a vast network of reciprocal, 'feudal' ties between patrons and their clients. Under the clientship system, known as *ubuhake* in Rwanda and *ubugabire* in Burundi, the client, usually a Hutu, offered goods and/or services to a patron, usually a Tutsi, in return for the latter's protection and the loan of a cow, the offspring of which became the client's property. Seen as a whole, the system was shaped like a pyramid with the king at the apex; all cattle belonged ultimately to him, and he exercised his rule by making and receiving gifts of cattle from his subjects. If any patron abused his client, the client could break the tie and seek a more congenial master elsewhere. This functionalist interpretation of the clientship system has come under attack from a younger generation of scholars, for example Claudine Vidal.[24] Her research into oral records of nineteenth century land and cattle transactions in Rwanda leads her to conclude that

the structure of pastoral clientship did not apply to all members of society and involved not so much individuals as family groups. In reality the theoretical liberty of choice of a *shebuja* (patron) was considerably restricted. Finally, the network formed by the *ubuhake* did not determine the general circulation of cattle and the Tutsi did not prevent the Hutu from having cows of their own.

Anthropologists, she continues, have been guilty of making a fetish of the cow. It was through their gradual control of the *land* rather than through their possession of beautiful long-horned cattle that the Tutsi came to achieve their hegemony; the leasing out of cattle was a consequence of dependency ties already based on land, and not the prior cause of such dependency. The colonial administration's rationalisation of the land-tenure system had the unintended effect of giving the cattle ties progressively greater importance. Thus, so the argument runs, the anthropologist's description of traditional society, relying often on the testimony of Tutsi informants, seized on the cow as the 'cause of inequality' and unwittingly served the purposes of the dominant group.

The anthropologists have also contributed indirectly to the development of ethnic stereotypes and subsequent discrimination by their technical use of the 'anthropological present.' Ethel Albert's account of the "culture patterning of speech behaviour" in Burundi is a particularly relevant example. Barundi might take offence at such undifferentiated comments as "There are no reservations about the desirability of flattery, untruths .... Whatever works is good," but the assertion that "boys in the upper social strata are given formal speech training" and "girls in the upper castes are also carefully trained" has the effect of sharpening the ethnic self-perceptions of the uninitiated Burundi reader today. He or she may not have the stamina to read through to the concluding pages where Albert admits that: "The potential for misunderstanding Burundi verbal behaviour is obviously high"![25]

III. The Evolution of Ethnic Stereotypes

If the professional anthropologists of the 1950s and 1960s are to be charged with unintentionally reinforcing patterns of discrimination already present in traditional society, the infinitely larger number of amateur anthropologists who as travellers, administrators and missionaries, have given their own account of these societies have wrought far greater damage.

The first Europeans to explore, evangelise and administer Rwanda and Burundi were predisposed by their academic training and their practical experience on the long march from the coast to emphasise the distinguishing physical features of the population groups they encountered and to speculate on their separate origins. When the Duke of Mecklenburg entered Rwanda he remarked that the only thing which the Negroes and the Tutsi had in common was their dark skin![26] K. Roehl hypothesised that glottal stops in Kinyarwanda were of Tutsi origin since they were not to be heard in the outlying areas which the Tutsi had not yet penetrated.[27] What is far less pardonable is that this style of analysis should have been pursued for so long and carried to such fanciful lengths. As late as 1948 a Belgian doctor, Jules Sasserath wrote:

In reality (the Tutsi) are Hamites, probably of semitic origin, or according to certain hypotheses can trace their origin back to Ham, even to Adam ....

They are 1.90m. tall. They are slender. They have a thin nose, high forehead, thin lips .... The rest of the population is bantu. These are the Hutu, negroes who have all the characteristics of the negro: wide nose, thick lips .... They retain a childlike character .... The Hamites came down from the North, doubtless from the Nile valley. Perhaps from Abyssinia. People link them with the Gallas and with the Tuareg peoples.[28]

A chapter sub-heading in *Ruanda* Volume I by Louis de Lacger reads: "The Tutsi, a branch of the Cushites, Ethiopians, or Hamites," and the text contains the memorable phrase, best savoured in French: "Avant d'être nigritisés, ces hommes étaient bronzés ...."[29]

This 'mythology' has certain serious consequences. First, the folk myths have acquired the status of historical fact to people who have had no time to do their own research. Thus mission literature, aimed at informing supporters at home, blithely says that, "About three hundred years ago the wave of migration of a mass of Ethiopian tribesmen arrived in Burundi and set themselves up as feudal lords over the Batwa (Pygmies) and the Bahutu."[30] ... "The Hutu probably originate from the Congo .... The Tutsi probably came from Ethiopia some time before the fifteenth century."[31] Children in school in Burundi and Rwanda, fed on such 'facts' in their history lessons, naturally identify themselves with the feudal lords or see themselves as serfs. In an oral history exam the question was asked, "Which people in Burundi today do the Hamites correspond to?" This was only days after the Hutu teachers in the school had been taken away and killed; the examiner was himself a Rwandese Tutsi. Significantly, the Tutsi pupils, interrogated separately, replied that the Hamites were Tutsi, but the Hutu pupils who had learned the same 'answer' by heart from the same notes, claimed that they did not know; they preferred to lose a point rather than risk real trouble by saying 'Tutsi' which was for them a taboo word. Teachers are just as much affected as the pupils. European teachers in Burundi and Rwanda fall into two categories: those who unquestioningly assume that the Tutsi are somehow 'more intelligent,' and those who under the influence of research findings on 'race and intelligence' elsewhere in the world try and exorcise the assumption of Tutsi superiority.

Another harmful consequence of this folk mythology is that later generations of Europeans have been predisposed to ask certain questions and expect certain answers. If one knows that Roehl back in 1914 reported that the Tutsi do not need food and milk but can live on beer and tobacco,[32] and a Tutsi guest declines a meal in your house, it is all too easy to draw the totally unjustified conclusion that Roehl was correct. The cliché that the Tutsi are herdsmen and the Hutu are agriculturalists can blind the foreigner arriving in Burundi to the evidence of his eyes that some Tutsi hoe and some Hutu own cattle.

In discussing the evolution of these stereotypes, the difficulty is to balance what we know to be the European's fondness for making distinctions with the Africans' keenness that such distinctions should be made. The current vogue for castigating the foibles of the white man overlooks how much Tutsi and Hutu alike have stood to gain and still stand to gain by the impression the white man receives. Here again the anthropologists are not immune from criticism. That Jacques Maquet's account of clientship in Rwanda[33] should highlight the reciprocal obligations of patron and client may be due to the fact that his informants were mainly Tutsi. Similarly, Helen Codere's insistence on the 'genuinely Rwandese' origins of the 1959 revolution, is understandable when one recalls that her research was being conducted with Hutu when the revolution in question was going on around them.[34] It is impossible to escape the same traps today. The Belgian journalists who promote the justness of the Burundi Hutu's cause reject the claim that a successful Hutu coup would be followed by the massacre of the Burundi Tutsi, but on what grounds do they reject it? Their convictions derive from the 'reasonableness' of the educated Hutu on whom they rely for information.

The other half of the equation – that ethnic perceptions which serve to strengthen discrimination may be reinforced by European categorisation, but have their own independent, truly authentic existence – is much harder to demonstrate. This is partly because so few Barundi or Banyarwanda have made written accounts of their traditional culture and made them available to foreigners, and because even fewer have tried to shrug off a European approach to the subject. Here, however, is one example: in a strikingly unselfconscious passage Michel Ntuyuhaga, now Bishop of Bujumbura, discusses the difference between a kraal with cows and one without:

Is not this what made a Mututsi laugh when he came across some Bahutu who had no cows? He found them talking together, smiling and laughing merrily. He withdrew from them and said to his friends: "These Bahutu are not even sad! They have no cows and yet they can find something to laugh about!" For a Mututsi the only thing of real value is the cow ....[35]

I.e. Ntuyuhaga, who must know that many Hutu actually have cows of their own, particularly since the suppression of clientage ties, chooses rather to promote the stereotype that it is the Tutsi who own cattle and that the Hutu are stupid unless they make their envy obvious.

The ethnic violence of recent years in both countries has thrown up remarkable examples of the degree to which stereotyped views control behaviour. Elderly Hutu in Rwanda who, even after masses of Hutu had risen against the Tutsi, said, "The Tutsi will always be the dominant race and the Hutu the dominated race,"[36] a belief demonstrated by many Hutu who followed their Tutsi masters as refugees into Tanzania and Uganda. The repression of the Hutu in Burundi in 1972 had already claimed several victims when a Hutu teacher at our school was called in for questioning; he had in fact openly expressed anger at the death of another Hutu colleague; and this 'provocative remark' had been reported by Tutsi pupils. He drove to the police post, was told to take the car back since he would not be needing it, and to return on foot. He meekly did so and came to bid us all good-bye, saying that there was no alternative but to go to his death!

The persistence of visual stereotypes is further evidence of underlying ethnic discrimination. The distinctive hairstyles of the Rwandese, *amasunza*, were a Tutsi prerogative. A tall European missionary teacher with an aquiline nose once overheard two Barundi women discussing whether she was a Tutsi! A very short friend of mine brushed his hair up and bought shoes with raised heels in an obvious effort to improve his height. 'Counter-cases,' where people deliberately wish to disassociate themselves from the stereotype, also serve to demonstrate its pervasive influence. The fact that King Mwambutsa of Burundi claimed to be 'above ethnicites' was often linked to his 'mixed' appearance – an advantage which his son Rwagasore inherited and turned to good use as UPRONA party leader in the 1961 elections.[37] President Micombero bluffs foreign journalists obsessed with ethnic categorisation by referring openly to his own 'non-Tutsi' appearance, while President Habyalimana's height visibly strengthens his claims not to be such a partisan president of the Hutu as was his diminutive and 'typically Hutu' predecessor Grégoire Kayibanda.

IV. BELGIAN RULE AND ETHNIC CONSCIOUSNESS

As certain aspects of Belgian colonial policy in Burundi and Rwanda are reviewed, the purpose is to point out the link between these policies and the development of ethnic tension. Each department of policy cited reveals a basic paradox: policies designed to 'civilise' what was seen as a backward society and bring it to a level where some measure of self-government could be entertained, unwittingly fostered the development of ethnic consciousness and tension.

Indirect rule was the cornerstone of Belgian administrative policy. Pierre Ryckmans, Belgium's first Resident in Burundi wrote in 1925: "The only smoothly functioning organ between us and the masses is the *legitimate* chiefs. They alone, because they are legitimate, can induce acceptance of necessary innovations."[38] However, it was precisely those measures which were designed to limit the 'excessive' powers of the chiefs and to tidy up what seemed to be inefficiencies and anomalies in the native administration which in fact had the effect of consolidating the power of a small cadre of chiefs. Tutsi chiefs from central and southern Rwanda were imposed on the northern regions which had traditionally been ruled by local Hutu lineages; the overall number of chiefdoms was drastically reduced; chiefs were forbidden to retain clients outside their own chiefdom, which made it much more difficult for an exploited client to seek a new patron; and "the balance of forces between cattle chiefs, land chiefs and army chiefs"[39] was destroyed. Moreover once chiefs became mere administrative officials their reciprocal obligations to their clients were dissolved; they were paid according to the amount of taxes they exacted from the population and had to organise forced labour for road-building etc. The Hutu peasantry had little redress against inevitable abuses by the chiefs of their authority. Similarly, the institution of 'native tribunals' where 'native' disputes would be settled by 'native' custom, thus keeping the native in his traditional environment, had the unintended effect of empowering the Tutsi magistrates to enhance their personal power. Jean-Pierre Chrétien summarises these administrative 'improvements' as "an almost general downgrading of the population in relation to a minority of chiefs integrated into the European circuit."[40]

A corollary of this administrative reorganisation was that since the Tutsi were deemed to be the only legitimate rulers, it was Tutsi boys who were selected for training as chiefs. Indeed the enrolment statistics at the Groupe Scolaire, which opened at Astrida in 1929, make this abundantly clear:[41]

Meanwhile as part of the policy to bring 'civilisation' to these 'dark' lands, the Belgian government was subsidising the educational enterprise of the missionaries. They were opening primary schools everywhere and promoting the ablest children into their seminaries and

Year	Tutsi	Rwanda	Hutu	Burundi	Congolese
1932	45	—	9*	—	14
1933	21	—	—	—	—
1934	26	—	13*	—	—
1935†	41	—	11*	—	—
1945	46	—		3	—
1946	44	1		8	—
1947	44	2		10	—
1948	85	2		11	2
1949†	85	5		9	—
1953	68	3		16	—
1954	63	3		16	3

* Territorial origins unavailable
† Enrolment figures for 1936–44, and 1950–52, unavailable.

higher seminaries on the basis of academic merit, regardless of ethnic identity. Thus by the mid-1950s a 'counter-elite' had emerged, educated in these seminaries, and composed mainly of disenchanted Hutu. They protested that the Belgian authorities discriminated against them in favour of less highly qualified Tutsi. Lemarchand cites the case of one Hutu, Anastase Makuza, who returned to Rwanda as a university graduate in 1955 but was forced to accept the post of typist because all other openings were barred to him.[42]

A similar paradox characterises the missionary enterprise. The European religious hierarchy, until World War II at least, was adamant that the Belgian administration should not attempt to 'eliminate the Tutsi class.' Mgr. Classe advised his powers temporal that

Generally speaking, we have no chiefs who are better qualified, more intelligent, more active, more capable of appreciating progress and more fully accepted by the people than the Tutsi.[43]

The conversion of leading chiefs was seen as the crucial step in winning the whole population; hence the church's recommendation that the administration should depose Musinga, the anti-christian king of Rwanda, in 1931. When his more promising successor, Mutara, requested baptism, he was told to wait until he had fathered a son, lest he be forced to reject his first wife in order to do so, and thus bring the christian religion into disrepute. Meanwhile the message that 'God requireth *all* men to repent and believe the gospel' was making its inroads into traditional society and values. Hymn No. 281 in the protestant hymnbook *Indirimbo* mentions specifically that the gospel is for Tutsi Ganwa, Hutu and Twa, – this verse is always omitted now –, and yet concern over injustices perpetrated against the Tutsi has been uneasily reconciled with the doctrine that 'the powers that be are ordained of God.' Lemarchand notes that "during the terminal phase of the Belgian trusteeship (in Rwanda), – unlike the Catholics, Anglican missionaries continued to give unrelenting moral and material support to the Tutsi group."[44]

A final paradox concerns the Belgians' belated attempts to modernise political institutions in Burundi and Rwanda, and indeed it was only as a result of intense pressure from the United Nations and developments elsewhere in Africa that anything was done at all. When A. A. Van Bilsen[45] first published his plan in 1955 by which the Belgian territories overseas would achieve self-government within thirty years, howls of protest arose from nearly all sections of the Belgian community. It was pointed out that so few Africans had become 'immatriculated,' the procedure introduced in 1952 by which Africans could climb the final rung on the ladder to 'Europeanness.' The paradox is that those whom the Belgian administration planned to bring into government in Burundi and Rwanda were almost exclusively Tutsi, in addition to their being 'civilised,' while other powerful forces at work, the Belgian trades unions notably among them, were campaigning for the introduction of adult male suffrage and consequently political rights for the Hutu. While the administration still retained its idealised goal of a competent African civil service, the emerging political parties, often with the encouragement of their European supporters, were busily recruiting members on a mainly ethnic basis.

In summary the charge brought against the Belgian administration is that their policies, carefully conceived and philosophically buttressed as they were, brought into being two opposed groups of educated people in Burundi and Rwanda, the one designated as rulers, the other excluded from positions of authority; and secondly that even those who were to rule were denied the opportunity of taking genuine administrative responsibility. If the deliberate policies of colonisation are said to have exacerbated pre-existing ethnic antagonisms, the completely unintended and sudden manner of the Belgian withdrawal from Africa or 'decolonisation process' made matters even worse. Burundi and Rwanda at independence were political vacuums. At least in the Congo the large private industrial sector was an attractive alternative employer, but in Burundi and Rwanda power lay only in government.

The hurried and undignified Belgian withdrawal had created a void
in which ethnic tension was bound to flourish.

V. Violent Discrimination against Tutsi in Rwanda

Although violence directed against the Tutsi in Rwanda from 1959 to
1964, and subsequent civil discrimination, appear to be 'mirrored' by
the fate of the Hutu in Burundi in 1972, what follows is an attempt to
avoid easy generalisations and to make certain important distinctions
between the ethnic discrimination practised to such excess in both
countries.

An attack by young Tutsi militants on a Hutu sub-chief was the
spark which started the violence against the Tutsi in all parts of
Rwanda in November 1959. Hundreds of Tutsi were killed, thousands
of homesteads burned, and the goods plundered. Two events provide
significant background information to this situation. The sudden installation of King Kigeri immediately after Mutara's death earlier in
1959 symbolised to the Hutu the determination of the Tutsi hierarchy
to preserve the ethnic basis of its privileges and to resist what it saw as
Belgian treachery. A letter written by a dozen Tutsi chiefs to the
Grand Council of Rwanda in 1958 had declared: "Since our kings
conquered the Hutu's country, by killing their little kings, and thereby
enslaved the Hutu, how can the latter now claim to be our brothers?"[46]
The other crucial factor is that the Belgian administration had indeed
already determined to tolerate and even facilitate what it judged to be
the 'conscientisation' of the Hutu; more significantly, it interpreted the
sporadic violence of November 1959 as 'evidence' of nationwide revolutionary discontent[47] and intervened decisively in the following
months as a 'midwife' who eventually brought the child Hutu republic
to full birth. The Belgian administration threw the full weight of its
propaganda behind the Hutu candidates in the communal elections of
June–July 1960. When as a result the Belgians were faced with the
unwelcome prospect of Hutu elected officials and a bureaucracy which
was still entirely Tutsi, they set about replacing Tutsi civil servants by
Hutu. The 'Gitarama coup' of 28 January 1961, at which the newly
elected councillors and burgomasters heard the Hutu leadership announce the abolition of the monarchy and call on Kayibanda to form a
government, could not possibly have taken place without the active
connivance of the Belgian authorities. The Special Resident of Rwan-

da, Colonel Logiest, told his staff on 11 January 1960:

What is our goal? It is to accelerate the politicisation of Rwanda . . . . People must go to the polls in full freedom and in full political awareness. Thus we must undertake an action in favour of the Hutu, who live in a state of ignorance and under oppressive influences. By virtue of the situation we are obliged to take sides. We cannot stay neutral and sit.[48]

The legislative elections held under United Nations supervision in September 1961 merely conformed the *de facto* advent to power of the Hutu. The UN Commission for Rwanda-Urundi had baldly set out their view in March of that year:

A racial dictatorship of one party has been set up in Rwanda, and the developments of the last eighteen months have consisted in the transition from one type of repressive régime to another. Extremism is rewarded and there is a danger that the (Tutsi) minority find itself defenceless in the face of abuses . . . .[49]

This extract from a missionary doctor's letters gives some indication of what these abuses were:

While I was doing the ward round, a tall Tutsi rushed into the ward and besought me to save him. He was followed by a gang of Hutu. I drove them out and took the man into the prayer room while a huge crowd collected outside. I refused to allow them to enter, but later Belgian soldiers came and took the poor man away. By afternoon the whole countryside was ablaze and the refugees began pouring in . . . . News came that Timoteyo, our pastor, had been attacked. Ted Sisley went right through the burnings to Timoteyo's house and met him being carried out, speared through the upper thigh. Then they came down this side of the hill and burned out our next-door neighbour and he has been beaten up and one ear is hanging . . . . It is now midnight and from my window I can count seven kraals burning. The gang has said if any of us missionaries are seen off the mission hill we shall be killed.[50]

It was against this background that the supposedly 'democratic' legislative elections were held.

The violence assumed even greater proportions in the months of December 1963 and January 1964, following the abortive invasion of Tutsi refugees from Burundi, known as *inyenzi* 'cockroaches.' These Tutsi were halted only a few kilometers south of the capital Kigali, and in the resulting panic and turmoil which swept Rwanda, some ten to fourteen thousand Tutsi were massacred in incidents of the utmost brutality. Several cases were attested of Tutsi having their feet chopped off so that they would be 'short like the Hutu'; a missionary reported that a group of Hutu "hacked the breasts off a Tutsi woman, and as she lay dying forced the dismembered parts down the throats of her children before her eyes.''[51] The number of Tutsi refugees who then and earlier had fled for their lives to Uganda, Tanzania, Zaire and Burundi, may be put at at least 200,000.

One completely unintended result of this Tutsi invasion was to convince the Hutu régime of the need to close up incipient divisions in their own ranks. Intra-Hutu divisions were evident both in the north among the peasantry at large, and in the centre-south among the educated elite. The northern dispute was between those whose claim to land was based on pre-colonial rights and those Hutu who had been installed on the same land more recently as clients to the imposed Tutsi chiefs (now expelled); the second rift involved the small number of Hutu fortunate enough to have been educated at the government school at Astrida and the Hutu ex-seminarists, because despite similar formal qualifications the former were given preferential access to employment.

Now that the very bloody phase was over, Rwanda's ethnic problems seemed 'solved' – by contrast with the situation in Burundi which is discussed below. The provision made before independence by the visiting UN mission that the Tutsi should have a minority voice in the Rwanda government was soon abandoned. The Hutu obtained a complete monopoly of local and central government posts and created an entirely Hutu army.

The recrudescence of ethnic violence in Rwanda in late 1972 and early 1973 may be attributed to several factors. One indication of Rwanda's lowly position in the league table of the world's poorest countries is the scarcity of new jobs in the already tiny private sector. Most clerical and supervisory positions were occupied at independence by Tutsi because of the educational advantages they had received during the colonial era. The frustration felt by unemployed school-leavers was exacerbated by the fact that, a whole decade after independence, many of these scarce jobs were still in the hands of Tutsi. Furthermore, the esteem of the Tutsi for formal education, fostered by colonial discrimination at the expense of the Hutu, has resulted in a disproportionate number of Tutsi schoolchildren surviving the very competitive scramble for places in the higher grades and at the tertiary level; the fact that many Hutu with intermediate qualifications were able to leave and enter 'middle-ranking' employment heightened the impression that the university of Butare in Rwanda, for example, had become a Tutsi preserve in the centre of a Hutu state. A third factor has been the predominance of Tutsi in the Rwandan church hierarchy, the reason again being that the church was one obvious avenue open to the Tutsi when the public and private sector were discriminating so ardently in favour of the Hutu. So when the church strongly resisted the decision of the state to 'nationalise' mission education, this opposition was interpreted by Hutu as Tutsi antipathy to the 'democratising' policies of the Hutu régime.

The frustration felt by Rwandese Hutu in 1972 at their inability to intervene in support of the Hutu in Burundi undoubtedly found its expression in renewed outbreaks of violence against the Tutsi in Rwanda. At the university, in banks and offices, lists of Tutsi students and employees were posted up with the demand that they be dismissed. According to press reports,[52] up to five hundred Tutsi were killed in the countryside and thousands more fled as refugees. It seems clear that President Kayibanda allowed this 'popular movement' to develop as a means of deflecting the mounting criticism directed against his own nepotistical, regionalist policies; for example, seven of the fifteen government ministers came from his own prefecture of Gitarama. This criticism had mainly been voiced by the Hutu northerners who felt discriminated against. The head of the army, General Habyalimana, himself a northerner, having survived an attempt on his life on 5 July 1974, assumed power in a bloodless coup d'état the very same day.

VI. The Growth of Ethnic Tension in Burundi from Independence to 1972

Until 1972 any discussion of Burundi politics of the period since independence tended to ask why Burundi, although apparently so similar to Rwanda, had not experienced the same violent ethnic strife. With at least 100,000 Hutu slaughtered in 1972 and a further 100,000 made refugees, the question has been reframed; it now asks why there was a delay of more than ten years, and secondly why the violence claimed such distressingly large numbers of victims.

Pre-1972 explanations[53] emphasised differences in the structure of the two traditional societies and differences in the political evolution of each territory under Belgian rule. The first Europeans to enter Rwanda encountered an absolute monarch presiding over a centralised kingdom (apart from certain areas in the north) and distributing power through a hierarchy of Tutsi chiefs dependent on his every word. By comparison the kingdom of Urundi was in disarray with the king disputing his supremacy with at least two powerful rivals. In Rwanda there was no equivalent to the *Ganwa* of Burundi, princes of the blood descended from earlier kings, and who considered themselves separate from and superior to the ranks of ordinary Tutsi. *Ganwa*, and not 'ordinary' chiefs as in Rwanda, were traditionally nominated to the powerful regional chiefdoms and used their independence to challenge the right of every new successor to the throne. There are good grounds for believing that King Mwambutsa is of Hutu extraction, having been substituted for the real son of King Mutaga who was killed by his rival uncles at birth. However, regardless of such biological considerations, the *Ganwa* were at pains to convince the early Europeans in Burundi that they were not Tutsi.[54] The cleavage between Tutsi and Hutu which widened in Rwanda in the 1950s was indeed present in Burundi but was overshadowed by the struggle between two parties, based essentially on the two main *Ganwa* families, the Bezi and the Batare.

The Belgians had consistently supported the christian, cultured, pro-European Batere chief Baranyanka, and made clear their displeasure with the unco-operative King Mwambutsa, whose close relatives formed the Bezi leadership. The UPRONA (Bezi) party, with the king's son Rwagasore at its head, campaigned for immediate independence on a traditionalist, anti-Belgian 'ticket' against the pro-Belgian Parti Democrate Chretien of the Batare and Chief Baranyanka. This situation was thus very different from the one in Rwanda where from his installation in 1931 to the late 1950s King Mutara was the ally of the Belgians, and where Belgian approval of the monarch and his traditional authority was extended much more visibly to the Tutsi administrative chiefs as a group than was ever the case in Burundi. Moreover in Burundi certain Hutu clans had traditionally occupied privileged positions at the royal court, and also there had always been many more Hutu sub-chiefs in Burundi than in Rwanda. The enrolment figures at Astrida, already quoted, show clearly that more Hutu were admitted to secondary education from Burundi than from Rwanda. Lastly, the general impression conveyed by foreigners with experience of both countries is that the clientship ties between Tutsi and Hutu or between Tutsi chief and Hutu subject involved greater oppression of the Hutu in Rwanda than in Burundi.

The next question is to ask how ethnic perceptions came to dominate political life in Burundi in so short a space of time. The ethnic composition of the UPRONA leadership at independence and that of the first few governments thereafter show a remarkable balance between

Tutsi, Hutu and Ganwa elements. Just as the Tutsi refugee invasion of Rwanda shored up the Hutu regime, the assassination of the UPRONA leader Rwagasore by members of the opposing Batare faction had the effect of temporarily uniting Hutu and Tutsi politicians around the UPRONA leadership. However, analysis of the upper echelons of the civil service in 1965 show that, just as in Rwanda, so too in Burundi the superior educational advantages of the Tutsi under Belgian rule had given them the lion's share of appointments, no matter how carefully the actual cabinet might be 'ethnically balanced':[55]

Total	Ganwa	Tutsi	Hutu	Other	Total
Directeur General	—	12	7	—	19
Directeur	3	36	14	1	54
Directeur Adjoint	—	35	22	3	60
	3	83	43	4	133

Several of the Hutu then governing Rwanda were former classmates in school of the Burundi Hutu who were smarting under unequal competition with the Tutsi, and from a comparison of the two situations a self-fulfilling prophecy was born:

By identifying their political aims and aspirations with those of PARME-HUTU (the governing Hutu party in Rwanda), they (Hutu leaders in Burundi) imputed to the Tutsi of Burundi motives which they (the Tutsi) at first did not possess but to which they eventually gave a substance of truth.[56]

The precedent for comparing Rwanda and Burundi was well established under the Belgian administration; civil servants and missionaries alike had consistently minimised or overlooked the essential structural differences between the two countries, with the result that foreign businessmen taking investment decisions in Burundi in the 1960s always bore in mind 'an eventual Rwanda-type revolution'. A Hutu and not a similarly qualified Tutsi was selected as first African bishop of the Anglican church in Burundi, because it was felt that a Hutu leader would have undoubted advantages politically, once the revolution had taken place.

The events in Rwanda not only affected the aspirations of Hutu in Burundi but prompted certain Burundi Tutsi, encouraged by Tutsi refugees from Rwanda, to take 'pre-emptive measures'; such incidents as the beating up of leading Hutu by Tutsi members of the Jeunesse

Nationale Rwagasore in Bujumbura in January 1962 had the effect of giving the spiralling ethnic tension a further twist. The assassination of Prime Minister Ngendandumwe, a Hutu and a known moderate, in January 1965 – allegedly the work of Rwandese Tutsi refugees – and the legislative elections of May 1965 finally brought into the open the fact that ethnic perceptions were now the dominant factor in all political matters. When the election result was known, the Hutu members occupying 22 of the 33 seats in the new parliament, the king abandoned his 'balancing act.' He recalled the *Ganwa* old guard to form a government and entrusted two Tutsi known to be 'hardliners,' Micombero and Butera, with control of the army and justice respectively; as secretaries of state they took their orders from the king and bypassed the authority of the elected parliament. The Hutu immediately realised that they had been manoeuvred out of their electoral gains. The mounting frustration broke out in the form of an abortive attack on the king's palace, and attacks on Tutsi in the interior, mainly in Muramvya province, the latter claiming approximately five hundred victims. Eighty-six leading Hutu politicians and officers were shot in reprisal. The king restored his *Ganwa* government but then left for what became permanent exile in Switzerland, abandoning his country to its increasingly threatening fate.

With the menace of the Hutu temporarily removed, however, the struggle for power now focussed on the radical and conservative Tutsi politicians who were attempting to control Ntare, the teenage son whom Mwambutsa had left to replace him. After only eight months, in November 1966, a group of army officers under Micombero stepped in and declared Burundi a republic. The *Ganwa* politicians were removed, as were some of the Tutsi 'young Turks' formerly prominent in the republican camp. The apparent return to an 'ethnically balanced' government in November 1967 (five Tutsi, five Hutu, and two Ganwa) masks the fact that the cabinet itself had little power, effective decisions being taken by the National Revolutionary Council composed solely of army officers who were, in Lemarchand's words, 'a ruling caste.' The disclosure of an alleged Hutu plot in 1969 and the immediate execution of some thirty leading Hutu confirmed the trend towards Tutsi supremacy. Of the 27 army officers making up the Supreme Council of the Republic, which was set up in October 1971 to supercede the National Revolutionary Council, only two were Hutu. Practically no Hutu received scholarships to study abroad after 1968, while a most bizarre 'girth by height' requirement was introduced as a patent pretext for excluding unwanted Hutu recruits from the army.

The ethnic identity of the participants doubtless influenced the outcome of a rural court case over land or cattle rights, but the statement is surely true that "racism was not born on the hills, it came from the capital."[57] The absence of remunerative employment outside the government sector, and the stark contrast between the lowest teacher's salary and that of a manual worker (about eight times) are pointers to this contention. The words of Martin Ndayahoze, a leading Hutu cabinet minister and army officer killed in 1972, are particularly worthy of quotation:

We can affirm that it is in the leisured class that the virus of tribalism is to be found. What happens is that the evil comes down from the top. It is the undeserving administrative staff who, in order to maintain their rank or to rise to a post they covet, need 'connections,' craftiness, and guile. It is the insatiable people in responsible positions who make a political strategy out of ethnic division in order to further their shameful ambitions. Thus if they are Tutsi they denounce a Hutu peril which must be countered. If they are Hutu they unveil a Tutsi apartheid which must be combatted.[58]

The allegation that as early as 1968 Arthémon Simbananiye, Foreign Minister in 1972, circulated a secret memorandum among Tutsi civil servants calling for a 'final solution' to the 'Hutu problem' becomes almost credible.

The 'judicial parody'[59] of 1971 is evidence of intra-Tutsi group discrimination. The Tutsi close to Micombero and in control of the army, mainly belonging to *Hima* clans and from Bururi province, wished to remove the suspected challenge posed by a group of Tutsi from more aristocratic clans in central and northern Burundi. The latter were suspected of only lukewarm support for republican government and of holding more conciliatory views on power-sharing with the Hutu. At the trial no credible evidence was forth-coming, and the prosecutor for the government, himself a Tutsi from Bururi, resigned and demanded that the case be dismissed. Then in a most dramatic turn of events nine of the accused were sentenced to death and seven to life imprisonment. This deep split in the Tutsi ranks raised tension to danger point all over the country, and the government finally bowed to this internal threat and to intense international pressure by quashing the original sentences. However, the Hutu revolt of April 1972 provides the unhappy sequel to these events: the all-out attack on the Hutu gave the Bururi Tutsi the 'cover' they needed to avenge this earlier setback, and several

Tutsi, among them the recently returned ex-King Ntare, were the first to be eliminated in the repression of May 1972.[60]

VII. The Violence of 1972 in Burundi and Its Aftermath

Crucial aspects of the 1972 'events' remain shrouded in mystery. However, certain facts are beyond dispute.[61] On the evening of 29 April, bands of Hutu, supported by Mulelist rebels from Zaire, attacked army posts in eastern and southern Burundi, while other Hutu attempted to seize the radio station in Bujumbura. Having gained control of arms supplies at Nyanza Lac and Rumonge, the rebels established their 'people's republic,' which lasted only one week before they were completely routed by government troops. Leading Hutu all over Burundi were arrested immediately, accused of complicity, and shot. After the first week of May, that is when the military situation was under full government control again, a wave of repression was unleashed against all educated Hutu and Hutu in paid employment, on a scale unparalleled even at the height of the violence in Rwanda. There had been almost no movement on the part of the Hutu population (other than in the far south of Burundi), certainly not in the provinces of Ngozi and Gitega where the proportion of Hutu is some 90%. The 'attacks,' claimed by the government to have occurred at Gitega, were merely a pretext for executing ex-King Ntare who was held under house-arrest there since being tricked into returning to Burundi 'as a private citizen.' The government radio broadcasts encouraged the population to 'hunt down the python in the grass,' an order which was interpreted by Tutsi in the interior as licence to exterminate all educated Hutu, down to the level of secondary and in some cases even primary school children. Army units commandeered merchants' lorries and mission vehicles, and drove up to schools, removing whole batches of children at a time. Tutsi pupils prepared lists of their Hutu classmates to make identification by officials more straightforward.

Two separate incidents based on the reports of eye witnesses known personally to me may be taken as representative of countless similar incidents which occurred during May, June and July 1972.

On 8 May 1972, ten days after the Hutu rebellion broke out, President Micombero announced on the radio that order had been restored throughout the country. What was meant by 'order' will be clear from this and the following incidents, representative of countless others during the repression of the Hutu from May 1972 onwards.

Six boys from the secondary school at Kibima who had fled in early May returned and were detained in the cells of the local police-post, together with the school secretary and his father who had been arrested. Foreign staff at the school were allowed to take them food twice daily. On 22 May they had gone. It subsequently emerged that the lorry transporting the prisoners had converged with three others on Gitega gaol at the precise moment when there was an attempted break-out inside the prison. The soldiers opened fire, tossing grenades into the prison courtyard. The prisoners in the lorries outside were liquidated on the spot, including a Murundi nun for whom a presidential reprieve had been signed. Sixteen prisoners escaped in the confusion. One, a teenage boy, returned to his school at the mission in Gitega and told his story. In a cell measuring 2m × 2m there had been about sixty prisoners, heaped up in layers. They had broken down the cell door by concerted brute force. This particular boy was later recaptured and killed. His headmaster, who left Burundi at the end of that school year, said that the boy could not have continued studying anyway since his experience had left him mentally deranged.

In mid-June 1972 teachers who had not collected their salaries for April and May were told by radio that if they had not done so by the end of June they would be considered either dead or to have fled the country. The surviving Hutu teachers suspected that this was a plot to identify and eliminate them. Two of the three remaining Hutu staff at Kibimba secondary school left for Bujumbura on 21 June in the company of a European teacher. The car was stopped at the military checkpoint at Muramvya and the two Hutu teachers taken out. Thirty minutes later they reappeared from the guardroom, their valuables gone, and themselves looking badly beaten. The European was escorted to the provincial governor and informed that his two colleagues were rebels. They were never seen again.

The Tutsi in power during those months of May, June and July 1972 admitted their prior knowledge of an impending Hutu attack, and it is surely significant that Micombero dismissed his ministers the very day before the attack was actually launched. It is also known that Shibura, a noted Tutsi 'hardliner,' was in southern Burundi the day before, distributing arms to local officials and warning "Tutsi to be on the watch." What is unclear is whether the extent of the repression should be attributed principally to the panic which gripped the Tutsi at the news of the atrocities perpetrated by the Hutu rebels, or whether more cold-blooded machiavellian tactics may have prevailed.

There is abundant evidence that the Hutu in Burundi have continued to suffer discrimination since 1972. An attempted invasion by Hutu refugees from Tanzania in October 1973 resulted in a further wave of killing of Hutu and devastation of their property. Although an amnesty has now been declared and all refugees urged to return, there are justifiable grounds for the fear that they will be treated as 'rebels.' In May 1972 a certain Hutu teacher was arrested late at night, and subsequently killed; a Tutsi friend accompanied his wife to the bank when it opened next morning to draw out the family's savings, only to find the account already closed and the money gone. In countless cases the furniture was removed from the homes of arrested Hutu, with the widows and orphans left sitting on the bare floor. The cars and lorries of wealthier Hutu became the property of those who arrested them. A considerable sum of money was raised by private subscription for 'victims of the events,' but I know of no Hutu widow or orphan who ever received a franc of that money; only the Tutsi along Lake Tanganyika who had suffered in the original Hutu attack benefited.

Discrimination in access to education, to employment and to the army since 1972 clearly operates. Blatant in 1972–73, it is gradually becoming less obvious. In September 1972 the local inspector came to our primary school, looked at the list of children requesting entry to Standard I and erased a number of names because the children were the sons or daughters of 'rebels.' The church leaders were told that their candidate for appointment as primary school headmaster – to replace one who had been killed – was unsuitable because he was a Hutu. If the academic year of 1975–76 may have seen one or two Hutu students admitted to the university, such cases are isolated exceptions, and even at secondary school level the Hutu are few and far between.

There appear to be no Hutu officers in the army, and after the recruitment drive to strengthen the army after its 1972 losses had taken place, the few Hutu rash enough to volunteer were sent home. Micombero has found two Hutu ministers to convey the impression to the world outside that his government has no ethnic bias, but below them in the 12,000 civil servant posts all Hutu have been eliminated. The leadership of the church shows a similar pattern: two Hutu bishops out of six in the catholic church, but a clergy composed almost entirely of Tutsi. The Hutu priests in training at the Grand Séminaire in Bujumbura fled en masse when their bishop, Mgr. Ntuyuhaga, told them that they had no right to expect his protection in the event of future ethnic strife.

However, the more subtle way in which discrimination operates is that many Hutu voluntarily refuse to compete for places in school; those who are at school take a basic qualification rather than go on to higher education; they seek employment in humble capacities in the missions rather than compete for government jobs. It may be true that some Tutsi in central government actively encourage the Hutu to apply for jobs – as countless official statements would lead one to believe – but once appointed, such Hutu are at the mercy of unscrupulous Tutsi; one hears, for example, of Hutu clerks not being allowed to use the office typewriter.

There is clear evidence of discrimination in the economy. Hutu peasant farmers bringing their coffee or cotton to market discover that they must buy a party card before their crops can be sold or are deceived into accepting a lower price per kilo for their goods than the official one. The result, which is currently of concern to Burundi's foreign economic advisers, is that many Hutu are reverting to subsistence agriculture only, deeming it not worth the extra work of producing cash-crops, only to be cheated out of their profit.

There is equally hard evidence that the international aid organisations who in general are disturbed at the ethnic discrimination obtaining in Burundi and wish somehow to guard against their aid being used to perpetuate it, are blocked at every turn by the Burundi government. Those foreigners impudent enough to ask who will benefit from a particular development project are told unceremoniously to mind their own business.

Some Hutu who fled in 1972 have indeed returned, for example to the plain along Lake Tanganyika. According to very recent reports,[62] however, a number of these people have been rounded up and are in Mpinga prison. One source claims to have seen a list with nineteen names on it. Also in May 1975 an army unit sent to patrol the border with Tanzania killed a whole group of returning refugees. Practically none of the educated Hutu who fled in 1972 or who were already abroad have responded to the President's appeal to return. They are understandably discouraged by the case of Vunuste Ntahondereye, a Burundi Hutu who was removed from a Sabena flight to Rwanda when it was diverted to Bujumbura airport; the man was never seen alive again.

Spokesmen for the Burundi régime since 1972 have constantly reiterated that ethnic discrimination does not exist. However, their argument has rested on the assertion that the Barundi are one tribe, evidence of which is the language, religion and culture which all Barundi share. Our initial discussion tried to make clear that although this linguistic, religious and cultural unity may exist – though with important qualifications which government spokesmen conveniently pass over – what matters is the subjective recognition of differences within the society. President Micombero is right in contrasting the linguistic diversity of Zambia with the linguistic unity of Burundi, but this does not alter the fact that some 85% of the population unanimously class Micombero as a Tutsi, someone apart from them, while the minority include him in their own ranks, as 'one of themselves.'

There are three main reasons for believing that Burundi government assertions about 'no tribalism' are a smokescreen destined to deceive foreigners and to induce ordinary Barundi to alter their perception of themselves. In the first place, while denying the existence of ethnic discrimination, the recently drafted Constitution is soaked in references to tribal or ethnic discrimination. Under *Titre II* ('Of Public Liberties and the Human Person'), it is stated that:

No law, no administrative decision can establish, in the rights and duties of the Barundi, distinctions based on race.
All ethnic propaganda, all manifestations of racial discrimination are punished by the law.
No grouping of whatever kind can make as its aim the defence of the interest of a race, nor make the nomination of its leaders of the recruitment of its members depend on belonging to a particular race. (Article 5.)[63]

Such emphasis makes it evident that the régime knows ethnic distinctions are perceived by the population at large; it is merely hoping to guard against the constant threat of a successful Hutu coup which would consciously introduce a Hutu tribal government, as happened in Rwanda under the First Republic.

The second point is that the President's oft-repeated three objectives for his new seven-year term of office are: social justice, national defence, and improvements to the habitat. The priority given to social justice suggests that serious social injustice must at present exist, and foreigners working in Burundi report that it is impossible for Hutu to get justice in the courts. And why should the régime need to raise the defence expenditure until it is the largest item on the budget, when Burundi's neighbours patently have not the slightest intention of unfriendly acts? One can only infer that the régime fears external or internal challenges which are of an 'ethnic' nature.

The third point of significance is the use made by the régime of the vogue for 'authenticity' now popular throughout Africa. The emphasis in Burundi is not so much on dancing and music as on the 'fact' that

'Burundi has its own mentality' which foreigners can never fully comprehend.

Instead of allowing any open debate on crucial political matters, the regime invokes 'authenticity' of Burundi tradition as a cloak to cover the totally dictatorial, undemocratic nature of its own authority. Thus, although the decision to extend the use of Kirundi as the medium of instruction throughout primary education is to be commended on general psychological and pedagogical grounds, the promoters of such policies are likely to be suspected of wanting to cut off the broad mass of the population from outside influences prejudicial to the régime's own survival. In this connection it is significant that Simbananiye, at present Minister of Education tried in 1975 to bring the *yama mukama* literacy classes organised by the catholic church under government control.[64] Many Hutu parents prefer sending their children to these 'safe' schools, despite the limited academic prospects offered there, but those in power are clearly concerned that these schools should not be allowed to foment dissent.

The other thrust of the authenticity campaign is to blame the Belgians for all the evils of tribalism:

The ditch in question (between the ethnic groups) was dug by the coloniser. Very simply and from earliest youth. The whole school system was marked by segregation. The children had to tell the 'good fathers' to which ethnic group they belonged – that is if they knew it, the poor kids. The very rare centres of higher education were exclusively reserved for the settlers' children to be sure, and for those of the royal family and for very rare Tutsi. No Hutu was admitted. And now there is astonishment that the percentage of employees in the administration does not resemble that of the population in general.[65]

It is suggested that Barundi and Banyarwanda were unaware of their ethnic identity until the Belgians forced them to write it on their passcards. The outside world is told, for example by Térence Nsanze,[66] that the number of Barundi of 'mixed' blood is very high, though everybody knows this not to be the case and confirms that the number of Hutu-Tutsi marriages has *declined* rapidly since the colonial era and has dwindled to zero since 1972. Hutu and Tutsi are said to have lived in a state of perfect symbiosis before the white man came to disturb them. Researchers who, like Rodegem, uncover such uncomfortable facts as the extermination of whole clans[67] are therefore not popular, while other foreigners who appear to bolster the régime's view of Burundi history are fêted. A recent publication of beautiful photographs[68] aimed to stimulate Burundi's tourist industry makes a claim which typifies this approach to the past: there were migrations of Twa, Hutu and Tutsi to Burundi in the distant past, but anyone who claims to know more about it than that is almost certainly telling untruths.

VIII. Discrimination in Contemporary Rwanda

One would expect the publicly stated attitude of the new Rwanda government on ethnic discrimination to be radically different from that of the Burundi régime. It is also different from that of the last Rwanda government. Kayibanda was preoccupied with the task of legitimising the authority of his Hutu, republican, régime, and an effective way of doing this was subtly to rehabilitate 'traditional' customs. The Rwandese President, like the Burundi President, allowed the trappings of the monarchy, to be transferred to them: the former royal titles were gradually introduced in their honour; those summoned for an audience with Mme. Kayibanda found that they had to wait in an ante-room just as was the custom at the royal court at Nyanza; Habyalimana's frank speaking on ethnic matters is a reaction to the veiled but pervasive influence which ethnic factors came to have under the Kayibanda régime. He justified his seizure of power on the grounds that these divisions had to be closed. His position is a strong one, not only because of his military background, but because he is a northerner. The 'premise of inequality,' to borrow Jacques Maquet's title, which the Kayibanda circle could not escape yet felt to be so humiliating, was not shared by the independent Hutu of the north. From his position of strength Habyalimana can attempt to 'exorcise' the latent ethnic factor and even go so far as to advise his 'brother President' Micombero on the subject:

We are lucky (in Rwanda) that the majority is now in command, but I must take into account the fact that all Rwandans are equal both in rights and duties.
  Burundi also has its problems; ... the Tutsi ethnic group is in power, but I am always telling my brother Micombero that he must see to it that he is not President of the Tutsi, but of the Barundi, and that therefore the Tutsi, the Hutu and the Twa must have the same rights and the same duties. I told him that when I went to Kitega recently.[69]

Recent visitors to both Burundi and Rwanda unanimously contrast the feeling of tension in Burundi, the cowed attitude of the Hutu peasantry and the suspicion manifested by the Tutsi, to the freer, more outgoing atmosphere pertaining in Rwanda. Leading Tutsi in Burundi now admit that 1972 was a terrible error and that by allowing the repression against the Hutu to assume such proportions they were digging their own grandchildren's graves. This awareness, however, also has the effect of encouraging the Tutsi in wage-earning positions to make their money while there is time; foreign advisers report that development projects essential to the long-term health of the economy, for example reductions in the cattle stock, are given no encouragement. In Rwanda, by contrast, where the problems of population growth and shortage of arable land are even more pressing than in Burundi, there is far more optimism. The difference can be summarised crudely by saying that the Rwandese Hutu believe that economic development could lead to the successful integration of the Tutsi minority in a unified polity, whereas the Burundi Tutsi fear that ethnic violence is far from over and that they will lose, possibly not the next round, but the final one.

IX. Discrimination against Foreigners

Evidence of a hitherto unknown form of discrimination has arisen in recent months in both countries. In Burundi it is directed against Tutsi refugees from Rwanda, and in Rwanda it affects Hutu refugees from Burundi. Many Tutsi who fled from Rwanda in the early 1960s or who returned to Burundi rather than Rwanda after studying in Europe have risen to positions of authority in their adopted country (as is the case in Uganda and Zaire). For example, several secondary schools, particularly in the interior of Burundi would collapse overnight without their Rwandese staff; at the two protestant church schools where I taught, Rwandese teachers outnumbered their Burundi counterparts by four to one. The university students and secondary school children who fled to escape the new wave of persecution in Rwanda in 1973 were admitted immediately to Burundi educational institutions, and in the case of university students, were given bursaries on a par with those given to Burundi students. Since then, however, the constantly increasing competition for a state number of employment openings has led to a deterioration in the situation. At least one school had to deal with a serious riot between Burundi and Rwandese Tutsi children during 1974–75. Then in August 1975 it was announced that the maxi-

mum number of foreigners allowed in any one school was to be cut
from 20% to 5% as from the start of the new school year; also, foreign
children had to reach 60% in the secondary school entrance exam to be
admitted, whereas Burundi children only needed 45%. Ironically, such
measures increase rather than dissolve the tension, because the Rwandese children remaining tend to come top of their class, a situation
which is then attributed to favouritism on the part of the Rwandese
teachers. There are even reports of Rwandese Tutsi leaving Burundi
for home, an unprecedented phenomenon.

A very similar situation has arisen in Rwanda where the Hutu
refugees from Burundi have discovered that their short honeymoon is
over. In Burundi, the slaughter of so many Hutu students and government officials in 1972 left spaces, into which the incoming Tutsi refugees from Rwanda could easily be absorbed, but in Rwanda the vast
Hutu influx merely increased the already severe pressure on educational and employment places. A condition of the tripartite agreement
between Presidents Mobutu, Habyalimana and Micombero was that
refugees should be removed to at least 100 km from the border of their
country of origin. For Burundi refugees in Rwanda this meant the
inhospitable swamps of the Bugesera or the arid plains of the north-
east. One of the ways to avoid being sent there was to gain recognition
as a student, and so the ranks of those besieging Rwanda's schools have
swollen accordingly.

X. DISCRIMINATION AGAINST THE TWA

The Twa have been omitted altogether from the discussion so far, and
indeed in many articles on Burundi and Rwanda they only receive a
one-line mention when the population figures are given. In the absence
of any reliable statistics they are always said to number 1% of the total
population. However, in a study whose title is discrimination, the Twa
demand detailed treatment.

All other Barundi and Banyarwanda claim to be able to recognise
the Twa on sight and to identify them by their accent. When asked
why the Twa are despised, a whole host of reasons are given, and it is
virtually impossible today to verify which of the customs the Twa
genuinely practise and what is merely attributed to them out of prejudice. What follows, therefore, is a collation of what a wide variety of
informants in different parts of Burundi and Rwanda told me. Twa

children are brought up without training in modesty and respect for their parents. The Twa will simply let their daughters be carried off without exacting the *inkwano* or 'bride-wealth.' It is the women who rule the household, the Twa men wander around the hill or go off hunting in a band for days at a time. They are greedy, they eat meat which other Barundi would never touch – rats, moles, sheep – and they prefer food to francs, they do not understand what money is for. The corpses of their dead are just thrown away in a deserted spot, whereas the Hutu and Tutsi are careful to bury their dead. They are inordinately fearful and smoke hemp to gain courage. They file their teeth and have a childish weakness for beads and ornaments; you will still find Twa women wearing copper wire rings on their legs. It would be defilement for other Barundi to eat, drink, or sit under the same roof as a Twa, and hence a Hutu or Tutsi would never take a Twa to court over a grievance. Just as gypsies in Europe are often reputed to be very rich, the Twa are said to have wealth – even to own cows.

The fate of the Twa has grown steadily worse since the abolition of the monarchy and the earlier abolition of feudal institutions in both countries. The majority of Twa scraped a bare living from making pottery or hunting, but a minority occupied traditional and specialised positions at the royal court, particularly in Rwanda, as jesters, executioners, undertakers, builders of the king's huts, etc., and at the courts of leading chiefs. The only instances I heard of where privileged positions had survived the change to modern political institutions were of a Twa deputy in Rwanda in 1961 and a Twa policeman in central Burundi in 1972. Sometimes Twa servants were rewarded with freehold land, or were allowed temporary rights on their masters' property; the Twa community adjacent to the Kibimba mission in Burundi had received their land as a gift from King Mwambutsa, while another group had received land after presenting a local chief with leopard skins. More commonly a group of Twa families would build very simple grass huts on an unoccupied piece of land and move on after a few months, partly to avoid paying the poll-tax, and partly according to custom if a child died while they were there.

Their story is one of continuous exploitation by the rest of Burundi and Rwanda society. Most of them have lost control of their own land, the group near Kibimba having been 'bought out' by local Hutu who then employed them as labourers on what had been their own land. The Twa women produce clay pots with great skill and at great speed, but the price the pots fetch at the local market indicates clearly who controls the transaction. An indication that their status is becoming increasingly 'marginal' in both societies, is that in the Rwanda violence of 1959–63 many Twa fought for their Tutsi patrons and in many cases accompanied them into exile, whereas the Burundi Twa played almost no part in the ethnic violence of 1972.

Discrimination against the Twa summarised in the earlier quotation "They are not people, they are Twa," is described in this extract from a missionary's letters in the 1930s:

The Vatwa, or Pygmies, mingle with the others only when selling pots, mats, etc. They do not come to our services or school, because they know the feeling against them on the part of the other classes . . . . The Vatwa are the 'scum' and the other tribes will not intermarry with them.[70]

An astonishing passage later in the same book shows that 'Twa' was a term of abuse, and secondly highlights the protestant-catholic discrimination practised at the time which this article does not cover:

The Catholic opposition is stronger . . . . The padre told the folks we do not know God; that he is not here; that we are Pygmies.[71]

A missionary told me that the best way for protestant Barundi to refute these charges was to tell the Catholics that King Mwambutsa had eaten lunch with the protestant missionaries, that the houseboys had seen this take place, and therefore that the missionaries could not possibly be Twa since the King would never eat with Pygmies!

The forty years since the above quotations have seen significant changes in ecumenical understanding between protestants and catholics, but the assessment of discrimination against the Twa remains just as valid. One hears of the occasional Mutwa in a seminary somewhere, but the few who start attendance in the primary schools rarely survive that far; they are driven out on the flimsiest of pretexts, for example that no other child will sit next to them and share their book, or that they smell badly and are unclean. When a Twa woman attended the crowded church at Kibimba, she was given a whole bench to herself. In northern Burundi, the decision of a catholic priest to live in a Twa community and teach them modern techniques of pottery and help them find markets for their products, was met with deep suspicion on the part of the local authorities. Rare efforts by other Barundi to 'civilise' the Twa have not met with success either; a catholic government official paid for a Twa boy and girl to be educated in Bujumbura in the hope that they would marry and produce a 'progressive' family, but once educated the boy said "I am a man now, I am not going to marry a Twa!"

The Twa huts at Kibimba actually adjoin the hospital compound, but hardly ever does a Twa come for treatment, and they go right down into the valley for water rather than use the tap in front of the hospital door. Their distinctive vocabulary and accent, substituting 's' for 'sh' and 'z' for 'j,' and their fondness for wearing charms causes great merriment among other Barundi. When formal encounters take place, for example when groups of children were taken to watch the Twa women making pots, or when individual Twa come begging at foreigners' houses, they readily conform to the stereotype which the rest of the community has of them, shouting, singing, and dancing in the uncontrolled manner which 'proper' Burundi and Rwanda culture so much despises.

NOTES

1. Burundi and Rwanda each has a population variously estimated at between three and four millions. The inhabitants, known respectively as Barundi and Banyarwanda, categorise themselves as belonging to one of three ethnic groups, Tutsi, Hutu and Twa. To be fully consistent, the forms 'Batutsi', 'Bahutu', and 'Batwa' should be used, but the Bantu prefix 'ba' has been dropped, in accordance with the prevailing usage. Censuses conducted under Belgian rule included a question on ethnic group identity, and the following figures generally emerged: Tutsi (14%), Hutu (85%), and Twa (1%), the proportions being approximately the same in both countries. The languages spoken, Kirundi in Burundi and Kinyarwanda in Rwanda, are considered to be varieties of the same basic language.
   The present government of Burundi, which has President Micombero at its head, is recognised to be predominantly Tutsi, while the present government of Rwanda, under President Habyalimana, is predominantly Hutu.

2. République du Barundi, Ministère de l'Information: *Livre Blanc* Bujumbura, 1972.

3. Emerson, Rupert, "The fate of human rights in the Third World", *World Politics* Vol. 27 No. 2, Jan. 1975, p. 206.

4. *New York Times*, 18 July 1973.

5. Korey, William, "The key to human rights implementation", *International Conciliation*, No. 570 (Nov. 1968), p. 17.

6. E.g. Newman, Frank, "The international bill of human rights: does it exist?" in Cassese Antonio (ed.) *Current Problems of International Law*, Milan: Guiffré, 1975.

7. United Nations: *International Covenant on Human Rights* (adopted by Res. 2200 (XXI) of 16 Dec. 1966) – *International Covenant on Civil and Political Rights*, Part II, Article 4.

8. *Flash-Infor* (Bujumbura), No. 1281, 8 Feb. 1975.

9. *Ibid.*, No. 459, 18 May 1972.

10. *Ibid.*, No. 472, 3 June 1972.

11. Huxley, Julian, Haddon, A. C., and Carr-Saunders, A. M., *We Europeans: a survey of 'racial' problems*, Harmondsworth: Penguin Books, 1939 p. 30.
12. Kirkwood, Kenneth, "Ethnic, cultural and racial pluralism: awareness, education, and policy," *Oxford Review of Education*, Vol. 1, No. 2, 1975, p. 113.
13. *Times Higher Education Supplement*, 26 Dec. 1975, p. 9.
14. Harrison, G. A. and Boyce, A. J., (eds), *The structure of human populations* Oxford: Clarendon Press, 1972, p. 3.
15. Ardener, Edwin, "Language, ethnicity, and population," *Journal of the Anthropological Society of Oxford* Vol. 3, No. 3, 1972.
16. Hiernaux, J., *Les caractères physiques des populations du Ruanda et de l'Urundi*, Brussels, 1954
17. Nsanze, Térence, *L'édification de la République du Burundi*, Brussels, 1970.
18. Forscher, Romain, "Les massacres du Burundi, le 'tribalisme' en Afrique Noire," *Esprit* (Paris), July–August 1972, p. 128.
19. Rodegem, F. M., *Dictionnaire Rundi-Français*, Tervuren: Annales du Musée Royal de l'Afrique Centrale, 1970.
20. Cyimana, G., *Plaidoyer pour le menu peuple au Ruanda-Burundi*, n.p., 1958 (?), p. 248.
21. Sandrart, Georges, *Cours de droit coutumier*, Part II, Astrida (Rwanda): Groupe Scolaire, 1951, p. 32.
22. Rodegem, F. M., "Burundi: la face cachée de la rébellion," *Intermédiaire* (Brussels), Yr. 4, No. 12, 15 June 1973, p. 17.
23. Among the standard works are:
    – D'Hertefelt, M., Trouwborst, A. A. and Scherer, J. H., *Les anciens royaumes de la zone interlacustre*: Tervuren: M.R.A.C. Monographies Ethnographiques No. 6, 1962. (*Ruanda, Burundi, Buha*)
    – Maquet, Jacques J. *The premise of inequality in Ruanda*, London: OUP for IAI, 1961.
24. See Botte, R., Dreyfus, F., Le Pape, M., and Vidal, C., "Les relations personnelles de subordination dans les sociétés interlacustres de l'Afrique Centrale," *Cahiers d'Etudes Africaines* No. 35, Vol. 9, 1969, especially part IV: Vidal Claudine, "Le Rwanda des anthropologues ou le fétichisme de la vache."
25. Albert, Ethel, "'Rhetoric,, 'Logic,' and 'Poetics' in Burundi: culture patterning of speech behaviour", *American Anthropologist*, Special Issue Winter 1964–65, pp. 35–54.
26. Mecklenburg, Adolf Friedrich, *Ins Innerste Afrika*, Leipzig: 1909, p. 101.
27. Roehl, K., "Die sozialen und wirtschaftlichen Verhältnisse Ruandas," *Koloniale Rundschau*, No. 5, 1914, pp. 27–287.
28. Sasserath, Jules, *Le Ruanda-Urundi: Etrange royaume féodal*, Brussels: Editions Germinal, 1948, pp. 27–30.
29. De Lacger, Louis, *Ruanda*, Vol. I, Namur: Grands Lacs, 1939, p. 49.
30. Choate, Ralph, *Dust of His Feet*, a short history of the Friends Africa Gospel Mission, Mweya (Burundi): 1965, n.p., p. 3.
31. Brown, Albert, *Getting to know Burundi*, London: Ruanda Mission (CMS), 1973, p. 4.
32. Roehl, K., *op. cit.*
33. Maquet, Jacques J., *op. cit.*
34. Codere, Helen, "Power in Rwanda," *Anthropologica*, Vol. 4, No. 2, 1962, p. 63.
35. Ntuyuhaga, M., "The return of cattle in Burundi" in Whiteley, W. H., (ed *A selection of African prose Volume II*, Oxford: Clarendon Press, 1964, p. 144.
36. Quoted in Lemarchand, René: *Rwanda and Burundi*, London: Pall Mall Press, 1970, p. 142.
37. The fact that Rwagasore, the king's son, married Marie-Rose Ntamwikevyo,

a girl from a Hima clan, considered very inferior by the aristocratic Nyaruguru clans, and in defiance of traditional custom, further improved his image as "a man for all the Barundi." However, after his assassination his wife was cruelly humiliated by her more illustrious rivals.

38. Quoted in Lemarchand, René, *op. cit.*, p. 66.
39. *Ibid.*, p. 119.
40. Chretien, Jean-Pierre, "Une révolte au Burundi en 1934," *Annales-Economies, Sociétés, Civilisations* (Paris), Yr. 25, No. 6, Nov.–Dec. 1970. p. 1704.
41. Table quoted in Lemarchand, R., *op. cit.*, p. 138.
42. *Ibid.*, p. 139.
43. Quoted by De Lacger, *op. cit.*, p. 522.
44. Lemarchand, R., *op. cit.*, p. 133.
45. Quoted in Chomé, J., *L'ascension de Mobutu*, Paris: Maspero, 1974, p. 8.
46. Cyimana, G., *op. cit.*, p. 245.
47. Lemarchand, R., *op. cit.*, p. 142.
48. Quoted by Lemarchand, R., *op. cit.*, p. 175.
49. *Ibid.*, p. 194.
50. St. John, Patricia, *Breath of Life*, London: Norfolk Press, 1971, p. 209.
51. Quoted in Lemarchand, R., *op. cit.*, p. 224.
52. Ugeux, Etienne, "Rwanda: un nouvel envol," *Remarques Africaines*, No. 457, 15 Feb. 1975, p. 9.
53. See especially Lemarchand, René, "Status differences and ethnic conflict" in Bell, Wendell and Freeman, Walter, *Ethnicity and nation-building: comparative, internal and historical perspectives*, Beverley Hills and London; Sage Publications, 1974, pp. 135–146.
54. Zuure, Bernard, *Croyances et pratiques religieuses des Barundi*, Brussels, 1929, p. 28.
55. Répartition ethnique des fonctionnaires de la categorie de direction en service au 1er juillet 1965, n.d., n.p., typescript.
56. Lemarchand, R., *op. cit.*, p. 344.
57. Forscher, Romain, art., *op. cit.*, p. 129.
58. *Ibid.*, p. 131.
59. See "Parodie judiciaire au Burundi," *Remarques Africaines*, No. 393, 10 Feb. 1972, pp. 9–14.
60. Greenland, Jeremy, "Black racism in Burundi," *New Blackfriars* (Oxford), Oct. 1973, pp. 441–433.
61. For a fuller treatment of the 1972 'events' and subsequent developments, see for example, Lemarchand, René and Martin, David, *Selective Genocide in Burundi* (1974), available in French and English from Minority Rights Group 36 Craven Street, London WC2; and the papers collected in Lemarchand, René and Greenland, Jeremy (eds.), *Les Problèmes du Burundi*, Colloque International, Brussels, 27–28 Dec. 1974, copies available from the authors.
62. *Liberazione* (Bonate Sopra, Italy), Yr. 2, No. 4, Oct. 1975, pp. 8–9.
63. Constitution of the Republic of Burundi, as published in *Flash-Infor* No.1107, 15 July 1974.
64. *Liberazione*, art., *op. cit.*
65. *Flash-Infor*, No. 506, 14 July 1972.
66. Nsanze, Terence, *op. cit.*
67. Rodegem, F. M., *Intermediaire*, art., *op. cit.*
68. Richer, Xavier, *Burundi Touristique*, Boulogne: Eds. Delroisee, 1975.
69. *Remarques Africaines*, No. 457, 15 Feb. 1975, p. 8.
70. Beals, Mildred, *Urundi for Christ* – a history of the Friends Africa Gospel Mission of Kansas Yearly Meeting 1933–40, compiled from missionaries' letters. Wichita, Kansas, 1941, p. 96.
71. *Ibid.*, p. 136.

The Balancing Act: Quota Hiring in Higher Education

GEORGE ROCHE

GEORGE CHARLES ROCHE III was for five years director of seminars at the Foundation for Economic Education in Irvington-on-Hudson, New York, and since 1971 has been the eleventh president of Hillsdale College in Hillsdale, Michigan. Before that, he taught history and philosophy at the Colorado School of Mines in Golden, Colorado. After receiving his A.B. in history from Denver's Regis College, he spent two years as a Marine Corps officer. His M.A. and Ph.D. – both in history – are from the University of Colorado, where he also taught for a year.

Dr. Roche is a member of the American Historical Association, the Philadelphia Society, the Textbook Evaluation Committee of *America's Future*, the Mont Pelerin Society, the National Advisory Board of Young Americans for Freedom, and the American Academy of Political and Social Science. He is also a consultant to the Center for Independent Education, vice president of the American Association of Presidents of Independent Colleges and Universities, chairman of the Academic Advisory Council of the Charles Edison Memorial Youth Fund, a member of the Advisory Council of the Freedom Education Committee of the American Association of Physicians and Surgeons, and a member of the board of directors of the Qualpeco Corporation of New York City. In 1972, Dr. Roche received the Freedom Leadership Award of Freedoms Foundation, Valley Forge, Pennsylvania.

He is a contributing editor of two magazines, *Private Practice* and *The St. Croix Review*. He writes a nationally distributed newspaper column, and his magazine articles have appeared in numerous publications. He is also the author of four books: *Education in America, Legacy of Freedom, Frederic Bastiat: A Man Alone,* and *The Bewildered Society*.

The Balancing Act: Quota Hiring in Higher Education

GEORGE ROCHE

I. What is Affirmative Action?

> We have a whale of a lot of power, and we're prepared
> to use it if necessary.
>
> J. Stanley Pottinger

In December 1972 Columbia University announced, "We would like
to have been able to make copies of the full-text edition of Columbia
University's Affirmative Action Programme available to interested parties without cost. However, because of the expense involved in repro-
ducing, collating, binding, packing, and handling this 316 page, 3-1/2
pound document, we are making it available at $17.25 per copy, which
includes postage."

If an interested party were to send for a copy of this document,
though it is difficult to imagine who might be interested, he would
receive a bureaucratized and computerized flood of trivia about the
inner workings of Columbia University – more than most observers
could conceivably want. The vast outpouring of time and energy necessary to gather and evaluate this information on institutional policy
symbolizes a major crisis for Columbia, a crisis given public airing by
its administrators.

Columbia University is not alone in its anguish. Other institutions of
higher learning across the nation are suffering similar problems as they
rush headlong to comply with the Department of Health, Education,
and Welfare guidelines imposing racial and sexual quotas on campus.
They find they are obliged to hire directors of Affirmative Action Planning at substantial salaries, and set up Affirmative Action programmes

This paper was originally published as a book, under the same title by the Open
Court Publishing Company, La Salle, Illinois, 1974. The Editors are grateful for
permission to reprint.

with policy influence over every aspect of campus life. Such schools as Cornell, Duke, Vanderbilt, Dartmouth, Johns Hopkins, the state universities of Illinois, Michigan, Missouri, and North Carolina, are among the growing number of public and private institutions already on the road towards Affirmative Action compliance.

A. *Federal Funding as a Weapon*

In a typical Affirmative Action project, the Department of Health, Education, and Welfare (HEW) has demanded that the City University of New York (the largest urban educational institution in the nation, with over 221,000 students and 16,000 staff members) comply with all HEW guidelines, set up an appropriate master plan, and provide complete information to the Office of Civil Rights (OCR), including access to all personnel files by OCR representatives. If this seems a substantial demand, substantial powers of enforcement lie behind the demand. HEW has warned the City University of New York (CUNY) that, should there be failure to comply, "sanctions may include the termination, suspension, or cancellation of existing contracts and subcontracts held by the university and debarment of the university from future receipt of contracts and subcontracts." In short, CUNY has been told by the Office of Civil Rights that complete employment information and evidence of institutional restructuring along HEW-approved racial and sexual lines must be forthcoming, lest HEW sanctions (involving loss of some $13 million in federal research contracts) be invoked.

For over a year before being put on public notice, CUNY had been attempting to move toward racial and sexual hiring quotas – not rapidly enough, however, for the man who was then chief administrator of OCR, Mr. J. Stanley Pottinger. Mr. Pottinger announced at a news conference that CUNY was being put "on clear notice" that "continued non-cooperation" would lead to sanctions.

Affirmative Action, under the auspices of HEW and OCR, has blossomed into a bureaucratic nightmare. Backed by the full force of Labor Department Revised Order No. 4, HEW and OCR have, since 1971, developed enforcement procedures which reflect a political attempt to mould the hiring practices for America's colleges and universities. American higher education is particularly vulnerable to this assault, since the federal government now disperses contract funds among colleges and universities which run to billions of dollars a year. The funding continues to grow. The Carnegie Commission on Higher Education has recently urged that federal funding to higher education be increased still further within the next six years to some $13 billion a year.

Some of America's most prestigious institutions are already deeply committed to the continued receipt of federal funding. The University of California budget calls for federal contract funds in the vicinity of $72 million a year, the University of Michigan is involved in federal funding to the tune of $60 million, and similar dependence is evidenced by other first-line schools on a level comparable with Princeton, Columbia, and Harvard.

According to HEW figures, federal funding necessitates compliance with OCR guidelines on 2,500 of the nation's 3,000 campuses. The majority of those campuses approached to date have been rushing to comply. This rush to racist and sexist quotas in higher education is being implemented on most campuses by men and women who think of themselves as liberal, who customarily (not to say ritually) voice their commitment to the open society in which individuals would presumably be judged exclusively on the basis of their merits. At least one of the reasons for the dramatic reversal which has occurred must surely be the increasing dependence on federal funding in recent years.

One of the first schools to feel HEW pressures for Affirmative Action was Columbia University, where roughly one-half of the $175 million annual dubget is federal money. The 1971 HEW assault astonished Columbia officials who felt that they ". . . had been making very serious efforts during recent years to keep the university abreast of rapidly moving patterns of social change in New York City . . ." As Columbia President William McGill put it,

In all respects Columbia's record in the field of Affirmative Action to remove employment discrimination seemed to me to be an outstanding one. Nevertheless the government chose to move against us . . . No one likes to be in the position of negotiating for his survival with Uncle Sam sitting at the other end of the table. Our instincts in such circumstances were to promise almost anything in order to get the government off Columbia's back.

The special irony of the present situation is that only a few years ago the very academics who today are under such enormous pressure from HEW were the same people who scoffed at the idea that federal money might bring federal control to higher education.

B. *The New Discrimination*

Nevertheless, control has come, and with flagrant discrimination on a
nationwide scale. HEW itself has been careful to avoid setting quotas,
since such quotas would be in clear violation of the Civil Rights Act.
Instead, colleges and universities have been setting their own quotas in
a feverish rush to comply with federal pressures. As the result, some
strange policies, new to the American academic scene, are now very
much in evidence. Vast amounts of time and money are being poured
into Affirmative Action programmes. Complicated surveys examining
the ethnic backgrounds of faculty members are being undertaken. Announcements of job openings appearing in professional circles openly
mention specific racial, sexual, or ethnic "qualifications" for employment. *De facto* discrimination is now commonplace:

The Department of Philosophy at the University of Washington is seeking
qualified women and minority candidates for faculty positions at all levels
beginning Fall Quarter 1973 ...
   We desire to appoint a Black or Chicano, preferably female ...
   Dear Sir: The Department of Economics at Chico State is now just entering the job market actively to recruit economists for the next academic
year ... Chico State College is also an affirmative action institution with
respect to both American minority groups and women. Our doctoral requirements for faculty will be waived for candidates who qualify under the
affirmative action criteria.
   Dear Colleague: Claremont Men's College has a vacancy in its ... Department as a result of retirement. We desire to appoint a black or Chicano,
preferably female ...
   I should very much appreciate it if you could indicate which of your 1972
candidates are either Negro or Mexican American.
   Dear ...: We are looking for females ... and members of minority grouds.
As you know, Northwestern along with a lot of other universities is under
some pressure ... to hire women, Chicanos, etc.
   Your prompt response to my letter of May 12 with four candidates, all of
whom seem qualified for our vacancy, is greatly appreciated. Since there
is no indication that any of them belong to one of the minority groups
listed, I will be unable to contact them ...
   Dear Mr. ...: All unfilled positions in the university must be filled by
females or blacks. Since I have no information regarding your racial identification, it will be possible for me to contact you for a position only in the
event you are black.

Only a few years ago, such hiring practices would have been denounced as racist and discriminatory, yet today they find wide accep-

tance throughout the academic community. How did this change occur?

C. Legal History

The Office of Civil Rights derives its claim to authority, via HEW, from the Department of Labor, which in turn bases its authority on Executive Order 11246 which was signed by Lyndon Johnson in 1965 pursuant to the Civil Rights Act of 1964. There are good reasons for doubting that President Johnson or anyone else connected with the original civil rights legislation and its implementation anticipated the extent to which middle-echelon bureaucrats would pervert anti-discrimination legislation into discriminatory programmes. Yet this is exactly what has occurred.

Originally "affirmative action" was little more than a political slogan, first used by President Kennedy to urge correction of various civil and economic handicaps experienced by minorities in federal employment. By the Johnson years, the slogan was beginning to appear with greater frequency during debate on the Civil Rights Act. During Senate hearings on the act, the fear was expressed that the powers being considered might be later used to force discriminatory hiring. At the time, the fears were dismissed and the act passed.

Though the final draft of the 1964 Civil Rights Act did not mention the phrase, "affirmative action" continued to find its way into discussions of enforcement tactics for the legislation. It was suggested that overall racial proportions should be used as evidence measuring intent and performance of institutions covered by the Civil Rights Act. Presumably such "evidence" would allow the enforcing federal officials to bypass the slow process of individual court cases and thus deal directly with discriminatory situations. In the mid 1960s, even the most outspoken proponents of the concept saw racial proportions as only one indicator of possible discrimination. "Equal opportunity" was still the ultimate goal and quotas were only a specific means to that general end.

As the 1960s wore on, that distinction between means and ends became increasingly obscure. When President Johnson issued his 1967 executive order calling for affirmative action to eliminate employment discrimination among federal contractors, the stage was set for increasing implementation of the quota system. Revised Order No. 4 was issued by the Department of Labor only months after the Johnson executive order, presumably as an "implementation" of the executive order. But Revised Order No. 4 did far more. It converted the executive order's original non-discriminatory intent into a weapon to enforce discriminatory hiring:

An acceptable affirmative action programme must include an analysis of areas within which the contractor is deficient in the utilization of minority groups and women, and further, goals and timetables to which the contractor's good faith efforts must be directed to correct the deficiencies and thus, to increase materially the utilization of minorities and women, at all levels and in all segments of his work force where deficiencies exist.

Affirmative Action now began enforcement of the same preferential discrimination on the basis of race and sex which had been expressly forbidden by the Civil Rights Act. Percentage hiring goals, first imposed upon the construction industry in the "Philadelphia Plan" and the "Long Island Plan," spread quickly to racial and sexual quotas for other industrial hiring and then moved throughout the American business community. Meanwhile, enforcement of Revised Order No. 4 in federal dealings with colleges and universities was delegated by the Labor Department to HEW. By late 1971, Affirmative Action had arrived on the campus.

The Office of Civil Rights has handled HEW enforcement of the programme for colleges and universities. Complete records for all employment practices are required of those institutions under examination. This in itself has caused consternation in many schools where confidential employment records have customarily been safe from external scrutiny. Another difficulty has arisen from the fact that most academic employment forms do not require racial information, both because laws in many states specifically forbid the practice and because most colleges and universities have in recent years shown little interest in questions of race or national origin when recruiting their professors. As the result, the Office of Civil Rights, exerting pressure for employment statistics which do not exist, has forced a number of schools into such bizarre antics as judging racial or ethnic origin by analyzing the name or physical appearance of a professor. For this reason, there has been great emphasis upon "candidates with Spanish or Indian surnames," "visual surveys" of faculty, and similarly penetrating means of analyzing a collegiate teaching staff.

However bizarre the means, the Office of Civil Rights has the power to push on towards its end. A college or university may have its Affirmative Action analysis and programmes rejected again and again, with the threat of contract cancellation always available as a club to insure compliance.

D. Resistance to Quotas

There have been some notable efforts within the academic community to resist OCR pressures. However, many institutions seem to protest less as a matter of principle than as the result of a feared inability to comply with HEW demands and thus risk loss of federal funding. The general feeling seems to be that the OCR demands are more objectionable in tone than intent. The bureaucratic arrogance which accompanies Affirmative Action programmes is apparently a new experience for many American educators and they have been almost uniformly unenthusiastic.

A protest with greater meaning has come from a relatively small group of educational leaders who are resisting the quota system on principle. Professor Sidney Hook's Committee on Academic Nondiscrimination and Integrity has attracted the support of some 500 scholars, including such major figures as Bruno Bettelheim of Chicago, Nathan Glazer of Harvard, and Eugene Rostow of Yale, all convinced that Affirmative Action as presently proposed will be extremely harmful to academic standards throughout higher education. Through the strong stand taken by these professors and by other groups such as the University Center for Rational Alternatives under the direction of Miro Todorovich, some reversals of Affirmative Action discrimination have been achieved.

The case of W. Cooper Pittman, a doctoral candidate at George Washington University who was caught in the web of Affirmative Action, shows what can be achieved by a principled stand. Pittman's story begins with a letter he received on 16 August, 1972, stating:

The recommendation for your appointment to the department of psychology at Prince George's Community College was disapproved by the board of trustees on August 15, 1972. The basis for disapproval was primarily that the position presently vacant in that department requires certain qualifications regarding the overall profile of the institution and department as well as educational qualifications of the individual involved.

The disapproval in no way reflects upon your professional preparation or specific background in the area of clinical psychology. The decision was based primarily on the needs of the department in accord with its profile and qualifications.

This reversal came on the heels of a series of earlier promising developments. While specializing in clinical psychology, Mr. Pittman taught during the preceding academic year, offering courses at Prince George's Community College. Planning to make college teaching his lifetime profession, he had applied for a full time teaching position in the school for the 1972–73 academic year. As the winter proceeded, the chairman of the department described Pittman's chances as "very good." In the spring of 1972, he was referred to as "the leading contender." By summer he was introduced as the man who would be "with us this fall." This seemed natural, since he was selected by the departmental committee from among 30-plus applicants as the department's "No. 1 recommendation."

Pittman's rank of assistant professor and a corresponding salary were approved by the dean of social sciences and the vice president of academic affairs. In July the department chairman asked Pittman for his preferences in the autumn teaching schedule. Mr. and Mrs. Pittman began their search for housing in the area of the college.

And so it went until August 3, when the department chairman broke the news orally that the president and the trustees, at a July 31 meeting, had disapproved Pittman's appointment to the department of psychology. At the same meeting, the trustees and president had also ordered that the two positions open in the department be filled by women, preferably black women. A woman applicant was subsequently hired. At that time, the board and president instructed the department of psychology to fill the remaining position with a black qualified in clinical psychology. In the opinion of the chairman, Pittman would have been hired without difficulty had he been a woman or a black.

This clear case of reverse discrimination has a happy ending. Through the good offices of the opponents of Affirmative Action, the Pittman case received national attention. On November 14, 1972, Pittman was hired by the college with pay retroactive to August 21. On November 15, the president of the college was replaced.

Similar results have been obtained in the area of student recruitment this past year at the University of Massachusetts. The applications of some 300 students were set aside by the admissions department since the students were not members of any favoured minority group and the school has an "affirmative action commitment to recruit minority students." Under pressure from outside the campus, the decision was hastily reversed and the 300 applications were reviewed on their individual merits.

Unfortunately such happy endings are all too uncommon in today's academic community. Many educators have been unwilling to take a strong strand. Not only have they acquiesced in the face of Affirmative Action pressures, but in many cases over-anxious administrators have raced beyond even the guidelines placed upon them by OCR, pushing reverse discrimination to shocking levels. Meanwhile, there has been all too little formal protest from the academic community itself. As of this writing, no group of academic institutions has yet gone to court seeking an injunction against implementation of the Labor Department's Revised Order No. 4 on the grounds that its enforced discrimination runs directly counter to the 1964 Civil Rights Act. This refusal on the part of most educators to take a strong stand amounts to tacit approval of discrimination on the basis of race and sex and a craven denial of equal opportunity in education.

E. Confusion on the Campus

This inability or unwillingness to stand on principle has left a wave of confusion and low morale in its wake. Elie Abel, dean of the Columbia Graduate School of Journalism, has agonized in the pages of the *New York Times*, "We can't, in essence, hire, promote, or give a raise to anyone without clearing it over there [HEW]. Are they really trying to tell us we cannot promote our own assistant professors without setting up a nationwide search?"

Educators who feel threatened in the self-determination and internal control of their departments and schools perhaps should also consider the implications which lie behind that threat. When a bureaucrat can threaten withholding virtually millions of dollars in funds from Columbia University, not because Columbia has been found guilty of specific acts of discrimination, but because Columbia, after a half-dozen attempts and the expenditure of tens of thousands of dollars in computer studies, has failed to come up with an Affirmative Action plan satisfactory to the bureaucracy, the results should be obvious to all: federal control of higher education now threatens to produce severe damage to those independent values which have meant so much for the preservation of our institutions of higher learning and the maintenance of an open society.

Many of those who have thought themselves most liberal and most committed to the idea of an open society which judged each of us on individual merit now find themselves involved in a process apparently designed to end any role for individual merit in higher education. These same educators now so vitally concerned about the continuance of federal funding for higher education should recall that their troubles actually began long ago, at the time when so many colleges and universities accepted the idea of large-scale federal aid for higher education. At that time, some observers warned that federal aid would ultimately produce government control over higher education. Anyone familiar with higher education in the past twenty years knows that those warnings were dismissed as absurd. Surely the well-intentioned supporters of higher education who were making federal funding available would never consider using that funding as the basis for control! Or so most American colleges and universities believed a few short years ago.

Today the question of federal encroachment on higher education is no longer a matter of speculation. Affirmative Action has a large and significant role in determining the future of American higher education. It is generally considered bad form to say, "I told you so," but even the most casual observer of current Affirmative Action programming on the campus, as he listens to the aggrieved outcry of so many educators, must be immediately reminded of the biblical warning to those who sow the wind. Few of us would today deny that the whirlwind has arrived.

II. Who's Discriminating?

> The adoption of quotas would be the most radical change one can imagine in the American ethos. The fact that it began to be implemented with no public discussion whatsoever and the fact this change began to be implemented through the activity of bureaucrats is an astonishing feature of the national life at this time.
>
> Norman Podhoretz

One of the goals which most Americans have shared, one of the cornerstones of the American self-assumption, has been that each person should be judged as an individual, on the basis of his own merits. Thus at first glance a programme such as Affirmative Action is potentially attractive to many people, since it promises "action" in eliminating discrimination. Most Americans agree that discrimination is wrong when it treats people as members of a group rather than as individuals. However, the question which needs to be raised concerning Affirmative Action is: who is discriminating? Is Affirmative Action the next step in achieving the American dream – or is it a new and particularly vicious form of discrimination?

A. Quotas or Goals?

In an effort to answer that question, we might profitably examine the definition of Affirmative Action provided by the programme's most eloquent spokesman, former head of OCR, Mr. J. Stanley Pottinger:

The concept of Affirmative Action requires more than mere neutrality on race and sex. It requires the university to determine whether it has failed to recruit, employ, and promote women and minorities commensurate with their availability, even if this failure cannot be traced to specific acts of discrimination by university officials. Where women and minorities are not represented on a university's rolls, despite their availability (that is, where they are "underutilized") the university has an obligation to initiate affirmative efforts to recruit and hire them. The premise of this obligation is that systemic forms of exclusion, inattention, and discrimination cannot be remedied in any meaningful way, in any reasonable length of time, simply by ensuring a future benign neutrality with regard to race and sex. This would perpetuate indefinitely the grossest inequities of past discrimination. Thus there must be some form of positive action, along with a schedule for how such actions are to take place, and an honest appraisal of what the plan is likely to yield – an appraisal that the regulations call a "goal."

Publications of the OCR go on to describe that "goal" and the required method for its achievement: "... the guidelines explicitly require that goals and time-tables be established to eliminate hiring, firing, promotion, recruiting, pay, and fringe benefit discrimination."

The Office of Civil Rights is quick to insist that "goals" are not "quotas." Mr. Pottinger has repeatedly announced that while he favours "goals," he opposes "quotas" which are "rigid" and "arbitrary." In the opinion of Pottinger and OCR, the quota question is nothing more than a rhetorical device in the hands of their critics:

Every crusade must have its simplistic side – a galvanizing symbol, a bogeyman, a rallying cry. The word "quotas" serves these rhetorical purposes in the present case.

Mr. Pottinger, who served as the architect for much of Affirmative Action before his promotion to the rank of Assistant Attorney General for Civil Rights, makes a valid point when he suggests that quotas *as such* are not required by OCR policy. But it is disingenuous to leave the matter there. It may be that a given policy will result in a quota system without its being called a quota system. This is precisely what has happened in Affirmative Action programming.

Certainly the college and university administrators faced with Affirmative Action have been badly confused in the process. "Goals" and "guidelines" have proven to be nothing more than confusing synonyms for numerical quotas. The college or university faced with proving its innocence by showing "good faith" has discovered that satisfying the bureaucratic task force is a supremely difficult undertaking. Those schools attempting to comply with Affirmative Action programming find themselves trapped in a mass of paper work, a labyrinth of bureaucratic guidelines, and an endlessly conflicting collection of definitions concerning "good faith," "equality," "minorities," "goals" and "quotas." A central fact in the confusion has been the discussion of goals versus quotas. Endless amounts of ink have been expended on this semantic distinction. But the distinction remains exclusively semantic.

Professor Paul Seabury of the University of California has been outspoken concerning the artificial nature of the distinction. In the process, he has developed two hybrid labels, which put the question in perspective: the *quoal*, a slow-moving quota-goal; and the *gota*, which is a supple, fast-moving quota-goal.

There is more validity in Professor Seabury's humour than HEW has been willing to admit. The "results-oriented goals and timetables" aspect of Affirmative Action simply results in a de facto quota system. As one highly placed OCR official recently commented: "The job won't get done unless the university is subjected to specific objectives that are results oriented."

HEW's insistence that it abhors quotas holds little weight when seen in the light of Mr. J. Stanley Pottinger's remark to the representatives of six Jewish groups. He said: "While HEW does not endorse quotas, I feel that HEW has no responsibility to object if quotas are used by universities on their own initiative." In practice, the central fact remains that both quotas and goals demand that our colleges and universities treat people as members of a group rather than as individuals.

B. Bureaucratic Quotas

The hiring record of the federal bureaucracy is itself a demonstration that the quota principle is approved and enforced, whatever the label. Although the federal government has now issued an order which presumably bars the use of quotas in hiring, the reality is otherwise. Quotas for hiring on the basis of race have existed for years in the Office of Management and Budget, HEW, HUD, the Agriculture Department, and the Labor Department, to name a few instances within the bureaucracy. During the past three years, within the ranks of the Equal Employment Opportunity Commission itself, there have been 85 complaints filed charging reverse discrimination in hiring brought about by a quota system. Since EEOC only has approximately 1,000 employees nationwide, these figures mean that almost 10 percent of the EEOC staff members have filed formal complaint, charging their superiors with discriminatory hiring quotas. This, I remind you, is the state of affairs in the very bureaucratic agency set up to insure no discriminatory hiring. Even since the presumptive federal ban on quotas, the direction of the bureaucracy remains the same. The Department of Justice has recently brought legal pressure to bear which proposes numerical goals for black state policemen in an Alabama case based on the Fourteenth Amendment.

There is little practical difference between saying: (1) "You must aim at a quota of 20 percent Lithuanians on your staff within the next three years," and saying (2) "You must set as your numerical goal recruitment of 20 percent Lithuanians within the next three years." It seems clear that the federal bureaucracy has every intention of enforcing quotas, and no amount of semantic confusion should be allowed to obscure the fact.

C. Double Standards

Under the guise of non-discrimination, Affirmative Action is actually pursuing a sharply different goal. One of the principal sponsors of that portion of the 1964 Civil Rights Act which has since produced the present situation, Senator Hubert Humphrey, denied that the quota idea would ever result from that legislation. Now, of course, those who have turned to quotas defend their position by asking, "How would social justice otherwise be achieved?" Such advocates of Affirmative Action are thus announcing their willingness to abandon non-discrimination in pursuit of another goal which they deem preferable.

This intention is clearly stated in the bureaucratic guidebook for Affirmative Action, *Questions and Answers for Higher Education Guidelines, Executive Order 11246*:

There are two basic concepts behind Executive Order 11246: (1) non-discrimination and (2) affirmative action ... Non-discrimination requirements of the Executive Order apply to *all* persons. *No* person may be denied employment or related benefits on grounds of race, colour, religion, sex and national origin. Affirmative Action requirements are designed to further employment opportunity for women, and minorities who are defined as Negroes, Spanish-surnamed, American Indians, and Orientals.

Remember that the original executive order insisted that affirmative action was to be taken to guarantee equal treatment without regard to race, colour, religion, sex or national origin. HEW, however, insist that Affirmative Action involves not equal treatment, but special efforts to recruit, employ, and promote some persons on the basis of race, sex, or national origin. Equal treatment is no longer the measure of compliance – proper "utilization" of women or minorities is to be the guideline. In practical terms this means that a college or university is required to make statistical analysis of its work force on the basis of sex and race. If "deficiencies" can be detected in the number of women or selected minority members employed, the university is then expected to establish numerical goals and take "affirmative action" to correct its statistical discrimination.

In other words, everyone is equal, but some are more equal than others. Discrimination is unacceptable, except when the bureaucracy orders schools to discriminate.

D. *Group Privilege versus Individual Merit*

At the heart of this matter lies a fundamental question concerning group rights vs. individual rights. The HEW directives which now attempt enforcement of group proportional rights are pushing towards a

major change in this nation's traditional conception of equality and opportunity. Affirmative Action, which evolved from an attempt to end
discriminatory practices, has now been elevated to the level of an ideology in its own right. The means has become the end. The bureaucracy
which pressed Affirmative Action upon the academic community does
so in the apparent assurance that discrimination is the means to
achieve true equality. Individual merit is to be set aside in favour of a
new, collective goal for the social order.

Reverse discrimination has been the direct and inevitable result. A
quota, goal, guideline, or whatever, which enforces hiring preferences
according to sex or race, can do so only by denying otherwise qualified
candidates proper consideration for the same position. Affirmative Action quotas are by nature inflexible. Such quotas can achieve their announced end only by enforcing the very discrimination they once set
out to stop.

Perhaps in this sense Affirmative Action is an ideal example of what
can happen when ideology runs amok. To draw a parallel, the civil
rights movement of the 1960s shared the same concern for minorities,
and was aimed at ending discrimination. After passage of the Civil
Rights Act, however, it soon became clear that equal opportunity,
though enforced by law, did not necessarily end all discrimination.
Cultural barriers were also involved; overcoming them takes time.

And it was precisely time that some ideologues were unwilling to
grant. Results had to come and come quickly – thus Affirmative Action
was born. It is an interesting historical footnote that the ideological lust
for quick results converted the quest for non-discrimination of the
1960s into the reverse discrimination of the 1970s.

E. *Academic Impact*

Nowhere have the results of Affirmative Action been more disappointing and damaging than in the field of higher education. In the earlier
stages of Affirmative Action, it was not yet clear to many people within
the academy what the programme involved or how far-reaching its effects would be. Many professors, secure in their own position by reputation or tenure, have only recently begun to appreciate the hiring difficulties of many schools and qualified scholars. Most of those same
professors have long recognized that blacks, members of other minority
groups, and women have been denied various opportunities without

proper regard to their qualifications. Those professors greeted with approval the federal civil rights acts of the mid-sixties and the executive order banning further discrimination. They looked forward to the day when all individuals would be judged on the basis of their abilities, not on the basis of their sex, race, or group membership.

By the early seventies, many of these professors were facing a painful disappointment. The news was beginning to circulate that the programmes presumably devised to fight the old discriminations were now introducing wholesale discriminations of their own. In the name of public policy designed to remove discrimination from the academic community, the thrust of HEW Affirmative Action programmes seemed to be demanding the deliberate introduction of discriminatory quotas. Affirmative Action, through a mixture of idealism, excess zeal, and political authority, seemed to be destroying precisely those values which it had been brought into existence to protect. Equality of opportunity had been increasingly set aside in favour of equality of result, thus denying the whole basis of professional qualification or individual achievement.

The new programmes were treating people as members of groups rather than as individuals, and the reaction within the academic community began to be increasingly critical. Columbia University philosophy professor Charles Frankel fumed, "We haven't had this kind of intervention since the days of Joe McCarthy." John Bunzel, president of California State College at San Jose, agreed: "I've heard cases of people hiring someone just to avoid a hassle with the federal government. I know of people who have gotten letters saying, 'Your qualifications are excellent but we are looking for a black or a woman this year'."

In the past two years increasing numbers of announcements for job opportunities within the academic community have appeared in professional journals and other academic outlets, making specific reference to race, sex, or ethnic background of the prospective applicant, usually in such a way as to suggest that such applicants will receive preferential treatment. The pressures for such preferential hiring are now an accepted fact in the American academic community.

In an effort to resist such pressures and force a re-examination of the entire underlying issue, several groups of scholars have made a determined effort to accumulate information of such abuses. These defenders of academic freedom and individual merit have been sufficiently successful in stating their case that an ombudsman has now been appointed by the Department of Health, Education, and Welfare to examine all complaints of reverse discrimination. Samuel H. Solomon, special assistant to the Office of Civil Rights, has already investigated some seventy cases and had discovered that a number of America's colleges and universities are engaging in reverse discrimination favouring women and minority candidates for faculty and staff jobs over equally qualified or better qualified white males. Solomon himself has commented, "I've been out on the campus trail in recent weeks and I am getting the impression that most of the institutions are engaging in some form of discrimination against white males." He also detected what he described as ill-advised recruiting practices, in which schools advertising faculty and staff positions identify them as "affirmative action positions" – which according to Solomon has become "a code phrase for minorities or women only." In the face of this pressure, HEW and other government agencies have been at pains to issue new "guidelines" and "clarifications" designed to stop such malpractices. Yet there seems little or no indication that the thrust of Affirmative Action has been turned from its original channel. In fact, the pressures for Affirmative Action compliance seem greater than ever.

The result is a rush of academic hiring practices based upon race and sex. It would require another book to publish the letters of inquiry, faculty minutes, questionnaires, and lists of available positions which have accumulated in past months, all reflecting such discriminatory hiring practices.

Several forms of damage have resulted. In the first place, quality and quotas simply do not go together. In the assault on academic quality which necessarily accompanies the imposition of minority quotas, the Jewish community has had most to lose because of its high concentration of students and professors in higher education. Jews make up some 3 percent of the general population, but a far higher percentage of the academy, including many of its most highly qualified members. Fortunately, something of the Jewish sense of humour has been retained in the face of this threat. Recently a spokesman for the Jewish Defence League commented with tongue in cheek:

Jews come from athletically deprived backgrounds. Irving is kept off the sandlot by too much homework and too many music lessons. He is now 25 and still can't play ball, but "he has the desire to learn." Therefore, the Jewish Defense League is demanding that New York City which has a 24 percent Jewish population, fill the city's ball teams with 24 percent Jews.

When we consider what this would do to baseball in New York, our reaction is a chuckle. When we consider what a similar approach in admissions and faculty hiring is doing to American higher education, the matter is a good deal less entertaining.

Another form of the erosion of quality that Affirmative Action has brought to higher education is the strongly anti-intellectual tone the programme has generated. Today on many campuses there seems less interest in a genuine life of the mind than in something that might be termed the "new pluralism." The new pluralism is based upon the assumption that the campus is fair game for whatever the various special interest groups may choose to demand. Any unwillingness to accept courses in free love, advanced bongo drum programmes, majors in homosexuality, or any of the other numerous and kinky demands made today in the name of the new pluralism, is usually put down to racism and sexism.

Today everyone wants greater representation on faculties, open admissions, funding for special programmes – in short, everyone wants a share of the already painfully limited academic resources. Any plea that standards and quality must be maintained is treated as an affront to the principles of participatory democracy.

These principles are coming to faculties now in the Affirmative Action assumption that racial and sexual faculty proportions should be identical to the racial and sexual proportions of society as a whole. Attaining such racial and sexual proportions is a practical impossibility. For example, there simply are not enough academically trained women to staff 50 percent of America's institutions of higher learning, though this fact does not deter the attempt. Nor does any concern over finding academically qualified persons in such large numbers seem to dismay the ideologues. Sacramento State College has sent out letters announcing, "Sacramento State College is currently engaged in an Affirmative Action Programme, the goal of which is to recruit, hire, and promote ethnic and women candidates until they comprise the same proportion of the faculty as they do of the general population."

The practical reality is, the enforcement of minority quotas on faculties is lowering professional and academic standards. The further Affirmative Action inflicts its ideology of statistics on the universities, the less they will be able to call themselves institutes of higher education.

III. What is a Minority?

A proper Sociological Caucus should contain: two blacks
(one man, one woman); one Chicano (or Chicana on
alternate elections); one person to be, in alphabetical
rotation, Amerindian, Asian, and Eskimo; and sixteen
white Anglos. Of the latter, eight will have to be men
and eight women; fourteen will have to be heterosexual
and two homosexual (one of these to be a lesbian); one
Jewish, ten Protestant, four Roman Catholic; and one,
in alphabetical rotation, Buddhist, Mormon and Muslim; fifteen will have to be sighted and one blind; eight
must be juvenile, four mature and four senile; and two
must be intelligent, ten mediocre, and four stupid.

Pierre L. van den Berghe

The word "minority" does not appear so much as once in either
Executive Order 11246 or in the 1964 Civil Rights Act. Yet in Labor
Department Revised Order No. 4, the key enabling document of Affirmative Action, the word "minority" is used in one form or another
65 times, but is never defined. "The Higher Education Guidelines"
issued by HEW in connection with its Affirmative Action programme
does provide a definition of sorts, including in that category "Negroes,
Spanish-surnamed, American Indians, and Orientals . . ."

Since neither the original civil rights legislation nor the related executive order ever mentioned the word, thus reserving "minorities" for
later Affirmative Action guidelines, the question naturally arises:
Where did the Affirmative Action zealots get their definition of the
word? The answer is frightening, especially for those interested in the
future of higher education.

The OCR has admitted borrowing its working definition of "minority" from the Department of Labor, one first used at the time the "Philadelphia Plan" was implemented. The Department of Labor had developed a definition of "minority" which, correctly or not, was felt to
be appropriate to hiring patterns in the construction industry. It was
this definition that OCR borrowed to apply across the board in developing Affirmative Action plans for higher education. However surprising this may be to the Washington mentality, it is likely that there
are differences between the construction industry and higher education.
These might well include differing patterns of discrimination, not to
mention differing patterns of job performance.

We probably need not be unduly concerned about the deficiencies in the OCR definition of "minorities" in higher education. The list of minorities is likely to grow very rapidly. As more and more groups discover the special privileges that can accrue to officially recognized "disadvantaged" minorities, colleges and universities will probably find themselves called upon to extend hiring quotas even further. As Senator James Buckley (Conservative-Republican, New York) told his colleagues,

And so our colleges and universities will find themselves forced to punch into their computer cards more and more categories of human beings so that they may achieve the exact mix of sex, race, religion, and national origin that will be required to satisfy their ever more fastidious inquisitors.

A. Pressures for Compliance

Certainly great pressure has already developed to compel the measurement of "minorities." Many administrators have simply abandoned any attempt to resist that pressure. Few academics are anxious to appear in opposition to a programme which purports to end discrimination. Even fewer are willing to jeopardize federal funding for their institutions. Brooklyn College, in direct violation of New York State law, has twice asked its faculty and staff to fill out detailed questionnaires which deal directly with individual race and ethnic background. In his covering letter, the school's president urged faculty and staff to provide the information since "... considerable sums which the university receives from the federal government are in jeopardy ... At this stage of the game, we have no choice but to perform this task as quickly and expeditiously as possible."

The same rush to conform to political pressures has also begun to occur in racial measurement of student bodies. Following a campus strike, President Robben Fleming of the University of Michigan caved in to demands for 10 percent black enrolment goals. Outraged faculty warned that present black attrition rates were running close to 50 percent at the university and that any attempt to triple the number of blacks (now about 3.5 percent of total enrolment) could be achieved only by lowering standards and thus sending the attrition rate even higher. Nevertheless, the University of Michigan has now accepted racial quotas for student enrolment.

As we move towards a period in which we measure faculty, students and academic standards by racial and sexual quotas, it is worth remembering that to date no comprehensive, statistically valid study has yet become available which demonstrates conclusively either the existence or the degree of discrimination in academic employment. In other words, even if we accept the vicious premise that faculty or students should be measured not by ability but by race or sex, we are still confronted with the problem of deciding which "minorities" should receive this special privilege.

B. What is a Protected Class?

Though it is fashionable today to discuss "oppressed minorities," the practical problem of identifying and distinguishing those minorities is very great. Dr. Aaron Wildavsky, dean of the Graduate School of Public Policy at the Berkeley campus of the University of California, has totalled all the currently fashionable "oppressed minorities" and concluded that the nation is composed of "374 percent minorities." In the same spirit, a departmental chairman of a large eastern university has posted the qualifications for a new faculty member: a woman Egyptologist, black, with a Spanish surname, born on a South-Western Indian reservation.

Even if we were to grant that some categories of faculty or students should receive special academic privilege, how do we decide which categories should be selected? Columbia University lists four protected classes: Black-Negro, Oriental, American Indian, Spanish-surnamed American. Brooklyn College originally listed five: American Indian, Black, Indian (Asian), Oriental, and Puerto Rican. Three months later, Indian (Asian) was dropped from the list and replaced by Italian-American. In the San Francisco area there seem to be seven groups singled out for special attention: Negro/Black, Chinese, Japanese, Korean, American Indian, Filipino, Spanish-speaking/Spanish-surname. Apparently definition of a protected class is subject to geography and institutional whim.

In practice, such categories quickly reach absurdity:

– Though a higher percentage of blacks than whites are poor, there are rich blacks; should the government insist that sons of well-to-do blacks should not receive preferential treatment?

– If the Spanish surname in question is Patino (former Bolivian tin mine owners), should preferential treatment be granted?

– Why include Chinese and Japanese as protected groups when the Japanese have a high rate of financial accomplishment and the Chinese have the highest per capita rate of Ph.D.'s in the country?

– If race is the standard for identifying an oppressed group, what about Appalachian whites?

As we select our oppressed minorities who are "underutilized" in higher education, we might remember that not only blacks, but also Irish, Greeks, Italians, Poles and all other Slavs (including Czechs, Croations, Slovenes, Slovaks and Serbs) are under-represented.

Perhaps we should also consider religious underutilization. Catholics comprise 30 percent of the population, but occupy a far smaller percentage of higher educational posts. As author, professor, and scholar Russell Kirk recently asked:

When will Harvard make a Dominican its president – a black Dominican, say? When will Brandeis appoint half a dozen nuns to professorial chairs? How many deans at the University of Texas are Mexican-American and Papist and maternal?

Many institutions of the learning allegedly higher already have converted themselves into theatres of the absurd. Why shouldn't we go the whole hog?

Indeed, why not go the whole hog? The State University at Purchase, New York, has been formally charged with discrimination against Italian-Americans. In a complaint filed with the state Human Rights Division, the Westchester County Federation of Italian American Organizations has charged the school with failure to offer Italian language courses or hire Italian faculty and administrators. The chairman of the federation, Mr. Raphael Riverso, has announced, "Since the population of Westchester County is 40 to 50 percent Italian, we are demanding that the university begin a programme to hire qualified Italians until they make up 40 percent of the supervisory, teaching and administrative staff."

Once the process is begun, once we grant special privilege to "oppressed minorities," the inevitable tendency will be towards an endless proliferation of oppressed minorities. If race or sex are suitable bases for determining special privilege, why not include groups with special physical characteristics? Professor Murray Rothbard recently took a humorous view of the prospect:

And how about a group in which I have a certain personal interest – short people? May we not maintain that "shorts" are the first to be fired and the last to be hired: and where in blazes are the short executives, the short bankers, the short senators, and presidents? There is surely no genetic evidence to prove that short people are inferior to talls (look at Napoleon). Shall we not call upon short pride, short institutes, short history courses; shall we not demand short quotas everywhere? Women have notoriously discriminated in favour of talls over shorts, and in how many movies have shorts – openly displayed as such – played the romantic leads? Professor Saul D. Feldman, a short sociologist at Case-Western Reserve, has now quantified some of this short-oppression ... and also points out the subtle corruption of our language (presumably as engineered by a tall-conspiracy); for people are described as "short-sighted, short-changed, short-circuited, and short in cash."

The whole idea of quotas, oppressed minorities and measurement by group rather than individual standards is ludicrous, nowhere more so than in the academic community. But as the laughter dies down, we might recall one painful and inescapable fact: it is impossible to achieve a quota for one group without reducing the "quota" for another. By pursuing justice too zealously, we are fostering an injustice.

C. The Problem of Measurement

Even after we have decided whom to reward and whom to punish, we are still faced with a problem: How do we gather information to measure quotas for various minorities?

There are a number of state and local laws specifically forbidding the requirement of racial, sexual, religious or ethnic information as a condition of employment. Presumably, all this is now set aside. *Questions and Answers for Higher Education Guidelines* states:

Under the principle of federal supremacy, requirements for information under the executive order supersede any conflicting state or local law. An individual, however, is not legally bound to report such information about himself.

The real problem lies in the fact that the institutions involved are required to provide that information under Affirmative Action, *whether or not the individual employees are willing to co-operate.* Columbia University conducted its inquiry into such matters in a way which would give the necessary A.A. information and still not involve individual faculty. "Census reporters" were appointed in each division of the school. These reporters were to make ethnic identifications "based upon the reporter's general knowledge and observation of the employee." Applicants for new positions (HEW requires that all applicants be classified, whether or not subsequently employed) were to be checked out by "visual survey." All of this was to take place without the knowledge of the individuals being "surveyed." This is ridiculous. It is hard enough, in some cases, to tell an individual's sex at a glance, much less ancestry or oppressed status. A few short years ago, had a novel described such a system of ethnic measurement at some fictitious university, it would have been received as a farce or a fantasy. Today such antics are undertaken as a serious enterprise.

Those institutions more open in their measurement techniques have also had their problems. A sociologist at Syracuse University, attempting to gather information on the status of black professors in predominantly white schools, quickly discovered the reason: many of those contacted in his national survey simply refused to co-operate. A number of the faculty members labelled black by the sociologist's informants returned their questionnaires with "white" indicated as their racial preference. Other professors wrote, asking for more information:

I would request you kindly to define more precisely what you mean by the term "black"? Am I right in supposing that you are seeking information regarding American faculty of African descent? Or do you wish West Indian and African faculty members to be included – or dark skinned faculty from other countries?

Michigan State University has also had its problems in computing minorities. Robert Perrin, vice president for university relations, has described what he calls "the numbers game," a game involving collection of vast amounts of statistical data concerning the employees and students of a school. He bemoans the lack of co-operation among those persons being counted. For example, some 150 MSU students categorized themselves as American Indians, fifteen times the actual number on campus. Others returned cards with additional categories marked: "Super Jew," "Texan," "50th Generation Hun," or "female." As Perrin describes the result, "One determined iconoclast not only mutilated and spindled his computer card, he stapled it as well."

D. Are We Helping or Hurting?

Meanwhile, what effect does Affirmative Action have upon the minorities we are trying to help? Here the story is saddest of all.

One of the casualties of Affirmative Action has been the black college and university. Competition has become so intense for qualified black professors that the black schools are losing their most qualified faculty members to those large, prosperous, predominantly white institutions that can afford to pay substantially higher salaries.

Meanwhile, qualified minority members are also penalized by Affirmative Action. What quotas and special privileges are saying all too clearly is that the minority member just doesn't have what it takes and as the result must be given what he is unqualified to earn. Even the minority member who earns his competence will surely be undermined as the result. The suspicion will be present in his mind and everyone else's that his success may be due to special privilege, not talent and hard work. No one resents this aspect of Affirmative Action more bitterly than the qualified minority member himself.

One of those highly qualified blacks is Professor Thomas Sowell of the University of California of Los Angeles, now on leave at the Urban Institute in Washington, D.C. In response to what has become known as an "Affirmative Action letter," Sowell stated his case plainly:

September 18, 1972

Professor Frank C. Pierson
Chairman
Department of Economics
Swarthmore College
Swarthmore, Pennsylvania

Dear Professor Pierson:

This morning I was pleased to receive a letter from Swarthmore College, an institution for which I have long had respect, and reports from which have added to my admiration.
Then I opened the letter and learned that "Swarthmore College is actively looking for a black economist ..." and the phrase that came immediately to mind was one from a bygone era, when a very different kind of emotionalism was abroad, and a counsel facing Senator Joseph McCarthy said, "Sir, have you no shame?"

What purpose is to be served by this sort of thing? Surely a labour economist of your reputation must know that unemployment among black

Ph.D.'s is one of the least of our social problems, and has been for many years – long before "affirmative action." In general, even, the salary is no higher at a top college than at less prestigious institutions for a given individual. So you are doing very little for black faculty members with broadcast recruiting campaigns like this (I note the letter is mimeographed). Maybe you think you are doing something for race relations. If you are going to find a Swarthmore-quality black faculty member, that is one thing. But Swarthmore-quality faculty members are found through Swarthmore-quality channels and not through mimeographed letters of this sort. *Many a self-respecting black scholar would never accept an offer like this*, even if he might otherwise enjoy teaching at Swarthmore. When Bill Allen was department chairman at UCLA he violently refused to hire anyone on the basis of ethnic representation – and thereby made it possible for me to come there a year later with my head held up. Your approach tends to *make the job unattractive to anyone who regards himself as a scholar or a man*, and *thereby throws it open to opportunists.*

Despite all the brave talk in academia about "affirmative action" without lowering quality standards, you and I both know that it takes many years to create a qualified faculty member of any colour, and no increased demand is going to increase the supply immediately *unless* you lower quality. Now what good is going to come from lower standards that will make "black" equivalent to "substandard" in the eyes of black and white students alike? Can you imagine that this is going to *reduce* racism? On the contrary, more and more thoughtful people are beginning to worry that the next generation will see an increasing amount of bigotry among those whites educated at some of the most liberal institutions, where this is the picture that is presented to them, however noble the rhetoric that accompanies it.

You and I both know that many of *these "special" recruiting efforts are not aimed at helping black faculty members of black or white students, but rather at hanging onto the school's federal money.* Now, I have nothing against money. I have not been so familiar with it as to have contempt for it. But there are limits to what should be done to get it, and particularly so for an institution with a proud tradition, at a time when the government itself is wavering and having second thoughts about this policy, and when just a little courage from a few men in "responsible" positions might make a difference.

Yours sincerely,

(s) Thomas Sowell

Professor Sowell has ample reason for his anger. A young black woman with an I.Q. of 142 and comparable grades and recommendations was told by a national organization that she would be eligible to receive financial aid for legal studies if her scores were low enough. The scores were *too high*; the aid was denied. Another young black applied for a well-publicized doctoral fellowship specifically for black students. The fellowship was denied to this student, despite his brilliant academic record, because his social and political views were insufficiently militant. The current thrust towards "helping" the minority member in pursuit of his education seems determined to penalize real achievement wherever it appears.

Meanwhile, the unqualified minority member is also cheated in the education which Affirmative Action promises. In the early 1960s, a great drive was under way to bring minority students to predominantly white schools. Between 1964 and 1970, the number of blacks on previously white campuses jumped 173 percent, from 114,000 to 310,000. The promise held out to a generation of young blacks was a lifetime of material success within "the system," a promise which higher education could not hope to deliver, especially since many of those minority students attracted to the campus were unprepared for the life and work which was thrust upon them.

Just as many of these students are ill-prepared to participate in higher education, so are many of their professors ill-prepared to offer a quality experience to their students. Affirmative Action has greatly aggravated this tendency. The attempt to achieve a statistically adequate representation of women and ethnic groups on college faculties has tended to produce a rush to discover sufficient numbers of well-qualified professors with minority credentials. In actual practice, the numbers demanded of such minority types far exceed the qualified people available. Thus a strange new word has entered the Affirmative Action dialogue. Today we talk about the appointment of persons who are not qualified, but who are "qualifiable." In point of fact, the guidelines state: "Neither minority nor female employees should be required to possess higher qualifications than those of the lowest qualified incumbent."

Has merit come to mean only equality on the lowest level of performance? Not only does this do an injustice to the institution and the students coming in contact with faculty members unqualified to hold their position, but also it excludes from consideration large numbers of an entire generation of young scholars, quite well-qualified to hold a position, yet often rendered ineligible by virtue of their non-membership in an HEW-approved minority group. Unfair discrimination and the lowering of standards go far beyond reverse discrimination. Today even well-qualified blacks are passed over for consideration – because

they are not from the ghetto. The search is not merely for blacks, but
for "authentic ghetto types."

Black professors and black students alike have been downgraded.
The first-rank performers have suffered this downgrading because
whatever accomplishment they attain is often assumed to be the result
of special privilege. Meanwhile, unqualified professors and students
from various ethnic groups have been cheated into assuming that they
were taking their place in a true educational framework, when, in fact,
all the standards which gave the framework any meaning have been
undercut. As one Cornell professor bluntly put it: "I give them all A's
and B's, and to hell with them." Surely this is not the "equality" which
we desire for higher education.

Such distortions are themselves the product of paternalistic recruiting quotas for minorities. Again to quote Professor Sowell:

Most people are unaware of the extent to which the severe educational problems of black college students are functions of the manner in which they are
recruited and selected, rather than simply being the inevitable result of
"cultural deprivation." There is no question that the overwhelming bulk
of black youth have been given grossly inadequate preparation in the public
schools. However, the overwhelming bulk of black youth do not go on to
college, and while the proportion of these youth who are educationally well
prepared for college is very low, in absolute numbers there are literally tens
of thousands of them who are, by all the usual indices – far too many for the
top universities to be forced to have as many inadequately prepared black
students as they do. The fact that standardized examinations may be less
reliable for ethnic minorities than for others has been used as a blanket
excuse for recruiting and selecting black students on all sorts of non-intel-
lectual criteria, from the ideological to the whimsical. Programmes for
black people tend to attract more than their fair share of vague humani-
tarians and socio-political doctrinaires seeking to implement some special
vision. Not all are as obtuse as the special admissions committee for black
students at one Ivy League university who objected to admitting three black
applicants with College Board scores in the 700's on grounds that they were
probably – God forbid – middle class, and that there were other blacks
applying who were more "interesting" cases – but this kind of thinking is by
no means rare. One consequence of this is that, despite the buzz of recruiting activity, there are many black students who belong in the best colleges
in the country who have not been reached with the information and financial
aid offers that would bring them there, and are languishing at some of the
worst colleges in the country. At the same time other black students are in
over their heads at the top colleges, struggling – or being manoeuvred –
towards a degree.

Plainly, the black students themselves have been the principal casualty of the system. The reaction is often a wave of anti-intellectualism and an orientation towards non-achievement, accompanied by a thirst for "relevance" and "black studies." How we can expect anything but racial antagonism and the posturing of black separatism when we have so effectively insured that genuine academic achievement is usually closed to the blacks in our colleges and universities? The situation cries out to recruit and educate young people, black or white, on the basis of their individual ability. Yet this is exactly what Affirmative Action and the patronizing zealotry lying behind it will not permit.

E. Overcoming Discrimination

Racial and ethnic forms of social engineering are always risky business. Witness the results of a century-long social experiment which treated the American Indian as a member of a "protected class" and ward of the federal bureaucracy. Yet something can be done to alleviate discrimination. The Jews have done just that in America. Long denied a place in the academic community, or granted only a small maximum quota, the Jews have carved a place for themselves through ability and effort until today they hold a major position on the American campus. This did not come about through government intervention or quotas favouring Jews. It was possible only because we enjoyed a system which recognized individual ability and emphasized individual achievement.

IV. How about Women?

> I envy the young and the young in heart, who do not experience my occasional difficulties in grasping that while American women, who are more than 50 percent, are a minority, American Jews, who are fewer than 3 percent, are not a minority.
>
> Milton Himmelfarb

Many of us would agree with such a common sense view. Most Americans, men and women alike, would perhaps go even further, regarding themselves primarily as individuals rather than members of some racial, ethnic, religious, sexual, intellectual, or economic group. They would probably agree that, sociology notwithstanding, there are no such things as "group rights." Only individuals have rights and only individuals can be discriminated against.

Still, when we discuss the question of discrimination and Affirmative Action programming, we should remember that the single largest category of all the "minorities" under discussion is women. Most of the problems which apply to other A.A. programmes apply with special force to women.

We also should remember that valid complaints do exist. There can be no question that women do not always receive equal treatment. Top starting salaries for men and women of equal qualification in the same profession are usually not equal. Employment opportunities are frequently not equal even in areas where little or no difference exists between men and women in their capacity to do the job.

The academic community is one of those areas. There are evidences that women, for whatever reason, have usually been less valued members of the academic community than their male counterparts. Women are still paid less as full time college and university faculty members. Women compromise some 22 percent of faculty and receive salaries on the average approximately $2,500 less than men. Undoubtedly there have been in the past, and still are at present, instances in which women of equal or superior qualification did not have an opportunity to equal pay for the same work or for a particular promotion which went instead to a man of perhaps inferior qualification. There are famous universities which have never chosen a woman as chairman of a department. On many campuses women teachers tend to be engaged to handle overload problems in undergraduate survey courses. Yes, there are reasons for valid complaint concerning unequal treatment.

A. Times Are Changing

Throughout society today, however, many positions formerly reserved for men are now attracting a growing number of women. Positions ranging from police officer to bank manager to truck driver are now more likely to be filled with women. Though only about 18 percent of managerial positions are currently occupied by women, the figure continues to rise and each year more co-eds are being interviewed for jobs with management potential. Even the unions are faced with growing pressure for providing women with a larger role, not only for promotion in industrial plants but also for a larger role in union leadership.

A higher percentage of total college enrolment is now filled with women. This is due in part to the removal of draft pressures, which has caused a decline in male enrolment. But many of those women now returning to school have been those who married young and who are now seeking the education which circumstances earlier denied.

Similarly, though naturally in far smaller numbers, women are taking a greater interest in joining college faculties. But it should be remembered, even by the most insistent partisan of equal rights for women, that most college and university teaching situations involve certain factors, common to the lives of many if not most women, that have a bearing on salaries and promotion. As a group, women have been less likely to complete terminal degrees, thus reducing their value in academic positions. As a group, women are far more likely to be affected in their careers by marriage and children, thus in some cases ending their desire for further education or for a continuation of their teaching position. Thus the tenure and qualification of many women are frequently less than those of their male counterparts. For those women who indeed have equal or superior credentials, equality of opportunity for various positions should certainly be available to them, but it would be incorrect to assume that the most pressing concern in the lives of all the women in the country is a desire to be a college professor or take a Ph.D.

Despite these factors, sharp gains have occurred in the number of earned doctorates for women. In a number of disciplines, especially in the social sciences, the number of women receiving terminal degrees has risen substantially faster than men since the mid-1960s. Even in those disciplines were the greatest growth of women's Ph.D.'s has occurred, however, women still account for only approximately 12 percent to 24 percent of the total degrees granted.

B. The Egalitarian Thrust of the Age

The same highly politicized lust for group-oriented "equality" which plagues other portions of Affirmative Action also is present in so-called women's liberation. Here again the political history goes back to the 1964 Civil Rights Act. The Southern attempt to obstruct the bill was failing, and Howard Smith, the "Virginia swamp fox" of the House Rules Committee, was casting about for a last-minute amendment which might make the whole project politically unpalatable to its

Northern supporters, so unpalatable that the bill would not pass. The amendment which he succeeded in attaching to the bill was an inclusion of women as an object of federal protection in employment. Sex was added to race, religion, and national origin as illegal grounds for hiring discrimination. Much to the surprise of the chivalrous Congressman Smith, the bill passed, amendment and all.

What neither Howard Smith nor anyone else might have guessed was that a decade later the Office of Civil Rights would seize on sexism as the most convenient means of bringing the campuses to heel. In the face of all the difficulties involved in measuring ethnic quotas and identifying minorities, sex appears to be a wonderfully simple and easily quantifiable factor for the enforcement of quotas. Outspoken advocates of women's liberation have not been slow to sense the direction of OCR thinking. We are now seeing sex as the rising egalitarian issue on campus.

In a time of tightened budgets and little hiring, those schools most deeply involved in A.A. compliance may soon be hiring only women, pushing blacks and other minorities entirely out of the picture. At least some 350 class action complaints were already filed by women on college campuses in the early months of 1973. The pressures have grown intense. Even Stanley Pottinger was considered to be an insufficiently aggressive champion for the cause of women's rights. Pottinger's promotion to assistant attorney general was opposed on that ground by the League of Academic Women.

One of the pressures thus generated is not merely for equality in hiring or pay, but is a demand for back pay and damages to make up for alleged prior inequality. Precedents already exist in the business world, where American Telephone and Telegraph, among others, have agreed to pay reparations to women.

The National Organization of Women and the American Nurses Association have filed complaints against several universities with the Equal Employment Opportunity Commission, on the grounds that the schools' retirement plans discriminate against women. The defence insists, of course, that women on the average *do live longer*, thus explaining the difference in the actuarial tables. Whether or not the courts will give legal recognition to this difference between the sexes remains to be seen.

Federal involvement in the area of sex discrimination also continues to expand. The U.S. Commission on Civil Rights, the monitoring agency for all anti-discrimination legislation, has now been empowered to investigate discrimination based on sex. The growing federal interest in sex discrimination, coupled with the current tendency towards litigation as a weapon for forcing various highly political issues, promises to have a large impact throughout society, an impact of particular importance for colleges and universities.

For example, the Equal Pay Act, as enforced by the Department of Labor, is a powerful weapon in forcing compliance. Complaint may be made against an employer by telephone or anonymous tip. No documentation is required. In a recent report in *The Chronicle of Higher Education*, Ms. Bernice Sandler, director of the Project on the Status and Education of Women for the Association of American Colleges, outlined the process with considerable relish:

Any person – employee or not – can look in the telephone directory for the phone number of the nearest regional office of the Wage and Hour Division, the Department of Labor, and report one's suspicion that there is a violation of the Equal Pay Act at X institution. A particular department or occupational classification or individual can be specified; no documentation is required. The identity of a complainant or person furnishing information is never revealed without that person's knowledge and consent.

An employer often does not know that someone has called the Wage and Hour Division. Under the act, the government has the power to conduct routine reviews, whether or not a complaint has been reported.

A woman might call, stating that she suspects she is being underpaid in the English department. Within a few weeks, a compliance officer will appear at the institution to do a "routine check." The investigator can review the entire establishment or may choose to limit the review to a few departments, apparently chosen at random but obviously including the English department.

If a violation is found, the employer is asked to settle on the spot: to raise the salaries of the underpaid persons and to give back pay.

It would be hard to imagine a more clear-cut exercise of raw administrative power, with wide latitude for discretion concerning what is or is not a violation, and with virtually no guarantees or legal safeguards provided for the employer. Of course it might be argued that the employer can always appeal against the decision in court, *if* he can afford the heavy costs and endless delays of litigation.

The women's rights movement moves rapidly on other fronts as well. Michigan State University has accepted the recommendations of the MSU Women's Steering Committee, authorizing salary adjustments of $118,658 to 138 women faculty members, establishing a Women's Advisory Council, establishing the position of director of women's athletics, and allowing women to compete on an equal basis for positions in the previously all-male MSU marching band.

Women activists occupied the central switchboard offices of Boston State College for fifty-two hours, leaving only after administrators promised co-operation in establishing space for a child-care facility, equalization of athletic expenditures for men and women, and establishment of a women's study curriculum.

The Women's Law Association at Harvard Law School has asked for a federal investigation of possible discrimination against women in hiring, admission, and recruitment, plus whatever other action may be required to eliminate discriminatory practices. And so it goes with women's rights on the campus front these days.

C. Impact on Colleges and Universities

As in the case of minority quotas, serious confusions and potential injustices are involved in academic quotas for women. How does a school determine that women are "underutilized"? The current recommended bureaucratic method is to measure the percentage of degrees granted nationally to women in a particular discipline against the percentage of total teaching positions held by women in that same discipline on a particular campus. Never mind whether those women available nationally wish to teach at your school; never mind whether you have positions available to offer those women; above all, never mind whether or not those women candidates interviewed for a job are the best qualified for the particular job in the opinion of faculty and administration. No, the only deciding factor is to be the quota.

And the quota for hiring women is in process of upward revision. Those zealots who think in quantities rather than personalities have decided that an insufficient number of women are entering academic life. Why not have as many women as men completing terminal degrees and assuming teaching positions? Why not indeed, unless women, for whatever reason peculiar to their individual taste and judgment, would prefer to do something else!

In an effort to force upward revision of the academic quotas for women, Title IX of the 1972 Higher Education Act contains provisions prohibiting sex discrimination in all federally assisted educational programmes. Under special scrutiny are institutions of professional and graduate education. HEW has yet to formulate complete guidelines for the project, but it seems clear that graduate schools will soon be required to establish sex quotas for admissions and for numbers of graduates. One such programme already contemplated by a Western university has been described in the following terms:

The university would be charged with the responsibility of conducting an analysis of its students to determine where women are under-represented, setting reasonable goals and timetables for correcting under-representation and designing a programme through which it would achieve these goals. Appropriate steps to take under this procedure would include: a review of admission procedures; the selection of admission committee members on the basis of their ability to be impartial with regard to the admission of women; a review of financial aid distribution; the development of affirmative recruiting techniques; and the integration of courses concerning women into the curriculum.

D. Frenzied Overreaction

It seems clear that in the case of women, as in the case of minorities, individual achievement is to be replaced with Affirmative Action quotas and group pressures. Unfortunately, there has been a frenzied rush of compliance which offers little or no leadership on behalf of the concept of individual measurement, for men or women.

The secretary of education for the Commonwealth of Pennsylvania has "committed the Department of Education to making the elimination of sexism in education a priority." Following a directive from the governor's office, the education secretary sent memoranda to all university and college presidents and deans, listing specific anti-discriminatory policies which would be enforced, including: development of women's studies as an integral part of the curriculum, including feminist literature in libraries, and elimination of all segregated classes and activities.

The Wisconsin Governor's Commission on the Status of Women has introduced a bill into the legislature which would require the Board of Regents to take steps integrating the student body of all undergraduate and graduate schools in the state university system, in an effort to insure that the percentage of women students more nearly reflects the Wisconsin population.

Dartmouth College recently became the last of the Ivy League schools to admit women as regular students, and is planning to admit some 800 women over the next four years. The nation's reputedly first women's athletic scholarship has been established at the University of Chicago. The scholarship is for full tuition, regardless of need, and became available to freshman women beginning in the autumn quarter, 1973. There is no stipulation that the recipient of the scholarship participate in varsity sports at the university.

The Air Force Academy has announced its intention to admit female cadets by 1975. Yale has increased its female enrolment by over 100 additional women in order to "work towards a better balance between the sexes in Yale College." The university also announced that it would abandon rigid admissions quotas for men and women and seek to achieve an eventual 3 to 2 ratio by recruiting efforts.

The faculty senate of New York State University at Buffalo has recommended that 50 percent of all new university appointments go to women or minority group members. Stanford University has created a Faculty Affirmative Action Fund, initially financed at $75,000, to provide a special means to increase the proportion of women and minority faculty.

Sarah Lawrence College has received a $140,000 grant from the Rockefeller Foundation for expansion of the master's degree programme in women's studies at the college. "Plans are to develop the programme into a model for the teaching of women's studies in colleges across the country." An ad hoc committee at the University of Minnesota has been set up to explore ways to establish a women's studies major. Perhaps this is in response to a recent report in *Women's Studies Newsletter* that more than a thousand women's studies courses are now offered in the nation's colleges and universities.

The rush to deny women their identity apart from the group continues at a fevered pace.

Despite all the haste, many institutions have been unable to move quickly enough to satisfy critics. The University of Michigan has been charged with sex discrimination by the Committee to Bring about Equal Opportunity in Athletics for Men and Women. The formal complaint to HEW points out that the school spends $2.6 million a year on men's athletics, but has no allocation for women's intercollegiate sports. The University of Michigan athletic director countered with the charge that the school spends more money on its nursing school "and you don't see any men there." No doubt this will soon be investigated.

Among the schools which have failed to move quickly enough to suit the *Zeitgeist* have been some 150 institutions in 33 states which have never been sexually integrated. Some have been reserved entirely for men, some entirely for women. These schools have now received a formal warning from the U.S. Office of Education, threatening withdrawal of all federal aid unless they open enrolment to both sexes immediately. Apparently no differences will be tolerated in the homogenized schools of the future.

E. Reverse Discrimination

In the midst of this sexist hysteria, the same reverse discrimination exists in quotas for women as in quotas for minorities. On campus after campus, the push to achieve hiring quotas based on sex has introduced a marked distortion and injustice to the hiring process. As one dean described the situation, "If you're a woman and preferably black, you can get any kind of job you want." President Robben Fleming of the University of Michigan has already agreed to engage female professors for 139 of the next 148 vacancies on the faculty. What this does for the job prospects of others, including minorities, should be self-evident.

What may be less evident is the impact which this and similar rulings are likely to have on academic standards. When only 13 percent of the doctorates in America are awarded to women, and when feminists on the campus are already advocating that women faculty members should be on a one-to-one basis with men, where are the qualified female faculty to be recruited to fill the positions? In a time of tight money and scarce resources on the campus, perhaps the champions of women's liberation do not intend to expand faculties so much as they intend to replace men with women. If so, presumably this would mean the discharge of nearly one-half of the male professors now employed. As one professor recently remarked, "Perhaps those chauvinist exiles could occupy posts in secondary schooling vacated by schoolmarms who desire elevation to professorial dignity."

At present, there are few signs that such questions of elementary justice or basic academic standards will be allowed to stand before the egalitarian juggernaut.

F. The Case for Women

Although we hear a great deal about discrimination against women, and though such discrimination undoubtedly exists in many quarters, it is interesting that only 8 percent of those women polled by the authors of a recent study, *Sex Discrimination against the American Working Woman*, thought themselves to be victims of discrimination. Perhaps the other 92 percent have recognized that steady progress has been made in according an even break to those women who choose to work. Certainly the professional position and pay of women in the academic world had already been progressing for years, in both relative and absolute terms. Perhaps the 92 percent are aware of the large number of women who have been able to distinguish themselves in academic life without special enabling legislation on their behalf. Perhaps the 92 percent also resist the tendency to homogenize their skills, energies, and personalities into an egalitarian group project.

Finally, the 92 percent may simply be exercising their prerogative to be women.

One of the most charming discussions of women and their place in society was first published in 1918. I refer to H. L. Mencken's *In Defense of Women*. Mencken pointed out several basic truths about the woman and her role and capacities that even the most ardent women's liberationist fails to consider only at great peril. In an essay which deserves a wider hearing today, Mencken pointed out that a lack of feminine participation in much of the world of commerce, industry, and education is less a matter of inability, or even prejudice, than it is a feminine reaction against the dull mechanical tricks of the trade that the present organization of society compels on the part of those who work for a living. As Mencken phrased it, "And that rebellion testifies to their intelligence. If they enjoyed and took pride in those tricks, and showed it by diligence and skill, they would be on all fours with . . . the men of society." Mencken insisted that women are consistently more intelligent than their male counterparts:

Women decide the larger questions of life correctly and quickly, not because they are lucky guessers, not because they are divinely inspired, not because they practise a magic inherited from savagery, but simply and solely because they have sense. They see at a glance what most men could not see with searchlights and telescopes; they are at grips with the essentials of a problem before men have finished debating its mere externals. They are the supreme realists of the race. Men, too, sometimes have brains. But that is a rare, rare man, I venture, who is as subtly intelligent, as constantly sound in judgment, as little put off by appearances, as the average women of forty-eight.

Of course, Mencken was the supreme iconoclast. He was also the supreme individualist, who might be criticized in this case for speaking of women, rather than taking his persons, male or female, one at a time. But he may have been right:

Women do not lend themselves to be regimented as men do – men find no problem in goose-stepping. The most civilized man is simply that man who has been most successful in gagging and harnessing his honest and natural instincts.

If women were indeed sufficiently perceptive to have avoided the regimentation of their male counterparts throughout history, one hopes they will be able to retain such common sense and individuality in the years immediately ahead, at a time when sexism seems to have replaced such older egalitarian causes as the war on poverty or the race question, as a dominant theme of the day.

V. WHAT IS EQUALITY?

There is a contradiction between the goal of an equal society and the methods of attaining it by means of unequal treatment of individuals

Paul Seabury

In a society which has long emphasized the concept of equal justice under the law, our recent tendency has been to carry that original doctrine far beyond equality of rights, until our present goal demands equality of condition. Of course, men are no more created equal than any other member of the animal kingdom – life is always unequal. Neither the Declaration of Independence nor the Constitution ever stated or implied an equality of condition. The guarantee of the 14th Amendment that no state shall deprive any citizen of "equal protection of the laws" is only another way of expressing what we in the American experience have viewed as each man's inherent right to equality in freedom under law.

The American experience has been consistent on that definition of equality. Even two such political rivals and crusty personalities as Thomas Jefferson and John Adams were in essential agreement on the point. Harkening back to the time they spent in the summer of 1776, labouring together in Philadelphia to produce the final version of the Declaration of Independence, Adams wrote to Jefferson nearly thirty years later:

Inequalities of mind and body are so established by God Almighty in His constitution of human nature that no art or policy can ever plane them down to a level. I have never read reasoning more absurd, sophistry more gross. . . than the subtle labours of Helvetius and Rousseau to demonstrate the natural equality of mankind.

It has been the American insistence upon an equality measured in freedom, independence and opportunity that has characterized our system. It is the accompanying inequality of individual talents, given full play by the legal guarantee of equal opportunity, which has led to progress in religion, intellectual affairs, the production of material wealth, and the pursuit of individual meaning in life. The social advances which we take for granted have their origin in allowing the individual the opportunity to give full play to his creative resources. It is precisely that aspect of American life which is now so heavily under attack. The assault upon the merit principle today is present not only in higher education, but throughout American society as a whole. The real danger of the social engineering now under way is that the drive towards mediocrity reflected in Affirmative Action programming has behind it not only the full weight of the United States government, but the unthinking support of most moulders of public opinion. One reason for this may be that equality of opportunity, as opposed to equality of condition, lacks the political attractiveness necessary for success in an age of group-interest politics. However the situation came about, the fact remains that merit is today being scrapped in favour of quotas. In the process, mediocrity is being institutionalized and equal opportunity suppressed.

A. Education as the Panacea

In our society's fevered search for equality we have turned increasingly to education as the panacea for our politically induced guilt feelings and confusions on the subject of equality. The Affirmative Action mentality seems to suggest that if equality of condition does not exist, then it is the obligation of education so to mould future generations that such equality is finally produced. Naturally, education has failed to deliver the egalitarian dream, since the schools cannot hope to set aside the inequalities of individual condition. The egalitarians' response to this is to resort to compulsion, using legal force and political interventions to bring the schools to heel.

This tendency to politicize education in the name of a false equality has been under way for some time. The U.S. Office of Education reports that roughly two million of the fifty-one million school children in America are "gifted," but the same report goes on to suggest that very few of these talented youngsters are being properly educated in our public schools. Nearly a century and a half ago, Alexis de Tocqueville pointed out that something of the sort was likely to happen in America, since democracies tend to resent and resist inequalities of talent.

One of those avenues of society most open to achievers of real talent has been the academic community. Those gifted students who survived the drudgery common to many elementary and secondary schools have at least had the opportunity to distinguish themselves in the higher learning. It is this avenue of performance which Affirmative Action now moves to close in the name of a politically enforced egalitarian dream.

Keeping pace with this trend towards politicized education has been the frantic search for "scientific" sociological proof of our newfangled egalitarian assumptions. The sociological speculations of Brown vs. Board of Education seemed to promise some hope for the achievement of our politicized egalitarian goals, but the evidence which has accumulated since that time has been embarrassing to say the least. The 1966 Coleman Report on the "Equality of Educational Opportunity" was the first of several studies demonstrating that scholastic achievement of students is not a matter of the quality of the schools they attend.

The Coleman Report stunned the environmental determinists. Then Christopher Jencks produced *Inequality: A Reassessment of the Effect of Family and Schooling in America*, demonstrating once again that economic inequality did not have a significant effect on educational inequality in America. According to Jencks, inequality is recreated anew in each generation. Thus the search for equality of condition can be fulfilled only by stifling the creative capacities of those who would be most productive in each new generation. One would suspect that this would hardly be in the interest of the body politic as a whole, but we must remember that policies are made by politicians, and that politicians often create their issues in areas of mythology rather than fact.

The effort to attain egalitarian goals in education has continued to receive growing criticism on a number of fronts. Many of those in the vanguard of the egalitarian thrust of the 1960s have begun to have their doubts in the 1970s. Those egalitarians who continue to have the courage of their convictions, despite all evidence to the contrary – such men as John Rawls, author of the recently published *A Theory of Justice* – are at least willing to take the process to its logical conclusion. Mr. Rawls suggests that the egalitarian ideal cannot succeed in education until enforced redistribution of wealth and total regimentation of society first destroys all special advantages in position or talent. At least Mr. Rawls is honest enough to admit that equality of result is fundamentally incompatible with equality of opportunity.

Can we achieve equality through education? The battle now rages, with such participants as Jencks, Moynihan, Coleman, Pettigrew, and Jensen. Whatever other generalizations might be made about the egalitarian ideal and its connection with education, it seems clear that the intellectual assumptions on which the egalitarian ideal has been built in modern America are losing support among the very social scientists who provided much of the ideological thrust for the idea in the period between 1930 and 1970.

B. Assault on the Merit Principle

Although fewer social scientists advocate egalitarianism today, the political, popularized version of the idea is just now coming into its own. Federal administrative involvement in higher education has been paralleled by a growing involvement on the part of the courts. Since 1955, nearly 4,000 decisions affecting education have been handed down by this country's higher courts. In some of these decisions, especially those of recent vintage, the egalitarian intent is unmistakable. For example, a recent federal district court decision abolished the "track system" in the Washington, D.C. public schools. The track system is a device to allow all the children in a given school to operate on their own level of aptitude and performance. The programme was ruled illegal and discriminatory since there were proportionately more white children in the higher tracks, and so the programme had to go. Education in the public schools of Washington, D.C. has now been made safe for egalitarian mediocrity.

The courts are handing down similar decisions under new Affirmative Action rulings. Mark DeFunis, a white student making application to the University of Washington law school, was denied admission even though thirty-eight black students with significantly lower qualifications were admitted as members of the same class. DeFunis, an honours graduate of the University of Washington, brought suit on the grounds that his rights had been violated under the 14th Amendment. He was denied satisfaction by the state supreme court, in a decision which reeked of the egalitarian lust to remake society. Denying that DeFunis' higher entrance scores and grades were relevant, the court went on to say:

It can hardly be gain-said that the minorities have been, and are, grossly under-represented in the law schools – and consequently in the legal profession – of this state and this nation. We believe the state has an overriding interest in promoting integration in public education. In light of the serious under-representation of minority groups in the law schools, and considering that minority groups participate on an equal basis in the tax support of the law school, we find the state interest in eliminating racial imbalance within public legal education to be compelling.

It has been suggested that the minority admissions policy is not necessary, since the same objective could be accomplished by improving the elementary and secondary education of minority students to a point where they could secure equal representation in law schools, through direct competition with non-minority applicants on the basis of the same academic criteria. This would be highly desirable, but 18 years have passed since the decision Brown vs. Board of Education, and minority groups are still grossly under-represented in law schools. If the law school is forbidden from taking affirmative action, this under-representation may be perpetuated indefinitely. No less restrictive means would serve the governmental interest here; we believe the minority admissions policy of the law school to be the only feasible "plan that promises realistically to work, and promises realistically to work *now*".

"Work and . . . work now" – to remake the face of society. The court seems less interested in dispensing justice than in social engineering. In its decision we have a graphic sample of the Affirmative Action mentality in action.

Even if the egalitarian society were possible to achieve, the effort to attain it by unequal treatment of individuals is not likely to succeed; such methods would surely become the means which destroyed the end. We in America are just beginning to face the nature of this powerful dilemma. There are other nations in the world which, further down the road towards a presumed egalitarian goal, are discovering the same inescapable truth. When all the "reforms" desired in pursuit of the egalitarian dream become law as they have in Britain and Sweden, we have an opportunity to view the outcome first hand. The reforms have satisfied no one and settled nothing. In Irving Kristol's words, "Above all, the passion for equality, so far from having been appeased, has been

exacerbated, so that there is more bitter controversy over equality –
and more inequalities – in Sweden and Britain today than was the case
5 or 10 years ago."

The Indian experience also gives first hand evidence of the final destination of the egalitarian dream. Nehru attempted to establish equality in the new-style egalitarian manner, institutionalizing reverse discrimination as the means to his end. What happened was that the disadvantaged beneficiaries of quotas came to view their situation as a
prescriptive right, while more and more Indians sought "the previous
designation of backwardness" as a means of gaining privilege. Once
established, quotas tend to perpetuate themselves.

What women, blacks, social engineers and all the rest of us might
keep in mind as we examine the slogans of the day, especially those
slogans of an egalitarian variety is one in which inequalities – of property, or station or power – are generally perceived by the citizenry as
necessary for the common good. At best, it is always difficult for a society to retain a sufficient sense of balance to work towards the common
good and not be turned aside into empty political promises concerning
absolute equality of condition. The corrective balance which kept this
nation and much of Western civilization on the right track has always
been what Irving Kristol describes as the "common sense" of the majority of the population. It is that common sense which is under such
heavy attack today.

One reason we suffer an erosion of common sense may lie in the fact
that we are generating a larger and larger class of "intellectuals." The
intellectual, as the word is increasingly used today, is not merely the
man who uses his intellect – we all do that, to greater or lesser degree.
An intellectual is best defined as a person whose work demands that he
devotes the bulk of his time and attention to abstract issues apart from
the normal business of daily life that occupies most men. For this
reason, or for some reason, today's intellectual class is deeply alienated
from American society, feeling itself superior to the common man, and
above the whole process of getting and spending. Thus many intellectuals are sharply critical of the world they see around them, generally
regarding that world as unfair and unjust because they feel it does not
provide them with an equal status in society. In fact, the status of the
intellectual is high indeed in our present society. He is able to live well
and pursue his own interests in a fashion never before possible. Despite
this, the theme of "inequality" persists. Those providing most of the
leadership towards enforced equality, towards what is now called Af-

firmative Action, prove to be members of the academic community and the professions. Yet a special irony lies in the fact that these reformers have now set in motion a process which subjects the standards and practices of their institutions to heavy attack from the newly empowered egalitarian bureaucracy they helped to create.

C. *The Fist of Government*

Stanley Lowell, former chairman of the New York City Commission on Human Rights, made a statement some time ago which indicates how far the doctrinaire can go in pursuit of the egalitarian goal: "The time has come when colour consciousness is necessary and appropriate ... The protection of human rights needs the fist of government." When we look to government for protection of human rights, we are relying upon an agency which has a very bad track record in defending anyone's rights. I suspect that very often when we invoke the power of government, we are acting in the belief that we have discovered some cause so noble it justifies using organized force to insure compliance on the part of our less enlightened fellow citizens, who otherwise might not co-operate. But there is scarcely any means of reform less effective than compulsion. The Affirmative Action zealots are already learning to their sorrow that the bureaucratic solution is worse than no solution at all.

Meanwhile, there is serious confusion at the heart of the egalitarian ideal. The thrust of Affirmative Action in all its forms is towards the homogenized society in which all are absolutely equal, and yet the means of attainment is to be through special group identity. We are all to be made identical by treating various interest groups in non-identical ways, giving some privilege and discriminating against others.

At the same time, the priorities among interest groups are continually shifting. The lust for Affirmative Action has caused a sharp decline in the intensity of feeling towards earlier causes. Not too long ago, the "poor" were presumably the central problem of our times. Now we hear very little about the subject. Race is also giving way to sex as the "trendy" cause.

D. *Pursuit of Opportunity*

Somewhere out there among all the fashionable causes, the old ideal of individual opportunity and identity has been lost. Politicized egalitarian rhetoric and enforced quotas cannot restore that opportunity. So long as we treat iron-clad, legally enforced group membership as the key to solving our problems, we may rest assured that individual opportunity will be progressively harder to rediscover.

Perhaps the problem in America is our success. In this nation the common man has generally enjoyed a substantial opportunity to do something for himself and his family. He has gone to work and built an astonishing level of prosperity, both in the wealth created and in the numbers of people sharing in that wealth. Surely this was the fruit of genuine individual opportunity. The system worked, but perhaps in working it created new appetites. Perhaps we were caught in an escalating world of achievement and expectation – the more we had, the more we wanted. Tocqueville told us to expect as much:

Among democratic nations men easily attain a certain equality of conditions: they can never attain the equality they desire. It perpetually retires before them, yet without hiding itself from their sight, and in retiring draws them on. . .

When inequality of conditions is the common law of society, the most marked inequalities do not strike the eye: when everything is nearly on the same level, the slightest are marked enough to hurt it. Hence the desire of equality always becomes more insatiable in proportion as equality is more complete.

Despite our problems, one of the central facts of American history has been the achievement of a high degree of individual equaltiy for most citizens. Perhaps the nation somehow sensed that human beings achieve their fulfilment in what they become. Certainly we are most fully ourselves as we aspire to further development, and enjoy the freedom to pursue it. It is in connection with our aspiration that we seek equality for each person. Surely race or sex is an inadequate basis for such equality. We do not aspire to be black, white, or yellow, male or female. These categories are facts of existence, but the achievement which we seek in life must lie elsewhere, and it is elsewhere that the definition of true equality must also be located.

What we all want, and what some members of society presently lack, is acceptance as an individual by others. It is that acceptance which constitutes genuine equality. Each of us wants to be a person in his own right. Such acceptance can hardly be produced by governmental compulsion. Compulsion smothers any creative response to a problem.

Quotas undercut acceptance for the individual. No matter how many legal guarantees enforce the quota, the primary effect is a stoppage of the acceptance and the opportunities for individual development which we seek. If a person lacks qualification for a position, it is a disservice to that person and to society as a whole to enforce a quota and compel legal acceptance. Quotas limit rather than enhance opportunity; they degrade rather than dignify. And as one pastor of a Harlem church put it, speaking for all quota-entrapped groups, "If we are going to be judged without discrimination then we will also be judged without pity." The only equality with real meaning is that based upon an absence of prejudgment. The quota is itself a prejudgment, institutionalized with the force of law, standing as a permanent obstacle to true equality.

Perhaps the route towards alleviation of our present discontents lies through a restatement and redefinition of the equality we seek. A vast majority of us want genuine equality of opportunity for all citizens. Discrimination on the grounds of race, sex, religion, or any other group oriented basis is simply unacceptable. But the course we now pursue is calculated to enforce a peculiarly American version of apartheid, an apartheid which not only sets race apart, but adds sex as another category of public regulation.

By every standard of simple equity, by the standards of the American dream at its best, in the interest of all individuals, especially in the interest of the "disadvantaged," and finally in the interest of society as a whole, we must understand that the egalitarian dream now pursued by Affirmative Action programming on the campuses of America's colleges and universities is undercutting the very structure of the open society. The commendable quest for equality of opportunity must not be confused with the shoddy, politicized quotas of Affirmative Action.

VI. Education vs. Egalitarian Politics

> ... there cannot be a university or college anywhere in the country today that does not know that where basic grievances exist, those who are aggrieved will turn to every available source for redress, including the federal government. And surely they must know that if the university does not *voluntarily* deal with the issue, a vacuum is created which the government, like nature, abhors.
>
> J. Stanley Pottinger

No one familiar with the bureaucratic mentality can be surprised to learn that Stanley Pottinger regards the power of the Office of Civil Rights to be on a par with the forces of nature. For that matter, Pottinger may be right. Already the Affirmative Action bureaucracy has so proliferated that the HEW "Contract Compliance" force alone has nearly 500 employees. And yet HEW is still not moving fast enough for some of the zealots. A coalition of various minority groups has charged that current guidelines "undercut and dilute" civil rights enforcements.

Such groups need not be concerned. It seems a foregone conclusion that more comprehensive and stringent pressures are on the way. The federal bureaucracy is supplemented by various state level actions. These state bureaucracies have moved to enforce changes in faculty hiring and promotion, curricular offerings, housing, hours, and other aspects of campus business in both public and private higher educational institutions. Worst of all, there is a sort of "do-it-yourself" Affirmative Action in operation on many campuses, where the administrators are running ahead of specific HEW guidelines in an anxious effort to avoid trouble.

All this is in addition to the main thrust of federal Affirmative Action, which continues to accelerate. The President's budget request for fiscal 1974 contained a substantial increase for the Office of Civil Rights. Some sixty new positions have been created in the office, producing a newly formed Division of Higher Education with the special responsibility of enforcing the executive order against sex bias in colleges and universities. Meanwhile, the Equal Employment Opportunity Commission, which already has jurisdiction over all educational institutions (whether or not they receive federal funds) is projecting a budgetary increase of nearly 50 percent, to a total of some $43,000,000. The United States Commission of Civil Rights, which now has enlarged jurisdiction including sex discrimination and is currently planning an investigation of bias on the campus, will receive an increase of some 13 percent in its budget.

Both the Equal Employment Opportunity Commission and the Equal Pay Division of the Department of Labor have also been co-operating with HEW campus investigations. A number of cases involving salary discrimination have already been pressed, both in and out of court. Suits have been filed against the University of Pittsburgh, the University of California at Berkeley, the University of Maryland, and Florida State University. The Florida State suit involves nine women faculty members suing the institution for $1 million in back pay and damages. These pressures have caused deans to take out personal liability insurance, since individual administrators may be expected to be named in an increasing number of suits.

Small wonder that the academic community is running scared. This climate of fear, generated by reverse discrimination against individuals and increasing governmental interference in the affairs of our colleges and universities, characterizes the present state of Affirmative Action on the American campus.

Of perhaps still greater consequence for the future is the development of a new federal agency, the National Institute of Education, with the announced function of promoting basic research in the processes of learning and teaching. As one university president has remarked:

When a federal institution begins finding the best methods of teaching, and is also associated with unrestricted support for instructional programmes in colleges and universities, it is just a matter of time – and a short time at that – until the conclusions of the institute on how teaching *ought* to be done are going to come over as requirements for those institutions that are receiving aid. These additional *requirements* will inevitably reach into the most sensitive area of the educational process – the content and manner of teaching.

The United States Office of Education has recently announced that it is engaged in developing new standards to apply to those organizations which accredit colleges and universities. Accreditation is a major factor in higher education. Without it, a school cannot hire qualified faculty, cannot guarantee students that scholastic work will be recognized on a transfer basis by other institutions, and indeed probably cannot long survive in the present academic climate.

And now it is proposed by the U.S. Office of Education that this life and death power of accreditation be made subject to a single national pattern. One of the suggested items in this new pattern would be that accrediting agencies have "ethical standards for institutions and programmes in such areas as discrimination in admissions and hiring ..."

Such total federal control for all schools, whether or not they receive federal funds, is not far down the road. The National Institute of Education has already received an initial grant of $92 million to facilitate research and central planning for the new national programmes.

A. Disregard for Basic Legal Guarantees

Another highly disturbing aspect of the present rush towards Affirmative Action has been the cavalier attitude adopted towards traditional legal guarantees. The OCR tendency has been to dismiss those abuses of legal rights which have arisen in A.A. programmes on many campuses as mere "excesses of zeal" on the part of local officials. In June 1972, Stanley Pottinger publicly declared, "I am convinced ... that the spectre of lost autonomy and diminished quality among faculties is one which obscures the real objective of the law against discrimination." As one commentator has observed, Pottinger seems to be implying that a law's consequences should not be allowed to "obscure" the intentions of its maker. For the zealot, good intentions are always enough. Presumably we may then overlook the harmful consequences of such laws.

And harmful consequences there are in abundance with Affirmative Action. For example, one of the root assumptions of Anglo-American jurisprudence has been that the accused is innocent until proven guilty. Not so with Affirmative Action, which assumes the educational institution guilty of discrimination until the school proves its innocence. Personnel records, previously considered confidential, are now regarded as fair game in Affirmative Action investigations, with no interest whatsoever displayed by the bureaucracy in securing permission from the persons whose personal files are thus converted into public property.

Affirmative Action pressures are also generating some highly questionable legal tendencies among the college and university administrators. Not long ago a document was circulated at a meeting of the North-East Regional Group on Student Affairs of the Association of American Medical Colleges, by the associate dean of a leading university in New York, recommending to fellow administrators a means for avoidance of moral and legal problems which might arise in reverse discrimination cases involving student admissions and faculty hiring. The dean described his secret consultation with several members of the judiciary, in which means were discussed whereby provisions for admission and hiring could "get around" constitutional and legal obstacles to reverse discrimination:

The purpose . . . is to explore in as concise a fashion as possible prevailing legal attitudes and how several distinguished jurists view this irksome problem. The heart of the matter is how the courts will treat the problem if and when presented with it, and their response, which may not be consistent, is the only tangible and dependable support available. Five justices of the New York State Supreme Court were identified for consultation. Three judges spent a considerable amount of their time discussing their own and what they thought the court's ultimate response would be to a law suit similar to the one now before the Supreme Court of the State of Washington. . .

Such collusion is clearly illegal as well as morally unacceptable. These same judges may one day hear such cases, and yet they are the same men now giving advice on the best means to deny redress for reverse discriminatory practices.

As a part of the same document described above, the associate dean admitted the intent of his recommendation was a quota system under another name:

Establishing given percentages or quotas of minority students to be accepted in a class represents predictable problems. This should be avoided at all costs. It is possible to achieve the same results without giving the appearance of restricting portions of the class for designated groups.

When representatives of higher education and members of the legal profession, including judges seated in responsible positions, meet in deliberate attempts to bypass legal guarantees for individuals penalized by the new reverse discrimination, the whole process becomes even more reprehensible.

Administrators today are also faced with the necessity of *deciding which law they will disobey*: the 1964 Civil Rights Act forbidding discrimination, or the Affirmative Action guidelines which carry the force of law and which specifically require discrimination on the basis or race and sex. In such a climate, it is not difficult to understand the confusion and lack of principle which characterize so many Affirmative Action programmes.

B. *The Latest Application of an Old Idea*

The quota system is far from a new idea. It is not the wave of the future; it is the putrid backwash of all the tired social engineering schemes of centuries. Both the Communists and the Nazis made prominent use of quotas recently enough that we should have no trouble remembering the result.

A departmental chairman in a large Eastern state university circulated a letter to a number of other departmental chairmen across the country, asking that the *curricula vitae* of new Ph. D.'s contain identifications of race and sex, since HEW hiring orders were impossible to follow in the absence of such information. To his credit, one of the departmental chairmen of a Western university replied:

If there were objective or legally established definitions of race, together with a legal requirement of full disclosure of racial origins, we would be in the clear. I understand that a number of steps in this direction were achieved by the "Nuremberg laws" of Nazi Germany. And in the Soviet Union, I am told, all individuals carry their racial identifications on their internal passports. Similarly for blacks in South Africa. So there are precedents.

I would suggest that the American Economic Association calls upon the Department of Health, Education, and Welfare (HEW) and other bureaucratic agencies now engaged in promoting racial discrimination for assistance. We should ask them to establish legal "guidelines" as to: (1) which races are to be preferred, and which discriminated against; (2) what criteria (how many grandparents?) determine racial qualifications for employment; (3) what administrative procedures must be set up for appeals against arbitrary classification.

With guidelines like these, you and other department chairmen would suffer neither embarrassment nor inconvenience in employing some individuals, and refusing to hire others, on the grounds of their race and sex. And you will have the peace of mind of knowing that the authenticity of racial labellings have in effect been guaranteed by an agency of the federal government.

If the President of the United States has the power to command colleges and universities to establish faculty quotas on the basis of race and sex, why not faculty quotas on the basis of ideology or party membership? Unless we answer definitely the questions concerning which portions of society are public and which are private, our inevitable tendency will be towards the totally politicized state.

Today federal power within the academy has already grown to life and death proportions. Federal funding already provides great leverage. The situation seems well on the way, through a variety of channels, to applying the same pressures to all colleges and universities, whether or not they receive federal money. This seems to be the assumption of much federal policy. Elliot Richardson, former secretary of HEW, defended Affirmative Action by claiming it was the federal government's vital interest to assure "the largest possible pool of qualified manpower for its project." As Professor Paul Seabury immediately asked, "Does HEW now regard universities as federal projects? If so, how far down the road of government control have we come?" In view of all the pressures discussed in these pages, pressures involving funding, accreditation, admissions, faculty hiring, and nearly every other aspect of campus life, to be administered by a variety of federal agencies, parallel state agencies, and the courts, it seems clear that we have come a long way indeed.

Not only is the power of self-determination passing from the academy, but in many cases the rise of Affirmative Action is destroying quality and standards as well. Higher education must have no priority ahead of the search for truth and the perfection of learning standards. When "social justice" supplants these goals within the academy, the result is likely to be a misdirection of attention and scarce resources from the primary goal of education. One effect of that misdirection has been the extremely expensive administrative costs which accompany Affirmative Action. One small college president announced: "To tell you the truth, my little college simply does not have the personnel to go through all our records and do the necessary homework." The Office of Civil Rights investigator replied: "Too bad. You'll just have to dig up somebody to do it."

The briefest examination of a completed Affirmative Action plan should make it abundantly clear how high the costs are in preparation of the original material. It has been estimated by the business manager of a large Mid-western university that $1 million would be necessary to make the transition to the new set of records and procedures demanded by Affirmative Action on his campus. This figure does not include the continuing costs involved in the maintenance and monitoring of an Affirmative Action programme.

One academic investigator deeply involved in studying the impact of Affirmative Action programmes on a number of campuses conservatively estimates that an ongoing Affirmative Action programme, operated within HEW guidelines, would consume 50 percent of the total administrative budget of a typical school. At a time when resources for higher education promise to be in increasingly short supply in the years ahead, such administrative costs are likely to have a great impact, probably further increasing dependence upon political funding.

Another problem arising within the academy as the direct result of Affirmative Action is the application of improper measurement standards, standards unsuitable to higher education. The language and practices developed by the Labor Department for application of Affirmative Action programmes in industry have been imitated by HEW and applied to higher education. There should be recognizable difference between a plumbers' union and a faculty. There is also the vital difference that the university is a highly decentralized institution which HEW now proposes to administer not only as though each school were a tightly knit unit, but also as though all schools were nothing more than interchangeable units of "the education industry." Such standards cannot be applied without doing lasting harm.

Lowered standards in admissions and faculty hiring, induced by HEW standards and such bizarre notions as the "qualifiable" candidate, will also inevitably have an effect throughout all segments of higher education. It should be obvious that the hiring of a faculty member, on any other basis than the particular merit of that individual faculty member, must in the long run be prejudicial to the quality of the institutional faculty so affected. The responsibility of every faculty and administration in this country is to find the most qualified person available for a particular post, regardless of race, sex, religion, or national origin. Any other basis for selection is not only discriminatory, but must necessarily be a downward step in the quality of the institution.

The same situations apply for admissions policies in academic institutions. Those institutions which have experimented with lowering their admissions standards to achieve racial balance have then found that the students admitted under the lower standards can only be retained in school if the institution is willing to lower its classroom standards as well. As in the case of discriminatory hiring, discriminatory admissions practices work directly contrary to the ideal of quality education.

Perhaps one of the most saddening aspects of the entire affair is the special damage which Affirmative Action inflicts upon the very people for whose benefit the programme presumably operates. The hiring of professors or the admission of students on any other basis than ability works a particular hardship on the "favoured" groups. The qualified, achieving students and teachers can never be sure of where they stand. How can one build an academic standing when neither he nor his colleagues will ever know for sure whether he is there because of ability or because he was part of some racial or sexual quota? The unqualified student or professor fares even worse. Such a person can be retained only by lowering standards and thus cheating those involved of the education they have been promised.

C. Proper Function of a University

The vagaries of politically pursued egalitarian dreams are hard to follow. We have considered the effects of Affirmative Action on individuals, black and white, man and woman. We have considered the effects of Affirmative Action on the various groups within society. Perhaps an appropriate closing note might be a brief look at the impact of Affirmative Action on society as a whole. Here are the thoughts of Professor Paul Seabury of the University of California at Berkeley, one of the outspoken and highly effective critics of Affirmative Action.

The case for merit and equal opportunity must also be seen in the light of common standards of a complex society which, after all, depends on the skills of the individuals composing it. Concerns of human safety, convenience, and the quality of our collective life are of as great consequence as our concern for equal protection of the laws. We do want a qualified surgeon when we need an operation. We assume we want a skilled pilot, especially when it is we who are on the plane. We want a clever lawyer when we are in trouble. We want the telephone to work, and our mail to come to us, and not to someone down the street. We want competent teachers for our children. In universities we want high standards of scholarship and research and we want them visible also as exemplars of excellence. In short, we want the entire complex of amenities and necessities in a condition which we can reasonably trust. Our existence places us at the mercy of persons, often invisible to us, who are certified for their qualities. While we may quibble about the arbitrary and fallible manner in which, in real life, skill and competence may be ascertained, we would hardly therefore argue that such standards are worthless, or that better ones could not be devised. Yet the erosion of standards, in the name of a form of equity, risks lowering the quality of existence and experience.

The merit system, which has made possible the retention of those norms permitting society to function effectively, has enjoyed an especially important place within the academic community. At its best, the academic community has consistently reflected a standard of professional excellence which is truly egalitarian. The egalitarianism of excellence offered opportunity for those able and willing to compete, with countless spin-off benefits to society deriving from that excellence. Now what is at stake in Affirmative Action programming is the end of that true equality of opportunity and the end of that excellence.

If we give way before the force which now menaces higher education and our society as a whole, we are not only opening the door to second-rate standards and a new and more vicious and permanent form of injustice. We are also passing control of tomorrow's leaders and tomorrow's dominant ideas from the privacy and independence of the academic community to the realm of egalitarian politics. If Affirmative Action gains the final say in curriculum, faculty, and admissions throughout higher education, effective control of society will have passed to the social engineers and the politicians, and America will have lost one of her greatest resources in the struggle to remain an open and effective society.

Race and Class in Indonesia:
Patterns of Discrimination and Conflict

JUSTUS M. VAN DER KROEF

JUSTUS M. VAN DER KROEF was born in Jakarta, Indonesia, was educated there, in Europe, Australia and the U.S.A., and holds a Ph. D. from Columbia University, New York. He has served as Consultant on South-east Asian affairs to the Special Operations Research Office, in Washington, D.C.; to the Center for Strategic and International Studies, Georgetown University; and to the Foreign Policy Research Institute, Philadelphia. He is now Charles Anderson Dana Professor of Political Science and Chairman of the political science department in the University of Bridgeport, Connecticut.

Professor van der Kroef has been a visiting Professor of Asian Studies at Universities in Singapore, the Philippines, and Sri Lanka, and since 1968 has been a Research Associate of the Society for Research in Indian Communist Affairs. In 1973 and 1974 he was in Thailand doing research on the problems of the Communist insurgency in that country.

He is the author of many articles in scholarly and popular periodicals and has also published six books, the latest of which is *Indonesia Since Sukarno*, (University of British Columbia Press, 1972). In 1970 The National Strategy Information Center of New York published his study on *Australian Security Policies and Problems*. He is a Director of the American-Asian Educational Exchange, a group of American and Far Eastern scholars concerned with freedom of communication and exchange of scholarly information in the Asian and Pacific region. He is currently engaged on a research project on post-Vietnam-war collective security problems and organizations in the Far East.

Race and Class in Indonesia: Patterns of Discrimination and Conflict

JUSTUS M. VAN DER KROEF

Analysis of inter-group conflict in Indonesia, particularly when such conflict may be rooted in actual or felt discriminatory treatment, should, at the outset, draw a distinction between conflict patterns operating at the *national* level (the primary concern of the following pages) and those of a *localized* or sub-systemic character the great number and variety of which exceed the limits set for this essay. There is a severe unevenness in the distribution of the total Indonesian population (estimated at 126,177,000 in 1970) in terms of the human occupation of the national archipelago territory of 3,000 or so islands, with the island of Java alone having one-thirteenth of the total land area but also possessing about 65% of the entire population of the country.[1] Consequently, a variety of social problems, including discrimination and class consciousness, found in Java, tend sometimes to be projected as characteristic of the nation as a whole. This may be true enough in some instances (as, for example, in Indonesian attitudes towards the three million, more or less identifiable, members of the Chinese minority today), but sight must not be lost of other, more localized, forms of ethnic or economic interest group confrontations (for example between Muslim and Hinduized Balinese, or Batak entrepreneurs and migrant Javanese estate labourers in North Sumatra).

I. URBANISATION

Similarly, concentration on Jakarta's growth problems have occasionally led to unwarranted generalizations about Indonesia's "urbanisation" as a whole, and about an allegedly attendant rise in social class (rather than traditional religious, ethnic, or other group) consciousness in Indonesia's urban population generally, which, if left unqualified, would create a wrong impression. Jakarta, to be sure, has witnessed a population growth from about 500,000 in 1940 to about five million in 1970 (with a realistically projected size of ten million by 1980).[2] But while many other Indonesian cities have also grown, such growth has to a significant degree taken place within the existing urban population, and with the exception of Jakarta is not necessarily or primarily to be ascribed to a continuous, permanent influx of people from the surrounding areas. The country as a whole, according to one calculation, has seen only a limited degree of spontaneous migration from the rural areas to the towns. Indeed, the flow of rural migration to the cities is said to have comprised only 2.6% of the population during the entire decade of the 1960s, for example, and "in 1971 only 17.5 percent of the popualtion was considered urban."[3] Some might be inclined to hypothesize that at least the matrix of a modern proletarian class consciousness could exist in those "desperately cramped" sections of Jakarta, like Senèn, where the local population density reaches fifty thousand or more per square kilometre, and to which, among a few other sections, many recent newcomers to the city tend to gravitate. Yet, most migrants to Jakarta, according to a 1973 report on Jakarta's urbanisation problems issued by the government's Central Bureau of Statistics and other agencies, are "short distance" migrants coming from regions (e.g. West or Central Java) relatively directly adjacent to the city.[4] Often driven by land shortages in their village areas, where they had already become accustomed to a variety of small-scale, part-time, intermittent and itinerant labour of all sorts – participants in a "scavenger economy"[5] – many of Jakarta's proletarian migrants retain strong familial, village, ethnic and other traditional group bonds that slow down a drift and immersion into a new class consciousness. Return visits for shorter or longer times, by these migrants, to their place of origin are common, as is permanent emigration again from the city.

This kind of migration to the Indonesian towns, a kind of traditional mobility in which the population is given to shuttling back and forth between its rural habitat and one or more towns in its vicinity for a stay of variable duration, probably has always contributed to the difficulty of determining the exact extent of urbanization in Indonesia, even in the colonial period. In 1930, in the whole of the "Netherlands Indies," with its total population then of nearly 61 million, there were only seventeen towns of 50,000 or more inhabitants (seven of which had 100,000 or more, six of them in Java), comprising just under 4% of that total pupolation.[6] Yet, it is likely that such data do not reveal the true degree of "urbanisation," in the sense that a segment of the population had by then already become more mobile, taking up residence in towns for periods of varying duration, and, in consequence, becoming subjected to the pressure of new social strata outside the traditional village environment.

II. Class Consciousness

The extent of this social mobility and its long-term effects on social class consciousness cannot even be gauged in circumstances of "planned migration," i.e. the decades-old programme of government-assisted migration from crowded rural Java to other rural areas in less densely populated islands of Indonesia. A recent analysis of the population structure of Lampung province in Southern Sumatra, a major area of government-sponsored Javanese migrant colonies, indicates that a decade ago the province had a population of only half a million, while by 1972 it had a population of 2.7 million of which only some 242,000 could be accounted for by government migration programmes themselves and suggesting that "spontaneous" migration might have been considerably larger than the government's own programme.[7] Some of the colonist-migrants eventually move to the towns in the area of their new settlement – what began as a planned rural migration ends as an unplanned form of urbanisation. Also, it is obvious that despite the urban-rural social interaction generally, which, especially in the islands beyond Java, may have acted as a barrier to the more rapid development of a distinctive class consciousness, in all the larger urban centres in Indonesia today a more or less permanently settled proletariat is nevertheless a distinctive social and political force.

There are other demographic factors which probably have, or will have, a long-term effect on social class and other forms of inter-group discrimination and conflict, although the exact nature of such effects is not yet wholly clear. One of these, for example, is the age composition of the Indonesian population. There are 56 million persons under the age of 15 in Indonesia today, and it has been estimated that those in the working age category (from 15 to 60 years of age) have the problem of caring for 85 out of every 100 people in the country (in the United States the labour force in the same age category must care for the needs of 45 in every 100).[8] At the same time, more Indonesians are becoming better educated than ever before, but in terms of economic opportunity that may mean little: no fewer than 72% or nearly 12,000 people of those who registered as unemployed at the government's manpower office in the city of Jogjakarta, Central Java, alone recently, were graduates of senior high schools.[9] Will a sense of proletarisation or group consciousness that is antagonistic to other social interest strata deepen under such circumstances? The effect of continuing high population growth rates (expected to remain around 2.5% a year during the next five years at least), and of an educated, youthful, but severely unemployed or under-employed population component, numbering in the millions already, on existing racial, ethnic, and economic antagonisms and other inter-group cleavages can only be surmised as likely to be severely unsettling.

III. Colonial Heritage

Much of the matrix of present day racial conflict, discrimination, and class confrontation dates from the colonial period in Indonesia's history. Dutch colonial public law divided the population of Indonesia into "natives" (the indigenous inhabitants), "foreign Asiatics" (i.e. typically Chinese and most other orientals), and "Europeans" (including Japanese).[10] "Assimilation," or "naturalisation," or other procedures, could see the transfer of native Indonesian or Chinese inhabitants to the "European" category. But even so, these public legal distinctions inherently had and retained extensive social and economic implications which tended to accentuate the racial character of a broad range of human relationships even where this was not intended, or where it was felt justified on humanitarian grounds. Thus, the public legal distinctions referred to were often explained as obviously necessary because of the cultural heterogeneity of the Netherlands Indies population and the correspondingly sharply divergent "legal needs" (*rechtsbehoeften*) which would allegedly render unification or levelling of legal rights into a serious injustice. Whatever the considerable merits of this contention, the fact that race and culture are not necessarily synonymous, but that the pattern of public legal distinctions had the effect of continuously making them so, even long after accelerating modernising economic and educational impulses in Indonesia were creating ever more unsupportable strains in the application of the distinctions themselves, seemed only to be realised rather slowly in some official colonial circles, and remained a matter of lively controversy in expert legal circles, including those noted as champions of native Indonesian legal rights.

One reason, perhaps, why the pattern of the three-fold racial public legal distinction persisted for so long was because the earliest structure of colonial administration in Indonesia was closely connected with it. Even in the seventeenth and eighteenth centuries, in the days of the gradually expanding power of the Dutch East India Company over the Indonesian archipelago, Dutch authority had identified itself with and made use of the forms and offices of the indigenous Indonesian feudal system and aristocracy, ruling through that system and the Indonesian nobility where it became necessary, and adopting suzerain-vassal relationships with Indonesian potentates. Even in the course of the nineteenth century, with the advent of a more systematic civil service as expression of the sovereign overseas power of the Netherlands Kingdom, the fusion of Dutch and feudal Indonesian administrative offices and policies continued, and as new groups of Dutch civil servants made their appearance in the course of development of a modern colonial "service state," the branches of public administration, "always confronted by Javanese feudalism, had to be feudalised" themselves as well.[11] All other social strata, or immigrant ethnic groups like the Chinese, took their appropriate social distance from the feudalised Dutch power élite. Thus, from its inception, Dutch colonial power preserved, perpetuated, and, in its administration through "indirect rule," relied on an aristocratic sub-class, commonly reffered to as *priyayi* or "regents," and in so doing set itself often athwart the aspirations to governance of a non-aristocratic, but schooled, group of Indonesians, which its own policies of emancipation in the twentieth century were also slowly beginning to create.

If the potentially destabilising consequences of such social strata compartmentalisation were obvious, those existing in the racial field would perhaps become even more disquieting. For, in the later nineteenth and early twentieth century, as the Dutch colonial community in Indonesia itself became more diversified due to the greater influx of individuals not connected with the government services but engaged in trade and the professions, the structure of relationships had hardened to the point that those with similar educational, including university, training, or with approximately comparable employment positions, but of different race, had reportedly but minimal contact with each other.

While, on occasion, Dutch colonial officials, along with unofficial but expert legal opinion, declared that racial criteria should be or, in fact, had been abolished, e.g. in the training for or appointment to various functions in the judiciary, in other respects the public legal differences based on race were officially offered as justification for the retention of certain restraints on the "foreign oriental" and "native" Indonesian categories, some of which remained well into the present century. "Foreign orientals" (primarily Chinese), even if subjects of the Netherlands Indies, could, as late as 1918, only take up their domicile, where, according to the government, "quarters had been designated for those of their ethnic origin," i.e. where Chinese ghettos already existed. Not until 1914 was the regulation eliminated requiring "native" Indonesians and "foreign orientals" to have passes or permits for travel within the Indonesian islands. Taxation, rendered in the form of labour services (the so-called *heerendiensten*), demanded of "native" Indonesians only, were not eliminated until 1918, the same year that a criminal code for all three ethnic categories came into effect[12] (though differences in application still remained). But a process of equalisation in the area of labour law provisions came to an end in 1927 with the promulgation of a new separate labour law code applicable only to the "Europeans." Differences between "Europeans" and "natives" in the feeding and clothing provided to those in prisons and government hospitals, and in salaries paid for the same ranks in the armed forces, and in grades of the civil service generally, remained sources of felt discrimination among the increasingly politically conscious Indonesian population group. According to the government's own classification system, 92.2% of the "higher personnel" in the government's services in 1938 consisted of "Europeans," as compared to 6.4% "Indonesians" and those considered as Indonesians, with the remaining positions (about 1.3%) held by Chinese and other "foreign orientals"; on the other hand, 99.1% of the "lower personnel" job classifications were held by Indonesians, 0.6% by Europeans, and 0.3% by Chinese.[13]

A. Preparation for Independence

In a collection of studies, written by civil servants knowledgeable of colonial Indonesian affairs, and published in 1946, one reads of a "feeling of racial discrimination" on the part of Indonesians in all manner of relationships, of a "general sense of being 'lower'" on the part of Indonesians,[14] and of the factual reality for those in the Indonesian community of always finding a member of the "European" group above them, particularly in matters of public administration, i.e. precisely that area to which the strong Indonesian desire somehow to participate meaningfully in the government of his own country tended to be directed. As one of these studies puts it:[15]

Every Indonesian government official, however high his rank or however able he might be, always found a Dutch government official above him and never a Dutch government official below him ... in a number of service branches there existed a kind of internal tradition, which resisted the incorporation of Indonesians in leading positions; of this the Forest Service and the Customs Service are probably the clearest examples ... It is especially this closing off of the native Indonesian society from above which explains the increasing tensions and which cannot continue to accompany a further political development and a further expansion of education.

In September 1940, with Holland already occupied by Hitler's Germany, and with concern in the Dutch government in exile in London as to the stability of the government's Indonesian possessions, an official inquiry was begun in Indonesia as to the future constitutional structure of Indonesia in relation to Holland, and as to the wishes, in this regard, of the different strata and social groups in the country. The report of this commission of inquiry noted that "in no area" were the voiced wishes and grievances of those who appeared before the commission of inquiry "so urgent" as in the area of "racial differences in law and society." It was reported that such "differences" made in society, i.e. racial discrimination, were felt to be "more grievous" than those made by the law. Those who appeared before the commission came from all the major racial categories – "European," "native" Indonesian, and "foreign orientals." According to the commission report, there was unanimity that social relationships between persons of a different racial background, but of similar education, were generally few; some of those queried were even of the view that in the last few decades there had occurred a growing social distance between the various population groups, including between Indonesian and Chinese. Racial barriers in European clubs and associations, in various public facilities like restaurants and swimming pools, deepened the Indonesian sense of racial discrimination, as did the personnel appointment policies of the bigger Western commercial enterprises and financial institutions in which "Europeans" only allegedly were appointed to the more significant positions. Not only Indonesians, but Eurasians too, according to this same inquiry, felt aggrieved that they were barred from consideration for staff jobs.[16]

B. Eurasians

This Eurasian grievance underscores the fact that even within the three broad population groups, there were social sub-segments and internal strata differentiations which also reflected extensive, if sometimes more subtle, forms of racial discrimination. Even before the arrival of the Dutch East India Company in the seventeenth century Eurasian groups had emerged in Indonesia as a result of the unions of Portuguese and indigenous women. Well into the nineteenth century, as the number of Eurasians steadily grew, a distinctive Eurasian colonial cultural element, sometimes styled as "*Indisch*", and reflecting the traditional, paternalistic relationships and the feudalisation of political power and life styles of the Dutch in Indonesia, developed. This development, because of its relation to those of elite or near elite status at the time, softened to a degree the sense of racial discrimination that existed within the European top group itself.

In the later nineteenth and first decade of the twentieth century, however, the Eurasians' position changed sharply for the worse. By the time of the end of Dutch colonial rule (1942) there were some 300,000 persons classified as "Europeans," and an indeterminate number of these were Eurasians, but the actual number of Eurasians in other, including the "native" Indonesian public legal categories probably numbered around eight million.[17] The increased communication with the Netherlands, the growth in the number of private Dutch settlers in Indonesia (i.e. those not having a government service connection), the modernisation of Dutch and other Western life styles, especially in the larger cities of colonial Indonesia, the demand for more specialised and technically trained personnel in the larger corporations – all these eroded the primacy of the "*Indisch*", life style, and the important role once played by the Eurasian in the colonial power elite structure. Inner strata differences in the Eurasian community now became more accentuated between, on the one hand, those of wealth, those commissioned members of the armed forces and civil servants, and, on the other hand, those holding the lower clerical or administrative positions, or in relatively less pecunious positions like teaching, or the petty professionals with postings in the smaller less attractive interior towns – in short, the world of *"de kleine bung"* (litt. "the small brother").

Relations between Eurasians and Indonesians could vary sharply; early in the twentieth century some Eurasians believed that their future lay in a common political struggle with emancipated Indonesians, and to a degree assimilation produced by common education and kindred modern life styles gave this belief some plausibility. For a much larger number of Eurasians, however, an almost desperate struggle to retain "European" status continued even after Indonesia had attained its independence, and a not uncommon Indonesian epithet of opprobrium for the Eurasian, *"blanda hitam"* (litt. "black Dutchman"), suggested something of the Indonesian's lack of appreciation for Eurasian pretensions. On the other hand, on the basis of one small sample of Eurasian attitudes towards the Indonesian taken in 1953, one researcher noted that Eurasians considered their own relationships with Indonesians as relatively better than those with Europeans, i.e. Dutch.[18] The strata differentiation within the Eurasian community probably sharpened with the growing diversification and modernisation of the colonial Indonesian economy in the first decades of the twentieth century, and a real sub-class consciousness, predicated on relative racial purity, developed. So that, as one reporter on colonial Indonesian political life in 1933 wrote, Eurasians living "in the lower city" (i.e. the less attractive residential areas), and those in the "upper" part of town (i.e. the better neighbourhoods), "are rather far apart from each other."[19]

C. Structure of Education

The structure of public and private education in colonial Indonesia undoubtedly provided important impulses towards a hardening of racially discriminatory attitudes as well. Proceeding, again, from a recognition of different *"behoeften"* (needs), i.e. the heterogeneous cultural and linguistic backgrounds of school-age pupils, and seeking to adapt particularly primary and popular education to the varying concerns of the pupils' environment, Dutch policy maintained racially differentiated schools for Indonesians, Chinese, and "Europeans." The policy, at one and the same time, failed to meet the growing demand for modern education of the Indonesian masses (thereby encouraging all manner of private or so-called "wild" schools, often of dubious quality), and also seemed poorly integrated with the demands of the developing labour market, thus creating a relative "overproduction" of graduates of modern, i.e. European oriented, primary schools.[20] In other words, particularly from the point of view of the emancipated Indonesian, the colonial educational system managed to have the worst of two worlds, offering neither sufficient access to the kind of modern preparation needed for advancement in a politically maturing and economically diversifying environment (in which the "European" element held the top positions, in any case), nor the rewards in employment opportunity once that training had been acquired.

While Indonesians and Chinese did, increasingly, begin to attend the better secondary schools in the years before World War II, in 1939, nevertheless, only 204 Indonesian, 116 Chinese, but 457 "European" students graduated from the senior secondary schools. Only a little over 6% of the population in Indonesia was literate in 1930 (according to the last major census taken before the end of the Second World War), although one colonial official refined this calculation so as to suggest an actual literacy rate nearly five times higher.[21] In a confidential 1940 report by the director of the colonial Indonesian education department one reads that Indonesia has a "shameful lag" compared to neighbouring countries in Asia in combating illiteracy, and that such a lag also had become apparent in the educational system generally.[22] There seems little doubt that the Indonesian's sense of racial discrimination, and that even of the latter situated Chinese in the country as well, could not but be accentuated by the principles of racial differentiation and the seemingly officially acknowledged superior needs for quality training for "Europeans" that seemed to permeate the entire colonial educational system.

D. The Chinese

Deserving of a brief separate mention, because it is, perhaps, the biggest and most enduring single feature of racial discrimination in Indonesia over the centuries, is the problem of the Chinese, the largest identifiable non-indigenous minority in the country, whose presence as merchants and craftsmen in the Indonesian coastal towns long precedes the establishment, early in the seventeenth century, of the Dutch East India Company's settlements, and whose numbers grew from 221,000 in 1869 to over 1.2 million in 1930, and to about 2.8 million in

1965. Over the centuries, unions with Indonesians and an overt assimilation process, often impelled by new official or popular outbursts of suspicion and hostility towards the Chinese (such as the one that followed in the wake of the abortive 1965 coup attempt in Jakarta), probably have created a much larger population group in Indonesia with some Chinese blood in its veins, and with varying degrees of Chinese consciousness. Competing with them in trade, the Dutch, already in the seventeenth century, "treated the Chinese as enemies and were not above piratical raids upon their shipping," and although the Chinese communities slowly grew and prospered in the Dutch East India Company colonies, with the Dutch even encouraging their immigration and relying on them in the promotion of their commerce (e.g. in the production of sugar) suspicion of the influx of the Chinese, coupled with hostility to their sharp business practices and the fear of their group cohesiveness, led to bloody outbursts, like the 1740 massacre of thousands of Chinese in Batavia (today Jakarta).[23]

Such, and other, forms of ambivalence in Dutch, and one hastens to add also in Indonesian, attitudes towards the Chinese continued over the centuries. As, subsequently, restrictions were placed on Chinese land ownership or tax farming, Chinese industry in the nineteenth century and following, focused heavily, though not exclusively, on the distributing trade. Here, on the one hand, their intermediary role in modernising the Indonesian consumer economy became virtually indispensable. On the other hand, usury and exploitative debtor relationships with the Indonesian peasant and urban dweller, however necessitated by the risk of financial transactions with the Indonesian became – often quite deservedly – synonymous with the Chinese.

Conscious and proud of their ethnic and cultural origins, confronted with serious restrictions on their freedom of settlement, movement, or means of earning a livelihood, despised, yet needed because of their essential service and commercial functions in an increasingly monetised and slowly and to a degree proletarianised environment, differentiated in citizenship and feeling forever defenceless, harassed and humiliated in a country where family forebears had already been settled for decades and generations, then again stirred by the modern Chinese nationalist *réveille* of the twentieth century in which the "overseas Chinese" play a critically supporting role – all these buffetings in time tended to harden the relatively self-imposed group exclusiveness of the Chinese, a development which, in turn, inevitably only deepened the suspicion, fear and enmity of the Indonesians and other population groups. In a general way, the relative similarity between the position of the Chinese in Indonesia and in other South-East Asian countries, and that of the Jews in most of the Western World, has been too often commented upon to require repeating here. Other "Oriental" minorities in Indonesia, like the Arabs (numbering about 71,000 in 1930), though often engaged in the same usurious money-lending and other sharp trading and business practices as the Chinese, have been comparatively protected from Indonesian animosity and suspicion because of their overt identification with Islam and with the country of origin of the Prophet Muhammad. No such aura of respect surrounds the Chinese, whose sense of self and group identity usually (though not always) underscores their physical distinctiveness in the Indonesian environment. The incomparable Fromberg, commenting on the Chinese sense of solidarity in an essay published in 1911 on the Chinese movement in Java, wrote:[24]

It has never happened that a Chinese on Java married an Indonesian woman as if she were an equal and so qualified as the head wife. Thus they never became one with the native Indonesian population. The fact that they (i.e. the Chinese) have Javanese blood in their veins did not prevent them from remaining Chinese. They have mixed, but not united themselves, with the native population. On the other hand, they have avoided contractual relationships with the Europeans (in Indonesia), at least on Java, which would have resulted in a continuous condition of subordination, in the manner of a relationship of servant and master ... As merchants and industrialists they have simply confined themselves to those contracts in which they are equal parties. Through such a deliberate course of behaviour, through their solidarity, their unity, through the power of their secret associations founded with the aim of providing mutual assistance, and through which, if necessary, the compelling pressure of passive resistance could be brought to bear, they have been able to maintain a separate position between Europeans and Indonesians as a *bangsa tengah* (middle people).

IV. IMPACT OF WORLD WAR II

The collapse of the Dutch power structure, and the ambivalent encouragement given by the Japanese occupation authorities to Indonesian nationalism, were, from the point of view of Indonesian social relationships, perhaps not as important as the Japanese attempts at ideological radicalisation and "massification" of the heterogeneous Indonesian population. Establishment by the Japanese authority, in Jakarta, in April 1943, of a *Pusat Kebudajaan* (Centre of Culture), committed not only to the "destruction of Western culture" in the country, and the promotion of "the true Oriental civilisation," but also to the mobilisation of the population in a "total war," in which "every song, every composition" created had to play an appropriate political role, was an example of this tactic.[25] Even in the more remote rural areas of Indonesia the ideological campaign was carried forward through a steady stream of propaganda messages via loudspeakers and other continuous mass mobilisation techniques, in which each day or each week was devoted to a political or ideological emphasis, whether a "counter-espionage week" or a "day of the Asiatics."[26] There is little doubt that the strata disruptive effects of these occupation tactics, though brief, if intense, were yet considerable, coupled as they were also to the humiliation and imprisonment of most of the "European" elite level of society, and to the preferments given in positions of governance and economic leadership to the small group of schooled Indonesians, including trained bureaucrats, professionals, political leaders and petty intelligentsia.

The small Indonesian middle class of traders and entrepreneurs, often of strong Muslim persuasion, were given advantages over the Chinese, and new prestige was accorded to the influential community of Muslim leaders and scholars of the writ, the *kiajihs* and *ulama*. By destroying the European elite, Japanese policy also effectively attacked the feudal Indonesian underpinnings of that elite, mainstay of Dutch power since the days of the East India Company. Though some members of the traditional aristocracy were confirmed in their position, the Japanese also encouraged the non-aristocratic lower ranking Indonesian civil officials and thus contributed, to a degree, to a "democratisation" of the future Indonesian national leadership.[27]

In a way, the course of the Indonesian Revolution could be said to have legitimised the Indonesian "commoner" as the new power elite in much of the country, though some, especially younger, *priyayi* and aristocrats made the transition to national Indonesian civil and public service with varying degrees of ease. Only in a very limited sense, however, was the successful end of the struggle for national independence accompanied by a social revolution deeper than that already accomplished as a result of the Japanese occupation. For one thing, the colonial heritage of racial heterogeneity exclusivity, and, therefore, of discrimination, continued to make itself felt, not only as regards the Chinese but also as regards the Eurasian. Opting for the uncertainties of *warga negara* status (i.e. Indonesian citizenship) was felt to be as difficult for many Eurasians as going to Holland or elsewhere and beginning a new life. In 1952, according to an official Dutch investigating commission, some 200,000 "Europeans," mostly Eurasians, had accepted Indonesian citizenship, but some 100,000 had not. Probably more than half of these, despite their formal Dutch citizenship, led an "Indonesianised" existence, despite European style pretensions, while a few of these held indispensable business administrative or professional positions. Most of the others lived in poverty or difficult circumstances, resisting assimilation, though now rarely an object of active discrimination in a new independent Indonesia where life was passing them by. Most of these eventually accepted "Indonesianisation." For some in this remaining Eurasian category, however, existence in Indonesia had particularly become an anomaly, in that their life style was essentially Dutch, adjusted to the Indonesian environment, "not a Dutchified Indonesian life style," as their situation was later described in a Dutch analysis.[28]

In December, 1958, all this changed, however, and as a result of Dutch refusal to hand the territory of West New Guinea (Irian Jaya) over to the Jakarta government, more than 50,000 Dutch citizens mostly Eurasians, were expelled from Indonesia and went to Holland, thus virtually ending one erstwhile racial minority problem that had lingered from the colonial past. In the immediate period preceding this explusion, there had become apparent in Indonesian political life, especially in the leadership of the influential Partai Nasional Indonesia, a kind of nativistic emphasis, reflected in a movement towards greater "Indonesianisation" of the country's economic leadership and towards ending the continuing dominance of Dutch business and cultural influences in Indonesian life. The expulsion of the remaining Dutch and Eurasian community thus was, in a sense, also a demonstration of the confident self-assertiveness of the new indigenous Indonesian political elite.

The Chinese problem proved more intractable, however. During the Indonesian Revolution a number of Chinese had supported the Indonesian nationalist cause, but an equal, if not larger, number had sided with the Dutch, and on more than one occasion, in the context of revolutionary fighting and the collapse of certain authority, Chinese (as well as Dutch and Eurasians) had been subjected to nameless horrors at the hands of Indonesian armed gangs and mobs. Suspicions of Chinese loyalty to the Indonesian revolutionary cause, whether or not justifiable, thus came to reinforce the existing negative stereotyping of the Chinese minority as a whole in popular Indonesian belief. Citizenship problems further complicated Chinese status. The revolutionary Indonesian government's citizenship act of 1946 was not coercive, essentially leaving choice of citizenship to the individual Chinese themselves.[29] The concept of free choice was reaffirmed in 1949, under the terms of the Dutch sovereignty transfer to the independent (federal) Indonesian Republic, but neither this formulation, nor the 1955 Dual Citizenship Treaty (not formally and finally ratified until 1960) with the People's Republic of China resolved the public legal ambiguities of the Chinese group. This was so because of attacks by Indonesian political groups on some of the provisions of the 1955 treaty, the continuing criticism of the Chinese economic role and the suspicion of their loyalties, Chinese reluctance to comply with the Treaty provisions and administrative confusion and bureaucratic delay, among other factors.[30]

Various estimates have been made of the number of Indonesian Chinese who, holding dual Chinese and Indonesian nationality in 1955 (probably more than one million out of a total Chinese minority of about 2.5 million) subsequently chose Indonesian citizenships. Most estimates range from 65% to 90%, but some official Indonesian assessments present a more confusing picture. According to one of these assessments in 1969 of the total number of then about 3 million identifiable Chinese in Indonesia, half considered themselves Chinese nationals, but only 100,000 of these held Chinese passports while, according to another analysis, some 300,000 of the Chinese nationals' group did not have permanent residence permits.[31] In the author's view, perhaps as many as half of the Chinese group in 1967 had no certain evidence of either Chinese or Indonesian citizenship.

V. INDEPENDENCE: THE CHINESE

Almost from the time that Indonesia officially acquired its independence at the close of 1949, various distinctions were developed by the government, especially in business activity and economic rights, between "indigenous" Indonesian citizens (*warga negara asli*), i.e. native Indonesians of the Malay race, and "non-indigenous" citizens (*warga negara asing*), i.e. primarily Chinese. Not until the later sixties did some mitigation occur in the application of these distinctions. But Chinese, admittedly with justification, complain until this day that even if they submit to new officially encouraged assimilation directives (e.g. by

adopting Indonesian family names) discriminatory treatment persists.
Such discrimination has, among other things, involved:[32] (1) barring
asing citizens from owning farmland (on the basis of an old colonial agrarian regulation dating from 1875 which prohibited alienation of such
lands to non-Indonesians); (2) barring, or severely restricting, *asing*
Chinese retailers and traders from settling in Indonesia's rural areas; (3)
extending favoured treatment to *asli* merchants, industrialists, and other
businessmen, at the expense of the *asing* Chinese, in the issuance of import licences, in obtaining credit for most enterprises, or in earning and
utilising foreign exchange; (4) establishment of quotas in government
universities and professional schools so as to favour *asli* students; (5)
severe limitations on the operations of private Chinese schools (even if
owned and operated by *asing* Chinese), and on the Chinese press or
other Chinese language media; and (6) a pervasive attitude among
Indonesian officials, particularly local military commanders, of suspicion and antagonism in dealing with local Chinese, justified on the
grounds of "national security" and the officially ever-emphasised danger of subversion by the Communist underground in the country,
which Peking is said to support. On the other hand, these patterns of
discrimination should not obscure the entry of Chinese (if, one has the
impression, sometimes only on a "token" basis), into participation in
all manner of recreational, sporting, artistic, or educational groups,
and into partnerships in business and the professions with Indonesians.
There is also a continuing intermarriage among Indonesian or Indonesianised Chinese, with varying racial genealogies and degrees of
lingering Chinese minority consciousness, although formal marriages
between *asli* Indonesians and *asing* Chinese are few, occurring, if at all,
mostly among intellectuals.

Despite some assimilation, a high degree of self-ghettoisation remains, even on the part of *asing* Chinese and including those living in
the smaller towns, thus reinforcing discriminatory reactions on the part
of Indonesians. Analysing attitudes towards the Chinese in 1956–57 in
the West Java city of Sukabumi (total population about 65,000, of
which 10,000 are ethnic Chinese, more than half of them Indonesian
citizens), one researcher reported "regret" by Indonesian officials that
many of the *asing* Chinese citizens in Sukabumi were "citizens in name
only," preferring their own Chinese schools, and remaining distant
from community activity to which they contributed preferably only by
a gift of money or one in kind.[33] Significantly, perhaps, this relative
isolation is noted also by some Chinese observers of the "overseas Chi-

nese" as constituting a distinct "major issue" or problem in their lives:[34]

Although most of the overseas Chinese in South-east Asia belong to the middle or upper middle class, receive average income and reside in relatively comfortable suburban sections of the city, yet a large number of them have a feeling of isolation, thus psychologically they are not truly happy. They are fully aware that they are not completely integrated into the local society nor accepted as full members of the community, and live on the edge only ... perhaps there is no discrimination against them in the strict sense, but they are convinced that no matter how hard they try, there will be no promotion; and they feel they belong to a different world.

There is in Indonesia, as in other South-east Asian countries, what might be called a kind of "free floating" popular hostility towards the Chinese, which expresses itself especially (1) in the ease with which a minor racial conflict involving a Chinese can balloon into a major conflagration, even at a time when there may be a relative improvement – because of political or diplomatic reasons – in the position of the Indonesian Chinese as a whole, and (2) in the Chinese in Indonesia becoming the target for various popular grievances for which they are not, or are only to a minimal extent, responsible. The latter is part of the classic "scapegoating" process in which a vulnerable, essentially defenceless, and readily identifiable, population group is blamed for all sorts of popular grievances and frustrations which do not appear to be soluble by existing means. An example of the first instance of "free floating" hostility was the anti-Chinese riots that began in the West Java city of Cirebon on March 27, 1963, and which, within weeks, had spread to other areas of Indonesia, indeed to places as far distant as Makassar, South Sulawesi (Celebes), and Medan, North Sumatra. The riots were caused by a traffic accident in Cirebon involving two youths, one Indonesian, the other Chinese, both with youth gang connections, and led to heightened tensions in and out of the courtroom, eventually spilling over into the town. Chinese stores and property were destroyed by roving gangs, and the Cirebon military commander declared, in the wake of the incident, that the Chinese should be blamed for conducting an ostentatious way of life during a time of economic difficulties for many Indonesians.[35] Riots, looting of Chinese property, street fighting, and demonstrations, spread rapidly elsewhere, and the tensions only gradually subsided. It is to be noted that this popular rage was vented at a time when Jakarta and Peking were beginning to move towards

a diplomatic partnership, and that no government, perhaps, was acquiring such prominence in official Indonesian regional and strategic
calculations as that of People's China. Did this new atmosphere perhaps have its effects on some Indoneisan Chinese, leading them to a
certain assertiveness that might strike hypersensitive Indonesians as unduly provocative? It is hard to tell, but alleged Chinese "ostentation"
in their life style or possessions, whether true or not, is an always available racial stereotype in Indonesia with which to mobilize and intensify endemic anti-Chinese discrimination.

An illustration of the second type of "free floating" hostility directed
at the Chinese were the mid-January, 1974, demonstrations in Jakarta
against the visiting Japanese premier Kakuei Tanaka. These demonstrations, preceded by several months of student unrest in the Indonesian capital, reflected widespread disenchantment over the economic
policies of the Suharto government which appeared to be benefiting
especially certain elite business, military and bureaucratic cirlces and
the upper social strata, but which seemed to be offering little to the
mass of Indonesians. The penetration of Japanese capital and enterprise, symbolized by Tanaka's visit, also was linked in popular Indonesian thinking with the Chinese who had become prominent business
partners of the Japanese. Even before Tanaka's visit, press reports
from Jakarta noted how Japanese business encroachments were stir-
ring Indonesians to anger and frustration, and went on to observe that
even according to the Japanese Embassy in Indonesia seventy percent
of Japanese investors in the country had associated themselves with a
Chinese, rather than an Indonesian, business partner, on the grounds
of Chinese superiority in management skills.[36] One Indonesian student
leader admitted shortly before the mid-January 1974 riots that previous demonstrations were not really against the Japanese, or even
wholly against the *Aspri* (President Suharto's powerful military assistants, widely suspected of too close involvement in the penetration of
foreign big business into Indonesia). Rather, the student leader said,
"We are really against the Chinese here who have corrupted our
leaders and sold our country. When a foreign country offers to invest in
a joint venture, who joins him? A Chinese! When the government
makes special domestic loans available, who gets them? The Chinese!"[37]

It is unnecessary to emphasise that if, after all the preferments and
special assistance already provided over the years to the *asli* entrepreneurs, the Japanese investor today still favours the *asing* Chinese as

partners, there may be sound business reasons for this, reasons which, moreover can hardly be held against the Chinese – certainly not by a government so hospitable to the massive sustained influx of foreign development capital as the Suharto government has been.

Another illustration of the "free floating," but readily targeted, anti-Chinese hostility were the pogroms following the abortive coup attempt of September 30, 1965, in Jakarta, and other parts of the country. This incident is usually referred to as the *Gestapu* affair (from *Gerakan Tiga Puluh September*, or Thirty September movement"), and while details of it are not relevant here, it must be noted that the failure of this coup attempt, in which elements of the Indonesian Communist Party (PKI) as well as dissident military were involved, triggered a wide ranging, indiscriminate campaign of mass executions of tens of thousands (and possibly hundreds of thousands) of Communists, PKI sympathisers, and, it is to be feared, innocents.[38] Elements of the Indonesian armed forces and anti-Communist Muslim youth groups assisted in this campaign. In this anti-Communist campaign, the Chinese community in Indonesia also became a victim, partly because of the ideological and tactical affinities at this time between Indonesian and Chinese Communism, the diplomatic collaboration between Peking and Jakarta, and, above all, because it was believed that China's leaders had had foreknowledge of and had encouraged the *Gestapu* coup attempt. In the period between 1963–65, as domestic political tensions between Communists and anti-Communists (the latter to be found especially in the top armed forces leadership) began to heighten, in what seemed to be a preparation for a final struggle over who should succeed the ailing President Sukarno, there was widespread Indonesian suspicion that some influential Chinese in Indonesia, through a variety of their own organisations, had formally or informally identified themselves with the PKI or its fronts.

Whether such suspicion was justified or not, the net result was that the officially encouraged anti-Communist campaign after *Gestapu* took on distinctively anti-Chinese dimensions as well, and it required very little to translate a popular militancy directed against the PKI and its sympathisers into yet another episode in the traditional persecution of the Chinese. In the first half of 1967, as the Chinese themselves took to the streets in protest against their harassment by the Army or against restrictions on their movement and business activities imposed by the civil authorities, tensions reached new heights, and violence continued to flare until the suspension of Sino-Indonesian diplomatic relations in

October, 1967, cooled things off.[39] Perhaps some 30,000 Chinese eventually made their way out of Indonesia in the course of 1966–67, more than half of them bound for People's China. By the close of 1967, the worst of the post-*Gestapu* pogroms were over, and new official "assimilation" procedures were being widely touted (ceremonies in which Chinese, en masse, adopted Indonesian names were much publicised by the Indonesian government). But Indonesian Chinese continue to complain that they must grease the palms of corrupt Indonesian officials, including the military, to facilitate the regularisation of their Indonesian citizenship and residence, and every step of their business or professional activity. In any case, the post-*Gestapu* bloodbath has not ended endemic anti-Chinese feelings: in August 1973, in Bandung, West Java, a traffic incident involving a Chinese, and an Indonesian pedicab driver, touched off a new outburst of anti-Chinese depredations, including extensive arson of Chinese enterprises and residences.

Meanwhile, of all states in South-East Asia, the Indonesian government remains perhaps the most reluctant to normalise relations with People's China, and the domestic problem of Indonesia's Chinese is given as one major reason. On January 11, 1974, for example, Indonesian Foreign Minister Adam Malik, commenting in Jakarta on reports indicating that Malaysia and Thailand would, in the near future, establish relations with People's China, said that a pre-condition for a normalisation of Sino-Indonesian diplomatic relations was not only that Peking would be required to stop her anti-Suharto campaign, as exemplified by assistance to the underground or exiled PKI, but also that Indonesia's domestic security would have to be sufficiently stable. Indonesia's state security, Malik said, could not be separated from the fact that the loyalty of the majority of the Indonesian born Chinese, even after they had adopted Indonesian citizenship still constituted a "weak point," thus necessitating a long "re-education" campaign by the Indonesian government. Within such a framework of policy it seems unlikely, indeed, that mutual Sino-Indonesian suspicions, Chinese self-ghettoisation, Chinese cultural pride or "aloofness," will disappear at any time in the near future.

It may well be that endemic anti-Sinoism in Indonesia is inextricably interwoven with, and a pre-condition for, consciousness of other, non-Chinese ethnic identities in the country, which have been prominent over the centuries. One recent researcher has reported, for example, that (1) "Many Indonesians of different regions are also resented while resident in other areas of the country, e.g. the West

Javanese culture discriminates against citizens from East Java or Sumatra," that (2) "Violence often occurs against other Indonesians," and that, (3) as one Chinese puts it, "Politics as perceived by Javanese culture has an anti-Chinese element built into it."[40] The brief history of Indonesia's national independence has been punctuated certainly by various manifestations of severe inter-ethnic conflict among indigenous Indonesian groups, and resentment of allegedly "Javanese" dominance of the outer Indonesian islands and their distinct population groups has been a factor, not only in the resistance of the South Moluccan population, and in the independence struggle still carried forward by the *Republik Maluku Selatan* since the early 1950s, but also in the partially military inspired regional rebellions in Sumatra and Northern Sulawesi (Celebes) against Jakarta's allegedly heavy hand.

VI. OTHER ETHNIC CONFLICTS

The extensive propagation of a panoply of national, integrative, political symbols during the Sukarno era, and in which the national doctrine of the "Five Pillars" of the nation state, or Pantasila (including belief in God, nationalism, democracy, social justice and, humanism or internationalism) still takes pride of place today, no less than the constant emphasis on the need for *ketahanan nasional* (national resilience) during the present Suharto era, may find their corollary in many other nations. Yet it remains true to say that ethnic self-consciousness, from that of the Achehnese and Batak of North Sumatra at one end of Indonesia, to that of the Keiese and Papuans of Irian Jaya on the other end, has not only not vanished but, amidst always persisting local feelings of resentment over neglect by a distant Java based (and allegedly Javanese dominated) government bureaucracy, appears even to have grown. In Irian Jaya bands of Papuans continue to struggle for independence from Indonesian rule. Even in the larger "melting pot" of Jakarta, ethnic self-consciousness and ethnic cohesion have persisted, and have indeed on occasion even acquired distinctive occupational dimensions as well for reasons that are not clear. In a recent study of Jakarta's poor and lower job holders, for example, it was found that North Sumatrans were predominant among bus conductors, that over twenty-five percent of persons from Central Java made their "living" from collecting cigarette butts (but less than ten percent of this group gathered other waste paper), that a fifth of all petty traders and a fifth of all kerosene sellers came from Bogor and Bekasi, respectively, and so on.[41] One can only speculate on the origins of such inter-group mutual accommodation in employment.

However, ethnic self-ghettoisation of the urban poor, and especially of rural migrants to the city, has been a long standing and often commented upon phenomenon, noticeable in Jakarta as well as in other Indonesian towns. In a less urbanised setting, migrations have sometimes resulted in a retreat of other ethnic groups, which seem to shrink protectively from contact with a potentially disturbing group, even if that group is part of the same broad ethnic stream. Thus, until the present century, Toba, Karo, and Simelungun Bataks in Sumatra's North Coast had but limited contact with each other, and when the Toba began their eastward migration in the second and following decades of the present century, the Simelungun "retreated rather than be assimilated with a group of people whom they felt to be offensive."[42] Such reactions have not been unusual, and have reinforced ethnic compartmentalisation in space, no less than discriminating stereotypes in thought. From his earliest years in Indonesia the present writer encountered such ethnic stereotypes from Indonesian as well as non-Indonesian quarters, e.g., the Central Javanese being "lazy" or "refined," depending on the perceiver, the West Sumatran Minangkabau "restless and rootless" or "enterprising and resourceful," the Madurese "loudly bellicose" or "keen to defend his honour," and so on.

VII. Impact of Religion on Social Class

Both religious and economic dynamics over the centuries, however, have continuously ruptured such ethnic strata, creating more clearly defined material indices of "social class." This is not the place to review the sociological impact of Islam and the, to all intents and purposes, still ongoing Islamisation of Indonesia, subjects that have already received extensive scholarly attention. Suffice it to note the significant historic intrusion into traditional, feudal, Indonesian social structure by the Muslim community, particularly its orthodox (*santri*) elements, as scholars and teachers, traders and landowners, and eventually as leaders of social betterment, business protection and political organisations. Just as race, in the particular case of the Chinese, could become an attribute, though not necessarily an exclusive determinant, of "middle class" status in colonial society, so could a *santri* religious orientation (not ignoring the *santri* element in other strata, e.g. the peasantry). To a degree, despite the rapid "middle class" social homo-genization process evident among schooled Indonesians (including "assimilated" *asing* Chinese) in business, the professions, and govern-ment services (a process that may weaken, or sometimes blur, but which is still far from having destroyed the ethnic consciousness and ethnic barriers among indigenous Indonesian groups referred to ear-lier), this racial or *santri* "middle class" attribute has remained evident until this day. The point is worth stressing, because it serves to under-score the difficulty that may be encountered in establishing meaningful social class categories, let alone class consciousness in contemporary Indonesia. The felt social distance between a landowning *kiajih* (Mus-lim scholar of the writ) and *pesantren* (Muslim boarding school) direc-tor, or an *asing* Chinese merchant on the one hand, and an *asli* Indo-nesian *serdjana hukum* (master of laws) and government bureau chief, whether Menangkabau or Makassarese, on the other, is likely to be as great today as a generation ago, precisely because of these racial and religious factors and notwithstanding the fact that by most material measurements all three would probably have to be considered as be-longing to Indonesia's "middle class." Only if our *asli* Indonesian law-yer were an avowed *santri*, or were to acknowledge a Chinese racial strain in his family background, would the social distance likely begin to lessen.

On the one hand then, the ethnicity eroding, politically and socially unifying effect of a *santri* religious life style (as opposed to a religiously more eclectic, though nominally Islamic, orientation) has long been evident in Indonesia.[43] On the other hand, modern economic develop-ment, whether at the urban trade union and rural proletarian levels, or – at the other end of the social specturm – at the level of the military, technocratic, and internationally oriented Indonesian business elite, that is the mainstay of the present Suharto regime, has had a distinc-tively class building and class consciousness raising effect. It may well be, that, considered in retrospect, in certain parts of Indonesia this economic class building process was facilitated in the first place by the disruptive role of the *santri* religious element in a traditional feudal en-vironment. The by now well-known case study of Acheh by A. J. Pie-kaar, describing the slaughter of many *uleebalangs* (indigenous tradition-al aristocracy) in a flare-up of violence instigated by their chief com-petitors in indigenous local power relationships, the *ulamas* (Muslim religious leaders), is a case in point.[44] But elsewhere, too, Islam and its

santri devotees have had a "levelling" – not necessarily a democratising
or egalitarian – objective, proving as inhospitable to non-Islamic structures of leadership as to the preservation of indigenous custom law
(*adat*) or – as recent Indonesian constitutional history shows – to the
idea of a modern, secular, pluralistic state that declines to make only
Islam the foundation of its public law.

VIII. Impact of Economic Modernization

Considering the dimensions of economic modernization, one should
point particularly to the pauperization and proletarianisation of rural
society, more especially in densely populated Java, as being, perhaps,
the most important aspect of developing class structure and its ideological and political correlates in the country today. In all probability
rural migration in Java itself including the movement of inhabitants
within a chain or cluster of contiguous village areas for reasons of employment, marriage, evasion of the law, and so on, has probably always
been far more extensive, even in the pre-colonial and colonial eras,
than modern conceptions and stereotypes of the relatively static, "in-
voluted," population-absorbing character of Javanese village society
have tended to permit. Well before the present century, serious *localised*
shortages of arable land in terms of the burgeoning farming population,
together with the steady monetization of economic and social life, new
tax patterns, the uncertainties of smallholders' subsistence agriculture,
the pervasive availability of credit on usurious terms through money
lenders (Chinese, Arab, but also Indonesian), among other factors, had
all combined to create a class of frequently debt ridden landless villagers, dependent on all manner of temporary or itinerant labour, and on
occasional sharecropping, for a very meagre living. At the same time,
there occurred concentrations of landed wealth in the hands of a few
landowners accompanied by the arrogation by such landlords of what
one Indonesian specialist describing agrarian conditions in the *ketjamatan* (sub-district) Udjung Brung, Bandung Regency, West Java, in
1954, has termed "seigneurial rights," by which tenants were being
kept "in servitude."[45] "Seigneurial rights" have included rendering
numerous forms of personal, unpaid, service to the landlord. Conditions
in Javanese villages, in which more than 72% of the arable land is
owned by absentee landlords, in which tenants along with their regular
rents must pay landowners a fee to obtain any land at all for just one

rice growing period within a given year (as well as provide fuel, fodder and watch services), in which 80% of households in a given village may hold rice-fields less than one-fourth hectare in size and family members are extensively engaged in various forms of other employment, or in which, indeed, as many as 69% of a village's households hold no arable land at all, necessitating extensive sharecropping, or trade on a commission basis – such conditions were already noted two decades ago.[46] Today two researchers of Indonesia's so-called "Agro Economic Survey," an inter-governmental research body for the formulation of agricultural economic policy in Indonesia, start a valuable preliminary analysis they have made of rural employment patterns in Java with the following observation:[47]

Can a major economic disaster be avoided in the villages on Java during the next ten to fifteen years? Even now in the major rice producing regions, large numbers of villagers cannot support themselves by working on their own farms. Almost one-third of these villagers must work either full-time or part-time as farm labourers on very small rice farms. If nothing is done to alleviate the population pressure in these villages, a majority of the villagers may not be able to survive by remaining in these villages in the future. Most will not have wet rice fields and will not be planting rice once the present farm operators divide their land among their heirs.

New, more efficient harvesting and marketing methods are cutting down drastically the numbers once needed in the labour-absorbing traditional method of rice harvesting. Customarily, rice harvesting has involved many itinerant labourers working for a fixed share, and cutting the individual rice stalk with the small rice knife (*ani ani*), which is rich in folklore. It has been noted that "literally thousands of landless families" used to "criss cross the Javanese countryside, following the harvest from west to east" in search of work and food.[48] This tradition is now disappearing, however, as fewer individual harvesters are needed with the spread of different harvesting methods in which even the use of a sickle, instead of the *ani ani*, speeds up production and at a lower cost to the landowner or rice producer.

The problem of the rural thousands no longer able to find employment in agriculture, even on an itinerant, "scavenger" basis, must be appreciated in the context of the evidence of widening rural poverty, as indicated by various careful individual case studies of village conditions. One such recent study of the village complex of Sriharjo, near the city of Jogjakarta, Central Java, discloses that in a span of seventy years the local population having tripled, the average amount of land per family had fallen to less than a quarter of a hectare, leaving two-thirds of the people with inadequate income with which to purchase the basic staple, rice, the year round; 37% of the 164 families in one of Sriharjo's hamlets held no irrigated land at all, another 47% only held plots of 0.2 of a hectare or less, while 16% (or twenty-seven families) controlled 67% of the total irrigated land area of the hamlet, truly a matrix of serious marginal employment and income problems for most of the inhabitants.[49] As intimated earlier, studies of population mobility in villages around Jakarta suggest a sizable, continuously drifting, migrant population looking for work, going to and from the capital,[50] and one might suggest that a similar pattern is developing around other towns in Indonesia. At the same time the rural *verelendung* process, in which the concentration of landownership plays such an important though not necessarily exclusive role, has polarised social relationships, making the problem increasingly exploitable in partisan political and ideological terms.

Such exploitation particularly took place under the aegis of the now banned Indonesian Communist Party (PKI) in Java the period between 1960–65.[51] Unquestionably there then occurred a radicalisation of the attitudes of landless peasants and a widening of class consciousness within the framework of PKI "land reform" agitation. The catastrophe that overtook the PKI in the aftermath of the *Gestapu* incident, however, rendered further politicised expressions of that class consciousness ever more dangerous to the peasant or landless worker, even though the problems of rural pauperisation and proletarisation remained, on the whole, as serious as ever. Class consciousness in this setting today had meant particularly a frequent confrontation of the rural proletariat and the peasant "scavenger," with the wealthier rural Muslim elite of landowners, *ulamas*, and leaders of Islamic educational and social institutions.[52] So that to a degree, in so far as one can speak of a rural "class struggle" in Java today, the previously noted contrast between those who are *santri* oriented, on the one hand, and those following a less orthodox, more eclectic religious life style appears to enter into (though not necessarily dominating) the confrontation.

The intrusion of this religious antithesis into social strata and class consciousness development, not just in rural Java, but also in West Sumatra (where in the Menangkabau region the struggle between the *santri* element and traditional non-Islamic elites and adherents of custom law is probably of more than two centuries standing), or in South

Kalimantan (where the developing rice economy shows a growing polarisation between *santri* distributing entrepreneurs and non-*santri* peasant producers) raises the controversy, by now of some years' duration, as to the place of the so-called *aliran*. By *aliran* is meant an ideological-cultural complex or stream, which in Indonesia involves Islam, divided into orthodox and reform orientations, Marxism, in various degrees of radicalism, and "Javanism," that is the world of the old *priyayi* aristocracy, but also including that of the Javanese commoner and his pre-Islamic religious lore, mysticism and social values.[53] Each of these, represented by political parties and by a plethora of allied interest groups, tended to unite individuals regardless of incipient or developed "class" concerns or needs of an economic nature. However, relationships within each of these *aliran* orientations have sometimes been viewed as traditional, i.e. as paternalistic, essentially feudal and patron-client oriented, and, therefore it has been suggested that the growing polarisation of modern economic interests in Indonesian society (as, for example in rural society, just discussed) is likely to efface *aliran* loyalties in favour of more clearly delineated materialistic class identities.[54] It has been pointed out also that those with different *aliran* orientations nevertheless may join the same political party, a party which, according to the *aliran* model, is more typically affiliated with just one *aliran* (e.g. *santri* landowners and non-*santri* sharecroppers joining the same conservative Islamic political party, the Nahdatul Ulama).[55]

The extent to which rising class consciousness now has begun to rupture "vertical" *aliran* loyalties is impossible to gauge in any case, in view of the paucity of empirical data, complicated further by the debilitations suffered by organised Marxism as a more or less distinctive *aliran* in the present Suharto era. Does a "Javanistically," non-*santri* oriented businessman in Indonesia feel greater identity of class interest today with a *santri* entrepreneur than in years past? Is it evident that rural labourers or urban workers are experiencing greater class solidarity, regardless of their religious, ethnic or perhaps even – subdued – Marxist perceptions? One may answer that it is probable, and one even should posit it as a likely development but which remains, however, to be validated satisfactorily. In the meantime, a distinctive social strata formation in Indonesia based primarily on economic interest and class consciousness, is likely to be retarded by the appeals to distinctive group loyalties emanating from Islamic orthodoxy, from the traditional Javanese culture and its social values, from other ethnic identities

prevalent in the Indonesian archipelago, as well as from an acknowledged racial (e.g. Chinese) identity. Whatever "social class" may
mean in contemporary Indonesia will have to accommodate these
competing appeals.

IX. Conclusion

The sharpest forms of social discrimination, prejudice and inter-group
antagonism in Indonesia today still reflect long-established racial, ethnic, and religious differences. Class conflict, while certainly demon-
strable in rural social and economic relationships, particularly in Java,
is relatively diffused and less intense, although strata differences based
on material circumstances are becoming increasingly more prominent
throughout the country. New and perhaps more transient forms of inter-group antagonism, e.g. between university students and the military bureaucratic elite of the state, which are not readily classifiable in
terms of existing models of social or class conflict, further tend to complicate the picture.

As this essay, by direction, has focused primarily on conflict conditions in Indonesia arising from race and social class, such conflict
stemming from religious difference has not received major attention. It
is necessary to stress, however, that patterns of inter-group antagonism
and conflict in Indonesia frequently show a mixture of racial, ethnic,
or class elements with religion, as well as with politics, so that feelings
of confrontation and hostility are reinforced from different sources, and
one can often not be sure if one is dealing with merely or even predominantly a racial, class, religious or other conflict situation. Hostility
to the Chinese may be racial, but clearly has an economic (that is to a
degree a class) cause as well, and, because of a suspected Chinese ideological orientation (as, for example in the period just before the *Gestapu*
incident) also has political implications. In and around Madiun, East
Java, the site of an abortive PKI coup attempt in 1948, antagonism
between *santri* Indonesians and non-*santri* or *abangan* (cf. note 43) Indonesians (the latter suspected of leftist or Communist sympathies) lingered into the early national independence period and probably beyond. Here the wealthier *santri* elements came to be portrayed as ten-
tacles of an international capitalist octopus threatening the democratic
and egalitarian aspirations of the Indonesian mass.[56] The *santri* versus
non-*santri* religious antagonism thus acquired an explicit economic and

even social class connotation, as it was to do elsewhere in Java until this day. Reported instances of Muslim resentment of the preponderance of Christian and other non-*santri* elements among senior military and bureaucrats in Suharto's *orde baru* (new order), to the point of the Muslim leadership feeling slighted and discriminated against, demonstrates the emergence of a religious antagonism in primarily political rather than economic or social class terms.

There is also the imponderable as to how recent reforms in the political structure, such as the merger and "simplification" of parties, and attempts to obliterate traditional partisan loyalties in favour of a bland, homogenized, general acceptance of the Pantjasila, will affect social strata development. Incipient syndicalism has become apparent in some of the Suharto regime's policies of "functional" reorganization of society, in which central government policies are transmitted through "vertical" occupational channels, i.e. interest groups and associations of peasants, fishermen, schoolteachers, and others.[57] Such interplays make of "race" or "class" impure categories of social analysis in Indonesia, today as in the past.

NOTES

1. Awaloeddin Djamin, "Manpower and Employment Problems of the 70's in Indonesia," p. 117 in *Manpower: Employment Growth and Economic Development* (Office of Labor Affairs, Agency for International Development, Washington, D.C., 1973). On Indonesia's demographic structure and development generally see Widjojo Nitisastro, *Population Trends in Indonesia* (Cornell University Press, Ithaca, and London, 1970).

2. John M. Goering, "Social Effects and Limitations of Development Planning: The Case of Indonesia and Singapore," *Human Organisation*, Winter, 1972, p. 387.

3. *U.S. Aid to Population/Family Planning in Asia*, Report of a Staff Survey Team to the Committee on Foreign Affairs, U.S. House of Representatives (U.S. Government Printing Office, Washington, 1973), p. 29. To what degree Indonesian urban growth is the result of the recent influx by rural migrants, and to what degree the result of the excess of births of the non-migrant population has not been accurately determined. In 1961 Indonesia's population was considered about 15.5 percent "urban," and between 1930 and 1961 according to census data the Indonesian "urban population" grew by 231 percent and the general population by 60 percent. Pauline D. Milone, *Urban Areas in Indonesia: Administrative and Census Concepts* (Institute of International Studies, University of California, Berkeley, 1966), pp. 3, 97.

4. T. S. S. Sutanto, "Migrants Threaten to Swamp Jakarta," *The Asian Student*, (San Francisco), April 28, 1973, p. 3.

5. Justus M. van der Kroef, "Centrifugal Economies," p. 203, in James W. Wiggins and Helmut Schoeck, eds., *Foreign Aid Re-examined. A Critical Appraisal* (Public Affairs Press, Washington, D.C., 1958).

6. *Verslag van de Commissie tot Bestudeering van Staatsrechtelijke Hervormingen ingesteld bij Gouvernementsbesluit van 14 September 1940*, no. IX/KAB (2nd edition, New York, 1944), vol. I, p. 54.

7. "Indonesia Sets About Moving People From its Overcrowded Central Island," *The Sarawak Tribune* (Kuching), December 25, 1972.

8. "Indonesia's Unique Population Problem," *The Indonesia Times* (Jakarta), June 23, 1975.

9. *Empat Lima* (Jakarta), August 14, 1975; *Indonesian Current Affairs Translation Service Bulletin* (Jakarta), August, 1975, p. 616.

10. W. E. van Mastenbroek, *De Historische Ontwikkeling van de Staatsrechtelijke Indeeling der Bevolking van Nederlandsch-Indië* (Dissertation, University of Amsterdam; Wageningen, Veenman Zonen, 1934), pp. 83–96.

11. D. H. Burger, "Structuurveranderingen in de Javaanse Samenleving," *Indonesië*, vol. 3 (1949–50), p. 104.

12. W. E. van Mastenbroek, *op. cit.*, pp. 97–105.

13. *Verslag van de Commissie, op. cit.*, (cited in note 6), vol. I, p. 56: vol. II, pp. 57, 58.

14. "Ambtelijke Adviezen. Nederlandsch-Indië en het Koninkrijk," p. 106 in W. H. van Helsdingen, ed., *De Plaats van Nederlandsch-Indië in het Koninkrijk. Stemmen van Overzee* (Leiden, Brill, 1946), vol. II.

15. *Ibid.*

16. *Verslag van de Commissie, op. cit.*, vol. II, pp. 85–87.

17. In this and the following paragraph information drawn from Justus M. van der Kroef, *Indonesia in the Modern World* (Bandung, Masa Baru, 1954), vol. I. pp. 275–308, and the literature there cited. The figure of 300,000 Europeans in Indonesia in 1942 is the estimate of A. van Marle in *Indonesië*, vol. 5, (1951–52), p. 106.

18. P. W. van der Veur, "De Indo-Europeaan: Probleem en Uitdaging," pp. 93-94 in H. Baudet and I. J. Brugmans, eds., *Balans van Beleid. Terugblik op de laatste halve eeuw van Nederlandsch-Indië*, (Assen, van Gorcum, 1961).

19. A. C. van den Bijllaardt, *Ontstaan en Ontwikkeling der Staatkundige Partijen in Nederlandsch-Indië* (Batavia, Kolff, 1935), p. 22.

20. M. Vastenhouw, *Inleiding tot de Vooroorlogse Paedagogische Problemen van Indonesië* (Groningen, Jakarta, Wolters, 1949), pp. 38–39.

21. R. Murray Thomas, "Literacy by Decree in Indonesia," *School and Society*, Summer, 1966, pp. 279–280.

22. S. L. van der Wal, ed., *Het Onderwijsbeleid in Nederlands-Indië. 1900–1940 – Een Bronnenpublikatie* (Groningen, Wolters, 1963), pp. 654–655.

23. Victor Purcell, *The Chinese in South-East Asia* (Oxford University Press, 1951), esp. 451–483.

24. P. H. Fromberg, *Verspreide Geschriften* (Leiden, Leidsche Uitgeversmaatschappij, 1926), p. 407.

25. I. J. Brugmans, et al., eds., *Nederlandsch-Indië onder Japanse Bezetting. Gegevens en Documenten over de Jaren 1942–1945*, (Franeker, T. Wever, 1960), p. 231.

26. M. A. Aziz, *Japan's Colonialism and Indonesia* (The Hague, Martinus Nijhoff, 1955), p. 234.

27. W. F. Wertheim, *Indonesian Society in Transition. A Study of Social Change*, (The Hague, Bandung, W. van Hoeve, 1956), pp. 153–156.

28. J. H. Kraak, et al., *De Repatriëring uit Indonesië. Een Onderzoek naar de Integratie van de Gerepatrieerden uit Indonesië in de Nederlandse Samenleving* (Staatsdrukkerij, 1956?),

p. 63, and Justus M. van der Kroef, *Indonesia in the Modern World, op. cit.*, vol. I, p. 291.

29. Donald E. Willmot, *The National Status of the Chinese in Indonesia, 1900–1958*, (Ithaca, NY, Modern Indonesia Project, Cornell University, Revised ed., 1961), pp. 21–29.

30. *Ibid.*, pp. 44–46, discusses the problems in the implementation of the 1955 Citizenship Treaty. See also David Mozingo, "The Sino-Indonesian Dual Nationality Treaty," *Asian Survey*, December, 1961 and *Peraturan Pemerintah No. 20 Tahun 1959 tentang Pelaksanaan Undang-Undang tentang Persetudjuan Perdjandjian Antara Republik Indonesia dan Republik Rakjat Tiongkok Mengenai Soal dwi Kewarganegaraan* (Jakarta, Departemen Penerangan, R.I., Penerbitan Chusus, 67, 1960).

31. *Antara Daily News Bulletin*, November 14, 1966, and July 5, 1967.

32. For an analysis of some of these discriminatory practices, as well as of patterns of integration noted below, see, e.g. G. William Skinner, "The Chinese Minority," pp. 112–117 in Ruth T. McVey, ed., *Indonesia* (Human Relations Area Files Press, New Haven, 1963).

33. Giok-Lan Tan, *The Chinese of Sukabumi: A Study in Social and Cultural Accommodation* (Modern Indonesia Project, Cornell University, Ithaca NY, 1963), p. 237.

34. Aloysius Chang, "The Chinese Communities in South-East Asia," *Chinese Culture* (Hwakang, Yang Ming Shan, Taiwan) December, 1974, pp. 44–45.

35. Mary F. Somers, *Peranakan Chinese Politics in Indonesia* (Modern Indonesia Project, Cornell University, Ithaca, NY, 1964), pp. 45–46.

36. Cf. Sydney H. Schanberg in *The New York Times*, December 20, 1973.

37. Peter Simms in *Asia Research Bulletin*, January 31, 1974, p. 2354.

38. "Indonesia – One Million Dead?", *The Economist* (London), August 20, 1966, pp. 727–728.

39. Justus M. van der Kroef, "The Sino-Indonesian Rupture," *The China Quarterly*, January–March, 1968, pp. 17–46.

40. David W. Chang, "Current Status of Chinese Minorities in South-East Asia," *Asian Survey*, June, 1973, pp. 590–591.

41. Gustav F. Papanek, "The Poor of Jakarta," *Economic Development and Cultural Change*, October, 1975, p. 15.

42. Clark E. Cunningham, *The Postwar Migration of the Toba-Bataks to East Sumatra* (Yale University, South-East Asia Studies, New Haven, Connecticut, 1958), p. 84–85.

43. The contrasting life styles between those Indonesians committed to strict adhesion to Islamic doctrine and ritual (variously called, in earlier days *bangsa poetihan* – the "white" or rather white garbed people – or *Kaoem* – the community – and, in recent decades, *santri*, which originally meant "follower" or "pupil," and those given to a more electic religious view (referred to as *abangan*, litt., the "red" or multi-coloured garbed people) had been noted by various writers in the colonial period, (see e.g. C. Poensen, *Brieven over den Islam uit de Binnenlanden van Java*, Leiden, Brill, 1886, p. 7, and C. Lekkerkerker, *Land en Volk van Java*, Groningen, Batavia, J. B. Wolters, 1938, p. 528). See also Clifford Geertz, *The Religion of Java* (The Free Press of Glencoe, Illinois 1960).

44. A. J. Piekaar, *Atjeh in de Oorlog met Japan* (The Hague, Bandung, W. van Hoeve, 1949).

45. R. Anwas Adiwilaga, *Ketjamatan Udjung Brung (Bandung Regency). An Agronomic Report* (Kantor Perantjang Tata Bumi Djawa Barat, Bandung, 1954, stencil), p. 29. Mr. Adiwilaga kindly provided a copy of his report.

46. Justus M. van der Kroef, "Land Tenure and Social Structure in Rural Java," *Rural Sociology*, December, 1960, pp. 414–430.

47. William L. Collier and Sajogyo, *Villagers' Employment, Sources of Income, Use of High Yielding Varieties, and Farm Labourers in the Major Rice Producing Regions of Indonesia* (Agro-Economic Survey, Indonesia, Research Notes No. 11, June 1972 stencil), p. 1. Grateful thanks to Mr. Collier for having provided a copy of this report, and those cited below in note 48.

48. Richard William Franke, *The Green Revolution in a Javanese Village* (Unpublished Ph. D. dissertation, Harvard University, Cambridge, Massachussets, June, 1972), p. 181, cited in William Collier et al, *Tebasan, HYVs, and Rural Change: an Example in Java* (Agro-Economic Survey of Indonesia, November, 1973, stencil) pp. 2–3. See also William L. Collier, et al., *Rice Harvesting and Selling Changes in Central Java Which Have Serious Social Implications* (Agro-Economic Survey, Indonesia, Research Notes, No. 14, January, 1973).

49. D. H. Penny and M. Singarimbun, *Population and Poverty in Rural Java*. Some Economic Arithmetic from Sriharjo (Department of Agricultural Economics, Cornell University, Ithaca, NY, May, 1973), esp. pp. 18, 70, and passim.

50. See, e.g., Koentjaraningrat, "Population Mobility in Villages around Jakarta," *Bulletin of Indonesian Economic Studies* (Australian National University, Canberra), July, 1975, pp. 108–119. See also note 4 *supra*.

51. Margo L. Lyon, *Bases of Conflict in Rural Java* (Center for South and South-East Asian Studies, University of California, Berkeley, California, December, 1970).

52. On this confrontation see, e.g., the articles by Jean Contenay in *Far Eastern Economic Review*, November 24, 1967, pp. 357–367, January 11, 1968, pp. 7072, and January 25, 1968, pp. 156–159.

53. On *aliran* see B. B. Hering, "Alirans," *Internationale Spectator* (The Hague), vol. 26, No. 12, pp. 1157–1171, and the literature there cited.

54. W. F. Wertheim, "From Aliran towards Class Struggle in the Countryside of Java," *Pacific Viewpoint* (Wellington, New Zealand), September, 1969, pp. 1–16, and Hering, op. cit., pp. 1166–1168.

55. Ernst Utrecht, "Class Struggle and Politics in Java," *Journal of Contemporary Asia*, vol. 2, 1972, No. 3, p. 278. Whether Nshdatul Ulama is truly a *santri* party considering its accommodation of more eclectic Javanese rural social values may well be argued.

56. Robert R. Jay, *Religion and Politics in Rural Central Java* (South-East Asia Studies, Yale University, New Haven, 1963), pp. 28–29, 72–76.

57. Dan Coggin, "Indonesia – Moving Away from the Old Culture," *Far Eastern Economic Review*, July 4, 1975, p. 15.

The Southern Sudan Civil War

ARYE ODED

DR. ARYE ODED is Senior Lecturer at the Department of Middle Eastern and African History, Tel-Aviv University. Born in Jerusalem in 1929, he received his M.A. from the Institute of Asian and African Studies, the Hebrew University, Jerusalem in 1959. In 1961–2 he was a postgraduate research student at Makerere University, Kampala, specializing in the history of Islam in Buganda. In 1973 he received his Ph.D. from Tel-Aviv University. During the years 1957–1973 he worked on the staff of the Ministry of Foreign Affairs and between 1962–7 he served with the Israel Embassy in Kampala.

Among his publications: *The Bayudaya*, A Community of African Jews in Uganda, published by the Shiloah Center for Middle Eastern and African Studies, Tel-Aviv, 1973. *Islam In Uganda – Islamization Through a Centralized State in Pre-Colonial Africa*, published by Israel University Press, Jerusalem, 1974.

The Southern Sudan Civil War

ARYE ODED

I. The 1955 Mutiny and its Causes

On the morning of 18 August 1955 a Company of the Equatorial Corps stationed at Torit in Southern Sudan and composed of Southern Sudanese soldiers mutinied, killing Northern officers and soldiers. News of the mutiny spread all over the South enkindling disturbances in which about 300 Northerners were murdered by the Southern rioters. Seventy-five Southerners were also killed in the clashes. The mutiny was suppressed with great difficulty with the help of Britain which was still responsible for the Sudan, but most of the rebels escaped to the bush forming the nucleus of the Southern guerrilla resistance. This mutiny triggered off an era of violence and civil war which lasted for seventeen years.[1]

Several reasons were mentioned as the immediate causes of the 1955 uprising. However, it would not be possible to understand the deep hatred which was reflected during the 1955 disturbances without taking into consideration the historical background of the 19th century. Indeed the mutiny was just another demonstration of a century old tension and traditional violence between the Southerners and Northerners strengthened by ethnical and geographical factors.

A. *The Geographical Factor*

The Southern Sudan consists of the three provinces of Bahr al Ghazal, Equatoria and Upper Nile covering an area of 250.000 square miles or about one fourth of the total area of the Sudan. The area is dominated by the swamps or the *Sudd* which are formed by the Nile river and which has always been a barrier between the North and South. The two areas have also different physical and climatic features, those of the South are difficult to live in and economically it lags behind the North.

B. *The Human Factor*

According to 1956 census, of the 10,263,000 persons who lived in the Sudan 2,793,000 or about one quarter lived in the three Southern provinces. The May 1973 national census has not yet been published. Unofficial reports fix the total population figures between 15 to 16 million.[2]

As in many countries in Africa also the Southern Sudan problem stems from the fact that ethnically, religiously, and politically the Sudan is a heterogeneous area. The people of the Southern Sudan have been classified according to their languages, physical types and tribes into three main groups:

1) The Nilotics comprising the Dinka, Nuer, Shilluk and Anuak who mostly live in Bahr al-Ghazal and Upper Nile Provinces.

2) The Nilo-Hamitics comprising the Murle, the Didinga, Boya, Topsa and Latuka who live mostly in Equatoria.

3) The Sudanic tribes comprising small tribes living in the Western parts of the South among them the most important being the Azande.[3]

Ethnically the Northerners claim Arab descent although some of them are mixed with negro tribes. The Southerners regard themselves as negroid and Africans. They regard the North as Arab and see the gist of the Southern Sudan problem as a fight for racial equality.[4]

The ethnical differences are reflected also in the languages. The North speak mainly Arabic while in the South about eighty different languages and dialects are spoken.

Religiously, the North is almost wholly Muslim with a small Christian minority while the South is pagan with about 10% Christian and with a Muslim minority.[5]

Politically, the North look primarily towards the Arab Middle East and the South towards Sub-Saharan Africa. In fact the main distinction between Northerner and Southerner is not colour as much as political orientation, language, customs and culture. Still, all the above-mentioned differences can't fully explain the identification of a Northerner to the North and a Southerner to the South.

The decisive, distinguishing factor between North and South seems, then, to be a sense of belonging which has its roots in history .... Completely isolated by the North until little more than a century ago, embittered by decades of subsequent hostility and administered separately until the threshold of independence the Southerner feels himself to be an African while the ruling Northerner is proud of his Arab connections.[6]

C. *The Historical Factor: Conflict and Terror in the 19th Century*

(1) *Slave traders.* From about the mid-nineteenth century, tribes of Southern Sudan were disrupted by the arrival of foreign invaders, European traders and their Arab armed servants who came up the Nile to acquire ivory and slaves. They plundered villages and enslaved the African local inhabitants. In his book *Ismailia* Samuel Baker who was during this period in Southern Sudan and Northern Uganda described the atrocities which the Northern traders had committed: "All is wilderness! The population has fled. Not a village to be seen. This is certainly the result of the settlement of the Khartoum traders."[7] The traders built fortified stations in the interior (*zariba* p. *zaraib*) from which they launched their attacks and used also to play one tribe against the other to obtain captives. While strong tribes like the Azande and the Dinka could resist the traders the small tribes were made slaves

Tens of thousands of people were lost and several tribes nearly vanished as cohesive political or social units.[8]

(2) *Egyptian soldiers.* In the 1960s and 1970s the invaders were the Egyptians. The ruler of Egypt at that time, Ismail, wanted to establish an African empire for Egypt and to monopolize the ivory trade. Indeed he announced that one of his main aims was to suppress the slave trade. Ismail failed in both aims. The Arab slave traders refused to recognize the Egyptian authority and continued their trade. On the other hand the Egyptians like the traders used force to suppress the resistance of local tribes who objected to the imposition of any foreign authority:

Chiefs were shot, their people killed, their cattle seized and their crops taken. The hereditary rulers of the people were lost and the traditional way of life further disrupted.[9]

(3) *The Mahdists.* In 1881 the Mahdi Mohammad Ahmad revolted against the Egyptian rule in the Sudan and in a few years conquered most of the South, annihilating the Egyptian army. He proclaimed a holy war (Jihad) in order to establish in the Sudan a purer form of Islam. The Mahdists fought both against the Egyptians and against the

Africans whom they considered as infidels and tried to force Islam upon them. The Southerners although they hated the Egyptian rule did not want to give up their tribal independence and resisted the Mahdists attempts to Islamize them. The Mahdists continued with the pattern of violence used by the slave traders and the Egyptian soldiers. Thus the second half of the nineteenth century was characterized by hardships and sufferings inflicted upon the South by invaders coming from the North. The Southerners reacted with resistance but generally they had to yield before the superior technology of the invaders. This tragic period developed in the South a legacy of hatred and suspicions towards the Northerners and a tradition of resistance which had a great influence on the future relations between the North and the South and were the roots of the 1955 mutiny.

Southern leaders and scholars used to emphasize that it was this period of slavery and conflicts that caused the Southerners to "surround themselves in a stockade of suspicion which has proved to be well founded."[10]

D. *The British Factor*: *Widening the Gap*

In 1898 the Mahdists were defeated at Omdurman by Anglo-Egyptian forces. On 19.1.1899 the Condominium agreement was signed providing for a joint Anglo-Egyptian rule in the Sudan. In practice it was the British who held the reins of power until Sudan independence in 1956. As a whole this was a period of pacification and order in the South and the British being more efficient administrators succeeded in establishing their authority over the local tribes. The main characteristics of what is known as "British Policy" in Southern Sudan was reflected in a Memorandum by the Civil Secretary of the Sudan Government stating:

The policy of the Government in the Southern Sudan is to build up a series of self-contained racial and tribal units with structure and organization based, to whatever extent the requirements of equity and good government permit, upon indigenous customs traditional usage and beliefs.[11]

From 1930 the trend of Africanization of the South was strengthened: Muslim Northern clerks and officials were transferred from the South and replaced by indigenous people; Arab policemen were removed; Greek and British traders were allowed to trade in the South while the

Northerners were excluded; native languages and English were encouraged while the speaking of Arabic was discouraged. The Christian missionaries were encouraged to establish mission stations to counteract the spread of Islam.[12] Nevertheless, by the end of the Second World War national feelings in the North grew stronger demanding greater participation in government and blaming the "British Policy" as aiming to cut off the South from the North. In 1944 an Advisory Council had been instituted and in 1947 another step towards self government was taken by the establishment of the Legislative Council. These political developments in the North raised the question of the status of the Southern Sudan. The British under the pressure of the Northern Nationalists and knowing that it was only a matter of time until they would have to evacuate the country, including the South, started in about 1946 to reverse their policy. Now they adopted the line that Sudan must be united on the basis of equality. Britain would see to it that adequate safeguards should be provided to the Southerners, to ensure

that they would by educational and economic development be equipped to stand up for themselves as socially and economically the *equals* of their partners in Northern Sudan.[13]

From that time on all restrictions against the Northerners in the South were revoked and the Southerners were pressed to agree to send representatives to the Legislative Council in Khartoum. But the Southerners were quickly disappointed when in the Ordinance of 1948 no specific safeguards for them were included because of the Northerners objections.

The British when reversing their policy assumed that the South would have ample time to catch up with the North and indeed from 1947 on great efforts were made in the economic and educational spheres, but it was as one historian remarked "too little and too late."[14] The political developments were much quicker than the British assumed. When in 1953 Sudan became self governing the Southerners were still far behind the more developed and dynamic North.

In conclusion, the British rule in the Sudan established security and order in the South and for several decades the pattern of violence which was so characteristic of the 19th century was stopped. But on the other hand it was, as Arnold Toynbee commented "not self-consistent nor far-sighted."[15] Its restrictions against the Northerners further prevented the understanding between the two parts of the country. On the eve of independence they were still ill prepared for union. The British policy widened the gap between the South and the North and thus turned to be another factor facilitating the tragic developments towards the Civil War.

E. *The Immediate Factors: Self Rule and Disappointments (1953–1955)*

In 1953 Sudan entered the period of Self Government which lasted until independence in 1956. This period of transition from colonial rule to independence was very crucial for the future because it provided the Southerners with first indications of the North's attitude towards them. These indications were disappointing and disastrous, constituting the immediate causes of the 1955 mutiny. Following the mutiny a commission of enquiry was appointed to look into its causes. Its report, widely commended for its fairness, is an important source for the understanding of the reasons for the uprising.[16]

In the elections for the first Sudanese Parliament in November 1953 twenty-two members were returned from the South out of a total of ninety-seven. In January 1954 Ismail al-Azhari of the National Union Party (NUP) became the first Sudanese Prime Minister. During the elections campaign the NUP pledged themselves if they came to power to give the Southerners vast responsibilities in running their internal affairs but in practice the al-Azhari Government disregarded the Southerners aspirations and tried to tighten its grip on the South by force of arms. Early in 1955 al-Azhari gave a warning:

Sudan is one integral whole ... the government shall not be lenient in this respect ... it has its army, its police and all its might.[17]

This and following events indicated that he believed that the Southern problem could be solved by military power and political restrictions. Among the main events that raised suspicions and distrust among the Southerners were:

The Sudanization Policy. On February 1954 a Sudanization Committee was appointed to replace British officials by Sudanese. The results startled the Southerners. The South, which was not represented on the Committee, was given only four minor posts of Assistant District Commissioner out of 800 posts Sudanized. All the key positions went to the Northerners.[18] Moreover, the Northern officials who were sent to the South were inexperienced and usually had little understanding and sympathy with the local population who regarded them as new invaders from the North. The Commission of Enquiry quoted a Southerner's letter to a Southern member of Parliament:

The result of Sudanization has been very disappointing .... However well intentioned, in fact it means our fellow Northerners want to colonise us for another hundred years.

The Commission commented:

Since the Southern Sudanese benefited very little from Sudanization they found little or no difference between conditions now and conditions previously; and independence for them was regarded as merely change of masters. We feel that the Southern Sudanese by finding themselves holding secondary positions in the Government of their country have a genuine grievance.[19]

Southern leaders like Oduhu attributed great importance to this event which they considered as the first deep disappointment after Self Rule and concluded that "from that time onwards relations between North and South deteriorated."[20]

The Zande Scheme killings. In July 1955 300 Southern workers in the Zande Scheme (a complex of agricultural and industrial projects to grow cotton and produce cloth in Yambio district on the Congo border) were shot down by the army and police when they demonstrated against their dismissal by the Northern management. The Commission of Enquiry pointed out

To the Southerners they (the dismissals) meant a deliberate attempt by the management to deprive Southerners of a livelihood and bring in Northerners instead.

The Commission also testified that some Northern merchants took part in the shooting at the demonstration.[21] This harsh action also helped to foment the rebellion.

Federation versus Unitary State. While the North attempted to impose strict unity on the South, Southerners advocated federalism. In 1954 the Southern Liberal Party was formed by educated Southerners who advocated regional autonomy for the South. Later in October 1954 Southerners held a conference in Juba in which it was decided that the South would remain united to the North only under a federal government. "Federation," wrote Oduho, "became a Southern watchword."[22]

The Southerner's suspicions of the al-Azhari strong hand policy was manifested in another event which became one of the immediate causes of the 1955 mutiny:

During July 1955 a telegram purporting to originate from the Prime Minister Ismail al-Azhari and addressed to Arab administrators in the South was circulated among Southerners. According to the Report of the Commission of Enquiry the text read as follows:

To all my administrators in the three Southern Provinces .... Do not listen to the childish complaints of the Southerners. Persecute them, oppress them, ill-treat them according to my orders ....[23]

The Northern Sudanese deny the authenticity of this telegram while the Southerners claimed that it was genuine. The Commission was of the opinion that the telegram was forged. But it also noted that the Southerners believed that the message was genuine because they felt "cheated exploited and dominated by the Northern Sudanese."

After this series of events came the order to the company of the Equatorial Corps, composed of Southern Sudanese soldiers, to proceed to Khartoum. It is believed that the soldiers mutinied fearing that the Northern Government was plotting to murder them.[24] It was this mutiny which sparked a new era of violence.

Northern scholars like Beshir admit that in this transitional period the Northern political parties committed many mistakes in their relations with the South but they explain that these

arose from inexperience and ignorance of conditions in the South rather than from bad intentions or designs. On the other hand they blame the Southern politicians for giving their regional interests greater value than the larger association with the Sudan as a whole.[25]

Indeed the two sides committed errors. Nevertheless, when considering the Southerners' feelings against the historical background of violence and suppression in the South it is no wonder that the tragic events that followed after Self-Rule revived their traditional suspicions towards the North and turned them into hostility. The hostility coupled with deeply rooted traditional suspicions led to the outbreak of the Southern soldiers rebellion in 1955 which lasted 17 years.

II. Areas of Discrimination

The rebellion in the South could last seventeen years because of the continued policy of subjection, restriction and discrimination against the Southerners. These were manifested in various fields.

A. *Islamization*

The Policy of Islamization was followed mainly during the Military
Government of General Abud (1958–1964) and the Civilian Governments of Mahjub (1965, 1967). They both tried to strengthen the unity
of Sudan and Sudanese Nationalism through Islamization and Arabization of the South. Propagation of Islam was done by:

(i) *Visits of Muslim Shaykhs in the South*
    Thus for example the Grand Qadi of Sudan during General Abud
reign, visited the Southern provinces in January 1961. The Qadi,
Mahjub Ishaq, distributed gifts to the people, dedicated new religious
buildings and propagated Islam among the tribes. In every place the
local chiefs were gathered to hear him, among them "a large number
of Nuer chiefs who had been embracing Islam since 1960." Speakers on
various occasions stressed such themes as "the importance of Islam as
the National religion of Sudan."[26] When he returned to Khartoum the
Grand Qadi stated that Islam was spreading rapidly in the South and
that encouraging the study of Arabic was an important means for
spreading Islam. During his tour "he had Islamized some 2000 people."[27] The Qadi of Wau stated that in his district alone more than 400
persons has been Islamized during the Shaykh's visit.[28] This is one
example of the many religious delegations which used to visit the South
for the propagation of Islam. Muslim political personalities, army officers and even Abud personally were also involved in this activity.
Abud used to visit the South accompanied by some of his ministers and
Muslim teachers. Again, many ceremonies and festivals were held in
the course of the visit. Abud distributed presents among the chiefs
while the Muslim teachers used to persuade people to join Islam.[29]
Events connected with Islamic activity and conversion in the South
received wide press publicity.

(ii) *Establishment of Muslim Religious Institutions*
    Koranic schools were established in different districts. During
Abud's reign six intermediate Islamic Institutes were opened in Juba,
Kodak, Wau, Maridi, Yei and Ruga. A Secondary Islamic Institute
was opened in Juba and centres for preaching and religious instruction
for adults were also established. The Government encouraged the construction of new mosques and granted the necessary funds.[30]

(iii) *Agents of Islam*

The government, particularly during Abud and Mahjub rule, played a large part directly in Islamic activity through various departments and institutions: The Department of Religious Affairs had a special budget for Muslim propaganda.[31] It was responsible for sending religious instructors to the South and for the construction of Koranic schools and mosques. It was also dealing with the training of high school students to serve as teachers of Arabic and Islam in the elementary schools in Equatoria province.[32] Other ministries such as the Ministry of Information and Labour used to send cultural and religious missions to the South.[33]

Conversion was mainly the concern of special missionary society *Jamiyat al-Tabshir* which had been working in the area since 1950 and raised its funds with the help and encouragement of the authorities. The Society established in various places local Islam groups to help Islamic activities.[34] Islamic activities were connected with the limitation imposed on the Christian missionaries.

The military governors and administrators devoted much of their time in the campaign "to raise the banner of Islam" and in suppressing the opposition of both the pagans and the Christian population.[35]

(iv) *The Issue of Islamic Constitution*

An Islamic issue which disturbed relations between the North and South since Independence was the Northerners continued effort to include in the constitution an article making Islam the official state religion. Time and again the problem was discussed in the Cabinet or the Parliament and the Southern politicians objected to it or walked out. They were afraid that by recognition of Islam they would lose their cultural tradition and would be subject to the Islamic law. Only the political crises among the Northerners themselves prevented the Islamic constitution from becoming law.[36]

B. *Arabization: Cultural and Social Subjection*

Besides Islamization, the governments of Abud and Mahjub used also Arabization as a means to eliminate the separatist tendencies of the Southerners. They believed that they could unify the country by the dissemination of the Arabic language and by propagating Arab culture, tradition and history to replace the local indigenous cultures based on African or Christian cultures. Most of the Southerners do not know Arabic, using indigenous languages, while the educated few speak English. To change this situation the Sudanese Government sent Arabic teachers and experts to the South and trained Southerners in teaching Arabic.[37] Northern Governors and Abud himself used to speak Arabic in tribal gatherings urging the tribal leaders and educated Southerners to study the language. Christian missionaries were asked to teach the New Testament in Arabic and all foreign schools were informed that they must include the Arabic language in their curriculum.[38]

Indeed Southern Sudanese leaders blame the Government for its efforts to annihilate the indigenous cultures, religions and customs by imposing "Sudanization" (SAWDANAH) which meant in practice Islamization and Arabization. They consider this attitude as one of the main reasons for the rebellion. Southerners also accused the government that by despising the tribal way of life they encouraged "open segregation policy."[39]

Indeed the Commission of Enquiry into the causes of 1955 mutiny indicated;

It is unfortunately true that many Northern Sudanese, especially from among the uneducated class, regard the Southerners as an inferior race, and the Gallaba (Arab traders) in the Southern Sudan are no exception to this, as the majority of them are uneducated. The traders refer to and often call the Southerners "Abeed" (slaves). This practice of calling Southerners "abeed" is widespread throughout the three Southern Provinces. It is certainly a contemptuous term and is a constant reminder to the Southerners of the old days of the slave trade.[40] In this connection Southerners claimed that while the Arabs kept their women from the Southern males "Sudanese Arabs are in continuous relation with African women and girls who are taken as concubines."

Indeed foreign observers testify to this.[41]

It should be noticed that the Northern government and Northern scholars, like Mohamed Beshir, denied allegations that the Southern Civil War was a *racial* conflict between Northern Arabs and African Southerners. Beshir indicated that ethnically the Northerners are not pure "Arabs" because they were mixed with African blood.[42] But Southerners still regard the Northerners as "Arabs" belonging to the Arab culture, tradition and religion. From a pure ethnical point of view it may be wrong to talk of *racial* conflict but surely there was social and cultural conflict between North and South.

C. *Restrictions against Christian Missionaries*

In the framework of Islamization and Arabization the Northern government, soon after independence, started to curtail the activities of Christian missionaries. During the Abud reign these restrictions had been intensified. The missionaries were accused by General Abud of keeping hostility alive and inciting the Southerners against the Government. They were deemed to be an adverse force toward the National integration of Sudan on the Islamic-Arabic basis.[43] All missionary schools were taken over by the government.[44] Missionary work was limited to purely religious functions.[45] Christian gatherings not in church were forbidden. Parents had to apply in writing to the police for permission to have their children baptized.[46] In 1961 missionary hospitals were taken over by the Ministry of Health in Upper Nile, Kordofan and in the Nuba mountains and their medical activities were curtailed. The government ordered the medical missions not to treat patients although there were no other doctors or nurses near by.[47] Already in 1960 missionaries who left Sudan on home leave were not permitted to return and new applications by missionaries to enter Sudan were refused.[48]

Another measure taken by the government against Christianity was a decree published in February 1960 fixing Friday as the official day of rest.[49] Until that time Sunday was the day of rest in the South. The decree caused unrest among Southern Christians. Leaflets opposing the measure appeared in a few Southern secondary schools and a student strike broke out. It was ended only with difficulty and the students were flogged on returning to school. A Southern priest and four students had been sentenced to 12 years and ten years imprisonment respectively for calling for a boycott of Sunday work.[50] Twenty missionaries were expelled for calling on the people to oppose the measure.[51]

In 1962 the Supreme Council of the Armed Forces promulgated a Missionary Societies Act which restricted the Missionary activities.[52] On February 27, 1962 the Ministry of the Interior announced the expulsion of all Christian missionaries in the Southern Sudan; 272 Verona Fathers and 28 Protestants were expelled. They were blamed for "instigating the people in the Southern provinces against the government."[53]

D. *Restrictions in Education*

The government activities against the missionaries were in line with its educational policy aimed at achieving cultural unification of the Sudan by Arabic and Islamic education. Education in the South was mainly provided by Christian missionaries and during the British rule they were helped by the government. By taking over missionary schools and expelling the Missionaries Southern education suffered. Moreover, education in government schools in the South after independence was based on Arabic culture and Islam which were not accepted by the Southerners who blamed the government policy for "rendering the Southerner permanently subject to Arab rule."[54]

Moreover nearly all new government schools were built in the North. Besides, in the North there were always non-government schools belonging to individuals or institutions and they were considered as a valuable supplement to the government schools. In the South a Southerner was forbidden to open a private school.[55]

The obvious implication of the system was that "African parents of the South irrespective of creed must accept the Islamic education provided by the government or do without education at all."[56] This increased the educational gap between North and South. According to Sudan Almanach 1961, p. 184–5, the number of schools in the North and South were:[57]

Type of Education	North	South
Intermediate (Boys)	180	17
Intermediate (Girls)	55	1
Technical intermediate (Boys)	14	3
Secondary (Boys)	49	2
Secondary (Girls)	14	—
Commercial secondaries	2	1
Technical secondaries	3	—
Universities	4	—

In 1960 Khartoum University had 1,216 students of whom only sixty were Southerners. In 1970 of 3000 students only about a hundred were Southerners.[58]

The introduction and compulsory use in the South of the Arabic language as a medium of instruction instead of English and the vernacular was resented by the Southerners and during 1961 and 1962 there were waves of strikes in Southern schools. The students protested against government educational policy and many of them never returned to school.[59]

E. *The Public Services*

As mentioned the "Sudanization" of the civil services in 1954 caused intense disappointment and resentment among the Southerners and was one of the immediate causes of the 1955 mutiny. Unfortunately the Commission of Enquiry conclusions in this regard were not taken seriously. The administration of the South continued to be mostly in Northern hands. There was no Southern Governor, Deputy Governor or District Commissioner in the South. There were few Assistant District Commissioners. There was no Southerner in the Sudan Diplomatic Service. There was only one Southern Minister in the Government. In the Southern Province Councils Southerners were represented but the more important Executive Councils were entirely Northern. The Army and Police were predominantely staffed by Northern Sudanese.[60]

Richard Gray, an expert on Sudanese affairs, who visited the South in 1960 remarked that there were many signs of discrimination against the Southerners

It was Arab traders and planters who enjoyed the confidence of Arab officials: it was Northern policemen who supervised convict labour on coffee plantations or beat boys in Juba in what had apparently become a routine procedure for instilling respect.[61]

(i) *Economic Neglect of the South*

From independence on nearly all development was carried out in the North. British development projects for the South were abandoned. Thus plans for growing sugar cane at Mangalla and Malakal where conditions were excellent were postponed in favour of another sugar project in the North. Projects for the construction of a sugar refinery, and other factories for cotton and tobacco were abandoned. A plan to set up a paper factory at Malakal and a meat packing in Bahr al-Ghazal were not carried out. A fish canning plant was transferred to the Jabal al Awliya in the North.[62] As a result Southerners had the feeling that the South was regarded by the government only "as a source of raw material for the North."[63]

F. *Political Discrimination*

Since Self Rule, there are many instances showing that the North disregarded the political opinion of the Southern leaders and Southern political parties. Below are a few examples. In 1953 when the Northern political parties signed the Anglo-Egyptian Agreement on the future independence of Sudan the Southerners were excluded. Thus "the South without being consulted and against its will was made dependent on the Arab North."[64] Immediately after Self Rule the Southerners established several political parties. These parties suffered from the disputes among the Southerners themselves but also from the harsh steps taken against them by the government. In 1953 the Southern Party was established by the Southern members of Parliament changing its name in 1954 to the Liberal Party. The Liberal Party was not supported by educated and more progressive Southerners who claimed that it has been bought off by the Northern politicians. Two intellectuals, Father Saturnino and Ezbon Mondiri founded in 1957 the S.S.F.P. (Southern Sudan Federal Party) which succeeded in defeating the Liberal Party and gained forty seats in the parliament. The S.S.F.P. insisted in parliament that the North should back its promises to give serious consideration to the Southern demands for Sudanese Federation. The government was not happy and Mondiri was arrested and imprisoned for seven years for allegedly threatening government officials. The Mondiri party disappeared from the political scene.[65] In 1958 the Military government of General Abud dissolved the parliament and banned the Southern political parties along with all other political bodies. The military regime silenced all talk about Federation "Every enlightened Southerner was classified as a politician and therefore a trouble-maker" wrote Oliver Albino, a Southern leader, in his book.[66] He noted, that enlightened Southerners ranged from "being neatly dressed to failing to behave as inferior to Northerners."

(i) *Persecution*

Arrests and escape into exile. When the Southerners expressed their indignation with government policy the authority tried to quieten them by repression. Abud's military rule intensified the wave of arrests in the South. Oduho gave a rough estimate of 5,000 Southerners arrested since independence until 1963 for political reasons and produced a list of eight Southern M.P.'s sentenced to imprisonment of 3 to 17 years. A further eight M.P.'s including himself succeeded in crossing the border into Uganda.[67] Escape of Southern politicians whom the government called "rebels" increased from 1960 on.[68] In December 1960 an alleged plot to carry out mass arrests in the South on Christmas Eve was discovered and many politicians fled the country to establish an organization in exile.[69]

Atrocities. The Southerners accuse the Government of burning villages and that in Equatoria alone up to 1963 at least 10,000 huts with all belongings were burnt by Northern forces. They claim that in eastern Equatoria the villages have been demolished completely or in part. They add that the administrators looted from the villagers at that time at least 500,000 head of cattle and goats.[70] Northern sources later on confirmed most of these charges.

Killings. As mentioned the Zande Scheme killings in July 1955 in which about 300 Southerners were murdered was one of the immediate causes of 1955 mutiny. Nevertheless, the policy of crushing the Southern political movements by brutal force continued. Thus in June and July 1965, during the Mahjub government, the Army tried to eliminate systematically throughout the South, politically minded and educated Southerners. Those who did not succeed in fleeing into exile in Uganda, Congo, Ethiopia or Kenya were killed. Some have attributed the murders to isolated incidents by ill-disciplined troops but the timing, geographical extent and the discrimination employed by the troops in singling out the educated Southerners remains as powerful circumstantial evidence that the army was acting on orders from a Prime Minister determined to annihilate "the terrorist gangs which abuse security."[71] News of mass-killing also reached the West during the first years of Numayri reign. The *Star* Nairobi, of 10 August 1965, reported from a refugee, an eye-witness, that on the night of 8 July 1965 about 1,400 Southerners were shot in Juba most of them clerks and intellectuals. The *Observer* of 30 August and 27 September 1970 and the *Times* of 20 November 1970 published corroborated accounts by eye-witnesses of mass-killings of civilians in the South.

Mr. Ateny Mudratemy Pajokdit, a Southern leader alleged according to a report from Nairobi in the *Christian Science Monitor* of 14 January 1971 that since 1969 Arab soldiers had massacred entire villages or segments of their populations in at least 212 cases. In Bahr al-Ghazal province all 700 inhabitants of a Dinka village Marial Aguog were machine-gunned; an estimated 2,000 people were reported killed in villages surrounding the police post of Ulang, nine miles south of Nasir, in Upper Nile province and their cattle were driven north; in November 1970 at Marta in Equatoria province, about 800 young men of the villages were allegedly killed and their women maimed. Scores of bombings were reported. Mrs. Cecil Epril who visited the Sudan in 1971 and also interviewed several Southern leaders in exile was informed of the "Akobo" affair of July 1971:

Akobo is a town in the Upper Nile province of Southern Sudan close to the Ethiopian border. The elementary school principal, Martin Mirich was forced into a car and shot outside the town. Angered at this the Anya-Nya launched an attack in the area. As a reprisal for the Anya-Nya attack 39 Southerners were taken out of prison at Akobo and machine-gunned. The soldiers then marched through the town turning their machine-guns on "all people who wore good clothes."

Mrs. Epril indicated that similar reports have been corroborated by other sources. "The Bonza church killings" in 1970 in which about 40 men women and children were burned to death while praying in a school room used as a church at Bonza – was confirmed according to Mrs. Epril by eye-witness accounts from survivors at a hospital in the Congo. The author concluded that in other cases confirmatory "evidence is difficult to obtain and some stories may be exaggerated."[72]

The Sudanese authorities refute this allegation and claim that brutality against civilians was forbidden and was a criminal offence. The Anya-Nya, for their part, did not deny carrying out ruthless attacks on Army posts and soldiers which they considered as an Army of Occupation.[73]

Concerning the number of victims who lost their lives during the Civil War there are various estimates. The difficulty of verifying the numbers stems from the fact that the South was most of the time closed to outside observers. Because of the immense size of the South even those who succeeded in crossing the borders clandestinely could cover only part of the country. They usually tell the same story with slight variations, i.e. destruction and atrocities.[74]

Estimates of the death toll of the 17 years Civil War range from 500,000 to 1,500,000 most of them civilian Southerners who died from diseases and starvation.[75] The Southerners accuse the government of "genocide."[76] Anthony Carthew, an English reporter who penetrated illegally into the Southern Sudan in 1966 published his report in the *Daily Mail* of 31 January, 1 and 2 February 1966 pointing out "Here an entire people is dying. Here a race war of immense ferocity is being fought." The Northerners refute such allegation and blame the South-

ern guerrillas for atrocities in the South. Mohamed Beshir, a Northerner, ex-government officer and later principal of the University of
Khartoum admitted in his book that although the Southern guerillas
did commit murders against their own people the Army has also been
responsible for the killing of innocent people and that "the Army's
repressive measures in the South drove thousands of Southerners out of
the country."[77] Government publications since 1970 emphasized also
the sufferings of the South although blaming only the previous regimes
"that for 14 years they did nothing to alleviate fears and suspicions."[78]

Although one can assume that the Southerner's stories and reports of
mass-murders and subjection are exaggerated they can at least manifest
the poisoned relations between North and South. It should also be
mentioned that some outside observers mentioned instances in which
the Northerners showed restraint and discipline as in the case of the
1955 mutiny when 250 Northerners lost their lives at the hands of the
rebels.[79]

III. The Anatomy of the Southern Resistance

The civil war which lingered on for seventeen years is characterized by
several factors:

(i) Most of the Northern governments, which suffered from internal
weakness and frequent changes, believed that they could settle the
Southern Problem by the use of force. Only when General Numayri
was ready to negotiate a compromise, an agreement was reached.

(ii) The Southerners resistance was manifested in the following
forms:

(1) A guerrilla war conducted with varying degree of strength and
success. It reached its peak in 1970. The fighters aim, most of the
time was complete independence for the South.
(2) Political activities of Southern politicians in exile. Their aim was
usually identical with the guerrilla leaders.
(3) Political campaign of Southerners within the Sudanese government. These politicians were more moderate. They demanded
Federation or other form of regional autonomy for the South in a
United Sudan.

(iii) The Southerners suffered from chronic personal rivalries which
weakened them and thus prolonged their fight. Only when they were

united under one capable leader did they succeed in getting most of their demands.

To clarify the complicated picture of the long civil war this chapter will be divided chronologically into several important periods. In each period the main features of the struggle will be described, up to the signing of the 1972 Agreement.

A. *From the Mutiny (18.8.1955) to Abud Military Coup* *(18.8.1955 – 17.11.1958)*

The 1955 mutiny shocked the Northerners. They were also afraid that the event might further defer their independence. Therefore they were ready to make some concessions to the South to regain its confidence. Several Southerners were given principal posts in the South and incompetent Northern officials were replaced. The 22 Southern members of parliament formed the Liberal Party and demanded a federal form of parliament. On 19 December 1955 the parliament passed unanimously a motion reading "Federation will be fully considered."[80] On the basis of this promise the Southern M.P.s agreed to the Declaration of Independence on January 1, 1956. On the whole these concessions had a tranquilizing effect which checked further deterioration in the relations between North and South. Between 1956–1958 only a few isolated attacks on government posts by the mutineers occurred. The struggle was mainly in the political arena. Nevertheless, the rift among the Southerners soon appeared. Some intellectuals accused the Liberal Party of selling out to the Northerners. In February 1958 a general election for the 173 seats of the Constituent Assembly took place. The North had 127 seats, the South 46. Ezbon Mondiri and Father Saturnino founded the Southern Sudan Federal Party which succeeded in defeating the Liberal Party by winning forty seats in the Parliament. They increased their pressure on the government to accept immediately Federal Constitution for the Sudan. Mondiri was arrested and the Party disintegrated. Father Saturnino then founded the Southern Block with 25 M.P.s. In May 1958 the Northern Parties presented a draft resolution rejecting federal status for the South and advocating Islamic constitution. The Southern M.P.s reaction was to withdraw from the Constituent Assembly in protest. In 1958 the whole democratic parliamentary system in Sudan was under great strain.

The governments that ruled after 1956 were neither strong enough to command respect nor enlightened enough to attract support of the intelligentsia in either North or South ... the Northern political parties were again too preoccupied with their intrigues and power-games to think and plan seriously for solving the Southern problem.[81]

The failure of the politicians to tackle the economic and national problems brought the end of democracy and in 17.11.1958 the Army under the command of General Ibrahim Abud took over control.

B. *Abud Military Regime (17.11.1958 – 29.10.1964)*

The Military Government banned all political parties and dissolved the parliament. It pursued a strong arm policy toward Southern Sudan wrongly considering the problem a military one and not political. General Abud objected to any talks on Federalism and attempted to unify the country by force and by imposing Islamization and Arabization on the South. Indeed, most of the atrocities and discriminations occurred during this period.

Abud's repressive measures increased the Southern resistance. Not able to use parties and political means to voice their grievances and demands, their underground and guerrilla activities were intensified. Thousands of Southerners went into exile. In February 1962 several educated Southerners and ex-parliamentarians founded in Leopold-ville, the Sudan African Closed District National Union which in 1963 became the Sudan African National Union (SANU). Joseph Oduho former member of parliament was President and William Deng, Secretary General. SANU declared that its policy was independence for the Southern Sudan, as they had failed to obtain Federation. Its activities consisted mainly of petitions to U.N. and O.A.U. and publishing the problem of Southern Sudan. Here again the personal conflicts among the Southerners in exile particularly between William Deng and Father Saturnino weakened SANU. On the other hand the Southern soldiers were now more effective.

In September 1963 the Anya-Nya ("snake poison") was founded at a meeting in the South organized by Joseph Oduho and from this event the organised resistance movement started. The Anya-Nya was composed mainly of ex-soldiers of the Equatoria Corps who fled to the bush after the 1955 mutiny and they were now joined by new recruits. It declared:

Our patience has now come to an end and we are convinced that only the use of force will bring a decision ....[82]

Immediately it launched a series of attacks by several hundred men on bridges, stations and army posts in Equatoria, Upper Nile and at the beginning of 1964 fighting spread also to Bahr al-Ghazal province. The Anya-Nya acted also against those Southerners suspected of collaborating with the government. In January 1964 the Anya-Nya ventured to conquer Wau in Bahr al-Ghazal with 43 uniformed fighters but the attack was repulsed. Abud's government reacted with harsher counter-measures. Some Southerners were hanged, others put in prison. Military dictatorship refused to recognize that there was a Southern problem and insisted that it was part of an imperialist plot carried out by the missionaries.[83] Only in 1964 when the war against the Anya-Nya became too expensive and with the unsolved economic problems there was an attempt on the part of the government to find a political solution and a Commission of Enquiry was established to make recommendations. Nevertheless, before the Commission could start its work the Army dictatorship was overthrown and a civilian government was installed. The failure of the Abud regime to solve the Southern problem was one of the reasons that precipitated its downfall.

C. The Second Period of Civilian Rule (29.10.1964 – 29.5.1969)

(i) The Transitional Government (October 1964 – April 1965)

After Abud's fall a transitional government was appointed until elections could be held. The government tried to establish good relations with the Southerners and two of their leaders Clement Mboro and Ezbon Mondiri joined the Cabinet. On December 10, 1964 the government declared a general amnesty for all Southern exiles. A search for a political solution through negotiations started. In 1964 a new Southern political party, the Southern Front was founded in Khartoum which called for "Southernization" of the administration in the South and appealed for renewed negotiations. SANU, moved its headquarters from the Congo to Uganda and renewed its contacts with Khartoum. The Southerners were riddled with devisions when the extremists led by Oduho demanded separation while the moderates led by William Deng advocated a federal solution. On February 1965 Deng heading a delegation of SANU members arrived in Khartoum to hold negotiations with the Government.

(ii) *The Round Table Conference*

On March 16, 1965 a Round Table Conference opened in Khartoum with forty-five participants: 18 representing the Northern political parties and 27 representing the South. Observers came from Uganda, Kenya, Tanzania, Ghana, Nigeria, Algeria and U.A.R.[84] All the participants expressed their desire to find a peaceful solution within a united Sudan. Nevertheless, when the Conference adjourned on 29 March 1965 agreement was reached only on several issues such as repatriation of Southern refugees, freedom of religion, but the main issue of the constitutional future of Sudan remained unsolved and the matter was referred to a twelve man committee representing all the parties. Beshir who was secretary to the Round Table Conference attributed its failure to reach agreement mainly to the divisions among the Southerners; while William Deng advocated federalism, another group of SANU led by Aggrey Jaden representing Joseph Oduho wanted nothing less than independence for the South. The Anya-Nya refused to participate and resumed its attacks on army and police stations in the South. The Conference ended with the understanding that it could be reconvened three months later to hear the recommendations of the twelve-man committee. But in the meantime there was a change of government and it was never convened. (Only in the beginning of 1967 the committee submitted its report recommending a system of regional autonomy to the South).

(iii) *Mahjub and al-Mahdi Governments (April 1965 – May 1969)*

In April 1965 elections for the parliament were held and a coalition government was founded under the leadership of Muhammad Mahjub. Mahjub was replaced by as-Sadiq al-Mahdi in July 1966 but in May 1967 Mahjub returned to power and his government ruled until General Numayri's Coup in May 1969.

The governments during this period, particularly Mahjub's, advocated firm and uncompromising policy towards the South based again on Arabization and Islamization and use of force. This policy was also reflected in a series of events; first the declaration of the Northern parties that their ultimate goal was an Islamic republic in the Sudan; then the incidents at Juba on July 8 1965 and at Wau on August 11, 1965 where an unknown number of Southerners were killed by the army while it was "searching for rebel symphathisers";[85] followed by the refusal of the government to re-convene the Round Table Conference to discuss the report of the twelve-man Committee. These events increased the fears and bitterness among the Southerners and increased their resistance.

The Anya-Nya intensified its fighting and it was strengthened by many new Southerners who fled to the bush. In 1965 it was also better equipped with weapons acquired from the Congo and it held large areas in the countryside. But the Anya-Nya attacks were usually not co-ordinated by central planning and they were launched by local groups. There were even instances when Anya-Nya groups attacked one another because of tribal and traditional animosities.[86]

As for the politicians in exile, in 1965 Joseph Oduho, George Kwanai and Aggry Jaden of SANU, who were more identified with the Anya-Nya, founded a new party called "Azanian Liberation Front" (A.L.F.). Its aim was

liberating the Southern Sudan and establishing a free and independent African nation so that the black man in this part of the continent may realize security, justice, welfare and his hitherto human rights and dignity.[86]

But in 1967 A.L.F. was dissolved because the rivalry between its leaders and Aggry Jaden established a new group in that year, the Southern Sudan Provisional Government. This organization was formed at a meeting in the South in which several Anya-Nya officers participated. But again the movement collapsed in 1969 because of personal antagonism among the leaders which hampered its effectiveness.

As for the Southern leaders who were acting in Khartoum – they believed that they could gain more by participating in the government than by fighting in the bush or quarrelling in exile. These were the moderates of SANU headed by William Deng and the Southern Front established in 1964 by Clement Mboro. They were ready for compromise and advocated Federalism. Nevertheless the civilian government was rendered ineffective at this period because of its firm line and repressive policy.

In the elections of 1968 SANU and the Southern front won only 25 seats out of the sixty southern seats, showing that most of the Southerners did not believe in their ability to find the solution. In May 1968 Deng was killed by the Army and the Southerners in Khartoum lost much of their influence.[87]

Thus, during this period the uncompromising attitude of the North towards the South's aspirations on the one hand, and the Southerners internal divisions on the other, blocked the way to peaceful solution and created a deadlock.

IV. The Numayri Military Regime
and the 1972 Agreement

A. *Resistance and Suppression*

On the 25 May 1969 a coup d'état was staged by Colonel Jafar al-Numayri and Sudan came under military rule for the second time since Independence. The army was frustrated by the incompetence of the politicians to solve the Southern problem and the deteriorating economic situation. In June 1969 Numayri announced a four point programme in which he offered the South regional self government within a united Sudan. On 19 June 1969 a special Ministry for Southern Affairs was formed headed by a Southerner, Abel Alier, and another two Southerners joined the government. In the South many key posts which were formerly reserved for Northerners were given to Southerners including the post of the Chief of Police. The three provinces of the South were put under Southern Commissioners. Numayri also promised that in working towards a political solution the special characteristics of the South would be taken into consideration.[88]

The Southern politicians in Khartoum regarded the new regime as the first since independence to make concrete concessions to the South. Therefore Abel Alier and his collegues were ready to collaborate with Numayri towards implementing his programme of reforms for the South. But now Southern exiles and soldiers were uncompromising and suspicious and insisted on complete separation from the Sudan. It seems that the Civil War could end at this stage if the guerrillas agreed to a compromise. Another factor which hampered at this time the efforts towards solution was the internal difficulties in the North and the plots to overthrow Numayri's regime hatched both by the Right Wing parties (March 1970) and the Communists from the Left (July 1971).

Therefore during the first two years of Numayri military rule, the armed conflict continued and even escalated.

By 1970 important developments occurred within the Anya-Nya when Joseph Lagu emerged as the Commander in Chief of the guerrillas. Lagu, of a Madi tribe and a Protestant, became in 1963 a Second Lieutenant in the Sudanese Army and immediately afterwards joined the Anya-Nya in Equatoria. Gradually he succeeded in bringing all military operations under unified command. Lagu also acquired from several Western countries greater military and financial support.[89] At the end of 1969 and during 1970 and 1971 the Anya-Nya could launch fierce attacks on army camps in the South and disturb the lines of communications. A new Southern political organization was also established by Lagu, The Southern Sudan Liberation Front which included most of the Southern leaders in exile. For the first time the military and political activities were united under one authority. The guerrilla force, at the end of 1971 was variously estimated at 5,000 to 40,000 men. In 1972 there were at least 20,000 Anya-Nya.[90] The Government, on the other hand also intensified its reprisals against the guerrillas and its offensive in 1970–71 absorbed half of the country's military budget and tied up three quarters of its army estimated at about 50,000 men. It's weapons included Soviet heavy tanks and Mig 21 fighter planes.[91] As usual, information about incidents in the South was contradictory and vague, coming mainly from Sudanese official sources or sources closed to Anya-Nya. Government sources used to belittle the guerrilla activities describing them as mere ambushes and sporadic unsuccessful attacks on army camps and bridges and as "terrorizing the villagers."[92] They reported successful attacks on guerrilla camps and the seizure of large quantities of weapons including anti-aircraft guns, machine-guns etc. supplied by "U.S., West Germany and Israel."[93] Government sources used to emphasize that the situation in the South was normal and under control. On the other hand the Southerners while announcing their successful operations[94] accused the Army of raiding villages and murdering innocent people in retaliation.[95] It seems that there were many ups and downs in the military situation and that particularly in 1970 the Army, strengthened by Soviet weapons had some successes in its operations against the Anya-Nya. British parliamentary delegations which visited the South in Oct. 1970 reported that Bahr al-Ghazal and upper Nile were quiet and that only in the Southern parts of Equatoria the clashes continued.[96] Ralf Steiner the West German mercenary who fled from the South at that time was arrested by the Ugandans and extradited to Sudan.[97] But the Army offensive could not completely crush the guerrillas and throughout 1971 skirmishes again continued with fury. The Anya-Nya although outnumbered and outweaponed enjoyed the advantages of the bush and terrain which particularly in wet weather caused the army many difficulties and much hardship. By the end of 1971 the Anya-Nya headed by Joseph Lagu, and gaining experience in the many years of fighting, became a more formidable and cohesive force and Numayri had to intensify the military operations against it. The ever mounting fierceness of the conflict caused both sides heavy casualties and eventually pushed them towards negotiations. Moreover, on both sides there were now strong key men and more realistic and talented leaders and this fact facilitated a solution.

B. *Negotiations and Agreement*

Towards the end of 1971 both Lagu and Numayri, who in the meantime had crushed his opponents in the North, tried to find ways to resolve the Southern Problem through negotiations. Numayri declared that his government was prepared to negotiate with Southern delegations, at any place, a political solution within the framework of a unified Sudan. On the other hand Lagu expressed also his readiness to find a compromise. Negotiations started at last with the assistance of the Ethiopian Government in Addis-Abeba at the beginning of 1972. The Sudanese delegation was headed by the Southern Minister of State for Southern Affairs, Abel Alier, while Laurence Wol Wol represented Lagu as the leader of Anya-Nya and Sudan Liberation Front. On 27 February 1972, after major concessions from both sides an agreement was reached. The North gave up the idea of a unitary Islamic State and the South abandoned its demand for secession.

The cornerstone of the Settlement was the Southern Province Regional Self Government Act of 1972 signed by President Numayri on 3 March.[98] Article 3 reads "The Southern Province of Sudan shall constitute a Self Government Region within the Democratic Republic of the Sudan and shall be known as the Southern Region." Regarding the sensitive issue of the language, Article 5 reads "Arabic shall be the official language for the Sudan and English the principal language for the Southern Region ..." The Act established that the Central Government in Khartoum was responsible for matters of defence, foreign relations, finance, communications, economics and education. The internal affairs of the South would be controlled by a legislative body, The Regional Assembly, and executive body, the Higher Executive Council headed by a President, who would act also as the National Vice President. The official ratification ceremonies took place in Addis-Ababa from 12–27 March 1972. On 19 March the amnesty for all the Southern guerrillas was issued and the state of emergency in the South was ended. Abel Alier was named as the President of the Higher Executive

Council of the Southern Region and as Sudan Vice-President. Joseph Lagu, the commander of the Anya-Nya, was given the rank of Major General in the Sudanese Army. A Southern Command was formed of 12,000 men of whom half came from the South. By January 1973 about 20,000 Anya-Nya were absorbed in the Army, Police and other government services.[99]

Thus, after seventeen years of fighting peace came to Southern Sudan. The blame for this prolonged civil war rests with both sides. The Northerners, because of their failure to understand the Southerners' aspirations to self-government and their struggle to preserve their local heritage. The Southerners grievances were simply attributed to "imperialists" and Christian missionary agitators. Moreover, the North believed during most of this period that by force of arms and suppression the problem could be solved. On the other hand the Southerners, although the main victim of the war, were not free of fault, particularly for their inability to overcome their inter-tribal and personal animosity and schism for the sake of the larger Southern cause.

Immediately after the Agreement was reached the enormous task of rehabilitation of the South and resettlement of the refugees started. With substantial donations from a large number of U.N. specialized agencies and voluntary organizations the Resettlement Commission had handled, until the end of 1975, the return of 148,000 refugees from neighbouring countries together with several times that number of displaced persons within the region.[100]

Until the end of 1973 these organizations provided about $ 21 m. The five-year $ 10.7 m. World Bank scheme for the region which covers research and improvement of food and cash crops, and livestock is expected to benefit 65,000 families. Industry too is being developed in the South and in Malakal for example, a $ 38 m. paper factory utilizing papyrus and bamboo as its raw materials is under construction. Foreign observers noted recently that reconstruction of the South, although slow, was continuing and that remarkable progress has been already achieved in agriculture, industry, in rebuilding the infrastructure, in health and education.[101]

Politically, from 1973 on, the Southern leaders were solidly behind the Numayri Government giving it strong support in the various crises which it faced. As a whole, the Numayri regime went a long way towards promoting co-operation and understanding between the North and the South.

C. *The Aftermath*

Following the 1972 Agreement, the South generally remained quiet although from time to time both Northern and Southern leaders had to face delicate situations emerging from a century old conflict and mutual suspicions. Here are a few examples:

At the beginning of March 1975 Southern troops mutinied at the Akobo garrison. According to a government communique, released only on July 30th 1975, the troubles erupted when the troops were informed that they were to be transferred to Juba. The communique added that eight soldiers were executed for participating in the mutiny. The Vice President Abel Alier claimed that the incident resulted from a "serious misunderstanding" and condemned the mutineers. But according to *Washington Post*, quoting refugees who reached Ethiopia, the incident in Akobo was much more serious. Ex-Anya-Nya soldiers and Northern troops were involved in fierce fighting and about 250 men were either killed in the battle or executed later.[102]

Another event which manifested the amount of carefulness and tact needed in dealing with the South was the Egyptian-Sudanese 280 km Jonglei Canal Project. According to the agreement signed in 1974 each side undertook to pay half of the estimated £ 150 m cost of the initial stage of the work. Although the project will primarily benefit the villages in the Upper Nile and Equatoria provinces, the Southerners demonstrated against it. Rioting and disturbances occurred in May 1975 mainly in Juba, the capital of the Southern region, where suspicions were easily excited by misleading propaganda that the project would benefit the Egyptians and attract large scale Arab settlement. Several demonstrators were sentenced to imprisonment, among them a former governor of Juba. In this case it was the government's failure to explain the purpose of the scheme which caused the troubles.[103]

Another source of danger threatening the delicate balance between North and South were the recurring attempts to overthrow the regime of President Numayri which disturbed the stability of Sudan as a whole.

The last (sixth in number) abortive coup against Numayri was on 5 September 1975 when Northern army officers tried to seize power but were quickly quelled by loyal troops. It is interesting to note that the Southern politicians and officers were throughout these crises loyal to Numayri and supported him.[104]

Despite the many dangers and obstacles threatening the 1972

Agreement it was a great tribute to Numayri and to the present Southern leaders, Joseph Lagu and Abel Alier, in achieving the settlement and in overcoming, up to these very days, the enormous difficulties which were involved in the task of reconstruction and rebuilding a peaceful Sudan.

In assessing the present situation in Sudan it should be taken into consideration that, after so many years of bitter fightings, suspicions and misunderstandings can't be easily eradicated. The future success of the settlement continues to depend on the ability of President Numayri and the Southern leaders to establish genuine co-operation between the North and the South based on compromise, mutual respect and equality.

V. Some African Reactions to the Civil War in Sudan

The long and cruel war between the Arab Muslims of North Sudan and the black animists of the South which continued for nearly 17 years is still one of the reasons for African resentment against the Arabs. During the war the Southerners published in Africa and in the world, leaflets, magazines and books in which they blamed the Sudanese Government and its policy aimed at Islamization and Arabization of the South and accused it of launching a war of genocide against the Southerners.[105] The *Voice of Southern Sudan's* issue of 15.3.1969, for example, wrote that during the years of struggle nearly 750,000 died in the South. The vast majority of Africans sympathized with the Southerners' struggle and expressed their support on various occasions. Some of the neighbouring countries, as mentioned, accorded them more than moral support and even gave refuge to their leaders. Radio Nigeria, for instance, in a broadcast to Africa on June 12, 1963 accused the Sudanese Government of "an accelerated plan to bully the South into accepting a thoroughly centralized system with a single education programme, a single language – Arabic, a single religion and a single Islamic way of life."[106]

It is true that the African countries although morally supporting the Southern Sudanese cause, generally avoided backing their demand for a separate state in international forums, out of fear of creating a dangerous precedent which might endanger their own unity. Many African countries, it should be remembered, have their inter-tribal conflicts. Still the Africans occasionally expressed their sympathy with the black African Southern Sudanese and blamed the Arabs for their atrocities. Even after the agreement was reached between the North and the South, in 1972, the period of bitter struggle and the atrocities against the Southerners left a sore which has not healed and on different occasions the Africans used it against the Arabs as a warning for the future. Thus the black African Archbishop of Abidjan, when warning against the *Jihad* ideology, also remarked "Moslems conquered Southern Sudan, destroyed its long established society and decimated its population."[107] In an editorial of the monthly magazine *Africa*, of January 1974 an African commentator pointed out that the civil war in Southern Sudan which lasted 17 years cannot be forgotten and is one of the factors "which keeps the historical and psychological gap between Arabs and Africans."[108]

TABLE OF EVENTS

1820–1884   Turco-Egyptian occupation of Sudan. Southern Sudan opened up from North.
1881   Muhammad Ahmad proclaims himself Mahdi of Islam and begins conquest of Sudan.
1885   Khartoum captured by the Mahdists who failed to conquer Southern Sudan.
1898   Mahdists defeated at Omdurman by Anglo-Egyptian forces.
1899–1956   Anglo-Egyptian Condominium providing for joint Anglo-Egyptian rule over Sudan. In practice Britain holds reins of power.
1930   Government proclaims "Southern Policy" separating Southern Sudan from Northern Muslim influence.
1946   Britain reverses "Southern Policy," convene Juba Conference (1947).
1948   Legislative Assembly opens with 13 nominated members from South, 76 from North and six British.
1951   Constitution Commission appointed to advise Governor-General on steps for granting Sudan self-government.
1953   Four main Northern political parties and Egyptian government agree to future independence of Sudan.
1953   Self Rule.
1955   Southern Corps Mutiny.
1956   Independence.
1958   General Abud Military Rule.
1964   Abud regime succeeded by civilian governments.
1969   Colonel Numayri Coup.
1972   Agreement reached between North and South.

NOTES

1. *Middle East Record*, Tel-Aviv, 1960, p. 418; Oduho, J., *The Problem of the Southern Sudan*, London, 1963, p. 29.
2. Legum, C. (ed.), *Africa Contemporary Record*, London, 1974–5, p. B103.
3. Beshir, M. Omer, *The Southern Sudan – Background to Conflict*, London, 1968, p. 5.
4. Oduho, p. 1; Beshir, p. 5.
5. Epril, C., *Sudan: The Long War*. Conflict Studies No. 21, London, March 1972, p. 1.
6. Richard Gray in his introduction to Oduho, p. 2.
7. S. Baker, *Ismailia*, London, 1974, Vol. II, p. 136.
8. Collins, Robert O., *The Southern Sudan in Historical Perspective*, Tel-Aviv, 1975, p. 18.
9. *Ibid.*, p. 30.
10. Oduho, p. 11; See also Oliver Albino, *The Sudan – A Southern Viewpoint*, Oxford, 1970.
11. Memorandum on Southern Policy, January 25, 1930, by Sir Harold Mac-Michael, Cited in Collins, p. 51.
12. Richard Gray in his introduction to Oduho, p. 5.
13. Sir J. W. Robertson, Civil Secretary, Khartoum 16 Dec. 1946 in a secret letter to Governors of Southern Provinces and other senior British officials, in Epril, p. 5.
14. Collins, p. 63.
15. Arnold Toynbee in his Foreword to Albina, p. VIII.
16. *Report of the Commission of Enquiry into the Disturbances in the Southern Sudan During August 1955–18 Feb. 1956*, McCorquodale and Co. (Sudan) Ltd.
17. *Report of the Commission of Enquiry*, p. 8.
18. Oduho, p. 25; Collins, p. 65.
19. *Report of the Commission of Enquiry*, p. 114.
20. Oduho, p. 25.
21. *Report of the Commission of Enquiry*, p. 99.
22. Oduho, p. 27.
23. *Report of the Commission of Enquiry*, p. 82.
24. Collins, p. 67.
25. Mohamed Omer Beshir, *The Southern Sudan*, London, 1968, p. 70.
26. *Sudan Daily* 15–29 Jan. 1961; *Middle East Record (MER)*, 1961, p. 475.
27. Radio Cairo, 9 Feb. 1961 – *MER*, 1961, p. 475.
28. *Sudan al-Jadid*, 20 Feb. 1961 – *MER* 1961, p. 475.
29. On similar visits see *Morning News*, Khartoum, 1 Nov. 1960, *Zaman* 16 Jan. 1960 – *MER* 1960, p. 418.
30. Beshir, p. 81; Collins, p. 76; *Ray al Amm*, Sudan, 15 Aug. 1961 – *MER* 1961, p. 475.
31. For example, see details in *Ayyam* 30 April 1960 – *MER* 1960, p. 419.
32. *Ray al Amm*, 18 Oct. 1961 – *MER* 1961, p. 475; Collins, p. 76.
33. B.B.C. 28 Oct. 1960 – *MER* 1960, p. 419.
34. *Ray al Amm*, 21 June 1960 – *MER* 1960, p. 419.
35. B.B.C. 28 Oct. 1960 – *MER* 1960, p. 419.
36. Collins, pp. 71, 93.
37. *Sudan al-Jadid*, 25 April 1960 – *MER* 1960, p. 418.

38. *Sudan al-Jadid* 2 May 1960 – *MER* 1960, p. 418; *Ibid* 12 March 1961 – *MER*, 1961, p. 468.
39. Oduho, p. 53; Albino, pp. 96–100.
40. *Report of the Commission of Enquiry*, pp. 123–4.
41. L. A. Fabuni, *The Sudan in the Anglo-Egyptian Relations*, London, 1960, p. 356 in Oduho, p. 54.
42. Beshir, pp. 4–6.
43. *MER* 1961, p. 475.
44. *Economist*, 19.11.1960; *Catholic Times*, 20.10.1961.
45. *Anba as-Sudan* 28.1.1960 – *MER* 1960, p. 419.
46. *Catholic Times*, 20.10.1961.
47. Radio Omdurman 24.7.1961 – *MER* 1961, p. 475; also *Economist* 19.11.1960.
48. *Saraha*, 25.5.1960 – *MER* 1960, p. 416.
49. *Zaman*, Sudan, 20.2.1960 – *MER* 1960, p. 419.
50. *Ray al Amm* 10.5.1960 – *MER* 1960, p. 420; *Daily Telegraph*, 29.12.1960.
51. *Universe*, London, 8.3.1960.
52. Beshir, p. 81.
53. *Ibid.*, p. 82; Collins, p. 72.
54. Oduho, p. 46.
55. Collins, p. 75; Oduho, p. 45.
56. Oduho, p. 46.
57. *Ibid.*, p. 46.
58. Albino, p. 100.
59. Collins, p. 76; Albino, pp. 96–100.
60. Beshir, p. 72; Albino, 101 ff.
61. Richard Gray's introduction in Oduho, p. 3.
62. Collins, p. 77; Oduho, p. 49; Albino, 88 ff.
63. Oduho, p. 49.
64. Oduho, p. 13; Epril, p. 8.
65. Collins, p. 70; Albino, p. 40.
66. Albino, p. 44.
67. Oduho, p. 64; see also on this Collins, p. 79.
68. *Sarahah*, 22.2.1960; *Ray al Amm*, 11.5.1960; *Sudan Daily*, 2.12.1960 – *MER* 1960, p. 418.
69. Epril, p. 6.
70. Oduho, p. 41.
71. Mahjub speech in Khartoum June 19, 1965 quoted in Collins, p. 84.
72. Epril, p. 8.
73. *Ibid.*
74. An Italian film producer Dino De-Laurentis in 1966 visited clandestinely the Southern Sudan and produced a film called "Strange Africa 2" showing the Sudanese Army atrocities against the civilians in the South. *Times of London* 8.2.1967 and *Le Monde* 10.2.1967 reported that the Sudanese Army burned in Torit at the beginning of Jan. 1967 six villages and murdered 400 people accusing them of collaboration with Anya-Nya. See also David Robinson's report in *Observer Magazine* 7. March 1971. Robison spent several months with the guerrillas.
75. *Times Magazine* 10.2.1965 quotes 500.000 dead at that time; Epril, p. 4., see also Appendix.
76. See Oduho, pp. 28–31; Albino, pp. 60–63. see also *Near East Report*, Washington, 21.4.71. on the "Genocidal War."
77. Beshir, p. 100.
78. "A revolution in Action" government publication cited in Epril, p. 7.

79. R. Gray in his introduction to Oduho, p. 4.
80. Oduho, p. 33; Beshir, p. 78.
81. Beshir, p. 78.
82. Beshir, p. 84.
83. See for example *Ruz al-Yusuf*, 6.3.1961.
84. Beshir, p. 92
85. *Ibid.*, p. 100.
86. Collins, pp. 85–86; Beshir, p. 100.
87. Collins, p. 87.
88. *Daily Report*, 2 June 1969 quoting Radio Omdurman 30 May 1969.
89. Numayri consistently accused West Germany, Israel and other Western countries of aiding the guerrillas. *Daily Report* 18 May 1970; see also *The Christian Science Monitor* of 14 Jan. 1971 on foreign aid to Anya-Nya.
90. *Africa Contemporary Record* 1972-73, p. B100.
91. *Near East Report*, Washington, 21 Apr. 1971; *The New York Times*, 28 Feb. 1972; *Washington Post* of 1 Jan. 1971 reported that there were about 100 Soviet advisers and also Soviet pilots helping the government in its offensive against the Anya-Nya.
92. *Le Monde*, 10 Nov. 1970.
93. *Daily Report*, 18.5.70.
94. I.e. *Sunday Times*, Nairobi, 1 Mar. 1970; *The Christian Science Monitor*, 14 Jan. 1971; see also on the Press Conference in Kampala given by the "Foreign Minister" of the Anya-Nya Mr. Barri Wanji on 13 Nov. 1969. Wanji spoke of the many successes of the guerrilla in "routing the government forces and capturing weapons" *Uganda Argus*, 14 Nov. 1969.
95. I.e. *East African Standard*, Nairobi, 4 July 1970. On massacres of entire villages as described by Southern refugees see *The Christian Science Monitor*, 14 Jan. 1971.
96. *Daily Report*, 26 Oct. 1970.
97. *Uganda Argus*, 11 Nov. 1970.
98. For full text, see *Africa Contemporary Record* 1972–73, pp. C154 ff.
99. *Africa Contemporary Record*, 1972–73, p. B100.
100. *African Development*, Feb. 1976, p. 27.
101. *Africa Contemporary Record*, 1973–74, p. B96. Detailed report on progress done in the various fields see *African Development*, Feb. 1976, pp. 27–28.
102. *Africa Research Bulletin*, 15 Aug. 1975, p. 3699; *The Guardian*, 11 Mar. 1975.
103. *Africa Research Bulletin*, 15 May 1975, p. 3599.
104. *Ibid.*, 15 Feb. 1976, p. 3904.
105. I.e. Joseph Oduho and William Deng's book *The Problem of the Southern Sudan*, London, 1963; Oliver Albino *The Sudan – A Southern viewpoint*, London, 1970; *Voice of Southern Sudan*, stencilled periodical published in London; *Grass Curtain* periodical published by the Southern Sudan Association, London.
106. Quoted in V. McKay "The Impact of Islam on Relations among New African States," in J. H. Proctor (ed.), *Islam and International Relations*, N.Y., 1964, p. 173.
107. Quoted by *New York Times*, 20 June 1974.
108. *Africa*, January, 1974.

Ethnic Discrimination and Conflict:
The Case of the Korean Minority in Japan

CHANGSOO LEE

CHANGSOO LEE is Assistant Professor and Director of the Asian American Studies Programme, University of Southern California, U.S.A. He received his B.A. from North-east Missouri State College in 1964; M.A. from Marquette University in 1966; Ph.D. in Political Science from the University of Maryland in 1971. He was born in Korea and served in the Army of the Republic of Korea for nine years, receiving military training from the U.S. Army Armour School, Fort Knox, Kentucky. His area of interest is minority affairs, Asian politics and government. He has published numerous articles on the problems of overseas Koreans and he is currently working on a book dealing with the Korean minority in Japan with Professors George A. DeVos and Hiroshi Wagatsuma.

Ethnic Discrimination and Conflict:
The Case of the Korean Minority in Japan

CHANGSOO LEE

I. THE FORMATION OF THE KOREAN MINORITY AND THE DEMOGRAPHIC FACTOR

As one of few ethnic minorities in a highly homogeneous and "closed" society of Japan, some 600,000 Koreans suffer from political, legal and social discrimination against them as well as from bitter political antagonism and internal conflict among themselves.

The presence of the Korean minority in Japan is clearly a colonial legacy and the product of the Japanese imperialism. The majority of the Korean population in Japan are composed of those who migrated to Japan after the annexation of Korea at the turn of this century. Prior to the annexation, only about eight hundred Koreans were residing in Japan. (Table 1) However, the Korean population in Japan continued to increase after the annexation and began to mark a sharp rise around 1939 corresponding closely with the spread of Japan's imperial scheme over Manchuria and the Chinese continent.

The Korean groups of migration to Japan could be classified under two broad categories, voluntary and involuntary. The former group were the students, free labourers and poor peasants who drifted into Japan in search of employment. Many farmers were compelled to leave the land as a result of the land survey and the subsequent reform undertaken by the Japanese to restructualize the political and economic system of the feudalistic Korean Kingdom under colonial rule. This marked the era of the Korean exodus abroad to Manchuria, Siberia and China as well as to Japan.

Second group were the forced labourers and military draftees who were brought to Japan against their will by the Japanese militarists and used to fill the manpower vacuum created by the expansion of the war economy. As Japan's invasion expanded deep into mainland

China, the Koreans were recruited under the "National Manpower Mobilization Plan of 1939" into the Japanese munition and other heavy industries, as well as coal mines. For instance, during the closing years of World War II, the Koreans constituted approximately 50 percent of the coal miners in Hokkaidō, and 31 percent of the entire labour forces in the mine industires in Japan.[1] Beginning from 1944,

TABLE I. *The Migration of Koreans to Japan*

	Korean population in Japan	Conscripted Labourers or Military Draftees
1909	790	—
1910	—	—
1915	3,989	—
1916	5,638	—
1917	14,501	—
1918	22,262	—
1919	28,272	—
1920	30,175	—
1921	35,876	—
1922	59,865	—
1923	80,617	—
1924	120,238	—
1925	133,710	—
1926	148,502	—
1927	175,911	—
1928	243,328	—
1929	276,031	—
1930	298,091	—
1031	318,212	—
1932	390,543	—
1933	466,217	—
1934	537,576	—
1935	625,678	—
1936	690,501	—
1937	735,689	—
1938	799,865	—
1939	961,591	38,700
1940	1,190,444	54,944
1941	1,469,230	53,493
1942	1,625,054	112,007
1943	1,882,456	122,237
1944	1,936,843	280,303
1945	unknown	160,427

Source: Naimushō, Keihōkyoku, 1945.

young Koreans were drafted to serve in the Imperial Armed Forces and shipped to the battlefields. Throughout the war period, the aggregated number of Koreans mobilized by the Japanese Government were estimated to be almost six million. Among them, 831,111 Koreans were draftees and labourers brought into Japan for the war effort. (See Table 1.)

To attain a complete subjugation and to perpetuate the colonial rule, the Japanese Government initiated an assimilation policy to turn the Koreans into Japanese. The assimilation policy was primarily designed to neutralize national consciousness of the Koreans and induce them to co-operate with the colonial rule. Speaking and teaching the Korean language was forbidden by law, the Koreans had to adopt Japanese family names and to worship Shintoism. From 1937 they were required to recite the "Oath of Imperial Subject" at all public and private gatherings. To theorize the assimilation policy, a few scholars like Kanezawa Shōsaburō and Kita Teikichi began to formalize a thesis that Japanese and Koreans shared the same ethnic and cultural origins. From the era of "Taishō Democracy" with the promulgation of the General Election Law of 1925, those Koreans who established legal residency in Japan were given suffrage and permitted to hold public office. Consequently several Koreans were duly elected to the Japanese Diet in 1932 and 1937. Through the systematic process of assimilation and political integration, the Japanese militarists attempted to give the Koreans a sense of participation in the Japanese imperial scheme. The Koreans in Japan were forced to co-operate with Japan's aggressive nationalism and aid the military venture for implementing the "Great Asia Co-Prosperity Programme."

When the War ended, more than two million Koreans were in Japan.[2] With Japan's surrender, "spontaneous mass exodus" back to Korea began in the middle of August 1945. Hakata, Senzaki and other ports of embarkation were swamped with homebound Koreans, with whatever belongings they could carry. They were free to leave Japan whenever they could find passage across the Tsushima Strait. All types of sea-going vessels were used to transport Koreans to their homeland, while the Japanese from abroad were brought back to Japan. This uncontrolled mass migration created chaos, as the facilities to accommodate the incoming and outgoing throng at the war-torn embarkation areas were totally inadequate. Within six months after the surrender, almost a million Koreans were repatriated to Korea and a

TABLE 2. *The Place of Birth of Koreans in Japan*

A Total Number of Koreans in Japan as of 1974	638,806
Born in Japan	483,185
Born in Korea	154,054
Born in China	96
Born in Sakhalin (U.S.S.R.)	262
Born Elsewhere	50
Unknown	1,159

Source: Hōmushō, *Zairyū gaikokujin tōkei, 1974.*

similar number of the Japanese soldiers and civilians went back to Japan from Korea.

Since then, many Koreans returned home. The present population of 638,806 Koreans in Japan as of 1974 are those who elected not to return home and their descendants born in Japan. According to the 1974 report published by the Japanese Government, 76 percent of them (483,185) are Japanese-born second and third generations. (See Table 2.) Many of them never set foot in their homeland, nor are they well versed in their mother tongue. And yet, though they have been raised and educated in Japan, they are not legally recognized as Japanese. One writer noted that they are "half-Japanese."[3] The younger generation of under age 30 is the majority, while the older generation who came to Japan during the war years will gradually decrease. The largest concentration of Koreans is found in the Osaka metropolitan area where 188,720 of them are widely scattered. Among them, some 40,000 live in the densely populated area in the northern section of Ikunoku, Osaka city, thus forming a hard core Koreatown. For any outsider, Ikunoku is the area where one can often notice some elderly people speaking Korean loudly at each other and exhaling a smell of garlic, or speaking broken Japanese shamelessly with a heavy Korean accent. Also this is the stronghold of the Ch'ongyryŏn[4] (The General Federation of Korean Residents in Japan) members who pledge their absolute loyalty to the Democratic Peoples Republic of Korea.

Two factors effectively kept Koreans apart from the mainstream of the affluent Japanese society: one a legal and the other a social barrier. Legally the status of Koreans in Japan is "alien," hence they are naturally excluded from the benefits reserved for Japanese citizens. The Koreans are also legally excluded from positions in the government, and from public schools and universities, and from the profession of notary public, attorney or pilot. In some cases, Koreans are not legally entitled to live in publicly owned houses and to use other social benefits, such as child welfare, aid to families with dependent children, disability compensation, workmen's compensation and the old age assistance programme, etc. The social benefits for the Koreans are limited to the national health insurance programme, daily labourers' insurance and unemployment compensation. According to the Japanese officials, these benefits are provided to Koreans not as a matter of right but as "privileges," based on humanitarian concern.

The avenue to become a naturalized Japanese citizen is not entirely closed to Koreans, but the legal process and eligibility rules are so complicated that only a very limited number of "good" Koreans can qualify under the provision of the Japanese Nationality Law. Recently the Ministry of Justice stated that, for reasons of privacy, they refused to make public the number of Koreans being naturalized. However, according to an unofficial report, the annual rate of naturalization of Koreans is said to be approximately 1 percent of the total population, but the rate of rejected applications for naturalization is reportedly very high.[5]

Another force working against Koreans in Japan is the Japanese ethnocentrism. The Japanese people are in general extremely ethnicity-conscious.[6] They look at themselves as a unique people with a history and culture distinctively different from those of other groups.[7] The Japanese prejudice is generally directed against four groups – the Koreans, Burakumin, the Okinawans and the Ainu.[8] Except for Koreans, the other three groups are Japanese citizens and the chances for Koreans to join the affluence of the Japanese society are much slimmer than for any other minority groups in Japan.

The Japanese prejudice against Koreans seems to have gradually developed through the years of Japan's domination over Korea. Through the period of subjugation of the Koreans as the "second-rate citizen" of Japan, stereotypes of the Koreans as "bad guys" have been built up and those prejudices and stereotypes continue to be strong even though Korea is no longer Japan's colony. Even today it is not unusual to find a Japanese grandmother scolding her grandchild about a bad sitting posture, by saying: "Don't sit like Chōsenjin do."[9] One writer, having examined some text books used by secondary schools in Japan, concluded that little effort had been made by the Japanese Government to minimize their prejudice against Koreans.[10]

The employment rate for Koreans has remained always low in Japan even at the time of economic prosperity. According to a report publish-

TABLE 3. *The 1974 Statistics of the Gainfully Employed Koreans in Japan*

Classification	Total Number of Koreans 638,806	
	Male	Female
	336,787	302,019
Engineer	615	16
Teaching Profession	756	283
Doctor and Medical Worker	544	323
Clergy	204	70
Writer and Author	108	8
Correspondent	162	21
Scientist	320	81
Artist and Entertainer	457	246
Other Professional	568	99
Managerial Worker	4,595	202
Officer Worker	16,796	3,973
Trader (Import & Export)	181	4
Scrap Iron and Ragpicking Business	7,112	382
Other Sales Work (retail and wholesale)	19,041	4,058
Agriculture and Forestry including Farmer	2,737	962
Fishery and Fisher	243	130
Miners and Stone Cutter	463	21
Transportation and Communication	804	22
Builders and Construction Worker	10,681	134
Other Technical Worker and Manufacturer	31,051	3,858
Simple Manual Labourer	15,177	1,744
Chef	1,422	116
Barber and Beautician	470	576
Receptionist in the Leisure Industry	697	98
Restaurant, Cabaret and Other Service Entertainment Business	2,069	956
Drivers	12,794	67
Housewife	—	724
Student	2,735	1,792
Unemployed	*155,929*	*218,711*
Unclassifiable	492	209
Unreported	47,564	62,133

Source: Hōmushō, *Zairyū gaikokujin tōkei, 1974*, pp. 42–49.

ed by the Ministry of Justice in 1974, 58.6 per cent of the Koreans in Japan are unemployed, though the job classification used by the report is too ambiguous to comprehend the precise nature of a Korean's employment. (See Table 3.) It is not uncommon for a university graduate

Korean to work as a scrap collector or as a manager of a pinball parlour. Most of the enterprises owned by the Koreans are small businesses related to entertainment and service industries such as restaurants, sauna baths, night clubs, pinball parlours and retail shops. It is a widely accepted notion among the Japanese public that the pinball parlour is an almost exclusive enterprise owned and run by the Koreans.

As the social conditions are highly unfavourable, some Koreans resort to illegitimate means to attain their personal ambition and gratification. Several infamous underground gangsters are said to be Koreans; and a two-volume story of their underground activities has become one of the best sellers in Japan.[11] Hence the poverty stricken Korean ghettos are often viewed by many Japanese as a seed-bed of all sorts of social evil, for the crime rate and unemployment is very high in these areas. For instance, according to the 1972 and 1973 reports, the crime rate of the Japanese is only 0.66 while the Korean is 2.98 per 1000.[12] Similarly juvenile delinquency among the Korean youth is said to be much higher than among their Japanese counterparts.

On the other hand, there are a few Koreans who have made fortunes in legitimate business competing with other Japanese industries, such as Shin Nak-ho's Lotte Chewing Gum, Son Wŏn-tal's Shin Nippon Tools and Machinery, and Sŭ Kap-ho's Sakamoto Textile Companies. The annual sales volume of each enterprise is reported to amount to more than $ 100 million with several thousand employees. A number of Koreans have also become extremely successful as singers of popular songs. It might be worth noting, however, that none of them uses their Korean names and they all "pass" as Japanese, at least in the mind of the Japanese if not in the mind of the Koreans. This makes a contrast with several Chinese singers from Taiwan and Hong Kong who are equally popular among the Japanese audience and from the beginning have made it clear that they are Chinese.

II. THE KOREAN COMMUNITY AND INTEREST ARTICULATION

The Korean community in Japan has been split between two major rival organizations ideologically opposed as in their homeland along the 38th parallel. Ch'ongryŏn (The General Federation of Korean Residents in Japan) is a group organized by the supporters of the North Korean regime, while Mindan (The Korean Resident Association in

Japan) supports the South. Each claims to be the sole representative body of all Koreans in Japan and has acted as a most influential pressure group to protect their interest in Japan. Each organization has its own followers and programmes maintaining its own educational system, cooperatives, credit unions and other voluntary associations to articulate their interest.

The presence of the two Koreans has presented a complicated diplomatic dilemma for Japan. The South and the North each insists that it alone represents the legal government of all Korea, hence each claims itself as the sole spokesman for the Koreans in Japan. Consequently, the Koreans' allegiance is divided between the two sovereign entities and the question of nationality for them has become a perplexing legal problem. The Korean community is entangled in the political rivalry between the two antagonistic regimes, vying with each other to secure their allegiance and support. The two Korean organizations, Mindan and Ch'ongryŏn, have clashed with each other, often resorting to violent bloodshed for the hegemony over the Koreans in Japan.

A. *Ch'ongryŏn (The General Federation of Koreans in Japan)*

Ch'ongryŏn is a highly nationalistic organization, supporting the principles and policies of the Democratic Peoples Republic of Korea (DPRK) and exercising little autonomous leadership at the higher levels of the organization. It has a rigid and centralized national apparatus which includes a National Convention, Central Committee and the Central Standing Committee composed of five members. The chairmanship has been held by Han Dŭk-su for the past 20 years since its inception and he is the most powerful figure who commands the Ch'ongryŏn members, estimated to be some 250,000. He is also an elected member of the Supreme People's Congress in DPRK. Therefore, his status as the Chairman of Ch'ongryŏn and a member of the People's Congress qualifies him to serve as head of a quasi-government agency representing the DPRK in Japan, though the two governments maintain no diplomatic relations.

The Ch'ongryŏn is actually heir to the earlier Korean organization called Choryŏn (The Korean Resident League in Japan) which was branded as a terrorist organization by the Japanese Government and was ordered to disband in 1949. When the Choryŏn was founded soon after Japan's surrender in 1945, it purported to be a non-political organization and merely a collective representative body of Koreans in Japan. In the spirit of these ends, the Choryŏn actively co-operated with the Japanese Government to facilitate the orderly repatriation programme for Koreans in Japan. The presence of the Choryŏn was largely credited with and admired for their endeavour to minimize the uneasy ethnic tension between the Japanese and Koreans as well as providing social services to the needy Koreans in Japan. The Choryŏn, however, did not long allow itself to remain merely a community organization. It was soon sucked into the vortex of revolutionary agitation along with the Japanese Communist Party (JCP). Influenced by the idea of world communism and proletarian internationalism, the left-wing Koreans in Japan were led to believe that the only way to secure fundamental rights in Japan would be to assist the JCP in the establishment of a "People's Republic" in Japan. The JCP also echoed the idea of a united front. The Korean communists in Choryŏn were useful supporters of the JCP whose leaders had just been released from many years of imprisonment and badly needed to recruit new party members.[13]

The Choryŏn's call for action had a profound impact upon the majority of the Koreans in Japan, especially those who felt a sense of deprivation and frustration by remaining in the hostile surroundings. The Koreans were ready to get involved with the crusade for the "people's liberation." They had plenty of reasons to protest against the Japanese Government policy which was rarely conciliatory in dealing with Korean problems.

The prevailing attitude among the Koreans at the early period of the American occupation was that they were "liberated nationals," whereas the Japanese were conquered nationals subject to the Allied Powers. The notion of "liberated" nationals was apparently derived from the Joint Chiefs of Staff directive to General MacArthur that Koreans were to be treated as "liberated nationals," if military security was not concerned. But they were treated as "enemy" nationals "in case of necessity," since they had been Japanese subjects.[14] However, a lack of any further clarification as to when the Koreans should be treated as "liberated" or "enemy" nationals seemed to have caused both Koreans and Japanese authority to misconstrue the extent of legal jurisdiction. The Koreans, therefore, believed that they were entitled to different treatment from the defeated Japanese. Such a mistaken notion, coupled with "the struggle for people's liberation" movement, led the Koreans to be outlawed, and tended frequently to entice them to claim prepos-

terous legal rights in Japan. As a result, the anti-Korean sentiment was
openly rekindled by the Japanese mass media and the general public.
The Japanese charges were directed at the black-market activities,
smuggling and illegal re-entry of Koreans into Japan. Similar anti-
Korean sentiment was wide-spread and open clamour against the
Koreans was heard from all quarters and finally reached slanderous
proportions. Surrounded by the hostile cries, it was a logical corollary
that the Koreans should become more receptive to the call for "the
people's liberation."

Whenever major political rallies were held, the Choryŏn members
never failed to participate along with the JCP advocating openly the
overthrow of the Emperor system. The Choryŏn was blacklisted as one
of the most militant organizations which was under constant surveillance by the Japanese law enforcement agency. The ever increasing
violence finally culminated in the Hanshin Riot Incident of 1948,
when the Japanese Government ordered all Korean schools to be closed
in compliance with the newly enacted School Education Law. The
issue was the Japanese Government's intention to control the extent of
the ethnic studies programmes conducted by the Korean schools, and
this the Choryŏn resisted. A series of violent protests sprung up all over
the nation where Koreans were situated; and the prefectural governor
was kidnapped in Kōbe and forced to rescind the school closing order.
Martial law by SCAP authority was proclaimed and the riots subsided after several thousand Koreans were arrested. To combat the
ever increasing left-wing inspired political unrest, the Japanese Government enacted the Organization Control Law in the following year,
the Choryŏn was ordered to disband charged with a terrorist and
undemocratic organization which was prejudicial to the American occupational policy.[15] The dissolution order of the Choryŏn served as a
prelude to the "red purge" which was to follow a few months later
against the JCP leaders.

After the outbreak of the Korean War, the young ex-Choryŏn members organized Sobōi (The Committee for the Defence of the Fatherland), an underground para-military unit to launch guerrilla warfare
against the American military base and munition supply depots. The
Sobōi co-ordinating closely with the JCP's "self-defence unit" planned
to develop a full scale guerrilla force and eventually to become a part
of the Japanese Red Army. Their strategy was to wage a guerrilla type
of war against the American "imperialists" and the Japanese reac-

tionary forces to bring about what they termed a "national liberation democratic revolution."[16]

Multiple factors contributed to the Koreans availing themselves of violent means to attain their goals. Frustrating conditions seem to have motivated a number of Koreans to act out their resentment in aggressive behaviour. Furthermore, their hope for a better life as "liberated nationals" after the defeat of Japan turned out to be a false expectation. This feeling of deprivation was skillfully exploited by some dedicated left-wing Korean leaders and the Japanese Communists. The unavailability for Koreans to channel their demands and unresponsiveness of the Japanese authority were the crucial factors which led them to resort to violence.

The present Ch'ongryŏn is the outcome of the policy change from the revolutionary struggle under the defunct Choryŏn. Some left-wing Korean leaders began not only to feel a sense of weariness regarding its militant posture but to doubt seriously its effectiveness while remaining within the yoke of the JCP. They questioned the legitimacy of its function as a kind of political party to struggle with the JCP which concerned itself solely with capturing political power in Japan. Since the Koreans in Japan were no longer Japanese nationals, they should not be involved with domestic politics in the host country. Instead, they argued that the Koreans as citizens of North Korea, should direct their primary allegiance to the fatherland. Their only political objective should be the attainment of the unification of Korea. The leading proponent of this position was Han Dŭk-su, the present Chairman, who master-minded the formation of Ch'ongryŏn.[17]

The first opportunity to test its organizational strength came with the Korean repatriation movement to North Korea. The Ch'ongryŏn was able to pressure the Japanese Government to open negotiations with the DPRK and the final repatriation agreement was reached in 1955. Throughout the following ten years, almost 100,000 Koreans had been repatriated to the North. Measured by Ch'ongryŏn's ability to persuade Koreans to move out voluntarily to the North, it was a success considering the fact that a majority of them were of South Korean origin. However, their predominant motive to be repatriated to the North seemed not ideological but rather the desire to escape from the misery of life and the hopeless situation in Japan.

Several favourable circumstances prevailed to assist the Ch'ongryŏn's cause. One was the absence of Syngman Rhee's policy concerning the Koreans in Japan, which alienated them and made them

look to the North Korean regime as their saviour. The DPRK's be-
nevolent gesture of remitting funds and expressing their willingness to
accommodate those who felt themselves abandoned by the Rhee regime (1948–1960) were the decisive factors in capturing the loyalty and
allegiance of the Koreans in Japan. Meanwhile the Japanese Government was pleased to find a convenient excuse to repatriate them from
Japan, as the presence of so many Koreans would become a potential
social problem.

The most effective campaign waged by the Ch'ongryŏn in securing
their right to conduct ethnic studies was well exemplified when they
obtained the official accreditation of Chosŭn University from the
Tokyo Prefectural Governor in 1968. Unlike the violence prone era of
the Choryŏn, they employed all conceivable means available within
the legal framework of the Japanese system to sway Japanese public
opinion in their favour. It has been the persistent Japanese official
position that they have always frowned on Ch'ongryŏn's insistence on
their ethnic studies programmes lest a minority culture could be nur-
tured in Japan. It was, therefore, an unprecedented move to establish a
Marxist-Leninist oriented 4-year university course and obtain accreditation to conduct what they termed "democratic ethnic education"
along with the Kim Il Sung thought. The Ch'ongryŏn has established
a total of 161 schools nationwide, ranging from kindergarten to university to conduct ethnic studies and indoctrinate the younger generations in compliance with the North Korean educational policy. It has
also set up elaborate networks in the finance system with 130 credit
unions to encourage ethnic business enterprises of the Ch'ongryŏn
members.[18]

Despite the impressive achievement after some 20 years of existence,
the Ch'ongryŏn seems to have entered a new era, or a transitional
period of great importance. The end of the long years of Han Dŭk-su's
leadership appears to be in sight and struggle for succession has begun.
This was manifested when his heir apparent the First Vice Chairman
Kim Byŏng-sik was purged in 1972.[19] His autocratic and unyielding
personality and his intolerance of any criticism have been the main
cause of the proliferation of dissenters within the Ch'ongryŏn hierachy. Especially the Ch'ongryŏn intellectual members are increasingly
sceptical and cynical about the growing emphasis of the deification of
Kim Il Sung and his *chuch'e* idea (independence and self-reliance)
which demands absolute loyalty and unbending dedication to the
North Korean regime. Some writers, scholars and activists, like Kim

Tal-su, Pak Kyŏng-sik, Kang Je-ŭn and others who had contributed a great deal to the founding of the present organization have left the Ch'ongryŏn. A number of seemingly high ranking members have also defected from the Ch'ongryŏn by criticizing publicly the Han's authoritarian leadership. They organized a separate organization called Chominryŏn (The Federation of Koreans in Japan for the Promotion of Democracy) in January 1975. The organization maintains an underground status and many of the leaders still wish to remain anonymous for the time being. The Ch'ongryŏn denounced the existence of Chominryŏn in public, refusing recognition on the grounds that it was a phantom organization and a plot fabricated by the Korean CIA in Japan to embarrass the Ch'ongryŏn.[20]

In September 1975, Han Dŭk-su was summoned to P'yŏngyang by the DPRK to attend the 30th anniversary of the founding of the North Korean Workers Party. At the banquet, he made a speech admitting some of his errors in leadership, as if implying that there was actual or impending stagnation and degeneration of the Ch'ongryŏn activities in Japan.[21] While he was still in P'yŏngyang, several hundred rank and file members of the Ch'ongryŏn accepted the invitation by the Government of the Republic of Korea to visit South Korea. It amounted to a mass defection from the Ch'ongryŏn organization. When the 4th session of 10th Central Standing Committee meeting of the Ch'ongryŏn was held on November 28, 1975, Han was said to have expressed his firm determination to prevent any further erosion and to set up a new policy to revitalize the organization.

B. *Mindan (The Korean Resident Association in Japan)*

The Mindan was organized soon after the War by those who were expelled by or dissidents against the Choryŏn's radical movement. The major contention raised by the dissidents was that the "democratic revolution" and the "overthrow of the Emperor" system were not the proper concern of Koreans in Japan. Rather they argued that the Choryŏn's emphasis should be on the promotion of Korean welfare. With the emergence of the two ideologically opposed organizations, the Korean community was split. Despite its ambitious launching against the Korean left-wing movement, the Mindan failed to convince the majority of Koreans why they should oppose the Choryŏn, which already had a nationwide organizational structure and was acting as a spokesman for the Koreans in Japan. From its inception, the Mindan's real concern was to enlist help from the Japanese Government to destroy its rival and to capture the hegemony over the Koreans already dominated by the Choryŏn.

The Mindan was a loose conglomeration of various factional groups divided on the basis of personal ties, regional origins and personal motives among the leaders. Constant factional discord and a series of scandals were to follow which seriously impaired the Mindan's activities during the most critical early period. One of the most persistent patterns that existed in the Mindan was that some of the leaders tried to use its organization as a springboard from which to build his political base in the home country. It used to be a customary practice to draft wealthy business men to important positions in the hierachy, as a means of raising funds. However, this policy usually failed to produce the desired results because each businessman, when recruited to a high position, tried to utilize the institutional machinery for his own personal ambition or for his own business enterprise. The Mindan used every conceivable means to raise funds for its expenses. For instance, when the Korean Mission in Japan delegated some of its administrative work to process the registration of the Korean nationals, the Mindan charged exhorbitant registration fees on the pretext that the funds would be used to finance Mindan activities. Subsequently the Mindan lost the confidence of the Koreans and was unable to regain their support for quite some time.

The irreconcilable ideological difference between the two rival organizations as in their homeland has often led to bloodshed and violence over the question of the hegemony of the Korean community in Japan. After the dissolution of the Choryŏn, the Mindan hailed the Japanese Government action in the hope that the demise of the Choryŏn might provide a unique opportunity to take over the leadership of the Korean community. However, the Mindan soon realized that the Japanese Government action was aimed not only at the left-wing Koreans, but was directed against all Korean activities in Japan. This prompted the Mindan and some ex-Choryŏn members to create a Committee for the Common Struggle to counter the forthcoming oppressive measures by the Japanese Government. However, the attempt to create a unified Korean organization has never fully materialized.

The Mindan's effectiveness was further incapacitated by a lack of support from the home government. Syngman Rhee's refusal to extend its protection over the Koreans in Japan was the major factor alienating many and causing them to pledge loyalty to North Korea. Rhee's position was that the Japanese Government must bear the responsibility for the well-being of all Koreans in Japan and pay due compensation to those who were forcibly taken there during the War. Hence, the Rhee regime did not establish any substantive policy to provide any protective measure for the Koreans.[22]

Even when the Normalization Treaty was negotiated with Japan, the Park regime failed to obtain adequate concession from the Japanese Government. The final outcome of the agreement determining the present legal status of the Koreans in Japan was almost entirely the work of the Japanese Government.

The Mindan maintains its own ethnic studies schools but the student enrolment is far less than that of the Ch'onryŏn. It has also its own credit union systems organized nationwide to help promote the small business owned by its members. Since the signing of the Normalization Treaty of 1965, the Park regime has appropriated the "overseas Koreans supplementary fund" to expand pro-South Korean education as well as to strengthen the Mindan organizational structure. However, the Mindan has offered neither cohesive ideological force nor a strong leadership to tie its members together. They have been always responsive to a variety of issues prevailing in South Korea and the members are often split between the anti- and pro- government elements. The split has become widened to a irreparable degree after the Kim Te-chung kidnapping incident in 1973. Since then, the splinter group from the Mindan called Hanmint'ong (The National Congress for the Restoration of Democracy in South Korea and Promotion of Unification) has spearheaded the anti-Park regime movement in Japan.

The assassination of Madam Park provided an opportunity for the Park regime to reassess the importance of the overseas Korean problems, particularly in Japan, as the assassin was a Korean youth who had grown up in Japan with a deep sense of hostility toward the South. The South Korean Government wasted no time in formulating a new policy to strengthen the Mindan organization and stepped up its PR campaign to the entire Korean populace in Japan. The current open invitation to all Ch'ongryŏn members to visit their family and relatives in South Korea is a part of this scheme. The Park regime now believes that winning the mind and soul of the pro-North Koreans in Japan should be considered a sort of victory during the present stage of the South and North Korean confrontation. South Korea has opened the door to all Ch'ongryŏn members to visit South Korea regardless of their past involvement. At the same time, their safe conduct and return to Japan are fully assured without any strings attached. Since the offer was made in the spring of 1975, more than a thousand rank and file members of the Ch'ongryŏn have responded and visited South Korea. Encouraged by the good response, the Mindan has pledged itself to raise a fund of 1 billion yen to subsidize the Ch'ongryŏn members' trip to Korea. The Mindan, for the first time in its existence, has undertaken an offensive position directly challenging the Ch'ongryŏn's hegemony within the Korean community in Japan. Meanwhile, the Mindan has taken a decisive measure by proclaiming "se Mindan" (New Mindan), a campaign to reorganize its structure to meet the new challenge.

III. Pak Chong-sŭk *V*. The Hitachi Company, 1974, and the Question of Ethnic Discrimination

The division between the two antagonistic regimes within the Korean community in Japan is so irreparably wide that a chance to unite as a single cohesive ethnic group is quite remote. The division has also seriously crippled the effectiveness to aggregate their demands as a single viable force to overcome the various discriminatory policies. Each Korean organization as a pressure group is bound to divert its attention to three different fronts. First, each has to mend its fences with the home government. Second, it has to compete with the rival organization. Third, it has to face the Japanese public and policy makers. These elements are so closely interwoven that none could be overlooked in formulating action policy. Such shortcomings of Korean organizations are well exploited by the Japanese Government so as to keep the Korean problem under control. The immediate disenfranchisement of the Koreans in Japan after the War was the most effective means to incapacitate them from becoming politically a potent ethnic group in Japan. By doing so, the Japanese Government used legitimate subterfuge to segregate Koreans in all aspect of life.

Two persistent patterns of the Japanese public in dealing with the Korean minority problems loom large: one is their desire to reduce the number of Koreans in Japan through repatriation and deportation. The other is to compel Koreans to assimilate into the Japanese cultural norms, yet refuse to accept them into the mainstream of society. Japanese society would not tolerate the presence of different ethnic, cultural and linguistic groups in Japan.

The Ch'ongryŏn, on the other hand, has firmly demonstrated its determination to preserve its members' ethnicity, culture and language through the establishment of their own educational system. However, the Mindan members and their children have generally been more amenable to the assimilation with the hope that through acquiescing they might escape discrimination and persecution. It is a widely accepted practice for non-Ch'ongryŏn members to carry two names: one is in Korean as it appears in the "alien registration card"; the other is a Japanese name commonly used in daily social contact in school or in business transactions. The children in such circumstances have often shown eagerness to be accepted by Japanese in order to secure a feeling of attachment and of belonging to a majority.

After sixty five years of subjugation, humiliation and mistreatment of the Koreans there are signs of the beginning of a new trend. Some Japanese have started showing sympathy for the Koreans and fighting with their own prejudice and discrimination. The so-called Hitachi Discrimination Incident is an example.

Pak Chong-Sŭk, plaintiff in this case, was born in Japan of Korean parents who had migrated to Japan in 1929. Until he finished high school, Pak used a Japanese name, Arai Shōji. He neither speaks nor reads a word of Korean. After his graduation from high school, he was briefly employed by a Japanese factory as a helper. In 1970, he answered the recruitment advertisement of the Hitachi Company and applied for a job. Then, he successfully passed the examination with above average marks and received an official notice of hiring. As is customary in Japan in order to complete his personal file, the Hitachi Company asked him to submit a certificate of *koseki* (family registration). It was then that the Company learned of his Korean nationality. When Pak initially filed his application, he had used his Japanese name and put down his place of birth in Japan as he intended to disguise his nationality, because he thought, the Hitachi would not accept an application from a Korean. Legally he should have used his Korean name as it appears on his "alien registration card" and instead of his place of birth in Japan he should have entered the address in Korea of his *koseki* (family registration). A few days later Pak received a letter of rejection from the Hitachi Company on the grounds that he deliberately intended to dece've them by using a Japanese name and providing false information in respect of the location of the family registry. The Hitachi Company deemed that Pak had committed perjury.

Pak insisted that the perjury charge was merely an excuse for the company's discriminatory hiring policy. He decided to file a civil suit against the Hitachi Company, demanding: (1) re-affirmation of his right to the labour contract; (2) payment of his back wages beginning from the date he was due to start working; (3) monetary compensation of $500,000 for the mental discomfort he had suffered through the discriminatory policy.

When he decided to file the suit, his only desire was to be reinstated by the company. He never intended to press the issue of discrimination in the way that the case developed. A few thoughtful young people began to gather around Pak in support of his lonely battle against one of the biggest businesses in Japan. In 1971, five Japanese and two Koreans became the founding members of a group called A Committee to Support Pak Chong-sŭk. When the trial ended after three years, the Committee had recruited more than 400 determined members. It was this group that played a key role in mobilizing public opinion to influence the final outcome of the judicial decision. They stood in picket lines; formally protested against the Hitachi Company; published a newsletter to disseminate up-to-date information on the progress of the case; raised funds for the legal defence; appealed to world public opinion by sending out letters to practially every known human rights commission in the world; opened a public forum to discuss the issues; and finally waged an extensive boycott campaign against all the Hitachi products. What the Hitachi feared most was this boycott which had already begun to spread in Korea. Hitachi was also extremely concerned with its own image abroad, especially in South-east Asia where they had substantial investments in Thailand, Indonesia and Philippines.

While the trial was still in progress, Hitachi privately made an offer to settle the dispute out of court. They agreed to reinstate the plaintiff with all the back wages plus the monetary compensation for which he had asked. However, Pak rejected the offer, arguing that the Company had failed to make an apology or acknowledgement in public of the discriminatory hiring practice used against Koreans.

Finally the matter was settled in court in June 1974. The decision was rendered by Ishifuji Ratō against the defendant. The judge read the decision, stating that "the court finds no apparent reason, other than the factor of the ethnic discrimination, when the defendant rescinded the contract to hire the plaintiff in the case." As to the usage of the Japanese name by the plaintiff, there was neither malignant motive nor was any harm inflicted upon the contending party. Rather, "the court's sympathy rests with the motive of the plaintiff," because it was Japanese society that compelled him to act in the way he did to escape somehow from the discrimination against Koreans. "The official is-suance of the hiring notice specifying the amount of salary and the date to report for work," said the judge, "constituted a consummation of the labour contract between the two parties." Therefore, the cancellation to hire the plaintiff should be construed as an arbitrary breach of the labour contract which was a violation of Article 3 of the Labour Standard Act and Article 90 of the Civil Code of Japan.[23]

This was a landmark decision in the postwar Japanese judicial system as it was a legal admission of the existence of discrimination against Koreans in Japan. A judicial decision of this nature has long been overdue. Not only should the case be considered a victory for the Koreans in Japan but also for the future democracy of Japan. It has set a cornerstone for the development of the civil rights movement in the decade ahead. The legal precedent has now been established to add a new judicial interpretation to the clause, "all people ..." in the Japanese Constitution. The meaning of "all people ..." is referring literally to all people who establish legal residence in Japan, who are equally entitled to the privilege of civil rights. Such entitlement is not reserved for Japanese citizens only.

Unfortunately, the two major Korean organizations, Ch'ongryŏn and Mindan, neither involved themselves officially with the campaign, nor did they make any significant contribution to help win the legal battle. The two Korean organizations viewed the Hitachi case from a different perspective which led eventually to the "benign neglect" by avoiding any involvement. Regarding Pak's intent to disguise himself as Japanese, they had questioned his moral integrity and judgement to negate his own ethnic identity which could mean the denial of the presence of his own ethnic group in Japan. This was considered to be disgraceful conduct regardless of whatever principle he was fighting for. It was inconceivable for the Korean organizations to render official support and endorsement to this man who was devoid of ethnic pride and national consciousness for which all Koreans in Japan stood.[24]

Instead, the bulk of support came from the Japanese, who were dedicated young activists, lawyers, students and scholars led by Satō Katsumi. Most of the Koreans were young second generation centred around a Korean Christian Church in Kawazaki city. This group was able to brief the best civil libertarian, Nakadaira Kenkichi who gave up his judgeship in order to take up this case and conduct it through to victory. The impact of this landmark decision has been profound. It appears that a long overdue civil rights movement in Japan is gradually gaining momentum.

It is conceivable that the Hitachi Incidence will serve as a precedent for the Korean individuals who choose to fight legally against social discrimination. It would be too optimistic, however, to hope that the campaign for the fundamental human rights of the mass of Koreans in Japan will yield a successful result in the near future. There are several factors that seriously work against such a hope. First of all, bitter antagonism between the Ch'ongryŏn and the Mindan badly interfere with the solidarity among the Koreans and prevent them from uniting their efforts in fighting against social injustice. Difficulties for the Japanese Government in dealing diplomatically with the "two Koreas" make the Ch'ongryŏn-Mindan rivalries a highly sensitive issue and complicate the Government policy toward the Koreans residing in Japan. Secondly, no possibility is visible on the horizon for the Koreans joining forces with other minority groups in Japan and fighting co-operatively against discrimination and prejudice. The political leadership among the three million Burakumin is badly split between the Socialists and Communists as described in the Wagatsuma article in this volume. Furthermore, the Burakumin, themselves victims of social discrimination, are generally prejudiced against the Koreans and indicate negative attitudes toward them. The Chinese prefer to be rather quiet and the Ainu are too few in number to be an influential group, although all these people suffer either mild or harsh prejudice and discrimination in Japanese society.

As mentioned elsewhere, the Japanese are a highly homogeneous nation living in a basically "closed" society. In a strict sense of the term, no one is allowed to "become" a Japanese, as they rigidly uphold the principle of *jus sanguinus*. If one is not related to the Japanese lineage by blood, no individual is "accepted" as a true Japanese, even a person who was born in Japan, speaking, thinking and acting like any Japanese. Japanese in general reject anyone who is not Japanese. This "non-acceptance" not only takes the form of social prejudice and discrimination but also creates serious identity problems for those who are born and raised in Japan, and yet cannot be defined as fully Japanese. Consequently, Korean youth in Japan suffer not only from the ideological conflicts between the two-Koreas and two rival organizations, but also from a painful dilemma regarding their self-identity.

NOTES

1. For further details, see the most authoritative studies on the Korean labourers in Japan, Iwamura Toshio, *Zainichi Chōsenjin to Nihon rōdōsha kaikyū* (A Study of Koreans in Japan and Japanese Labour Class), (Tokyo: Kyōkura shobō, 1972). Pak Kyŏng-sik, *Chōsenjin kyōsei renkō no kiroku* (The Record of the Forcibly Conscripted Koreans), (Tokyo: Miraisha, 1975).

2. William J. Gane, *Repatriation: from 25 December 1945 to 31 December 1945* (Seoul: United States Military Government in Korea, 1947), p. 14.

3. Chang Tu-sik, "Kikoku to han-Nihonjin" (The Repatriation and the Half-Japanese), *Sekai*, (October, 1959), pp. 198–199. It is important to note that the Japanese Nationality Law does not recognize the principle of jus soli as a requisite for legal acquisition of citizenship.

4. There are several ways of calling this organization. Some Japanese writers abbreviate it as Chōsoren or Chōsensoren. Other Koreans call it as Choch' ongnyŏn or Chosŭn Ch'ongnyŏn. As it is a proper noun, the author follows the way the General Federation of Korean Residents in Japan wishes to be called and abbreviates it.

5. *Tōyō Keizai Nippō*, January 17, 1975.

6. Wagatsuma Hiroshi and Yoneyama Toshinao, *Henken no kōzō: Nihonjin jinshu kan* (The Prejudice Formation: The Japanese View on Race), (Tokyo: Nihon hōsō shuppan kyōkai, 1973). And Hugh H. Smythe, "A Note on Racialism in Japan," *American Sociological Review*, Vol. XVI, No. 6, (1951), pp. 823–825.

7. However, the traditional theory and origin of their culture has currently been challenged by many archeologists as a result of the excavation of the Takamatsu-zuka tomb. See, Kim Tal-su, *et al.*, "Nihon bunka to Chōsen bunka" (Japanese and Korean Civilizations), *Keizai Hyōron*, (Autumn, 1972), pp. 16–30. And Kim Chŏng-chu, "Kodai bunka no Kannichi kōryū" (The Ancient Cultural Intercourse Between Korea and Japan), *ibid.*, pp. 31–37.

8. For further details, see William Wetherall and George A. DeVos, "Ethnic Minorities in Japan," Willem A. Veenhoven, ed., *Case Studies on Human Rights and Fundamental Freedoms: A World Survey*, Vol, II, (Hague, Netherlands: Martinus Nijhoff, 1975), pp. 333–375.

9. Hatada Takashi, *Nihonjin no Chōsenjin kan* (Japanese Views on Koreans), (Tokyo: Keiso shobō, 1969), pp. 72–73, 79–80.

10. Chŏn Chun, "Ilbon kyokwasŭ e nat'anan Han'guk kwan" (The Japanese Views on Koreans Reflected on the School Text Books), *Sasangge*, No. 5, (May, 1965), pp. 167–173. And Endō Toyokichi, "Kyōkasho no nakani yugamerareta Chōsen zō" (The Distorted Image of the Koreans Reflected in the School Text Books), *Atarashii Sedai*, (March, April, 1975), pp. 30–33.

11. Iiboshi Kōichi, *Yamaguchikumi sandaime*, Vol. I, II, (Tokyo: Tokuma shoten, 1970). As of 1974, the publisher printed 28th edition of these books, as they were the best sellers.

12. The 1972 figure is from the Prime Minister's Office, Statistics Bureau, *Japan's Statistics*, and the Japanese Supreme Court, *Annual Report of Judicial Statistics*. And also see, Takahasi Masami, "Haisengo no Nihon ni okeru Chōsenjin no hanzai" (The Crimes Committed by Koreans in Japan after the Surrender), *Keihō Zasshi*, Vol. I, No. 2, (1950), pp. 119–144.

13. Changsoo Lee, "Chōsōren: An Analysis of the Korean Communist Movement in Japan," *Journal of Korean Affairs*, (July, 1973). Nakanishi Inosuke, "Nihon tennōsei no datō to tōyō minzoku no minshu dōmei: Chōsenjin Renmei he no

yōsei" (The Overthrow of the Emperor System and A Democratic League for Asian Races: An Appeal to the Choryŏn), *Minshu Chōsen*, No. 7, (July, 1946).

14. "Basic Initial Post-Surrender Directive to Supreme Commander for the Occupation and Control of Japan," J.C.S. 1380/8, November 3, 1945, Report of Government Section, Supreme Commander for the Allied Powers, *Political Reorientation of Japan, September, 1945, to September, 1948*, Vol. II, (Grosse Pointe, Mich: Scholarly Press, 1968), p. 432.

15. Lee, *op. cit.*, pp. 11–13.

16. Hōmu Kenshūsho (The Research Institute of Legal Affairs in the Ministry of Justice), *Zainichi hokusenkei senjin dantai shiryōshū* (The Collected Data concerning the Pro-North Korean Organizations in Japan), Special Report No. 16, (Tokyo: Ministry of Justice, 1952), pp. 404–456.

17. Han Dŭk-su, *Zainichi Chōsenjin undō no tenkan ni tsuite*, (Concerning a Change of the Direction of the Korean Movement in Japan), (Tokyo: Gakuyū shobō, 1955). His thesis concerning the Korean movement in Japan was already published in 1952 under a pseudonym, Paek Su-bong, *Aekuk chinyŏng ŭi sunwha wa kangwha lŭl wihayŏ* (n.p. 1952).

18. "Zainihon Chōsenjin Sōrengōkai ni tsuite kiku" (Listening to What Ch'ongryŏn is About), *Atarashii Sedai*, (May, 1975), pp. 6–18.

19. Tōitsu Chōsen Shinbun Tokushūhan, Ed., *Kim Byŏng-sik jiken* (The Kim Byŏng-sik Incident), (Tokyo: Tōitsu Chōsen Shinbun, 1973).

20. *Korean Central News*, November 24, and December 12, 1975.

21. *Tōitsu Nippō*, September 30, and October 1, 1975, and *Korean Central News*, October 2, and October 6, 1975.

22. Some 100,000 Koreans repatriated to North Korea from Japan should be understood within the frame of the absence of Rhee's policy. It was partly this reason that the Mindan officially denounced the Rhee regime and declared a vote of no confidence in the home government. On this point, see Cŏng Chŭl, *Mindan* (Tokyo: Yōyōsha, 1967), pp. 56–57, and 198.

23. For the detailed accounts, see The Committee to Support Pak, ed., *Minzoku sabetsu* (The Ethnic Discrimination), (Tokyo: Akishobō, 1974).

24. Author's conversation with the officials of the two Korean organizations during his visit to Japan, July, 1975.

Uganda: The Expulsion of the Asians

CHARLES HARRISON

CHARLES HARRISON was born in Manchester, England. Educated in Manchester, he entered the field of journalism there briefly before the Second World War, returning to journalism in Manchester after serving in the Royal Navy for six years during and after the Second World War. In 1953 he moved to East Africa, and after representing the Nairobi newspaper, East African Standard, in Uganda, he helped to found the Uganda Argus, Uganda's first modern newspaper, in 1955. Serving with the Uganda Argus for 15 years, he resigned from the post of editor in 1970 to run his own business in Kampala, as a public relations consultant and free-lance journalist. He remained in Uganda until August 1973, and is now a resident of Nairobi, Kenya. He has broadcasted frequently for the BBC, and has contributed articles to a wide range of publications.

Uganda: The Expulsion of the Asians

CHARLES HARRISON

Uganda has become widely known throughout the world because of an exercise in discrimination which was applied to its inhabitants of Asian origin in August 1972, when President Amin, who had come to power in a military coup in January 1971, ordered that all people of Indian, Pakistani or Bangladesh origin, and who were not citizens of Uganda, must leave the country within 90 days.

If President Amin's original order had constituted the totality of the anti-Asian operation, it would have been serious enough, because it singled out a particular group of people, for no other reason than their racial origins, for expulsion from Uganda within a space of time which was bound to cause hardships. But in fact there were a large number of additional factors, some of which appeared only incidentally and in the course of a very brief space of time, which increased the discriminatory aspect of the entire affair. It also became clear that a principal element in the affair was that it was designed to deprive the Ugandan Asian Community of most of its very considerable material possessions, without any clear plan of who precisely was to benefit from the appropriation of assets which ranged from personal effects and cash to motor cars, houses, businesses and other property.

I. Historical Background

To consider the situation applying in Uganda since 1972, it is necessary to take into account the earlier history of discrimination in that country. Although there was nothing in Uganda on the scale of the 1972 operation, discrimination had existed in different forms throughout the country's modern history. Uganda's modern history, however, extends over a comparatively short period, as it was only in 1882 that the first white explorers, John Hanning Speke and James Grant, reached Uganda. There was then a gap before non-Africans came to be established in Uganda, but by the time that British influence was established there in 1890, English Protestant missionaries and French Roman Catholic missionaries had started operating.

There is no clear information about the first Asians to reach Uganda, but Asian traders were well established on the East African coast long before they appeared in Uganda. One of the first historical references to Asians in Uganda dates from 1897, when 30 Sikhs were recruited in India to form a military transport service for the British administration in Uganda.[1] And later in the same year, 150 men of the East African Indian forces, who had been stationed in what is now Kenya, were sent to Uganda to contain a critical situation arising from the mutiny of Sudanese troops there.[2]

Very shortly afterwards, there is a record of the pioneer Indian trader, Alidina Visram – who had arrived in Zanzibar in 1877 – establishing a branch of his firm in Kampala in 1898. By 1902, the British Commissioner, Frederick Jackson, was noting the important role being played in the development of the economy of Uganda by Alidina Visram, since there were no banks in the country. Jackson wrote: "Our present difficulty lies in the circulation of specie, but I am doing all I can to induce the people, through their chiefs, to cultivate sugar cane and simsim (sesame). An Indian trader named Alidina Visram is already prepared to buy up as much as the natives like to cultivate of each ... and this should materially assist in the circulation of specie rupees, and pice if the people can only be induced to cultivate."[3]

A. *The "Railway Coolie" Legend*

There is no historical basis for the claim which has often been made, and which was repeated by President Amin in 1972, that the Asian community in Uganda grew up under British rule from the coolies who were brought from India to build the Uganda Railway around 1890. Although it was called the Uganda Railway, it did not reach the present-day Uganda until much later, and the original railway, for which many Indian labourers and skilled tradesmen were used, was built entirely in what is now Kenya.

From the first, Asians went to Uganda as traders. Alidina Visram was not typical of the others, as he was a man of great resources. Most of the Indians who subsequently arrived as traders were in business in a small way, although some did develop into bigger things, laying the foundation for most of Uganda's commerce and industry, and particularly of the cotton industry which was the mainstay of the Uganda economy from the early days of the 20th century. The Indians did not themselves grow the cotton – this was restricted to Ugandan Africans, since Britain's policy was that land in Uganda should not be made available to non-Africans for agricultural purposes – but they bought it from the African growers, processed it in ginneries, and exported it, mainly to India.[4]

The restriction of non-African land holdings was a discriminatory policy, but it was justified by the British Government as necessary to protect the indigenous people of the country.

B. *The Post-War Period*

By 1948, there were 35,000 Asians in Uganda, of whom 5,065 were engaged in commerce (including wholesale and retail trade), 2,875 in manufacturing industry, 716 in public service, 452 in transport and communications, 330 in building and construction, and 221 in agriculture.[5]

By 1963, the year after Uganda achieved independence, the Asian population had reached 82,100.[6] The big increase in the Asian population between 1948 and 1963 was partly a result of a high birth-rate, but also partly due to the entry of more Asians, usually from Kenya or from India, to work in commerce and industry, which expanded significantly over this period.

The total population of Uganda expanded considerably over the same period. The 1948 census showed a total population of 4,958,520 (of whom 35,000 were Asians); the 1959 census showed a total population of 6,536,531, and the 1969 census showed a total of 9,548,847, which included 74,308 Asians and 9,533 Europeans.[7]

Under British rule, which ended with independence in 1962, Asians were not at first discouraged from entering Uganda or from making a living there. In fact, the British administration welcomed the Asian efforts to develop the economy of Uganda. However, from 1948 onwards increasingly strict controls were placed on immigration, with the aim of preventing the entry of non-Africans who might compete with the indigenous Africans of Uganda. The immigration laws were strict, and no Asian or European was permitted to enter Uganda to take up a job which could be filled by a Ugandan African – and this was later made even stricter by a requirement that the authorities had to be satisfied that it would be in the interests of the African people for a non-African to be allowed to enter the country.

In effect, this law recognised the need to preserve the African nature of Uganda, but it also recognised the need for people with special skills to live and work in Uganda.

II. Early Signs of Discrimination

There was, then, a strong element of discrimination, particularly against Asians. Equally, there was discrimination against both Asians and Europeans during British rule, since non-Africans in Uganda were subject to income tax, while Africans were exempt from this tax until 1962. On the other side, discrimination was practised against Ugandan Africans until the 1950's, in that they were not permitted to buy non-African liquor – such as whisky and gin – while non-Africans were permitted to do so. This was a result of the Congo Basin Treaty – the Berlin Act of 1885, and the Convention of St. Germain en Laye of 1919 – which required the colonial powers in the Congo Basin area to exercise paternal powers to protect the African people of these countries.

Frequent allegations have been made that the Asians in Uganda had only one aim, to make as much money as possible. And since the majority of the population was African, it was from their trade with the African population that the Asians made most of their profits. To some extent, this allegation is justified, but the profit motive was and is an essential part of all trade, and without it, there would have been no economic development in Uganda.

A. Social Exclusiveness

The Asians' social habits are also cited as reasons why resentment has developed against them from the African people of Uganda. Their exclusive attitudes were certainly resented.

An Asian study of this question produced the conclusion:

In part, the isolation of the Indian community was the product of its rigid communal and caste traditions. While the caste system as such could not operate in East Africa, the social mobility of the individual, and frequently his choice of employment, continued to be influenced by considerations of caste and creed. This was true, for example, of much of Indian commercial enterprise in East Africa where the traditional trading groups – Bhattias, Khojas, Lohanas, Bohras and Vanias – continued to play the dominant role ....

The general compartmentalization of the Indian community into religious, communal, sectional and caste groups largely reinforced, rather than created, their isolation in East Africa. For this, in essence, was the product of the 'historical process' in East Africa, which has tended to be one of communities for the most part living separately, and not one of partnership in development.

In the circumstances, while the social and economic progress of the community underlined its racial and cultural distinctiveness, the limitation of their role, on account of restrictions, to the urban areas and to middle-grade employment – especially as shopkeepers and traders – exposed the Indians to continuing criticism for exclusiveness and economic 'exploitation'.

The position of the Indian settlement in East Africa, as it had emerged by the end of this period (1945) presented in fact a marked parallel to that of Jewish communities elsewhere – for, like them, the Indians, though constantly under scrutiny, had played a crucial role in the general process of development.[8]

III. Citizenship

With the approach of independence for Uganda in 1962, the big question affecting many of the Asians was that of citizenship. Most of the Asians were British subjects, having chosen British, rather than Indian, citizenship when India became independent after the Second World War. But a significant proportion of the total automatically became Ugandan citizens under Uganda's independence constitution, because they were born in Uganda, and at least one of their parents had also been born there. As a result of British insistence (although it was accepted with some reluctance by Uganda's African political leaders), the independence constitution also provided that any non-African born in Uganda, or who had become a naturalised British subject while in that country, could acquire Ugandan citizenship by applying for it within two years of independence.[9] Probably no less than 20,000 Asians in Uganda made this choice, and applied for Ugandan citizenship, and under the terms of the country's constitution they should have received that citizenship automatically.

It was soon obvious, however, that even a constitutional safeguard of this nature was no guarantee of the preservation of the rights of a minority group in an African-ruled state, as Uganda became on October 9, 1962. A large number, certainly many thousands, of the Asians who applied under this provision for Ugandan citizenship, and who should have received it automatically, did not receive it, as their applications were simply not processed. This was naturally interpreted as a conscious decision by the Uganda Government, which was headed by Milton Obote, the leader of the majority party, the Uganda People's Congress.

It can also be assumed that such a decision was taken simply because the African leaders in Uganda were not ready to accept the continued existence of an Asian minority of that size, although it was not until several years later, after the 1971 military coup, that this issue was taken a great deal further by the introduction of measures to remove the Asians from Uganda.

A. *Civil Service Recruitment*

A further measure of discrimination against the Asians in Uganda at this period was to deny them recruitment or promotion in Government posts, even when they were Ugandan citizens. To some extent this was a conscious policy to avoid having a civil service in which Asians were present in a bigger proportion than they represented in the country's population. If there had been no such discrimination, Asians, having more highly qualified people, would certainly have filled a great many senior posts in the Government and in Government-owned organisations, such as the Uganda Electricity Board.

Whatever the political justification for this policy (and there was obviously a strong case for ensuring that a minority group did not dominate the scene), it was nevertheless a case of conscious discrimination.

The next assault on the Asians in Uganda occurred in 1968, when the Obote Government cancelled the Uganda citizenship of several thousand Asians who had obtained it. The reason given was that a check of citizenship documents had shown that many Asians had not formally renounced their previous (British) citizenship within 90 days of the approval of their applications for Uganda citizenship. This was technically correct, in that because of the large number of cases, there were delays on the part of the British authorities in completing the formal registration of such renunciations, with the result that the 90-day period was exceeded. However, this was not the fault of the Asians concerned, and their applications had been officially accepted as valid in the first place.

By deciding to apply this rule strictly, several years afterwards, a large number of Asian residents of Uganda were declared not to be Ugandan citizens. Even the Speaker of Parliament, and other Asians who were Members of Parliament, were affected in this way.

The British Government undertook a period of patient negotiation with Uganda on this matter, and President Obote finally agreed to restore the Ugandan citizenship of these Asians at the end of 1970. But he was ousted in the military coup in January 1971, and the military regime of President Amin soon showed that it had no wish to make life easy for the Asians in Uganda.

In fact, very shortly after taking power in January 1971, President Amin showed a hatred of Asians in General. It is not clear whether this was due to any particular set of circumstances – most probably it was not, but was a reflection of the reaction of a large number of Ugandans who resented the Asians for their commercial success and business acumen, and for their social exclusivity. To this extent, the troubles encountered by the Asians in Uganda in 1972 can be regarded as a result of the transfer of power to an individual who was not subject to the sanctions against the arbitrary use of power which had existed, to some extent at least, with his predecessors.

The situation of the Asians in Uganda had changed first when the country became independent in 1962, when Britain ceased to have power over Uganda. While Britain was in power, the Asians had a strong safeguard in the British Parliamentary system, since the British Government itself was fully aware of the power of that system, which allowed allegations of discrimination to be aired at the highest level in Britain. The existence of such power certainly acted as a check on the British-controlled Government of Uganda, particularly in respect of any policies which could be considered to be discriminatory.

After independence in 1962, the British sanction disappeared, but Uganda had its own Parliament, and although the ruling party, the Uganda People's Congress, was in a strong majority there, there were opposition members, and questions of discrimination could still be raised. This sanction was respected more in the early days of Uganda's existence as an independent state, when there was an understandable anxiety to establish a favourable reputation in the world, than it was in subsequent years – and in fact the denial of citizenship rights to Asians was not raised in Parliament with any effect.

IV. Military Regime Assumes Arbitrary Powers

But with the military coup in January 1971, Parliament was abolished, and all power, in effect, was placed in the hands of President Amin himself,[10] who had spent his entire adult life in the army, and who was quick to declare that he was not a politician and that he had no political ambitions. Clearly, the absence of a Parliamentary sanction made it possible to introduce forms of discrimination which had not appeared before 1971.

There was no longer any provision for the questioning of decisions taken by the President – even when, as in the case of his decision to expel the Asians, it was taken as a result of a dream.

It is significant that the first statement made on behalf of the Uganda Army on January 25, 1971 – the day of the coup – listed 18 reasons for the coup, but made no mention of the word "discrimination," nor of any matters concerning Asians or other non-Africans living in Uganda.[11]

V. A Catalogue of "Grievances"

By the end of 1971, President Amin had revealed his own feelings about the Asians in Uganda, and had shown his resentment of their presence. On December 6, 1971, President Amin summoned a meeting of leaders of the Asian community, a meeting which was presented as a means of exchanging ideas with the Asians on their role in Uganda. But no effective notice was taken of the declarations made by the Asians, declaring their loyalty to the country and their anxiety to play an appropriate role in its affairs. Instead, President Amin delivered a speech which had been prepared before the meeting. He said:

This particular Conference has been convened as a follow-up of the many public statements and letters in the press complaining against the Asian community in this country. At this Conference you as representatives of Asian groups throughout Uganda can brief the Government about the different aspects which have made Africans in this country complain against the Asians.

My aim is to ensure that like a father in a family, understanding and unity between the different communities in this country is established on a permanent basis.

I am sure that, having received your views as expressed through this conference, and the memoranda which you produced to the Chairman, Hon. A. C. K. Oboth-Ofumbi, the Minister of Defence, whom I directed to chair your Conference, and having listened to what I am going to tell you this afternoon, I hope the wide gap between the Asians and the Africans in the different economic and social fields will narrow down, if not disappear altogether, so that all of us, whether citizens or non-citizens, African or non-African, can live a happier life in the Republic of Uganda.

No one doubts the various positive contributions which you Asians have made since the arrival of your forefathers in East Africa as railway builders. Some of the Ugandan Asians even received Government assistance to undertake different types of courses, including post-graduate training in medicine, engineering, law and other professional fields. Whereas some of these people after completing their training joined Government, and have done a good job, I regret to point out to you that many of them have shown total disloyalty to the same Government which financed their training and enabled them to use other training facilities.

For instance, between 1962 to 1968, the Government of Uganda sponsored as many as 417 Asians for training as engineers. To date, however, only 20 of the 417 Asians work for the Government. Within the same period, Government sponsored 217 Asians to train as doctors, but to date not more than 15 doctors of these are working for the Government.

Finally, within that same period, Government sponsored 96 Asians to undertake law courses, but of these only 18 are now serving in the Government.

You can ask yourselves the question as to where the majority of the Asians trained by the Uganda Government have disappeared. My information is that many of them either took up private practice immediately after their training or joined the Government but resigned to go into private practice. In view of the fact that it is extremely expensive to sponsor a student to undertake a professional course at graduate level, I consider that these Asians who deliberately refused to return to serve the Government, or who did so briefly and then left, have cheated this nation.

I am further informed that some of these Asians who were sponsored to take courses abroad refused to return to Uganda after they qualified, which means that they have contributed absolutely nothing in return for the training benefits which they have received from this Government. Moreover, I am told that some of them who resigned from Government service did so on very selfish grounds, such as working in Government on condition that they would not be transferred away from either Entebbe, Kampala, Mbale or Jinja to up-country stations.

Although some of them gave the excuse that they would not agree to be transferred up-country because of lack of schools, housing, appropriate medical facilities etc., yet we know fully well that in most cases their refusal was due to the fact that a good number of them have side businesses outside the Civil Service, such as shops, garages, transport businesses etc., from which they get extra huge sums of money, and which therefore they dislike to leave behind while they go on up-country transfer.

My government deplores this attitude and I wish to direct all the Ministries in which Asians are employed at any level to report to me from now on any Asian who refuses to go on up-country transfer for any reason at all.

I am particularly disturbed in this matter because according to reports which the Minister of Health has given me, some of the Asians who refused to be transferred to hospitals such as Gulu, Apach, Aturtur, Iganga, Soroti and even Butabika Mental Hospital, and who in some cases resigned in protest against those transfers include some consultants on whom the Government obviously heavily relies for the improvement of the medical services to residents of Uganda at large. This is but one of the many disturbing aspects of your community.

Having made the above point on the general disloyalty of some members of your community to the Government, I now wish to turn to probably the most painful matter around which public statements and correspondence in the press have centred. That is the question of your refusal to integrate with the Africans in this country.

It is particularly painful in that about 70 years have elapsed since the first Asians came to Uganda, but despite that length of time the Asian community has continued to live in a world of its own; for example, African males have hardly been able to marry Asian girls. For example, a casual count of African males who are married to Asian females reveals that there are only six. And even then, all the six married these women when they were abroad, and not here in Uganda.

In the cases where there have been moves by Asian girls to love Africans, it has been done in absolute secrecy. I as well as you yourselves certainly know that these girls are under their parents' strict instructions never to fall in love with Africans.

On the other hand, it is interesting to note that many Asian men in this country are loving and living with African girls without favourable pressure from the parents of those girls. This is the sort of attitude which I would welcome because it points the way to integration between Africans and Asians. Asian parents should leave their sons and daughters free to integrate with Africans, instead of imposing against them social restrictions that are completely out of date.

Although I am aware that this lack of integration between the Africans and the Asians is due to the extension of the Asian caste system and ways of life generally, the Government of the Republic of Uganda is of the firm view that if there is goodwill on the part of the Asian communities it is possible for you to reach an understanding whereby integration among all the people in this country would be easy. I am therefore appealing to you here as the representatives of all the Asian communities in Uganda to consider this point seriously in the interest of integration between you and the Africans at all levels. I am saying this because I know that if we do not integrate in this country the situation which would be built up could easily lead to serious racial disharmony.

I am aware that one of the causes of the continuing distant social relations between the Asians and the Africans in this country was the policy of the colonial Government which ensured that the Africans, Asians and Europeans had entirely separate schools, hospitals, residential quarters, social and sports clubs and even public toilets – with the facilities to serve the Africans being of the poorest quality and hopelessly inadequate. We have, of course, now changed all this, but there are Asians who still live in the past and consider, like the former colonialist Government, that the Africans are below them. This living in the past cannot help Asians in any way, nor can it foster the desired harmony and unity.

One sector which greatly disturbs my Government are the numerous malpractices which many of your community members are engaged in. We are, for instance, aware of the fact that some Asians are the most notorious people in the abuse of our exchange control regulations. Some of you are known to export goods and not to bring the foreign exchange back into Uganda. On the other hand some of you are known to undervalue exports and overvalue imports in order to keep the difference in values in your overseas accounts. Another malpractice for which many of you are notorious is that of smuggling commodities like sugar, maize, hoes etc. from Uganda to the neighbouring territories.

This has on many occasions created an artificial shortage of those commodities within Uganda, with the result that whatever was left here at home was finally sold at unduly high prices.

You are all aware of the recent importation of sugar from India. In this particular case, Government was told that the shortage of sugar within the country was due to the drought which had hit sugar production at Kakira and Lugazi. What we know, however, is that the sugar shortage which we suffered was mainly due to the fact that a number of Asian business men had smuggled sugar into the neighbouring countries.

Another bad practice which many Asian businessmen practice is the hoarding of goods in order to create an artificial shortage, again resulting in higher prices for these goods. A typical example is the recent court case in which Hussein Shariff Velji Mawji was convicted for hoarding oil and selling it at black market above the Government controlled price.

These malpractices show clearly that some members of your community have no interest in this country beyond the aim of making as much profit as possible and at all costs. As I have already said on other occasions, my Government will not tolerate those malpractices and will take all necessary measures to stamp them out. If any businessman is found smuggling or hoarding goods in this country, such businessman should not expect any mercy and he will permanently lose his trading licence whether he is a citizen of this country or not.

My government also feels strongly about the practice of some of your traders in deliberately sabotaging Government policy by, for instance, renting to African traders only the front room in the shops in controlled areas, while retaining the back rooms, toilet and the cooking facilities.

Your community made use of the policy of establishing their own commercial and trading organisations which played a big part in the economic life of the nation. Here I am thinking of thousands of shops which the Asians built all over Uganda to deal in a wide variety of goods. I am further thinking of big industrial concerns and farming activities which, for example, have all along been spearheaded by such outstanding families as the Madhvanis, Mehtas, etc. All these activities have assisted employment opportunities without which some people might have been forced to take up criminal activities.

Besides your contribution to the commercial and industrial life I must also mention the part some of you have played in the expansion of educational and medical facilities in Uganda.

I should also like here to pay tribute to some of your members who have served and are serving in the different fields in the Government. There is no doubt, therefore, that the work of some of your people as judges of the High Court, Magistrates, doctors, engineers, teachers, accountants, etc., has been vital in the development of the country.

But, and this is a big but, there are several disturbing matters which I now want to point out to you frankly as, indeed, this is the purpose of this Conference. Firstly, I want to say that it is a well-known fact that the Uganda Government has made available facilities for the training of Ugandans as well as non-Ugandan Asians in the local and overseas educational institutions.

Some Asians have deliberately locked up their premises in areas which have been declared restricted areas, and have refused to rent them to African businessmen. It is also common knowledge that some of you who decided to rent their premises to the African traders did so at inflated rates.

I must remind you that any Government worth its name cannot sit back and allow a minority group of any kind deliberately to work against the policies of that Government, which are aimed at the overall national development of that country. I therefore intend to instruct the Ministry of Commerce, Industry and Tourism to double its efforts in tracking down such offending Asian traders in order to completely wipe out these malpractices that are aimed at defeating government policy.

Another malpractice I may mention is that of under-cutting African traders, and unfair competition. It is well known that you are generally importers, wholesalers and retailers at the same time. Many of you have taken advantage of this position to frustrate aspiring African businessmen in every possible way. Again, many of you practise price discrimination against African traders, in that you supply your fellow Asians with goods at lower prices than those at which you supply African traders. In this respect, it is up to you Asian businessmen to do everything possible to see that the competition between you and the African businessmen is conducted fairly, with the aim of balanced commercial and economic development of this country, otherwise here again Government will be forced to take action.

While still on the subject of malpractices in trade, I should like to mention the tendency of Asians to keep all their business within their family circles.

When Government insisted that you should absorb as many Africans as possible into your businesses, some of you started to employ some outstanding Africans in the posts of, for instance, managing directors, personnel managers, sales managers etc. What we know, however, is that all these appointments were mere window-dressing, and that those Africans whom you have employed, although they earn fat salaries, know next to nothing as far as the secrets of your enterprises are concerned.

Apart from this, I also regret to note that you have been most reluctant to trust Africans in your different trades. Thus you find that even the Africans you employ at your counters in your shops have to consult you practically every time a customer approaches them, to ask the price of whatever you sell. This shows that, apart from your giving them the jobs in your shops, you have not given them the necessary authority and trust to finalise even simple deals with customers.

It is also disturbing to note that some of your members have carried out practices which are meant to evade the payment of income tax. They do this, for example, by keeping two sets of books. One set is specially for in-spection by the Income Tax Department, whilst another, which shows the true and correct accounts of the business, is kept for your own use. Of course, one of the advantages which you derived from the colonial Government in this case is that you were also permitted to keep your accounts books in your Gujarati writing which cannot be read by your African directors and the officials of the Income Tax Department. It is not my intention to direct the Minister of Education to introduce Gujarati in our schools yet, but I urge you to refrain from such practices which made the reading of accounts by the authorised officers impossible.

It is also very well known that many Asians in this country believe that they cannot get any services rendered to them by any Government depart-ment or para-State organisation without their extending favours to the officers who are dealing with their problems. There appears to be a belief that, unless one corrupts somebody one might not get such things as licences, passports, tenders, applications for citizenship, medical treatment, a plot in the town, or eating-house licence approved at all, or approved quickly enough.

This malpractice has unfortunately generally been accepted by some of the public officers in this country, because of the constant pressure they receive from the members of your community who practise corruption. This practice of corruption by some Asians has, therefore, interfered with some of the officers' decisions which should otherwise be based on truth, equality, nationality and justice.

As I appealed to the taxi-drivers to report any cases of policemen who asked them for bribes, I appeal to you to report any cases where any public officer asks you for a bribe. Equally, I expect all of you to stop tempting public officers with bribes.

I now turn to the question of citizenship. As already stated on many occasions in the past, my Government is committed to upholding all the binding legal obligations inherited from the previous Government. This means, in short, that in the matter of citizenship my Government will respect all citizenship certificates which were properly issued before the 25th January 1971. However, with respect to such certificates as were illegally obtained, these will not be respected and will be cancelled in accordance with the provisions of the law.

Concerning old applications for citizenship which were outstanding as on the 25th January 1971, my Government does not consider itself in any way bound to process such applications and regards them as having been automatically cancelled by lapse of time. Some of them had been outstanding for as many as seven or eight years.

For the future, all those who are interested in obtaining Uganda citizenship will have to make fresh applications, and these will be processed in accordance with new qualifications which my Government is in the process of formulating and which will be announced in due course. In this respect, information and particulars which Government will obtain from the recent census of Asians, when finally worked out, will be relevant and of much use. However, my Government is disturbed because it is clear that many of you have not shown sufficient faith in Uganda citizenship. This is indicated by the fact that the vast majority of you refused to apply for citizenship which was offered after independence. Another point is the practice whereby one family is composed of individuals all of whom are citizens of different nationalities.

For example, whereas a head of the family may be a British passport holder, his wife may turn out to be an Indian or Pakistani citizen, whilst their children might be citizens of either Kenya, Uganda or Tanzania. Sometimes two brothers are registered as different citizens. This shows clearly that many of you have no confidence at all in Uganda or any of the other countries, for that matter. I will not hesitate to say that you are gambling with one of the matters which any Government takes most seriously, and that is citizenship.

Therefore I will remind you that, if there is any blame which you might later on wish to bring against my Government about your citizenship, the persons responsible for any confusion were yourselves.

Having drawn your attention to the above points, I now strongly wish to appeal to you to come together as a single community and discuss these points and present to Government a memorandum showing clearly what you are going to do in order to eliminate the complaints I have made against your community. My government is going to take steps to see where the malpractices stated above are a breach of the laws of this country or exploitation of loopholes.

Those laws will then either be amended so that they work more tightly, or their enforcement will be strengthened. What I do not want to convey to the group whom you represent here this afternoon is the impression that Government considers your community as an abandoned child. It is you yourselves, through your refusal to integrate with the Africans in this country, who have created this feeling towards you by the Africans. But as far as my Government is concerned, and until the issue of the Asians who hold British passports is cleared, I consider you as one of a family of this nation.

Therefore, when you discuss what to do in order to eliminate the misunderstanding which has been created between you and the Africans in the country, you should remember that the solutions you are looking for are for the improvement of the relations within this family – Uganda. Furthermore, I wish to reassure those of you who might be panicking because I called this conference, that this Conference, like the Uganda Development Master Plan Conference, the Baganda Elders' Conference, the Muslim Leaders Conference, the Church of Uganda Leaders Conference, and the Agricultural Officers Conference, is meant to fulfil the aspirations of this Government, which is to improve the unity, understanding, love and racial integration among all the people of this country.

In other words, this is not an isolated Conference which is aimed at attacking your community because of the malpractices which I have outlined above. What I want of you is self-examination and the correction of any weaknesses which affect your community and which have made the Africans speak and write against you. I am doing this because I believe in God and in being frank. That is why I did not discuss the public allegations against you secretly with my Cabinet or the Defence Council, but I decided to put it to you as prominent leaders of the Asian community in this country.

I, therefore, hope that you will take my address to you this afternoon and probably the whole night counting the various malpractices which are common among the Asian community, particularly in commerce and industry, but as it is not my intention to accuse, but rather to remedy an unsatisfactory situation, I consider that the examples I have given are sufficient to illustrate the concern of the public and of my Government over the activities of your community in this country.[12]

This was a serious warning to the Asians of Uganda, indicating the depth of the resentment against them – from no less a person than the President himself. Most of the allegations were general in nature and while they probably had some substance, at least in the mind of President Amin, they were, at the same time, an admission by President Amin that his Government was unable to enforce its own regulations, such as the exchange control rules.

Despite the obviously serious situation indicated by President Amin's speech, which clearly showed his own resentment against the Asian community, few Asians in Uganda expected to see the drastic measures which were later to be introduced against them.

In fact, before the Asian expulsion, President Amin turned his attention to another group of people, the Israelis. Early in 1972, he left to visit West Germany, and on his way back visited Libya, Chad and Ethiopia. In Libya, President Amin and Col. Gaddafi signed a communique affirming their support for the Arab people in their struggle against Zionism and imperialism, and for the right of the Palestinian people to return to their land and homes.

VI. Israel Becomes a Target

Until this time, relations between Uganda and Israel had been close and cordial. Some Israeli companies were carrying out large building contracts in Uganda for the Government, and Israel had a close link with the Uganda Army which dated from 1964, when Israel supplied material and assistance to form a Uganda Air Force.

Now, however, President Amin alleged that Israel was planning subversion against Uganda, and ordered first the Israeli military training personnel, and then all Israelis, out of Uganda. Uganda broke diplomatic relations with Israel on March 30, 1972, and something like 700 Israelis were expelled. President Amin has since stated that he took this action because Israel was insisting on being paid for work done in Uganda, and for material supplied to that country, and he has said that this is the reason he expelled them.

The expulsion of Israelis, however, was clearly discriminatory, because it made no distinction, apart from the distinction of race or citizenship, or of religion.

VII. The Asian Expulsion

It was then only a matter of months before the Asian expulsion was ordered. There is no evidence that any of these actions by President Amin resulted from pressure from his army, or from any other group in Uganda. In fact, he says that his decision to expel the Asians came as a result of a dream. The morning after his dream, he told an army unit at Tororo, in eastern Uganda, that he would ask Britain to "assume responsibility" for her Asian citizens in Uganda. It is not significant that by no means all of the Asians in Uganda were British passport holders; President Amin is not the man to concern himself with such details.

The following day, in a broadcast speech, he elaborated further on the same subject, and this time said that all non-citizen Asians would be expelled. The official description of this announcement states:

The President announced, much to the disbelief of his listeners' ears, that he would summon the British High Commissioner in Uganda to make arrangements to remove the 80,000 Asian British passport holders within three months. He said the Asians were sabotaging the economy of the country, and did not have the welfare of the country at heart. He explained that nearly all shops in Kampala, Jinja, Mbale, Fort Portal, Arua and many other towns are in the hands of Asians.

The figure of 80,000 Asians mentioned here is interesting. A special census of all Asians in Uganda was ordered in 1971, but the results of the census were never announced publicly, although President Amin must be presumed to have had them available. Leading Asians in Uganda placed the figure much lower than this, at between 40,000 and 50,000, as there had already been a considerable outflow of Asians from Uganda both before and after the 1971 military coup, and there had been virtually no further entry of Asians into Uganda.

A few days later, on August 9, 1972, President Amin summoned the British High Commissioner and other diplomats, plus representatives of the Asians, to his residence, and announced the details of a decree requiring all Asians who were not Ugandan citizens – except for those in essential jobs – to leave the country within 90 days.[13]

The immediate reaction of the British High Commissioner, Mr. Richard Slater, was to state that the British Government would find it extremely difficult to cope with such an influx of British passport holders – although it had, all along, made it clear that it accepted the final responsibility for them. This made no impression on President Amin, but relations between him and Mr. Slater were strained to such an extent that Uganda soon afterwards demanded Mr. Slater's recall to Britain – and in accordance with diplomatic custom, this was done.

The British Government's reaction was to announce that all aid for Uganda would be halted, and over 1,000 British experts, including teachers, doctors and others, who were serving in Uganda under British technical aid schemes, were informed that their contracts would not be renewed by Britain, and that if they wished to leave Uganda before their existing contracts ended, Britain would ensure that they did not suffer financially. As a result, most of the British experts working in Uganda prepared to leave the country, and other countries took similar action – partly prompted by many incidents in which expatriate personnel in Uganda were molested or maltreated by soldiers.

As far as the Asians of Uganda were concerned, while they were not completely unprepared for trouble, they were surprised by the drastic nature of the order for their expulsion.

A. *No Prior Preparation or Planning*

The decree was issued without giving thought to the many questions which the expulsion of tens of thousands of people, many of them having lived in Uganda for long periods, was bound to arouse. These included the fate of their considerable assets – houses, businesses, stocks in their shops, motor cars, and even cash in the bank. As a result, a series of obviously hastily drawn-up regulations was issued.

The Asians were required to appoint agents who would assume responsibility for ensuring the transfer of their property. But, clearly, there were not sufficient people available to undertake such a complex task. At first, when it appeared that Asians who were Uganda citizens would not be required to leave the country, many of these people agreed to act as agents for the non-Ugandan Asians who had been ordered out. But it soon became clear that these Asians would not, in fact, be allowed to remain, and so they could not perform such tasks.

Further, there was insufficient time to carry out audits, stock-taking, and valuations to ensure that up-to-date records existed of the Asian property being taken over. Since most of the qualified auditors and accountants in the country were Asians, they, too, were leaving, and their time was fully occupied with their own affairs.

There was also the physical problem of moving 50,000, 60,000 or 70,000 people out of the country within a matter of a few weeks, and of arranging accommodation for them elsewhere. The Uganda Government tended to use the highest of these figures, and in fact states that over 70,000 Asians did leave the country in 1972. However, Asian representatives then in the country maintained that the total was, in fact, much lower than 70,000.

Although a special census of Asians had been carried out by the Government in 1971, no figures for this were ever made public.

B. *Action against Ugandan Asians*

The problems for the expelled Asians were increased and complicated when orders were issued in August and September 1972, requiring all Asians with Uganda citizenship to produce all the documents pertaining to their citizenship, and to prove physically that they were entitled to hold Uganda passports. They were called on to produce their original birth certificates and those of their parents, plus citizenship and other documents – all in the original, since copies, even certified ones, would not be accepted.

It soon became clear that this exercise was designed to ensure that most, if not all, these people left the country along with those holding British, Indian, Pakistani or Bangladesh passports (in fact, there were no Bangladesh citizens in Uganda, but they were specified in the expulsion order).

For no apparent reason, perfectly valid citizenship documents were rejected and torn up. As a result, most of the Asians who held Uganda passports were deprived of their citizenship in this way. As if this were not enough, a further physical check was then ordered of the few Asians who had survived the first checks[14] – and in the process, very few of them emerged with their Ugandan citizenship recognised, even if they had been born in the country, and their parents, too, had been born there.

As a further measure to ensure that Uganda "solved" her Asian problem completely, President Amin then announced that Asians who were accepted as Uganda citizens would not be allowed to live in the towns, but would be required to go and live in remote rural areas – and specifically in the near-desert area of Karamoja.[15] This was completely at variance with any normal human rights provision, since it appeared to treat one class of Ugandans differently from the others, and specifically to deny them their basic rights. But the statement was not questioned in Uganda – simply because there was no way in which a pronouncement by President Amin, however questionable, could be criticised.

In private, many Ugandan Africans made it clear that they did not support such naked discrimination. But they also admitted that they could not express their views publicly. President Amin explained his decision by saying that it would be necessary for the Asians to learn how to cultivate the soil, in the same manner as the majority of other Ugandans, and that they could not integrate with the rest of the population if they continued to live in the towns and to carry on their traditional trades there.

Understandably, this order had the desired effect, and the few Asians who had been planning to stay in Uganda quickly decided, in almost every case, that there was no future for them there.

No legal order was ever promulgated to give effect to President Amin's announcement that Asians remaining in Uganda would not be permitted to remain in the towns. It is likely that no steps were, in fact, ever taken to draft such an order, simply because the effect sought by President Amin had been achieved without a legal order.

Similarly, in September 1972, when the Asians had moved out in only small numbers (mainly because of the sheer impossibility of uprooting themselves, fulfilling all the required formalities in such a limited period), President Amin declared that any "non-citizen Asian" who was not out of the country by the deadline, November 4, would be transferred to special camps under military guard until he or she could be moved out of Uganda. His statement declared that arrangements had been made to convert some new, but unopened, rural hospitals for this purpose. Here again, there was no evidence that any such measures were in fact put into operation – but once again the technique was to frighten the Asians into leaving the country without delay.

The Asians were faced with numerous practical problems. For one thing, they had to obtain clearance from the Income Tax authorities in Uganda, and this was not granted until their tax returns for the whole period of their residence in Uganda had been checked and counter-checked, often with the result that arbitrary assessments for tax allegedly underpaid were produced. The Income Tax authorities were completely unprepared for the avalanche of extra work that this involved, and many Asians spent days, and even weeks, waiting patiently at the tax offices in an effort to obtain the necessary clearance to leave the country.

VIII. Military Invasion Brings Complications

Matters were further complicated when, on September 17, 1972, Uganda was invaded by a guerrilla force from neighbouring Tanzania, with the aim of overthrowing President Amin and his regime.[16] The attack, in fact, took place on the precise day on which the main airlift for the Asians was to start, and President Amin declared that it had been planned to disrupt the Asian expulsion, as well as to unseat him.

The guerrilla force was mainly made up of Ugandans who had fled from the country after the 1971 military coup, and who were supporters of former President Obote, who had been living in Tanzania since the coup. The invasion was obviously undertaken with the knowledge and support of the Tanzanian Government, but it had no real chance of success, and within a few days the Amin regime had overcome all resistance.

In some respects, the guerrilla invasion served to strengthen the Amin regime, by demonstrating its ability to overcome opposition. It also created suspicion that the invasion was backed by an "imperialist plot," in which President Amin alleged that both Britain and Israel were involved – although both these countries denied any such suggestion, and there was, in fact, no evidence that they were in any way involved. But because the guerrilla invasion coincided with the Asian exodus, it also helped to make life even more difficult for the Asians then in Uganda. There were numerous reports of Asians being robbed and assaulted, and allegations of rape were also made. In many cases, it was alleged that the attackers were members of the Uganda Army. But no official action was taken to prevent such incidents, and inevitably they increased; probably many of them were the work of ordinary criminals, but it is also more than likely that a considerable number were, in fact, carried out by soldiers, either on their own initiative, or on being told that no action would be taken against them.

IX. No Action to Stop Attacks on Asians

Asian families travelling to Kampala from their homes in different parts of the country were a particular target for attacks. Almost without exception, they claimed that they had to bribe soldiers who stopped them on the road to "examine" their luggage.

Often, goods were stolen by the soldiers while they were ostensibly "checking" the belongings of the Asians, and no attempt was made to conceal these thefts.

Personal effects consigned by the Asians for transport by Air – with the permission of the Ugandan authorities – were frequently plundered and looted, and the Ugandan press published an official picture of broken packing cases, suitcases and other items of baggage, lying in the open air at Entebbe airport, where they had been thoroughly looted. Before any goods could be taken or sent out of the country, the Asians were required to submit them to meticulous investigation, which was carried out by soldiers or police. Each box, suitcase or other container was opened, every single item in it was taken out and examined, and even clothing was meticulously searched, apparently to ensure that no money or valuables were being taken out by the Asians.

X. Cash Remittances are Reduced

Until the Asian exodus was ordered, Uganda's exchange control rules allowed a departing resident to take with him a quantity of cash and assets. The limit was 50,000 shillings per family – about £3,000 sterling at that time. With the expulsion of thousands of Asian families, Uganda clearly did not have the foreign exchange to stand such a considerable drain. So the limit was arbitrarily reduced to one thousand shillings – a little over £50 sterling. Extra measures were taken to prevent the Asians from taking with them more than a small quantity of personal effects, and particularly to prevent them from taking out any significant items of jewellery. It is the custom of many Asians to possess items of gold, such as bangles, necklaces and ear-rings, as well as finger rings. The Ugandan rules, again made arbitrarily, and clearly directed only at the Asians, imposed strict limits on the amount of jewellery that could be taken by persons leaving the country. A single gold bangle was permitted, but items above this were roughly seized or confiscated at the airport.

Special search booths were erected at Entebbe airport, through which all Asian passengers had to pass – after they had had their baggage meticulously checked, and their papers and documents checked. As a result, Asian families who left the country had to spend many hours at the airport, in conditions of great discomfort, before they were allowed to board the planes taking them out.

Securing places on the airlift was only part of the problem for the Asians, as they had to obtain numerous documents, including entry certificates for Britain (for the majority who were leaving for Britain), or for other countries, health documents, and so on.

XI. The Stateless Asians

Further complications were caused as a result of the action taken by the Uganda Government to deprive thousands of Asians of their Ugandan citizenship. Most of these people were entitled to no other citizenship, and they effectively became stateless, once Uganda had declared that she no longer recognised them as her citizens. This situation was not made easier by the fact that not all members of the same family had the same citizenship. The parents, having been born, for instance, in

India before that country achieved independence had chosen British nationality, but their children, having been born in Uganda before Uganda achieved independence, had the right to become Uganda citizens in many cases, and had exercised that right.

Most of the Asians now rendered stateless would have wished to go to Britain, along with those who already held British passports. But Britain, partly because of the size of the political issue raised on her domestic scene by the unprecedented influx of Asians, would not agree to accept those who were not British subjects. This meant that the stateless Asians had to look elsewhere.

The United Nations, partly through the U.N. High Commission for Refugees, was able to bring the matter sufficiently to the attention of other countries, however, and as a result the stateless Asians were eventually able to move to other European countries, whose Governments had agreed to admit them on humanitarian grounds. But the Asians had no traditional links with those countries, and the process of transformation for them was particularly difficult.

Apart from Britain, a number of countries helped to solve the problems of the Uganda Asians by agreeing to admit them. Canada, for instance, was willing to take a considerable number – and, in fact, admitted stateless Asians, and even some who still held Ugandan passports, as well as many with British nationality. The United States and Australia took some Asians in, while India and Pakistan admitted much larger numbers. In fact, the Indian Government was ready to admit virtually any of the Ugandan Asians who wished to go to India – although, for those with British passports, she insisted that Britain should concede their eventual right to live in Britain if they wished to do so. India's attitude was dictated largely by humanitarian considerations, but partly also by a realisation that the Asians of Uganda had originated from India, and that their numbers (large as they were in the Ugandan context) were small in relation to India's own population. Most of the Asians from Uganda, however, did not wish to move to India if they could find other destinations. One reason was the heavy taxation in India, another was the comparative lack of employment and career opportunities for people who, in Europe and North America could expect to enjoy higher living standards than they would have had in India.

Despite tremendous difficulties, the exodus of Asians from Uganda was completed. Only a small number remained to be moved when President Amin's 90-day deadline expired early in November, and the

United Nations assumed responsibility for them by extending its protection; and they were not molested when travelling to the airport in
buses carrying the United Nations flag, and with U.N. officials as escorts.

Volunteers from the small European community in Uganda helped
to look after the Asians, and many members of the Asian community
themselves worked to help the others – organising accommodation and
food, and providing help and advice with the many problems of documentation and so on. Many diplomatic missions in Uganda moved in
extra staff to help to handle the unprecedented operation.

XII. The Scramble for Asian Assets

The Asians were hardly out of the country before the scramble began
to gain possession of their motor cars. Thousands of cars had been left
by the Asians, who were unable to sell them or otherwise to dispose of
them. Members of the Uganda Armed Forces pressed for, and were
given, the first chance to obtain cars, and the others were then auctioned to the general public, often being sold for nominal sums. Businesses and houses were taken over in the name of the Departed Asians
Property Custodian Board, or by Uganda's Ministry of Commerce and
Industry, and were "allocated" to Ugandan Africans, usually by allocation committees on which the Uganda Army was well represented.

The object, in President Amin's own words, was to make the indigenous Ugandans rich. "There was nothing racial in what I did. I
merely transferred the economy from the hands of non-Ugandans into
the hands of the indigenous Ugandans," he declared on numerous
occasions.

XIII. Britons Expelled

The Asians were not the only people to be affected by President Amin's
"economic war." In December 1972, in a midnight broadcast, he
announced the taking over of 30 companies, most of them British-
owned, and soon afterwards 24 tea estates, also mainly owned by Britons, were similarly taken over.[17] In no case was the word "nationalisation" used; President Amin, in fact, declared that he did not believe
in nationalisation, and would never allow it.

The comparatively small number of Britons who were required to leave Uganda at this time had few of the problems experienced earlier by the Asians. They were, in many cases, required to leave the country within a matter of hours, but they did not, in general, have to cope with chaotic conditions when obtaining income tax clearances, or when leaving Uganda.

The question of compensation for the assets taken over from Asians and others was clearly not considered at the time the people concerned were forced to leave the country. But as a result of international pressure, and of a realisation that Uganda's international reputation was suffering, President Amin later stated that compensation would be paid for all assets taken over, and rules were later promulgated for the valuation of such assets.

Partly as a result of pressure from Britain for the payment of compensation to the Asians, a team of experts from London visited Kampala during 1975, for discussions with Ugandan representatives. Only limited progress was made at this meeting, and it became obvious that the size and complexity of the matter was likely to result in considerable delays before any final settlement could be reached.

During 1975, however, payment was made to the one American businessman whose property in Uganda was taken over. The amount paid was not announced. Towards the end of 1975, discussions took place between representatives of the Ugandan and Indian Governments on compensation for the Indian citizens who had been expelled. It was then announced that the Indian Government had accepted the figure suggested by Uganda, and on January 25, 1976, a cheque for compensation was handed to an Indian Government representative. The Ugandan announcement merely described the cheque as being for "millions of dollars," but reports from India said that it was for £700,000 sterling – a very small figure if it represented compensation for over 1,000 families, some of whom had extensive business and private assets in Uganda up to 1972.

XIV. International Commission of Jurists' Report

Early in 1974, the International Commission of Jurists produced a report on conditions in Uganda under President Amin's military regime. It listed the names and details of a number of Ugandans who had been killed, apparently by the military regime, since January 1971.

The report estimated that many thousands of Ugandans had, in fact, been killed, and it alleged that the rule of law was no longer observed in Uganda, and that there was a denial of basic human rights there.

Despite opposition by the Uganda Government, the International Commission of Jurists report was passed to the United Nations Commission on Human Rights. There it waited for some two years, until, in March 1976, the Uganda Government announced with obvious delight that the report had been rejected by the U.N. Commission on Human Rights.

A comment by an unnamed Government spokesman, published in the government-owned "Voice of Uganda" on March 9, 1976, stated:

The verdict of the U.N. Commission on Human Rights meeting in Geneva has cleared Uganda of dirty smears which were calculated to mar what would otherwise be a most favourable international image of this country.

The London-based International Commission of Jurists' attempts to bring Uganda into disrepute seem to have failed. Instead, the so-called watchdog for international law and order by jurisprudence seems to have lost credibility on a matter they ought to have known better.

On the expulsion of non-citizens, the U. N. Commission on Human Rights ruling in the matter stands as a clear testimony to the reasons why President Amin took the decision to act in the interests of this country. In other words, the Commission has upheld Uganda's right to eliminate economic exploitation of its citizens by non-citizens.

Uganda's 70 years of hospitality should have been reciprocated in more favourable terms than being taken to an international court of law. In any case, there can be no more justification for prolonged exploitation, and yet on top of this Uganda has pledged to pay compensation for whatever property that was taken over from the departed non-citizens.

It should have been too obvious to the learned jurists in London that non-citizens have no right to stay in a country except at the express pleasure and hospitality of the country concerned.[18]

Other views on the readiness of the U.N. Commission on Human Rights to deal with the basic questions implied in its title have, however, been expressed. The *Sunday Times* of London published an article on March 14, 1976, no doubt as a result of the rejection of the International Commission of Jurists' report on Uganda. It states:

The record of the Commission's 29 years shows that it has been more concerned to cover up than to expose human rights violations. It is neither farce nor tragedy, in the proper senses of those two overworked words. But it is, perhaps, the most poignant and disgraceful of false international pretences that the governments of the world have yet had the temerity to devise. To millions of people its name offers a glimmer of hope for justice – that hope is founded on, quite literally, nothing. The Commission is an almost total lie. It plays a vital part in what Sean McBride, U.N. Commissioner for Namibia and 1974 Nobel Peace Prize winner, has described as "the conspiracy of governments" to deprive the people of their rights.[19]

NOTES

1. Foreign Office Records, Public Record Office, London: F.O. 2/143 (India Office to Foreign Office, 11th August 1897).
2. Uganda National Archives, Entebbe: "Staff Correspondence inward 1898."
3. Foreign Office Records, Public Record Office, London: Foreign Office Confidential Print No. 7946, page 197.
4. Colonial Office Archives, Public Record Office, London: C.O. 533/79, Confidential report on Uganda cotton industry, by S. Simpson, Director of Agriculture, dated 31st July 1912.
5. Non-native census reports for Kenya, Uganda and Tanganyika, 1948.
6. "Portrait of a Minority: Asians in East Africa," edited by Dharam P. Ghai, Oxford University Press 1965, page 92.
7. 1971 Statistical Abstract, Government Printer, Entebbe, page 17.
8. *A History of the Asians in East Africa*, by J. S. Mangat, Oxford University Press 1969, pages 141–143.
9. Constitution of Uganda, Government Printer, Entebbe, 1962.
10. "The First 366 Days," Government Printer, Entebbe, 1972, page 39.
11. *Ibid.*, pages 1, 2.
12. "Uganda, Second Year of the Second Republic," Government Printer, Entebbe 1973, pages 101–107.
13. *Uganda Gazette 1972*, Governnent Printer, Entebbe.
14. "Uganda, Second year," pages 66, 67.
15. *Ibid.*, page 67.
16. *Ibid.*, page 71.
17. Decree 32/72, Government Printer, Entebbe.
18. "Voice of Uganda," 9th March 1976.
19. *Sunday Times* (London), 14th March 1976.

Gender Discrimination

CLARICE STASZ

CLARICE STASZ recently dropped the name she has published under (Stoll) in support of a woman's right to maintain or choose her own name. She received her Ph.D. at Rutgers and is currently Associate Professor of Sociology at Sonoma State College in California. Her early work includes co-authorship of two books on simulation, *Simulation Games for the Social Studies* and *Simulation Games* (both Free Press), as well as numerous papers on the topic of social control, such as "Images of Man and Social control." Her work on sex roles includes *Sexism: Scientific Debates* (Addison-Wesley) and *Female and Male: Socialization, Social Roles, and Social Structure* (Wm. C. Brown). Her work has become increasingly humanistic and political in orientation, with ongoing projects including a biography of Charmian Kittredge London, research into the politics of nutrition, and theoretical essays on the social control of love and intimacy. She is actively involved with an informal group of sociologists who are developing a visual sociology based upon the use of photography and film, and in this regard teaches photo documentary courses and is preparing several large documentary essays.

Gender Discrimination

CLARICE STASZ

I. Definitions

Discrimination against the female gender is a universal feature of human societies. While considerable variability exists, in all societies there are at least several activities which women are discouraged from participating in, and punished or ignored if they do participate. In virtually all contemporary societies women are almost completely excluded from meaningful political leadership roles. In most, their social identity is made with reference to a male, usually their father or husband. In many, they are denied education beyond primary skills, and subsequently fill only menial and unskilled jobs in the labour market. The major religions exclude women from ministerial roles and the world artistic institutions often ignore their creative contributions. In everyday life, social practices in most societies cast women in a passive, dependent and inferior role. Consequently, a common female psychology in many cultures is that of a weak, worthless, insecure ego.

These discrimination patterns form a social complex known as *sexism*. While generally speaking, the term would apply to discrimination against either gender, it almost always implies the female. A corollary ideology that supports these social practices is *androcentrism*, which refers to a world view or gestalt that presumes the superiority of masculine activities and values. Just what values are "masculine" or "feminine" depends upon the culture being studied. In 1935, Margaret Mead's study of sex roles in three primitive cultures illustrated how three small New Guinea village cultures produced three distinct sets of gender role expectations.[1] In two societies the Arapesh and Mundugumor, sex typing was minimal. That is, few activities or personality traits were considered to be "masculine" or "feminine." The Arapesh females and males alike were gentle, maternal, emotionally warm, and passive. The Mundugumor males and females alike were violently aggressive, acquisitive, rivalous, and non-maternal. These societies are unusual for their low degree of *sex typing*, that is, the expectations they assign to gender categories. The third culture, the Tchambuli, had a strong system of sex typing. In this case, males were expected to be artistic, emotional, and delicate, while women were to be the economic providers, energetic, and unadorned.

Mead's research implies that concepts of masculinity and feminity are not universal, and that culture can inhibit or redirect any innate differences between female and male. However logical this conclusion, it appears nonetheless that certain values attach to femininity and masculinity across the largest, most powerful societies. Namely, femininity carries connotations of receptiveness, passivity, intuitiveness, emotional expressiveness, maternal and personal caring, while masculinity implies power, expansiveness, intellectuality, and manipulation of objects. These polarities permeate the religious and philosophical influences in both Eastern and Western thought. For example, in *I Ching*, the "male" symbols represent creativity, strength, movement, danger, and such, while the "female" symbols represent devotion, adaptability, and joy. Similarly, Christian theology repeatedly views the feminine as antithetical to the spirit, the earthbound temptations of life. (Mariolatry is a notable exception, though even it casts women in a very narrow role.)

The wide acceptance of these very general feminine-masculine concepts is evident at international state events, wherein males are the prime actors and females are merely supportive or decorative. During international visits, wives of heads of state are given jewelry and shown humane institutions, such as hospitals, schools, or cultural settings. The men attend all-male meetings, view military shows, and make speeches for the international media. No wife, however closely she works with her husband in his work, could ever be considered an appropriate member at the "serious" state gatherings. Similarly, it would be considered frivolous, even insulting, for the male leader to express interest in attending the women's activities. This scenario repeats itself regardless of the political, religious, and cultural mixes of the countries concerned.[2]

Very likely the men from these different countries would not agree unanimously as to the definition of masculinity. For example, Mao and Nixon would not have agreed upon the importance of competitive sports as an expression of manhood. Nor would an Arab leader and a

Western European agree that a stolid suppression of emotional feelings is a major quality of masculinity. Nonetheless, their public behaviour suggests they do agree that men are to be powerful, important, active beings. Perhaps their greatest area of agreement would be on the treatment of women as subordinate, supportive, decorative, domestic creatures. Their behaviour typifies sexist patterns, while their taken-for-granted attitudes are androcentric.

To summarize, in spite of considerable cross-cultural variations, societies exhibit sexist practices toward women based upon belief in the superiority of the masculine principle. The degree of sex-typing – the extent to which female and male are viewed dissimilarly – will vary from culture to culture as well. The specific content of gender-based definitions will vary so much so that what is considered to be masculine in one society will be viewed as feminine in another. However, when the largest or most influential societies are looked at there is some commonality across cultures as to what qualities are feminine and which masculine. This implies that patterns of discrimination against women in various cultures will exhibit certain similarities and that indeed is the case.

II. Identifying Discrimination

"Discrimination" connotes a systematic denial of rights or opportunities to a minority group. So the first thing one must do in deciding upon whether discrimination occurs or not in a society would be to select some *social indicator*, a measure of those rights, opportunities or costs that accrue to particular sub-groups in a society. Very common examples are suffrage (a right), educational options (an opportunity), or morbidity data (a cost). This paper will elaborate on the wide range of these indicators.

In practice, a social scientist or political activist will gather data on an indicator and compare the distributions for females and males in that regard. For example, Table 1 presents the proportion of barristers or lawyers in various countries by sex, as collected by Sullerot.[3] Law is a prestigious profession in these countries, so its labour force data provide one measure of individual opportunity to achieve success and power. Sometimes, in place of the actual proportions, a *sex ratio* is computed, based upon the ration of female to male frequencies. If equal numbers of women and men are in a position, the ratio is 1.0; if fewer women are occupants, the ratio is less than 1.0; if more women, more

TABLE 1: *Proportion of Barristers by Country and Sex*

	Female	*Male*	*Sex ratio*
U.S.S.R.	38	62	.61
France	19	81	.23
Denmark	10	90	.11
Austria	7	93	.08
Sweden	7	93	.08
Federal Germany	5	95	.05
Great Britain	4	96	.04
U.S.A.	3	97	.03

Source: Sullerot, 1971, p. 152

than 1.0. Although it does result in loss of much specific information, the sex ratio is a convenient summary measure of possible discrimination. In this example, one can see how all the countries save the U.S.S.R. are far from achieving equal representation of women in the legal profession.

This statistical approach to identifying discrimination is perhaps the most common for the apparent clarity and precision of the findings. Yet it has several sources of potential misinterpretation. First, the only way to ascertain inequality is to compare the social indicator proportions to the proportion of females and males in the base population, or the *base ratio*. For example, currently in the U.S.A. the sex ratio is 52 : 48 or 1.08, and consequently an equitable distribution of female lawyers should be in the area of 1.08 and not 1.0. Second, some might question just what the base ratio should be. In many of these countries the proportion of female higher education graduates – those eligible for legal training – is low. By choosing these data as a base, one could see exactly to what extent law schools are the source of discrimination. Currently in the U.S.A. the sex ratio of higher education graduates is approximately 40:60 or .67. Even using this corrected ratio, one can see that considerable blockage of opportunity for qualified women exists. The choice of an appropriate base population for comparison can thus provide a more systematic guide to the possible sources of discrimination.

Furthermore, a political meaning attaches itself to these choices as well. No doubt those with strong feminist leanings are biased towards selecting the sex ratio of the largest size as a way of emphasizing the discrepancy. Were this data accompanied by the smaller higher education comparison base, some would feel that the issue was being minimized. It is difficult neatly to separate scientific and political interests. A writer can set aside personal "biases" and select base ratios on purely "rational" grounds, but such data will seldom be perceived purely in a "scientific" way, and one should be willing to accept the validity of accompanying political attacks. The choice of a small ratio as the base ratio *is* conservative in a sense, however good the reasons for using it for the study at hand.

Another problem with this statistical approach has to do with the usual fallacies inherent in surveys and counts. Such data is often collected and provided by the institution under scrutiny, not in an independent manner by the scientist or activist who needs the information. Thus, the data on lawyers came from government agencies in the case of the U.S.S.R., and from lawyers' associations in the case of other countries. It is known that the U.S.S.R. likes to publicize its equal treatment of women to other countries, so no one can be sure that *all* the women included in their count have the same training and title as the average male barristers. This is not to discredit this particular datum from the U.S.S.R., so much as to indicate potential biases from the data sources, namely one planned and designed by the agency so as to foster a most favourable image. (Currently in the United States, some companies count anyone with a Spanish surname as a minority, when in fact many of these individuals are not members of the Spanish-speaking poor minority being oppressed. This manner of counting favourably exaggerates the appearance of their minority hiring practices).

A related error concerns whether the institution is in fact an efficient data collector, regardless of any systematic biases it chooses to introduce. Exactly how do the legal associations of these countries develop and maintain files? That some bias exists is indicated in the case of Britain. Sullerot notes in her discussion that another survey of professions in Britain presented a figure of 8.5 percent women, not 4 percent. What could account for the difference? In one case the count may have been of practising attorneys as against trained attorneys. Or perhaps the lower count comes from an organization where membership is not accepted by all attorneys, as often happens. Since women tend to be outsiders to begin with it should be expected that fewer of them will be involved in professional organizations. This questioning is the type one must explore in making sense of statistical evidence for discrimination.

Statistical evidence is useful, yet reliance upon statistics can prevent recognition of other sources of discrimination. That is, various patterns of oppression occur which are often missed in simple number counts. Similarly, ignorance of these other forms may cause the numbers to be misinterpreted.

A most frequent type of discrimination occurs when a society simply ignores a woman's contribution to an activity, and thus does not count it. For example, the economies of certain African states include a large segment of female activity in the form of farming production, small crafts production, and the trading thereof.[4] Yet because these activities involve local informal exchanges of commodities, they are not counted in official data on economic productivity. So, while the women in these societies are the primary household providers, their contribution is not often acknowledged. In the U.S.A. and Western Europe, the economic contribution of the housewife is similarly ignored because she is not paid in actual money. The same goes for charitable and volunteer activities. A more blatant example occurs in France, where statistics on part-time women workers have simply not been collected.[5] Those social scientists who design models of the economy do so from an androcentric position – ignoring women's contribution because it is "not important," not paid for (which hardly makes it uneconomic), or not easily measured.

The statistical analyst confronting this problem would note that women are excluded from the economic realm because they are under-represented in the labour force, in banking decisions, in trade agreements, or whatever. Of course, this conclusion is premised upon the androcentric model of the economy, and leads one to argue merely that women be encouraged and allowed to have more labour force participation. In rejecting this model, one is able to look for sources of contributions that already exist and thus suggest ways of including these contributions in a more formal scheme of things (e.g. giving women volunteer workers tax credits or special old age benefits).

A second pattern of discrimination occurs when a society counts women's contributions and then devalues them. For example, in many countries one might find equivalent participation of women and men in various sports. Yet upon closer examination one would learn that the men's sports receive favoured treatment in the form of money, equipment, media publicity, and so on. The male sports figures would be celebrities more often than female. In effect, the culture merely *allows* women to be athletes, while it *encourages* and rewards men to do so.

A related pattern gives both sexes equality up to a point, and then allows only men to achieve the top position. Thus, one finds in the

U.S.A. that women are well-represented in teaching, social work, and library science, while hardly any women become major administrators in these professions.[6] Consequently, a statistician in such cases may or may not find discrimination, depending upon the indicators selected. Does she, for example, break down the job categories by rank or does she look merely at the jobs overall?

Another type of discrimination missed by most statistical analyses occurs when the wife or female relative of a man is the equal partner and collaborator in a job, yet he, being the official office holder, receives credit. This is not an unusual occurrence in the academic world, where highly educated women apply their training and skill in their husband's research with little acknowledgement thereof. It also occurs in art, politics, indeed any job where some individual initiative and creativity is granted the job holder. This pattern hurts the female in the short run by denying immediate feelings of pride and sense of accomplishment for her work. More insidiously, in the long run she lacks any legitimate record of her accomplishments. Thus, the wife of a noted historian who has collaborated in all his work will have no standing in the academic marketplace if divorced or widowed, however accomplished and experienced she be. (In politics, there is some precedent in the U.S.A. for a few wives to step into their deceased husbands' offices, but this is most unusual.)

In this third case, the statistician will note many male achievements. Indeed, it is precisely data of this kind that leads anti-feminists to conclude that women lack the talent and drive of men and are not so deserving of important responsibility!

Another type of discrimination is more subtle. It is possible to identify select societies wherein sex typing is minimal, such as the Arapesh or China. This does not automatically mean that sexism is not pervasive. Women and men may be permitted the same rights and activities. Yet distinctions may be made as to the male contribution being more necessary, essential, important, or whatever. The attitude of masculine superiority brings with it psychic costs to the female, not to mention additonal pressures on the male to meet high performance standards. The converse case is also possible. For example, in some peasant societies an elaborate sex-typing occurs, so much so that female and male are virtually separated during their lives.[7] Yet the attitude of male superiority need not be great (although it always exists to some degree). In such societies one may find two hierarchies of power – the men in the fields, the women at home – with the male hierarchy having only a slight edge over the female. Indeed, these societies with their severe role expectations strike one for the harsh restrictions *each* sex faces.

A variation of this pattern can be found in the U.S.A. and societies where a feminist movement is forcing social change. One variety of feminism continues to support male values as superior in that it discredits feminine activities (domestic and volunteer work) and argues that a "fulfilled" woman must succeed in areas previously dominated by males. Young girls are thus encouraged to develop initiative, self-assertiveness, career orientation, and such previously male qualities. (This is not the only variety of feminism.) One must wonder whether discrimination is eliminated by having *both* sexes adjust to the standard previously applied to males. The statistical approach would answer "yes," but this is not the only possibility.

A second category of problems in the use of statistical data is often ignored by investigators. This concerns the use of significance tests. One problem is that researchers rely too heavily on significance levels to distinguish "important" trends in their data. Two errors of interpretation follow. First, many times the significance values are attached to differences that are not terribly larger in size. Researchers tend to group all "significant" findings in one category, rather than examine the range of differences and move on to distinguish the more important ones. The result of this error is to exaggerate the real appearance of gender differences, implying that they are very great. Similarly, researchers often fail to examine the variances in their measures. These can be important for the understanding of phenomenon relating to gender because often the variances have special characteristics. For example, in research on children's game play, the data repeatedly show less variance in boys' game behaviour than girls'. This is an important fact in itself for making sense of sex role socialization. Gender roles are such that one of the gender categories will often have considerably more or less variance than the other.

The tendency to lump all significant findings together means that the negative findings are typically ignored. Yet in the area of sex differences and discrimination, these negative findings are of particular value. If one administers twenty psychological tests to women and men, noting differences in five, the fact of no differences on fifteen others is hardly unimportant. An example from childrens' play behaviour is relevant here again. If one reads surveys on child's play and sex roles, often one will read how girls are more passive on the playground and boys are more active. Similarly, it is said that girls play with dolls and boys with trucks. Yet a careful reading of the play research reveals that girls' and boys' play behaviour is more often *alike* than not, that the amount of time spent with certain toys other than dolls and trucks is the same.[8] *The usual style of social science research reporting with its emphasis on "positive results" seriously distorts the phenomenon of sex roles by exaggerating the differences between women and men.* Such an approach results in data that support the stereotypes of sex roles that exist among social actors in a society, as well as oversimplifying the subtlety of the processes that are operating.

III. A Multi-level Model of Gender Discrimination

Another serious problem with purely statistical analyses of discrimination is that they tend to tap into only certain types of activities that are indicative of sexism. They require that one be able to codify and quantify fairly discrete sets of behaviour. Consequently, one is left with a static view of the situation, a cross-section of society. This is probably the most useful initial approach to a problem, but it fails to allow for the many behaviours that do not readily fit into a statistical mode. As we shall see, provocative qualitative studies have and can be done.

In additon, the statistical studies read to date fail to utilize these techniques such as regression analysis, path analysis, and such, that enable one to ferret out some of the processes that may be operating. Until the statistical sophistication of these studies increases to include social process or causal networks, then the statistical study of gender discrimination will remain tied up on a simplistic level.

In order to indicate the importance of extending research techniques and of moving beyond mere documentation of gender discrimination, the elaboration of one model will serve to illustrate one of the many facets of this topic. In spite of the sub-discipline known as "sociology of sex roles," the concept of sex role is not the most helpful for conceptualizing the problem. A role is a pattern of behaviour associated with a position in society. The study of gender structures extends far beyond the actual elaboration of roles. It includes the distribution of rewards and opportunities available by gender, the processes through which these opportunity patterns develop and are maintained, the cultural mythologies and ideologies that relate to these processes, the peculiar form sexism takes within particular social institutions, the socialization of persons to gender expectations. In addition, the idea of "sex role" suggests that gender is the primary basis for individual identity, when in fact we know from many studies of the self that it is only one of many available guides to self-definition. Thus, to speak of "sex roles" is to miss the complexity of how gender identity systems operate in real life.

The model is developed from a conceptualization originating with Benoit-Smullyan.[9] Three structural categories are defined: (1) *status*, or the relative position in a hierarchy; (2) *locus*, or the social position that arises from the function an individual's performance provides for a group (e.g. sister in a family); (3) *situs*, or the aggregate category of persons socially distinguished by any common characteristics except status and locus (age, race, gender). Three social psychological structures correlate with these social positions.[10] *Personal status* refers to an individual's rank in a hierarchy; *role*, to the position one plays in a social situation, and *identity*, to the situs categories one bears. Figure 1 illustrates the interplay of these systems.

Gender is a situs category that provides a basis for personal identity from birth. All cultures provide supporting beliefs and expectations that persons within one gender category will behave in a similar, predictable way. The criteria applied may be either real or imaginary, in the sense that they may or may not correspond to objective characteristics of the persons so distinguished. Thus, regardless of situation, women in American society are typically expected to be more passive than men, less analytical in their reasoning, less physically agile, and so on. This system of beliefs influences an individual man's woman's conception of femininity as it applies to herself and other women. However, in developing her conception of femininity, the woman will also take into account her other identity categories – her race, ethnicity, religion, age – all of which further delineate the meaning of "woman." In a pluralistic society such as the United States, many definitions of "woman" result (e.g. old Chicana, young Protestant white, etc.).

The status system in all societies is such that a male is usually considered to be superior in rank to a female. Also, gender is one determinant of the social roles an individual may be permitted to play. An obvious example is the economy, where in most countries one finds that any one job category is predominated by one sex.

The lines in Figure 1 suggest a logical order that appears to underlie these relationships. The dotted lines remind us that the process has feedback; that is, it is self-reinforcing. Thus, if men are seen primarily in positions of high rank or in certain types of occupations, then this fact can be used to support the notion of natural differences.

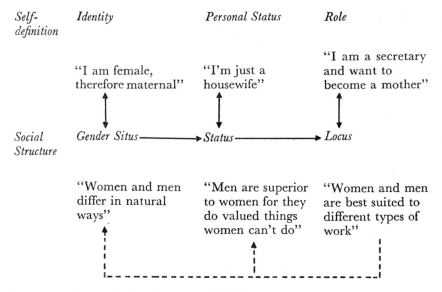

FIGURE 1: *Gender, Stratification, and Self-definition*

The process described here resembles what Merton has defined as the "self-fulfilling prophecy."[11] which is

... In the beginning, a *false* definition of the situation evoking a new behaviour which makes the originally false conception come true. The specious validity of the self-fulfilling prophecy perpetuates a reign of terror. For the prophet will cite the actual course of events as proof that he was right from the very beginning. (Merton 1957, 423).

The "errors" that perpetuate sexism usually concern an argument that women and men are "naturally different" or "inherently suited to different types of tasks." Yet the weight of evidence is against such assumptions. Repeatedly arguments of natural differences are being discredited by a variety of investigators: sociologists, medical researchers, anthropologists, psychologists. That differences do seem to occur are not strong enough to or unusual enough to account for the large differences in social behaviour of women and men. Even though some of this research is becoming part of the common culture of some societies, sexist attitudes prevail nonetheless.

Sexism is deeply pervasive because the process occurs on all levels of social activity. On the interpersonal level, or micro-order, it influences the way people define both themselves ("I am a man, and therefore I should be domineering.") and others around them ("She is behaving too aggressively.") As the famous dictum by W. I. Thomas (1928,572)[12] explains, "If men (women) define situations as real, they are real in their consequences." When humans interact, they do so on their understandings of what is going on and what is to be done. The meanings attached to social positions, in this case gender, are one component of their view of social reality.

When one moves up to the level of informal groups, expectations concerning gender pattern themselves further. Knowledge of the sex composition of a group of people would be sufficient for placing good bets on a number of predictions. Consider this situation. In a mixed work group, who would: be first to speak up, offer advice, remain silent, provide supportive statements, touch other members? Or consider all-male and all-female groups. How would you characterize the differences in co-operativeness, formality, warmth, status hierarchy?[13] In many societies you would be able to make such distinctions. Of course, these predictions would not hold in specific cases because many other features of the situation would come into play as well, such as the group task, member personalities, and so on.

When the overall social order is considered, the macro-structure, again as expected, it is found that the patterns reflect the daily interactions of societal members. The participation of women and men in various activities will be reflected throughout data on the power structure, the leisure sphere, religious life, and every other institutional arena. These distributions hint at the welcoming and supportive opportunities, as well as the closed or forbidding activities, what women and men face in that society.

In many contemporary societies sexist processes have resulted in a situation whereby the segregation of individual activities by gender pervades virtually every institution. Fair-minded persons can point to the division of labour and exclusion of women (or men) from various activities as support for policies that perpetuate such practices. They are not being prejudiced in the sense that the facts permit them no other conclusion.

Merton used examples from racial and ethnic prejudices to illustrate his argument, but the analogy to gender discrimination holds as well. In fact prior to Merton's article, Hacker[14] detailed the numerous ways in which women can be considered a *minority group*, which is defined as

... any group of people who because of their physical and cultural characteristics, are singled out from others in the society in which they live for different and unequal treatment, and who therefore regard themselves as objects of collective discrimination.

According to Hacker, one can show this objectively, by pointing to many instances of discrimination against women in a society. The definition also has a subjective element, that is, a woman's own recognition of her minority status. One could argue that until the recent feminist revival, few women held minority group status in the subjective sense, either because they were blind to the treatment or presumed that they warranted it.

Hacker argues further that the sex role structure in our society is analogous to a caste system. Berreman[15] defines *caste* as a "hierarchy of endogamous divisions in which membership is ascribed at birth and unalterable." Women's condition is ascribed at birth, but the rules of endogamy do not apply. That is, women are not, for obvious reasons, prohibited from marrying out of their caste (all other women). A more precise term to apply to women as an indication of their inferior status would be to call them a *subordinate class*. Class divisions do not have rules concerning marriage, as minority group and caste divisions do.

Nonetheless, one can also identify caste-like characteristics among women. Individuals in the low castes are considered to be inherently inferior, regardless of their behaviour. Whether racially or religiously based, caste systems are very stable because they maintain themselves with little effort. The inferior caste member accepts her fate, which means she avoids taboo contacts and displays deference to high caste persons. Considerable economic interdependence binds the group with the benefits (economic, sexual, prestige) going to the superior group. As Berreman notes, "high persons gain, *by virtue of their status alone*, deference from others, constant reinforcement of a feeling of superiority, and a permanent scapegoat in the lower castes."

Hacker elaborated the many similarities between the status of American blacks and women. The stereotypes (childlike, emotional, unintellectual, primitive) applying to each are similar. The rationalizations (natural differences) are the same. Consequently, blacks and women developed patterns of accommodation of similar manner (supplicatory presentation, concealment of real feelings, outwitting the superordinates, fake appeals of ignorance or helplessness). This relation can also be seen to have historical roots, in that the legal status of slaves was borrowed from the notion of *patria potestas*, the subordination of women and

children under the male family head. During the 19th century, the
suffrage and abolition leaders worked closely together. Furthermore,
the historical movement from a pre-industrial, paternalistic society to a
technological imperialism has affected the status of blacks and women
in similar ways (e.g. relegating them to unskilled labour, isolating them
from decision-making centres, encouragement of infighting).

Of course the analogy does not hold perfectly. Women can use marriage as a vehicle for social status (though not freedom). And most societies shape strong needs that drive women and men towards each
other. Racial minorities cannot call upon the leverage of sexuality or
reproduction, particularly given strong anti-miscegenation ideologies
in many societies. In spite of these important differences, Hacker implies that much of theoretical understanding of gender discrimination
can be extended from the base of our available work on racial and ethnic minority discrimination. To my knowledge, no one has seriously
continued a more sophisticated extension of this view, though it seems
most promising.

This model only hints at the complexity of structure and processes
surrounding gender discrimination. Yet it is more sophisticated than
the taken-for-granted model one finds in much current research. It
seems more likely than not that studies use a monocausal theory. For
example, Figes[16] traces the rise of sexism to religious beliefs. Radical
theorists point to the economic order. Others point to the schools, the
media, and so on. Typically too, the independent variable, the measure
of sexism, is narrowly circumscribed to one level of social activity. For
example, a wealth of material is appearing on labour market statistics,
but scarcely any studies have examined the work culture, the peculiar
nature of women's and men's work, and even fewer have explored the
social psychology of the woman worker. These studies will come in
time, as awareness of the problem is just beginning.

A. *Some Examples*

Though feminism as a social movement has existed for some centuries
in Western societies, its specific aims and activities have changed with
the historical situation. Early American feminists challenged feminine
oppression purely on moral grounds and did not present much "scientific" documentation of sexist evils. One quality that distinguishes the
most recent feminist activity from prior ones is a reliance on data-

gathering as a means of providing evidence for the cause. Feminist social scientists in particular have recently examined many aspects of sexist discrimination, yet only the broadest outlines of the process are discernable.

Five institutions have received the most attention: politics, the family, the economy, education, and health. Interest in these areas is both political and theoretical. Politically speaking, many women in the United States and other countries have become active supporters on such issues as child care centres, equal pay for equal work, the right to abortion, equal rights in marriage, equal education for their daughters, more female representation in government, and so on. These issues grew out of the practical needs of well-educated women living in an urban, anomic society where life expectancy had recently extended considerably, and marital security was becoming less guaranteed. On a theoretical level, much contemporary feminism takes root in the writings of Marx and Engels, both of whom emphasized the interplay of the economy, the family, and power. Consequently, social scientists are prone to examine these institutions as the primary ones in sexual oppression.

Less often considered are those institutions that concern themselves with "quality of life." Included here would be the role of gender in the creative and performing arts, leisure activities, religion, and informal activities. On another level, one can ask about the role of women and men in everyday life – that is, the taken-for-granted practices and customs that affect women and men in a culture regardless of the particular setting they are in. Finally, one can examine the role of women and men as deviants in society – their treatment by the criminal justice system or other agencies of control, such as mental hospitals.

Currently it is possible to locate such an overview of gender discrimination and differences for virtually any country in the world. But social scientists, should also wish to know why it occurs, why it continues, or why it is not present in particular societies. Why do humans build such structures of differentiation? What do they do to us individually? Here a series of middle-range theories emerge. That is, in examining discrimination patterns in any one institution, a pattern for studying others typically suggests itself. Here three diverse areas of investigation should be examined. The study of discrimination in politics shows how diverse research and theory can be fit together to form a general model of discrimination in achievement areas of life. The study of one occupation, the cocktail waitress, suggests a set of unspoken everyday rules about female-male interaction that fit across many situations. And the data on crime and punishment remind us that gender discrimination is a complex process that implicates the oppression of certain groups of men in society as well as women.

Politics. One indicator of political participation is suffrage. In 1900, only one nation (Australia) allowed women the right to vote in all elections.[17] By 1945, women had the vote in forty nations, and today suffrage is virtually universal. Currently, only some Moslem countries and Switzerland deny women the vote or right to hold office. This is clearly an indication of major social change, that women should after centuries of denial suddenly be granted the vote. It was in fact not so sudden, for feminists have been active in some countries for centuries. Why did this occur? Was it related to the rise of industrialization, changes in life expectancy, secularization, the development of a world media? It is not known. This is an important question for the comparative sociologist to explore.

In spite of suffrage, the most blatant and readily visible form of sexism is on the political level. Almost always heads of state are men, legislative representatives are men, mayors are men, high court judges are men, and so on. When African countries developed independence in the sixties, women received more participation in government than was common in Western countries. Many feminists took this to be a sign that the developing nations would become models for the emergence of women in power, but they were unduly optimistic. Once these various nations "settled down," women were no longer granted high offices, and today African nations, like most in the world, are patriarchal. One need only examine lists of office holders around the world to see this.

Why has this occurred, given suffrage and the right of women to hold office? Here one can examine many types of studies and theories. Data on the United States, for example, shows that the large majority of major office holders begin as lawyers. Since so few women achieve any profession, and particularly law, they are cut off from the important contacts such as professional membership brings. The political parties operate so as to thwart women further. Women contribute primarily on the "grass roots" level, that is, as local organizers and campaigners. Men quickly move into the "backroom," where decisions are made as to who should be supported by the party. These gatherings until recently have been all-male and operating from a sexist bias. Currently, the few women in major offices in the United States today have achieved that position by circumventing the party until their vote-getting power was proven in some way. They have had to rely upon their husbands' financial and political contacts to assist them.[18]

A frequent explanation for the lack of women office holders is that no one will vote for them. This may operate in a minor way, but the data suggest, first, that women simply aren't given the opportunity to run, and second, that they can win if they have an effective campaign staff, suitable financing (and obviously, have competence). Recent public opinion polls in the United States have shown an increasing willingness to accept women as major office-holders. Furthermore, the old folk belief that a woman wouldn't vote for another woman fails to be supported by such data.

Duverger[19] studied the role of women in four countries intensively (France, the German Federal Republic, Norway, and Yugoslavia), along with fifteen other countries in less detail. He found that the participation of women *decreased* following suffrage. Furthermore, women in administrative posts in government have over the years come to specialize in such areas as health, welfare, motherhood, and such, so that their major impact is increasingly narrow. In left-wing parties, which ideologically advocate female equality, women are not very active. Thus suffrage did not, in the countries studied, result in getting women in office or in high administrative posts.

Tiger and Fox[20] have examined Duverger's data along with others and conclude that the extensive exclusion of women must result from a species-wide patterning. They argue, for example, that child rearing and low education alone cannot explain the poor participation of women. In addition, they believe that women neither aspire to leadership as a species characteristic, nor do they inspire followership. Also the proclivity of men to band together, the "male bond," prevents women from being accepted in the secret settings where major political decisions are made. Tiger and Fox predict that were women to dominate a set of offices, the other powerful men would circumvent them and in effect take away their power through informal, secret procedures. Though some will not accept their theory on many points, it remains an important source of ideas and issues for anyone interested in sexism in political life.

Were one to explore the topic more thoroughly, one could locate the many levels of social interaction that interact to effect the outcome. That is, the low proportion of women in political office in America (and very likely in many other countries) can be traced ultimately to these factors:

1. Female psychology. Women do not view themselves as powerful, efficacious, or worthy of high position. Hence, a low motive to seek power results.[21]
2. Family socialization. The mother has less power within the family, and thus presents a model of women as less efficacious.[22]
3. Educational socialization. Young girls are given less opportunity in schools to practice political roles. Their attitudes toward politics are more idealistic and simplistic than boys. Consequently, girls will have less interest in political roles, whether as voters or as office holders.[23]
4. Prerequisite opportunities. Most office holders in the United States have legal training, which has been denied many women.
5. Unequal participation. In spite of socialization, many women become political workers, but are excluded from decision-making roles in parties.
6. Competing demands. Political office holding typically requires expenditures of time and effort that conflict considerably with family activities. Women with domestic responsibilities find these dual roles impractical to manage.
7. Economic support. Office seeking and holding often requires financial support, both for the campaign and the demands of the office. Women have much less access to personal wealth or to those institutional sources that traditionally provide such funds.
8. The stigma of the female executive. In most cases a women is the only candidate for an office, thus plays the deviant role as an atypical candidate. She must act against existing sexist views of powerful women, thus is initially handicapped in her efforts.
9. Ongoing political processes. Those in power work to perpetuate their power. A woman who cannot hook in to the existing structure (e.g. being a widow or relative of a politician) must organize against it.

Although it is now possible to identify such variables, the importance of each and the way they interact is not yet known. They do, however, seem to form an underlying developmental sequence, as Figure 2 illustrates. Most women are removed from the process in the early stages. Of those who do become active politically, most do not aspire to office. Those who do, face significant barriers to running and winning. And those few who do win are thrust into the role of female office holder,

FIGURE 2: *Development Sequence of Female Political Involvement*

which may not be helpful to their performance and subsequent re-elections.

What this example leads to then is a possible model for the *study of female participation in non-familial or achievement roles,* including the professions, the arts, leisure pursuits, occupations, and such. In all these cases a developmental sequencing appears to result in the continual elimination of women from prestigious, powerful, or financially rewarding endpoints. Such a model is of course quite compatible with statistical studies of discrimination.

But what of nonquantitative work? This refers to features of discrimination that affect one's humanity: one's self-image, one's opportunities to express one's self to full potential. It would seem that much social science research on this problem overlooks the human dimension. The statistical approach encourages a focus on power, achievement, or money, for these outcomes are readily quantified. But in many countries the ruling class is small, and the majority of men as well as women are relatively powerless. What does discrimination mean for the lives of the "common people," those who seek a "decent life," however they define it?

Woman's Work. Economic data on many nations show how women are directed into "women's jobs" for which they receive considerably less income than men.[24] Many of these jobs have a "service" quality to them: secretarial and receptionist positions, sales work, waitressing. Women are the visible "front line" or "on stage" workers in many establishments. As such they must present a "good front" and suppress many of their feelings as representatives of the organization. While on the surface one can identify a variety of demands inherent in such jobs, scarcely any systematic research has been performed.

Recently Spradley and Mann[25] reported the work of their ethnography of cocktail waitresses at one bar. This intensive study produced a model of female-male relationships that may apply to many other settings. As such, it is an outstanding example of how a seemingly narrow and "unimportant" topic, when creatively explored, can generate major theoretical guidelines.

Bar jobs are traditionally divided by sex in America, with women as waitresses and men as bartenders. Spradley and Mann found no logical reason for the division of tasks. For example, waitresses carried heavy beer cases and trays, while waiters did lighter work. Waitresses could not announce "last drinks" to customers unless bartenders told them so. The deeper meaning of the assignment of these tasks was to restate continuously through work the taken-for-granted concepts of femininity and masculinity.

The following patterns could be discerned among the workers:

1. The handicap rule. Females are consistently put at a disadvantage through impediments, embarrassments, or restrictions that are not applied to men. For example, females do not drink before work, while males do. If the bartender gives a female a drink, she is to take it with pleasure and much gratitude.

2. Cross-over rules. Females can do male tasks, when ordered to do so, but not vice versa. Further more, females are to *thank* males for the opportunity to do their more valuable work.

3. Keeping busy. This is a form of the handicap rule that says the same activity may be labelled non-work if it is done by women, but some special form of work if it is done by men. For example, if a waitress talks to someone, it is broken up because they are "gossiping," while a bartender who talks is doing PR (public relations) work.

4. Taking orders. The job of taking orders involves a complex sequence of activities because it is done in such a way as to make the bartenders' job as easy as possible.

5. Responsibility for work. Although a wrong drink is the bartender's

fault, failure is attributed by clients to the waitress. Similarly, clients praise the bartender for success, not the waitress.

Overall, the division of labour is structured so that waitresses continually accommodate, serve, and reward the bartender. As Spradley and Mann summarize, "For bartenders in general, the waitresses have one fundamental principle; *don't assert yourself but let the bartender's wants determine the course of the encounter.*" (p. 72) In doing so, they acquire the reputation for being a "good waitress," a label girls diligently work toward.

Waitresses do bond together in some dealings with bartenders, help teach newcomers, gossip and socialize together. Yet the male workers are more tightly bonded. This is because ultimately the women are dependent upon bartenders and male customers for social support, while the converse is not true. Consequently, competition for male favours produces tension among females and creates divisions among the waitresses.

Spradley and Mann discuss many other features of the situation. Space, for example, is divided so that waitresses can continually be touched by male workers and customers alike. Rules of ordering drinks are such that they become male presentation devices, often inconveniently so for the waitress. Thus, a "regular" customer may order one drink and the waitress is supposed to know he really wants another kind. Dominance displays by males toward waitresses (taunts, invitations, physical invasions) are to be received demurely, passively, patiently, and with a smile. Through this behaviour, they reaffirm the sexual identity of the customer.

Many of the concepts and rules revealed by Spradley and Mann seem to have applicability to many other settings. Examples of handicap rules and cross-over restrictions in offices between secretaries and bosses, and in stores between clerks and managers have often been noticed. Indeed, it has often been seen to apply more subtly between female and male workers of the same rank, such as in the academic professions. These impressions suggest that some meta-rules in a sense apply to the everyday structuring of female-male inequality. We have only to look closely to see if they are in fact present.

Discrimination against males. It is easy to overlook how the cocktail bar system presents a set of restrictions on some of the males. In emphasizing certain behaviours as evidence of masculine display and prowess, a ranking system and competition results. Men who know the subtle complex signs for ordering drinks gain special status. In fact, an under-aged male who uses this special system will be served as a reward, even though the bartender recognizes the misrepresentation. Dominance displays, control of liquor, joking skills and such are part of the repertoire of actions to which the male must accommodate. Some men do not meet the standards, obviously, for there is no "winning" of this game, just a relative jockeying for position.

Status competition is an insidious feature of sexism that affects males. Control of women becomes one measure of masculinity, and restrictions from access to women are a punishment for undeserving men. But what is defined as "male?" Here one must examine the stratification system of the group or society as a whole. In America, the white Protestant business-oriented male of a certain inheritance sets the standards. Were artists or intellectuals the determining group, our vision of masculinity, and the effects of its enforcement, would be quite different.

The value preferences of this elite group govern all areas of life, dress (neat and conservative), appearance (hair trimmed), work ("clean" and inside), personal style (unemotional, competitive), intelligence (high educational achievement), and so on. These values automatically exclude large groups of men, e.g. minorities, compassionate men, homosexuals, artists, and so on. Consequently, it is not surprising that the laws and practices of the country are defined so as to harass and punish men from such groups, as well as keep them from achieving power, prestige, or money. It can be shown that this general principle pervades all institutions: work, family, leisure, religion, and so on. Take, for example, the areas of health and crime.[26]

With regard to health, American men suffer considerably more from health problems than women. Their life span is over seven years shorter. The reasons for these problems are multiple, including:

1. Worker protection laws have traditionally applied to women in many areas. In general, worker safety practices are not encouraged or regulated by the government. Consequently, many men suffer work accidents.

2. American men suffer many more accidents, which typically can be traced to their failure to observe safety precautions. Being safe or cautious is considered unmasculine.

3. Accidents are also related to alcoholism. In America, male alcoholics outnumber female by 3 or 4 to 1. The debilitating physical effects of heavy drinking on the body are well known.

4. American men are raised to deny bodily feelings and are threatened by bodily manipulations. Consequently, they see doctors in later stages of disease and resist many therapeutic practices.
5. American men even suffer more dental disease, which is again related to their poor preventative practices.
6. Although physical activity is encouraged, the competitive features are so great that most men are relatively inactive and become sports spectators rather than participants.

The reasons for this complex of behaviour relate to the medical delivery system and economics. The medical system has not been prevention oriented, nor are its activities scheduled well to serve large numbers of persons after work. (Do men in countries with other health delivery systems fare better?). The liquor industry has long had considerable political and economic clout, so that today one essential component of American masculinity relates to alcohol consumption and the accompanying rituals surrounding it. By raising men to ignore their health and then failing to provide health and safety support structures, the male stratification system becomes a deadly one indeed. Even the privileged men are not exempt, for the pressures on them to meet a narrow and rigid role model are most severe.

In the area of criminal justice, one finds more direct evidence of male oppression of other males. In the United States, crime is such that women currently comprise only about 12 percent of those arrested. Twenty men to every woman are imprisoned. Most of these men are poor, minority, or otherwise disadvantaged. Curiously, criminologists overlook the enormity of these data, taking them for granted. Often they argue that socialization explains the gender differences, but research on this point has not been convincing.

When one examines the criminal justice system, one finds that it is a masculine domain. Establishment males write the laws and run the courts. Police jurisdiction is narrowly restricted to fairly public and visible acts of personal harm or property loss. White collar crime is relegated to special law enforcement groups, often created for a temporary life span and to focus on one particular establishment. White collar criminals go to special minimum security prisons (*vide* the Watergate criminals). So the system selectively intimidates and harasses men who are most threatening to the ruling males. Such men for various reasons do commit deplorable acts, and crime should not be discounted. However, the system serves to mishandle many innocent minority men, mistreat the guilty, and serve them questionable justice, particularly given that other groups of men committing deplorable acts are ignored or lightly admonished.

The case of rape provides further illumination here. It is well-known that the Southern states for years have used the rape laws inequitably to murder many black males of questionable guilt as a means of perpetuating racism. But inter-racial rape is quite rare, and the vast majority of rapists are not prosecuted because the rules of evidence and court procedures in most states treat the female victim as guilty, a wanton seducer.

There is no certainty as why this system of male oppression has developed, the ramifications it takes, and the exact linkage it has to female discrimination. It seems, however, that this is a most fertile and promising area for further research. At the very least, it leaves the perspective that the gender stratification is intersticed with other stratification systems so that being male is no automatic guarantee of privilege.

IV. Sources of Gender Discrimination

Much work to date has dealt with the related questions: Why sex differences? Why gender discrimination? This search has led to a range of answers. The search for "real" sex differences has revived a sophisticated variation of the old nature-nurture debate, with investigators examining body physiology, anatomy, personality traits, and such. Those who search for the causes of gender discrimination presume these differences are negligible and examine the historical-cultural roots of the stratification system. Here are some of the major themes of these inquiries, though again it should be understood that this is not a comprehensive summary.

The comparative psychologists and ethologists have examined sex differences among other species for possible general laws that apply to humans as well. Much of this work has been misinterpreted and distorted in a variety of popular books. Beach[27] has extensively studied sexual behaviour of various species, demonstrating in particular the role of hormones in sexual motivation. De Vore[28] has described the importance of hormonal cycles on the dominance hierarchies of baboons. And Harlow[29] has noted a variety of sex-based behaviour in monkeys, e.g. the more rough and tumble play of young males, the grooming activity of females. Yet such studies are fraught with the

possibility of over-simplification. Much research in this area is contradictory. For example, more recent primate studies are beginning to
question the pervasiveness of the male hierarchy both across species and
within a species across locales.[30] Furthermore, we know from this research that the more one advances up the primate ladder, the more
diminished the role hormonal variables play. So this approach to date
has uncovered more problems than answers.

Biological studies of humans have been more helpful. The numerous
studies by Money and his colleagues[31] have suggested that the very
measurement of gender is not a simple matter. Their studies of hermaphrodites were most illuminating here. Hermaphrodites have mixed
sex characteristics, when measured in terms of chromosomes, gonads,
hormones, internal organs, and external appearance. They discovered
that maleness and femaleness did *not* correlate with any of these phy-
siological characteristics. Rather, assigned sex, an indicator of sex role
learning, was the determining variable in behaviour. Persons with very
discrepant body-label combinations (e.g. a "woman" with a penis)
functioned according to assignment, and often functioned well by their
own standards. Consequently, Money and his associates argued
"There is no biologic entity as sex. What exists in nature is a dimor-
phism within species into a male form and a female form."[32] As their
work continued, the investigators extended this view to argue that sexual identity is neutral or undifferentiated at birth and that a person
becomes masculine or feminine in the course of growing up. Although
some have criticized this work, empirical disproofs have not been offered.[33]

Some social theorists have built from the biological work to develop
a general model of sexual stratification in society. In all cases, the proponents have turned to ethology, not Money's investigations, so the
theories tend to be offered as "general laws" based upon cross-species
findings. Perhaps best known here is the work of Tiger and Fox,[34] who
argue that the human "biogrammar" is a hunting one, one based upon
male bands with their accompanying male politics, and the female-
child bond. More recently, Goldberg[35] argues that hormones play a
major role in the development of patriarchal power structures. Less
well-known is Collins'[36] sophisticated relating of male size superiority,
female dependence on biology (childbearing, nursing), and economic
development. Such theories tend to ignore damning evidence, yet they
are provocative syntheses of much ethnographic and anthropological
material.

A similar strand of theory claims the biological and historical superiority of the female, one that has been corrupted by recent societal developments. The superiority of the female in terms of mortality, resistance to infection, inherited weakness, developmental growth, and such has been well-documented.[37] Diner and Reed, among others, have argued that women were the leaders and creators of early society, and indeed much evidence points to the contributions of women.[38] Yet whether women were rulers (Read: superior) is another matter not answered to date in a satisfactory way. Anthropologists and historians have tended to underplay and ignore much of female contributions to culture, so the revival of this approach (originated by Bachofen a century ago) has resulted in an intellectual re-examination within these disciplines.

Certainly the most coherent theory of sex stratification is that of Engels.[39] He argued that women reigned in primitive times because they dominated the household. Descent was through the female line, so a father's children did not receive his property. Engels suggests that somehow maternal law was overthrown. Early marriages, such as those found in communal living groups, were easily dissolved by either party and the child belonged to the mother. With the advent of private property and wealth, the primacy of the male overthrew the mother's right to her children. Engels refers to those Greek civilizations where it was explicitly stated that the exclusive aim of monogamous marriage was to make the man supreme in the family and to propagate children of his own. Monogamy ensured that the children were indeed of his own seed.

Thus marriage has moved from a matter of sex-love, a natural bonding, to an unnatural one of economics:

Monogamous marriage comes on the scene as the subjugation of one sex by another; it announces a struggle between the sexes unknown through the whole previous prehistoric period... The first class opposition that appears in history coincides with the development of the antagonism between man and woman in monogamous marriage, and the first class oppression that coincides with that of the female sex by the male. Monogamous marriage was a great historical step forward; nevertheless, together with slavery and private wealth, it opens the period that has lasted until today in which every step forward is also relatively a step backward, in which prosperity and development for some is won through the misery and frustration of others.

A careful reading of Engels shows that he does not condemn marriage or monogamy in toto. Rather, he disapproves of the system of monogamy as it actually occurs, a system of controls over the woman, though not the man. As a result, there is an inherent contradiction in the family, where the appearance of equality is subverted by the fact of female subjugation. The first condition for the liberation of the wife would be to "bring the whole female sex back into public industry, and that this in turn demands the abolition of the monogamous family as the economic unity of society."

Gough[40] has examined Engels in light of current anthropological knowledge. She disputes the existence of group marriage or communal living groups, and points to the likely preponderance of nuclear family varieties in very early societies. She also notes that "matriarchy" in the home or society does not mean absence of male privilege systems. She agrees that the key element of the argument – the development of private property – has served to enhance the superiority of male status systems with their consequent despotic effect upon the role of women. Accordingly, those countries that abolish some private property, provide women with economic power, and reorganize the domestic realm are those that have advanced the most with regard to the rights of women.

The most recent theoretical development has been more empirically guided. Comparative sociologists are exploring the relationship between female rights and various structural arrangements. Sullerot[41] has explored this in historical terms as well as current ones. As a result of her study of European societies, she concludes that urbanization more than any other variable has resulted in the gradual eroding of female rights. The changing demographic characteristics in recent years (longer life expectancy, birth control, fewer children) have required societal changes to provide women with renewed opportunities. Safilios-Rothschild[42] made a cross-cultural examination of available census and other official data to investigate the relationship between social modernity and women's options. No linear relationship was found. For example, the option to marry is greater in less economically developed countries; the option to education was greatest in medium-development countries; the option for professional jobs was greatest in medium development countries. No clear configuration of conditions provide women with the maximum options, although feminist ideology appears important regardless of the country's development.

The other thrust in empirical work has been the study of child development. Over the years, much research on early sex differences in skills and personality traits have accumulated. Maccoby[43] has performed careful and detailed reviews of this material. She finds that many of the reported differences do not hold up under critical scrutiny. However, several (e.g. the male superiority in mathematical reasoning) appear to be real, though not sizeable in extent.

From this review it should be clear that the issue of why gender discrimination is unanswered. Some of the research – Money's in particular – makes its existence most puzzling. If gender is a social variable, if women are biologically superior to men, then how can a system have developed that forces bipolar sex-typing and exploits at least half of those typed?

V. Social Change

Those concerned with gender discrimination may find themselves frustrated at times because the system is under change in many countries. This change in itself is a worthy topic of investigation. Who is organizing for change, through what tactics and principles, with what success? Who is organizing against change?

Close studies of American feminism, combined with observation of some other societies, suggests that there are common themes. Early feminism aligned itself with other moral crusades of the 19th century, namely abolition of slavery and temperance (anti-liquor). Leaders and members of one cause typically espoused one of the others. With the Civil War, abolition became the focus of energy. Once slavery was abolished, feminism and temperance became more separate. Feminism itself developed particular strands, which remain to date. In the 19th century the split was along suffrage versus broad social change. The latter group desired especially changes in the family structure.

Currently, the split is along equal rights (legal establishment of "equal protection" of women and men) versus "liberation" (the elimination of gender as a basis for social identity and distinction). This is of course a simplification, but it exists sufficiently to make feminist coalitions difficult in some political situations. These ideological differences are undercut by other identities – race, class, ethnicity, religion, education – that work against a ready joining of interests among women. Consequently, change is occurring in many ways, not through a clearly visible central force of effort. A variety of individual women's organizations serve as lobbies and information resources; a feminist media is growing; many informal feminist self-help groups exist throughout local communities. The aims of these efforts range over all institutions: health, family, work, church, art, leisure. Given this conglomerate of activities, it is impossible at this time to measure the actual direction and scope of change, though its existence seems indisputable.

In considering social change as it is in the U.S., there are several forces that serve to obstruct the move toward female equity. Although the import of these variables will vary with particular countries, they will be found to be relevant in most.

First, women as a group are not united by other common bonds *except* their caste-like status as women. Being caste-like, they are not quick to recognize the role gender plays in their life. Rather, they may refer to other identities (race, class) to prove that they are *not* alike. Clever opponents of feminism manipulate these differences. For example, the media in the U.S. typically present feminist women as ugly, "unfeminine," lesbians so as to discredit their message. This is an example of the old principle of divide-and-conquer.

Second, women who do achieve success will go through changes that can dampen their feminist potential. The mobile person typically disassociates herself from the group of origin, thus loses sympathy and understanding of that group's difficulties. This can be seen amongst academic colleagues who tend to view many "women's problems" from their special privileged view, one that is not realistic for the average working woman. This is not a necessary consequence of mobility, but it does occur, to the point where some women in power, identifying with the sexist system they have beaten, are more exploitative of other women than many men.

Third, men tend to dissociate themselves from the movement. Two reasons among many are prevalent. One is that men fail to see how they suffer from the system of sex-typing. This applies especially to those men who are most oppressed by other men. For example, the situation for contemporary black women is exacerbated by the demands of some black men that they "move over" and not be so strong.[44] Again, the blue collar male tends to be very accepting of the standards of masculinity imposed that are used to "fail" him.[45] He admits to being a failure rather than acknowledge the problem as a political-economic one. The other reason is that men tend to perceive a gain in women's rights as a loss of their own. That is, they view power as of constant amount. This is again common among men who are the most powerless, who would have the most to gain with any social change.

Finally, changes in sex roles tap at changes in sexuality, which in a puritanistic society such as the United States, is particularly threatening. The use of homosexuality as a derogatory label ("sissy," "queer") is a major deterrent for men who would break from the bonds of masculine expectations. Similarly, the necessity to identify one's self as belonging to a male sexual partner is a major component of female identity. Many Americans confuse gender identity with sexuality and the security of family life, and this touches upon profound insecurities built into the American psyche.

What will happen? Can feminism, in which should be included male liberation, come about? This can be seen as an accompaniment of what appears to be a value shift in world culture. Certainly in the Western world there is currently a questioning of the primacy of technocratic values, with a renaissance of a new humanism promising itself. This shift will not occur smoothly, and may ultimately be precipitated by ecological catastrophes that prove many current political-economic systems inviable. Many would like to think that no such external threat and destruction will be necessary, that differences will be settled by negotiation, in recognition of common human needs.

NOTES

1. Margaret Mead, *Sex and Temperament in Three Societies*, William Morrow and Co., 1931.
2. An interesting current exception to this principle involves the Shah of Iran, who has in recent years greatly increased the power of his wife Farah Diba, so that she fills more than a figurehead role on her state visits. This example is curious in that Iran is a Moslem country, where legal and social discrimination against women is perhaps at its greatest.
3. Evelyne Sullerot, *Women, Society, and Change*, New York, MacGraw-Hill, 1971.
4. Denise Paulme, *Women of Tropical Africa*, Berkeley, Ca., University of California Press, 1971.
5. Sullerot, *op. cit.*
6. *Women in Labor*, U.S. Department of Labor Report, 1969.
7. A good example here is peasant Greece. See J. K. Campbell, *Honor, Family, and Patronage*, New York, Oxford University Press, 1974.
8. See, for example Robert Herron and Brian Sutton-Smith, *Child's Play*, New York, Holt, Rinehart, and Winston, 1973.
9. Emile Benoit-Smullyan, "Status, Status Types, and Status Interrelations," *American Sociological Review* 9 (1944), pp. 151–161.
10. Clarice Stasz Stoll, *Female and Male*, Dubuque, Iowa, William C. Brown Co., 1974.
11. Robert K. Merton, *Social Theory and Social Structure*, Rev. ed., New York, The Free Press, 1957.
12. W. I. Thomas, *The Child in America*, New York, Alfred A. Knopf, Inc., 1928.

13. The classic study here is Robert F. Bales and Philip Slater, "Role Differentiation in Small Decision-Making Groups," in T. Parsons and R. F. Bales, *Family Socialization and Interaction Process*, New York, Free Press, 1955.

14. Helen Moyer Hacker, "Women as a Minority Group," *Social Forces*, 30 (1951), pp. 60–69.

15. Gerald D. Berreman, "Caste in India and the United States," *American Journal of Sociology*, 61 (1960), pp. 120–127.

16. Eva Figes, *Patriarchal Attitudes*, New York, Stein and Day, 1970.

17. A good summary of political data is provided by Sullerot, *op. cit.*

18. For example, Edmond Constantini and Kenneth H. Craik, "Women as Politicians," *Journal of Social Issues*, 28 (1972), pp. 217–236; Ingunn Norderval Means, "Women in Local Politics," *Canadian Journal of Political Science*, 5 (1972), pp. 365–388.

19. Maurice Duverger, *The Political Role of Women*, Paris, UNESCO, 1955.

20. Lionel Tiger and Robin Fox, *Men in Groups*, New York, Random House, 1969.

21. For more on this, see Judith Bardwick, *Psychology of Women*, New York, Harper and Row, 1971.

22. Dair L. Gillespie, "Who Has the Power: The Marital Struggle," *Journal of Marriage and the Family*. 33 (1971), pp. 445–458.

23. For example, Fred Greenstein, "Sex-related Political Differences in Childhood," *Journal of Politics*, 23 (1961), pp. 353–371.

24. A sampling of such economic studies include Elena Haavio-Mamnila, "The Position of Finnish Women," Journal of *Marriage and the Family*, 31 (1969), pp. 339–347; Pawel Horoszowski, "Women's Status in Socialistic and Capitalistic Countries (II)." *International Journal of Sociology of the Family*, 1 (1971), pp. 160–180: William M. Mandel, "Soviet Women in the Work Force and Professions," *American Behavioral Scientist*, 15 (1971), pp. 255–280.

25. James P. Spradley and Brenda J. Mann, *The Cocktail Waitress*, New York, John Wiley and Sons, 1975.

26. This section is based upon data and references provided in Stoll, *op. cit.*

27. Frank Beach, *Sex and Behavior*, New York, John Wiley and Sons, 1965.

28. Ivan De Vore, "Male Dominance and Mating Behavior in Baboons," in F.A. Beach, *op. cit.*, pp. 266–289.

29. Harry Harlow, "The Heterosexual Affectional System in Monkeys," *American Psychologist*, 17 (1969), pp. 1–9.

30. One example of this work is J. F. Eisenberg, N. A. Muckenhirn, and R. Rodran, "The Relation Between Ecology and Social Structure in Primates," *Science*, 176 (1972), pp. 863–874.

31. This work covers a 20 year period, and has recently been synthesized in John Money and Anke Erhardt, *Man and Woman, Boy and Girl*, New York, Signet, 1974.

32. John Money, "Sex Hormones and Other Variables in Human Eroticism," in W. C. Young (Ed.), *Sex and Internal Secretions*, Vol. 2, Baltimore, Wilkins and Wilkins, 1961, p. 1340.

33. M. Diamond, "A Critical Evaluation of the Ontogeny of Human Sexual Behavior," *Quarterly Review of Biology*, 40 (1965), pp. 140–175.

34. Lionel Tiger and Robin Fox, *Men in Groups*, *op. cit.*; also *The Imperial Animal*, New York, Harper and Row, 1972.

35. Stephen Goldberg, *The Inevitability of Patriarchy*, New York, William C. Morrow, 1974.

36. Randall Collins, "A Conflict Theory of Sexual Stratification," Social Problems, 19 (1971), pp. 3–21.

37. See Chapter One of Stoll, *op. cit.* for data and references.

38. Helen Diner, *Mothers and Amazons*, New York, Julian Press, 1965; Evelyn Reed, *Problems of Women's Liberation: A Marxist Approach*, New York, Pathfinder, 1971.

39. Friedrich Engels, The Origins of the Family, *Private Property and the State*, Chicago, Charles Kerr and Co., 1902, Many contemporary feminist theorists of note have been influenced by Engels, notably Shulamith Firestone, *The Dialectic of Sex*, New York, Bantam, 1970; Juliet Mitchell, *Woman's Estate*, New York. Vintage, 1971.

40. Kathleen Gough, "The Origin of the Family," *Journal of Marriage and the Family*, 33 (1971), pp. 760–771.

41. Evelyne Sullerot, *op. cit.*

42. Constantina Safilios-Rothschild, "A Cross-Cultural Examination of Women's Marital, Educational, and Occupational Options," *Acta Sociologica*, 14 (1971), pp. 96–113.

43. Eleanor Maccoby, *The Development of Sex Differences*, Stanford, Stanford University Press, 1961, and *The Psychology of Sex Differences*, Stanford, Stanford University Press, 1974.

44. This is discussed in Pauli Murray, "The Liberation of Black Women," in M. L. Thompson (Ed.), *Voices of the New Feminism*, Boston, Beacon Press, 1970.

45. See Jonathan Sennett and Richard Cobb, *The Hidden Injuries of Class*, New York, Random House, 1973.

The Manhunts: Aché Indians in Paraguay

MARK MÜNZEL

Dr. Mark Münzel is a German ethnologist, born in Potsdam in 1943. He studied ethnology and romantics in Frankfort/Main, Paris and Coimbra (Portugal). From 1966–68 he was in Brazil for research on the Kamayurá and on the Makú in the North West Amazon territory. He obtained his Doctor's degree in 1970 from the J. W. Goethe University, Frankfort/Main, where he became a lecturer on South American ethnology. From 1971–72 he went to Paraguay for research on the Aché, and from there he went to the Cuzco territory for research on the Peruvian Indians. Since 1973 he has been the curator of the Frankfort Museum for ethnology and lecturer in ethnology at the University of Giessen.

Dr. Münzel's publications include "Notas preliminares sôbre os Kabori (Makú entre o Rio Negro e o Japurá)" in *Revista de Antropologia* XVII–XX, 1, 137–181, Sao Paulo, 1969–1972; "Tortuga Persique a Tortuga – Por qué los Axé 'mansos' persiquen a sus hermanos 'salvajes'?" in: *Crisis*, 4, 9–12, Buenos Aires, 1973; "Kwere veja puku. Notas preliminares sôbre cinco canciones axé" in Suplemento Antropológico, VI, 1–2, 177–259, Asunción del Paraguay, 1971; "The Aché Indians: Genocide in Paraguay," IWGIA Document 11, Copenhagen, 1973; and "The Aché: Genocide Continues in Paraguay," IWGIA Document 17, Copenhagen, 1974.

The Manhunts: Aché Indians in Paraguay

MARK MÜNZEL

Alexander K. Macdonald, British traveller in Paraguay observed in 1911:

If a party of native hunters hear the tapping of the Indian's axe, they sneak up quietly and murder the poor wretch up in the tree with no more compunction than if they were killing a monkey. I asked one of these fellows why they killed these people without provocation. He shrugged his shoulders and replied, "Quien sabe. Don't you know that the skin of an Indian is tougher than any other for making hammocks?"[1]

In 1968, Juan Alfonso Borgognon, a senior officer of the Paraguayan armed forces and a member of the ruling political party, then Vice-Director of the Native Affairs Department of the Ministry of Defence, wrote that the Aché were close to extinction due to the repressive action which follows any Aché effort to resist the occupation of their lands,[2] In December 1971, Justo Meza, a distinguished reporter for *abc color*, the most important pro-Government newspaper[3] in Paraguay wrote of

murders of fathers and mothers as the only way of seizing Aché children who are then sold and brought up as servants ... They even tell of prizes for those who manage to kill the Indians.[4]

Meza cites the following as legally valid proof:

The bullet traces on many of the Indians ... One of them cannot use his hand any more, another has bullets stuck in his thigh, one woman has shrapnel in her shoulder. We have seen all of that.[5]

The Paraguayan anthropologist Miguel Chase Sardi confirmed this in an interview in the same newspaper in 1972:

They are hunted, they are pursued like animals. The parents are killed and the children sold ... and there is no family of which a child has not been murdered.[6]

How these hunts are executed, we are told by another Paraguayan anthropologist, Luis Albospino, former head of the Paraguayan Indigenist Association, a semi-official organization that includes national figures interested in Indian questions:

With the "mboca-nuhá," a trap made of a fire-arm that is hidden in the woods and that fires automatically when the victim passes; with poisoned meals; with "senuelos" (Aché captured during childhood and sent into the forest as adults, in order to attract their free brethren) .... They put on their trail Indian scouts from other tribes or dogs.[7]

In 1971, I taped the statement of a manhunter, who described to me how he would go about proceeding against the Aché:

Grab them by the arms, drag them behind us. Attack them at night, stamp out their campfire, strike them down. We'll force the damned women, who don't want to be carried off by truck, to run in front of it until they collapse with exhaustion. We'll have to break the arm of the wild chief "Tortoise-man." He, "Tortoise-man" will cry out with pain, and we'll finish him off with the machete. The White Man says, "Tortoise-man" will cry out with pain.[8]

Since 1968 several cases can be verified with documents which, taken together, result in a dismal picture and which are nevertheless surely only the tip of the iceberg. Here are some examples:

1. Letter of Gumersindo Ayala, a respected Paraguayan intellectual and delegate of the Ministry of Public Works and Communications to his Minister, dated "Asunción, January 2nd, 1969":

Dear Mr. Minister:
As a delegate of the Ministry of Public Works and Communications to the Department for Native Affairs of the Defence Ministry I have the honour of applying to Your Excellency in order to bring the following to your kind attention:
Mr. Roque Jacinto Lovera, an acquaintance of mine who was in the Telegraph Department of the ANDE for the Department Alto Paraná came to my apartment expressly for the purpose of informing me that the rural laborers of Mr. Retamozo's estancia "La Golondrina," which lies between Itakyry and Yhü, had killed 7 Aché – Women, old people, children – apparently without any cause whatsoever, and that they had kidnapped a little girl about six years old whom they held captive in the aforesaid estancia. Furthermore, he told me that this incident took place in September/October of last year (1968) and that the above mentioned Mr. Lovera called for the foreman to account for the unpardonable crime committed. Whereupon the foreman replied that he had orders to liquidate these "savages."
I am bringing this case to your attention, Your Excellency, so that you

can decide what should be done and so that a repetition of such actions by "civilized" persons can be prevented.[9]

2. On June 29, 1973 a spokesman for the Paraguayan Episcopal Conference informed the press that the Paraguayan bishops were deeply alarmed about massacres committed against Indians:

One of the massacres of Aché Indians took place last year near Laurel, on 12 to 20 persons .... The incident is even more terrible because the massacre of the Aché, which was not the first, was executed in cold blood in the course of a manhunt. Five children were brought back, of which two have already died.[10]

Exact details about this incident are to be found in a document compiled on the basis of eyewitness reports by the Department of Mission (that is, for Indian Affairs) of the Paraguayan Episcopal Conference. The statement made by Father Meliá, Executive Secretary of the Mission Department, superior of a Jesuit community at Asunción, and President of the Centre of Anthropological Studies at the Catholic University of Asunción, is based on this document:

At the end of August 1971 two dead cows were found which belonged to the estancia "Naranjito." This deed was attributed to the Aché. Thereupon a retaliatory expedition was organized against them. For several days they pursued the traces of the Aché until they finally found them on a tract of land belonging to the government called "Zona F" .... Those participating in this manhunt were: the foreman of the estancia, his brother, who had organized a hunt in 1967, from which he had brought back two girls and a boy who at present live in Itakyry and Hernandarias respectively – and a well known forest guide nicknamed "Teyú" (Lizard), and two or three more in addition .... Several (Aché) were stabbed to death with machete knives, including women, probably the mothers of the children brought back from the hunt.[11]

3. On August 13, 1973 the Paraguayan daily newspaper *La Tribuna* published an interview with Father Meliá in which he reported on indications, which he himself had seen of an additional massacre:

On an estancia north of Itakyry there is ... a whole stock of bows and arrows. Two or three Aché children lived on the same estancia – all of them quite obviously the yield of a previous massacre.[12]

4. 3 September 1970 on the Itaimbey River approximately 35 to 40 kilometers up river from Puerto Santa Teresa, a working group of the UN-FAO and the Paraguayan Ministry of Agriculture Project on Forest and Forest Industries Development, including Donald Wood, the field supervisor of the Forest Inventory Section of this project, and

David Griggs, a Peace Corps volunteer attached to this section met and photographed a man-hunter:

This man is shown proudly displaying a 4 month old Guajaki (= Aché) arrow wound which he received, approximately 12 kilometers further up the Rio Itaimbey, after he and a group of Paraguayans attacked a group of Indians. He boasted of killing several Indians on this occasion before he was wounded. (Letter from David Griggs to me.)

5. On September 21, 1973 the Paraguayan weekly magazine *Aquí* published a report on "tracking down" a group of Aché, which is especially interesting because of what is between the lines and what is left out:

(In Hernandarias) the natives and the persons who found them – or captured them, as you wish – spent the night ... The Aché[13] were found by Hilarion Vera, who described his experience in the midst of the tropical forest of Alto Paraná to us:
"On Thursday, August 30th I set out with my companion .... We rode on a tractor and pushed on into the forest until we came to a place called Soó-i about 80 kilometers from the bank of the Paraná River .... There I saw a completely naked man run past us .... We stopped the tractor, but then we pushed forward another 50 meters and saw another completely naked man run past us in the same place .... I shot into the air with my rifle. When the Aché saw us they began to run. I stopped the tractor and shot into the air again. Then they stopped in their tracks, threw away their bows and arrows, and held up their hands.[14]

The report continued that shortly thereafter a larger group (10 to 20 Aché) "came out of the forest" and surrendered. A few days later, however, the reporter only came across 3 Aché. What happened to the others was not stated.

Everything seems to indicate that manhunts are still being carried out today. As late as September 1973 Antonio Oddone Sarubbi, the head of the administration and police department of Alto Paraná, declared that there were people there "who kill them (the Aché) very calmly and without any compunction."[15] In 1974 an article in the *New York Times* quoted a North American Protestant missionary living in Paraguay as saying that it was still not certain that an Aché "can walk up to a Paraguayan and not be shot at."[16] The Paraguayan anthropologist Chase Sardi, in a report of the Centre of Anthropological Studies dated January 16, 1974, which was directed to the Defence Minister authorized to handle Indian Affairs, stated:

The groups of hunters, woodcutters, and palmito collectors have developed into veritable punitive expeditions against them (the Aché) .... (The well-known slave hunter Manuel de Jesús Pereira) is constantly on expeditions in the forest with the objective of enslaving additional Aché groups.[17]

Again in 1974 the Paraguayan Episcopal Conference protested against the continuing massacres. On April 22, 1974 Msr. Alejo Ovelar, President of the Department of Missions declared in a letter to the editor of the daily newspaper *La Tribuna*:

Our Secretariat has in its possession a documentation about cases of massacres ... against Paraguayan Indigenous.[18]

8 May 1974, the same Department stated again:

The Department of Mission of the Paraguayan Episcopal Conference
- has denounced and denounces, based upon concrete data which have been duly investigated, the existence of cases of genocide;
- has received information about other cases, with data which have only partly been studied and must still be completed;
- desires there be a large investigation, especially about the situation of certain indigenous groups of Paraguay who are especially threatened in their ethnic survival.[19]

What injury is really being inflicted upon the Aché becomes evident to the person who sees how Aché children are taught from an early age not to cry, so that they will not betray their location to the manhunters – or who talks to survivors who list the names of those murdered in a monotonous voice and who describe their lives in the last years: always fleeing, almost constantly forced to look for cover in the jungle, reduced to hiding places like a swamp without fresh water, where, for example, a group of over 100 people vegetated for months in 1971/72.

Running, fearing, screaming, hastily burying the dead, digging up roots to eat, running further,

was the resumé, which, Indian-like, a laconic Aché gave me of his life fleeing from the manhunters. These reports, taken together, show clearly that it is no longer a question of single infringements originating from a traditional contempt of Indians, but a systematic combing of the forests for Indians, specifically since about 1968.

What kind of nightmare, what permanent state of fear that must mean for the Aché is intimated in a report by the Italian-Paraguayan anthropologist Luigi Miraglia, who in 1972 observed an Aché group which had just been captured: these Indians had had to get so used to the precautionary measures necessary for survival that they still heeded them even during the first few days after their capture. When it gets dark (nightfall is according to the concurring testimony of many Aché the hunting time of the Whites)

They don't talk. They ask and answer in sign language .... They have a cover of branches over the fire, and on top of that a woven mat so that no smoke can rise up.[20]

Whoever survives this life is usually psychologically disturbed. The case of the approximately 25-year-old Nambúgi, with whom I lived on a reservation in 1971/72, is typical. He wanted to tell me things about his life again and again. He always began with a description from his childhood of how he set out together with the adults on a hunt. When he was about 10 years old, his people killed a tapir. At this point he always broke off his narrative, like a tape that has been erased in the middle. A friend of this man finally gave me the explanation. "The adults left Nambúgi to guard the dead tapir. There the Whites attacked him by surprise and shot him. He fled, bleeding profusely, was pursued, and got lost in the forest. That is what he wanted to tell you." Nambúgi himself never succeeded in telling me that. But the Aché possess a poetic language which helps the Indians retain and express their thoughts and dreams. Nambúgi is the author of a poem in which the shock of the attack by the Whites on the small boy guarding the tapir has obviously been assimilated into a mystical nightmare vision:

> I, when I was still a man,
> I shot great wild boars with my arrow,
> on the hunt I pierced wild boars.
> I, when I was still a man –
> until the tapir was shot,
> until I died and with me all men,
> until a great trembling caught hold of me.
>
> Then I began my roving far far away
> through the rain, on my shoulder the tapir.
> The tapir wandered with me,
> he bore me away.
> I and the tapir – he bore me into the forest of the dead.
> The tapir bore me into the forest of the dead.
>
> In the forest of the dead we shot wild boars,
> wild boars in the rain.
> In the forest of the dead I mounted the truck,
> in the forest of the dead I was driven away
> on the truck full of dead.

The truck of the dead bore me to Asunción.
I, when I was dead, I visited the city of the Whites.
I when I was dead, with my friends the Whites,
in the city of the dead we shot
at the dead bodies of Aché, at the many dead bodies.
Dead bodies in the rain.
I, when I was dead, I roved far away,
on the truck of the Whites I rode,
in the airplane of the Whites I flew,
into the splendid, great shining white house of the sun,
I, when I was dead, I flew there,
I, all alone, with me only the Whites,
I with my rifle shot at the corpses of Aché,
I threw a flaming billet into the white house of the sun,
I killed our great Mother, who lives at the sun.
I, all alone, with me only the Whites.[21]

While listening to some tapes I possess of Aché describing their lives, I discovered that the most frequent key word is "fear." And an Aché myth relates:

At the beginning of all things when the Great Jaguar told all the people what they were supposed to do on earth, he left the Whites out. He was afraid of them himself.

I. THE SLAVERY

"Slavery Just One Hazard Facing Paraguayan Tribe" is the headline of an article of the *New York Times* about the Aché in 1974. It reports from Paraguay:

Examples of slavery abound even today in eastern Paraguay and occasionally here in the capital .... "It's still a sign of status around here to own your own Aché," Mr. Stolz (a North American Protestant missionary interviewed in Paraguay) explained. "Many Paraguayans consider them the fiercest Indians in the country, and I guess for some of them it's like having a tiger at home to show off to friends."[22]

Slavery is defined as the state of someone over whom any or all the powers attaching to the right of ownership are exercised. In the case of the captured Aché the possibility of sale and of lending out for money should be especially emphasized in this context. On March 8, 1974, in the US Senate, Senator James Abourezk declared:

Recently, I received a copy of a receipt made out for payment for work done by Aché slaves.[23]

Mr. Luis E. Pena, Research Affiliate at the Peabody Museum, Yale University, who recently travelled through the interior of eastern Paraguay was offered an Aché child. In 1972, I was told by rural dwellers that the price of Aché children was falling, due to the great supply and the current price was the equivalent of $5.00 for an Aché girl of about five years of age. Rabbi Rosenthal, Director of the Latin American Division of the ADL in New York reported that the going rate for Aché slaves had dropped to $1.25 in late 1973. The ethnologist Clastres touches on the psychological background of slavery when he tells of the case of a large group of captured Aché who could escape because their hunters had put them into a cattle corral, with no one to guard them:

The ingenuousness of their logic made the Paraguayans treat the Indians like a herd of cattle.[24]

The daily athmosphere of slavery is described in an article published in a Paraguayan pro-Government newspaper:

Two hunters penetrated into the forests of the Paraná. They killed an Aché "male" and wounded a "female," his wife, taking possession of her children, a little boy of ten years of age and a baby girl. The boy was sold to a wood cutter of the Paraná, the girl to a village family. These data we obtained from Kandégi, the Aché "male", now an adult, 15 years after he was hunted: data confirmed by his "master" . . . .
(His sister), after having served as a slave for many years, . . . was put in the street when advanced pregnancy made it impossible for her to perform her tasks. As a reward for years of slavery, she bore on her shoulders a shirt . . . almost too short to cover her nakedness. . . . When, after giving birth, she offered her services to another family, the latter insisted that she get rid of her daughter – a condition which she accepted in order that they should not both die of hunger. She gave her daughter to a family without children[25].

Different cases of enslavement of Aché can be verified by the accounts of witnesses in Paraguay, as for example:
1. In the newspaper interview of August 13, 1973 already cited, Father Meliá mentions:

a blood-bath in 1966/67 in which two girls and a boy were taken captive. The girls are in Itakyry and the boy in Hernandarias.

As can easily be verified in the above-named places, the killers were directed by Mr. Jorge Enciso, a well known hunter of Aché from Laurel and a relative of Mr. Margeal Enciso, the foreman of the already mentioned "naranjito" estancia. The girls seen by Father Meliá are Magdalena, some 4 years old when captured, sold to Guillermo Colmán, a shop owner at Itakyry; and Margarita, about 6, sold to the Samudio family, likewise shop owners at Itakyry. The boy, of perhaps 12 years of age, was first kept in the house of the leader of the raid, Jorge Enciso in Laurel, and later passed on to a brother of Mr. Enciso, who used him as a servant in his "Bar-Pensión La Guaireña" in Hernandarias, where Father Meliá saw him.

2. On July 2, 1972 the Director of the Native Affairs Department of the Ministry of Defence, Colonel Infanzón, mentions in a newspaper interview an Aché girl who was separated from her parents and given to a married couple of Japanese immigrants. He adds that this is confirmed by the report of a country parson.[26]

3. The report already mentioned of the Paraguayan anthropologist Chase Sardi of January 16, 1974, states:

About 15 kilometers from Yhü is the estancia "Kurusú"of Mr. Manuel Cáceres. Somehow, we don't know how, about 30 Aché, and in addition several Aché children who had been separated from their parents and relatives were brought there. Among them the following could be identified: Tomasa, 13 years old; Emilio, 7; Reina, 10; Miguel, 5, easily identifiable because of a large burn on his buttocks .... The administrator of the estancia refuses to give the children back to their parents .... The adults have to work without any sort of wage, only for their food. I could also see that some of the especially strong-bodied Aché Indians who were submissive to their master served as prison guards of the other Indians and kept them from returning home ....
(On another estancia with about 20 Aché) according to the statements of the inhabitants of Yhü, soldiers are employed to prevent the Aché, who have to work for deficient and filthy food, from escaping. They are punished very severely if they do not do the work they are charged with .... The neighbours told us very fearfully in private that three of them (of the Aché), Lila, Juanita, and Lucía, had been sold to people who came from Asunción to fetch them.[27]

4. The officially recommended "solution" of these "problems" does not include the limitation of the massacres and liberation of the slaves by means of legal pressure, but the installation of a "reservation" to which the Aché, who are a "problem" elsewhere, may be deported. September 1973, in an interview in the German radio station "Hessischer Rundfunk," Chase Sardi explained that the inmates of this "reservation" are "real prisoners."[28]

5. In his report of January 16, 1974, the anthropologist names several cases of children who were carried off the reservation, for example:

Father Jorge Romero from Cecilio Báez took the little boy whose photograph I am enclosing and who is called Cleto-í. He is about ten years of age, and his Indian name is Takuángi. His mother, Elena, whose Indian name is Pichúgi, cries very often over the absence of her son. The priest refuses, however, to give him back, on the pretext that he is giving him a Christian education.[29]

6. I possess the photocopy of a letter, which a Paraguayan farmer, Arnaldo Acosta Kant, wrote to Nélido Ríos, a health officer working on the "reservation" and an employee of the Paraguayan Ministry of Health, on May 1, 1973. It is clear from this letter that the state employee "herded together" (the expression used here is generally used when referring to driving livestock together) a group of Aché Indians on the "reservation" and handed them over to the farmer. The two had agreed upon giving as a reason for this act that they wanted to protect the Indians from slavery.

II. Hunger and Disease

It was also reported in the above mentioned letter that the Indians tearfully refused to return to the "reservation" because, as they declared, "they didn't get anything to eat there." In a letter of July 26, 1973, a very dependable witness wrote to me:

There was an Aché (on the "reservation"), who in order to be able to buy food, sold his son to a settler for 80 Gs.[30]

Famine seems to occur only periodically on the "reservation." The bad position of the "reservation," however, is permanent, and because of it future famines can be expected. It has been situated on soil of such poor quality that it has but

little agricultural value. The forests of the reservation have a limited potential . . . . (Quantity and quality of the water on the Reservation) will possibly turn out to be of no use to the necessities of the inhabitants,

as explained in the section "Soil and Use of the Land" of the UN-FAO and Paraguayan Ministry of Agriculture Project for Forest and Forest Industries Development.[31] Moreover, the 4500 hectares on the reservation are no longer intact. The letter already mentioned of July 26, 1973 states in addition:

Before the reservation was founded about 10 families of white settlers lived on this land. In the last few years, however, about 100 families have penetrated into the land, about 30 in last several months.

That means that the Paraguayan administration deported the Indians to a tract of land which it knows will not be able to support them for long, and it even allows this small patch to be cut up further.

The change of diet brought about in the "reservation" is one of the factors which foster disease among the Indians. Added to that comes the well known biological shock of the first contact with the microbes of the white man. At present, the policies of the "reservation" help to widen the effects of these shocks, that is they help to increase the mortality rate of the Indians. This occurs by first bringing the Aché on to the "reservation," and then allowing them to leave it after a while. The inevitable consequence of this is the spreading of the diseases which the Aché encountered in the Reservation to those still living in the forest, thus weakening such free Aché as remain.

III. THE DECULTURATION

Since September 1972 the "reservation" has been run by missionaries of the North American Protestant "To the New Tribes" group, who were commissioned by the Paraguayan authorities. In comparison with earlier years, when the "reservation" was under the direct auspices of the Paraguayan military officials, this means the end of open brutality towards the Indians and more concern for their physical welfare. Nevertheless, one still cannot speak of a mission policy of their own. Basically, the missionaries carry out in detail the still unchanged reservation policies of the Paraguayan authorities, but with certain humane reforms. In one important aspect they pursue the official line of the Indian policy of the Paraguayan Native Affairs Department with even greater severity than the former administrators: they try to achieve rapid cultural "integration" of the Aché. This is motivated, on the one hand, by the basic attitude of the "To the New Tribes" missionaries in particular, who fit into a special category among all the different mission groups that work with South American Indians. They are known for "civilizing with a sledge hammer" (as the ethnologist W. Haberland states) because they (as Chase Sardi formulates)

confuse the essential principles of Christianity – which as we understand it, are above every culture and have universal value – with the particular values of Western culture, and teach the latter as though they were the former .... (They) regard the Indians as degenerate and given to dealings with the devil ... (and therefore) systematically oppose the few remaining tribal customs and ceremonies, which they regard as pagan.[32]

On the other hand, in the case of the Aché there seems to be added pressure from the Native Affairs Department, which probably chose just these very missionaries for the "reservation" because it perceived them to be possible allies in the rapid erasure of the Aché culture. Under this influence, the missionaries' contempt for the Aché culture seems to be greater than is otherwise the norm of the "To the New Tribes" group. While elsewhere the members of this group are noted for carefully studying the languages of the natives to whom they are assigned (the missionaries receive language training), this is obviously not the case on the Aché reservation. After over a year's stay there the reservation administrator still spoke no Aché and evidently did not think of learning it.[33] Imagine, here is a man who practically has the power of life and death over people with whom he does not even seek linguistic communication. Just as lacking also is the missionaries' understanding for the primitive culture of the Aché.[34] The result is a relentless destruction of the old culture, accompanied by the inability to help the Indians build up a new culture. David Bidney's observation is appropriate here:

For many native peoples brought involuntarily and reluctantly into contact with Western civilization, acculturation is all too often "deculturation," since the old, partially discarded cultural forms and institutions are not superseded by functional new forms. Such cultural crises may be regarded as the products of cultural inertia and of the withering away of native institutions when brought into contact with alien patterns of culture which they can neither resist nor assimilate.[35]

The destruction of the Aché identity has already been noted by the Paraguayan anthropologist and linguist León Cadogan, by Vivante and Gancedo, Argentinian scientists, and by the Bishop of Coronel Oviedo, Mr. Pechilo and by Father Meliá.[36] Cadogan has stated that

a people, now that its miserable remnants have been obliged to "integrate into civilized life," is deprived of . . . what it considers its dearest possession, its identity . . . . What has happened on the human level merits the designation of tragedy.[37]

I could observe what he meant when I was on the "reservation" in 1971/72. Everything indicates that this deculturation is continuing or is even getting worse.

Without regard to the hunting habits of the Aché, the "reservation" has been situated in an area where hunting is difficult if not altogether impossible. The result is a complete disorientation, as admiration for the great hunter was the main basis of the cultural values of these people. In the absence of their traditional subsistence base, with the resultant need to become wholly dependent upon their captors for food and shelter, the authority of the traditional chiefs, which was the basis of the social and political life of the Aché, tends to disintegrate in the face of the growing economic and psychological dependence which the Aché develop in relation to the white men who control the "reservation."

One of the most important aspects of the Aché world view is the giving of names and the name one has is intimately related with one's soul. The "reservation" Indians are forced to give up their Aché names and Christian names are imposed upon them by the administration and the Aché are not even allowed to participate in their selection. Because of the importance of the name of an individual, together with the name-soul connection in their beliefs, they now believe they are losing their souls.

The Aché are prevented from celebrating their traditional feasts and their music is being eradicated. They have been forced to change their hair styles and the men have been forced to remove the "betá," a lip ornament which for the Aché is an indication of manhood. The Aché are supposed to give up their own language. They are constantly exhorted to become more like the whites, and they now start to think that anything connected with their own culture is shameful.

To illustrate the cultural disorientation suffered while on the "reservation," the story of a couple, Torági and Kvevégi-Chachúgi, whose child died of hunger shortly after capture is indicative of the extent of the cultural disruption in the every day lives of the people. According to the custom of the Aché, the couple wanted to bury their child in the forest according to their traditional rites, but the administrator interfered and obliged them to bury their child close to the house and in accordance with a specific Christian rite. The implication of this, according to the Aché belief, was that the spirit of the child remained close to the house and constituted a grave danger to the mother should she engage in sexual intercourse. Thus the couple abstained from sexual relations, waiting for the chance to fulfill the necessary rites which had been forbidden. The fact that the woman was obliged to have intercourse with the administrator and other men presented not only a marital threat to the couple, but also a religious danger from the spirit. This is not an isolated example.

This is not the place to discuss the theoretical and real issue of whether primitive cultures should be preserved or modernized. What is taking place, however, is not modernization but the destruction of the identity and self-respect of the Aché. This destruction begins from the moment the free Aché is captured and is forced to become sedentary. And from this very moment the Aché himself is well aware of what is happening to him. On March 8, 1972 I was present on the "reservation" when a new group of captives arrived. I asked one of them what his name was. He answered evasively, speaking in the poetic metaphors typical for the Aché:

I am one who shot at the Whites with my arrows when they penetrated into the forest. I am a dead man, who once hated the Whites, I am a White Man.

Even this newcomer to the "reservation" expressed here a thought quite clearly, which preoccupies those who have stayed on the "reservation" for a longer time: that capture with the consequent transition to the mode of life of the Whites is like death. I recorded on tape many songs lamenting the end of the Aché, in which the singer regards himself as no longer an Aché and not even a human being, but rather as a dead man. The French ethnologist Clastres describes a song he recorded on the "reservation":

Every strophe, psalmodied on a sound of deep sadness and nausea, ended in a lamentation that was then prolonged by the delicate melancholy of the flute. He sang that day of the end of the Aché and of his despair in realizing that it was all over:

> "The Aché, when they were real Aché, shot many animals
> in the woods.
> And now, the Aché are Aché no more.
>
> The Aché in the woods joined their arrows
> against the wild boars, gaily they ate the wild boars' meat.
> And now, the Aché lie down in the ashes,
> and do not leave their houses any more,
> when outside they hear the animals' cries.
> Then the Aché hit the big anteater in the woods.
> Now the Aché will never hit the big anteater in the woods.
>
> The Aché, oh, the Aché are no longer Aché at all –
> woe, woe to me!"[38]

In their own names, the Aché express their rejection of this transition. Usually they have animal names, but with an ending which indicates that the bearer is a human being. On the "reservation," however, they often leave off this ending, thereby showing that they themselves believe they have lost all human dignity and have become animals. In the same way songs demonstrate a very clear perception of the situation in which they now live. I translated a song about the contrast between their old free life in the forest (when the Aché only worked for themselves and the Great Father of their religion) and their present life on the "reservation" where they serve the Whites and where their old chiefs and the Great Father are displaced by the Big Bosses.

> We, who were once men,
> never, never will we
> rove freely between the trees of the forest.
> We will never leave
> our Big Boss,
> who put on a big chieftain's headdress.
>
> Now we will never again
> find sustenance between our forefathers,
> the trees of the forest.
> Now we have forever left
> our grandmothers, the great anteaters
> far, far behind
>
> Now, out of the radiant shining great house of the sun
> of our Great Father
> the wide sleeping mats have been brutally ripped out.
>
> Now my daughters
> live in big houses of the masters.
> We will never weep together.
>
> Now my daughters
> live in big houses of the masters
> already completely tamed.
>
> Now, our mothers, the stately women,
> have long been buried.
> They, the magnificent anteaters,
> have all been left behind.
>
> Now those who once were our fathers
> have already turned into magnificent anteaters
> and have all been left hastily far behind.
>
> Now the Big Boss
> is our Big Boss
> Master of the corn;
> his is a big house,
> his is power over us all.

Between the trees of the forest
I will never again find my sustenance –
all the corn for the Boss!
We will never leave him again.

Between the trees of the forest
we will never again
carry away with us things taken from the Whites
in our baskets.

Now our daughters, women in their blossom,
are in the big houses of the masters,
where they are shouted at, so that they do their work,
the work of the Whites.

Our daughters, already beautiful young girls,
are now in the houses of the big masters
completely tamed
from being shouted at so much.

Our girls, who were beautiful flowers
were stepped on by the Whites
were carried off violently from far away
to the big houses with the whitewashed walls,
those who had thrown their heads over their crossed arms.

This song is for those, who will never again be human,
the aged,
they grow with the rain,
those whom we have left far behind,
their heads thrown over their crossed arms.[39]

Another song, which can only be understood if it is remembered that the Aché call the Whites "Jaguars":

The Whites hold the women in captivity,
prey to the jaguars.
Those who have fled the road construction
of the Whites
have already turned into magnificent dead creatures.
Already the splendid masculine adjuration against
the jaguars
has been extinguished.

The trunks no longer stand upright,
we hastily left the trees far behind,
our heads thrown over our crossed arms.

The forefathers of distant times,
who were trunks,

the splendid spines of the forest
their bold call has been extinguished.

Our aged grandmothers,
we have left them,
as we were carried off far away,
our heads thrown over our crossed arms.[40]

Another song tells how the forefathers, seeing that the Aché have left
the forest, have decided to destroy them for their infidelity. In fact, the
singer tells, the animals and trees of the forest, forefathers of men, can
no more be visited by the Aché:

He, who is like an Aché,
who will never again be young,
the nausa,
they won't permit us to see him,
how he embraces the trees in which the likes of us live
– what a beautiful sight that was!

He, who is like a young Aché,
with the roaring body of the tapir,
who was once an Aché,
they won't allow us to see him.
We have left our own blood-sisters,
as if they no longer belonged to us.
We carry the iron axe,
whet it,
do the work of the Whites.

But, the singer goes on, it is not the fault of the Aché. They were
forced to a life far away from their home forest:

One after the other we turn into Whites,
we, who never worked the fields stooped over
– we do not exist anymore.
We are no longer hunters,
we are field workers.
Our Big Boss wants to order us all to the fields,
even the Aché in the forest cannot stand upright any more.
But a body, brown like mine,
will not yet turn white and tame –
At the Big Boss's place I will not yet settle.

The singer goes on, telling that he will substitute the White Man's
iron axe for a traditional stone axe, and return to the forest – in the
land of the dead. To be killed by angry forefathers will be salvation.

At the end of this tragic song which resumes the story of an Indian
nation, he asks his dead sisters to accept him – it is not his fault that he
does not live like an Aché anymore.

> My body was taken captive by the Boss
> when I was a young stripling.
> Therefore I carry the iron axe
> on to the field, whet it,
> and speak the language of the tamed,
> in the tracks of my Boss Pereira.
>
> But in the tracks of the dead women of our people
> I will set out,
> I will soar up
> as if on a rope
> to the sun.[41]

Death is the solution hoped for in many Aché songs which tell about the
end of their culture: It will return life to them. Modern psychiatry
knows few methods more likely to induce a refusal to survive than the
destruction of an individual's sense of identity. The Aché, although no
modern psychiatrists, have understood this. In a word, the right to be
different appears to them as essential to survival as the right to food.

IV. Who are the Wild Men?

The Aché are contemptuously called "Guayaki" = "wild rats" by
their neighbours. But their sorry fate, caused by the Whites, makes
clear why they on the other hand think we, the Whites, are the wild
men and correspondingly call us jaguars. Since anthropologists have
researched the world view of the Aché it is known why they "on sight
of their fellow men fly like a wild animal" (Macdonald 1911): not out
of wild, primitive fear of everything unknown, and not alone because
they are afraid of being instantly shot at by the Whites, but also out of
the calculated decision to live their own lives in their own way, instead
of subjugating themselves to the White Man's Way, which they consider wild and barbaric. Here lies the challenge for us: the refusal of
the Aché to integrate themselves into our civilization is based on their
mistrust in us and our culture – and what is worse, this mistrust is all
too well justified, as the Aché's history of suffering shows.

This history, with all of its petty, foolish cruelties, which our civilization brought in, is the topic of this essay. But, for better understand-

ing, let us now cast a glance at the victims of this history, the Aché and their "wild" culture.

> I am one, who once killed anteaters!
> That which I killed with my well-aimed hits,
> the animal with the big stripes, the wild loner,
> this heavy burden I carried home on my back.
>
> That which I killed with my well-aimed hits,
> the fat, savoured animal,
> this heavy burden I carried home on my back,
> I, all alone, when I was still a young man.
> — Song of an old Aché

The Aché of the hilly forest zones of the Paraguayan Eastern Region are the prototype of a hunting and gathering group. Hunting is the central theme of their life. In the beginning of all things, according to an Aché myth, the Great Jaguar commanded man to hunt from then on. The animals were ordered to fight with the hunters, and to let themselves be killed by them at the and of a fight. Woman was ordered always to eat the meat the hunters would give to her, and to get pregnant with the man who would bring her the best meat. The soul of the child is believed to be formed by the meat the pregnant mother eats. The name of the child denotes the species of animal which its mother ate, expressing thus a mystical relation between the animal and the soul of the child. Changing an Aché's name (as occurs today) would be tantamount to destroying this relation and depriving the soul of its connection with nature and of its after-life. The animals and trees of the forest are ancestors of men, and one part of the human soul will re-integrate into the forest after death – but only if men keep on hunting. The feeling of a close relationship with the forest is expressed in the Aché conception that the forest is a big, kind animal whose spine is formed by the trees and in whose belly animals and men live. The Aché perceive themselves to be a kind of soul of this animal.

The social life of the Aché can be characterized by the description of three classes: the mothers of the families, the chieftains, and the young warriors. The middle-aged women (which means here between 20 and 30), often married to two or even three husbands, are the fulcrum of the family. They have the last word in all decisions to be made and are the actual rulers of the Aché. The favourable position of the women

appears in their general attitude which ... often shows a tranquillity, a self-assurance .... The relations between spouses are usually excellent, with mutual confidence and unconcealed affection,

as the French ethnologist Pierre Clastres notes.[42]

Each group or sub-group has its leader, normally a good hunter with a big family, for instance many brothers, to support him. The characteristics of such a man (who is usually married to a woman of the first-named class) are not expected to be, as might be supposed, warlike ferocity or a domineering demeanour, but rather sensitiveness in associations with other people, courtesy towards women and tenderness towards children. In the opinion of the Aché a true chieftain does not have to shout or give orders to get his way, but rather convinces others by his kindness and cleverness.

During wartime the bold young warriors become more influential, from whom not wisdom but courage and cunning are expected. They are also the most zealous hunters, but according to the Aché they often lack the patience and experience necessary for a successful hunt or for a leading role as chieftain. Many of these young men are secondary husbands (that means, they are allowed to sleep with their heads on the shoulder, not on the hip, of the woman) of the matrons. The Aché women tend to say that these men still lack the equanimity and tenderness of the truly great men for a higher rank of marriage. So occasional feelings of envy are not unknown to the young towards the old. They are more restless, more discontented, and need perhaps for that reason as compensation the occasional, seldom very serious disputes with neighbouring groups, the skirmishes, during which not much blood flows, but where manly courage can be shown.

The necessities of hunting limit the size of the traditional Aché band to little more than from 40 to 60 persons which appears to be the ideal number for a nomadic existence in the forest. Several bands, totalling perhaps from 200 to 400 persons, form a tribe united by a common feeling, linguistic uniformity, and peaceful relations. At a particular time in the year different bands come together and celebrate a time of feasting, during which news is exchanged and marriages are arranged. The Aché compare this meeting in their language to the merger of many honeycombs to a hive. Sometimes the honeycombs do not separate again after the celebration but remain together in a new larger unit, which then only occasionally breaks up into hunting parties. Within one group Clastres was struck by

the perceptible, constant effort to eliminate all violence from the relations between comrades. The most extreme courtesy always prevails, ... the common will to understand each other, to dissolve in the exchange of words all the aggression and grudges which inevitably arise during the daily life of the group .... Never do the adults strike each other, except for ritual reasons .... There are no impetuous gestures, no box on the ear from vexation.[43]

Between different tribes, on the contrary, the common all-Aché feeling is very weak, and has not prevented battles. There exist not only linguistic but also remarkable cultural differences.

Let us keep in mind what is important to understand the present lot of the Aché. Their society is (or was) stable, based on the power of the mature women and the chieftains, and supported by a religion which explains the hunting life ideologically and glorifies it. Dissociative factors exist – the occasional discontent of the young men, the conflicts between hostile groups – but they are kept in check by harmonizing tendencies. As will be seen further on, this traditional society is today being destroyed by White Men who deliberately take advantage of the dissociative factors and weaken the harmonizing tendencies. They promote the discontent of the young men and the inter-tribal conflicts, and subdue the power of the chieftains, the dignity of the women, and the traditional religion.

V. The Trail of Tears

How did it all start? The Mbyá who are sedentary cultivators of the land account for the Aché situation by explaining that

In the beginning, Aché and Mbyá Indians lived together under the rule of the Sorcerer Whose Body is Like the Sun. But one day, the Aché appeared at the ritual dance ceremonial without the prescribed feather dresses, totally naked. The Great Sorcerer got angry and shouted: "Disperse through the woods!" and from then on, the Aché dispersed through the woods and did not settle down any more.[44]

The intentional theme of the Mbyá myth manifests the view that it was not blind destiny on the part of the Aché to be relegated to the life of nomadic hunters, but rather the conscious decision on their part to disobey the rules of the Sorcerer by appearing at the ceremonial sans the required ceremonial dress. In juxtaposition, the Aché mythical tradition stresses that the restless mode of existence (adopted only recently, the Aché agree) is due to the White Man's invasion:

In the olden days, the Whites had practically nothing, whereas our forefathers owned all the goods of civilization: metal axes, knives, woollens,

big houses, streets . . . . But one day, two white men entered the forest of the
Aché. They happened to possess mental knives which they had no right to
own, since manufactured goods were solely meant for the Aché. The whites
slept while the Aché approached silently, killed one and buried the other
alive in order to appropriate the knives. Then the Aché slept and during
the night the white man who was buried alive began to move within the
earth and like an armadillo he scratched the earth with his fingernails in
order to get out. He scratched and scratched and moved violently until
dawn when not one, but many white men appeared – angry, terrible
whites. When the Aché awoke in the morning, most of their forest had
disappeared and in its place, the endless green plains of the white men's
fields appeared, covered with horses, cattle, houses and white men armed
with guns. And all of a sudden, the Aché had no more metal axes, no more
houses nor woollens. It had all passed to the whites during the night. Full of
fear, the Aché fled far away lamenting the fact that they should have killed
the other white too.[45]

The significance of the Aché myth cannot be underestimated. It
reflects the impact of the encroachment of the Aché forest lands in
such a way as to bespeak the resultant psychological and cultural
disorientation the Aché have suffered. The myth manifests the traumatic turn about of events within the recent memory of the Aché. In
the span of a weird night, the Aché become dispossessed of their lands
and their rights.

Historical research may reconcile the Mbyá and Aché versions. The
white invasion has pushed the Aché back to the more remote areas
and to a wilder life, yet the Aché were not wholly passive in the face
of the encroachment because they consciously decided to withdraw
into the interior. This conscious choice is inextricably related to their
need to hunt. The soil of their land is better suited to hunting and
gathering forest products than to cultivation. Thus there could be no
rational basis for the Aché to relinquish their traditional mode of existence. The Whites and the various Indian groups allied with them chose
the path of aggression: they took the land they wanted. The Aché chose
the path of non-violence: by retreat and the preservation of their
identity and freedom in an environment essential to their culture.
Thus, to repudiate a way of life around which the Aché have developed
social, familial and indeed theological institutions is no more conceivable to Aché or to any other group suffering from a form of
Babylonian exile.

In the 18th century, the Aché and related Indian groups inhabited
the woody interior, from North-east Argentina through the Eastern
Paraguayan Alto Paraná Valley and Central Plateau, to the northern

part of what is today the Brazilian state of Paraná.[46] Colonization and
the resulting contacts with the Indians proceeded more rapidly in
Brazil and Argentina than in Paraguay where it was delayed by the
lack of roads and the low population density which left much land
undeveloped.

These Indians were friendly and helpful towards the first colonists.

Their character is extremely gentle, and so sociable are they ... that one
has never heard of even the most trifling harm done by them ... – to the
contrary: they help to collect maté tea, they look for and show the places
where there are many maté tea plants, and they come to the rescue with
food when this becomes scarce.[47]

However, the Indians soon discovered that the colonists intended
to keep their land and use them as indentured labourers. This is the
background of the words of an Indian who, in 1781, was asked why
his people did not want to stay in the Christian villages:

He said that the smallness of their lands (in contrast with) the nearby
forests where they found everything for their nutrition, and their unwanted-
ness with labour were the motives which made those who had come to the
Christian villages withdraw again; and that the unbelievers, although they
all wanted to become Christians, understood that in the Christian village
they had nothing to eat and therefore did not want to come there; ...
and that only if they were given no good land somewhere else, it would be
possible to increase the population of the Christian village.[48]

Further, the missionaries could not prevent their enslavement, and
counselled against self-defence. The Aché finally chose to fight the
colonists in a futile attempt to save themselves and their land. Already
weakened by European diseases transmitted by the colonists, and by
a change in diet brought about by the missionaries, the Aché and
related groups in Argentina and Brazil gradually decreased in number
until all had either died or been killed.[49]

During the 19th century, the sparsely populated wild Interior of
Eastern Paraguay was an ideal retreat for the Aché. Outside the woods
during the same period racial mixture created a Paraguayan culture
with as many Indian as European roots. The strength of Indian influence can be seen in the bilinguality of most of the population, in
Spanish and Guarani, an Indian idiom related to Aché. The desire of
the Paraguayan half-Indian nationalists to create an empire where
whites and Indians could live in harmony together was one of the
factors leading to war in 1864. Paraguay was defeated and conquered
by her white neighbours Argentina, Uruguay and Brazil; her country-

side was devastated and the population was reduced by almost 70 percent, in what Paraguayans today call the greatest genocide which ever occurred in America.

Reconstruction was funded by foreign capital, Paraguay's resources having been wiped out by the war, and was carried out by South American and European Whites who arrived in the wake of the foreign troops. It was these "gringos" and their descendants who formed the new upper class which dominated the commercial sphere. They attempted to crush the spirit of resistance of the Paraguayan nationalists. Recognizing the role of the Indians in the nationalist consciousness, they hated the Indians as well. The Guarani language, unintelligible and barbarous to their ears, became a symbol of the country's passive resistance to the white domination.

These events explain the position of the Indian, including the Aché, in Paraguay, from the end of the 19th century to the present. To the Paraguayan nationalists, the Indians are the "truest Paraguayans." To the "gringos," who have continued to play a leading role in the economic sphere, the Indians represent a distillation of the characteristics hated in the Paraguayans.

The laws of 1883 and 1885 concerning the Sale of State-Owned Lands promoted the development of large cattle ranches in Eastern Paraguay, often owned by foreign investors from Argentina, Brazil and Europe. The poorer farmers and ranchers could not meet the conditions of staying on the lands, either as renters or as purchasers; they were forced to work for the resulting large land owners. Thus, the foreigners ended the political and economic dominance of the half-Indian mestizo settlers, who inhabited the edges of the forest. While the mestizos sometimes considered the Indians "younger brothers," the foreign landowners saw them as standing in the way of progress. The Aché did not respect the new land property divisions, which had not been explained to them, and sometimes stole cattle which grazed on pasture land they considered their own. And it is at this moment that the documents about the Aché begin to resemble a 20th Century thriller. By the end of the 19th century, hunting of the Aché was widespread.

One day ... we perceived ... a group of Aché hurrying from an isolated thicket .... We took up the pursuit. The savages reached the forest well before we caught up with them. Only one of them had not been able to follow. But, in spite of the rather large distances he still had to overcome on foot in order to reach the forest, neither ourselves, on good horses, nor the

dogs accompanying us, would have managed to overtake this savage, had
not one of our group had the presence of mind to use the boleadoras (balls
used for throwing down cattle) with which the Aché was thrown down to the
earth and could thus be captured.[50]

(Close to the farm of a well-to-do German immigrant) the administrator
of the farm saw a smoke column rising in the forest. Going there, he discovered a woman with two children. Without any provocation ... he
wounded the woman, who nevertheless escaped. One of the two children,
an 8 year old boy, fell dead. Mr. Endlich managed to obtain the skull and
rest of the skeleton, which he sent with other artifacts of the Aché to the
Ethnographic Museum of Leipzig. The other child, a little girl of four or
five years of age, was taken to San Bernardino (a German settlement),
where she ... experiences the first benefits of Christian civilization.[51]

Beginning in 1902, cattle ranchers, largely German immigrants,
advanced to the small Savannah areas, "potreros," in the South-
eastern corner of Paraguay, close to the town of Encarnación. These
areas had always belonged to the Aché, who preferred them to the
woods. When ranchers began to clear the "potreros" for the cattle,
the Aché fought back. They shot and ate cattle that were driven onto
the "potreros," and attacked the "tame" Indians, who had surrendered to the whites and served as pathfinders for pursuit of the
"wild" Aché. Immediate retaliation followed.

In 1903, Paraguayans shot several Aché, and even cut one of the bodies into
pieces and put it in a cage trap as jaguar bait. Mayntzhusen saw a settler
pull the finger of an Aché out of his hunting bag and boast about it.[52]

I am ashamed to say that one European estanciero up there, now owning
several large cattle ranches, who arrived in Paraguay without a cent, has
been urging the local authorities to destroy these Indians, threatening to
withdraw his interests from the country. Only six months ago, some
estancia peons ... made a night raid upon a group of sleeping Guajakis
(= Aché). The first man seen was shot, the rest stampeded in all directions.
Two of the children were seized. These screamed pitifully, and the father, a
fine bearded man, came back to the rescue brandishing a club. The poor
fellow was mercilessly shot.[53]

The Aché counterattacked; their aggressiveness was limited in
comparison to warlike acts of other Indians such as the Chilian Ma-
puche or the North American Sioux, but shocked the Whites since it
was performed by the Aché, who were thought of as passive and
defenceless victims. Numerous police expeditions went out to hunt
the Aché.

In one of these (expeditions) Rosario Mora participated in 1907, who later
on ..reported the following: They had followed the traces of the Aché, and

they reached the Indians the very first evening of their journey .... They arrived at the camp of the Aché slaughtered 7 women and children, and caught 7 small children. When leaving next morning ... the captured children cried and lamented; their mothers, hidden in the forest, called for them. The manhunters felt threatened, although they had burnt all the bows and arrows left behind in the camp by the fleeing Aché. In his excitement and fear, Elijio Zarza, the local police chief, gave the order to cut the throats of all the children, so that their lamentations would not reveal to the Indians where the Paraguayans were.[54]

Private killing parties joined in. Today, the traveller who is admitted into the houses of the German settlers of Hohenau, Capitán Meza, or Obligado will still find many trophies from those pioneer days: Aché bows and arrows, sometimes even a skull. In 1911, after years of being hunted down, the Aché of that zone were near to extinction: some 300 only were left. By 1930, they had disappeared. Only some skulls in houses of German settlers, some collections of Aché utensils in Paraguayan, Argentine and German museums still keep their memory alive.

Now it was the turn of the Central Aché, more to the north between Caazapá and the Paraná rivers.[55] They, too, clashed with the expanding cattle ranches. The French ethnologist Vellard wrote after his visit to the Central Aché zone in 1932:

Guided by expert trackers from the submissive Indians, they (the ranchers) try to take some small Aché encampment by surprise, killing without mercy all they can find. In their view the Aché are vicious animals, stinking brutes that have to be destroyed.[56]

The scientists Luigi Miraglia, well acquainted with the region and its inhabitants, tells:

The Paraguayan Maximiliano Villalba told me that when acting as a guide in the neighbourhood of Ajos he used to receive a premium of 300–500 pesos for every Aché he killed ....
Among his tales I was much struck by the case of an Aché surrounded in a high tree, who refused to come down and surrender, preferring to throw himself down and fracture his skull. In the house of a maté grower, I saw the skull of a young Aché girl. She has been abandoned by her fleeing family because she limped, was brought in by a peasant who raped her and then killed her.[57]

As early as 1925, Mayntzhusen had published, in a review read by all German ethnologists, that in the Central Aché zone every adult Aché found in the woods was immediately liquidated. He mentioned the case, verified by the written testimony of a priest, of an Aché band attacked by maté collectors; some escaped wounded, but most were killed; several children were taken away by the aggressors.[58] The ethnographic details about the Aché culture in the same article were greeted with great interest by the scientific public, but the cry of human misery Mayntzhusen tried to transmit was not heard: Not a voice of protest rose against what was happening to the "interesting" savages. The French ethnologist Vellard, who considered "true man-hunting" as the only way of studying the Aché, was assisted by French cattle ranchers of the region in the preparation of an expedition which led to the driving away of Aché bands, to the brutal capture and subsequent "scientific study" of two Aché children, and to the death of other Aché. Vellard himself describes one of the episodes of his fatal party:

(He and his men approached a camp of resting Indians in silence). Before the Aché could recover from their surprise, we were in the midst of them. (Most of the Indians managed to escape, but two of them got caught in the fire of Vellard's men, who immediately seized one, a small boy, while the other, an adult), groaned on the ground and did not survive more than some minutes .... As we could not take the corpse with us, I contented myself with measuring it. The little Aché boy looked at us with his astonished eyes, without a shout, without a tear, without a gesture of emotion in front of the dead; he obeyed our signs without saying a word.

Upon returning to the ranch of the French settlers, Vellard proceeded to "tame" (as he called it) the captured boy in the sense of transforming him into a source of information for science about the Aché idiom and culture.[59] Vellard's expedition was praised by the scientific public for the interest of his observations, but nobody asked what was the further fate of the kidnapped children.

Opposition to genocide was left to the Aché themselves, among whom by now at least some younger warriors had made resistence a part of their lives. It was quite logical of them to attack mainly the horned cattle in the interest of which they had been driven off their lands and which, moreover, was good meat for the hunters.

The ox-hide seems to be a valued trophy, and their chiefs make helmets from it. They also plunder the corn and sweet manioc plantations ....
One of my Mbyá Indians (allies of the Whites against the Aché), who often served as my guide, had one day withdrawn for hunting alone, when he perceived an Aché up in a tree who aimed at him with his bow. He himself raised his own bow at once, but before he could shoot, the Aché's arrow twisted together his two hands. The aggressor and the wounded both took to flight and my guide met one of his comrades who freed him from the

arrow. Close to Caraya-ó, a punitive party was surprised in a creek canyon by an Aché band and had to take great pains to get away. The leader of this party had his chest pierced by an arrow.[60]

One hour before dawn, we approached the Aché noiselessly in the hope of surprising and befalling them. Suddenly, some 60 meters from their encampment, an Indian rose from amidst the ferns, brandishing a piece of burning wood and uttering loud shouts. Immediately, a swarn of arrows arrived close to us. Before I could give an order my men shot. The man with the torch let it fall down, wounded, and ran away howling. Horrible cries arose from all sides. Some moments later, we were in the encampment its occupants had just abandoned taking with them only their bows and arrows. The day broke while we made the inventory of what the Aché had left. These, returning noiselessly, attacked us twice, shooting quite a few arrows at us that penetrated into the trees near to us and broke there. My men replied; this was inevitable ....

We beat our retreat, taking with us a beautiful collection of objects for the Trocadéro (Museum at Paris).[61]

Such an adventure was anthropology when it served the gathering of "beautiful collections" – and so little did the scientists care for the Indians.

In 1950, the Office of Indian Protection was founded, with the scientist León Cadogan at its head. Backed by a group of Paraguayan intellectuals, Cadogan led a desperate struggle against the hunters of the Aché. This courageous attempt of a persistant campaign by many Paraguayans, who often risked revenge from powerful slave-masters and dealers, did not put an end to persecutions, but obliged the criminals to be more careful. The situation was propitious because if the remotest parts of the country were to be opened to foreign investment and to international roads, as was the government's intention, the anachronism of slavery had to be eliminated in order to make the country exhibitable to foreign eyes.

At this time, the Aché slaves of Paraguay's biggest slave-holder, López, aware of the change in their favour, revolted. López was brought to trial, accused of having ill-treated his "labourers." He was soon released, but was urged by the police to leave the country voluntarily. The background of the revolt will lead to a better understanding of the function of the "reservations." The oral deposition of Kybwyrági, leader of the revolt, follows:

A long time ago, we were captured by white men who found our encampment with the help of captured Aché who had been transformed by their masters into Aché hunters. We were sleeping when they surrounded us in silence and aimed at us with their fire-arms. Then they woke us up – rifles

all around us! We shouted fearfully: "Oh! Oh! White men all around!"
All our women started running in many directions, but they captured us and
brought us to their house. Soon however, we fled back to the forest again.

Later, we were made captives once again, by a man whom we called
"Captor" (the above-named López). I am Captor's ex-slave. During the
time of our enslavement we tilled many fields, as we were numerous. The
white man, Captor, owned me. I lived in his house, worked in his fields
which was very hard work, for many days on end.

Captor had brought to his house Hawk Woman, the wife of Puma Man.
Captor had made her his wife and he took her with him into the forest to
make her show him the hiding place of Monkey Man, who was my brother.
When she perceived my brother's traces she said: "Soon you will be
captured!" Then they got him. They fettered his wrists, his feet, it was like
fettering his wings. My brother tried to hit Captor, but could not reach
him. Captor killed him with a shot in the head.

The next morning, Hawk Woman returned and told me: "Captor has
killed an Aché!" I left the house and assembled many many Aché. We went
into the forest where I found my dead brother – he smelled putrid already.
Captor had fled. We followed his trace and finally got him in the woods. We
were a big band and they marched behind me. We brought Captor back
to his house where we guarded him. I fettered his wrists and many took
part in doing this. Then we delivered him who captured us to the white
men's police, who came with rifles. The police took Captor with them, but
they also took with them the son of one of us.

After that I fled back to the woods, far away.[62]

Kybwyrági told his story in the usual Aché manner, quietly smiling
and with a terse, impersonal tone as he obviously tried to remain
objective so as not to be overtaken by his feelings. Only once did he
lose his self-control – when he recounted how he fettered his master's
wrists. His smile was gone for a moment and beneath his external calm
one could sense a mixture of triumph and hatred. It was a time of hope
for the Aché.

This was an illusion. Let us listen to the dry, objective description
Kybwyrági gives of what followed:

Later on, Big Boss Pereira came to my, dwelling place. He kidnapped
Toucan Man. Puma Man was captured, Fish Man, they were all kidnapped.

What had happened? Since 1958, and especially since 1968, the
Aché situation has turned worse again. This coincides with the foundation of the Native Affairs Department of the Ministry of Defence –
the Indians were put under military control, as part of the general
transfer of power from civilians to the military – in 1958, and with
the subsequent retirement of Cadogan in 1966. The military installed
a rule over the Aché which, partly relieving the private oppression,

ceased being as obsolete and colonial as the ancient manhunts had been, and turned sadly modern. It combined a carefully measured genocide (scandal was prevented by not permitting too many deaths at one time) with an appearance of good will and an effort to tranquillize public opinion.

VI. The Soft Extermination

Listen once more to the story of Kybwyrági:

I still managed to escape. Later, Fish Man returned to my place and informed: "Big Boss Pereira is different from Captor. He is already on his way to our encampment, but if we take the first step, going to his place, he is willing not to kill us." So we came, shortly after the new moon, in the moonlight we arrived at his house.
We told him: "Captor liked to kill." We told him all our griefs: "When they took away our children from us, we fled back to the forest again!" Now Big Boss Pereira spoke: "I will sell nobody. I will not sell your children." Then he added: "I do not kill." That's how he spoke. That's why we stayed.

Big Boss Pereira was a killer. In his youth, he had been guard of a forced labour camp for Indians in the woods of the Alto Paraná, where Indians had to collect and prepare maté tea plants. During the Paraguyan Civil War, he had become an intimate friend and collaborator of Patricio Coleman, a torture specialist (who, from then on until his death in 1972, remained the régime's shady character being called upon every time political adversaries were to be eliminated. Coleman has become a kind of mythical figure. The man in the street did not like to pronounce his name in public and told phantastic-sounding stories about him in private, like the one that Coleman owned an enormous collection of body parts cut off from prisoners). After the war, Pereira had turned to the hunting and selling of Aché, becoming a junior partner of Captor López. His brutality and cold blood had made him almost a legendary figure in his region, but the Aché ignored this. A physical defect permitted him to gain their confidence: Pereira was unable to have children. Aché philosophy connects closely the giving and taking of life: an Aché will not kill if he is not able to produce new life, therefore an Aché man unable to engender can be no killer. Transposing this to Pereira, the Aché thought he would not kill, either. Moreover, his defect meant more tranquillity for their wives and daughters than with other slave owners.

The hunting range of Kybwyrágu's band had been so severely restricted as to prevent the continuation of their free existence. These Aché were not only pressured by the creation of estancias, farms, and new land boundaries, but they were being hunted besides. They believed that surrender could mean survival. They hoped that thus they would be in a good bargaining position so as to be able to keep their children, which they would surely lose if caught by the manhunters by surprise in the forest. The first group that had come to Pereira on a night in August, 1959, consisted of only 20 Indians, but Pereira foresaw the opportunity for enterprise. Fearful of legal prosecution, he did not dare sell his new Indians, but used them instead as indentured labourers on his farm. He informed the authorities that he was willing to "protect" the Aché, provided he received financial aid. The authorities, while aware of his reputation as a slave dealer, accepted his proposal hoping that they could control his farm in this way, which otherwise threatened to become the central market for the sale of Aché. Later on, some of these officials collaborated with Pereira in his scheme for financial gain. Pereira was nominated a functionary of the Native Affairs Department of the Ministry of Defence, and his farm was transformed into a "reservation." His first administrative act was to plunder the goods of his wards in order to sell them as tourist souvenirs. Cadogan remembers:

When I visited the camp for the first time, on the occasion of the arrival of the Aché, they were all wearing their weapons, ornaments, etc., in full; but when I returned for the second time all this had disappeared ... the total value of the objects had gone into the purse of Pereira.[63]

It is important to know the character of this Manuel de Jesús Pereira, who was officially presented and favoured as the solution of the Aché problem, admitted to a special audience with the President of the Republic, glorified in the pro-government press. The ethnologist Clastres who lived on his "reservation" for 9 months, gives a vivid description of him:

His absences sometimes extended for weeks on end, which he devoted to endless bouts of drunkenness in the villages of the area. When he returned, almost unable to keep himself on the saddle, he would explode in a fury impossible to understand, pulling out his gun and firing it in all directions, and shouting vague threats ....
From his new power he drew direct advantages, not the least of which was access to the young girls of the tribe .... If the salary he received was modest, the quantity of food – flour, grease, sugar, and powered milk – sent

for the Indians from Asunción, was, on the other hand, rather important.
The Aché certainly received part of it, but the rest was diverted by the
white chief, who sold it, for his exclusive profit, to the farmers of the region.[64]

Kybwyrági bore witness to the evolution of the "reservation" into
a manhunt centre and how captive Aché were used to capture their
still free brethren:

There were those Aché of another tribe, our enemies. We captured them all.
We brought here that Big Wild Cat Man, we dragged them all in. First we
followed their traces. Then finally we saw them. We started weeping. We
painted our faces (as for warfare). Then we told them: "We do not want to
hurt you!" But when some of them resisted, we fettered them. Wild Boar
Man the Courageous One, oh, he has been dead for such a long time now,
we fettered him and dragged him by his wrist, because he had too much
courage.

Jesús Pereira induced such action by advising the captive Aché that
to become like white men, they had to hunt the free Aché like the
whites. Compelling the "tame" Aché to fratricide is accomplished
easily because of the demoralization of individuals on the "reservation"
and the denigration of their cultural heritage with the consequential
attempt by the captive Aché to become more like their white captors.
Thus, the "tame" Aché identify strongly with their captors and their
Aché identity is further weakened by a forced separation of families and
groups upon capture. The young Aché warriors, who in the traditional
Aché society, as described before, play a somewhat subordinate role and
who are not always content, have a special function in the manhunts.
The destruction of the traditional society and of the authority of the
chieftains in particular gives the young men new opportunities: as
manhunters in the service of the Whites they can capture the older
men whom they often envied in earlier times and humiliate them. It
was Pereira who comprehended this aspect of inner discord within the
Aché society and who knew how to use it. The chief is usually subjected to undue humiliation so as to break down his political authority. Those who participate in this humiliation are rewarded. In
the case of one chief who arrived on the "reservation," for instance,
his little son was taken from him and the father informed that his son
would suffer maltreatment should there be any resistance on his part.
In another case, the resistance of a chief was broken by driving the
sensitive desperate man to mental disorder; ridiculed for that by the
white masters, he could nevermore be a symbol of resistance, but became a poor devil.

In June, 1962 the Reservation Indians numbered perhaps 110. In July 1968, only 68 Indians were left, although in the meantime many new captives had been brought in and new children were born.[65] Clastres remembers:

When I arrived at Arroyo Moroti (the "reservation"), there were about 100. I left them one year later; no more than 75 were left. The others had died of diseases, had been eaten by TB, lacking care, lacking everything.[66]

One of the main reasons for the decline of the Aché "reservation" population is malnutrition and the diseases associated with it. Hunger among the Aché was the intentional result of the withholding of essential foods which were available because the "reservation" itself produces food and has received outside aid. Another reason for the population decline is attributable to the sale of the Aché. This is manifest in the numerical disproportion of male and female inhabitants on the "reservation," observable however (in 1972), only among individuals over 5 years of age. The tragic explanation is the disappearance of small girls at what is regarded as the age of maximum commercial appeal, specifically when they have ceased being babies and are thus not difficult to care for, but are not yet old enough to be rebellious. For its masters, the "reservation" was a source of profit, even more so because the Indians were forced to produce a sizable agricultural yield.[67]

By 1966, no free Aché remained in the area where the camp was situated. And in the camp, the number of Indians had been reduced sufficiently to ensure that they could never again be a hindrance to "progress." But the cattle ranches and forest industry companies were extending their field of action into the until then rather untouched forests of the San Joaquin-Curuguaty region. Here lived the Northern Aché, who call themselves the "Aché-who-hit-on-the-heads." They are different from their relatives farther to the south. They constitute bigger bands, they have permanent villages hidden in the forest, and they are more warlike. Those Whites accustomed to the sporadic, inefficient resistance of other Aché experienced a bad surprise when they penetrated the forests of the "Aché-who-hit-on-the-heads." Suddenly, they met organized resistance. Manhunters who wanted to catch some poor, isolated families camping in the forest found themselves surrounded by warriors.[68] This was a shock to all those who had hoped the game would be as easy as with other Aché. And it is since this shock that the Aché policy of the military authorities has really changed.

VII. "Saving" the Aché

In 1966, Jesús Pereira and his superior, the Vice-Director of the Native Affairs Department of the Ministry of Defence, undertook an expedition to the new problem area, in order to localize the problem-creating Aché. The party was guided by five "tame" Aché specialized in hunting their free brethren. In 1968, the "reservation" was relocated in the problem area. So doomsday approached for the free Northern Aché living there.

Years later, one of them, Great Wild-Boar Man, told me his story which I reproduce here because I consider it typical. Great Wild-Boar Man was a village chief of the Northern Aché, married, two children. On a hunt for game in the woods, the family spent the night outside the village, when white manhunters discovered them, immediately opened fire against the sleeping family, and killed the woman and the two children. Great Wild-Boar Man managed to escape, but felt ashamed that he had been unable to protect his family and therefore did not dare return to his village. For months on end, he stayed in the forest, then finally joined another Aché village, where 200 to 300 persons lived under the leadership of Tortoise Man, the most powerful chief of the Northern Aché. Great Wild-Boar Man married again in the new village, and soon was father of a daughter again. His hatred against the Whites who had killed his first family made him a great warrior, assistant to the chief Tortoise Man.

One day, he led his and some other families to Jesús Pereira's "reservation," in order to pillage a corn field. Great Wild-Boar Man hated the Indians on the "reservation" who had surrendered to the Whites and let themselves be forced to manhunt. On their way, already within the "reservation" territory, Great Wild-Boar Man and his people met a group of "tame" Aché with fire-arms, sent out to search for the traces of free Aché. The manhunters (who as Aché felt pity for their Aché victims) would probably have permitted the free Aché to escape, had Great Wild-Boar Man not fired an arrow at one of them and wounded him. The "tame" Aché knew their white masters would notice the wound, ask them what happened and punish them if they failed to pursue Great Wild-Boar Man and his group. Great Wild-Boar Man had given the order to retreat immediately after his shot, but the "reservation" Indians caught a woman who carried a baby with her. They let the others escape.

When Jesús Pereira saw the captive, he immediately informed the Native Affairs Department, which in its turn informed a military compound nearby (of these details, I was not informed by Great Wild-Boar Man, but by the Whites involved). The officers put at the disposal of Jesús Pereira trucks and provisions. The captured woman was forced to reveal where Great Wild-Boar Man would probably flee. The manhunters approached the place in trucks. Although they did not take the direct way through the woods, the vehicles were quicker than the fleeing Indians. Finally, the manhunters climbed down from the trucks and continued on foot (details about this hunt were given to me by "tame" Aché who had participated). They prepared an ambush for Great Wild-Boar Man, with the captured baby as bait. The hunted free Aché managed to escape narrowly, but were now tired after the long treck, whereas the hunters had travelled on trucks and felt still fresh. A pursuit of days through the forest followed. Several free Indians died during their flight. When Great Wild-Boar Man and his wife felt too tired to carry their daughter, they killed her and went on running.

She was too small a baby. We did not want her to fall into the jaguar's power. We did not want her to cry in the houses of mighty white bosses, working for white men, walking with a stoop instead of walking upright. So we both killed her. So her soul was taken away by a tapir who took her to the Great Mother's house. The tapir run quickly, so tapir and baby could escape from the jaguar and will never have to work for the mighty white bosses.

Finally, Great Wild-Boar Man, his wife, and 34 other Aché were caught. Other Aché groups from the same village were also kidnapped and transported to the "reservation" on military trucks, shortly before or after this; in total, some 80, between October and December 1970.[69] In August 1971, 26 of them were left.

The pattern of what happened in 1970/71 can now clearly be seen as repetitive. First, Indians are captured and transported to the "reservation." There, they do not receive enough food and are ill-treated. Although it is well known that Aché who arrive from the forest are very susceptible to diseases like flu, no medicines are given to them. The shock of capture, consequent utter despair, hunger and ill-treatment make the newcomers even more susceptible to diseases. The death of many of them inevitably follows, and destroys their hope of one day being able to reconstitute their old life in the forest. Those who survive the purgatory of suffering, are finally defeated: without any more hope, physically and psychologically weakened, they cease to think of resistance.

Once their spirit of freedom is broken, those surviving are suddenly subjected to a flurry of kindness. This method is a familiar one (refined in countries where torture and brain-washing are combined to elicit the co-operation of the captive: after a period of deprivation and suffering, the prisoner is suddenly presented with gifts of cigarettes and other desirous things, and it is then that he finally confesses in the aftermath of a fleeting benevolence). In the "reservation" the Aché, shocked by the sudden change from being free and independent hunters, suddenly find themselves dependent for their very subsistence upon their captors, who in turn elicit their full co-operation in the capture of other Aché. Suddenly when food once again appears and medicine is available, the captives tend to identify with their captors, if only to insure their continued physical survival. While the general athmosphere is opressive in terms of the prohibition of anything re-sembling their old ways, certain liberties are conceded to those Aché who co-operate. Journalists are sometimes invited to "see for them-selves." The visit's shortness, the language problem and the Indians fear of being punished for critical words would guarantee that the journalists would leave the "happy" Indians (who are smiling because smiling in spite of misfortune is part of the Aché etiquette and because they have survived hell) with not too bad an impression. Sometimes, good tamed Indians are taken to Asunción and shown to the public. Later on there is a new manhunt and the pattern repeats itself all over again.

A thousand technical difficulties would arise and prevent any more visits to the "reservation," while in Asunción responsible functionaries would start a series of press interviews etc., in order to hide what is really going on.

It would be hard to believe that this pattern is accidental. I must explain that even during the repeated periods of hunger and disease, the "reservation" disposed of victuals and medicine in great quantities, while these were withheld from the Indians: that those responsible were fully aware of the danger to newcomers which arises from a change of diet and contact with European diseases. In fact, one of those responsible, a doctor in charge of health in the camp, has pub-lished scientific notes about this danger: that, in one case at least, an influenza epidemic was already raging in the "reservation" when the manhunters went out again in order to bring new captives into the infected place. This was, as a spokesman of the Paraguayan Roman Catholic Church put it in 1972:

the most secure and less openly violent way of killing a considerable number of them.[70]

A noteworthy aspect of the authorities' Aché policy is their preoccupation with the good image. To this purpose, in 1971 several foreign business men living in Paraguay joined the Director of the Native Affairs Department of the Ministry of Defence in order to constitute an "Indian Aid Commission." It was declared that the function of the Commission was to provide for a better image of Indian, but in fact the better image it provided was exclusively of the official Indian policy, mainly with regard to the Aché "reservation." This seemed necessary as the Paraguayan public opinion had since 1965 become sensitive to denouncements of what was happening in the "reservation." Church dignitaries had joined in the protest. In December 1970, the pro-government daily newspaper *abc color*, reputed to be serious, had published a series of articles denouncing the private killing parties in violent terms. The articles were more cautious with regard to the official "reservation," yet a careful reader could find between the lines that there, too, violence and capture were used, and that the Indians were lacking food and medicines.[71] The "Indian Aid Commission," founded immediately after these publications, started with a publicity campaign in favour of the "reservation," for which purpose the business men put at the disposal of the authorities their advertising experience.

Their main argument was that the Aché had to be "saved" from persecutions by transporting them to a "secure" camp. The manhunters going out from the camp were described as "rescue squads." As the Paraguayan public is practically un-informed about the fact that the Aché themselves are divided into many different tribes, often hostile to each other, the fact that Aché participated in these expeditions seemed to be a good argument: one Aché group, it was declared, wants to help the other by "saving" it.

The business men also organised the collection of "aid for the Indians," thus creating the impression that something was being done. In 1971, they took over part of the official functions of the Native Affairs Department with regard to the "reservation." Vis-à-vis public opinion, this was an advantage, as people in Paraguay tend to mistrust the military authorities and are therefore inclined to expect that any money collected by military functionaries could disappear into their own pockets. The foreign business men do not suffer this suspicion, because people consider them to be rich enough already. (In 1971-2, a sum corresponding to US$ 36,500 was collected, according to these business men, although the Indians certainly never saw much of it.)[72] Moreover, if ever the truth came out and a scandal followed, the Paraguayans implicated in the "reservation" could always put the blame on the foreigners, who had taken over the responsibility but were immune from effective reprisals.

In 1972, the scandal finally came into the open. Paraguayan journalists and intellectuals forgot their fear and presented proofs of a planned genocide in full operation. The Roman Catholic Church joined in the protests. At the same time, visitors to the "reservation" noticed the Indians, usually resigned and obedient, showing signs of recalcitrance. I myself, at that time pursued by the administrator's wrath (because I had denounced the treatment of dying Indians), was shown, for that very reason and intentionally, in the view of the administrator, a manifest sympathy even by those Indians who had not been my friends before. In May 1972, a revolt seems to have broken out, but was repressed at once. Nevertheless, the unexpected resistence meant a shock to the masters accustomed to docile slaves. The change was probably due to the increased number of Northern Aché (displaced there in March/April), who, more warlike and united, were more difficult to tame.

Consider for a moment the white masters' view. One possible solution would have been the liquidation of the refractory Indians by open violence; but this was difficult, as public attention was now focused upon the camp. The problem could best be resolved if: 1) Public opinion were tranquillized, not by denying what had happened (that was by now impossible, in the face of too much evidence), but by giving the impression that the past mistakes were now being corrected. 2) The Indians, once they could not be killed, were divided, in order to counteract the increased number of restive Northern Aché. 3) The manhunts were continued (in order to destroy the free Indians' resistance), but not from the "reservation," in order not to upset public opinion. In fact this was the way the problem was resolved:

1. The Reservation was given into the charge of North American Missionaries. So, to the superficial observer, things really seemed to have changed.

2. The tamest Indians – mainly the longest-staying camp inmates – were deported by the old administrator Jesús Pereira to a new camp.

They were thus withdrawn from the influence of the less tame Indians
On the other hand, those considered especially refractory were allowed
to flee, withdrawing thus their "negative" influence. With the most
courageous having fled back to the forest, and with their total number
reduced by two thirds, the Reservation Aché (who, moreover, had
passed through the brain washing purgatory phase described above)
lost the hope of successful resistance: the Missionaries could talk of
love and be less brutal.

3. Far away from the official Reservation, old manhunter Jesús
Pereira was allowed to transform his new "private" camp into a manhunt centre, where he could again count upon the tamest Aché and
upon the Armed Forces. His new camp was strategically better situated
than the official Reservation – closer to the most important military
compound of the zone from where trucks and arms can easily be
brought in. With public opinion focused on the official Reservation,
Jesús Pereira could act more freely outside.

It seems that since Jesús Pereira's removal from the official Reservation in 1972 until today, 1974, a new pattern has been repeated
several times: new Indians were captured by Jesús Pereira or other
hunters, the tamest kept with Jesús Pereira, the others brought to the
Reservation, where the missionaries permitted the most untameable
to flee back again to the forest. Many of the re-escaped are hunted
down again, or take refuge voluntarily with Paraguayan farmers who
give them shelter in exchange for slave-labour, or they even return to
the missionaries. The latter have thus assumed a role which can be
compared with that of the "nice fellows" (those, who finally offer cigarettes to the prisoner) in the above mentioned torture system, while
the private manhunters and especially Jesús Pereira are comparable
to the "ugly fellows" of the same system. Both missionaries and manhunters are, in fact, part of a system which, whether its participants be
aware of it or not, contributes to the destruction of the Aché nation.
Desperately, these Indians sing about their end:

> Now
> I am going far away
> in order to disappear
> with my brothers, in the land of my brothers.
>
> With the Aché from other bands who were our enemies,
> we will form a band
> in a new and perfect homeland.

The brother of my mother
was once a great warrier,
he is now a magnificent anteater
who has found his way to the light.
He will carry my soul away
while I am being saved, being squeezed to death
by the earth.

The only brother of my mother,
much I have wept over him,
and his mocking songs about me
have long faded away.

The terrible bird of bitterness will carry me away
as he always does.
Over my grave he will sweep the dust meticulously
and I will finally be happy
when I hear his mocking songs.

Like us, but without misery and malice,
stand the dead with their great animal faces,
upright and proud,
in expectation of the Aché.[73]

VIII. Demography of the Dead

It will never be known how many captives in total have been brought
to the "reservation," how many Aché have been killed by manhunters
from it, and how many died or were sold. But the minimum figures can at
least be established from documents examined, though the real figures
may be higher. From October 1970 until June 1972 (a period covered
by official statistics and by the testimony of "reservation" inmates),
at least 138 Aché have either disappeared from the camp (in all probability by death) or been killed by manhunters from there. Furthermore, 122 others have been kidnapped and deported to the camp.[74]
The minimum figure of free Aché killed or captured during private
raids from Sept. 1968 until Nov. 1971 is 83, according to the existing
evidence[75] – but of course this is only the tip of the iceberg, as most
crimes of that kind are never documented. Summarizing these figures
it can be stated that – at least 343 persons have either been killed or
deprived of their liberty (or deprived of their liberty and then induced
to die) between September 1968 and June 1972.

Turning from these minimum figures (for which documentary
proofs can be presented) to what may be reasonable estimates (based

partly upon documents and partly upon scientific evaluation), and taking into account that at least 3 Northern Aché tribes have disappeared between 1968 and 1972, be this through killing or kidnapping, by private or official hunts: this might mean the killing or kidnapping of some 900 persons.[76]

All these figures refer exclusively to the Northern Aché, no exact data being available to me about those Aché living farther to the south. It seems quite likely that they, too, have been the victims of massacres and kidnap parties, which would mean that the total number of victims is higher than indicated above.

From 1972 until 1974, more Aché have disappeared. Spokesmen of the Paraguayan Roman Catholic Church and of several international organizations have required an exact investigation about the proportions of the crimes committed during this period. Such an investigation could furnish more reliable data than I am able to publish at this moment. At least some 66 Aché seem to have disappeared from the Reservation, most likely by death, during this period,[77] although I believe the real figure to be much higher. About the number of free Aché captured or killed between 1972 and 1974 I possess no exact data.

As for the number of Aché still surviving today, 1974, estimates can at present be only very rough. Chase Sardi's detailed report about Aché living in 4 different camps under the control of White Men[78] gives a total of 150. To this must be added a group of 10 who since 1973 live under the protection of a Roman Catholic priest at Arroyo Guazú near Curuguaty.[79] Of those Indians mentioned by Chase Sardi, some 50 seem to have fled back to the forest in the first half of 1974; they are said to have joined with a group of perhaps 20 free Aché; this new group of 70 Indians joined the Aché of Arroyo Guazú in June, 1974.[80] Summarizing, it can be said that in June, 1974 some 180 Aché lived at 4 different places under White Men's control.

An unknown number of others was scattered as slaves all over the East Paraguayan countryside. Moreover, there still survived several free Aché groups in the woods:

1. More than 50 Aché in the forests close to the Reservation, in contact with the Reservation Indians.[81]
2. The Ywyrarovaná Group, estimated at some 80 or 100 in July, 1972.[82]
3. The Mbaracayú Mountain Group, estimated at "at least 400" in July, 1972.[83]

4. A recently discovered group in the Department of Amambay, between Ypanemi and Arroyo Guasú. No figures are available, but, as it was discovered only in 1974 and therefore has not been the victim of persecutions in the past, its number could well be some 300 or 400.

No data are available about the actual situation of the Hondo Creek and the Monday River Groups, who in 1970/71 totalled at least some 80 persons.[84] I do not know if these groups still exist. Summarizing, as a very rough estimate, there may be between 800 and 1200 Aché still free in the woods.[85]

IX. In the Way of Whom?

The Aché are just a few weak savages, without fire-arms, without social or political connections that could make their existence dangerous to those ruling. Yet, the genocidal policy directed against them can only be explained by the fact that they are in the way. In the way of whom?

In recent years, Paraguay has experienced an economic boom. The road from Asunción to Puerto Pres. Stroessner, through Eastern Paraguay, was completed in 1965; the road from Coronel Oviedo to the Guairá cataracts, which cuts through the forest of the Northern Aché, was completed in 1968. Prices for land are rising in the areas which have become more accessible, as well as the prices for forest products (timber, tannin, palmetto, etc.) and especially that of cattle, which means that more land is reserved for horned cattle, and less for the Indians. The plan of building one of the world's most massive hydro-electric power plants in the area has further increased prices. As land values rise, and more land is acquired by entrepreneurs, Aché are forced into smaller and smaller areas. There have been instances of Indian resistance.

Thus, the Aché become inconvenient elements. Father Meliá explains the results of an inquiry directed by the Mission Department of the Paraguayan Episcopal Conference:

The new invaders of the forest: wood cutters, palmetto collectors and land-owners, want to have the forest "clean"; they are bothered by the presence of the ancient owners of the forest.[86]

But who, in fact, are these new invaders? In contrast with the Far West of the United States in the 19th Century, Paraguay today lacks a multitude of free settlers who could be trained and independant enough for directing colonization. Paraguay's "wild frontier" consists, mainly, of tropical forest that is more attractive for companies which specialize on the extraction of forest products than for old style pioneers who till the soil. The extraction and transformation of forest products is executed mainly by companies, whereas independant settlers are rarely engaged. These companies are closely bound up with the "estancias" (big farms specialized in stock farming) which often have no individual owners, but belong to joint-stock companies. It is these estancias and companies whom Father Meliá connects with the Aché problem:

Sometimes they say that it is the settlers who commit these killings ....
This is false. It was not the settlers who carried out the massacre, but rural workers, rural workers from big estancias. The Aché do not interfere with small farmers, but with big landowners.[87]

A closer look at land property in the zone in question will confirm this opinion. In Eastern Paraguay, according to a North American USDA/USAID report,

106 ownership units of more than 10,000 hectares each account for more than six million hectares, which together with about 600,000 hectares owned by the state account for about 40 percent of eastern Paraguay.[88]

Cattle, those intruders into Aché land, are raised on big farms rather than by small settlers:

According to the 1956 census almost 70 percent of the cattle were on units of 1,000 hectares and more and the 1961 census shows that ... about 150 operators account for a third of the total cattle in Paraguay.[89]

The situation is even clearer in that part of Eastern Paraguay where the Aché live, the forest zone: In 1972, the forest industries companies and the state ("tierras fiscales") accounted for 48% of the total forest soil. Great parts of the remaining land belonged to the estancias. The forest can further be divided into parts already exploited, and parts still virgin. The Aché have mostly retired to the virgin zones where they are being persecuted now. Here, 64% of the total soil is owned by the forest industries companies.[90] Obviously, it is the forest industries companies, the state, and the estancias, who could be interested in having the forest "clean".

This leads to the question who owns the companies and the estancias? The Paraguayan Rubén Bareiro-Saguier, in a rather well documented book about his country, affirms that twenty enterprises with a majority of foreign shares own 30 percent of the Paraguayan territory, and fifteen enterprises with a majority of foreign shares own more than 20 percent of the total Paraguayan stock of cattle.[91] The economist Fretes Ventre writes about those branches of the Paraguayan industry which promote the penetration of the forest:

Foreign capital accounts for almost all important branches of industry – tannin, meat, wood; these constitute, in fact, islands which give little dynamism to the economy as a whole, as their investments are not directed in a sense of favouring Paraguyan interests.[92]

But the distribution of land property just described also leads to the question of the role of the state, which is one of the big landowners in the Aché region and on whose land several of the massacres have been committed. According to the Paraguayan authorities they are not implicated in these acts, but have on the contrary established a Reservation as a shelter for the persecuted Aché.

The genocidal role of this "reservation" has been dealt with already. Possibly, more Aché have died these last years on the "reservation" than outside. Reliable sources, like the scientists Chase Sardi and Cadogan, or the Church dignitary and scientist Father Meliá have called the "reservation" a "concentration camp," a "dirty pigsty," or simply an Aché "graveyard."[93]

The Reservation Administrator until September 1972, Mr. Jesús Pereira was a non-commissioned officer in the Paraguayan Army and as such was subject to military orders. As Administrator he was (as the present Administrator still is) directly under the jurisdiction of the Native Affairs Department of the Defence Ministry, whose Director, Colonel Tristán Infanzón has in his turn stated repeatedly that all his actions regarding the Aché were determined exclusively by the military orders he had received.[94] The hierarchical structure of Paraguay's authoritarian political and social order would make it impossible for Infanzón or Pereira to disregard the orders of their superiors. Pereira was relieved of his functions as an Administrator in 1972, yet he was allowed to take a group of Aché slaves with him upon leaving the "reservation."

The participation of the military has been even more active. The manhunts going out from the "reservation" were partly accompanied by military vehicles operated by soldiers subject to the orders of the Ministry of Defence. The manhunters have had access to military compounds for rest purposes. At least in 1970, transport of captured Indians to the "reservation" was accomplished on military trucks.

Moreover, the argument (used by the Paraguayan authorities, and today also by the missionaries in the "reservation") that the military can only protect the Aché from persecutions by gathering them together in a Reservation, is cynical. Taken seriously, it would imply that the Paraguayan Army is unable to protect the Indians against manhunts outside the Reservation. In fact, the Paraguayan military have proved their efficiency and absolute control over the country for 20 years now, having crushed any serious political opposition movement. They would certainly be able – if they were willing – to crush the manhunt parties as well, or even to prevent their organization. As Father Meliá wrote, the Reservation policy

means to put into prison the innocent, in order that the wrongdoer may continue to rove wheresoever he wants.[95]

REFERENCES

Albospino, Luís
    1960 La Caza del Guayakí. Trágico Resabio de la Conquista. *Ñandé* I, 22 (29 Febr. 1960): 6–7, 26. Asunción.
Arnold, Adlai F. (Team Leader USDA/PASA, USAID/Asunción)
    1970 *An Agricultural Policy Statement for Paraguay: A Case Study*. Foreign Development and Trade Division, Economic Research Service, U.S., Dept. of Agriculture/PASA/USAID, Asunción.
Baldus, Herbert
    1972 Die Guayakí von Paraguay.
        Anthropos LXVI, 3/4, 465–529. St. Augustin.
Bareiro-Saguier, Rubén
    1972 Le Paraguay.
        Bordas études 201. Paris.
Bidney, David
    1967 *Theoretical Anthropology*.
        Schocken Books, New York.
Borgognon, Juan Alfonso
    1968 Panorama Indigena Paraguayo.
        Suplemento Antropológico de la Revista del Ateneo Paraguayo III, 1–2 (octubre): 341–371. Asunción.
Gadogan, Léon
    1959 Ayvu Rapyta, Textos miticos de los Mbyá-Guarani del Guairá.

Universidade de Sao Paulo, Faculdade de Filosofia, Ciências e Letras, Boletim 227, Antropologia 5. São Paulo

1968 Chonó Kybwyrá: Aporte al conocimiento de la Mitologia Guarani.
Suplemento Antropologico de la Revista del Ateneo Paraguayo III, 1–2 (*octubre*): 55–158. Asunción.

1971 Ywyra Ñe'ery, Fluye del árbol la palabra.
Suplemento Antropológico, Universidad Católica, V, 1–2 (corresp. al a. 1970): 7–111. Asunción.

Chase Sardi, Miguel
1972 *La Situación Actual de los Indigenas en el Paraguay.* Asunción.

Clastres, Pierre
1968 Ethnographie des Indiens Guayaki.
Journal de la Société des Americanistes de Paris, LVII: 9–61. Paris.

1972 *Chronique des Indiens Guayaki.*
Paris.

Doblas, D. Gonzalo de
1970 Memoria Histórica, Geográfica, Política y Económica sobre la Provincia de Misiones de Indios Guaraníes.
in: *Pedro de Angelis ed.: Colección de Obras y Documentos,* V: 7–187. Buenos Aires.

FAO – Proyecto de Desarrollo Forestal y de Industrias Forestales Paraguay:
1974 Inventario Forestal de Reconocimiento, Informe preparado para el Gobierno de Paraguay por la Organización de las Naciones Unidas para la Agricultura y la Alimentacion en su carácter de Organismo Ejecutivo del Programa de las Naciones Unidas para el Desarrollo.
FO: DP/PAR/66/515, Informe técnico 1, Roma.

Gorham, J. Richard
1973 Portraits of Paraguay.
in: Gorham ed.: *Paraguay: Ecological Essays:* 209–275. Miami, Florida.

Lehmann-Nitsche, Robert
1899 Quelques Observations sur les Indiens Guayaquis du Paraguay.
Revista del Museo de la Plata, 9: 399–408. La Plata.

MacDonald, Alexander K.
1911 *Picturesque Paraguay.*
London.

Mayntzhusen, F. C.
1925 Guayaki-Forschungen.
Zeitschrift für Ethnologie, 57, 3–6: 315–318. Berlin.

Meliá, Bartomeu
1973 Yo, indio guayaki, acuso a los hombres vestidos.
in: Meliá – Miraglia – C. & M. Münzel: *La agonía de los Aché-Guayakí:* 79–82. Asunción.

Meliá, Bartoneu & Münzel, Christine
1973 Ratones y Jaguares, Reconstrucción de un genocidio a la manera del de los Axé-Guayakí del Paraguay Oriental.

in: *Suplemento Antropológico, Universidad Católica* VI, 1–2 (corresp. al a. 1971): 101–147. Asunción.

Miraglia, Luigi

1941 Gli Avá, i Guyakí ed i Tobas.
Annali Lateranensi V: 253–378. Città del Vaticano.

1973 Dos Capturas de Aché-Guayakí en el Paraguay en Abril 1972.
in: *Suplemento Antropológico, Universidad Católica* VI, 1–2 (corresp. al a. 1971): 149–171. Asunción.

Münzel, Mark

1973a The Aché Indians: Genocide in Paraguay.
IWGIA Document 11. Copenhagen.

1973b Kware Veja Puku, Notas preliminares sobre cinco canciones Axé.
in: Meliá – Miraglia – C. & M. Münzel: *La agonía de los Aché-Guayakí*: 83–165. Asunción.

Vellard, Jehan

1933 Une Mission Scientifique au Paraguay.
Journal de la Société des Americanistes de Paris, n.s. XXV. Paris.

1934 Les Indiens Guayakí.
ibid. XXVI: 223–292. Paris.

1935 Les Indiens Guayakí.
ibid. XXVII: 175–244. Paris.

1939 *Une Civilisation du Miel, Les Indiens Guayakí du Paraguay*. Paris.

Vivante, Armando & Gancedo Omar Antonio.

1968 Sobre el arco y la flecha de los Guayakí.
Revista del Museo de la Plata n.s. sección Antropología VII: 39–52. La Plata.

NOTES

1. MacDonald 1911, quoted in Gorham 1973: 246.
2. Borgognon 1968: 360.
3. *abc color*, Asunción, 16 Dec. 1970, p. 13; 17 Dec. 1970, p. 32.
4. These Indians call themselves *Aché*, but are often also called *Guayakí*, which is a contemptuous name from the Guaraní language, meaning most probably "rabid rats" (Clastres 1968: 52). In this paper, I have used the name *Aché*. In order not to confound the reader, I have used this name even in translated quotations where the original reads "Guayakí."
5. *abc color*, Asunción, 17 Dec. 1970, p. 32.
6. *abc color*, Asunción, 14 March 1971, p. 7.
7. Albospino 1960: 6.
8. Deposition of the "tame" Aché Nambúgi regarding the orders he had received from the Administrator of the Aché Reservation about how to proceed on a manhunt. Taped by me in the Reservation, October 1971. The manhunt was finally realized in February/March 1972.
9. Copy of this denouncement was sent by the Minister to General Leodegar Cabello, Minister of Defence, on 3 January 1969. No measures were taken either against the killers or in defence of the captured girl.
10. Cf. *La Tribuna*, Asunción, 30 June 1972, p. 5.

11. Meliá in: Meliá-Münzel 1973: 134.
12. *La Tribuna*, 13 August 1972, p. 12.
13. See note 4 above.
14. *Aquí*, Asunción, 21 September 1973, No. III–139, p. 11.
15. *Ibid.*
16. *The New York Times*, 21 January 1974, p. 8.
17. Report of the Centre of Anthropological Studies, signed by Miguel Chase Sardi, dated January 16, 1974 and directed to the Minister of Defence. I own a photocopy of this report.
18. Extracts of this letter were published in *La Tribuna*, Asunción, 28 April 1974, p. 4.
19. I own a copy of this letter which was not published in the Paraguayan press.
20. Miraglia 1973: 162.
21. Abbreviated, very free translation.
22. *The New York Times*, 21 January 1974, p. 8.
23. *Congressional Record*, Proceedings and Debates of the 93d Congress, Second Session, vol. 120, No. 30, Washington, Friday, March 8, 1974 – Senate.
24. Clastres 1972: 72.
25. *Patria*, Asunción, 31 July 1957, section "Antena." This description is still valid today.
26. *La Tribuna*, Asunción, 2 July 1972, p. 13. In Münzel 1973a: 15, I mentioned this case, but adding that it was perhaps the same already referred to, *ibid.*, p. 15, section 3. In the meantime, I was informed that these are two different cases.
27. Report of the Centre of Anthropological Studies.
28. On the air October 5th, 1973, 1st programme 9 p.m., transmission "Uns ist davon nichts bekannt – Ein Bericht über Indianermord in Paraguay."
29. Report of the Centre of Anthropological Studies.
30. "Ha habido algún Guayakí que para poder comprar de comer, ha vendido su hijo – por ochenta (80) Gs. – a unos Colonos." I will not reveal the name of the writer to a greater public, for reasons of security of this person who still lives in Paraguay.
31. In a report written in 1971 by Ing. Miguel A. Rico, FAO Soil Expert, and based on fieldwork in the area and exhaustive interpretation of aerial photographs. The report was sent to the Paraguayan Native Affairs authorities in December, 1971.
32. Chase Sardi 1972: 59.
33. Cf. report "Una Experiencia Entre los Guayakíes," signed Santiago Stolz (the Administrator). The report, which was sent to me on February 25th, 1974, describes the conduct of a group of "wild" Aché in the Reservation in September 1973. Mr. Stolz and the other North Americans with him were not able, according to this report, to speak with the "wild" Aché in their own idiom, although the "tame" Aché from the Reservation were. That "tame" and "wild" Aché were able to communicate in Aché shows that they belonged either to the same or to linguistically related tribes. That the missionaries were unable to communicate with the "wild" Aché shows, therefore, that they were unable as well to communicate in Aché with the "tame" Reservation Aché. The report, written by the Administrator, also shows a remarkable ignorance of Aché phonetics in spelling Aché names. Obviously, Mr. Stolz did not perceive that what he took to be the "name" of one of the "wild" Aché was, in fact, the Aché word for "Indian who adapted to the White Men's ways."
One of the photographs accompanying the report has a comment by the missionary who asks what could it be that the Aché shown is thinking. He adds

that he will know this, once the Aché will have learned "our idiom" – as if the other way round was out of the question.

34. Cf. the report cited in note 33. The most important and very frequent Aché rite of ceremonial salute is noted as "this seems to be some kind of ritual of theirs, because after it they kept quiet." The report shows that the missionaries did not catch at all the sense of the cultural expressions of the Aché observed by them.

35. Bidney 1967: 360.

36. Cadogan 1971: 12–13; Vivante-Gancedo 1968: 40; Msr. Pechilo, in a memorandum presented to the Papel Nuncio in February 1971; Meliá, in the interview cited in note 12, and in *La Tribuna*, Asunción, 2 July 1972, p. 13.

37. Cadogan, cf. note 36.

38. Free translation of a fragment of a longer song quoted in Clastres 1972: 348–349.

39. Abbreviated, very free translation. For a literal translation and translator's notes see Münzel 1973b.

40. *Ibid.*

41. *Ibid.*

42. Clastres 1968: 22.

43. Clastres 1972: 233–234.

44. Cadogan 1959: 48; 1968: 133.

45 Münzel 1968b: 86.

46. For further details about the history of the Aché, cf. Melia-Münzel 1973.

47. Doblas (1836) 1970: 91.

48. *Ibid.* 93

49. For further details about the history of the Aché, cf. Meliá-Münzel 1973a.

50. Account of a Paraguayan quoted in Lehmann-Nitsche 1899: 8.

51. *Ibid.* p. 9–10.

52. Baldus 1972: 468.

53. MacDonald 1911, cf. note 1.

54. Cf. note 52.

55. I refer to the "Northern" Aché of Mayntzhusen and other authors who still ignored the existence of a third Aché group even farther to the north.

56. Vellard 1939: 39–40.

57. Miraglia 1941: 343

58. Mayntzhusen 1925: 316.

59. Vellard 1933: 317, 316, 324, 329; Vellard 1935: 176; Vellard 1939: 136.

60. Vellard 1934: 228.

61. Vellard 1933: 319–320.

62. Deposition of Kybwyrági taped by me in 1971, confirmed by other Aché witnesses who in 1971 inhabited the Aché Reservation and by Mr. León Cadogan. Aché original and literal translation of the deposition in Münzel 1973b: 95–98.

63. Letter to the Editor, *La Tribuna*, Asunción, 28 August 1972, p. 10.

64. Clastres 1972: 189, 78.

65. For a detailed explanation of the figures, see Meliá-Münzel 1973: 139–142, and Münzel 1973a: 22 (with notes 41–43 on p. 70 there).

66. Clastres 1972: 347.

67. For a detailed explanation of the aid theoretically sent to the Indians and of the agricultural yield of the Reservation cf. Meliá-Münzel 1973: 142, 137–138; Münzel 1973a: 23, 58.

68. Cf. Cadogan 1968: 141; *La Tribuna*, Asunción, 29 Oct. 1963.

69. This figure of 80 captives is based upon an official publication of October, 1972, by the "Indian Aid Commission" which had taken over official responsibility

for the Reservation and its demographic census: "La Civilización de la Miel," in *La Tribuna*, Asunción, 1 October 1972, p. 12. It seems, in fact, that one group of 36 was captured, plus another of 11 (making a total of 47), plus another of some 33. Cf. also Chase 1972: 41. Before, it had been believed that the number of captured Aché was lower.

The figure of 26 is based upon my own eye-witness count.

70. *La Tribuna*, Asunción, 13 August 1972, p. 12.

71. *abc color*, Asunción, 4 Dec. 1970, 5 December, 7 December, 9 December, 13 September, 14 December, 15 December, 16 December, 17 December, 18 December, 21 December 1970.

72. Paper titled "Comisión de Ayuda al Indígena," edited by the "Aid Commission," Asunción, August 1971 (I own an exemplary of this paper). Interview, *La Tribuna*, Asunción, 2 July 1972. Publication in *La Tribuna*, quoted in note 69.

73. Abbreviated, very free translation. For a literal translation and translator's notes see Münzel 1973b.

74. Figures based upon the source quoted in note 69, upon Meliá-Münzel 1973: 143 and upon Münzel 1973a: 35–56. For detailed explanation, see there.

According to a census I made in the Reservation in 1970/72, the camp must have had 80 inhabitants in October, 1970. From October until December 1970, some 80 more were brought in, which should have resulted in a rise of the population to 160 persons. Nevertheless, in August 1971, only 106 Aché in total lived on the Reservation, which means a loss of 54 persons. In March/April 1972, another 171 (approximately) Aché were brought to the Reservation, which should have resulted in a rise of the total population to 277. Nevertheless, only 202 lived on the Reservation in June, 1972, which means a loss of 75 persons. Moreover, according to depositions of "tame" Reservation Aché who participated in manhunts, at least 9 free Aché died or were killed during manhunts from the Reservation. $54 + 75 + 9 = 138$.

Supposing that those who died were all or almost all new captives, the number of surviving captives makes 122.

75. Cf. Münzel 1973a: 14–19. There, several massacres are mentioned, each of which is classified by a number. Following the order I used there, we have: Massacre 1: 7 dead, 1 captured. Massacre 2: At least 2 captured. M 3: at least 3 captured. M 3a (cf. above note 26): 2 (the parents) killed, 1 captured. M 4: 12 At least killed, 5 captured. M5: 3 captured. M6: 3 captured. M7: At least 3 ("several") killed. M 8: According to depositions we heard, at least 7 killed and 3 captured. M 9: 8 killed, at least 3 captured. M 10: at least some 20 killed or captured.

76. Believing that an Aché tribe which has not yet been too much decimated could number between 200 and 400 persons. This figure is based upon demographic research I carried out in the Reservation in 1971/72. In the course of this research, I compiled a list of those persons who, according to the depositions of Aché, had composed tribes in the last years before they had come to the Reservation. The result was that the number of these persons must indeed have been close to 400 about 1968 in the case of the Northern Aché group living in the Reservation. As the Aché themselves do not count further than 3, this kind of statistic is, of course, only a very rough estimate. Taking the Reservation as a point of comparison, an Aché told me that some time before (about July/August 1970) his village had had "much, much more inhabitants)" – at the moment of this declaration (March 1972) the Reservation had about 180 inhabitants.

77. June 1972, the Reservation numbered 202 inhabitants. (Cf. Münzel 1973a: 55). January 1973, another 18 Aché were brought in (according to several

sources in Paraguay; the truth of this affirmation can easily be checked in the Reservation). September 1973, another 46 Aché were brought in (according to page 4 of the report by the missionary Administrator Mr. Stolz, quoted above in note 33). Thus, the population of the Reservation should have risen to 266. Nevertheless, in January, 1974 there were only some 100 Aché on the Reservation or in the forests close to it. This means a loss of some 166 persons. Supposing that the 100 inhabitants of 3 other camps mentioned by the report of January 1974 (cf. above note 17) had all come from the Reservation, there still remain some 66 Aché who have simply disappeared.

78. Report of the Centre of Anthropological Studies.
79. According to a paper edited by Procuradoria das Missões, Missionários do Verbo Divino, Ponta Grossa-Paraná, on August 7th, 1974, and entitled "Um relance histórico sobre as Missões do Verbo Divino entre os Indios do Paraguai," page 3, chapter "Os Guaiaquis."
80. According to the source quoted in note 79 and to private information I received from Paraguay.
81. According to the report quoted above in note 17.
82. According to Colonel Tristán Infanzón, Director of the Native Affairs Department, in *La Tribuna*, 15 July 1972, p. 8.
83. *Ibid.*
84. Cf. Münzel 1973a: 67.
85. Adding up in the following way the figures just given: Minimum estimate: Group 1 (some 50 persons) + group 2 (some 80) + group 3 (some 370) + group 4 (some 300). Maximum estimate: Group 1 (some 60) + group 2 (some 100) + group 3 (some 550) + group 4 (some 400) + Hondo Creek and Monday River groups (together, some 90). These estimates are only very rough.
86. *La Tribuna*, 13 August 1972, p. 12.
87. *Ibid.*
88. Arnold 1970: 165, 160.
89. *Ibid.*
90. Statistics elaborated by the joint UN-FAO and Paraguayan Ministry of Agriculture Project on Forest and Forest Industries Development, 1972. Published in FAO 1974: 334.
91. Bareiro-Saguier 1972: 74.
92. Fretes Ventre (1969) quoted *Ibid.*, p. 67.
93. Chase Sardi and Meliá in interviews published in *La Tribuna*, 13 August 1972, p. 12. Cadogan in his letter to the Editor quoted above in note 63.
94. As he is quoted, for instance, on page 2–3 of the report mentioned above in note 17.
95. Meliá 1973: 80.

Discrimination in Northern Ireland: The Protestant Response

SARAH NELSON

SARAH NELSON, born in Scotland in 1949, is a Junior Fellow at the Institute of Irish Studies, Queens University, Belfast. She was educated at schools in Scotland and England, and obtained her M.A. degree (first class honours) in politics from Edinburgh University in 1971. She then spent ten months as a local authority social worker in Belfast. In 1972 she began her Ph.D. thesis research at University of Strathclyde, Glasgow, where her Supervisor was Professor Richard Rose. Title: *Images of the Northern Ireland Conflict among Protestant Political Groups in Belfast, 1969–1975*, to be completed September 1976. Her publications include "Protestant Ideology Considered: the Case of Discrimination," *British Political Sociology Year Book, 1975* and "Ulster: Gunmen in Politics," *New Society*, May, 1975.

Discrimination in Northern Ireland: The Protestant Response

SARAH NELSON

After the last five years' events in Northern Ireland, it is now almost easy to forget that 'discrimination' was the central issue of Ulster politics during the early stages of the present unrest. Arguments about it filled the literature and utterances of all parties to the conflict. Despite their policy differences, all but one of these parties broadly accepted that certain kinds of discrimination in the political, social and economic spheres had taken place against the minority Roman Catholic population in Northern Ireland since Partition. 'Discrimination against Catholics' was thus seen as a major element of 'the Northern Ireland problem', and its eradication was viewed as a prerequisite to a 'solution' of this problem.

I. POPULAR THEORIES OF ULSTER PROTESTANT BEHAVIOUR: THE NEED FOR SUBJECTIVE APPROACHES

Large sections of the Protestant community, however, appeared to dissent from this analysis. That many of them refused to acknowledge the *fact* of discrimination had already been made clear by the findings of Professor Richard Rose's 1968 opinion survey which formed the basis of his book 'Governing Without Consensus'.[1] In reply to the question 'do you think Catholics in Northern Ireland are treated unfairly' 74% of Protestants replied 'no' while an equal percentage of Catholics replied 'yes'. This was the question which produced the highest degree of polarisation between the two religious groups. While, between 1968 and 1970, Unionist politicians were publicly denying the existence of 'discrimination', supporters of the Rev. Ian Paisley were demonstrating by their opposition to political reform measures that they would fiercely oppose any initiatives giving increased power or opportunities to their Catholic fellow countrymen.

By their refusal to accept premises which other parties shared, and which provided a common means of communication, many Protestants as it were excluded themselves from the kinds of discussions that were going on about Northern Ireland and its inhabitants; these were unreal to them. But plenty of people were eager to theorise about the motives for their 'discriminatory' behaviour, while few seemed to think that actually talking to Protestants about their perceptions of the situation would substantially aid their understanding of this behaviour.[2]

Some observers suggested the existence of a 'racist' or 'supremacist' ideology among Protestants, which provided rationalisations for discriminatory activity. That Protestant behaviour has been linked to the desire to retain superior power and economic resources in Ulster has been a long-held and much-publicised viewpoint of many left wing and republican groups in both Ireland and Britain. Such a view tends to encourage hasty comparisons between Ulster and countries as diverse as Algeria, Rhodesia or the Southern states of the U.S. Such comparisons are also made by those who see in Northern Ireland a 'caste situation' or a 'race relations situation'.[3] Contradictions and uncertainties which exist in the literature of 'race' itself present problems to anybody trying to define a 'race relations situation'. There are differences of opinion about the very definitions of 'race', of 'caste' of 'pluralism' and so on. This does not deter Robert Moore, who contends that in Northern Ireland Protestant privileges 'are based on racial considerations which are more salient than the economic ... the basis of the order lies in ... beliefs about others ... the parties to a race relations situation believe certain behaviour by others is inevitable'. He considers, though he does not demonstrate, that 'a considerable body of deterministic theory about Catholics' exists, which includes a view that '99% of Catholics are disloyal' and a religious theology which 'ascribes unchanging characteristics to Catholicism and Roman Catholics'.

In his interesting and informative paper 'protestant Ideology and Politics in Ulster',[4] Frank Wright examines fundamentalist Protestant theology and suggests that it does indeed give rise to deterministic views about Catholics and their church, which is seen as a monolithic and aggrandising force which must inevitably direct and influence the activities of its members even when the contrary seems the case (as when priests have spoken out against the actions of IRA members).

He also claims that these doctrines actually provide a justification for discriminatory treatment of Catholics: i.e. that Catholic influence must be opposed in order to prevent the liberties for which Protestantism has fought being undermined or destroyed.

However, many observers have linked supposedly 'deterministic theory' less with Protestant religious beliefs than with the kinds of beliefs which are often said to surface in groups which dominate others politically, socially and economically and which fear the loss of their privileges. They claim that Protestants tend to see Catholics as lazy, dirty, untrustworthy and given to excessive breeding, and that they use such images to justify denying them equal political and economic opportunities.

These theories tend to play down the salience of the 'national question' in Northern Ireland – the problem of two communities with conflicting national loyalties. From Moore's paper, and several other writings on Northern Ireland politics,[5] one would hardly guess that this problem had existed historically at all, except as a 'bogey' or 'delusion' in the minds of certain Protestants, or as a mere mask for other motives of a more material kind.

In reaction to this tendency, a recently-formed group (the British and Irish Communist Organisation) has turned much traditional theorising about Irish politics on its head. It challenges republican one-nation theory and claims that two nations developed historically in Ireland due to the uneven development of capitalism. The Southern bourgeoisie and the Catholic church refused to accept this situation and continued to divide the northern working class by imperialistic claims to northern territory. Catholic workers were led to believe their economic interests lay with a unified Ireland rather than in the more prosperous British-linked north, while Protestant workers were forced into an alliance with their own ruling class through the constant threat of antipartitionist movements. The organisation implicitly claims that if the antipartitionist threat were removed, Catholic and Protestant workers in the north could unite in a socialist movement and the economic and religious fears kept alive in Protestants by this threat would disappear; so also would the discriminatory practices which Protestants had used as a means to national self-preservation, when the legitimacy of the northern nation was denied by their opponents.[6]

In my own research I have been concerned with trying to answer the question: can a coherent Ulster Protestant 'ideology' or set of ideologies be said to exist? Does it make sense to describe it as 'racist', or 'colonialist' or in any other of the terms which analysts of Ulster politics have commonly employed? Protestant interview responses about one of the key issues of Northern Ireland politics, 'discrimination', might be expected to provide at least some indications of how these questions should be answered, and suggest reasons why so many people in the majority community could not, or would not, accept premises about the 'Ulster problem' which other parties to the conflict took for granted.

I draw throughout on statements made by activists in the Unionist, Democratic Unionist and Vanguard parties in Belfast, and the Protestant para-military groups, the Ulster Defence Association and Ulster Volunteer Force during open-ended interviews held in 1973 and 1974.[7]

My research led me to several major conclusions: first, that 'discrimination' is an issue of great concern to many Ulster Protestants, who think and talk about it a great deal. Secondly, it is something about which many people hold confused, ambiguous or contradictory opinions – about whether it exists or not, what it means, and whether it is justified or unjustified. Thirdly, views that could reasonably be described as 'racist' were only employed by a small minority of respondents, and it would be true to say that the confusion many respondents demonstrated arose in part from the fact that they held one set of beliefs which implicitly condemned discrimination, and another set which implicitly justified it. Fourthly, it could be argued that intransigent Protestant response to the Civil Rights Movement and political reform was caused by a variety of factors peculiar to the situation in Ulster, only some of which were related to 'ideology'.

II. Interview Responses Analysed

A. *Denial Responses: A Range of Contributory Influences*

I opened my discussion of 'discrimination' with the question: 'there has been a lot of talk in Northern Ireland about discrimination against Catholics. Do you think this existed or not?' Almost without exception my respondents replied 'no' thus apparently confirming the findings of Professor Rose's survey. However when encouraged to talk further about the subject, these people usually qualified their original denial almost immediately. It was also obvious that many respondents were very eager to talk about it and to defend their viewpoint; the subject tended to make people angry and defensive. A few gave the impression that the whole world was ranged against them, pointing accusing fingers with quite unjustified venom.

Such reactions might be interpreted as the expected response of a guilt-ridden person trying to rationise his complicitly in unjust acts. Whatever the truth of this assessment, alternative or additional contributory factors to this response are worth discussing here.

World attention came very suddenly to Ulster, from people the Ulster ruling class had always encouraged (possibly to its later regret) to remain in considerable ignorance about its historic conflicts and community problems. The claims and demands of the civil rights movement were widely accepted without question and any protesting noises by Protestants (for example, at the apparent hypocrisy of Catholics with well known Irish Republican sentiments calling for 'British standards') were construed as attempts to rationalise injustice. Protestants tended to be 'tarred with the same brush' as this girl, who supported the reform measures, illustrates:

I went over to England just after the trouble started. Someone was talking about Northern Ireland and one of the group asked me what religion I was. When I said 'Protestant' their whole attitude to me changed and they said we were a lot of bigots.

The feeling of powerlessness produced in many Protestants at this time by the fact that no-one listened to anything they had to say produced anger and frustration and encouraged irrational responses, which in turn persuaded observers that they were indeed faced with a bigoted and inarticulate group of people. Protestants could count on no articulate left wing intellectuals to put their case or write their pamphlets, either to correct mistaken impressions (e.g. that 'one man one vote' meant Catholics were totally disfranchised) or to suggest that Catholics had contributed to their own exclusion from public office (until the 1960s Catholic religious and political leaders tended to discourage their community's participation in this.) Many Protestants I have talked to give the impression that they are still reacting to the fast-moving events of this civil rights period, and it is relatively recently that the belief in the mass media as a deliberately hostile force has begun to diminish, especially in working class areas.

If some aspects of the way the campaign and the political situation in general was interpreted by groups outside Northern Ireland contributed to intransigent Protestant reaction, the response of radical reform groups to this intransigence tended to diminish further any opportunity of building up a strong reform movement which spanned the religious divide. That disappointment led, in general, not to an intensification of effort to win Protestant support, but rather to a 'giving up' on this group – at least until the 'dialectics of the struggle' or whatever had worked themselves out – became increasingly obvious to everyone as time passed.[8] This tendency reinforced many Protestants' beliefs that the civil rights movement was somehow a 'front' for a Catholic anti-partitionist campaign, rather than a non-sectarian political and social movement.

Thirdly, the implicit demand of reformers – that Protestants accept both the need for reform and the reforms themselves unless they were to be considered bigoted or supremacist – was quite a considerable one in view of historical developments in Ulster, and possibly unrealistic. A high degree of segregation existed between the two religious groups in most spheres of life, while hostility, suspicion and fear had been kept alive or rekindled by sporadic periods of political unrest, which left memories of real conflict as well as a store of mythology. Many people rarely came into contact with the 'other side' and were relatively unaware of the conditions in which they lived, drawing most of their information about this from their own community leaders.[9] As the type and degree of anti-Catholic discrimination varied between areas and in different types of employment, many Protestants could go through their lives without finding 'proof' of Catholic complaints, unless they were sufficiently concerned with the welfare of people who had traditionally been enemies to go out of their way to investigate. What their accusers were demanding was that all Protestants accepted on trust what these traditional enemies claimed to be true. Given the circumstances of such a historically divided society, it is perhaps more surprising that the reformists gained as much Protestant support as they did.

Lastly, the concessions the reformers demanded were not simply material ones; the first necessity was an admission of past misconduct, which necessitated a profound questioning of lifelong beliefs and personal integrity, by everyone who had supported the government of Northern Ireland. It is likely that people placed in this kind of situation will try and preserve their self image in the face of such a threat rather than face up to the possibly painful reality of the situation, or at least they will delay doing this as long as they can; for admission implies personal complicity. Hence some respondents went to extraordinary lengths to defend their community's conduct, and became angry and upset by my questioning. Others grasped eagerly at stories they had heard or read, which quickly became 'catch-phrases' or 'community myths', and repeated them to me.[10] For example, the burning of the Catholic Bombay Street, Belfast in August 1969 evoked guilt and shame in the Protestant community. A community myth grew up that 'the Catholics burned it down themselves' which some of my respondents had clearly made themselves believe. Defensive and intransigent reactions did not necessarily come from those respondents who were clearly hostile to Catholics; indeed, they often came from the kinds of people the civil rights movement probably hoped to embrace. One moderate Unionist with a long record of public service to both sections of the community always reacted fiercely to the mention of 'discrimination' and clearly saw the accusations as a profound threat to his own 'honour' and to his trust in colleagues whom he believed had acted as impartially as himself. Unable to bring himself to question his beliefs, he assumed that prominent Catholic politicians must be lying in order to further some ulterior motive and to stir up animosity between the two communities.

I have discussed some factors which may have increased the likelihood of an intransigent Protestant response to the civil rights demands, but which are not directly related to material considerations or to ideological pre-conceptions about Catholics. When we consider further comments made in interviews by my respondents, questions about 'ideology' become more pertinent, but we may still find that the accuracy or adequacy of conventional views about 'protestant ideology' are open to doubt.

After respondents made an initial denial I then asked 'why do you think some people said there was discrimination against Catholics?'

During the civil rights campaign conscious efforts were made by some unionist leaders to identify it with republican or 'extreme socialist' agitation. Belief in a 'troublemakers' theory is still widely found in the Protestant community, enabling them to identify a ready scapegoat and again to avoid facing up to the possible truth of the accusations. There are three other reasons why such a view is likely to be readily adopted. First, community relations in the late 1960s appeared superficially to be improving considerably, and the two groups seemed to be losing their hostility. Many people therefore believed that trouble could only come from 'agitators' bent on destroying the new spirit. For example, some Protestants I talked to believed that the

Southern Irish government must have been getting worried that Catholics were coming to accept and work for the Northern Ireland regime, and that they therefore decided to inspire a campaign of revolt before the chance of uniting Ireland with northern Catholic support was irrevocably lost!

Secondly, my interviews were conducted at a time when, after the downfall of the Stormont government, a devastating IRA bombing campaign and continued Catholic alienation despite 'paper' reforms, it appeared to Protestants that their worst suspicions and fears about the motives of the civil rights movement had materialised: 'we gave them what they asked for and look what happened'.

Thirdly, poor Protestants in particular found it hard to accept many of the claims of the civil rights movement, and found it easier in consequence to believe that it was an 'IRA plot'. In Ulster, working class Protestants outnumber working class Catholics, though the great majority of wealthy people are Protestant.[11] Though these workers suffered less unemployment than their Catholic fellows, they were more likely to be out of work than British workers, and were lower paid. Many have taken temporary jobs on the mainland and are well aware of these facts. Yet they felt they were being identified as part of the 'Protestant ascendancy' and that the civil rights movement was presenting to the world injustices which they too had to suffer, as things purely inflicted on Catholics:

I had worked beside RC's all my life and this Catholic friend of mine lived in the same kind of house as me. Therefore I couldn't see the civil rights case and blamed it on the students. They had their grants while I had to bring up a family on a widow's pension ... but things just seem to get worse whatever we do, which is what makes you think there must be some foreigners behind it all.

(working class housewife, Belfast)

Both working class and middle class Protestant reactions to the civil rights movement were influenced by other beliefs, about themselves and about Roman Catholics.

It was common for people to reply to my second question that the situation had been misinterpreted: that if Catholics were disadvantaged, the fault did not lie with Protestants, but somewhere else. They, were, therefore, still denying 'discrimination'. Responses suggested, however, that the great majority of Ulster Protestants who believed this neither saw Catholics as a distinct 'race' separate from themselves, nor believed the faults or inadequacies they attributed to Catholics were innate. Rather, they believed that Catholics were under the influence of malignant forces, notably the Catholic church and the Irish Republican movement:

It's not surprising they couldn't get on in life. How can a woman in Bally-murphy[12] keep her house clean or get a good education for her children when the church says she must have ten or twelve of them? She's bound to be poor.

(Unionist respondent)

Their own people get them if they take part – e.g. the IRA. There was a third of the places reserved for them in the police. The church always discouraged them from joining. If they did they might be shot by the IRA-look what happens in the Ulster Defence Regiment now.

(DUP respondent)

When I worked in the post office there was this lad of 17 who had to tie string round the bundles of letters. I noticed he was tying a whole ball of string round each bundle. I said, Patrick what are you doing? He was muttering "break the state, break the state." It's criminal the notions they put into them at that age.

(Unionist repondent)

Thus the notion that Catholics 'don't work' or 'don't want to work', which has anguished many a trade union activist in Northern Ireland in the past, derives from the idea that Catholics don't want to work for the Protestant Northern Ireland state but would rather milk it of benefits without contributing to it, rather than because they are lazy or workshy by nature (an important distinction, though again trade unionists may feel the first belief has worked as effectively as the second would have done to hinder effective joint working class action on social issues):

UDA respondent   1: I employed them on a building site, half of them didn't turn up and most of the others were drawing assistance at the same time ...

UDA respondent   2: Yes but RC's in Scotland don't behave like that do they? I've worked with them there ... they support the state don't bring it down.

UDA respondent   1: That's right ... but you people don't under-stand what they're like here ...

It is difficult to describe these beliefs as 'racist' in any accepted sense, though they would become 'deterministic' if and when people believed Catholics could not escape the influence of their church, or republican leaders, nor act independently from them. Frank Wright[13] discusses this issue at length; it is possible that he exaggerates the extent to which Protestants feel Catholics are 'tied' to their church. Most so-called 'extreme' Protestants to whom I have talked clearly have ambiguous feelings about this. On the one hand their upbringing has influenced them to believe in the tremendous power of the RC church and its 'hold' over its flock. On the other hand, they tend to believe in the existence of a large if vague body of 'good Catholics' who could be wooed away from 'disloyal' activities, leaving a small group of IRA activists whom they (the loyalists) could 'deal with no bother'.

Northern Protestants do not, on the whole, have any well-defined conception of themselves as a 'race', nor even as a 'nation', despite the fact that at a 'folk' level images of Protestants as more industrious, thrifty and self-reliant than other Irishmen are often apparent. This is not to deny that one of the reasons Protestants have opposed Irish unity has sprung from a feeling that the Southern state is 'different' and culturally alien; but northern Irish Catholics will also express the feeling that southerners are 'different' from themselves, while Rose[14] found Protestant respondents were more likely to say that the English were 'much different' to themselves than that northern Catholics were. As many Republicans believe Protestants have been "artificially" separated from them by a scheming imperialist power, so many Protestants believe Catholics have been "artificially" separated by a scheming church.

The minority of respondents who introduced specifically 'racial' concepts into their discussion of the conflict belonged almost entirely to William Craig's right wing Vanguard movement, a group which has flirted with ideas of 'U.D.I.' and which has tried to develop a theory of 'Ulster nationhood'. These people often talked to me at length about the supposed 'racial' characteristics of the 'Scots-Irish' in Ulster and gave rather implausible accounts of their historic origins and development, with great enthusiasm. This political philosophy of this party suggests a desire for an authoritarian and puritanical type of society which rejects the 'permissiveness' of modern Britain. It should be borne in mind, however, that the same members of this largely middle-class group who criticised the supposed characteristics of Catholics (and even they were often uncertain what racial group *northern* Irish Catholics now belonged to) also tended to show distaste for the political pretensions and abilities of working class Protestants, despite their supposedly admirable 'Scots-Irish' characteristics.

Many people to whom I talked appeared to be strengthened in their view that 'discrimination' must have been someone else's fault' by a belief that 'Protestants just wouldn't do things like that'. Here we are entering the realms of 'Protestant ideology about *Protestants*', which, if it exists, as I want to suggest – has perhaps been ignored or overlooked by students of group relations in Ulster.

Protestants in Ulster tend to see themselves as law-abiding and peaceful people, in contrast to the Catholic 'rebels' who have sought to oppose British and Protestant rule by bomb and gun. The Protestant housewife who said incredulously to her neighbour as she actually watched a loyalist mob burn shops and shoot at firemen, 'but it can't be Protestants, we don't *do* things like that' revealed in extreme form beliefs I have commonly found in talking to Protestant people in Ulster, especially on the subject of Protestant violence.

As they are law-abiding people, so they are just and tolerant people who believe in 'fair play for all'. The first contributory factor to this belief springs from the influence of 'official propaganda' about the nature of the Northern Ireland government before it was prorogued. It had all the trappings and constitutional and electoral procedures on the British model; at national (rather than local) level it could not, apparently, be faulted in its constitutional methods. (The only, and rather substantial, problem for Catholics was that they could never hope to have anything but a minority of MP's democratically elected!) If British children could be socialised into beliefs about British democracy like 'fair play' and 'integrity', so could members of the Ulster Protestant community; indeed, their schools probably placed more emphasis on the supposed virtues of the 'Mother of Parliaments' and its 'model' in Ulster than did British schools.

A second factor made it almost compulsory for Protestants to believe these things about themselves. Their forefathers opposed Home Rule for Ireland not simply because they claimed British identity but also because, for them, Home Rule was synonymous with tyranny and clerical-dominated government: 'Home Rule is Rome Rule'. If they were fighting to escape injustice and preserve freedom, they could hardly be guilty of the very malpractices they claimed to oppose, once that freedom was granted.

But does not the Calvinist view of the relationship between religion and politics not make justifiable the denial of free speech and other

political rights to those who threaten 'Protestant liberty'? This was
one argument used by Ian Paisley and those who opposed the ecumenical and pro-reform movements of the late 1960s. However, I
have found very few Protestants who are willing to use this kind of
argument to support 'discrimination', though in other countries such
as South Africa or Rhodesia, those who comply with discriminatory
practices against the native population will frequently draw on biblical
or pseudo-biblical arguments to justify their defence of 'Christian society' and values. I only met one respondent who openly declared that
discrimination against Catholics was 'right' in order to safeguard
Protestant liberties. To prove his point he read to me the whole of the
1707 Act of Union between Scotland and England, which he appeared
to have standing by for such emergencies as my visit, and declared
that Britain, not Ulster, had now departed from her Protestant principles. (The Act debarred Catholics from holding certain prominent
public offices).

It is possible that Wright exaggerated the importance of the Protestant 'religio-political' interpretation of Irish politics because his interviews were conducted solely with members of Paisley's own political
party (the D.U.P.). Because Paisley, with his powerful personality,
became the beacon round which all the anti-reformist forces tended
to gather in the late 1960s, it does not follow that all his supporters
shared his knowledge of, or commitment to, the principles of 'Bible
Protestantism' which he enunciated.

I am not trying to suggest here that Protestants do not fear the
extension of power of the Catholic church, for many of them clearly
do; nor that they do not condone or rationalise anti-Catholic discrimination; merely that their religious beliefs about Protestantism may
make it more difficult, rather than easier, for them to justify such discrimination.

'Where Protestantism flourishes liberty flames ... Protestantism is
the torch-bearer of liberty'.[15] The number of my respondents who drew
on religious principles to claim that discrimination was 'wrong' was
far greater than the number who drew on these to rationalise it. Even
among Protestants who are not regular churchgoers or even believers,[16]
the idea that Protestants are somehow 'free men' of independent
mind, who unlike those in the hold of the RC church do not oppress
others, still exerts a powerful influence. *Despite* the hierarchical and
authoritarian nature of the Orange/Unionist system which most
Protestants accepted and supported, and *despite* the findings of Rose's

survey which suggested a high degree of deference to authority in both communities, many Protestants perceive themselves as 'free men' who neither allow themselves to be 'bossed around' nor to treat others unfairly:

I think one reason why we can't get unity on our side now is ... people always think they know their own minds and won't be told what to do ... this is a traditional Protestant idea ... sometimes I feel it can be our un-doing.

(D.U.P. respondent)

'The Protestant ethic is equal rights for all, special privileges for none' has almost become a catch-phrase in arguments about 'discrimination' in the loyalist press.

Such ideas may be useful as 'whitewashing' propaganda on behalf of the Unionist system, but they will be even more effective if supporters of that system actually come to believe them, for they may prevent people understanding a political situation or making redefinitions of it. As beliefs about 'individual freedom' may have acted as an additional barrier to the realisation of the *lack* of freedom in traditional Protestant society, so beliefs about the 'tolerance' and 'fair-mindedness' of Protestantism may prevent people from looking closely at 'Protestantism in practice' or at the criticisms made by others about Protestant treatment of Catholics in Northern Ireland.

B. *Discrimination as 'Natural': Sectarian Political Traditions in Ulster*

I have been talking about 'responses of denial'. Quite often, people would indignantly indulge in such responses and then say something like 'anyway, they were as bad': thus implying that 'discrimination' did exist:

What about the Nationalist councils? You never hear about them do you. Let a Protestant try to get a house in Newry!

(Unionist respondent)

Did you ever hear of a Protestant getting a job in the Falls Road? Or living in the Falls!

(Unionist respondent)

British society sometimes came under attack:

They're hypocrites, with their race relations problems. And all the politicians do it too you know. Harold Wilson is in the Masons – how do you think he got where he did?

(UVF respondent)

The responses suggested that in pre-'68 Northern Ireland society there was widespread acceptance that certain forms of discrimination by one community against the other were somehow 'natural' and 'inevitable' (especially in private employment) as were certain corrupt electoral practices. (This does not mean people felt they were 'right'.) I asked why the two communities seemed to give preference to their own side in this way:

well–fear partly. People just liked to be with their own, you just felt more at ease obviously.

(Vanguard respondent)

Look, it was just people's way of doing things here till everyone started interfering. Given time, it would have died out naturally – in fact it was doing so.

(Vanguard respondent)

Now why did people just not admit this at the beginning? This extract from a group interview with D.U.P. activists suggests a reason, 'we were all getting along great just before the troubles – all the working class people. How could we be 'discriminating' when we let them live and go shopping in our area? (Shankill Rd) ... look, we knew we couldn't get a job in (X) bakery but we didn't complain, we just accepted it. Then they started complaining about 'discrimination'!

The answer is that many Protestants did not look upon certain practices as 'discrimination' at all – for example, in private employment. They just accepted them as an inevitable, if sometimes regrettable, part of life. (Easier for Protestants to do, as there were many more 'Protestants-only' than 'Catholics-only' firms.) The precept 'each looks after his own' is not seen as shameful, even if it is regrettable – it is merely natural, given the historic conflicts, segregation and suspicion of Northern Ireland society.

Why do we find this high degree of acceptance that such forms of discrimination are 'inevitable' in Northern Ireland? Why am I confronted with a respondent who tells me that as a socialist he believes people should get jobs on merit, and who later on appeals to me that it is surely natural that people give jobs to their friends; and is obviously confused and upset when I point out the contradiction? It is likely that many Northern Irish people were simply not aware of the extent to which they unconsciously accepted values which the Stormont system was always liable to foster in the population. On the one hand, Protestants were given to believe that their system, modelled on the British democratic 'ideal', represented values that would make discriminatory practices impossible. On the other hand, realities often diverged sharply from the ideal, so that over the years people developed more than one set of expectations of 'what politics is about'. For fifty years the two conservative parties, unionists and nationalists, played the same sterile 'game'[17] – 'looking after your own', the use of patronage, 'cutting up the sectarian cake', the great 'numbers' obsession with its consequent electoral and local government corruption, including the 'vote early and often' syndrome on polling day. Some of my respondents obviously found it hard to believe that other countries like Britain didn't indulge in these practices because they seemed a 'natural' part of politics. I met several activists from the whole spectrum of Ulster political parties who roundly condemned corrupt electoral practices then explained confidentially 'of course it's shocking but if they do it you have to do it too'. Some ran highly organised 'flying squads' of personators on polling days, equipped with boxes of disguises.

'Everyone did it'; or if they didn't, they were liable to lose out. Catholics had first and foremost a practical reason for rejecting corrupt electoral practicies and gerrymandering of electoral boundaries: their gains were small, and overall they could never 'win'. Put crudely, Protestants could best secure 'Protestant power' through discriminatory practices and gerrymandering. Catholics, in the minority, could best increase 'Catholic power' through demanding an 'open society'. I am not suggesting that reformists were merely making cynical use of idealistic principles like 'human rights for all', but rather suggesting that it may be naive to assume that all Catholic politicians and voters have been able to 'shake off' some of the socialised assumptions about politics that some of my respondents demonstrated here:

a) that the interests of Protestants and Catholics as groups will often be in opposition, even if not in a 'zero-sum' situation.
b) that each side's politicians will naturally 'look after their own' first. They cannot really be 'impartial'. Similarly, firms will tend to give jobs to 'their own'.
c) that each 'side' will therefore do best to build up a strong sectarian political bloc to safeguard their interests (the present UUUC and SDLP?).

What many Protestants fear today is that despite the reassuring noises beloved of Catholic politicians, the reality of increased 'Catholic power' will not be a 'nonsectarian society' but one in which Catholics merely have more powers of patronage. They may be right; it may be that beyond Ulster's narrow 'centre' most Northern Ireland people think like each other about what politics is about – a 'sectarian cake' – without – and I stress this point – necessarily realising consciously that they do so, or being able to face up to the fact openly.

C. *Discrimination as 'Justified': Catholic Faults and Protestant Fears*

It will have become evident by now that many people were confused about the precise meaning of 'discrimination'. Perhaps both reformers and anti-reformers have tended to 'lump together' all the injustices which have been claimed to exist in Northern Ireland; certainly many Protestants subsume these under the heading 'discrimination', yet they often take different attitudes to different parts of the 'package'.

At the most general level, what upset my respondents was the suggestion that the Protestant community had treated the Catholic community *'unfairly'*. It is the precise meaning they attached to 'unfairly' that we have to try and elucidate. The moderate Unionist who believed discrimination was 'wrong' literally believed that the Unionist government had treated Catholics exactly as it had treated Protestants, and considered that if the latter were under-represented in the professions it must be because their lay and religious leaders had discouraged them from accepting the Northern Ireland regime. He admitted that local councils, notably in Londonderry, had not always behaved with impartiality but ascribed this to bigotry and fear on the part of less-well educated people; it was regrettable, but could be put right with government reforms and 'enlightened' administration. He also thought the practice of 'giving jobs to your own' – of which Catholics, he considered, had been as guilty as Protestants – was also regrettable but could be eroded by enlightened leadership and a growth of trust between the communities. To him, 'treating Catholics unfairly' meant treating them differently from Protestants, to their disadvantage.

The respondents in loyalist groups were as indignant as he at being called 'discriminators', and did as much as they could to convince not only the interviewer but themselves that, if Catholics were disadvantaged, it was not the fault of Protestants. However, the sum of their comments on 'discrimination' suggested that they tended to have more ambiguous attitudes about it, and that they tolerated – albeit with some discomfort – rather than actively supported certain discriminatory practices, either because they felt Catholics had 'asked for it' or because they feared the consequences reform might bring.

For example, working class Protestants in depressed areas of Belfast tended to assume that if so many Catholics were unemployed, it must be because they didn't want to work; after all, they themselves suffered high unemployment but didn't complain about it: they 'went and looked for work'. They assumed they must be recognised as more reliable workers, so that if firms preferred to employ them, it did not particularly worry them. It was up to Catholics to change their attitude to the state!

Their feelings might be summed up in these lines from a loyalist song:

> And when their babies learn to talk
> They shout "discrimination"
> Their dad just lies in bed all day
> And lives upon the nation.[18]

Thus Catholics annoyed Protestants, not only because they were always complaining about 'ill treatment', but also and more especially because they did *deliberately* inflammatory things, like waving Irish tricolours, insulting the Queen or singing nationalist songs in public. Having both insulted Protestants and demonstrated their disloyalty, how could they expect either community relations to improve or the majority to place them in positions of trust in the state? Thus some of my respondents were implicitly saying: do you expect me to concern myself investigating these people's complaints when they openly insult me? If they are true, and they are probably propaganda, then they must have asked for what they got.

This kind of 'gut' feeling may co-exist with other, contradictory, feelings about discrimination. The very reason many Protestants tend to feel like this is illustrative of one aspect of political development in Ireland. When the civil rights movement implied that the term 'democracy' involved the rights and the protection of minorities, it was introducing an argument that was unfamiliar in Ireland. The Irish nationalist movement demanded Home Rule because they claimed the majority of Irish people wanted it. The nationalist argument against Partition has at its centre the claim that Partition denies the democratically expressed wish of the majority of Irish people to govern themselves; that the minority in the north east corner has no right of secession. Ulster Protestants, on the other hand, feel they have only preserved their small piece of land through constant struggle and under constant threat. As the majority in their area, they have constantly reaffirmed their desire to remain separate from nationalist Ireland, yet 'the enemy' cannot be content without trying to take their territory as well. Ulster Protestants, too, have adopted the equation of 'democracy' with 'majority rule', with the idea that those who oppose the last are also opposing democracy. Thus many Protestants cannot see the flaunting of Orange banners as 'provocative', but rather as symbolic of the ideals of the majority in its own territory; parading of tricolours, however, is insulting and provocative, indicating an undemocratic disrespect for the legitimate values of the society which, it is felt, the minority are free to leave if it is unacceptable to them. This kind of thinking should be more understandable to Irish nationalists than to Protestant or Catholic 'centrists' in Ireland.

We have seen that some people managed to hold several contradictory viewpoints, without necessarily realising that they did so: 1) that discrimination was 'wrong' and not something that Protestants did; if Catholics were disadvantaged, it must be because they had excluded themselves. 2) that some forms of discrimination, notably in private employment, existed; they were inevitable if regrettable, but the way people in Ulster 'did things'. 3) that if Catholics had suffered injustices and there was some truth in what they were saying, they deserved it for rejecting the state which kept them: 'loyal to the half-crown not the Crown'. (Thus: it is up to Catholics to prove their 'loyalty' first. *How* they are to do this, and *which* Catholics are to be trusted when they do, has been one of the central issues dividing Protestants during the present political unrest).

D. *Discrimination as 'Necessary': Protestants as All-Ireland Minority*

A fourth possibility suggests itself: that some Protestants believed discrimination was *necessary*, which is something slightly different from believing it was right, wrong, inevitable or justified. Nothing becomes more quickly obvious to an outsider working in Northern Ireland than the fact that many Protestants are deeply afraid of being 'taken over' or outbred by Catholics and of being physically oppressed by them, and feel nervous about entrusting them with any kind of power; that they see themselves as a constantly threatened minority in an all-Ireland context. It is actually unusual to hear Ulster Protestants talking of Irish unity who do not speak in terms of being 'taken over by' or 'absorbed or incorporated *into*' the Southern Irish state (the present Republic of Ireland) which suggests that many people have difficulty even of *conceiving* of a different form of unification. Now this kind of situation makes it likely that even if some Protestants have felt that discrimination was 'wrong', and that Catholics were treated unjustly, they would hold back from actively fighting unjust practices (notably gerrymandering) which at least delayed the dreaded 'takeover' of their province by nationalists. Similarly, those who were concerned by the disproportionate level of Catholic unemployment also knew that the higher Catholic emigration which resulted offset the fact that, at any one time, almost half the children of primary school age in Northern Ireland were Catholic.

Why are many Protestants so afraid of a 'takeover'? Why did several of my respondents, for example, see Catholics as aggressive people, continually plotting to subvert their territory?

Look at this map of Belfast. I'll show you all the districts they have taken over since the troubles started.[18]

(Vanguard respondent)

We opposed mixed housing because what they do is this. First they get in enough voters to elect a nationalist councillor, then enough to put out a loyalist if not to elect a nationalist MP. Then gradually they will take over all of N. Ireland.

(D.U.P. respondent)

Religious ratios in Northern Ireland, and the higher birthrate of Catholics there, has always meant that the 'numbers game' assumed continuous importance for Protestants who feared the consequences of Catholic power. The reasons for these fears have been explored or suggested by both partisan and non-partisan commentators in varying degrees of depth; but whatever decision is reached, and however much talk is raised about 'myths' and 'shibboleths', it is unlikely that all these fears can be removed, either by reassuring words, structural and economic change, or 'education', because their roots lie only partly in 'ideologies' about Catholics which can be changed. What many Protestants fear most, at root, is simple physical oppression of their group by the other religious group, of being literally 'driven into the sea'. (One respondent, on hearing I came from Scotland, asked me anxiously: 'are you ready to take us when (sic) we come?') Thus, if 'myths' about, for example, the aggrandising and monolithic nature of the RC church can be changed, it is unlikely that memories of atrocities perpetrated by one group upon another in the past can be easily eradicated. 'Ideology' contributed to the fact that the atrocities happened, but what is relevant is that they are historical facts, which themselves serve to increase group hostility and suspicion. History provides several sound reasons why one community should not trust to the goodwill of the other: the present conflict has provided many more, and an infinite number of bitter memories. In my discussions with Ulster people of both religions I often asked their recollections of what they were told about 'the other side' as children. I expected to hear 'character stereotypes' of Prods and Micks, who were snobbish or who didn't wash their faces. Some people talked in this way, but far more described historic incidents of which they had been told – the 1920's 'troubles', the burning of relatives' houses or the shooting of relatives by the police or 'the other side'. Protestants and Catholics were, first and foremost, people who fought each other.

III. Conclusions: Some Outstanding Questions

My interviews with Ulster Protestants in the Belfast area[20] on the subject of 'discrimination' were conducted with members of 'loyalist' parties, the Unionist party and 'centrist' parties (Alliance and Northern Ireland Labour). However, I have concentrated my attention in this paper on members of groupings which have tended to oppose political changes which the British government and reformist Ulster politicians have attempted to implement since 1969. I wanted to begin to look at the way such people themselves saw the demands for change, why they thought these should be opposed, and how they rationalised their opposition to reform.

'Objective' analyses of the kinds of inequalities which exist in a society like Northern Ireland are important, and yield much valuable information about the nature of the social situation which pertains there.

In Ulster, especially during the early years of the present conflict, a number of studies have been attempted which seek to examine the exact nature and extent of 'discrimination' against Catholics in different fields–housing, employment, (public and private) and so on[21] and in different geographical areas of the province. Examination of Ulster's economic structure, or of Protestant-Catholic ratios in different types of employment, may also assist the student who is trying to answer questions like: 'can Northern Ireland be described as a 'caste society' or as a 'colony' of Britain?

However, unless such 'objective' studies are supplemented by 'subjective' ones, which examine how conflicting groups actually see their relations with each other and understand what is going on, any pronouncement on the *kind* of social situation which exists will be difficult to make with accuracy, and is more likely to be influenced by the cultural or other biases of the researcher. (Robert Moore, for example, decides that 'racism has an active role' in Northern Ireland and quotes in 'evidence' three nineteenth century writers, a journalist from Le Nouvel Observateur and 'A Catholic recently interviewed by the Sunday Times').

I have only been able to discuss briefly here some of the responses made by Protestant respondents about the issue of 'discrimination' in N. Ireland, and my study as it stands has only the most limited usefulness to our understanding of Ulster politics. I have divided respondents by political group allegiance; group membership indeed had significant influence on response, but others may feel division of respondents by some other criterion, for example occupation, might have provided as useful or more useful information about the perceptions of anti-reform groups. That much new work in this field suggests itself is an indication that relatively few researchers in Ulster to date have concentrated their attentions on the 'subjective', especially where Protestants are concerned, while they have not always been so reticent in constructing simplistic theories about the 'nature' of the Ulster political situation.

Perhaps some of the issues discussed in this paper at least raise questions which need to be explored in greater depth.

1) How usefully in fact can the Northern Ireland 'situation' be compared with 'race relations situations' (either the 'deep South' variety, or the 'settler-native' variety); first in terms of structure (extent of inequalities, which have no legal sanction:) secondly of parties to the situation (which include two 'outside' governments, both claiming the territory;) thirdly of ideology? Is it really possible to claim with any validity that a widely held and recognisably 'racist' ideology about Catholics exists among Ulster Protestants?

2) Can a coherent ideology be found at all which rationalises discriminatory treatment of Catholics by Protestants? How does fundamentalist Protestant religious belief in Northern Ireland influence attitudes to such treatment – does it facilitate or undermine it, or may it do both?

3) To what extent do the majority of Protestants and Catholics in Northern Ireland share certain beliefs about 'what politics is' which have important consequences for their political behaviour, and which establish barriers in communication between themselves on the one hand, and British and Ulster 'centrist' politicians on the other?[22]

4) Were the political events of recent years in Northern Ireland in some sense 'inevitable' given the cleavages and latent tensions which existed, and the views each group held of the others; or did 'the way things were done' in itself help to produce polarizing outcomes which might have been avoided – in particular, reactions of intransigence in a substantial section of the Protestant community?[23]

NOTES

1. Richard Rose, *Governing Without Consensus*, Faber and Faber 1971, page 497, question 43.
2. Social workers in Catholic areas of Belfast told me of the numerous research students, psychologists etc. who flocked there during 1969–71. However, the bias towards Catholics was partly the result of the suspicious and unco-operative attitudes of 'loyalists' to pressmen and researchers at this time. See Max Hastings, 'Ulster '69,' London, Gollancz, 1970.
3. Cf. Robert Moore, "Race relations in the Six Countries', in *'Race'*, 1972, XIV, 1.
4. Frank Wright, 'Protestant ideology and politics in Ulster,' In *European Journal of Sociology*, Vol. XIV 1973, pp. 213–80. He challenges some conventional viewpoints, suggesting that 'extreme' Protestant ideology has sometimes functioned to regulate conflict and facilitate co-operation; and that the greatest hostility to Catholics is not necessarily found among Protestants most threatened by economic competition.
5. Especially the 'instant' post-'68 variety; see David Boulton, *The UVF*, Torch books 1973; the writings of Andrew Boyd; Rosita Sweetman, *On our Knees*, Pan 1972; Liam de Paor, *Divided Ulster*, Penguin 1970, which remains a most useful work nonetheless.
6. British and Irish Communist Organisation, 10 Athol Street, Belfast 12.
7. The Unionist Party itself has been seriously divided on a "moderate-loyalist' basis since 1969. The Democratic Unionists are led by Ian Paisley, Vanguard by William Craig. For background information, not always accurate, on UDA and UVF see David Boulton, *op. cit.*
8. The Official Republican movement remains committed to the necessity of building a working class revolutionary movement of Protestants and Catholics. My comments apply particularly to People's Democracy, but most of its

original members now appear to have left the movement. See Paul Arthurs, *The P.D.*, Blackstaff 1974.

Conor Cruise O'Brien in *States of Ireland* (Panther, 1974) gives some useful insight into "Catholic psychology" and its influence on reformist, antipartionist and revolutionary groups in Ulster.

9. See Frank Wright, *op. cit.*, D.P. Barrit and C.F. Carter, *The Northern Ireland Problem*, Oxford University Press 1962; D. P. Barritt and A. Booth, *Orange and Green*, Northern Friends Peace Board 1972.

10. The role both of politicians, and of 'street newspapers' and news-sheets of the kind which have proliferated in Belfast since 1969, in providing these 'community myths' may be important and deserve further study.

11. See Richard Rose, *op. cit.* Barritt and Carter, *op. cit.* Barritt and Booth, *op. cit.*

12. A Catholic housing estate in Belfast, noted for its poor amenities, deprivation, delinquency and large families.

13. *Op. cit.*

14. *Op. cit.* Appendix, Loyalty questionnaire, questions 18d and 41.

15. Quoted in Frank Wright, *op. cit.*, page 224.

16. Not a contradiction, as anyone familiar with Ulster politics will know, and the subject of numerous anecdotes. Cf. 'Wanted, reliable cook general, Protestant, (Christian preferred)' quoted in Barritt and Booth, *op. cit.* The labels 'Protestant' and 'Catholic' may indicate several other things besides religious belief: likely voting habits, cultural and national outlook.

17. Cf. Peter Gibbon, 'The dialectics of religion and class in Ulster,' *New left review*, No. 55, May–June 1969.

18. Orange Cross Book of Songs and Verse (2nd ed.) obtainable from Orange Cross, 10 Upper Charleville St. Belfast 13.

19. Cf. CRC research unit, Bedford House, Belfast 2: *Flight: a report on population movement in Belfast during August 1971*, 1971. As Catholics tended to crowd into inner city areas while Protestants evacuated to the suburbs, Protestants tended to interpret Catholic movement as 'proof' that they were taking over the city.

20. An area where Protestants greatly outnumber Catholics. In counties like Fermanagh and Tyrone where the Catholic population approximates or exceeds 50% the Protestant population is more immediately threatened, and it was in these areas that Catholics claimed some of the most flagrant abuses of Protestant power.

21. The literature is extensive; but see e.g. *Campaign for social justice*, (Castlefields, Dungannon), *The Plain Truth*, 1969, 2nd ed.; Fermanagh C.R.A., *Fremanagh facts*, 1969; Aidan Corrigan, *Eyewitness in N. Ireland*, Voice of Ulster publications, 1969; Cameron Commission. *Disturbances in N. Ireland*, Belfast, H.M.S.O., Cmd. 532, 1969.

22. Cf. Peter Gibbon (*op. cit.*); 'moderation and extremism are moralistic notions of bourgeois democratic politics which have no meaning in Ulster.'

23. Gibbon's paper suggests an 'inevitability' about what took place while Conor Cruise O'Brien (*op. cit.*) seems to suggest that people with so many misperceptions of each other were likely to boob right along the line. The volume of adverse comments from all factions which I have received on Terence O'Neill's personality and tactics, at least raises questions about the possibility that another reformist leader in the same situation might have carried through political change with more success.

The Arabs as Slavers

JOHN LAFFIN

JOHN LAFFIN is an Australian-born journalist and historian, presently residing in England. In his writings he specialises in military history and current world affairs, particularly in the Third World, with special emphasis on the Middle East. He is a prolific writer and his works include: *Links of Leadership* (Harrap), *Swifter than Eagles – Biography of Marshal of the R.A.F. Sir John Salmond* (Blackwood), *One Man's War* (Angus and Robertson), *The Walking Wounded* (Amalgamated Press), *Anatomy of Captivity – Political Prisoners* (Abeland-Schuman), *Letters from the Front* (Dent), and more recently *Fedayeen – The Arab-Israeli Dilemma* (Cassell).

The Arabs as Slavers

JOHN LAFFIN

One of the strangest aspects of the long and terrible history of the slave trade is that the Arabs have never had to accept as much responsibility for it as the English and the Americans. Yet they were engaged in slaving – as a trade – for more than 1000 years before the Anglo-Saxons took it up and for more than a century after they had abandoned it. The imbalance of responsibility is easily explained. Slavery between Africa and the Americas – the source and the market respectively – was well known and it always obscured, in the Western world, the practice of slavery in other regions. Sales of African negroes in the Americas were public affairs and since slavery took place in the most common languages, English, French and Spanish, it was a popular topic in speech and literature. Publicity was inevitable. Also, the great European reformers, such as William Wilberforce, were so concerned with the infamy of their own nationals being involved in the trade that they gave little attention to the part played by slavers of other races.

The enslavement by Arabs of African negroes and other peoples was geographically concealed. The slavers were operating in a vast area of jungle, desert and mountains, all remote from the civilised world and for centuries the only foreign witnesses were the few explorers, consuls, naval officers and missionaries who encountered slave caravans or dhows, compounds or markets. They reported what they saw but not until 1876 with David Livingstone's impassioned cries from Africa – "this open sore of the world" – did Europe take much notice. Even then the matter seemed to have no direct relevance and until modern times it has appeared to many people that Arab slave trading and slave owning was some kind of spasmodic aberration.

History must now record that Arabs have played the major role in the world slave *trade* and one of the major parts in the use and exploitation of slaves. An author faces the linguistic problem of whether to use past or present tense, since some slavery still exists. For clarity, the present tense is used only when referring to the Koran – for to Islam the advice of the holy book remains as valid now as it did 1300 years ago – and in reference to slavery in modern times.

It is essential to distinguish commercial slaving from that of the age-old and universal custom of using as slaves those enemies defeated in battle. The second type was so much the norm, with its roots going back into antiquity, that perhaps a case could be made out for not regarding it as slavery in the modern sense. Slavery as a trade or commercial enterprise was first begun in Africa by the Arabs, who were both the procurers in the field and the suppliers in the markets. Soon after the Arabs began to conquer North Africa the first written record was made of their desire for African slaves – in an agreement with Nubia after the conquest of Egypt in AD 641, which stated that the Nubians should pay yearly "300 slaves to the leader of the Moslems, of the middle class of slaves with healthy bodies, males and females..."

The history of Islam, from its earliest period, contains many mentions of slaves as tribute or taxes to be paid to political superiors. Some Arab conquerors imposed on vassals an annual tribute of as many as 1000 slaves for possession of slaves was even then a status symbol. (The Arabic word for slavery is *rikk* and for slave *abd* or *abid*.)

I. DEFINITION OF SLAVES

If slavery requires definition, that of the League of Nations in 1926 will suffice: "Slavery means the status or condition of a person over whom any or all of the powers attached to the right of ownership are exercised." This description is accepted by the Anti-Slavery Society and by the United Nations. Four other forms of servitude condemned by the U.N. are significant in the Arab experience – debt bondage, serfdom, sham adoption of children, servile forms of marriage.

Debt bondage occurs when a debtor pledges his own services or those of another person under his control as security for a debt. If unable to pay the interest, the debtor must surrender himself or some other person – usually the latter in Arab countries – to the money-lender. Bond servants are most frequently boys aged nine years and over but they include some girls before the age of puberty.

A serf is a tenant bound by custom or agreement to live and work on land belonging to another person and to render some service.

Sham adoption is a way of concealing slavery. In Libya, Egypt, Saudi Arabia and Iran children have been "adopted" not for their protection but for their exploitation.

Three servile forms of marriage are known to be widespread. (*a*) A woman, without the right to refuse, is promised or given in marriage on payment of money or goods to her parents, guardian, family or other people. (*b*) The husband of a woman, his family or clan has the right to transfer her to another person. (*c*) A woman on the death of her husband is liable to be inherited by another person.

II. Earlier History and the Islamic View

Before the year 622, when the prophet Mohammad came to prominence, many Arab merchants had grown rich through slaving, especially in Mecca, which Mohammad was to establish as Islam's holy city. Most of the slaves until this time were Ethiopian but white slaves were also brought to the area by Arab caravans, some from as far away as south-central Europe. Since Arab scholars and theologians tend to separate slavery before the establishment of Islam from slavery after that time it is essential to see what differences Mohammad and the *Koran* effected.

The *Koran* does not, in so many words, either condemn or sanction slavery. It regulates the position of slaves, and with some apparent equity. The only legal cause of slavery is prisonership of war or birth from slave parents. Some scholars (see Snouek Hurgronge, *Mohammadanism*, London, 1956) believe that according to Koranic principle, slavery was an institution destined to disappear. This is debated but certainly Islam made some unequivocal statements. For instance, by freeing a slave a Moslem could gain direct benefits; he could atone for certain crimes including the causing of accidental death and he could absolve himself from perjury. To free a slave at the time of an eclipse was particularly commendable and could atone for breaking the fast of Ramadan.

We can accept then, that the Koran advised against slavery and introduced the new idea that to set slaves free is highly meritorious. This produces the most fundamental difficulty of interpretation: Many Islamic savants say that *you cannot set slaves free unless you first own them* — therefore slavery is sanctioned by God and almost certainly is directly commanded by him. As further evidence and as precedent, they say

that although Mohammad and certain of his close associates freed
their slaves some leaders possessed slaves until death. Yet other Moslem
scholars draw attention to the sections of the Koran and the hadiths –
the accepted traditional truths of Islam which supplement the Koran –
which advocate kindness in the treatment of slaves. This must indicate,
they say, that slavery is sanctioned under certain conditions. Again.
the Koran stipulates that the slave has obligations: He is to give loyal
service, he is the "shepherd of his master's wealth" and he will be asked
for an account of it in the next world. All this, the Islamic argument
runs, indicates the existence and acceptance of the institution of slavery.

This form of logic permeates the Islamic view of slavery. Islamic
specialists on slavery accept that the Prophet told Moslems that, "Your
slaves are your brothers" and that he advised a master to feed and
clothe his slave with the same kind of food and clothing as his own and
not to ask the slave to do anything that was beyond his ability. But
these specialists point out that the Prophet added, "If you do ask your
slave to carry out a task beyond his ability you must help him." This is
taken to mean that a master is fully entitled to drive slaves to the limit
of endurance provided the master gives some assistance, no matter how
slight.

The concept of a slave as "property" is paramount. In many parts of
the Arabian sub-continent slaves have been branded on forehead or
cheek with their master's mark of ownership. In civil and religious law,
a slave could be the object of all legal proceedings usually connected
with property – sale, gift, hire, inheritance, claims for damage. In some
regions where the Makili law is dominant a buyer of a slave had an
automatic guarantee of three days and if he discovered fault in that
time he could return the slave to the seller; the guarantee against
leprosy or madness held good for a full year. Most schools of Islamic
thought allow the master to do as he wishes with property in possession
of his slave.

The law gave slaves some protection. For example, no man could
lawfully have sexual intercourse with a female slave except her master
or her husband. But whatever "rights" the slave may have had under
the spirit of Koranic law, in practice these rights were subject to
approval by his master. For instance, while the adult male slave may
marry of his own accord he needed his master's approval of the woman
he chose. Similarly, Koranic law states that once a master announces
that he plans to free a slave he cannot revoke this emancipation – but
he can insure against any uncertainty by saying that the freeing is to

take place at some future date. Complete circumvention can be achieved by selling the slave before the waiting period expires; the emancipation is then legally nullified.

Much has been made of the notion that under Arab masters many slaves have had a reasonably happy life, and often a more comfortable one than they might have had in their forest or savanna village in Africa. This type of rationalisation has not impressed most Arabists, one of whom, Eldon Rutter, has said:

Let there be no contended slaves. A social system which rears men to be so ignorant and devoid of spirit that they are contented to be bondsmen and which rears others so insensitive that they are contented to own, to buy and to sell their fellowmen like cattle, carries its own condemnation. (Lecture to Anti-Slavery Society, March 15, 1933).

However much the 20th century might condemn slavery, the Arab world has never read condemnation into the *Koran* or into the hadiths. In any case, even in major matters the Koran's injunctions have often been circumvented. Since the *Koran* permits the enslavement of enemies captured in war, many Arab tribes and nations have declared large-scale *jihad* (holy war) against foreigners for no other purpose than to acquire slaves.

While white Christian slaves were often ransomed by Church or family agents, until modern times the negro or Arab slave had only one effective way of becoming free and that was by contractually buying his freedom. Such a method is advocated by the *Koran* (Sura xxiv, 33) although slave owners have never regarded such advocacy as a strict obligation. To achieve such freedom the slave had to be given the opportunity to earn money and his payments were usually spaced out, though some owners accepted a single payment. On gaining his liberty the freedman was supposed to enjoy the same rights under law as freeborn men, but – and this point is crucial – he and his male descendants must remain forever attached to the former owner or his or her family. In practice this meant that while the owner might treat the slave differently he expected from him the same services, and perhaps even more of them. It was never possible for a female slave to buy her freedom since Arab owners believed that the only way a woman could earn money was by prostitution.

III. The Source of Slaves

Principally, the Arab slavers collected their raw material from black Africa, in an area stretching from Mozambique to Somalia and Ethiopia on the east and north, through the interior to the vast Congo basin and in a wide band across the continent south of the Sahara to take in the Sudan and the countries which are now Chad, Mauretania, Mali, Senegal, Guinea, Nigeria, Ghana, Ivory Coast. Secondary collection areas were south-east Europe, Turkey, India, Spain, Italy and the Mediterranean islands. Supply from these areas was intermittent and except for India gradually dried up, apart from occasional white-slave traffic. Yet a third source, until the end of the 18th century, was provided by the Christian crew and passengers taken from merchant ships captured in the Mediterranean and the east Atlantic. Overall, the supply must have seemed inexhaustible, which accounts for the slavers' brutal methods which killed so many people during capture and transport. The attitude was, "There are plenty more in the African forests and savanna." A fourth source was – and still is – among other Moslems. This is supposed to be against Islamic law, but much evidence shows that various tribes of the Arabian peninsula enslaved the people of enemy tribes, notably in the Hadramaut – the region which is now Saudi Arabia and the two Yemens. Also, Moslem Arabs have enslaved Pakistani Moslems, African Moslems and Indonesian Moslems.

IV. Methods of Collection and Transport

Techniques varied according to terrain, vegetation and the strength of the slaving gang. A common method in forest country was for a gang to surround an African village, fire the huts, drive off the cattle and destroy the crops. Firing their guns into the flames the raiders created a panic and easily rounded up the terrified natives. Destruction was so widespread that explorers such as Livingstone and Richard Burton speak of "miles of ruined villages." Livingstone witnessed the massacre at the village of Nyangwe on July 15, 1871, when Arab slavers under Tagamoio opened fire with rifles at point-blank range. Many of the villagers took to the river where the Arabs picked them off, killing about 400 by their own reckoning. "No one will ever know the exact loss on this bright sultry summer morning," Livingstone wrote, "It gave me the impression of being in hell." Such massacres, which were frequent, are inexplicable and can only be seen as bloodlust.

Sometimes the slavers would pretend to be harmless merchants until they had gained the villagers' confidence and would pounce when the people had gathered to inspect the colourful merchandise the slavers carried. Other slavers would promise one tribe immunity in return for help in trapping the people of an enemy tribe. Promotion of inter-tribal warfare became a fruitful source of slaves in the Congo and Sudan.

Only captives of great age were considered worthless; other impediments could be profitable. Deaf and dumb slave girls were much sought after, until well into the 20th century, as servants for Moslem magnates in Europe, Asia and Africa. Part of their value lay in their novelty but more importantly they could neither hear secrets nor relate them. A deaf mute was especially desirable. Dwarfs, favourite playthings for young Moslem princes, were only a little less costly than eunuchs.

Formed into a "caravan" the captives were marched to the coast, a journey of perhaps 2000 kilometres which might last several weeks. While in the forests, where they might attempt to escape, slaves were roped or chained together in gangs with their hands behind their backs. A "difficult" man would have a piece of wood tied into his mouth, or his neck would be secured into a heavy cleft stick – a sheba – and locked by a crossbar. Sometimes a double sheba was used with a man locked into either end. The women were usually roped together by the neck and the children trailed behind. During the 19th century, when the slavers were also dealing in ivory, a woman might have a baby on her back and ivory or some other burden on her head. Such a caravan "presented a moving picture of utter misery ... Our own inconveniences sank into insignificance compared with the suffering of this crowd of half-starved, ill-treated creatures who must have longed for death." (A. J. Swann, Fighting the Slave Hunters in Central Africa, London, 1890.)

When a woman could no longer carry both baby and ivory, the baby was killed. Slaves who became too ill to travel were shot or speared to discourage others from pretending to be ill in order to be left behind. In the long marches across the hot grasslands or desert, chains and ropes were not necessary; only the slavers knew the location of the waterholes and with whips they drove their captives from one to the next.

Livingstone describes many instances of men, women and children being killed or left behind tied to a tree for animals to eat when they could not keep up with the caravan through illness, exhaustion or starvation. Mostly, Livingstone recorded, they were finished off with a blow from a rifle butt or their skull smashed with a rock. The German doctor, Gustav Nachtigal, an eye-witness, believed that for every slave who arrived at a market three or four died on the way. He knew a spring on the road to Tibesti where the ground was carpeted with human bones, the remnants of a slave caravan which had found the spring temporarily dry.

Keltie (*The Partition of Africa*, London, 1920) believes that for every slave the Arabs brought to the coast at least six died on the way or during the slavers' raid. Livingstone puts the figure as high as ten to one. On average, his estimate could be the most accurate since some caravans were wiped out in cholera epidemics or when caught between waterholes in drier country. Casualties were sometimes very high when a tribe resisted slavery. Nachtigal once watched impotently while 170 negro men bled to death after being wounded in a fight with slavers.

Many slaves who survived the marches were destined for the plantations of Zanzibar and Pemba and were shipped from Kilwa or Mombasa. The dhows used for transport were lightly built sailing boats, sometimes partly decked but generally open and weighing 80 tons. When engaged in slaving these vessels had temporary platforms of bamboo, leaving a narrow passage in the centre. The negroes were then stowed in bulk, the first layer along the floor of the vessel, two adults side by side with a boy or girl resting between them or on them, until the tier was complete. Over them the first platform was laid, supported an inch or two clear of their bodies; then a second, third and fourth tier would be laid until they reached the gunwale. Here the slaves remained for at least three days; many died from asphyxia, thirst or cholera. Attempts by the British Royal Navy to control the trade sometimes increased the slaves' hardships. With prices going up throughout the 19th century it paid the dealer to cram more and more negroes into the dhows; if one vessel in four evaded the British warships it was enough to make a profit.

Since the 1950s, aircraft have been used to take slaves to the principal markets of Arabia; instances of this form of transport continue into the 1970s.

V. Main Markets and Methods of Sale

In earlier centuries, Arab dealers had great slave compounds at Almeria in Spain, Darband on the Caspian and Taranto, Italy; as the Arab invasion of Europe was stemmed and reversed these market places disappeared. Until late in the 19th century every big Moslem town had its slave market and some persisted until late in the century and in some cases until modern times. Historically, the most important markets include Cairo, Tripoli (Libya), Marrakesh, Fez, Ghadames, Tunis, Zanzibar, Khartoum, Jedda, Mecca, Medina, Jibouti, Oman, Bokhara.

Records exist of enormous sales. In the year 1077 many thousands of women of a Berber tribe were sold at public sales in Cairo; most Arabs have long regarded Berber women as best for housework, sexual relations and childbearing and prices are high.

A sale of 1000 men, women and children was not uncommon in the late 19th century, especially when Arab dealers were selling by quantity for plantation labour rather than by quality for domestic purposes. Astute dealers perfumed and oiled girls and women to make them more desirable and therefore more expensive; weak men were given drugs to enable them to lift heavy weights. Unsightly scars were painted over. Young women were taught how to pose seductively for potential customers and were beaten if they were not seductive enough.

Some of the more commercially minded slavers offered to fulfil specific orders placed by the merchants or private buyers but generally slaves were offered at particular prices. At times, when slaves were in short supply – perhaps because caravans had been reduced by disease – they were auctioned. At a sale in Jibouti in 1956, this author saw several slaves auctioned, presumably because they were exceptionally powerful men and the dealer realised that competition among buyers would bring a higher price than in a normal transaction.

Captain A. Smee, Royal Navy, describes a Zanzibar sale in 1811.

The slaves were set off to the best advantage by having the skins cleaned and burnished with coconut oil, their faces painted with red and white stripes, which is here esteemed elegance ... and ornamented with a profusion of bracelets ... When any of them strikes a spectator's fancy the line immediately stops and an examination ensues which is unequalled in any cattle market in Europe. The intending purchaser examines the person, the mouth and feet first and every part of the body, not even excepting the breasts etc.

of the girls, many of whom I have seen handled in the most indecent manner ... Women with children newly born hanging at their breasts and others so old they can scarcely walk are dragged out ...

Richard Burton was present at the Zanzibar market in 1856;

Lines of negroes stood out like beasts, the broker calling out a description of his wares. The least hideous of the black faces were surmounted by scarlet nightcaps. All were horribly thin with ribs protruding like the circles of a cask and not a few squatted sick on the ground.

Rudolf Slatin – one of General Charles Gordon's lieutenants – who spent several years in the Sudan as a prisoner of the Mahdi or Islam's "Chosen One," was all too familiar with the market at Omdurman in the 1880s.

Round the walls numbers of women and girls stand or sit. They vary from the decrepit and aged half-clad slaves of the working class to the gaily-decked concubine ... They are carefully examined from head to foot without the least restriction, just as if they were animals. The mouth is opened to see if the teeth are in good condition. The upper part of the body and the back are laid bare and the arms are carefully looked at. They are ordered to take a few steps backward or forward so that their movements and gait may be examined ... When the intending purchaser has completed his scrutiny he then refers to the dealer and asks ... if he has any better wares for sale. He will probably complain that she is not pretty enough, that her body is not sufficiently developed and so on with the object of reducing the price ... Among the various 'secret defects' which oblige the owner to reduce the price are snoring, bad qualities of character, such as thieving ... (*Fire and Sword in the Sudan*, London, 1896).

On any one day at Omdurman market about 60 women and 30 men would be offered.

At the sale in Jibouti, previously referred to, the author saw about 200 negroes from around Lake Chad offered to about 50 Arab buyers. Dealers paraded the slaves on a raised platform and forced them to show their teeth or display their muscles. Young women were made to expose their breasts and boys their buttocks. At least one young woman was crudely examined for evidence of virginity.

Of course, much private trading has taken place and today this is perhaps the most prevalent form of buying and selling because it is hidden from authorities who might wish to take action. A particularly significant case was reported by a French woman doctor, Claudie Fayein, working in the Yemen during the 1950s. It is described here

not because of any uniqueness – such sales are commonplace – but
because it is reliably attested and concerns men of senior rank. A high-
ranking diplomat from Saudi Arabia wished to buy a slave girl from
a Yemeni prince as a gift for his own prince, with whom he was
travelling in Yemen. The prince was a son of King Ibn Saud. The price
had been agreed (£ 700) but before the deal could be concluded the
girl had to be medically examined and Dr. Fayein was the only doctor
available. She had already spent a year in the Yemen and she knew
that for a girl to be worth so much money she had to be white. Dr.
Fayein was collected by one of the prince's aides who took her to the
palace and sent for the slave girl, whose age, the doctor estimated, was
15. She had been told nothing about the transaction and let herself be
examined but then apparently understood the purpose of the inspection and protested. The prince, holding her down by force, wanted to
know if the girl was free from venereal disease. Scared and shamed,
the girl kept struggling; Dr. Fayein was, in other ways, as outraged as
the girl. The slave was quite healthy but Dr. Fayein was able to say
with honesty that the skin of her arms and legs was grainy as the result
of poor vitamin balance in her diet. She wrote this on the certificate
and returned home but soon the Yemeni and Saudi princes and the
diplomat arrived. All deeply disturbed, they wanted to know if the
girl's condition was syphilitic, contagious, curable. How long would a
cure take and would it be permanent. By describing in detail the
horrible symptoms of pellagra, the vitamin deficiency disease from
which the girl suffered, the doctor prevented the sale and the Yemeni
prince later renewed his attachement for her. (Claudie Fayein, *A French
Doctor in the Yemen*, Anti-Slavery Reporter, June 1960.)

    It is not possible to say how many people have been enslaved by
Arab traders over the centuries but the figures which are known or
have been carefully estimated suggest an enormous total. Romolo Gessi,
the Italian explorer – who impresses the historian with his unemotional
style – estimated that between 1860 and 1873, when Gessi himself was
continuously in the Sudan, at least 5,000 Arab slavers were operating.
They had, he says, taken 4,000,000 women and children from the area
to be sold in Egypt and Turkey, a figure which may seem unrealistically
large but simple calculation shows that on average, each slaver would
only have to snare about 60 slaves each year. Royal Navy records
show that between 1867–1869 its naval patrols off East Africa inter-
cepted and freed 2,645 slaves and estimate that another 37,000 were
smuggled through. British consuls in Zanzibar reported that between

20,000 and 40,000 slaves were imported into the Zanzibar market
every year for much of the 19th century. In 1856 about 5,500 Arabs
lived in Zanzibar and some owned as many as 2,000 slaves. The
British High Commissioner in Nigeria in 1901 reported that the Arabs
were taking "tens of thousands of slaves." In 1964, James Wellard, an
experienced Saharan traveller, estimated that on one route alone Arab
slavers had taken out 5,000 slaves a year for so many years that the
Lake Chad region was virtually depopulated by 1900. Wellard, from
modern anthropological investigation, believes that between 1510 and
1865 at least 12 million negroes were taken out of Africa as slaves.

VI. The Purpose of Slave Trading and Slave Owning

The principal motive in slave trading was profit and in this sense the
Arabs were as much colonialists as any of the European "imperialists"
if colonialism means – as it generally does – the forceful conquest and
exploitation of one nation by another and the keeping of the native
people of that nation in a socially, culturally, economically and racially
inferior state. The significant difference between Arab colonialism and
that of say, Britain, France and Holland, was that the Western nations
had something to give their conquered peoples in the form of education, enlightenment and employment. The Arab colonialists gave
nothing and, when they departed, they left nothing of any cultural,
educational or constructional value. The classic case is that of Zanzibar,
where Arab slavers and many other Arabs who had profited from
slavery lived for three centuries. They never became assimilated with
the local population, which they regarded as low and inferior. Their
racialism had been so intense that when Zanzibar secured independence in 1962 the negro population massacred the entire Arab aristocracy and the Oman dynasty, which had dominated the African east
coast for so long, was destroyed. The only Arab legacy remaining in
Zanzibar is a slave mentality and social structure among the descendants of slaves.

Slave owning has different motives from slave trading, although the
profit aspect is also noticeable. King Ibn Saud, of Saudi Arabia, told a
Western interviewer in 1945 that he kept slaves as a divine right, a
right he shared with any Moslem Arab able to afford to buy slaves,
since the Arabs are the chosen people of God and all others are sub-
servient to them. While other Arab slave owners might agree with this

rationalisation, they have kept slaves for more mundane purposes. Being too proud to stoop to menial labour, the Arab's principal requirement has been for service for commercial, domestic and labour needs. Many slaves so employed have been worked extremely hard in gardens, plantations or workshops but countless others were engaged in frivolous tasks for their entire lifetime; they did nothing but sit by a door and open it as the master approached; they waved fans, peeled fruit, held horses or weapons. Women and girls have been mainly bought for sexual use as personal concubines or professional prostitution. When age ended their attractiveness – and a negro slave woman was generally regarded as old by 30 – they became domestic workers. Arab women often possessed their own female slaves and some observers, such as Rudolf Slatin, believed that they were more cruel than male owners, being more likely to stab or strike their slaves.

Some wealthy Arabs have collected slaves as another man might collect varieties of stamps. Al-Haj Bashir, ruler of Bornu, Sudan, in the mid-19th century and a friend of the German explorer Heinrich Barth, had a harem of perhaps 400 which Barth thought he regarded as a kind of ethnological museum. Bashir made great efforts to acquire a perfect specimen of each tribe; he even had a Circassian woman, a rarity in that region.

Child slaves have been coveted because of their long slave-life expectancy; a healthy child of five years was regarded as a good investment, since it could easily be trained to the standards expected by the master. Sedasi from Bornu – boys who measured six spans from the ankle to the tip of the ears – were considered particularly valuable. Sedasi (the word comes from the Arabic) were usually aged from 12 to 15 years and are mentioned in much popular poetry and song. Bornu also provided a brisk trade in boys and girls of the five-span group (10 to 13 years). Seven-span boys (15–20 years) while they brought good prices, were difficult to train and were more likely to run away. Many boys were used for homosexual purposes and at market were always carefully examined for any symptom of disease. Certain Arabs could achieve sexual satisfaction only with young girls, who have always been highly priced. Many a principal concubine in a harem has been no older than 13 years.

VII. SLAVES AS SOLDIERS

The military aspect of slavery is a phenomenon peculiar to Middle-Eastern Islam. From the first Arab conquests, military guards and vast negro and white militia were made up of slaves. The armed slave replaced the Arab, Berber and Iranian soldier and the military strength of the Ottoman empire depended on its slave battalions of Janissaries. These units were established in 1370 and recruited from white children stolen from Christian families in Eastern Europe, the Balkans and the Slav countries and sold in the slave markets of the Islamic world. Having been converted to Islam, often forcibly, they were kept in special barracks and moulded into fanatical Moslems and highly skilled and disciplined soldiers to serve their entire lifetime in the army. For 500 years they played a leading role in Ottoman and Islamic history until massacred by the Sultan Mahmud in 1826. Other Islamic rulers used the Mamelukes, Turkish slave-soldiers, from the 12th century onwards. Systematically indoctrinated and trained, almost to the point of automation, the Mamelukes were the striking force of many Arab armies until 1811 when Mohammad Ali, then governing Egypt for the Ottomans, believed they were a threat to his rule and had them massacred. Later Mohammad sent slavers to capture big, strong Sudanese blacks and created his own slave army which was kept in huge barracks in Upper Egypt. Most Arab rulers have had negro bodyguards or larger armed forces under Arab or Turkish officers or trusted eunuch slaves.

VIII. INFAMOUS SLAVERS

Some slavers' names have survived because of particular ruthlessness or power. They include:

The Princes of Muscat. Although they came from Muscat and Oman, these princes operated from Zanzibar. Sa'id, active in the earlier part of the 19th century, turned the island into a great slave entrepôt. His son, Bargash, made enormous profits from slave "royalties" −£ 30,000 a year by British estimates in 1875. (Modern equivalent approximately £ 500,000).

Hamed bin Mohammad, better known as Tippu Tip. One of the last "great" slavers of the 19th century, Tippu Tip ruled vast areas and his name was known and feared in East and Central Africa. Explorers such as Livingstone, Cameron, Stanley and Wismann made extensive use of his power; Leopold, King of the Belgians, appointed him Governor of the Congo Free State in 1887. In his 30 years of trading, Tippu Tip handled about 500,000 slaves.

Agad the Egyptian. Before direct British intervention, the Sudan was controlled by Egypt, whose Khedive, Ismail, was one of the largest slave owners. In the 1860s, the chief of the 15,000 Arab slavers then operating was Agad, who had a government contract granting him slave-trading rights over an area of 90,000 square miles; he commanded a small private army.

Rahman Zobeir. Head of a family slaving business, Zobeir was the supreme slaver of the Sudan in the last quarter of the 19th century and carved for himself territory far larger than France. He had a strong private army and was so wealthy and influential that the British Government at one time considered giving him Sudan if he could save the life of General Gordon, then besieged in Khartoum.

Ibrahim Wad Mahmoud. Active for 25 years until 1904, Mahmoud practically depopulated some regions of the Sudan. The Borun tribes were particularly hard hit and an official British report from the Blue Nile Province stated, "It is pitiable the devastation wrought by Mahmoud ... There are no children left, the proportion of adults is about seven men to one woman, and the villages are devoid of sheep, goats, poultry and cattle." The British caught and hanged Mahmoud the following year.

Ibn Gruraib. A leading slaver of modern times, Gruraib operated in Arabia and the Persian Gulf, frequently importing slaves from India. Gruraib's technique when raiding in Africa and the Yemen was to promote inter-tribal rivalry. Having selected a village, he would arrange a fair, complete with musicians, jugglers and dancers, and strike a deal with a neighbouring tribe to make a raid during the performance. Gruraib would pay the attacking chief for his work and the slaves would be handed over to him. Other Arabian slavers, such as Al Mirri, Jabou Ibn Hadfa and Ibn Ard Rabbo, used the same technique.

IX. Eunuchs

Castrated male slaves have for centuries been prominent in the palaces of all nobles and in the home of any ordinary Moslem able to afford them. The price has always been high since the operation, which was always forcible, caused many deaths. It was carried out by the slaver at the point of capture, by the dealer before a sale or by the buyer afterwards, though either dealer or buyer might employ a professional castrater, who had no implements other than a knife and tongs. The victim would be knocked out or held down, though chloroform has been used in this century. White slaves were usually treated with more care than black ones and were left with some penis, which apparently has enabled them to perform coitus with concubines. The blacks were left "level with the abdomen," in slavers' parlance. They were considered to have ungovernable sexual appetite, hence the complete castration. Increasingly during the twentieth century, slave traders paid skilled surgeons to perform the operation, thus reducing the risk of losing valuable property.

Prevented by castration from succumbing to sexual temptation, the eunuch's main duty was to guard the harem. Moslem rulers have also found eunuchs attractive as senior politicians and government officers since they could not found a rival dynasty. Eunuchs are also employed for religious purposes in mosques. Sometimes women illegally enter the mosques in Mecca and must be chased away and as a Moslem is not supposed to touch any women other than his wives, his slave women or females in his family, eunuchs are entrusted with this important task. The negro eunuchs of the Grand Mosque in Mecca, called *aghas*, wear enormous green turbans to signify their status.

Some travellers insist that eunuchs were being "produced" in the 1970s. No clear evidence supports this allegation but the position of the eunuch is inextricably woven with that of women and as long as Arab males have a harem to guard, eunuchs will be needed.

Some women slaves bought as concubines have also been subjected to "de-sexing," the purpose being to safeguard their chastity by removing the means of sexual satisfaction. Accordingly, clitoridectomy – removal of the clitoris – was practised. This horrible mutilation was commonplace until the 1920s and is still occasionally reported, more frequently as a means of ensuring a wife's fidelity. The result is that the wife becomes frigid and the husband then turns to slave women for enjoyment.

Sir George Macmunn, who spent many years in Arabia, explained why Arab men desired a negro woman.

She is very popular as a concubine in the summer for her black skin keeps

surprisingly cool while that of an Arab does not. When during the Great
War the British forces came to the Tigris, the word went around among the
Arabs that now the British had come all the slaves would be freed. The
Arabs petitioned the British not to free the women because of the advantages
of coal-black skin. (*Slavery Through the Ages*, London, 1938).

X. Decline of Slavery

Any recession in slavery is difficult to measure, since declines in the
traffic have been intermittent and local and influenced by war. For
instance, the trade was in suspension during the years 1939–45 because
the world war swept across the traditional lines of supply. However,
it can be affirmed that Tunisia was the first Moslem state to bring in
an edict of emancipation for slaves. This occurred in 1846 but another
44 years elapsed before French pressure forced implementation of the
edict. In general, British political and military initiatives gradually
reduced the power of the Arab slavers in East and Central Africa,
eastern Sudan, Egypt and the greater part of Arabia. Similarly, the
French reduced slavery in Morocco, Algeria, Tunisia, Syria, the western Sudan and parts of the Sahara. Perhaps the most potent force was
the Royal Navy which, until 1939, patrolled the Red Sea, the Persian
Gulf and East African waters and deterred many slavers from operating. It is important to realise that in no part of the Arab world did
the decline come about "naturally"; it was everywhere enforced by
political and military pressure supported by world opinion, though the
latter should not be overstressed since it rarely penetrated into the
slave-owners' world and when it did was largely ignored.

Slavery was legally abolished in Iraq in 1924, Persia (modern Iran,
not an Arab state but buying from Arab dealers) in 1929, Transjordan
the same year, Bahrein 1937, Tanganyika 1922 – coupled with penal
sanctions in 1930, Morocco 1930, Ethiopia, through Italian armed
intervention, 1936. But, as the next section shows, slavery is deep-
rooted and persistent.

XI. Modern Slaving

Sudan. After 1899, when the British and the Egyptians set up a condominium in eastern Sudan, the British could more actively restrict
slavery but the area was too vast – 3,000,000 sq. km. – to police effec-

tively and some slavery persisted into the 1950s. The British administered the country in two sections – the Arab north with about 9,000,000
people and the Negro south with 3,000,000. After independence in
1956, the Moslem Arabs seized control of the entire Sudan and the
"southern slaves" – as the Arabs called the Africans – came under
racial and economic discrimination. Black schools, churches, missions,
orphanages and hospitals were closed and Africans, including the
highly educated 250,000 Christian negroes, were excluded from all
positions of authority. During the 1960s, hundreds of Sudanese blacks
were transferred to the north to become slaves there or to be sent to
Saudi Arabia, Yemen or the Gulf oil states. Even Joseph Odubo, a
member of parliament before Sudan's independence, was arrested as
an agitator and put up for sale at 1,600 dollars, but escaped. In the
mid-1970s, most black Sudanese, if not outright slaves, were being
kept in a state of servile repression and debt bondage was increasing.

Egypt. Slavery is illegal but in 1960 an Egyptian wife sued her husband in the Egyptian courts and obtained compensation from him for
selling her to a Saudi prince. The husband admitted that he had
received £ 3,300 for this wife but in mitigation said that for the other
65 wives he had sold he had received only half this price.

Lebanon. Slavery declined here to the point of extinction under
French administration but Beirut remains a principal centre for the
white slave traffic and girls kidnapped from Europe are passed through
this city. In 1970, Mr. Sekyiamah, a member of the U.N. Sub-Commission on Prevention of Discrimination and Protection of Minorities,
reported to the Anti-Slavery Society that 50 schoolgirls from his own
country, Ghana, had been sold into unpaid service in Lebanon.

Zanzibar. In 1975, the Anti-Slavery Society had been campaigning
for five years for the release of Nasreen Hussein, a girl kidnapped and
subjected to forced marriage in Zanzibar in 1970.

Muscat and Oman. Slavery survived openly here until 1970. In 1973,
Lord Wilberforce, descendant of the anti-slavery pioneer, cited exam-
ples of modern slavery in Muscat and Oman and other parts of the
Persian Gulf. Debt bondage is common in parts of the Gulf.

Syria. When World War II ended in 1945, slavery had a resurgence
in Syria. The organisers were a well-known group of merchants from
Latakia who exploited the official prohibition of prostitution. In one
year, these men bought 3,000 girls and sent them to secret brothels in
the country. To the present day, in the Alaouite Mountains, poor
parents hire out their children for five or ten years. An unknown

number of Syrian girls have been enticed to Saudi Arabia by Arabs posing as princes. It appears that these girls often undergo a form of marriage with the "princes" but in Saudi Arabia find themselves no better than concubines. The Syrian Government protested to Saudi Arabia in 1955, 1960 and 1966.

Iraq. Slave trading and ownership is illegal in Iraq but some dealers are at work. In 1960, Mohammad Hussein was caught slave smuggling and sentenced to 15 years in prison; at the moment of arrest he had 50 young girls he was taking to sell in Riyadh, Saudi Arabia. In 1975, rebellious Kurds, captured in fighting with the Iraqi troops were being enslaved to prevent further uprisings.

Among the Tuareg. The Tuareg tribes of the Saharan region hold about 470,000 slaves; a UNESCO survey states that one person in seven is a slave in the Adrer region, between one in six and one in three in the Ahaggar and one in three in Air. Among the Tuareg of Gourma, south of the Niger bend, three out of four are slaves.

Moors of Mauretania. Some Moorish groups have a system of slavery little different from that of their ancestors in the 17th century. The term *abd* has been juridically abandoned and *hartani* (freedman) substituted but this does not hide the continued existence of slavery. When Mauretania became independent (1960) UNESCO reported that about a quarter of the Kounta people were slaves.

Saudi Arabia. The importance of Saudi Arabia in the history of Islamic slavery is that the country was the most resistant to reform and slavery has been persistent and widespread. The International Bureau of Slavery set up by the League of Nations in 1926 could effect no reforms in Saudi Arabia, though in 1927 King Ibn Saud told the British legation at Jedda that all slaves who claimed their freedom could have it. But some slaves who did so disappeared or were beaten and between 1930 and 1935 only 150 slaves were freed. As a gesture to the British, the king abolished the customs duty which had been imposed on all slave imports since the establishment of the kingdom in 1926. One researcher in the field has alleged that in the 1920s and 1930s in Arabia and Yemen, corps of slave men and women were maintained and bred like cattle to produce children to swell the slave trade. (G. C. de Jong, *Moslem World*, April 1934.)

On October 2, 1936, the Saudis introduced a law to end slavery but it was ineffective. By the 1960s, slavery, financed by oil revenues, was flourishing as never before. In the British House of Lords on July 14, 1960, Lord Maugham reported: "Vice is unrestrained and the means to gratify unusual lusts can easily be procured by money. There are sheikhs who can achieve sexual satisfaction only with young children. Slaves are often horribly abused for pleasure or mutilated as a punishment and castration of young boys is practised." Prince Faisal was appointed Prime Minister of Saudi Arabia on November 2, 1962, and four days later issued a programme of slave reform but his decrees did not end slavery and slave identity cards were still being issued in 1963, when the slave population was estimated at 300,000. In its Economic and Social Document on Slavery, July 16, 1965, the United Nations reported that King Ibn Saud himself still owned hundreds of slaves. Some royal Baluchee slaves who ran away were captured and executed, three of them in the main square of the capital, Riyadh. After King Ibn Saud's death, slavery lost some of its strength but in the mid-1970s it seemed likely that Saudi Arabia was still the principal importer of slaves, despite the legal end of slavery.

Because of their great wealth, Saudi Arabians could afford to employ large numbers of workers in the normal way, but this has no attraction. Hiring people is neither as exciting nor as satisfying as buying the human commodity. Habits die hard and this habit is almost as old as Arab history.

Yemen and South Yemen. Probably the most backward of all Arab countries, the Yemens discourage travellers, so evidence of slavery is difficult to produce. The one fact is that slavery has never been abolished by law. Much inter-tribal fighting takes place and as a result it is believed that perhaps as many as 100,000 Yemenis are slaves in their own countries. Sales of African slaves have been reported in Aden, the capital of Southern Yemen, since the British gave Aden its independence in 1967, and at Sanaa in Yemen. Yemen has a predominantly agricultural economy and slaves are said to be used in the fields and in the copper, coal and salt mines.

XII. Mecca's Role in the Slave Trade

Mecca, the holiest of Islam's cities and the focus of the great Moslem pilgrimage, was also Arabia's main slave marketing centre from the 18th to the 20th centuries. The more astute slavers posed as escorts for negro Moslems making the pilgrimage, only to turn them into slaves on arrival in Saudi Arabia. (Corroborated by Mohammad Haikal, editor of the Cairo newspaper *Al Ahram*, January 27, 1961.) Other

Moslems, not slavers by profession, take black slaves with them on pilgrimage and use them as a form of human traveller's cheques to defray expenses along the way; children are used more than adults in this way. Some slave traders visit African Moslem countries where they pose as missionaries entrusted with the delicate mission of guiding black Moslems to the holy places of Islam and of instructing them in the *Koran*. Men, women and children have fallen into this trap and have happily allowed themselves to be taken across the Red Sea to the port of Lith, where they are declared illegal immigrants and imprisoned. Sale at markets in Jedda or Mecca is the inevitable end of the journey. The Governments of Nigeria and Ghana have complained to Saudi Arabia.

XIII. Authoritative Comment since 1900

"It is the most serious charge against Islam in Africa that it has encouraged and given religious sanction to slavery." Lord Lugard, *Africa*, London, 1933.

"Pilgrimages to the holy places of Arabia are said to provide the principal opportunity for the slave traffic." From the *Report on Slavery* by the League of Nations Committee of Experts, 1932.

"Slavery is a traditional part of the social structure. It is congenial. The peninsular Arabs are too proud to work as servants ... so that the well-to-do have either to do the work themselves or employ slaves. In the unabatement of slavery, Arabia has been false to her prophet." Bertram Thomas, one-time adviser to the Sultan of Oman, *The Arabs*, London, 1938.

"Among the bedouin of the Arab peninsula and its fringes black slaves may intermarry and acquire property but however intimate they may be with the master and his family ... they are never regarded as equals, even after enfranchisement; they are *abd* and *abd* they remain; and marriage with the sons and daughters of them is considered a come-down, by the lowliest of whites." R. Brunschvig, ed. *Encyclopaedia of Islam*, 1954.

"Throughout the whole of Islamic history ... slavery has been an institution tenacious of life and deeply rooted in custom." *Ibid.*

"The fact, brought out in the Koran, that slavery is in principle lawful, satisfies religious scruples. Total abolition might even seem a reprehensible innovation, contrary to the letter of the Holy Book, and the exemplary practice of the first Moslems." *Ibid.*

"The survival of slavery and the existence of concubinage in parts of the Arabian peninsula is to a large extent due to the specific need to co-habit with non-circumcised, sexually keen women who echo the man's desire and derive pleasure from love-making." Wendell Phillips, *Unknown Oman*, London, 1955.

"There is no need to feel that slavery is a 'dying institution'. The millions in oil royalties have given the industry a new lease of life in Saudi Arabia." Roderic Owen, *The Golden Bubble*, London, 1957.

"Castration is the most revolting consequence of slavery." C. W. W. Greenidge, one-time director of the Anti-Slavery Society, in *Slavery*, London, 1958.

"Nothing more monstrous or cruel than this traffic had happened in history." Alan Moorehead, *The White Nile*, London, 1960.

"Slaving was in the Arab blood. No Arab regarded the trade as any more evil or abnormal than, presumably, a horse-dealer regards as evil or abnormal the buying and selling of horses." *Ibid.*

"Under the efficient direction of the Arabs slavery involved the whole civilised world ... The ancient world was based on slavery but not on African slaves. The exploitation of black labour was the contribution of the Arabs to mankind, for it was they who organised the vast traffic in human merchandise out of Africa to the Atlantic and Mediterranean ports." James Wellard, *The Great Sahara*, London 1964.

"All this ruthless savagery [slavery] was perpetuated in the name of religion." E. W. Bovill, *The Golden Trade of the Moors*, Oxford, 1968.

XIV. ENDURING EFFECTS OF ARAB SLAVERY

A. On Africans

Since the "end" of slavery, relationships between the Arab and black African states have not been easy, as shown by much hostile political and press comment from the African states, many of them newly established. During the 1974 conference of the Organisation of African Unity held in Mogadishu, several African delegates, led by Ghana and Ethiopia, criticised the Arab oil producers' refusal to treat OAU countries as a special case by allowing them a price reduction in oil. Kenya, Zaire, Tanzania, Ethiopia, Ghana and Madagascar described the difficulties and economic hardships resulting from Arab oil policy, which they bitterly attacked. Strong feelings, brought to the surface by the oil issue, indicate a deep-rooted historical resentment which many Africans feel towards the Arabs. African newspapers are quick to comment on any signs of a resurgence of slavery.

It is revolting and bewildering to note that Ghana is being used for a revival of the slave trade ... We recall vividly the uncertain days when Lebanese and Syrian merchants in Ghana constituted themselves into a volunteer force and with barons cudgelled down freedom fighters in the streets of Accra in open daylight. It appears that we have taken our tolerance too far and they have taken our leniency for weakness and are now adding insult to injury by trading our young daughters like apples or any other commodity ... Our children must be defended against slavery. (Ghana *Weekly Spectator*, February 17, 1973).

Again:

After the departure of white colonial rule, the onslaught of the Arabized version of Islam in Black Africa is making inroads with predictable penetration. A new form of colonialism, this time thinly disguised and even more devastating in its impact ... is enveloping black Africans. The winds blowing across the Sahara [from Arab nations] do not bring blessing and rain to black Africa. These are the winds of destruction and herald altogether new ominous signs of anxiety and worry. (*Kenya Mirror*, May 1974).

In African minds, imperialism/colonialism is almost synonymous with slavery and the fear that the first will bring the second finds frequent expression. "Military Pan-Arabism is essentially racist and is therefore bound to favour slavery. It should not appeal to black Africans." (*Daily Times*, Nigeria, September 9, 1969.) Other writers are even more forthright.

Refusal by Arab countries to sell oil to African states at a reduced price is a tacit example that Arabs, our former slave masters, are not prepared to abandon the rider-and-horse relationship. We have not forgotten that they used to drive us like herds of cattle and sell us as slaves ... (Zambia *Daily Mail*, June 21, 1974).

One of the most pertinent comments has come from Professor L. H. Ofosu-Appiah, Director of the Encyclopaedia Africana Secretariat. "When Arab leaders cannot understand the hostility of some Africans to their regions, it may be worth reminding them that their part in enslaving Africans is a festering sore which cannot be easily cured."

B. On Arabs

A race of people accustomed to the use of slaves as part of a way of life cannot adjust in a few decades to the absence of slaves. The mere thought of life without slaves is intolerable to the wealthy and more traditional Arab. Status, comfort and custom are involved, as well as a profound psychological need to dominate. That this domination is sometimes benign, in the case of favourite slaves, makes it no less powerful. The religious aspects of slavery must not be overlooked. Islam is a religion of pride and it teaches Moslems that they are superior to "unbelievers" – people of other religions. It is only right, Islam teaches, that Arabs should be the masters and overlords. This is why, in their colonial areas, the Arab masters did everything in their power to maintain their exclusive power and social and religious distinction. Such an attitude, which persists, inevitably produces a need for slaves in some form. Some prominent Arabs concede that their economic dominance of much of the world, through their oil power, is a form of modern slavery. Underlying all this is the resentment among Arabs that they were *forced* to abandon slave trading and to relinquish many of their slaves. Compounding this insult is the fact that the force came from *dar al-harb* (foreign territory) and from Christians. "The West forced Islam to give up its slaves, do you suppose that Islam will forget and forgive that?" (Algerian diplomat to the author, February 1975.)

XV. SLAVERY, THE UNITED NATIONS AND THE ANTI-SLAVERY SOCIETY

Paradoxically, it is easier to conceal slavery in the late 20th century than it was fifty years earlier, for slaves can be flown from source to market or buyer with only a slim possibility of their being seen by people who might talk. Also, the once great powers, such as Britain and France, no longer accept any responsibility for suppressing slavery. The newly great nations, the United States and the Soviet Union, have no international anti-slavery tradition. The Soviet Union, in any case, has much forced-labour slavery within its own borders. Since Britain and France left the arena, no other nations have stepped in. No machinery exists to implement the United Nations' abolitionist policy nor is there any office, or even a single individual, at the United Nations, engaged full-time on recording instances of slavery. Further, no government has instructed its U.N. delegates to call for an observer or an enforcement agency on anti-slavery. Conditions could hardly be better for slave-dealers, of Arab or other race.

It has been left to the Anti-Slavery Society, 60 Weymouth Street, London, to publicise cases of slavery and to ensure world awareness of a continuing problem. The Society's president, Sir Douglas Glover, in his annual report of 1966, attempted to find in history the reasons for continuation of the trade after 1945. He believed that this period resembled that of 1834–1890 – that is, before the date of the Brussels Convention on Slavery and the establishment of the International Bureau for Slavery – in that both were periods during which slavery was condemned but without any effective means for its abolition being put into practice. The progress achieved by the League of Nations Committee of Experts, between 1933 and 1939, was swept away by the upheaval of the Second World War. In addition, the resolution by the United Nations in 1956 to outlaw slavery had resulted in a Convention on Slavery which only 62 of the 115 countries of the U.N. signed in 1965. Saudi Arabia was one nation which did not sign.

The period since 1945 had been a "sorry story," Sir Douglas said.

There is no doubt that as a result of the growing richness of the Arabian Peninsula, owing to the discovery of petrol in regions where slavery is an accepted practice, and has been for thousands of years ... slaves have become a status symbol and their price has gone up drastically ... Consequently, there is an ever-increasing fleet from Nigeria, Mauretania, Mali and other parts of the world to the Arab peninsula because people are willing to pay a much higher price than ever.

Sir Douglas was reacting to the frustrations caused among reformers by the report issued by the U.N. Economic and Social Council in May 1965. The "Special Rapporteur," appointed to produce the report, was Dr. Mohammad Awad of Egypt, who submitted a questionnaire to the governments of all U.N. member nations. No fewer than 63 failed to respond to the questionnaire. These countries included the Arab states of Algeria, Ethiopia, Lebanon, Libya, Mauretania, Morocco, Saudi Arabia, Somalia, Syria, Yemen. Dr. Awad confessed to disappointment, but thanked "this great Society" – the Anti-Slavery Society – for services rendered. Some of the questions were direct: "Does slavery or any institution or practice similar to slavery exist in the country?" And: "What measures have been or are being taken to assist persons freed from servile status?"

That so many Arab countries failed to reply to the questionnaire or even to acknowledge it, is not in itself proof of slavery but the silence must be taken at least as evidence of difficulty in answering some of the questions.

Some Arab diplomats and politicians felt that the questionnaire was "too searching," by which they really meant that it left no room for equivocation. For instance, "What measures have been taken to ensure that the ports, airfields and coasts of your country are not used for the conveyance of slaves? Have such measures proved effective? If not, what were the reasons?" And: "What provisions exist under your laws placing responsibility on either the pilot/master or the owners of an aircraft/ship or on both for carrying slaves?" Arab politicians believed that to have any such laws was too frank an admission that slavery existed.

As the Anti-Slavery Society had already shown, Buraimi Oasis in Arabia was the staging point for a brisk traffic in airborne slaves. The fact was first brought to the Society's attention by an officer of the Trucial Scouts, an Arab desert military force led by British officers. Buraimi was for several years a neutral zone, administered under an agreement between Britain and the Saudi government. By arrangement, each side was allowed three flights a month to supply their respective army contingents. These planes were forbidden to carry civilian passengers and could be used for no purpose other than military supply. The Trucial Scouts officer noticed that when the Saudi aircraft was about to leave, usually at dusk, lorries loaded with people arrived in a rush and they would be hurried aboard the plane, which took off at once. A Saudi official told the Englishman that these were Buraimi residents going to visit relations in Saudi Arabia, but investigation showed that they were slaves who had arrived by truck from Dubai and were then flown to buyers in Saudi Arabia. Each plane carried 30 to 40 slaves in a flight, an annual load of up to 2,000 slaves.

In May 1974, the Anti-Slavery Society, after 18 years of continual campaigning, succeeded in inducing the U.N.'s Economic and Social Council to approve the appointment of a working group of five experts "to review developments in the field of slavery and slavery-like practices, the traffic in persons and the exploitation of the prostitution of others." The experts, the Council decided, would meet on three days each year. No doubt, much of the three days will be taken up in discussion of forms of slavery in south-west Asia, including Arabia, and in Africa.

The Anti-Slavery Society, as a recognised United Nations consultative body, seems destined to remain its principal source of information, but its funds are too limited to permit complete and sustained investigation.

REFERENCES

Apart from references under "XIII. Authoritative Comment"

H. Barth, *Travels and Discoveries in North and Central Africa*, London, 1858.
R. F. Burton, *Zanzibar, City, Island and Coast*, London, 1872.
R. Coupland, *The Exploitation of East Africa 1856–1890 – The Slave Trade and the Scramble*, London, 1968.
Pierre Crabitès, *Gordon, the Sudan and Slavery*, London, 1933.
Jonathan Derrick, *Africa's Slaves Today*, London, 1975.
Leda Farrant, *Tippu Tip and the Eeast African Slave Trade*, London, 1975.
Allan and Humphrey Fisher, *Slavery and Muslim Society in Africa*, London, 1970.
David Livingstone, *Last Journals*, London, 1874.
Robin Maugham, *The Slaves of Timbuktu*, London, 1963.
Gustav Nachtigal, *Sahara und Sudan, Ergebnisse sechsjähriger Reisen in Afrika*, Graz, 1967 edition.
C. G. L. Sullivan, *Dhow Chasing in Zanzibar Waters and on the Eastern Coast of Africa*, London, 1873.
Rudolf Slatin, *Fire and Sword in the Sudan*, London, 1896.
J. S. Trimingham, *Islam in the Sudan*, London, 1965.
Peter McLoughlin, *Economic Development and the Heritage of Slavery in the Sudan Republic* – article in the magazine *Africa*, October 1962.
All issues of the *Anti-Slavery Reporter*, journal of the Anti-Slavery Society.

The Problems of National Minorities in the Soviet Union

EDWARD J. ROZEK

EDWARD J. ROZEK is a professor of political science at the University of Colorado where he has taught since 1956. Born in Poland, Dr. Rozek fought during World War II as a tank officer from Normandy to Germany, was wounded several times, and received the *Cross of Valor* three times. A member of Phi Beta Kappa, he was graduated magna cum laude in 1951 from Harvard where he also took his M.A. and Ph.D. His book, *Allied Wartime Diplomacy*, published in 1958, received a National Book Foundation Award. He contributed a section to the book *Soviet Foreign Relations and World Communism*, published in 1965, and to *The Idea of a Modern University*, published in 1974. He is co-author with Professor Walt W. Rostow of *The Dynamics of Soviet Society*, published in 1967. During 1961 and 1962 he was a research associate with the Russian Research Center at Harvard University. Dr. Rozek has been repeatedly cited by students of the University of Colorado for teaching excellence, receiving a "Professor of the Year Award" and a "Distinguished Faculty Member Award." Dr. Rozek is the director of the Institute for the Study of Comparative Politics and Ideologies and president and executive director of the Center for Science, Technology, and Political Thought.

The Problems of National Minorities in the Soviet Union

EDWARD J. ROZEK

> None of the evils which totalitarianism ... claims to remedy is worse than totalitarianism itself.
>
> Albert Camus

In the *Peking Review* of March 5, 1976 the Chinese Communists stated the following:

The new tsars in Moscow have thrown into concentration camps Soviet people of all nationalities in large numbers who dare to oppose or resist their fascist rule, thereby subjecting them to torment mentally and physically.

The Brezhnev clique's oppression of the people of non-Russian nationalities is even more ruthless. Reports show that political prisoners of non-Russian nationalities are imprisoned in remote areas and they are forbidden to use their own national languages when addressing officials, corresponding with others, or meeting their families. Following in the footsteps of the old tsars, the new tsars are pushing ahead with Great Russian chauvinism.

Three women political prisoners from the Ukraine sent a letter to the United Nations in May 1973. In it they disclosed that the Soviet authorities launched a "new wave of repression" in the Ukraine in the previous year. Their letter said: "We have been persecuted and imprisoned simply because we, as Ukrainians, advocate the preservation and development of the Ukrainian national culture and language in Ukraine." The Western press reported that the number of so-called "nationalists" arrested in 1972 by the Soviet authorities was greater than in any previous year.[1]

What are the facts?

The Soviet Union is unique as a multinational power in that the dominant nationality, the Great Russians, comprise only 53.4% of the total population (241,720,000), the rest of the people consisting of Finnish, Turkic, Asiatic and European ethnic groups. Whereas in pre-Soviet Russia, Russian colonists settled among isolated and scattered ethnic groups, the Soviet Russians confront more than a dozen strong ethnic groups, most of them with a considerable degree of national consciousness and a desire for national self-realization. Since the Russians are declining demographically vis-à-vis ethnic minorities it is unlikely that Russian colonists will be able to penetrate, as they have in the past, throughout the republics of the Soviet Union. Rather, they will be increasingly regarded as outsiders by the ethnic groups of the republics other than the Russian Soviet Federal Republic.

Ethnic consciousness is also reinforced by competition between the Russian colonists in the various republics and the native ethnic groups for services (e.g. housing, schooling, etc.) and resources. In the face of reduced ability to continue the emigration to areas outside the Russian Soviet Federal Republic and increasing competition for services and commodities, the Great Russians may experience a greater growth of national sentiment, particularly since the identification of the Soviet regime with the Russian people and Russian history has been intensifying.[2]

In the first phase of Soviet imperialism Lenin imposed Communist control on numerous nationalities which dwelled within the boundaries of the Soviet Union. The Communists of Russian nationality were in a position of control over other nationalities and their predominance remains the same at the present time.

I. Nationalities Predominantly in the USSR in Europe

Russians

Although the Russians with a population of 129,015,000 are the largest national group in the USSR (53.4%), their weight in the population has been declining due to a low rate of natural increase. Their weight in the population of their own republic also declined from 83.3% to 82.8% between 1959 and 1970. Originally migrating because of poor economic opportunities from rural to urban areas within Russia as well as to non-Russian areas, the Russians have, increasingly in the last decade, emigrated to non-Russian republics because of industrial development accompanied by the inability or reluctance of the native population to provide manpower for industry. In addition, bureaucratization throughout the USSR as a result of the introduction of the Soviet system has brought an influx of Russians into all the republics.

Although all the republics and their ethnic populations are theoretically equal, the Russian Soviet Federal Republic comprises three-fourths of the territory, over half the population and almost two-thirds of the Communist party membership of the whole USSR. Russians tend to predominate in the party organizations of non-Russian republics and often hold a disproportionate number of important positions in non-Russian republics in higher education, large-scale agriculture and key industries. This dominance reflects the facts that Russian is the language of business everywhere in government and economic organizations and that a larger percentage of Russians receive higher education than most other national groups.

Except for a few years at the beginning of the Soviet era, Russification and the encouragement of Russian nationalism continues to be official government policy. Political and cultural autonomy of minority nationalities is carefully contained while Russian language and culture is brought into non-Russian areas (e.g. Russian is encouraged as a "second" language; books, magazines and newspapers in Russian outnumber those in other Soviet languages by three or four times). This intense pride in Russian culture is reflected on all levels of the Russian population and Russian nationalism has been expressed in varying degrees of intensity by the Russian intelligentsia. Although not all non-Russians are hostile to the Soviet government's policy of Russification, there has been keen resentment among many non-Russian nationals, which in turn evokes resentment among the Russians. Thus, "Russian ascendancy breeds nationalism among minority nationalities, which intensifies Russian nationalism and drives for dominance."[3]

Ukrainians

The first historic state in Ukraine was Kievan Rus (ca. 800–1000 A.D.) which later disintegrated into provinces dominated by Poland and Lithuania. Most of present Ukraine came under Russian domination during the eighteenth century due to the successive partitions of Poland. After a brief period of independence (1918–1919), Ukraine was incorporated into the Soviet Union in 1919, with further territory added from Poland, Bukovina and Ruthenia as a result of the Second World War.

Ukrainian, like Russian and Belorussian, is an east Slavic language with writing based on the Cyrillic alphabet. It is the second most widespread language in the USSR. 73% of the population of Ukraine (including non-Ukrainians) spoke Ukrainian as a native language in 1959; this percentage decreased by 1970 to 69%. The proportion of native Russian speakers has increased from 6.5% in 1959 to 8.6% in 1970, with 28.6% of the population speaking Russian as a second language.

Population in Ukraine (48,200,000 in 1973) rose by 13% between 1959 and 1970, but the proportion of ethnic Ukrainians decreased from 76.8% to 74.9% while the Russian population increased from 16.9% to 19.4%. This is due to low natural increase on the part of the Ukrainians and to immigration by the Russians.

An important economic area in both pre-Soviet Russia and the Soviet Union, Ukraine, with 3% of the territory and 19% of the population of the USSR, is a major producer of coal and metals such as iron and steel as well as diverse agricultural products.

Unable to establish a stable government during the brief period of independence in 1918–1919, Ukraine was incorporated into the Soviet Union. After the Second World War, Ukrainian guerrillas, who had hoped to regain independence when Germany attacked the Soviet Union, fought against the Soviet regime until finally crushed by the KGB in the late 1940s. Today, Ukrainian nationalism is based on the existence of a modern Ukrainian language, literature, art and music as well as awareness of the long Ukrainian history. After the severe repression of Ukrainian culture under tsarist Russia, Ukraine enjoyed a brief Golden Age during the 1920s. During the Stalinist era, however, Ukrainian culture was severely repressed and many writers and artists were arrested and executed between 1933 and 1937, while others, such as the artist Dovzhenko, were banned from Ukraine. Between 1965 and 1972 many of the Ukrainian literary and academic intelligentsia were arrested and imprisoned because of writing and disseminating nationalist literature. Modern Ukrainian dissent is based on a desire for an independent Ukraine separate from the USSR or, at least, transformation of the USSR in accordance with Marxist-Leninist principles as well as abandonment of Russification (e.g. resettlement, discrimination against the Ukrainians in the education system and relegation of Ukrainian culture to a provincial role).[4]

Belorussians

Although the name Belorussia is of fairly recent origin, the forebears of the Belorussians, east Slavic tribes, settled in the area around the sixth century A.D., assimilating or displacing the local east Baltic tribes. In the thirteenth and fourteenth centuries, Belorussian lands became part of the Grand Duchy of Lithuania and later of Poland. Incorporated into Russia by the partitions of Poland in the eighteenth century, Belorussia became independent briefly in 1918, but in 1920 was divided between the USSR and Poland. Western Belorussia was re-annexed from Poland and incorporated into the republic in 1939.

Belorussian, an east Slavic language, came into use before the thirteenth century and was the official language of diplomacy, business and literature in the Grand Duchy of Lithuania until 1700. In 1970 Belorussian was considered their native language by 90.1% of the Belorussians, a decrease from 93.2% in 1959. 52.2% indicated Russian as their second language. The percentage of those who regard Russian as their native language has risen from 6.8% in 1959 to 9.8% in 1970. Russian is used throughout higher educational institutions as the language of instruction, except for some courses in philology and literature.

In 1970 the population of Belorussia was 9,002,000. The percentage of Belorussians to the rest of the population in the republic has remained constant since 1959 (81%), while the percentage of Russians has risen to 10.4%. Other people living in Belorussia are Poles (4.3%), Ukrainians (2.1%) and Jews (1.6%).

Traditionally a rural and agricultural area, Belorussia specializes in farming and light industries. The republic produces a significant portion of the USSR's small machinery as well as agricultural products such as grain, meat and milk.

Unlike Ukraine, in which there is evidence of a desire for independence, Belorussia "seeks to consolidate and strengthen a national identity within the Soviet Union."[5] Though discrimination against the Belorussian language and culture by the Soviet government does exist, there has not been severe repression of Belorussian culture as there was in tsarist Russia. The main concern of the intelligentsia has been to preserve and cultivate the Belorussian language, literature, art and history.

Estonians

The Finnic forebears of the present Estonians arrived around 5000 years ago in their present location. Under German and later Swedish domination, Estonia was conquered by Russia in 1710. Independence of a fully literate and nationally conscious Estonia was achieved in 1917 after the February Revolution and lasted until 1940 when the country was incorporated into the Soviet Union as a result of the Molotov-Ribbentrop Pact.

Estonian is a Finno-Ugrit language and thus of a different language family from Russian and the languages of the other western Soviet republics. Over 99% of the ethnic Estonians consider Estonian their native language, with 27.6% speaking Russian as their second language. Estonian is predominantly the language of instruction in most schools and institutions of higher education.

Though the population of the republic grew from 1,197,000 to 1,356,000 between 1959 and 1970, the Estonian share of the population dropped from 75% to 68% due to low natural increase and massive immigration, primarily of Russians, whose share increased from 20% to 25%. This immigration is due to the need for manpower for industry which Estonia cannot supply and to attractive "westernized" living conditions.

Despite a lack of natural resources, Estonia, with a highly skilled work force, is heavily industrialized and produces 75% of Soviet oil shale. Agriculture, primarily (80%) animal husbandry, has among the highest yields in the USSR.

The Estonian language, the use of the Latin rather than the Cyrillic script (used by the Slavic and most other republics) and the predominance of the Lutheran rather than the Orthodox religion are basic factors in Estonian nationalism. So is the continuous development of Estonian literature, music and art since the nineteenth century. During the Stalinist era there was forced collectivization and mass deportation involving about 10% of the population. In 1950 native-born Communists were purged for alleged nationalism and replaced by Estonians raised in Russia, who still retain all major government and party posts. In the post-Stalin era many deportees returned. Estonia has been the focus for union-wide quests for civil rights and rapprochement with the West. Although Estonians were arrested in the 1960s for sympathizing with Solzhenitsyn and for protesting against the invasion of Czechoslovakia, Estonian cultural nationalism (e.g. preservation of the Estonian language, literature and art) is in the main accepted by the Soviet regime. There is apparently a movement, which may be spreading as recent attacks in party organs indicate, to establish a separate Communist Estonian state.[6]

Latvians

The Baltic forebears of the present-day Latvians entered Latvia about 2000 years ago and, for the most part, maintained their independence until the thirteenth century when they became dominated successively by the Germans, Poles and Swedes and finally in the eighteenth century by the Russians. Remaining under Russian rule until World War I, Latvia established its independence in 1920 and remained free until 1940 when the country was incorporated into the Soviet Union as a result of the Molotov-Ribbentrop Pact.

Latvian, with Lithuanian, is one of the two surviving languages belonging to the Baltic branch of Indo-European languages and is quite different from Germanic and Slavic. More than 98% of the Latvians in the republic consider Latvian their native tongue; 45.3% speak Russian as a second language, while 1.9% consider Russian their native language.

Although the total population of the republic increased from 2,093,000 to 2,364,000 between 1959 and 1970, the Latvian population decreased from 62% in 1959 to 56.8% in 1970, while the Russian population increased from 26.6% to 29.8% and other Slavic peoples increased from 7.2% to 9%. Moreover, more than 94% of the Latvians in the USSR live in their republic. This demographic distribution indicates the steady erosion of ethnic Latvia, which in 1935 was comprised of over 75% Latvians. The factors which created this situation are a high number of casualties during World War II, the execution, deportation or emigration of innumerable Latvians during the imposition of the Soviet system and, more recently, the extremely low natural increase (2.9 per 1000) in Latvia, the lowest rate of natural population growth in the USSR.

One of the most industrialized areas of the Russian empire, Latvia's industrial plant was either destroyed or moved to Russia in World War I. During independence Latvia's government developed the country as a source of high-quality agricultural products for western markets, but since incorporation in 1940 the Soviet regime has re-developed industry so that, as of 1971, Latvia was the most heavily industrialized republic in the USSR. In addition to being the most productive of the republics, Latvia has one of the highest standards of living in the USSR.

Like Estonia and Lithuania, Latvia differs from the rest of the Soviet Union in being traditionally oriented toward west-central Europe due to influence by Germans, Poles and Swedes, religion (the religion in Latvia is predominantly either Lutheran or Roman Catholic rather than Orthodox), the use of the Latin rather than the Cyrillic alphabet and historic trade ties with the West. Latvia did not accept Sovietization freely. The imposition of the Soviet regime in 1940–1941 led to the execution, deportation or emigration of most of the Latvian political leaders and educated population. Following the expulsion of the Nazis, nationalist guerrillas were destroyed only after much fighting. Collectivization, forcibly accomplished between 1947–1950, led to the deportation of thousands of kulaks to Siberia and severe disruption of the economy. In the 1960s and 1970s arrests of the intelligentsia and other Latvians for expressing nationalist views or distributing anti-Soviet literature has continued. Concern over denationalization and Russification of Latvia was revealed in the most important dissident document to come from Latvia, "Letter of 17 Latvian Communists" (1972),[7] which cited six aspects of Soviet policy in the republic: 1) Russian control of second secretary and second cadres secretary posts, 2) importation of labour, 3) location of major military bases and all-union health resorts, 4) Russian domination of many government departments, 5) use of Russian for two-thirds of all radio and television broadcasts, 6) insistence on conducting meetings in Russian even if only one Russian is in the group. Resistance to this policy has led to purges, one example of which was the Berklavs affair in 1959. When a majority of the Latvian Politburo members supported Berklavs in opposing Russification, the Politburo and numerous government and party officials were removed.

Lithuanians

For a brief period in the fourteenth and fifteenth centuries Lithuania was a great Eastern European power, but from the mid-fifteenth to the eighteenth centuries, the country was dominated by Poland. Occupied by Russia in 1796, Lithuania achieved independence following World War I. During independence the government brought about land reforms and instituted public education. As a result of the Molotov-Ribbentrop Pact, Lithuania was incorporated into the Soviet Union in 1940.

One of the oldest living Indo-European languages, Lithuanian, with Latvian, is one of two surviving Baltic languages. In 1970 over 99% of the Lithuanians in the republic considered Lithuanian their native language; only 0.2% considered Russian their native language although 34.8% speak Russian as a second language.

In 1970 with a population of 3,128,236, 80.1% of the population in the republic was Lithuanian, 8.6% Russian, 7.7% Polish and 1.1% Belorussian. Unlike most of the European Soviet republics, the Lithuanian population increased between 1959 and 1970 and 94.1% of the Lithuanians in the USSR live in their republic.

Unlike Estonia and Latvia, Lithuania remained undeveloped in tsarist Russia. During independence the government pursued a consciously agrarian policy though industrialization in textiles, luxury goods, timber, clay and stone products proceeded slowly. After World War II and the imposition of the Soviet system Lithuania made remarkable economic growth and surpassed much of the Soviet Union in industrialization in light industry.

Lithuania, like Estonia and Latvia, is a western-oriented state with a language, alphabet and religion which differ from its Slavic neigh-bours. These factors, in addition to a long history and a strong literary and artistic tradition, are sources of national pride to the Lithuanians. In the aftermath of World War II Lithuanian guerrillas fought against the imposition of the Soviet regime for several years until destroyed by the KGB. This event and the massive deportation or execution of Lithuanian political leaders and intelligentsia in 1940 is still part of the personal experience of most Lithuanians. Although the present-day Lithuanian leaders have done much to protect Lithuanian culture from Russification, there seems to be a well-organized dissident under-ground and there has been considerable protest against the Soviet system, a large part of which centers around the Roman Catholic Church (Catholicism is the dominant religion in Lithuania). This protest has ranged from refusal to speak Russian to self-immolation. This last means of protest touched off the Kaunas Riots in May 1972. Another form of protest are the innumerable petitions against religious persecution (e.g. arrest and imprisonment of priests for such offences as "'systematically' teaching the catechism to children"[8] which ap-peared between 1968 and 1973.

Georgians

The Georgians, who settled in the Caucasus between the twelfth and the seventh centuries B.C., have had a long and turbulent history of periods of independence and imperial greatness interspersed with periods of domination by Romans, Mongols and Turks, finally coming under the rule of Russia in the nineteenth century. During periods of independence, Georgia, on the caravan route linking Europe with India, attained high economic and cultural levels. In the nineteenth century with the rise of the intelligentsia, nationalist political groups were formed and, unlike most nationalist groups were very closely identified with Marxism.[9] Georgia asserted its loyalty to the Russian Provincial Government after the Bolshevik coup in 1917 and declared independence only after the Treaty of Brest-Litovsk ceded the Trans-caucasus territories to the Axis. Although Soviet Russia recognized

Georgian independence in 1920, the country was invaded and conquered by the Soviets in 1921, incorporated into the Transcaucasian Soviet Republic in 1922 and was granted union status in 1936.

Georgian, an Ibero-Caucasian language distinct from Indo-European, Turkic and Semitic languages, is spoken as a native language by 99.4% of the Georgians living in the republic, with only 20.1% considering Russian their native language. The Georgians have their own script, said to date back to Alexander the Great, and it has not been altered or replaced by the Soviet regime.

The population of Georgia in 1970 was 4,686,000, a 15.9% increase over 1959. Of that number, 66.8% were Georgian, 9.7% Armenian and 8.5% Russian. Among the most densely populated of the Soviet republics, Georgia has 176 persons per square mile.

Though coal and oil deposits were developed during the tsarist period, Georgia remained a predominantly agrarian region until the Soviet era. Today industrial production (Georgia is third in the Soviet Union in metallurgical production) comprises 59% of the "total social product." The economy is also dependent upon agricultural production (fruits, tea) and industrial processing of food.

With a 3000-year history, a strong literary and artistic tradition and a Christian Church that binds them to western Europe and to Russia, the Georgians have a strong sense of ethnic identity. The most famous Georgian, Stalin, who became a Great Russian chauvinist and imposed extremely harsh suffering on Georgia during the purges of 1937–1938, is still a Georgian hero and the 1956 riots in Tbilisi were a response to the initiation of de-Stalinization. Stalin (as well as Beria and other Georgians prominent in the Communist party) is blamed by the Soviet regime for strengthening nationalistic feelings. On the other side of the coin, many Georgians (who are considered to be shrewd and tricky businessmen) engage in illicit commercial dealings to such an extent as to rouse critical comment in the Soviet press. Since the accession of E. A. Shevardradze as first secretary of the Georgian Communist Party in 1972, many have been arrested for such illegal activity. Georgians have also been censured for nationalist tendencies expressed by the intelligentsia in books and articles, such as a desire that native Georgians fill important posts. It is not known to what extent Georgians are eager for independence; opinion appears to be divided at the present time.[10]

Jews

The Jews settled in Eastern Europe in the era before Christ, but enjoyed their greatest freedom and expression under the Kingdom of the Khazars (eight to eleventh centuries A.D.). In succeeding centuries, the Jews lived not only around the Black Sea and in Ukraine, but also in Poland and Lithuania, coming under Russian rule by the three partitions of Poland in the eighteenth century. Always subject to discrimination under the strongly anti-Jewish tradition of the tsars, the Jews of the Pale, established in 1791 by Catherine the Great, suffered from a seesaw between times of greater and lesser restrictions imposed by the tsars in the nineteenth century. Massive pogroms in 1881, 1884 and 1903 resulted in the emigration of many Jews to Palestine, western Europe and the United States. Many of those who remained in Russia joined the revolutionary Bolsheviks and reached high positions in the early Soviet government (e.g. Trotsky). After the Bolshevik revolution Jewish organizations were reorganized under the Soviet regime, but were destroyed in the 1930s. In 1934 Birobadzhan in the Far East was created as a Jewish Autonomous Province, but Jewish colonization has never been heavy due to the backwardness of the area and greater opportunities in the western republics. During World War II between 1,000,000 and 2,000,000 Jews were massacred by the Nazi invaders and by anti-Semites in Nazi-occupied areas. After the war purges of Jews by Stalin continued. To this day official policy, excluding Jews from diplomacy, foreign trade, party and security apparatus and responsible state positions, has not changed.

Yiddish, derived from medieval German, is considered their native language by only 17.7% of all the Jews in the Soviet Union. 78.2% consider Russian their native language, while another 16.3% speak Russian as a second language. Thus, 94.5% of the Soviet Jews know Russian. In addition, 28.8% of the Jews know languages of other Soviet nationalities, one of the highest percentages for any ethnic group.

It is difficult to determine how many Jews there are in the Soviet Union. There are an estimated 165,000–300,000 Oriental Jews (those living in Georgia, the Caucasus Mountains and Central Asia) and approximately 393,000 Jews living in the western republics. As a group the Jews are more highly educated than their ethnic counterparts. In the Russian Soviet Federal Republic 68.2% of the Jews are specialists with higher or secondary education, while approximately

50% of the Jews in Ukraine, Latvia and Belorussia had higher education. In the May 3, 1970 *New York Times Magazine* it is stated that the 1959 official Soviet census listed 2,267,814 persons who declared themselves Jewish. Unofficial estimates run all the way to 3,500,000.

Traditionally an urban people, the Jews were artisans and businessmen before the Bolshevik Revolution. During the 1920s and 1930s a major socio-economic change took place among the Jews and they became managers, bureaucrats, engineers, educators and scientists, an occupational pattern which persists today.

Because of continued Soviet discrimination, many Jews have become assimilated to Soviet culture. The Jews have a low rate of natural increase and no viable cultural institutions. The reaction of a large number of Jews to the pressures of discrimination, however, is to emigrate. This trend has increased dramatically in the last decade. In the first six months of 1974 an estimated 10,000 Jews emigrated from the Soviet Union, primarily to Israel. Between 1964 and 1974 an estimated 100,829 Jews left the Soviet Union because they had come to the conclusion that the anti-Semitic policy of the Soviet Union would never change.[11]

Tatars

The Tatars are Turkic in origin and became Moslems in 922 A.D. Coming under Russian domination in the nineteenth century, the developing Tatar intelligentsia were at first Bolshevik supporters when the Tatar-Bashkir republic was formed in 1918, but became disillusioned when the republic was split into two Autonomous Soviet Republics without union status. Agitation and unrest were severely repressed under Stalin. Although Tatars have increasingly held important political and economic posts within the republic, they are restricted because the republic does not have union status, which is a source of dissatisfaction.

Tatar is a Turkic language. In 1940 in an attempt at Russification, the script was changed from the Latin to the Cyrillic alphabet. 99.5% of the Tatars in the republic speak Tatar as a native language while 54.8% speak Russian as a second language.

As of 1970, 5,931,000 Tatars were living in the USSR, an increase of 19.4% over 1959. In 1970 the population of the Tatar ASSR was 3,131,000, of whom 49% were Tatars and 42.4% were Russian.

Tatars took a large part in the industrial development of Russia as early as the eighteenth century, especially in textiles. Good transport facilities, a large labour force and a secure geographic location led to speedy industrialization in the Soviet era and the discovery of oil after World War II has made the Tatar ASSR one of the Soviet Union's most important economic areas. In 1969 industrial production had increased 337 times over that of 1913. Agriculture (wheat, oats, hemp, vegetables and dairy cattle) is also an important part of the economy.

The most westernized of the Turkic people in the USSR, the Tatars with a rich cultural heritage are firmly attached to their national values. Russification does not seem to have made any significant headway, but the unavailability of higher education in the republic as well as the advantage of knowing Russian prompt many parents to send their children to Russian schools. The Tatars, however, are ardent defenders of their culture and language against Russification.[12]

Moldavians

Conceived as an instrument of Soviet protest against the incorporation of Bessarabia into Rumania and thus as a means of political action against Rumania, the Moldavian Autonomous Soviet Socialist Republic was created in 1924. In fact, although Russia did possess Bessarabia during part of the nineteenth century, Bessarabia historically and demographically was part of the Rumanian principality of Moldavia and the Soviet Union was able to annex the province only militarily as a result of the Molotov-Ribbentrop Pact in 1939. Moldavia was then granted union status. The Soviet Union's possession of Bessarabia was finally legalized by the Rumanian peace treaty of 1947.

The "Moldavian" language is actually a dialect of Rumanian which is an Indo-European language derived from Latin. The Cyrillic rather than the Latin alphabet is used. In Moldavia where 85.4% of all the Moldavians in the USSR live, 97.7% consider "Moldavian" their native language with 33.9% speaking Russian as a second language. Of the 1,264,957 non-Moldavians resident in the republic, only 13,790 consider "Moldavian" their native language and only 173,612 speak it as a second language.

The population of Moldavia in 1970 was 3,568,873, an increase of 24% over the population in 1959. The Moldavians constitute 64.6% of the population while Ukrainians comprise 14.2% and the Russians 11.6%. Other minority groups are the Turkish-speaking Gagauzy (3.5%), Jews (2.7%) and Bulgarians (2.1%). 82% of the Moldavians still live in rural areas, while 77% of the Russians live in cities. Only about 31% of the Moldavians have a higher education.

Primarily an agricultural area producing grain, livestock, wine and related products, Moldavia has also developed some light industry, though food processing remains the most important industry in the republic. Moldavia has the lowest industrial production, lowest capital investment and lowest rate of industrial employment of all union republics.

Historically, the nationalism of Moldavia has been characterized by anti-Russianism, anti-Semitism and anti-Communism based on tsarist Russification and Communist activities in the area between the wars. Collectivization, discrimination against Moldavians with regard to educational and professional opportunities and the imposition of Soviet culture have exacerbated the anti-Russian and anti-Soviet attitude of the Moldavians. Although supposedly cut off from Rumania, Moldavian nationalism has been encouraged by the revival of historic nationalism in Rumania and the USSR's negative reaction to it. Repeated statements by Communist Party officials condemning the intrusion of "harmful phenomena" (i.e. bourgeois-nationalist sentiment) into Moldavian literature and the apparent necessity of continuous reiteration that the Moldavians welcomed incorporation into the Soviet Union in 1940 (a patently false statement) reveal Moldavian dissatisfaction.[13]

Mordvins

Scattered across the plains and forests of the Upper Volga, Mordvins have recently developed their own distinctive literature, despite the use of two dissimilar regional dialects. Mordvins are famed as master bee-keepers. Largely an agrarian people, with grains and vegetables their main crops, the Mordvins now also work in factories, manufacturing electrical components.

II. NATIONALITIES PREDOMINANTLY IN THE USSR IN CENTRAL AND SOUTHERN ASIA

Armenians

The Armenians, who arrived in the Caucasus around the sixth century B.C., developed an empire in the second century B.C., but soon fell under the sway of the Romans, the Byzantine Empire, the Otto-

man Turks and the Persians. Though Islam has dominated the Trans-
caucasus since the eleventh century, the Armenians have maintained
their Christian Gregorian Church as a strong national institution since
conversion in 301 A.D. Conquered by Russia in 1828, Armenia enjoyed a brief and unstable period of independence between 1918 and
1920 when it was incorporated into the Soviet Union. A part of the
Transcaucasian Soviet Republic from 1922 to 1936, Armenia became
a separate union republic in 1936.

Armenian, an independent branch of Indo-European, has many
resemblances to Georgian, a non-Indo-European language, perhaps
due to the merging of the Armenians with the indigenous Hurrian-
speaking peoples. The language is written in a unique script invented
in 406 A.D. and, although the Soviet regime has made changes in
orthography, it has not attempted to replace the alphabet. 99.8% of
the Armenians in the republic considered Armenian their native language in 1970 while only 23.5% claimed to be fluent in Russian. Although Russian is mandatory in the schools and Soviet Armenians
seem to have a reading knowledge of the language, as of 1971 little
Russian seemed to be spoken by the Armenians.[14]

Of the 2,491,873 persons living in Armenia in 1970, 88.6% were
Armenian, making the republic one of the more homogeneous republics in the USSR, even though only 56% of the Armenians in the
whole Soviet Union live there (the smallest figure of any republican
nationality). Unlike the European Soviet republics, Armenia has a
high natural increase of 19.5 per 1000 compared with 9.8 per 1000
for the USSR as a whole. The population of the republic has increased
three-fold under Soviet rule.

Since under Ottoman and Persian rule, political, military and agricultural pursuits were closed to them, most Armenians became merchants and artisans and are known to be canny businessmen. Under
tsarist rule, little was done to develop this backward area, but industrialization was introduced in the Soviet era. Between 1913 and 1969
the value of industrial production increased 162 times, the second
highest rate in the Soviet Union. Armenia today is one of the most important centres in the USSR for scientific research and production of
calculators, computers and measuring instruments. The food industry
produces wines, cognac, fruit preserves and juices for export to other
Soviet republics and abroad.

A long oral, literary and artistic tradition has been an important
factor in Armenian national culture, but the most important element

is the Armenian Church which has been a symbol and a cohesive force in Armenian nationalism through centuries of foreign domination, particularly by the Turks. Under Soviet rule, the Armenian Church suffered persecution in the 1920s and 1930s in the form of confiscation of property, harassment of the clergy and distribution of atheistic propaganda, but today Echiamidzin, world centre of the Armenian Church, is permitted to hold services and to train a small number of clergy under close surveillance.[15]

Recent manifestations of Armenian nationalism have been expressions of the Armenian hatred of the Turks, whose massacres of the Armenians in 1896 and especially in 1915 are bitterly remembered. In 1973 central Soviet leadership replaced two Armenians with two Russians in major positions in the republic because of alleged manifestations of nationalism and economic slackness.

Azerbhaidzhanis

Azerbhaidzhan, ancient Media, has suffered repeated invasions by Persians, Greeks, Sassinids, Moslems and Turks and is inhabited by a people of Turkic-Iranian origin. Finally passing under Russian rule in the early nineteenth century, the region remained backward until the 1870s when the introduction of foreign enterprise in oil, Turkish revival of national feeling and various other factors encouraged Azerbhaidzhani national awareness. After a brief and unstable period of independence from 1918 to 1920, Azerbhaidzhan was incorporated into the Transcaucasian Soviet Republic in 1922 and achieved union status in 1936.

Azerbhaidzhani is an Altaic language closely related to Osman Turkish. In 1922 the Soviet regime changed the writing of Azerbhaidzhani from the Arabic to the Latin script and in 1937 again changed to the Cyrillic alphabet. Between 1959 and 1970 the percentage of Azerbhaidzhanis speaking their native tongue rose from 97.6% to 98% with only 16% speaking Russian as a second language in 1970. The language of commerce, politics and business is Russian and Russian is often the language of instruction in secondary schools, but most Azerbhaidzhanis drop out of school before completing a secondary education, which may explain the low fluency in Russian.[16]

The population of the republic grew by a dramatic 38.4% between 1959 and 1970, reaching 5,177,100. Of thus number 73.8% were Azerbhaidzhani. During these years the Azerbhaidzhani population rose 51.4%, the Russian 1.8%. This increase is due to the high natural growth rate of the Azerbhaidzhani people. Although urban population growth has been steady, the increase in rural population has also been great, creating a labour reserve which is not likely to be absorbed into industry or urban enterprises and may create tensions since most Transcaucasians are unwilling to emigrate to distant parts of the Soviet Union.[17]

Oil and oil-related industries have dominated Azerbhaidzhani industry since 1871. After the oil boom of the pre-World War I years, oil production declined and today, due to diminishing reserves, high expenses and technological problems, Azerbhaidzhan produces only 7% of the oil in the USSR. Although agricultural production – especially cotton – has tripled since 1913, its future is restricted due to limited arable land, competition from other republics and lack of mechanization. The Soviets have diversified productions into oil-related industries and mining, but nothing can substitute for the sluggish oil industry and the outlook for Azerbhaidzhani industry is not bright. Azerbhaidzhan surpasses only the Moslem republics of Central Asia in standard of living and level of industrialization and is last of all the republics in rate of economic growth.

Azerbhaidzhan differs from the European Soviet republics and its Transcaucasian neighbours in not having a unified national, historical or cultural tradition. Until the 1930s Islam was the dominant political and social force, but purges destroyed Islamic political leaders who have not been replaced. Lacking the cohesive force of Islam and cut off from Azerbhaidzhanis in Iran, there is no political nationalism, but rather an ethnic consciousness expressed chiefly through a distinctive Moslem life-style.[18]

Kazakhs

A mixture of Turkic tribes which emerged in the fifteenth century in Central Asia, the Kazakhs submitted in 1731 to Russia which was expanding eastward to Siberia. Thereafter, however, the Kazakhs repeatedly and unsuccessfully rebelled against the Russians. Although at the beginning of the twentieth century a nationalist movement began to develop as did modern industry, almost all modern institutions were in the hands of Russians, Ukrainians, Germans and Jews while most of the Kazakhs (nomads and small farmers) were ruled by a tribal-feudal nobility. Following the Bolshevik Revolution, Kazakhs demanded independence and became involved in the struggle in Central Asia between the Red and White Russian armies. Although some Kazakhs remained active against the Soviets into the 1920s, Kazakhstan was incorporated into the USSR in 1919 and was granted union status in 1926.

Kazakh, a Turkic language, is spoken as a native language by 98.8% of the Kazakhs living in the republic, with 41.8% speaking Russian as their second language. Non-Kazakhs, who are also non-Russian, overwhelmingly choose Russian as their second language rather than Kazakh. As a result of the Russification effort, the alphabet, changed from Arabic to Latin in 1922, was again changed to the Cyrillic (i.e. Russian) alphabet during the 1930s.

With 5.3% of the population in the USSR, Kazakhstan with a population of 12,849,000 in 1970 ranks third in population behind the Russian Soviet Federal Republic and the Ukraine. Its population doubled between 1940 and 1970. However, Kazakhstan is unique among the Soviet republics in that its native population comprises only 32% of the population as of 1970, while the Russians comprise 42%, Ukrainians 7.2% and Belorussians 1.5%, so that the Slavic European population comprises over 50% of the republic's total population. Moreover, most of the republic's growth in urban population and in industrial labour force has resulted from non-Kazakh immigration; most Kazakhs have remained in rural areas. The large non-Kazakh immigration has been compensated somewhat by the high rate of natural increase (17 per 1000), almost twice that of the average increase in the USSR (9.8 per 1000).

Overall production in Kazakhstan increased 146 times between 1913 and 1970 and the republic is third in the USSR in production. Kazakhstan is a major producer of chemicals, but basically produces energy and raw materials to industries outside the republic. Kazakhstan is also a major supplier of agricultural products, such as meat, grain, cotton and wool, to other areas of the USSR, importing finished products. This pattern is similar to economic relations between colonial/underdeveloped countries and highly industrialized countries.[19] Most economic and political positions are filled by non-Kazakhs and most industrial labour is supplied by non-Kazakhs.

To a nomadic people, the influx of Russian immigrants as bureaucrats and technicians, the imposition of the Soviet administration and collectivization were traumatic since such systems were entirely foreign and disruptive of the tribal system and the traditional political structure. There are three demographically and culturally distinct divisions in the republic: 1) traditional Kazakh nomadic and small rural areas, 2) mechanized farm areas settled by Slavs with a predominantly Slavic culture and 3) industrial and administrative towns where Russians and Europeans with modern culture predominate. Islam is the strongest traditional force in the republic and is an inhibitor of Sovietization.[20]

Kirghiz

The Kirghiz as the dominant people in present-day Kirghizistan date back to the sixteenth century. Russia extended control over the area in the mid-nineteenth century, making it an area for Slavic resettlement, thus restricting grazing land and reducing the size of the nomadic people's flocks. The Bolsheviks, establishing control in 1918, followed a similar policy until the Basmachi revolt in 1919 forced them to exercise a different land policy.

Written in the Cyrillic script, Kirghiz is an east Turkic language. 99.7% of the Kirghiz living in the republic consider Kirghiz their native language, while 19.8% speak Russian as a second language.

The population of Kirghizistan increased 42% between 1959 and 1970, reaching 2,933,000. This growth is due to a high rate of natural increase (35–40 per 1000) and immigration from other republics. Except for Uzbekistan, Kirghizistan had more immigrants than any other Central Asian republic during this period. Though the Russians remain predominant in the cities, their overall weight in the population has declined from 30.2% to 29.2%, reversing a long standing trend, while the Kirghiz population, which had been declining in weight, rose from 40.5% to 43.8%.

Like the other Central Asian republics, Kirghizistan is less industrialized than the western republics and its relative standing is low, but the republic has industrialized significantly since World War II, especially in the non-ferrous metal industry. Agriculture, especially livestock husbandry (traditional Kirghiz occupation), provided 30% of the national income in 1969. The economic roles of ethnic Kirghiz are predominantly unskilled agricultural work, while non-Kirghiz comprise 81.7% of industrial, skilled agricultural and non-agricultural labour forces.

The Kirghiz have a strong ethnic-nationalist movement as has been manifested from the time of the Bolshevik take-over to the present day. The Basmachi revolt 1918–1919, which involved all the present Central Asian republics, forced the Bolsheviks to introduce more conciliatory policies. During the 1920s the Kirghiz attempted unsuccessfully to form a Turkic Communist party and a Turkic republic in Central Asia. They also tried unsuccessfully to prevent collectivization. During this period the Soviets repressed the greater part of the native political and intellectual elite, whose ranks were decimated. In spite of the great purge of the 1930s, however, Kirghiz nationalism has been continually expressed in attempts to preserve and encourage the Kirghiz language and customs and to protect the republic's constitutional rights.[21]

Turkmens

The Turkmens, a branch of the Seljuk and Ottoman Turks, established themselves in Central Asia during the eleventh and twelfth centuries. Maintaining a precarious independence for centuries, the Turkmens offered stiff resistance to Russian expansion during the late nineteenth century and were not conquered until 1885. During World War I the collapse of the tsarist government left a power vacuum in Turkmenistan, to be filled by the Soviets only after much fighting in 1925 when the republic was incorporated.

Like Azerbhaidzhani, Turkmen is a southwest Turkic language with a close relationship to Uzbek and Kazakh. The Arabic alphabet, used until 1929, was replaced by a Latin alphabet closely adapted to Turkmen, but in 1940 the Latin alphabet was replaced by a modified Cyrillic alphabet. Like the other Central Asian republics there is high retention of the native language: 99.3% of the Turkmens in the republic consider Turkmen their native language. Turkmen is the native tongue of 65% of the total population, while 17.1% consider Russian their first language. Only 14.8% of the native Turkmens speak Russian as a second language.

Like the other Central Asian republics, Turkmenistan has a high population growth (42% between 1959 and 1970) due to high natural increase (27.3 per 1000). In 1970 the population was 2,159,000 of which Turkmens comprised 65.6% and Slavs (Russians, Ukrainians and Belorussians) 16.3%. Urbanization has been high compared to other Central Asian republics due partly to large desert areas and to the tendency of the Slavic settlers to locate in cities.

One of the least developed areas in tsarist Russia, Turkmenistan still remains largely a producer of raw materials, but oil, gas and mineral production is of union-wide significance. In the last decade, increased irrigation, reclamation of land, mechanization and greater production of mineral fertilizers have brought major expansion to

Turkmen agricultural output. Cotton, for which Turkmenistan has always been famous, remains the most important crop, followed by production of livestock.

The Turkmens actively resisted both tsarist and Soviet rule. In 1931 Turkmen rebellion, a result of forced collectivization, was crushed and the nomadic peasants were forced onto collective farms. Nonetheless, Turkmenistan has been repeatedly accused of "nationalism" by the Soviet regime. The Turkmens want a larger representation in the republic's government and resent the fact that Turkmen cotton, gas and oil are sent out of the republic for the benefit of other areas in the Soviet Union. Dissidence, however, is not tolerated as is shown by the case of Annasoltan Kekilova, a poet, whose 56-page criticism of shortcomings in her republic led to such harassment that she decided to give up Soviet citizenship and emigrate. In 1971 the Soviet regime committed her to a mental institution in an attempt to force her to take back her criticism.

Uzbeks

Incorporated as a union republic in 1925, Uzbekistan, inhabited by a Moslem Turkic-Mongolian people closely related to the Kirghiz, Turkmens and Kazakhs, has been successively invaded and was part of the empire ruled by Tamarlane. Subsequently with the shift in trade routes, Turkestan, from which modern Uzbekistan emerged, fell into decline and was conquered by Russia in the late nineteenth century. Although Russification was not pressed, the heavy influx of Slavic immigrants caused resentment culminating in the Basmachi revolt during World War I, which was not crushed until 1921. In order to delimit nationalities and to inhibit the Pan-Turkic movement in Central Asia, Turkestan was split into separate republics for major ethnic groups of which Uzbekistan was one.

Uzbek is a member of the Turkic language family. In an attempt to "nationalize" the language, the Soviets changed from the Arabic to the Latin alphabet in the 1920s and then to the Cyrillic alphabet in the 1930s in order to undermine the Pan-Turkic, Pan-Islamic unity and to further assimilation to the Soviet Union. Today, however, over 98.6% of the Uzbeks in the republic consider Uzbek their native language while only 13% speak Russian as a second language.

With the fourth highest population of all the republics in the USSR (11,960,000), Uzbekistan is comprised of 64% native Uzbeks and 12.5% Russians, with substantial minorities of Tadzhiks and Kazakhs. Like the other Central Asian republics, Uzbekistan has a high rate of natural increase. That the Slavic element of the population plays a key role is indicated by the 1961 figures on specialists with a secondary specialist education (42% Slav, 32% Uzbek).

Uzbekistan, third largest producer of cotton in the world after the United States and China, is the Soviet Union's chief source of that crop and also leads the USSR in production of cotton-related equipment. Industrialization of the republic has been intensive under the Soviet regime and recent gas strikes in the republic have increased the importance of Central Asia as a source of fuel and power.

There was abundant opposition to tsarist and Soviet rule. Resistance, however, was local and religious in scope rather than national. Since most of the uneducated religious peasants did not respond to the appeals of the modern and reformist intelligentsia during the troubles following World War I, the intelligentsia collaborated with the Bolsheviks. The Uzbek intelligentsia were wiped out, however, in the purges of 1937–1938 because Stalin feared "bourgeois nationalism," i.e., any attachment to the past and to local Moslem culture. Though local customs and Moslem culture have persisted, there has been no concerted effort within the government or the intelligentsia to express dissatisfaction with Soviet rule. The Tashkent riots of 1969 were an expression of resentment by ordinary people rather than the intelligentsia. While Russians hold key posts in politics, local Uzbek intelligentsia have risen in politics and economics to hold important positions.[22]

Tadzhiks

The Tadzhiks, unlike the inhabitants of the other Central Asian republics, are an Indo-Iranian people, but as a result of the seventh century Arab conquest, they are Moslem. The Perso-Arabic civilization was destroyed by the Mongol invasions and the area was cut off from the West. A part of Turkestan until granted union status in 1929, Tadzhikistan took part in the Basmachi revolt of the 1920s, engendered by the Soviets' "colonial" attitude and repressive policies toward Moslems. Resistance to enforced collectivization and industrialization in the 1920s and 1930s led to the purge of Tadzhik leadership and to the placing of political and economic leadership in the hands of the Russians.

Tadzhik is an Indo-Iranian language close to Persian and is written in the Cyrillic alphabet. 97.2% of the native Tadzhiks speak Tadzhik as their native tongue while only 16.9% speak Russian as a second language. Uzbek is the second official language since a large number of Uzbeks live in the republic, while Russian, the third official language, is the language of all political, administrative and economic activity except on the rural level.

Tadzhikistan has the highest natural increase rate (31,1 per 1000) in the USSR due primarily to a high birth rate. Tadzhiks comprise 56.2% of the total population (2,899,602), Uzbeks 23% and Russians 11.9%. Although urbanization has increased (38% of the population in 1971), the high birth rate in rural areas has created a large unabsorbed labour reserve.

Extremely backward when incorporated into the USSR, Tadzhikistan's economic role in the Soviet Union has been the production and processing of cotton, coming second in rate of production to Uzbekistan. Industrialization began in the 1940s and progressed significantly in the 1960s, but Tadzhikistan remains low, in comparison with other republics, in industrial production and occupies a "colonial" position of exporting raw materials and importing finished products.

Persistent shortcomings in fulfillment of economic goals established by the Soviet regime, adherence to their native tongue and recent rediscovery of their classical Persian heritage show that the Tadzhiks have not been assimilated into the Soviet body politic. The separateness maintained by the Tadzhiks is enforced by the cohesiveness of Islam and the unequal political and economic positions of Tadzhiks vis-à-vis the Russians. At the same time the Tadzhiks desire a larger share of their government and of benefits.[23]

III. Nationalities Predominantly in Northern and Eastern Asia

Tuvans

The Turkic-speaking Tuvans were early introduced to education through the teachings of Buddhist missionaries. Their homeland in the Sayan Mountains was originally a province of China. Traditionally pastoral nomads, many Tuvans have settled and now raise livestock.

Buryats

Inhabitants of the areas around Lake Baykal, the Buryats were once a nomadic hunting and cattle herding people. Due to collectivization and industrialization, the Buryats have become farmers and workers. They have achieved a high level of education which helps equip many for work in regional industries such as aircraft manufacture.

Yakuts

Originally a nomadic people, hunters and herders of horses and cattle, the Siberian Yakuts have become farmers and recently have begun to sow wheat that is highly resistant to cold. The Yakuts pursue a traditional love of learning. Graduates from their own university and scientific research institutions hold key administrative and educational positions in the region.

Chukchi

The Chukchi, numbering only 13,000 live in shoreline villages and in the Siberian tundra. As reindeer farmers, the Chukchi tend 10,000 to 20,000 head.

Evenks

Widely dispersed throughout Siberia, the Evenks are a semi-nomadic people. They are hunters, reindeer herders and cattle and horse breeders. Many Evenks have settled in permanent communities, tending plots of grain and vegetables and farming pelt-bearing animals.

Chuvash

A Turkic-speaking people who claim descent from the ancient Bulgars of the Volga, the Chuvash have been ruled by Russians since 1552 when Ivan the Terrible destroyed the Kazan Khanate of the Tatars. A farming people modernized by collectivization, the Chuvash's main crops are rye and potatoes.

IV. Russian Domination in the Soviet Regime

The special place of Russians in the power system is due to the fact that for Russians the Soviet regime is largely their own regime. For other nationalities in the Union it is a Russian, alien regime.

> Valery Chalidze, Russian publicist and charter member of the Moscow Human Rights Committee under Academician Andre Sakharov, in *To Defend These Rights* (1974)

In the courting stage before the October Revolution of 1917, Lenin described the Russian Empire as the "Prison of Nations." He promised the right of self-determination for all nationalities and ethnic groups which had suffered under Russian domination. Lenin maintained that the Russians were oppressors of all non-Russian people. Unfortunately, Lenin never implemented those promises once he captured power.

The national problems in the Soviet Union of today are far more acute than in old Russia. If you used a twelve-point seismic scale to register the degree of national differences, in old Russia it could be put at about the second point; in the USSR today it is about force ten

> Aleksandr Solzhenitsyn, at a press conference in Zurich, November 16, 1974.

Krushchev's speech at the Twentieth Party Congress of the CPSU, *Samizdat* (unofficial producer and distributor of manuscripts), writings of the three Soviet Nobel Laureates, Boris Pasternak, Aleksandr Solzhenitsyn and Andrei Sakharov, and reports of *Amnesty International* prove that the Soviet regime is intolerant, oppressive, arbitrary and indifferent to all its citizens. Stalin and his successors succeeded in establishing equality in servile conditions for all citizens. To paraphrase George Orwell, some slaves are more equal than others. Over 75% of all policy-making and administrative positions throughout the USSR are in the hands of the Russians.

There are at least two stages in Communist colonialism and enslavement of its victims. From 1917 to 1939 the Russians enslaved 129 different national and ethnic minorities. The Jews were the eleventh largest of the national groups in the USSR. Between 1939 and 1944 the Soviet Union conquered and incorporated into the USSR the following:

	Area in Square Miles	Population
Rumanians	19,446	3,700,000
Slovaks	4,900	731,000
Poles	70,000	11,800,000
Finns	18,000	450,000
Tanna Tuva Republic	64,175	65,000
Kuriles Island and Sakhalin	17,850	483,000
Estonians	18,353	1,122,000
Latvians	25,500	1,951,000
Lithuanians	2,953	2,957,000

In addition, the Red Army of the USSR imposed Soviet control over the following Captive Nations:

	Area in Square Miles	Population
Albania	11,100	2,019,000
Bulgaria	42,845	8,370,000
Cuba	44,218	8,074,000
Czechoslovakia	59,370	14,362,000
East Germany	41,500	16,100,000
East Berlin	155	1,100,000
Hungary	35,919	10,284,000
Poland	120,632	32,207,000
Rumania	91,660	19,721,000
Outer Mongolia	604,090	1,174,000

The Iron Curtain descended over those nations which were longing for their own 1776. The right of nations to self-determination became the right of the Soviet Red Army to "liberate" any nation from its previous condition and make it dependent on the USSR. The Four Freedoms and The Atlantic Charter were cast into the dustbin of history in order to appease Stalin and to gratify his imperialistic drive for domination of other people.

Between August 1941 and June 1944 Stalin's troops rounded up and deported to eastern Siberia eight nations of the Soviet Union. Approximately one-and-a-half million people – men, women and children – were packed into cattle trucks and sent near the Chinese border. These uprooted and helpless people were the Crimean Tatars, the Volga Germans, the Kalmyks, the Chechens, the Ingush, the Balkars, the Karachais and the Meskhetians. In less than twelve months approximately 500,000 of them died from hunger, cold and disease. Stalin unjustifiably suspected his tragic victims of disloyalty toward the Soviet Union.

No effort was made by the United Nations to protect the national minorities in the Soviet Union or those under the control of the Red Army in adjacent areas.

It is all the more contradictory that the Soviet Union should continue to press for the creation of more and more independent nation-states in Africa and Asia while manifestly aiming at the abolition of national distinctions inside the Soviet Union itself and at the fusion of all nationalities in a unitary state with one uniform culture.

> Geoffrey Wheeler, Director (retired)
> of the Central Asian Research Centre,
> London, in *The Modern History of Soviet
> Central Asia* (1964)

The record of the 58 years of the Soviet regime proves that there is no relation between their pious allegiance to noble ideas of freedom, self-determinations, etc., and their actions. Soviet practices contradict and repudiate all their claims. The most striking contrast between theory and practice in the Soviet Union is their treatment of the blacks.

In 1963 African students picketed Red Square in Moscow hauling signs which read "Moscow Is Another Alabama."

Most of the African and Third World students in the Soviet Union attend Moscow State University or Patrice Lumumba Friendship University. They find race prejudice so obvious, and in many cases so brutal, that they have formed protection societies to ward off attacks by the Russian students.

The blacks in the Soviet Union like neither the people nor the climate, and the only reason many of them remain there is that they believe erroneously that no other country will have them. The Russian Communists insist there is no race prejudice in the Soviet Union, but let a white female take up with a black student, and she is immediately ostracized.

In the fall of 1975 the Czech government withdrew a scholarship from a Czech girl who married a Nigerian. Black students in Kiev and Ukraine, thereupon rioted. It was the first demonstration by black students in the Soviet Union since 1963.

> Parade Magazine Jan. 9, 1976.

It is unfortunate and tragic that international organizations, like the United Nations, are only preoccupied with the real or imaginary sufferings of people in other parts of the world, but conveniently overlook much greater suffering of humanity under the Communist yoke. Let us hope that one day free men will heed the appeal of the last Nobel Laureate in the Soviet Union, Andrei Sakharov, who said the following:

I would hope that representatives of the Western intelligentsia would play a more active role in defending human rights in our country to choose one's country of residence; the Tatars, the Germans, the Lithuanians, the many others; the rights of persecuted religious groups; and the right to defend prisoners of conscience.

> Andrei Sakharov, Russian scientist,
> winner of the 1975 Nobel Peace Prize
> in *My Country and the World* (1975).
> From Radio Liberty Report 16/76,
> Jan. 9, 1976.

TABLE I. *Republic Populations, 1959–1970, Ranked by Growth Rate*

Rank Republics	Population (in thousands)		% Growth 1959–1970	% USSR Population	
	1959	1970		1959	1970
USSR total	208,827	241,720	16	100.0	100.0
1 Tadzhik SSR	1.981	2,900	46	0.95	1.20
2 Uzbek SSR	8,261	11,960	45	3.96	4.95
3 Turkmen SSR	1,516	2,159	42	0.73	0.89
4 Kirghiz SSR	2,066	2,933	42	0.99	1.21
5 Armenian SSR	1,763	2,492	41	0.84	1.03
6 Kazakh SSR	9,153	12,849	40	4.33	5.32
7 Azerbhaidzhan SSR	3,698	5,117	38	1.77	2.12
8 Moldavian SSR	2,885	3,569	24	1.38	1.48
9 Georgian SSR	4,044	4,686	16	1.94	1.94
10 Lithuanian SSR	2,711	3,128	15	1.30	1.29
11 Estonian SSR	1,197	1,356	13	0.57	0.56
12 Latvian SSR	2.093	2,364	13	1.00	0.98
13 Ukraine SSR	41,869	47,126	13	20.05	19.50
14 Belorussian SSR	8,056	9,002	12	3.86	3.72
15 RSFR	117,534	130,079	11	56.23	53.81
16 Tatar ASSR	2,850	3,131	10	1.36	1.29

Sources: *Izvestia* (April 17), 1971; CDSP, 1971: XXIII: 16: 16–18; *Itogi* 1970: I: 12.
Cited in *Handbook of Major Soviet Nationalities*, Zev Katz, Rosemarie Rogers, Frederic Harned, eds., The Free Press (New York: 1975), p. 442.

TABLE II. *Speakers of Languages of Major Nationalities of USSR, 1970, Ranked by % Identifying Language as Mother Tongue*

Rank Language	Native Speakers	Fluent as Second Language	Total Speakers	% Nationality Identifying Language as Mother Tongue
1 Russian	141,830,546	41,937,995	183,798,559	c
2 Turkmen	1,514,980	50,996	1,565,976	98.9
3 Kirghiz	1,445,213	41,493	1,486,706	98.8
4 Uzbek	9,154,904	543,023	9,697,727	98.6
5 Tadzhik	2,202,671	261,248	2,463,919	98.5
6 Georgian	3,310,917	190,115	3,501,032	98.4
7 Azerbhaidzhani	4,347,089	263,160	4,610,249	98.2
8 Kazakh	5,213,694	146,057	5,359,751	98.0
9 Lithuanian	2,625,608	152,523	2,778,131	97.9
10 Estonian	947,649	69,520	1,044,169	95.5
11 Latvian	1,390,162	215,376	1,605,538	95.2
12 "Moldavian"	2,607,367	283,426	2,890,793	95.0
13 Armenian	3,261,053	147,727	3,408,780	91.4
14 Tatar[a]	5,493,316	344,414	5,837,730	89.2
15 Ukrainian	35,400,944	5,618,837	41,019,781	85.7
16 Belorussian	7,630,571	903,024	8,533,031	30.2
17 Jewish[b]	381,571	166,571	547,649	17.7

Source: *Itogi* 1970: IV: 20, 76, 331–332, 333–359.

[a] Complete data available only for RSFR, Kazakhstan, Georgia and Central Asia.
[b] Includes Yiddish and other languages of Jews in USSR. Data not available on non-Jewish speakers of the language except in Jewish national region (Birobidzhan); however, number of such speakers is estimated to be negligible.
[c] Precise statistic not available; all other evidence indicates that virtually all who identify themselves as of Russian nationality speak Russian as their native language.

TABLE III. *Urban-Rural Distribution, 1959–1970, by nationality ranked by Urban Percentage*

Rank Nationality	1959		Rank Nationality	1970	
	% Urban	% Rural		% Urban	% Rural
1 Jews	95.3	4.7	1 Jews	97.9	2.1
2 Russians	57.7	42.3	2 Russians	68.0	32.0
3 Armenians	56.5	43.5	3 Armenians	64.8	35.2
4 Latvians	47.5	52.5	4 Estonians	55.1	44.9
5 Tatars	47.2	52.8	5 Tatars	55.0	45.0
6 Estonians	47.0	53.0	6 Latvians	52.7	47.3
7 Ukrainians	39.2	60.8	7 Ukrainians	48.5	51.5
8 Georgians	36.1	63.9	8 Lithuanians	46.7	53.3
9 Lithuanians	35.1	63.9	9 Georgians	44.0	56.0
10 Azerbhaidzhani	34.8	65.2	10 Belorussians	43.7	56.3
11 Belorussians	32.4	67.6	11 Azerbhaidzhani	39.7	60.3
12 Turkmen	35.4	74.6	12 Turkmen	31.0	69.0
13 Kazakhs	24.1	75.9	13 Kazakhs	26.7	73.3
14 Uzbeks	21.8	78.2	14 Tadzhiks	26.0	74.0
15 Tadzhiks	20.6	79.4	15 Uzbeks	24.9	75.1
16 Moldavians	12.9	87.1	16 Moldavians	20.4	79.6
17 Kirghiz	10.8	89.2	17 Kirghiz	14.6	85.4
USSR AVERAGE	47.9	52.1	USSR AVERAGE	56.0	44.0

Sources: *Itogi* 1959: 190–196; *Itogi* 1970: IV: 20, 27, 28.
Cited in *Handbook of Major Soviet Nationalities*, Zev Katz, Rosemarie Rogers, Frederic Harned, eds., The Free Press (New York: 1975), p. 447.

NOTE: Highest urbanization: Jews Russians, Armenians, Latvians, Tatars (highest Islamic group), Estonians. Lowest urbanization: Central Asians plus Moldavians. Only three nationalities – Jews, Russians and Armenians – are above USSR mean level of urbanization. They and Tatars are only peoples exceeding urbanization levels of their respective republics. Tatars are far more urbanized than other Moslem peoples who, with Moldavians, are grouped at bottom of urbanization ranking. In 1970 urbanization ratio between lowest group (Moldavians) and highest (Jews) was 1:6.7 and second highest (Russians) 1:4.7. The gap closed somewhat in comparison with 1959.

TABLE IV. *National Composition of CPSU, January 1, 1972, Union Republic Nationalities Only, Ranked by Weight Index*

Rank Nationality	No.	%	Weight Index[a]
1 Georgians	242,253	1.66	1.24
2 Russians	8,927,400	61.02	1.14
3 Armenians	223,372	1.52	1.04
4 Ukrainians	2,333,750	15.95	0.95
5 Belorussians	511,981	3.50	0.94
6 Azerbhaidzhanis	206,184	1.41	0.78
7 Kazakhs	246,393	1.68	0.77
8 Estonians	45,454	0.31	0.74
9 Latvians	60,843	0.42	0.71
10 Lithuanians	93,271	0.64	0.58
11 Kirghiz	45,205	0.31	0.52
12 Uzbeks	282,918	1.93	0.51
13 Turkmen	43,111	0.29	0.46
14 Tadzhiks	57,271	0.39	0.44
15 Moldavians	58,062	0.40	0.36
Other Nationalities	1,253,821	8.57	1.28
Total	14,631,289	100.00	1.00

Source: *Kommunist vooruzhennykh sil*, 1972: XXIV: 12.
Cited in *Handbook of Major Soviet Nationalities*, Zev Katz, Rosemarie Rogers, Frederic Harned, eds., The Free Press (New York: 1975), p. 449.

[a] Weight Index: Nationality's % of party divided by % of 1970 population.

TABLE V. *National Composition of CPSU by Geographic-Ethnic Group, January 1, 1972*

Group	% of Party	Weight Index[a]
All Slavs	80.47	1.09
Russians	61.02	1.14
Other Slavs	19.45	0.94
Other Europeans	1.77	0.43
Islamic	6.01	0.48
Armenian-Georgian	3.19	1.14

Source: Calculated from data in Table IV.
Cited in *Handbook of Major Soviet Nationalities*, Zev Katz, Rosemarie Rogers, Frederic Harned, eds., The Free Press (New York: 1975), p. 449.

[a] See note in Table IV

TABLE VI. *Scientific Workers by Nationality, Ranked by Relative Weight Index, 1971*

Rank Nationality	1960			1971			Point Change In Weight Index 1960–1971
	No.	% of Total	Index[a]	No.	% of Total	Index[a]	
USSR	354,158	100.00	1.00	1,002,930	100.00	1.00	
1 Jews	33,529	9.47	8.69	66,793	6.66	7.48	−1.21
2 Armenians	8,001	2.26	1.70	22,056	2.20	1.50	−0.20
3 Georgians	8,306	2.35	1.82	19,411	1.94	1.45	−0.37
4 Russians	229,547	64.81	1.19	666,059	66.41	1.24	+0.05
5 Estonians	2,048	0.58	1.23	4,959	0.49	1.17	−0.06
6 Latvians	2,662	0.75	1.12	6,262	0.62	1.05	−0.07
7 Lithuanians	2,959	0.84	0.76	8,751	0.87	0.79	+0.03
8 Azerbhaidzhani	4,972	1.40	0.99	13,998	1.40	0.77	−0.22
9 Ukrainians	35,426	10.00	0.56	107,475	10.72	0.64	+0.08
10 Belorussians	6,358	1.80	0.47	20,538	2.05	0.55	+0.08
11 Tatars	3,691	1.04	0.44	12,619	1.26	0.51	+0.11
12 Turkmen	707	0.20	0.42	1,946	0.19	0.40	−0.02
13 Kazakhs	2,290	0.65	0.38	8,629	0.86	0.39	+0.01
14 Kirghiz	586	0.17	0.37	2,100	0.21	0.35	−0.02
15 Uzbeks	3,748	1.06	0.37	12,928	1.29	0.34	−0.03
16 Tadzhiks	866	0.24	0.36	2,550	0.25	0.28	−0.08
17 Moldavians	590	0.17	0.16	2,624	0.26	0.23	+0.07

Source: *Nar. khoz.* 1972: 105.
Cited in *Handbook of Major Soviet Nationalities*, Zev Katz, Rosemarie Rogers, Frederic Harned, eds., The Free Press (New York: 1975)[i] p. 457.

[a] Index = $\dfrac{\text{Weight (\%) of total USSR population}}{\text{\% of USSR scientific workers}}$

NOTE: Jews, Armenians and Georgians with a very high weight ratio, have gone down considerably. Russians have gone up, though considerably "over-represented."

TABLE VII.

The following are the 53 ethno-administrative units of the Soviet Union:

Armenian S.S.R.
Azerbhaidzhan S.S.R.
  1 Nakhichevan A.S.S.R.
  2 Nagorno Karabakh A.O.
Belorussian S.S.R.
Estonian S.S.R.
Georgian S.S.R.
  3 Abkhaz A.S.S.R.
  4 Adzhar (Ajar) A.S.S.R.
  5 Yugo Ossetian A.O.
Kazakh S.S.R.
Kirghiz S.S.R.
Latvian S.S.R.
Lithuanian S.S.R.
Moldavian S.S.R.
Russian S.F.S.R.
  6 Bashkir A.S.S.R.
  7 Buryat A.S.S.R.
  8 Chechen-Ingush A.S.S.R.
  9 Chuvash A.S.S.R.
  10 Daghestan A.S.S.R.
  11 Kabardin-Balkar A.S.S.R.
  12 Kalmyk A.S.S.R.
  13 Karelian A.S.S.R.
  14 Komi A.S.S.R.
  15 Mari A.S.S.R.
  16 Mordovian A.S.S.R.

17 Severo Ossetian A.S.S.R.
18 Tatar A.S.S.R.
19 Tuva A.S.S.R.
20 Udmurt A.S.S.R.
21 Yakut A.S.S.R.
22 Adygey A.O.
23 Aga Buryat N.O.
24 Chukchi N.O.
25 Evenk N.O.
26 Evrey (Jewish) A.O.
27 Gorno Altay A.O.
28 Karachay-Cherkess A.O.
29 Khakass A.O.
30 Khanty-Mansi N.O.
31 Komi-Permyak N.O.
32 Koryak N.O.
33 Nenets N.O.
34 Taymyr (Dolgan-Nenets) N.O.
35 Ust' Orda Buryat N.O.
36 Yamal Nenets N.O.
Tadzhik (Tajik) S.S.R.
  37 Gorno Badakhshan A.O.
Turkmen S.S.R.
Ukrainian S.S.R.
Uzbek S.S.R.
  38 Karakalpak A.S.S.R.

NOTES

1. "Soviet Concentration Camps," *Peking Review*, March 5, 1976, pp. 15–16.
2. Richard Pipes, "Introduction: The Nationality Problem," *Handbook of Major Soviet Nationalities*, Zev Katz, Rosemarie Rogers, Frederic Harned, eds., The Free Press (New York: 1975), pp. 1–4.
3. Dina Rome Spechler, "Russia and the Russians," in Katz *et al.*, *Handbook of Major Soviet Nationalities, op. cit.*, p. 19.
4. Roman Szpoluk, "The Ukraine and the Ukrainians," in Katz *et al.*, *Handbook of Major Soviet Nationalities, op. cit.*, p. 45.
5. Jan Zaprudnik, "Belorussia and the Belorussians," in Katz *et al.*, *Handbook of Major Soviet Nationalities, op. cit.*, p. 64.
6. Rein Taagepera, "Estonia and the Estonians," in Katz *et al.*, *Handbook of Major Soviet Nationalities, op. cit.*, pp. 87–91.
7. Frederic T. Harned, "Latvia and the Latvians, in Katz *et al.*, *Handbook of Major Soviet Nationalities, op. cit.*, p. 115.

8. Frederic T. Harned, "Lithuania and the Lithuanians," in Katz *et al.*, *Handbook of Major Soviet Nationalities, op. cit.*, p. 138.

9. Richard Pipes, *The Formation of the Soviet Union: Communism and Nationalism 1917–1923*, rev. ed. (Cambridge: Harvard University Press, 1964), p. 17, cited in "Georgia and the Georgians," by Richard B. Dobson in Katz *et al.*, *Handbook of Major Soviet Nationalities, op. cit.*, p. 165.

10. Richard B. Dobson, "Georgia and the Georgians," in Katz *et al.*, *Handbook of Major Soviet Nationalities, op. cit.*, p. 186.

11. Zev Katz, "The Jews in the Soviet Union," in Katz *et al.*, *Handbook of Major Soviet Nationalities, op. cit.*, pp. 378–386.

12. Gustav Burbiel, "The Tatars and the Tatar ASSR," in Katz *et al.*, *Handbook of Major Soviet Nationalities, op. cit.*, pp. 410–413.

13. Stephen Fischer-Galati, "Moldavia and the Moldavians," in Katz *et al.*, *Handbook of Major Soviet Nationalities, op. cit.*, pp. 429–432.

14. Mary K. Matossian, "Armenia and the Armenians," in Katz *et al.*, *Handbook of Major Soviet Nationalities, op. cit.*, p. 151.

15. *Ibid.*, pp. 148–149.

16. Frank Huddle, "Azerbhaidzhan and the Azerbhaidzhanis," in Katz *et al.*, *Handbook of Major Soviet Nationalities, op. cit.*, p. 199.

17. *Ibid.*, p. 194.

18. *Ibid.*, pp. 205–207.

19. Zev Katz, "Kazakhstan and the Kazakhs," in Katz *et al.*, *Handbook of Major Soviet Nationalities, op. cit.*, p. 215.

20. *Ibid.* pp. 231–232.

21. Allen Hetmanek, "Kirghizistan and the Kirghiz," in Katz *et al.*, *Handbook of Major Soviet Nationalities, op. cit.*, pp. 256–258.

22. Donald S. Carlisle, "Uzbekistan and the Uzbeks," in Katz *et al.*, *Handbook of Major Soviet Nationalities, op. cit.*, pp. 302–311.

23. Teresa Rakowska-Harmstone, "Tadzhikistan and the Tadzhiks," in Katz *et al.*, *Handbook of Major Soviet Nationalities, op. cit.*, pp. 345–350.

Cyprus: The Greek and Turkish Confrontation

MICHAEL AND EIRWEN HARBOTTLE

BRIGADIER MICHAEL HARBOTTLE was commissioned into the British Army in 1937 and during his 31 years military career served in many parts of the world, including three tours in Cyprus. He was there in the peaceful days of 1950, during the period of the EOKA guerilla campaign in the late 1950s, and finally as Chief of Staff of the United Nations Peacekeeping Force from 1966–68. Since his retirement in 1968 he has made his main work the study and teaching of the skills required in international third-party peacekeeping and the related techniques of peacemaking and peace building. In this connection he has been a Vice President of and is now a senior consultant to the International Peace Academy and has helped to structure and direct its transnational seminars since 1970. He was appointed a Visiting Senior Lecturer in Peace Studies at the University of Bradford, England in 1973. He is the author of *The Impartial Soldier*, *The Blue Berets* and co-author (with Rikhye and Egge) of *The Thin Blue Line: International Peacekeeping and its Future;* he is a contributor to a number of institutional and military journals in Britain, USA, Canada, Holland, Austria and Australia, writing on the use of military forces in non-enforcement roles. Since 1974 he has been continuously concerned with the Cyprus dispute.

EIRWEN HARBOTTLE was born in Cyprus and lived there for almost fifty years. Her father was for many years Manager of the Ottoman Bank, a founder of the Agricultural Bank and the Cyprus Chamber of Commerce. For seventeen years she was a flower farmer in northern Cyprus, during ten of which she combined her work with that of newscaster and announcer for Cyprus Broadcasting Corporation. From 1963 she was administrator of the inter-communal Junior School in Nicosia. Her work brought her into touch with Cypriots of all communities and at all levels of society. Since coming to England she has assisted her husband in his peacekeeping studies and has worked with the Centre for Human Rights and Responsibilities. Currently she is secretary to the British-Kurdish Friendship Society.

Cyprus: The Greek and Turkish Confrontation

MICHAEL AND EIRWEN HARBOTTLE

Cyprus has experienced an alternating history in which rule and power supremacy have changed hands many times. The phenomenon that impresses itself on the reader of Cyprus history is that it has been, in the main, the major ethnic community which has been subjected more to oppression, violence and discrimination over the centuries than the minority groups. For more than 3,000 years the original Hellenic settlers and their Greek descendants, basically the indigenous people of Cyprus, suffered from the whims and excesses of conqueror after conqueror. It has been only in the twentieth century that the emphasis has shifted and the majority have discriminated against the minority. It is only since the end of the Second World War that the discrimination has embraced violence and suppression. Yet in the event it has been the majority who once again has become the victim, while the power supremacy has passed back into the hands of the conqueror.

This exposition therefore is not so much directed at the nature and consequences of discrimination against a particular ethnic group; nor is it a commentary on the denial of human rights and freedoms in a majority/minority interaction. Rather, it is an analysis in depth of the antecedents that have led to the present ethnic confrontation, of its structural and manifest causes and of the differing cultures and life styles which have helped to create the circumstances in which the people of Cyprus – Armenians, Greeks, Maronites and Turks – currently find themselves. It underlines the personal relationships between Greek and Turk that could in time heal the wounds and give birth to a unified Cyprus.

* * *

Cyprus has been described as 'a place of arms'; in the sense that it was a military defence base providing an arsenal of military strength in the eastern Mediterranean. The comment was Benjamin Disraeli's, British Prime Minister at the time that England assumed control of Cyprus from Turkey in 1878,[1] and was intended as an indication of its importance in the safeguarding of Turkey's interests against the threats and ambitions of Russia, as well as British interests in the Suez Canal. Using a different context and bearing in mind Cyprus' turbulent history, the description could be interpreted as meaning 'a place of conflict', though this would neither be accurate nor wholly precise. It cannot be questioned that in the course of its history Cyprus has witnessed many periods of acute and excessive violence. Yet, when studied in deeper perspective, that history has a chameleon quality about it, during which the different ethnic groups have lived more years in relatively peaceful co-existence and inter-relationship with one another than in violent confrontation; in fact Cyprus has never been more divided than it is to-day.

Until 1974 a policy of total separatism had never been a part of the island's physical or material structure. Even in the early Middle Ages when Cyprus was divided into as many as nine 'kingdoms', economically it had remained a single entity. The territorial demarcations neither imposed rigid frontiers nor denied completely freedom of movement. To-day a new geopolitical structure is being created with the two main communities of Greeks and Turks separated under military duress and occupying two thirds and one third of Cyprus respectively. This division, coming as it does as the direct result of war, is to a large degree the consequence of the political, ethnic, social, cultural and military confrontation, lasting from the second half of the 1950s into the early 1970s. What has now occurred is that with military support from Turkey there has been a reversal of the old domination of majority over minority – a domination that depends entirely on the continuing presence of large numbers of Turkish soldiers on the island. More significantly, however, is the emergence of a new geopolitical and demographic structure in Cyprus, resulting from the immigration of mainland Turks into Cyprus as a colonisation process, directed at increasing their ethnic ratio in the island.

Though the present complexities of the Cyprus situation and its communal problems relate in no small way to its historical past, there is merit in beginning with the present and putting into proper perspective the differences as they exist to-day, before turning to the past to study the antecedents which brought them about; antecedents which were fundamental in destroying two life styles and in causing the breakdown of inter-communal communication. Our starting point therefore is July 1974 and Turkey's military intervention to protect Turkish Cypriot interests.

I. Contemporary Perspective

In July 1974, in response to a direct threat to the Turkish Cypriot community, occasioned by the armed coup which deposed President Makarios and his government, Turkey intervened unilaterally with military forces.[2] By the middle of August those forces had occupied a third of Cyprus, displaced 200,000 Greek Cypriots, who fled their homes and became refugees in the unoccupied southern part of the island, and rendered ineffective the Greek Cypriot National Guard. In the twelve months that followed, those Turkish Cypriots who had till then lived in the south, moved or were moved on Turkey's demand to the north, leaving behind their property and most of what they possessed; creating in effect a double refugee problem, for not all found accommodation on arrival in the north.

The presence of 30–40,000 Turkish soldiers at least assures the physical security of the Turkish Cypriots against any form of attack from within or from outside the island. It does, however, create social problems which are inherent in any military occupation. Military controls and security priorities inevitably bring in their wake restrictions and deprivations for the civilian population, particularly in terms of freedom of movement and of choice. This in effect has been the situation that has faced the Turkish Cypriots since their 'liberation'; though safe from attack they do not have the freedom to move at will in the north.

Military priorities in situations like Cyprus will always affect the personal freedom of individuals and it is yet to be seen how long the authorities in the north intend that these priorities should be overriding. But one paramount factor arising out of the large military presence is that overnight the Turkish Cypriots have, so to speak, reversed the balance of power and can now dictate or deny from a position of strength – the minority calling the tune to which the majority must dance. Already they are in possession of a territorial third of Cyprus whilst only accounting for just over one sixth of its population. Backed by an overwhelming military superiority they have the potential to extend that territorial control. On the face of it it would seem that the Turkish Cypriots not only hold the initiative but also hold almost every card in the pack. But there is always the danger in such circumstances that it is the interests of the supporting external power that are the better served than those of the people themselves; so easily can the interests and aspirations of the inhabitants be over-ruled or ignored for the sake of international and national political expediency. In our analysis and later evaluation of the basic structures of inter-community life in Cyprus, it will be evident that this is what is now happening in Cyprus.

But military power is not everything. It cannot in a matter of months remove an innate psychological feeling of inferiority experi-enced by a minority group over more than a century; for psychologi-cally among the Turkish Cypriot community there remains deep down the same sense of inequality which existed before the present change in relationship. The outward manifestation of attitude and approach to the new relationship conceals a basic consciousness of their still being the minority, despite their recently acquired power superiority. But there is an added complication in the Cyprus scenario. For the Turkish Cypriots, the inferiority complex is double-edged; for it not only evolves from the inherent sense of being the minority group but also from the fact that without the strength of the Turkish army to back them their present equivocal position would be untenable. They are not therefore masters of their own destiny, nor are they wholly in control of their day to day affairs. No one can feel secure in such circumstances.

For two decades the Turkish Cypriot community has lived with a sword of Damocles hanging over its head. It has lived with an abiding and by no means wholly unjustified fear that the Greek Cypriots would one day drive them out of Cyprus. This fear and deep sense of insecu-rity governed their reactions and attitudes in the years between 1958 and 1974, and now dictates their approach to any measure of relation-ship between them and the Greek community. The uncertainty of the present and the future means that the Turkish Cypriots cannot relax their vigilance, cannot trust, cannot co-operate with their opposite community. Until they can, the chances of full communication and thereby inter-communal reconciliation, political and social, remain a matter for the future.

Possibly the most important factor dominating the Turkish Cypriots' consciousness is their desire for an identity and status. Probably it is this absence of identity that has affected the Turkish Cypriots most.

It could account for the refusal on their part to move towards any process of inter-communal understanding, co-operation and co-ordination of effort since separation took place two years ago. But identity is a very precious and sensitive possession and in this case for the Turks it is not so much a question of the Greek Cypriots according them their rightful recognition, but of the international community recognising that the Turkish Cypriot community exists as an established ethnic group with its own identity and status. It is understandable that the Turks should seek to be accorded a status and identity equal to that of their Greek Cypriot counterparts. However, it can be said with equal certainty that the lack of a Cypriot identity as such has aggravated the problems arising out of the 1960 Constitution and has emphasised the differences between the two communities. It is to be hoped that ultimately an acceptance of a common national identity will be forthcoming; for so long as inter-community rivalries exist and so long as there is inequality, socially and economically, between communities, the discriminatory factors in the present separatist situation will persist.

The effect of the 1974 events on the Greek Cypriot community was far more traumatic than that experienced by the Turks. Nearly one third of its people were displaced and turned into refugees, losing in the process most if not all that they possessed. In terms of real estate the rich agricultural area of the north came under Turkish control while the less fertile area of the south remained in Greek Cypriot hands. The booming economy from which the community had become rich collapsed overnight and became stagnant. From being total masters of their destiny the Greek Cypriots were suddenly at the mercy of others. The initiative was no longer in their hands, their bargaining position was negligible and they were faced with a 'dead' economy, the future viability of which was in doubt. The task of reconstruction and rehabilitation was one of immense proportions and could only be tackled slowly. Characteristically, however, the Greek Cypriots reacted positively from the beginning, though the Government proceeded cautiously with industrial and economic development projects for fear of giving the impression both to its own refugees and to the Turks that it had accepted the status quo. Now, two years after their world crashed around them, the Greek Cypriots have progressed some way along the road of economic recovery and have begun to re-establish their industrial potential. Analysis will show that it is in the nature of the Greek Cypriot's character to create, develop and expand, whereas the Turkish Cypriot is more inclined to wait and see. For the moment it is sufficient to remark that it is the Greek Cypriots who are working to overcome their disadvantages while the Turkish Cypriots are failing (or are unable) to profit from their advantages. Therefore in contrast to the Turkish Cypriots, Greek Cypriots have retained their sense of superiority despite all that has happened to them.

There is another psychological difference that commands consideration – the quality of fear. For the Turks it is very personal and relates to their individual safety and survival, whereas for the Greeks it has a collective quality, relating as it does to the threat of destruction of their whole community. The difference is not surprising when one appreciates that the period of personal danger for so many Turks has lasted since the middle 1950s, during which time the Greeks, except for two occasions when Turkey might have intervened, have experienced no physical threat at all. Though aware of the danger of further advances by the Turkish army and the possibility of an islandwide occupation, the personal safety factor was never mentioned during a visit we made to Cyprus in September 1974 (only weeks after Turkey had completed its second phase occupation). It was the fear for their continued existence as a community which was uppermost in their minds which they voiced to us. The Turks had never expressed their anxiety in quite the same way. Naturally they were fearful for their community's continued existence, but it was the more personal dread of "We will all be murdered in our beds" that impressed itself on the observer's mind; and it is this sentiment that will motivate the kind of attitude and approach that the Turkish Cypriots will adopt in securing viable safeguards for future peaceful co-existence in Cyprus.

Cyprus' current problem has not arisen simply from an act of discrimination by one ethnic group against another, but from a sequence of cause and effect in which both communities have suffered in turn; the evils of discrimination and denial of human rights which have generated both structural and manifest violence. External influences have played a significant role in shaping the present destiny of the Cypriot people, as they did in bringing about the catastrophe that befell their island. Regrettably, political and strategic interests being what they are, it does not appear likely that in the foreseeable future the island will be permitted to formulate its own future. Communication between the two communities is discouraged, only at the negotiation table and when Greeks and Turks meet outside Cyprus only then is the former friendly rapport temporarily re-established.

Because communication is denied, reconciliation will take longer and will be more difficult. Cyprus is a story of miscalculation and missed chances in the years since the second World War, partly intentional, partly unwitting, but all detrimental to the Cypriots. It has been the people of Cyprus who have been the sufferers, for communally they have been allowed to grow apart instead of together. The question is whether it is too late for them to come together to establish a viable unitary state.

Because of the predominance of the Greek-Turk confrontation there is a tendency when studying the Cyprus issue to overlook the existence of two other and much smaller ethnic groups, the Armenians and the Maronites. These two groups first settled in Cyprus in the 6th and 9th centuries AD and in the Middle Ages comprised a significant proportion of the population. The Maronites suffered severely at the hands of the Turks when they conquered Cyprus in the 16th century and have never regained their former position; instead the size of their community continued to dwindle. By 1960 Armenians and Maronites together represented less than 5% of the total population. Turkish discrimination against the Armenians has followed a similar pattern in Cyprus to the treatment they have received in Turkey itself; while escaping actual massacre, since 1963 they have been displaced from their homes, their property, their places of worship and their business. The tangled skein of Cypriot relationships does not confine itself therefore only to those between Greeks and Turks but can be seen within and between the different minority ethnic groups.

II. Historical Perspective

History has not permitted Cyprus to achieve an identity of its own, as has been the case in most other sovereign states that have obtained their independence from colonial rule since 1946. Some comment is clearly necessary to explain how the course of history in Cyprus has affected what would be the expected outcome of a country's fight for self-determination – a unified state. The lack of unity that has characterised Cyprus' short independent life stems from two distinct patterns in its demographic development. The first, the violent and turbulent nature of its history of conquest and liberation covering more than a thousand years, and second, the permissive attitude adopted by those who conquered towards the development of individual ethnic cultures.

Despite oppression and suppression the various ethnic were permitted to establish their own separate identities and to manage their own social and cultural affairs. But even from the beginning there was no attempt by those who ruled nor by those who were ruled to create a single Cypriot identity.

Cyprus' history breaks down into a number of distinct phases. Though historians would probably interpret them differently, for the purpose of this study they have been divided into six. Of these, five will be considered in the next section, while the sixth, which covers the period from July 1974 to the present day, will be considered separately at the end. The six are: *Years of Conquest: 294 B.C.–1571 A.D.; Under Turkish Rule: 1571–1878; British Administration: 1878–1960; Independence and Constitutional Crisis: 1960–1963; Civil War: 1963–1974;* and *The Divided Island: 1974.*

A. *Years of Conquest: 294 B.C.–1571 A.D.*

Cyprus' strategic position in the eastern Mediterranean gave it both a military and economic importance situated as it was 'at the crossroads of the civilisations of Europe, Asia and ancient Egypt'.[3] It is not surprising that it was a prize coveted by many a potential conqueror and experienced a constant procession of conquests and 'liberations' over the centuries. Each, however, though stamping its own particular mark on the cultural development of Cyprus, neither materially altered nor sought to tamper with its unitary structure, created by the Ptolemies of Egypt in 294 B.C. But despite this unification the ethnic pattern on Cyprus remained diffused and diversified. None of its early conquerors were over concerned about this. They were content to profit from its resources and to defend it against those seeking to snatch away the valued prize, rather than to colonise Cyprus and develop it. It was easier to allow the native population to manage their own affairs and religions and to leave them alone, so long as they paid their tithes and taxes. As Sir Harry Luke wrote, it was 'a land of antiquity and diversity of experience ... a land where races have met but never really mingled'.[4]

In succession over a period of 3,000 years, Egyptians, Romans, Lusignans and Venetians all came and went – conquering and in turn being conquered – while the indigenous people, largely of Hellenic origin, became the constant ethnic element in Cyprus' ever changing demographic structure. But the occupying powers were not the only influences that helped to mould and shape the future destiny of Cyprus. During the period of Egyptian rule the Phoenecians crossed the hundred miles of sea that separated their land (now the Lebanon) from Cyprus and established trading posts and settlements around the island which later expanded into towns and cities. Being a seafaring race they capitalised on the rich resources of Cyprus and developed profitably its trading capacity with neighbouring Mediterranean countries. The influence that the Phoenicians had on Cypriot culture was considerably greater than that exercised by the Egyptians or any of the subsequent occupiers. It was, however, settlers from the Aegean, of Mycenean origin, who founded the first indigenous colony in Cyprus in 1400 B.C. From these first settlers there developed the Greek community which to-day forms the major proportion of Cyprus' population. They never surrendered their Hellenic identity, and over the centuries strengthened and fostered ever closer cultural and emotional ties with their 'motherland'. When Alexander the Great created the Hellenist, empire the Hellenes on Cyprus offered him their allegiance and loyalty. This sense of unity was held together by the power of the Eastern Christian church which became the symbol of solidarity between Greeks and Greek Cypriots, unshaken by the ebb and flow of power politics and the violent sufferings that the latter experienced throughout their history. Absorbing one cultural experience after another, the Greeks in Cyprus remained ethnically aloof, avoiding fusion in any sense or form with the successive occupying powers.

It was from this inheritance that there emerged the hellenic dream of enosis (Union – with Greece) which dominated Greek Cypriot thinking in the 19th and 20th centuries, which led to the fight for self-determination and independence from the British in the 1950s, and ultimately became the issue on which Greek Cypriot supremacy, divided and disunited, foundered in July 1974.

B. *Under Turkish Rule: 1571–1878*

The Turkish conquest of Cyprus began in 1570 and was completed the following year. It was part of an expansionist programme in the Aegean and had been preceded by the capture of the island of Rhodes. The Venetians, the deposed rulers of Cyprus, had neglected the island for almost all of their 82 years of occupation, showing scant interest in its prosperity or the welfare of its people. Trade had been allowed to languish and cultivation had been neglected. Cyprus was therefore a relatively easy prey for the invader; even so when the attack came it was resolutely resisted by the Venetian defenders.

Initially the Cypriot islanders welcomed the arrival of the Turks for they had suffered much under the Latin Christians during the preceeding three centuries of their serfdom; being forced in the process to witness the luxurious life style enjoyed by the European traders and travellers whose wealth was built on the natural resources of their island. Their Orthodox church had been viciously persecuted. The Turks set them free of their serfdom and, somewhat ironically, reinstated their archbishop as head of the autocephalous church of Cyprus. Under the *millet* system of the Ottoman empire the various religious communities were committed to the care and authority of their church leaders, who were answerable in turn to the Ottoman authorities but who otherwise enjoyed comparative freedom providing that they remained loyal and dutiful subjects. Nevertheless, their rescue from the Venetians brought only relative relief for, as Christians, they were considered to be of inferior status to the Turks; they were referred to as *rayahs* ('human cattle') and treated as such. For the privilege of keeping their faith they were required to pay an additional tax – which gave rise to a category of person known as *lino-bambaki* ('flax-cotton-wool': i.e. a fabric woven of two different fibres) who were those who varied their faith as expediency demanded between Christianity and Islam.

Turkey governed Cyprus through an annual succession of governors. The Orthodox archbishop and his clergy co-operated with these gentlemen whom they assisted with the collection of taxes and other fiscal duties, acquiring increasing power and position until by the end of the 17th century they had become, in the eyes of foreign travellers and to the Turkish peasantry, equal in authority to the Governor himself.

In its 300 years of rule Turkey settled 20,000 of its people in Cyprus, most of whom remained after Turkey had ceded the island to Britain and were the forebears of the present generations of Turkish Cypriots. Turkey, however, achieved little else in terms of development and social change. Turkey to-day is not a rich nation, nor does it enjoy a thriving foreign trade. In Cyprus at the end of the 19th century the deterioration was almost as great as that inherited by Turkey 300 years previously. The initial honeymoon period did not last and soon the Greeks were experiencing similar degrees of persecution and neglect to what they had suffered from their former conquerors. The Turks quickly appreciated the superior skills and craftsmanship of the Greeks and their greater energy and employed them to do their work for them; even so, though the two races lived in relative harmony with each other the *millet* system precluded them from coming together. So far as the development of resources was concerned it seems that the Turks were no better than their predecessors. When Britain acquired responsibility for Cyprus in 1878 it found the island in a poor state. The land was impoverished, the forests had been devastated by human and animal depredations and soil erosion was extensive. A combination of drought, plague and locusts had further affected the deterioration so that the new administration was faced with daunting ecological, economic and social problems.

C. *British Administration: 1878–1960*

Whatever may be said in subsequent years about Britains' handling of the 1974 crisis and its attitude towards Turkey's second occupation of Cyprus, the period of Britain's administration was, economically at least, the most beneficial and secure in the island's history; it was also the most peaceful. Of the 82 years of British rule, 77 of them were peaceful, including those of both world wars. Within the colonial administrative system Greek and Turkish Cypriots, with members of other communities, shared civil service responsibilities, the legal profession was open to all and for the first time an inter-relationship outside the rigid conformity of ethnicity emerged and prospered; to a point where Greeks and Turks lived quietly together in the same villages, sometimes totally intermingled. The sense of security increased year by year and community life took on a new dimension.

In material gain Cyprus benefitted from the considerable expertise of the British in road and bridge building, harbour construction, communications and transportation services. Education improved with the building of schools and technical training raised standards in farming, forestry, animal husbandry and public health. A police force was formed under British officers and included members of all communities. The economic and ecological situation was established and improved consistently over the years. In the tradition of the British colonial system a High Commissioner was appointed (subsequently to become Governor) and in due course, with Britain's annexation of Cyprus in 1914, the Cypriots found themselves a part of the British

Empire – a transformation not to the liking of Greek Cypriot nationalists whose ultimate ambition was to belong to Greece.

Cyprus flourished during this period of colonial rule, becoming
economically more productive and more soundly established. Its
people benefitted from the increased wealth of the island and enjoyed
a higher standard of living than that found in most other eastern Mediterranean countries. By the time it obtained independence Cyprus
could claim that its living standards were comparable to those of many
European countries. It is therefore difficult to understand why the
British government was so totally reluctant to encourage, or even
permit, the Cypriot people to advance to independence; in fact its
policy was quite the opposite, as is shown by a statement in Parliament
in 1954 in which an Under Secretary of State[5] at the Colonial Office
declared that, whereas other colonial territories would in due course
receive their independence, Cyprus could 'never' expect to do so. Such
an obdurate intention to continue indefinitely the administration of
Cyprus as a Crown Colony could only derive from a belief that there
were other claims on the island which Britain could not ignore. On the
one hand there was the considerable proportion of Greek Cypriots
whose aspirations were for *enosis*. (In 1915 Britain had offered Cyprus
to Greece as an inducement to join the Allies against Germany but
the offer had been refused). On the other hand there had to be balanced Britain's post war relations with Turkey and its responsibilities
for the interests of the Turkish Cypriot community with which Britain
had always had considerable sympathy. The outcome was that Britain
decided that its proper course was to retain its dominion over Cyprus.
It therefore took no steps to mould and develop a core of Cypriot
unity, nor a sense of Cypriot identity. It is doubtful whether Britain
ever even contemplated doing so, but by this omission it missed totally
the opportunity of developing a pan-Cyprian attitude; preferring to
continue indefinitely to administer the different ethnic groups within
the crown colony.

On the surface during the first half of the 20th century all appeared
peaceful enough, but the frustrations that such a possessive attitude
provoked became increasingly unbearable. The Greek Cypriots'
underlying allegiance to Greece and their much proclaimed demand
for *enosis* began to assume larger proportions. Though many reacted
simply to the emotional appeal there were others, more militant,
prepared to fight for self-determination. By the early 1950s their voices
were being heard more and more. On the Turkish side the reaction

was one primarily of apprehension that, were Britain to accede to the demands of the enosists, Turkish Cypriots' lives would be at risk. Some insisted that if Britain were to give up Cyprus, the island should return rightfully to Turkey from whom it had been ceded as part of the secretly concluded Cyprus Convention of 4 June 1878.[6]

Britain, confident in its ability to govern Cyprus indefinitely, tended to ignore the Greek Cypriot manifestations as being inconsequential and frivolous. But in 1955 the Turks' fears were given a fresh impetus when under the leadership of Archbishop Makarios and General Grivas, the Greek Cypriots launched a guerilla campaign against the British, which lasted for four years and resulted in many Cypriots and Britons being killed. It did not, however, have the hoped for outcome for the Greeks – it achieved independence but not *enosis*. The Greeks saw this as only a temporary setback; *enosis* was still their ultimate goal and they continued to work for it. For the Turks independence was no final solution to their problem. In 1958 they had experienced a back-lash from the campaign against the British, when fierce inter-communal violence erupted in the capital of Nicosia and elsewhere during which a considerable number of people were killed and villages burned.

No Turk was sanguine about the prospects for the future, for the whole security of the community was at stake and many believed it was inevitable that sooner or later the Greeks would turn on them and destroy them.

D. *Independence and Constitutional Crisis: 1960–1963*

Cyprus became independent on 16 August 1960; an independence guaranteed under treaty by Britain, Greece and Turkey. By the terms of the 1960 Treaty of Guarantee, the three guarantors undertook to 'recognise and guarantee the independence, territorial integrity and security' of the new republic. Collectively or unilaterally they were empowered to act in the event of that independence, integrity or security being threatened. No other country had enjoyed such a guarantee on its decolonisation. It is to be regretted therefore that when implementation of the treaty's provisions was called for fourteen years later, this unique compact failed to stand the test of time. However, it was to be the constitution which was to crumble first. When it collapsed it opened the door for the inter-communal violence which so many had feared and which the architects of the Constitution had hoped to avoid.

First in Zurich and then in London representatives from Cyprus and from the three guarantor powers endeavoured to find an equitable constitutional compromise acceptable to all concerned. Proportionate representation in government, the House of Representatives, the civil service, police and the planned (but never constituted) defence force was insisted upon by the Greek Cypriots. This representation was agreed finally to be in the ratio of 7:3, except in the police and defence force where it was to be 6:4. In government, cabinet posts were allocated in the same manner, with the Turkish Cypriots opting for the Ministries of Defence, Health and Agriculture. This system of proportionate representation extended down the chain of administrative control to districts and municipalities. In the House of Representatives, in order to safeguard Turkish interests and status, it was agreed that separate majorities within each representative group would be required to enact certain laws and bills concerned with major issues and policies; foreign affairs and internal security were among these. This procedural arrangement meant that if eight of the fifteen Turkish members voted against a motion the bill, though passed by 42 votes to 8 against, could not become law.

The Constitution was full of anomalies and it soon became clear that there were parts of it which would be very difficult to implement. Discrimination by the Greeks against the Turks further aggravated the issues and heightened the latters' frustrations and fears. From the start the Greeks did not wish to recognise that the Turks deserved special consideration in respect of financial assistance. The Turkish community, by nature less enterprising, energetic and hard-working, was and always had been much poorer than the Greeks. But now, in order that the community could contribute to and share in the prosperity of Cyprus, it needed encouragement and help. It needed considerable investment in education, welfare services and economic development to bring the Turks up to a parity with the larger community. The financial aid allocated did not measure up to the requirement. To be effective it needed to be as much as 40% of the total development aid and educational programme, but it was restricted by the Greeks to 20%; equating with the proportionate size of the Turkish community's share of the total island population. This was subsequently raised to 28½% but it was still not enough for the Turks.[7] The Greeks being the richer community contributed most in taxes and they saw little reason why their money should be expended upon bolstering up a part of the population whom they considered to be indolent and idle. Had they been more far sighted they might have recognised not only the fairness but also the long term advantages to Cyprus in assisting to increase the potential of the less prosperous community.

It was, however, a different issue which more than anything else triggered off the ultimate breakdown of the Constitution and opened the way to violence. At the London and Zurich constitutional conferences it had been envisaged, and at that time strongly advocated by the Greeks, that there should be separate municipalities for the communities living in their own quarters of the five main towns. Such divided municipalities already existed under British law (1958). When, however, it came to the point of implementing the arrangement the Greek Cypriots reversed their opinion, declaring that it would be uneconomic, unworkable and certainly less efficient to excercise administrative control in this way, and that it would be preferable for there to be a single municipal authority for each of the towns, structured on the same proportional basis as had been agreed for the central government. The Turkish Cypriots certainly saw the single control system, and their inevitable minority status in it, as being a direct threat to their community's security. They saw in the Greeks' insistence a confirmation of their deep seated fear that the Greeks were determined so to weaken their position that their existing security and safeguards under the Constitution would eventually disappear. The immensely complex tax laws were an added complication which had not been resolved at the time of independence. Under the Constitution two communal chambers were set up to manage particular cultural, religious and ethnic matters affecting the respective communities. Among other responsibilities each communal chamber had been granted certain taxation rights over their communities. Neither was agreeable to the idea of additional taxes being imposed by central government. The issue of single municipalities immediately raised the question of municipal taxation. The Turks not surprisingly suspected that in a single municipal system their right to collect and disburse taxes from their own community would disappear; instead they feared that all taxes collected would be pooled for general purposes and that they, the Turks, would find themselves discriminated against. To prevent this from happening they vetoed, in December 1961, the income tax laws contained in the budget, thereby bringing about a constitutional impasse.

The argument for and against single municipalities remained unresolved until January 1963. Throughout that period the constitutional structure became more and more fragile.

The issue of the municipalities has been presented in some detail because it was the major single issue that led to the breakdown of the constitutional arrangements created in the London-Zurich Agreements. The issue was never settled and was to be reactivated nearly a decade later as part of the inter-communal negotiations. Then again it became a predominant and thorny issue which no amount of talking could resolve.

As year succeeded year from 1961 onwards, the constitution became more and more inoperable. Frustration on the part of Greek Cypriots intensified as the veto tactics of the Turks made it increasingly difficult to get important legislation through the House of Representatives. The Turk Cypriots on the other hand were stubborn in their resolve not to endorse any legislation that might weaken their already precarious position. In this constitutional vacuum the militant elements in both communities prepared themselves for the day when argument would end and fighting would begin.

Although a political confrontation and a degree of political and economic discrimination was being exercised, the public in general had not reacted openly to the problems arising out of power sharing. Peaceful co-existence was still very much in evidence in most parts of the island. There were those who tended to 'shout in the market places' that Greeks and Turks could never live together in peace; they were not much heeded for the fact that they could was there to be seen and for many was a part of their life style. There were, however, those who believed in and welcomed the inevitability of civil war between the communities. There was no shortage of arms. The Greeks had stored those used in their fight against the British, while the Turks had received consignments from Turkey. The more the political situation deteriorated the more prepared became the fighter groups. A few days before Christmas 1963 the first shots were fired and the first casualties resulted. It was five years before a stable ceasefire was achieved, but even then peace and a peaceful solution remained elusive.

The more one studies the story of Cyprus the more one becomes aware of its schizophrenic character. It is a pattern of imposed violence and peaceful co-existence interwoven like a patchwork quilt. Strangely enough, of the two it is the overspill of violence which is the more out of character, while it is peaceful co-existence which is the predominant feature of the life style of Cyprus. This is emphasised by the fact that despite the fighting which followed the 1963 outbreak of inter-communal violence, co-existence continued in parts of the island. Even after joint government had ceased and the Turkish Cypriot politicians had withdrawn to their quarter of Nicosia and set up their own administration under the Vice-President, communication did not entirely break down. Old friendships were honoured and former colleagues exchanged messages – sometimes even doing business together. This inbred relationship had been fundamental for so long that it was difficult to destroy; peaceful co-existence remained (and still remains) the spontaneous desire of a very large majority of the population. It is therefore hard to understand the failure of the two communities to arrive at an acceptable modus operandi; it is easy to say that opportunities were missed and that there was a lack of foresight during the period of British rule. The omissions were far more serious after independence when the Greek Cypriots failed completely to respond to the needs of the Turks, creating in them not reassurance but accumulating fear.

In Cyprus one cannot separate the history of the past from the history of the present. They are too closely related. School history books do not minimise the oppression and suppression of the past but tend to play them up. All Greek Cypriots are aware of their historic struggle against conquest and how despite it they acquired a self sufficiency and a superiority from which their considerable economic capacity grew. They sustained their cultural and social development and forged deep hereditary ties with mother Greece. The indifference and, in some cases, the scorn that they showed to the Turks was not unlike that of master to servant. (It was once described to us in these terms, "the Greeks are the employers, the Turks are the employees.")

The Turkish Cypriots' experience is very different. At first they came to Cyprus as conquerors, ruling the island for longer than anyone else. They were relatively unskilled and relied heavily on the Greek inhabitants for labour and expertise. When Britain replaced Turkey those Turks who remained on represented a minority community, lacking the military support to which they were accustomed. It would probably be true to say that the seeds of doubts as to their lasting security were sown then. It was not, however, until the EOKA[8] campaign towards the end of Britain's mandate that the Turks first came face to face with anything comparable to what the Greeks had experienced over the centuries, but it was enough to leave them with considerable disquiet about the future.

In the latter half of the 1950s the Turkish Cypriots saw that salvation lay in Britain's continuing presence in Cyprus. The intercommunal violence at the beginning of June 1958, in which over 50 Turks and an equivalent number of Greeks were killed, brought into clear focus what could happen were the status of Cyprus to change. It can be said with certainty that from that day fear really took hold and thereafter governed the Turks' every action. Every decision, every ploy, every proposal by the Greeks from then on was viewed against the perspective of Turkish Cypriot security and survival. From the moment that the constitution showed itself to be unworkable the Turks adopted a clear policy of 'no concessions to security'. In an atmosphere of impatience and indifference on the one side and obdurateness based on physical fear on the other, it is not difficult to appreciate how the breakdown came about. It remains, however, a matter of fact that the foundations existed on which a Cypriot entity could have been built had either side wished it and had indifference and fear not been such overriding factors in the dispute between the two. Had sympathy and encouragement replaced indifference and had trust and confidence replaced fear, a totally different scenario might have been played out in Cyprus over the past 16 years. As it was 1963 heralded the beginning of yet another period of turmoil for its people which is still far from being ended.

E. *Civil War: 1963–1974*

The fighting that began in Nicosia on the night of 21 December 1963 spread quickly to all corners of the island. In Nicosia and the other large towns Turk Cypriots fled their government and civil service posts and their places of business and withdrew within the confines of their own community quarters. The national army contingents of Greece and Turkey, permitted in Cyprus under the provisions of the 1960 Treaty of Alliance, left their assigned barracks and joined in the fighting (the Turkish contingent remaining thereafter inside the Turkish Cypriot enclave north of Nicosia). This action rendered both contingents ineffective so far as third party peacekeeping was concerned; a task which had to be shouldered in the first instance by Britain until the role was taken over by the United Nations in March 1964.

After the initial outbreak of acute violence which lasted some three months, the military situation crystallised into a classic intrastate conflict. Violence continued but was less excessive. There were incidents every day but, except in two major instances, they were contained and resolved by the United Nations peacekeeping forces before they could escalate into more serious eruptions of violence. Gradually over the next four years the UN peacekeepers lowered the temperature of the conflict and created an increasingly peaceful atmosphere, bringing about a defusion in tensions and a return to a situation of military sobriety.

During the course of the first few months of fighting Greece infiltrated clandestinely more than 5,000 of its national armed forces into Cyprus to support the newly formed National Guard.[9] (When these illegal troops were finally expelled in 1968 they numbered nearly 7,000). They were equipped with tanks and artillery. Turkey in comparison only deployed a handful of its officers and non-commissioned officers to lead the various fighter groups dispersed around the island using the six monthly rotations of their national contingent as the means by which they could be infiltrated into Cyprus. Militarily therefore Greece and Turkey participated in the fighting and para-military operations which followed, though it is clear that Greece's contribution was by far more comprehensive and laid the basis for the Greek army influence in Cyprus which in 1974 was to provide the backlash against Archbishop Makarios and his government.

The National Guard itself was not constitutionally authorised. It grew from a grouping together of all the Greek Cypriot guerilla and fighter groups that went into action in December 1963. It became the conscript army in which all Greek Cypriot youth was required to serve as a form of national service. It totalled over 10,000 at any one time and could call on a reservist resource of four times that number. Greek Cypriots, however, could only aspire to the more junior officer and non-commissioned officer ranks – the higher being held entirely by Greek army officers. The Turkish Cypriots had nothing comparable; they could only hope that Turkey would come quickly enough to their aid in an emergency to save them from being annihilated.

Between these two opposing 'armies' stood the United Nations peacekeeping force. During the four years of active conflict it fulfilled its mandate, preventing the annihilation that the Turkish Cypriots feared. Its mandate was not to make peace but to keep it. It did that and in the process created the atmosphere in which it was possible in June 1968 for the representatives of the two communities to come together and begin negotiations for a peaceful settlement of the dispute. It was not a failure on the part of the UN peacekeeping force that these negotiations did not succeed.

Military action aside and the potential threat that it posed to the physical survival of the Turkish Cypriots, there was another element of violence which imperilled their day to day lives and livelihoods; the structural violence of blockade. From the moment that the Turkish Cypriots withdrew into their enclaves and shut themselves up in their villages, their normal freedom of movement and the free movement of economic supplies into their areas ceased. An embargo was placed on the movement of any materials which in the broadest sense could be described as having a military use. The movement of Turks was strictly controlled and checked; police checkpoints and roadblocks being established on many roads. Schools and education in general in the rural areas suffered because the restrictions made it extremely difficult for children and teachers to attend school and for examination candidates to travel to the examination centres in the towns. Hospitalization of emergency medical cases was affected because of the reluctance of the Turks to travel under the threat of police arrest or detention en route. Postal services to the Turks were discontinued among other public service facilities. In those areas close to the forward confrontation lines agriculture came to a halt because the owners of land or grazing animals were either unable or unwilling to tend their land, harvest their crops or vines and graze their herds.

The economic blockade and embargo on the movement of materials into the enclaves and villages was almost total; for when one considers what does or does not have military use, most items fall into the former category – bricks, timber, cement, straw, building materials of all kinds, diesel oil, lubricants, machine spare parts, tools, gasoline; even clothing such as boots, denims, greatcoats were subject to rationing. In time the United Nations Force succeeded in easing the restrictions and acted as the honest broker in negotiating with the Cyprus Government for the release of reasonable quantities of all categorised goods, so that the Turks were subsequently able to receive the essential needs of livelihood. UN escorts supervised seeding and harvesting of crops, the grazing of animals in the confrontation areas and the marketing of produce. UN policemen observed at government roadblocks and checkpoints to ensure that there was no ill treatment of the Turks passing through them. Even so and even though the UN were successful in negotiating a relaxation of many of the other problems affecting education, medical treatment, postal and other public services, the degree of structural violence exercised against the Turks was considerable. It lasted four years and left its indelible mark; for a further six years after 1968 its effect dictated the lack of progress in the intercommunal talks. Though in 1968 the blockade and the embargoes came to an end and the right of freedom of movement was restored, the Turks remained apprehensive and suspicious. Having been subjected to violent discrimination for so long it was not to be expected that their Leadership would reciprocate with a return to normal understandings with the Greeks. The barriers around the enclaves remained up and though Turks could move freely around the island no Greek could pass into or through a Turkish controlled area unless escorted by the UN.[10] This restriction remained in force until 1974 when the whole of the north of Cyprus came under Turkish army control. It cannot be wondered at that the Turkish Cypriots should have remained so stubborn. They believed that any concession on their part would be taken as a sign of weakness. They felt no more secure than they had for the previous four years and were certain that were they to open up their enclaves they would be infiltrated and taken over by the Greeks. In all such situations the minority group has the most to lose in the way of human rights and personal freedoms; and it is therefore not surprising that it should fight every inch of the way to preserve them. The Turks were no exception.

In November 1967 the National Guard made a full scale assault with artillery and mortars on two neighbouring unprotected villages of Ayios Theodhoros and Kophinou in the southern part of Cyprus. Though Turkish Cypriot fighters had provoked the incident the attack and the degree of force used were wholly unwarranted. While failing to prevent the assault, the UN succeeded in bringing about a ceasefire within a few hours, but not before 22 Turks had died and 9 had been wounded.

Internationally the repercussions were considerable with major conciliation initiatives being taken by the UN and the USA to prevent a war situation developing between Greece and Turkey. (Turkey mobilised a sizeable invasion force and her air force flew sorties over the island). Ultimately the conciliators succeeded and the situation was defused; the illicit Greek army units on Cyprus were withdrawn and the Cyprus Government ended its four year blockade of the Turkish Cypriots. The November incident to all intents and purposes marked the end of the fighting between the National Guard and the Turkish Cypriot fighters and from then on it was to be political negotiation not military action that dominated the Cyprus scene. As a postscript to this tragic episode in November 1967, it is of interest that while the international placatory manoeuverings were proceeding, while a Turkish sea invasion appeared imminent, while war between Greece and Turkey was still a distinct possibility, the inhabitants of the mixed village of Ayios Theodhoros, both Greek and Turk Cypriots, were back together in their coffee shops not only exchanging conversation but also Christmas gifts. As so often in the past, the violence had been imposed by outside elements upon the ordinary Cypriot people. The aftermath, however, stiffened attitudes on the Turkish Cypriot side and further alienated the two communities, but an inter-relationship persisted at the personal level which not even the more devastating events of 1974 could entirely sever.

The remaining years of the civil war period were spent in intermittent political bargaining. The inter-communal talks made some progress in solving peripheral problems but solutions to major issues remained unobtainable. More than once the talks broke down and were discontinued only to start up again either by mutual agreement between the chief negotiators or as a result of third party initiatives. The aim was to create a unitary state but the suspicions were still too strong and, from the Turkish Cypriots' standpoint, the safeguards too weak for agreement to be reached on anything but general principles and the lesser issues. The major issues affecting the running of government, security and human rights and freedoms remained unresolved though some progress was made. Once again it was the difference of opinion over whether municipalities should be under a single or bicommunal control which represented an immovable stumbling block. Underlying the reservations of the Turkish Cypriot Leadership was the reluctance or intentional refusal of Archbishop Makarios and his government to declare unequivocally that *enosis* was no longer an issue and that it was no more the policy of the Greek Cypriots to seek union with Greece. Though statements were made by the Archbishop and others from time to time that *enosis* was an unrealistic proposition, there was left in the mind of the hearer the unspoken qualification that 'some time in the future' it might be. For the Turks the declarations never rang true, and so long as the uncertainty of purpose existed they remained suspicious of Greek Cypriot motives and anxious for their safety as a community.

III. COMPARISON OF LIFE STYLES

Before moving to an analysis of the final phase of Cyprus' history – the present – and to an appraisal of the possibilities of the future, it would be useful to consider in a little more detail the life styles of the two communities; for it is from these have emerged the inequalities which have conditioned the atmosphere in which the communities have grown up side by side. The solution of the present problems and the future prospects of co-existence will depend to some considerable extent on the mutual understanding and acceptance of these differences.

Any attempt to analyse ethnic or national characteristics must inevitably be subjective and provocative. In the case of the Cypriots it becomes additionally controversial because of the domestic anomaly, i.e. physical cohabitation but ethnic separation. Fundamental to the sociological dissimilarity is the variance in tempo in the approach to life of the two communities; a variance which is of deep significance for it reveals a sharp contrast in their respective life styles. Non-Cypriots often mistake the effects of this contrast as arising from discrimination, but such an interpretation is inaccurate, even though discrimination has more recently been a major factor in the exercise of the Greek Cypriots' attitude towards the Turks. Since it is so fundamental to basic attitudes and since the contrast in the two life styles is conditioned by the tempo level of the two communities, we use it as the starting point for this part of our analysis.

"Cunning and keen" was how a British diplomat[11] described the Cypriot Greeks, shortly before Britain took over Cyprus in 1878. 'Cunning' is an ambiguous word but there is nothing equivocal about the word 'keen'. It accurately discribes the Greeks, who, had they not been energetic and tenacious, would never have survived intact a millenium of suppression. They have developed an inborn energy, volatility and resourcefulness which has assured them of success in their economic enterprises. Before the collapse of their 'boom' world in 1974 the Greek Cypriots had created a wealth potential which could in time have matched that of the most prosperous of the eastern Mediterranean countries. The island's export capability had been growing fast; even so the limit of its economic capacity had not been reached but was still expanding. Enterprise and initiative, the readiness to take a gamble, the insatiable appetite for work and profit gave the Greeks a raison d'être which was above politics. They felt secure, confident and invulnerable and saw no reason why they should not continue that way. This prosperty did not touch only the upper levels of Greek Cypriot society, it was available to the hitherto poorer and less endowed. Land holdings in the 1950s and 1960s increased enormously in value. There was an increasing demand for land for development as well as for building. Foreigners wishing to settle in Cyprus or to own a holiday home were anxious to buy and were willing to pay inflated prices. Suddenly a new social strata of wealth began to emerge. The former poor villager or even peasant who owned anything from 5–20 donums (one third of an acre) found that he or she had a saleable commodity and many took advantage of the opportunity to profit from the rush to buy land. Nowhere was there unemployment.

In contrast the Turks of Cyprus are less venturesome and not so energetic as their Greek counterparts. It is not their nature to exert themselves in the same way and though they are enterprising in developing small business interests (it was noticeable on our visit to the Turkish quarter of Nicosia in September 1974 that a number of traders had opened new shops and businesses), for the most part they have not built up big businesses or major export enterprises. Unlike the volatile and impulsive Greek, the Turk tends to take an appreciable time to make up his mind; as a result, opportunities are lost and he misses out on the benefits. The progress made by the Greeks has not been paralleled by the Turks, even when the same opportunity has been available to both. As an illustration of this there was an occasion some years back when a prosperous Greek Cypriot owner of extensive vineyards in the south of Cyprus decided to improve the quality of his wine by introducing a new strain of vine. This entailed digging up and replacing all the vines on his estate. Financially it would mean forgoing several years of profit from the harvest of his existing crop. It was a sacrifice he was prepared to make. So far as the villagers were concerned to whom he offered cuttings of the new strain, it meant putting their existing livelihood at stake. The Greek villagers, though reluctant to give up their immediate source of income, believed nevertheless that if the owner considered it worth doing then it must be so. They therefore dug up their old vines and replanted with new ones. The Turkish villagers on the other hand were not so convinced and refused the offer; they could see no advantage in changing from what seemed to them to be a perfectly satisfactory system. Ten years later they became aware of the obvious success of the change and the increased profits enjoyed by their fellow Greek villagers. Only then did they decide to accept the offer of new cuttings, which in this case was still open.

From the differences in their respective natures and thereby the life styles of the two communities, has come an inequality not only in financial terms but also in living standards. In the back streets of Turkish quarters in the main towns one finds conditions similar to those in the less sophisticated Arab and Asian societies. Not having created the same wealth potential it is not surprising that the Turkish Cypriots appear so underprivileged. Where Turks and Greeks lived together or as neighbours in mixed villages, or in mixed village communities in the rural areas, the distinction was not so marked. However, since the largest proportion of the land of Cyprus was owned by the Greeks the opportunities of advancement open to them were very much greater than those open to the Turks. While Greek Cypriots were growing richer and more affluent, the Turks dropped economically further behind.

A. *Education*

Education has been another divisive factor, as it has been in other countries where the ecclesiastical authorities have been in control of the schools. Under the Ottoman *millet* system education was on denominational lines, with each ethnic community responsible for its own. When the British took over there was hardly a village in the island in which one could find a single literate person.[12] In 1878 there were 63 Moslem schools receiving financial support from the Evqaf (Turkish office in Cyprus administering Moslem religious property), and 83 Christian schools supported by voluntary contributions. In the former the principal subject was the recitation of the Qoran, while in a few schools some elementary reading and writing was taught. All were poorly attended. In the Christian schools education was far more comprehensive with teaching in sacred history, arithmetic, geography and ancient Greek. In some Nicosia schools English, French and German were included in the curriculum.

The contrast was summed up at the end of the first year of British rule by the then Chief Inspector of Schools, Canon Newham, as "a vivid contrast between races; the Moslems conservative, contented with little but some organization; and the Christians eager after some new thing and alive to the advantages of a liberal education ..."[13]

Gradually every village in the island came to have its school, but denominational segregation continued as it had under the *millets*. The prime need as the British saw it was to establish a satisfactory system of primary education throughout the island under the Department of Education. Village authorities were given grants and loans to assist in this process and schools when established were subject to regular departmental inspection. Secondary education on the other hand was less rigidly controlled, remaining under community direction. A shortage of sufficiently trained Greek Cypriots necessitated secondary school teachers being brought in from Greece. Thus there developed in British controlled Cyprus an anomalous situation in which most of the Greek gymnasia and their curricula came directly under the aegis of the Ministry of Education in Athens. In allowing this, Britain had opened the door to the propagation of Greek nationalism and the fostering of the 'hellenic dream' – *enosis* – within the school system in Cyprus. Nothing comparable occurred in the Turkish Cypriot schools but the insemination of Turkish history and the glories of the Ottoman Empire became in time as important an aspect of the young Turkish Cypriot's education as learning the Qoran.

It was not until much later when institutes for higher technical training were established that there was any real opportunity for Greeks and Turks to study together in a place of education. There had been certain inter-communal secondary education available at the English School (founded 1900) and later at two American mission schools; but these were largely for fee paying students, although grants were available to intelligent children from poorer backgrounds. The higher training establishments and the inter-communal schools were forums of learning in which harmony and co-operation existed between all students. It is ironic that in the years of strife and confrontation immediately preceeding the 1974 July coup and its aftermath, these integrated educational systems were increasing in popularity and membership, enrolling a proportionately greater number of Greeks and Turks each year, despite a decade of apparent separation of the two communities.

For their university education young Cypriots in the main went either to Ankara or to Athens, but many found their way to the universities in Britain and the USA – scholarships, public grants or private wealth permitting. At the higher level of secondary education the disparity between Greek and Turk was less. It did, however, provide a side effect which has a relevance in more ways than one to the out-come of events in Cyprus. Within the communal society of Cyprus, Turks were competing with Armenians and Greeks for the jobs in the public services and government departments. In Turkey, where educational standards were far below those in Cyprus, there was a major deficiency of suitable people to fill responsible posts. Turkey therefore recruited for these posts young Turkish Cypriots whose secondary education had given them among other qualifications a fluency in English as great as that in Turkish. In educational profi-ciency they outmatched their mainland contemporaries and in Turkey they enjoyed a superiority that they could not command in Cyprus. It was small wonder that with the field wide open to them, many young Turkish Cypriots emigrated to the country which to many of them was their motherland. It resulted in a steady 'brain drain' of talent away from Cyprus and has deprived the Turkish Cypriot community of a resource of expertise that it could ill afford to lose; either in the politi-cal, the economic or the social sense.

To-day, because of a history of inter-denominational segregation in education, because of the stillbirth of the inter-communal institutes, because of a decade of inter-community conflict in which Turkish school age children suffered from disruption of their education, there are many young Cypriots in each community who have never met with young members of the other. In the situation existing to-day it is inevitable that a whole new generation of Greek and Turkish Cypriots will grow up without knowing each other, except as enemies. For an island whose people are by nature happy and generous hearted, and whose older generations cherish long standing friendships with each other, such a reversal of behaviour would be a tragedy. It poses a permanent threat to peaceful co-existence, in whatever form, were hate rather than friendship to become the criterion by which young Greeks and Turks assess their relationship to each other in the future.

B. *Co-existence*

Co-existence has been the measure of life on Cyprus ever since the first settlers arrived on the island. It has been the pattern of its history despite its turbulence. It has been the structure of inter-community life for more than a century and was a matter for comment by the British Vice Consul in 1874 when he noted that "the Moslems . . . live in harmony with their Christian neighbours in town and country."[14] Though in the towns and in some of the mixed villages each community lived separately in their own quarter, freedom of movement and the opportunity to communicate prevailed throughout the island. Greeks and Turks worked side by side in the fields, in the vineyards and citrus groves, in the mines and in the factories. They served together in the administration and in the police force. In the days when there was a Cyprus Regiment they soldiered together.

Peaceful co-existence depends upon inter-communication and that element existed in community relations during the first half of the 20th century, despite ethnic differences. The level of communication in certain situations was such that a group of villages would create their own mixed society, developing a co-operation and relationship which defied outside pressures to disrupt it. The same can be said about the mixed villages where the two communities were wholly inter-mingled. In these villages the inhabitants developed a mutual sym-pathy and respect for each, shared each others' coffee shops (the village meeting places) and came to the assistance of each other in time of need or in an emergency. There are many instances of this happening during the years of violence and during the war of 1974 when Greek helped Turk and Turk helped Greek when threatened. It was more than a mere rapport engendered through many years of living to-gether; it was a much deeper bond than that which activated a kind of loyalty one to the other.

C. *Local Government*

Neither under Ottoman nor British rule was Cyprus given an oppor-tunity to develop a system of local government. The British established an excellent civil service in which all communities participated. There was a measure of self administration within rural areas where villagers elected from within their own ranks members to committees responsible for all aspects of village life: church, education, water rights and co-operatives for marketing of produce. But in all other respects govern-ment was centralised. This policy was the cause of deep resentment, particularly to the Greeks, since in the Legislative Council the com-bined vote of expatriate, government appointed and Turkish members, when supported by the Governor's casting vote, was sufficient to block any controversial measure put forward by the Greeks. "This power pattern became a permanent feature of the administration of Cyprus, even when the proportions of the population changed more heavily in favour of the Greeks. It became a source of intense frustration to the Greek Cypriots and served to widen the gulf, politically between them and the Turkish Cypriots.[15] On the Turkish side the frustration was of another kind. The Turks' share of official appointments was considerably less than that given to the Greeks. Their frustration to a certain extent was of their own making, because many of the appointments required technical qualifications which no Turk in Cyprus at that time possessed but which Greeks did. Though there was no act of discrimination at the time, the passage of years helped to obscure the circumstances and it became another cause for jealousy and resentment.

In the light of this background of co-existence and inter-relationship separation is a new and unnatural phenomenon. It has meant that whole families and urban/rural communities have been driven or uprooted from their homes and from the environment in which the family had lived for generations. Mass transference of population poses considerable problems of physical and mental adjustment. Loss of home and property, perhaps for ever, has its personal traumatic consequences, but the consequences of the destruction of a way of life are far greater. It would therefore be unrealistic to suppose that all those Turks who moved from the south to the north of the island will be satisfied in their new environment and content never to see their homes again; sooner or later they will wish to return. However, set against this there will be a majority who will see in the move a guarantee of greater personal security – and who can blame them after suffering the fears of a decade of violence. Nevertheless, the general consensus of the latter category, expressed to us during our conversations with them in April 1974, was that primarily they were looking for safety in numbers; but that once their security was assured and firmly established, they were anxious that old inter-communal relationships should be restored so that members of both communities would be able to work together again. They recognised this would necessitate a restitution of freedom of movement throughout the island, and it was this that the majority of those to whom we talked wanted, as a prerequisite to the basic human right of freedom of choice.

Even though the Greek Cypriots' plight at that time was different, many in the community deeply regretted the departure of the Turks with whom they had lived in friendly neighbourliness and harmony for so long, expressing the hope that one day they would return to their homes. Many of those Greek Cypriots who are now refugees from the north and who have lost everything are hoping that one day they will be repossessed of their own homes and property. They are, however, well aware of the weight of guilt and responsibility that the Greek community has to bear for what happened to their world in July 1974. In effect they too look for the day when the two communities can co-exist and collaborate again. They speak of the Turks with whom they lived and worked in the north as friends and on the whole without malice. Co-existence therefore is what the Cyprus problem is all about. It has been shown in the past that it can work; time will tell whether it is to be the pattern for the future.

D. *The Divided Island: 1974*

Within one year of the coup that temporarily overthrew the government of Archbishop Makarios, complete separation of the two communities had taken place and the dividing lines had been drawn so far as the Turks were concerned. In the process all but a handful of the 60,000 Turkish Cypriots living in the area controlled by the Greeks had moved or been moved to the north. With physical inter-communication at an end, except at the negotiation table, the immediate chances of reconciliation and a renewal of former relationships were slight. As time passed and no progress was made at the negotiation table those chances became more and more remote.

On the face of it it would appear that the Turkish Cypriots are determined to pay back the Greeks threefold for the indignities and discrimination they suffered in the past. If this is their policy then they have kept the pressure on the Greeks, demanding concession after concession from them without making a single concession themselves. They have given up none of the territory that was occupied during the fighting in 1974 and have indicated that if they decide to do so the amount will be peripheral. In the political context they have stood firm on a bizonal structure for Cyprus within a loose central government system; in which Turkish Cypriots would share equal responsibility on a basis of complete parity.

These are just the bare facts and do not take into account the influence and supporting strength of Turkey in the outcome of events in Cyprus since 1974. Turkey's proximity and its considerable military strength, which enabled it to station 30–40,000 troops in Cyprus, has been the dominating factor. It is doubtful whether the Turkish Cypriot leadership can make any significant political decisions without first obtaining clearance from Ankara. It is also questionable to what extent it has a free hand in managing its day to day affairs, bearing in mind the overriding military presence on the island. The Turkish military authorities have isolated the north from any contact with the south; even foreign diplomats and pressmen are restricted in their freedom of movement. The Turkish Cypriots themselves do not have free access to any part of the north, being substantially limited in their movements outside their home towns or villages. In effect the northern part of Cyprus has become, at least for the time being, an armed camp under military control.

As a result of this self imposed isolation it is difficult to obtain any clear idea of what is the situation in the north. It is, however, possible to assess some of the effects that the isolation has had on the social, economic and demographic structures of Cyprus as a whole. Since the beginning the normal public services have operated separately. Even though there have been negotiations and frequent meetings between parties on political issues, the Turks have not agreed to take part in any comparable discussions between the respective authorities on the joint or co-ordinated management and functioning of the public services. One of the more valuable legacies of the British administration was the high standards it created in animal husbandry and the control of malaria and plant disease. As a result of strict discipline, foot and mouth disease, swine fever, fowl pest, rabies and Mediterranean fruit fly were unknown in Cyprus for the last fifty years. Turkey on the other hand is less fortunate and most of the diseases from which Cyprus remained free were endemic there. So the uncontrolled movement of large bodies of men, animals and the importation of meat and offal from Turkey into Cyprus presented a major threat to the island's former immunity. Similarly the anopheles mosquito had been effectively eliminated from Cyprus; now because an island wide control programme no longer operates malaria too could sweep the island – for a ceasefire line is no barrier to the mosquito. So far none of these potential dangers has manifested itself, but the threat remains so long as there is no central organisation to ensure that the old disciplines are perpetuated.

The determined opposition by the Turks to any co-operation in the essential island services extends into realms of public health and medical treatment. Even the treatment of Turkish cancer cases by the cancer clinic in Nicosia was denied because it was staffed and operated entirely by Greek Cypriots, although no facilities for treating cancer existed on the Turkish side. It is the same story in respect of treatment for kidney disease.

It is difficult to understand how such apparent inhumanity can be condoned for the sake of political ends unless one attempts to understand the motivation behind it. At the beginning of this chapter we commented upon the importance to the Turkish Cypriots of identity and status and how their attainment pre-empted all other considerations. It is relevant to refer back to this underlying premise on which the Turkish Cypriots so clearly base their geopolitical future. They have for so long been relegated in their eyes to an inferior position in Cyprus and treated as a minority. They now insist upon parity and having achieved dominance they are determined, as a community, never again to be looked upon or classified other than as a people with an identity and an international status. It is this preoccupation with their destiny that could be behind their resolve not to accept any form of assistance from the Greeks or to co-operate in joint endeavours however beneficial they may be to their own people. For by doing so they could very well feel that they would be weakening their position and making themselves vulnerable to Greek superiority. Clearly they are determined to avoid placing themselves in the position of being under the thrall of the Greeks and becoming submerged to the extent of losing their identity and status.

It is the economy of Cyprus that has suffered most from the separation of the two communities. Cyprus has never before had a divided economy – a factor that has been its strength throughout the vicissitudes of its history. It has been said that the island cannot survive were it to lose its economic singularity. Certainly it is doubtful if it could achieve the kind of prosperity that is potentially there for the taking, were there to be separate economic systems for any length of time. It is equally a fact that if the people of Cyprus are to enjoy that prosperity there needs to be inter-communal economic understanding and co-operation. The point has already been made that the Greeks were the architects and creators of the boom economy of the 1950s and 1960s. That economy derived most from its agricultural assets and from tourism, both of which depended heavily on the northern part of the island, where the majority of citrus groves and farmland were to be found and where the beaches were the most appealing to the tourist trade. To-day the Greeks are left with the far less fertile land in the south and a virtually undeveloped tourist potential. As one might expect, they have already begun to make a start at creating something out of a little and one has little doubt that in the light of their nature they will make progress. On the other hand, the profitability of the north is likely to diminish because of the difference in potential between the Turk and the Greek. This does not mean that the land will become fallow and the groves will die, but considerable damage can be suffered from the failure to harvest; during the first year after separation took place unpicked fruit was left to rot on the citrus and olive trees. This disinclination on the part of the Turkish Cypriots to leap at the opportunity to profit from such assets stems not so much from laziness as from an innate reluctance to work someone else's land.

Respect for property rights is a deep seated moral issue for most Cypriots. The right of ownership is recognised as a fundamental principle of social ethics, rising above political considerations. The confiscation and redistribution to Turks of Greek owned houses and property completely cut across all that had hitherto been accepted and cherished as a social dictum. One appreciates that necessity may have forced many Turks from the south to occupy Greek owned property because the alternative was an open field; even so the sentiment of other Turks still in the south in April 1974 was that it was tantamount to stealing. The reluctance therefore to work on land and to harvest crops which are the property of another, and to accrue financial benefit from so doing, indicates that the principle is not dead. It is a matter of conjecture as to how long it will remain alive.

The Greeks on their part have held to the principle and continued to respect the property rights of the Turkish Cypriots who have gone north. Very little squatting has taken place in consequence of the Government's policy that Turkish Cypriot property will not be taken over or confiscated. Where occupation has been permitted the occupiers are required to pay rent into a government holding account against the day of the rightful owner's return. Despite the continued presence of 18,000 Greek Cypriots in the refugee camps, this policy is being respected and in many mixed villages the Turkish houses have been locked up, inventories of their contents recorded, and the Greek mukhtars (headmen) hold the keys and make periodic inspections to ensure that all is in order. Again it is conjecture how long this philanthropic gesture will last, for one must assume that it is a matter of expediency for the Cyprus Government to avoid in every way the suggestion that the Turkish Cypriot property is being exchanged for the Greek Cypriot property in the north. So far as some Turkish Cypriots are concerned they leased their land on a 1–2 year basis to their Greek neighbours before leaving, obviously believing or at least hoping that they would be able to retain ownership or return to it later.

It is difficult at the present time to see how the issue of property ownership is going to be resolved. The answer might be a form of moratorium on ownership of all land vacated by members of either community during and after the fighting. The moratorium could be for a period of up to ten years during which time the right of ownership would not pass from the legal owner, who would receive some form of compensatory rent where land was being worked. However, any solution of the problem will depend upon some form of inter-communal collaboration being established.

Possibly the matter of greatest significance during the post 1974 period has been the reported influx in large numbers of Turkish nationals from the mainland. It is a fact that some immigration has taken place, what is uncertain is its extent. Whether it is part of a major colonisation plan of Turkey remains to be seen but if, as is widely reported, it is continuing, some concern is natural – for two reasons. First, any colonisation programme endangers the demographic structure of Cyprus and, if continued indefinitely, could change it radically. Second, an extensive immigration programme could create a Turkish province in Cyprus in which the Turkish Cypriots could easily become a minority group within a Turkish community. The repercussions from such a development would be considerable and far reaching though quite impossible to assess at this time. It is not, however, a possibility that should be ignored.

It is not our intention to make an evaluation of the possible future developments in the Cyprus situation. It is too much in a state of flux at this time to make any fine judgments or forecast the future. What this chapter has attempted to do has been to present a scenario in which two communities have confronted each other over four centuries, lived for long periods in an atmosphere of peaceful co-existence and finally have broken apart. It has been an attempt through a series of perspectives to analyse and comment on the many aspects of their histories and life styles so as to help the reader to understand how it is that Cypriots are not a race of people but an arrangement of ethnic groups. Set against those perspectives it is perhaps possible more readily to comprehend the motivations that have led Cyprus to the situation that it finds itself in to-day.

'Saki' probably had it right when he wrote "Cyprus is an island in the eastern Mediterranean which persistently produces more history than it can conveniently consume locally."

NOTES

1. Benjamin Disraeli's comment was made at the Congress of Berlin in June 1878.
2. Article IV of the 1960 Treaty of Guarantee provided for its guarantor powers (Britain, Greece and Turkey) to take collective or unilateral action to uphold the independence, territorial integrity and security of the Republic of Cyprus.
3. *Cyprus: An Appreciation*, by Sir Harry Luke, p. 20.
4. *Ibid.*, p. 20.
5. Mr. H. Hopkinson (now Lord Colyton) in House of Commons debate on 24 July 1954.
6. *A History of Cyprus*, by Sir George Hill, Vol. IV, p. 269.
7. *Cyprus: A Place of Arms*, by Robert Stephens, p. 173.
8. Ethniki Organosis Kyprion Agonistou (National Organisation of Cypriot fighters) was the organisation that fought the British and of which General Grivas was the leader. It was its successor EOKAB which led the coup against Archbishop Makarios in July 1974.
9. Formed from Greek Cypriot irregular fighter groups by General Grivas on his return to Cyprus in June 1964 and officered by Greek army officers. *The Impartial Soldier*, by Michael Harbottle, p. 169.
10. A twice daily convoy was permitted by the Turkish Cypriot Leadership to travel under UN escort between Nicosia and Kyrenia through the Turkish main enclave. *Ibid.*
11. P. H. White, British Vice Consul in Larnaca, Annual Report for 1862. *Cyprus Under the Turks*, by Sir Harry Luke, p. 210.
12. Luke, *op. cit.*, p. 94.
13. *Handbook of Cyprus (1913)*, by H. C. Lukach and D. J. Jardine, pp. 133–34.
14. White, *op. cit.*
15. Stephens, *op. cit.*, p. 107.

The Persecution of Christians in the U.S.S.R.

KESTON COLLEGE STAFF STUDY

edited by

MICHAEL BOURDEAUX

REV. MICHAEL BOURDEAUX is Director of Keston College, Kent, England, the Centre for the Study of Religion and Communism. He has spent twenty years studying in communist countries – especially in the U.S.S.R. where he was a student at Moscow University.

His writing has established standards of objectivity, and his books *Religious Ferment in Russia*, *Patriarch and Prophets* and *Faith on Trial in Russia* have been read in many countries.

He recently returned from a visit to Russia, where he was repeatedly told by Christians that Keston's work was *invaluable* and must be *expanded at all costs*.

The Persecution of Christians in the U. S. . .

KESTON COLLEGE STAFF STUDY

edited by
MICHAEL BOURDEAUX

Soviet delegates at international conferences
crimination in South Africa, Chile and other c
of discrimination in the U.S.S.R. is ever raised
Soviet delegates are present, severe problems
sphere, this rarely seems to happen. When the su
against believers and others was raised at a re
Central Committee of the World Council of C
European representation, led by the chief Sovi
another rose to deny the accusations.[1]

There appears to be a conspiracy of silence in the
regarding discrimination in the U.S.S.R. Yet the f
The present essay will deal solely with the pers cu
the U.S.S.R., although there are many other are
nation in need of investigation.

I. Religion and the State

Communism, first conceived as an economic
evolved into a system claiming the right to legisl
area of life: economic, political, social, artistic,
This is certainly the case in the Soviet Union whe
that socialism has been achieved and communism is

The existence of the Communist Party of the S
dominant force in Soviet society automatically f
(whether active or passive) any individuals or g
the current Party line in any area. In some sen
huge number of people. At the same time, the
population has probably inherited a good deal of

sivity of the Russian nation. Over centuries of tsarist rule, the Russians have been accustomed to non-participation in the governing process, and have mostly contented themselves with exploiting an arbitrary system wherever possible.

Since the Communist Party claims the right to legislate for all Soviet citizens in the ideological sphere, it is clear that there must be some kind of clash with religion. In fact, religion is the only ideology other than communism which is officially tolerated in the Soviet Union. But the tolerance level is low, and often breaks down completely.

Most Christian communities in the U.S.S.R. today offer no deliberate opposition to their national power structures. Most Soviet Christians take seriously the biblical command to obey secular authority (at least, where it does not directly command disobedience to God). A few years ago, there was a group of Orthodox-oriented intellectuals in Leningrad who talked about overturning the government and establishing a new rule based on Christian principles. It was, however, an idealist circle that offered no real threat to the state. The group was betrayed and its leaders given ridiculously harsh sentences. This incident is the exception which proves the rule.[2]

In the main, Christian communities – even those which suffer the worst persecution – maintain a high degree of loyalty to the Soviet authorities. The Russian Orthodox Church for centuries was closely associated with the tsarist rule and today, in a curious way, it continues to see itself – and even seems to be regarded by some communist functionaries – as the "ruling Church." All non-Orthodox confessions knew some degree of discrimination or persecution before 1917, and have thus been able to adapt to the Soviet situation without immediate disorientation. In fact, for a few years immediately following the October Revolution, evangelical Christians experienced a previously unknown liberty, which they exploited to the full. But whether tolerated or persecuted, most Christian communities retain a basic loyalty to the Soviet state – they only ask for internationally-recognised human rights and for the religious freedoms guaranteed under early Soviet law.

A Pentecostal pastor, Ivan Fedotov, was sentenced in April 1975 to three years in strict regime labour camp. The main charge against him was "slandering the Soviet state and social order." In his post-trial appeal, Fedotov described his difficult early years and exclaimed: "All this shows that I was born under the Soviet power, I grew up and went to school under it, I served in its navy and worked in state enterprises –

how could I slander the Soviet state and social order? This is my country, I live in it, I breathe its air, I make my small contribution of work and mental effort along with everyone else."

More lyrically, here is a poem written by a Baptist pastor while in labour camp in 1968:

MY LOVE AND MY SONG IS RUSSIA

A bleak land of forests and snow...
Garlands of snow tenderly embrace the firs...
Between its snow-covered banks the taiga river
Dreams of spring and the April floods.

The white sails of the clouds across the sky
Bear a gift of great snows to the south.
On frosty days I whisper with tears in my eyes:
"My love and my song is Russia!"

The time will come: the rays of spring
Will melt the snow, and the tree-tops in the forest will straighten
The taiga streams will run
To bow in greeting to the great rivers.

The river banks will turn green
And the wind will play above the waves,
The meadowlands will be clothed with children,
Like lush, bright flowers.

A flock of cranes descending to a stream
Will cry out in greeting to its native haunts;
On a spring day, I whisper rapturously:
"My love and my song is Russia!"

Accustomed from childhood to bear misfortune,
I have endured partings, waited for meetings.
Protectively, I bore my dream
Of your happiness, my native land.

Believing in a supreme Love,
Which comes to us across the storm of ages,
Today I repeat again and again
That man's happiness is in Christ alone.

For your happiness I am ready to give up
My whole life and my young strength;
To say with joy as I die:
"My love and my song is Russia!"[3]

more moving when one realises that the author,
nded from Western European immigrants to

n of loyalty and indeed love from the Christian
horities have exercised a constant discrimination
s varied from cool tolerance to outright persecu-
ntemporary exigencies and on local factors. But
ny genuine relaxation in their basic drive against

INDOCTRINATION AND ITS CONSEQUENCES

ies have demonstrated with their intensive pro-
ctrination how highly they assess the ideological
ristianity. This indoctrination pervades the entire
nd also affects public life at every possible point –
es of work, atheist programmes on radio and tele-
ys, materials in newspapers, magazines and books,
to has also implemented a wide range of ineptly-
ng," secular ceremonies to replace Christian ritu-
marriage, funeral, First Communion, Harvest
new traditions" are often rejected by the people,
tle enthusiasm.
iet Constitution in theory guarantees freedom of
tians have rightly pointed out that in practice,
n denies this. In fact, Anatoli Levitin, a Russian
living in the West, has even argued that neither
s free under this system. He wrote in 1965:

not free, just as religion is not free. The situation of
strongly recalls the situation of the Orthodox Church in
Russia. Orthodoxy at that time, as is well known, was the
ll disputes with it were categorically prohibited. The
because it was under compulsion. Atheism is not free in
recisely because it is under compulsion, obligatory and
n. Therefore the struggle for religious freedom is also a
m of atheism, for methods of compulsion (direct or in-
sing atheism, depriving it of all ideological significance,
nation. Therefore, long live free religion and free

On a more down-to-earth level, Aida Skripnikova, a young Baptist from Leningrad, once suggested:

It is absurd to announce that if believers were to be given freedom, then this would be an infringement of the workers' freedom of conscience. How could it constitute such an infringement if a Christian periodical, such as "The Young Christian" or "Joyful News" were to lie beside "Komsomol Truth" in a kiosk? Only those who wished to would buy our periodicals. This is no more than justice and only in this way can one interpret freedom.[5]

We have already quoted Levitin's judgment on the "freedom of atheism." There can be no doubt that the supremacy of atheist propaganda sometimes backfires. Petras Plumpa, a Lithuanian Catholic, stated at his trial in December 1974:

In reading the works of the philosophers, I saw the constant battle which atheists waged against God. I began to think – if God does not exist, why should anyone fight the non-existent? But what if he does exist? ... Wanting to hear the other side of the question, I began to read religious books. In this way I found God and came to believe. Until 1961, I despised religion and never went to church; I understood nothing of God. Since 1969 I have never been deceived in my faith, and I firmly believe to this day.[6]

During an interrogation at the Moscow Procuracy in the summer of 1972, Orthodox priest Dmitri Dudko remarked:

Young people are interested in religious questions.

(INTERROGATOR:) But only because you're indoctrinating them.

(DUDKO:) You can't indoctrinate in this. I don't like proofs of religion. I mean I'm not against them. But you can't indoctrinate people with religion, you have to feel it. Young people are beginning to feel it. In 12 years I have already baptised about 1,000 adults. And I know how they came to accept God. The main weakness of atheist propaganda is that it tries to indoctrinate. So it's produced the opposite effect: everyone is fed up with atheism. No-one reads atheist literature.[7]

In attacking the ideological viability of Christianity, Soviet propagandists have one crucial problem: the Christian communities tend to turn out better citizens than the communists. In August 1973, a group of Lithuanian Catholics (the document is signed by 540 people) addressed an appeal to the Lithuanian Supreme Soviet. They said, among other things:

Religion is condemned, while atheism is forcibly sold to everybody. What are the results? Lenin taught that only practice confirms the correctness of ideas, theories and science. For almost 30 years now the young generation and the whole of society have been educated and conditioned in the spirit of atheism. Atheism is propagated and religion denigrated in schools during classroom hours and in all events outside the classroom. Cartoons mocking believers are exhibited in school displays. Churchgoing pupils are interrogated, intimidated, sometimes even penalised.

What has this lengthy practice of atheist education demonstrated? While before the introduction of atheist education in Lithuania juvenile thieving, robbery, homicide attempts, sexual profligacy were very rare, now they are constant phenomena. Special children's rooms have been set up in police stations to combat juvenile delinquency. Alcoholism, crimes against property, murders, lies, dishonesty and the absence of a sense of duty were never before so widespread in Lithuania as in recent years. We meet with callous consciences wherever we meet workers and officials: in shops, factories, offices, clinics, everywhere. Practice has demonstrated that atheist education is incapable of fostering strong moral principles among the young and that atheist propaganda is unable to alter the society's moral level.

Christian morality, that has passed the test of the ages, that sensitises the conscience, that urges man to assume self-control, to conquer his negative inclinations, to fulfil his duties conscientiously and to feel an inner responsibility for his own actions – that morality is negated and obstructed. The believers are under attack, but they are not allowed to defend themselves.[8]

This is a strong indictment. It is the more impressive when one remembers that the greater part of the Soviet Union has been subjected to enforced atheism for about twice as long as Lithuania, which was not annexed until the last war. This assessment has been confirmed many times over, also in other socialist countries. The criminal population of the U.S.S.R. is estimated at over one million out of a population of some 250 million. This is a very high percentage.

This is clearly a severe embarrassment to the communists, whose ideology claims to produce a superior human product. Communist theory also claims that the building of a communist society will automatically cause regressive phenomena such as religion to disappear. After almost sixty years' experience in the Soviet Union, this is manifestly untrue. The same is again true in other socialist countries. Ideologists try to explain this situation in various ways, but the plain facts are against them.

There is a tension in the Soviet approach to religion between the ideological purists, who maintain that religion must disappear of its own accord, and those who take the more pragmatic view that its demise, being delayed, must be helped along. Soviet policies towards religion tend to vacillate between these two poles, but being based essentially on current trends and needs, they are more truly pragmatic. Lenin himself was usually a pragmatist, despite his sometimes ferocious attention to doctrine. Theoretical atheist articles in the Soviet media usually defend the former view, but practice at local level often adopts the latter. This is only one example of the dichotomy between theory and practice in the Soviet Union, between what is said on paper, and what actually happens. This is a fact of Soviet reality which must be kept constantly in mind when dealing with subjects of this kind.

III. Denominations and their Groupings

The situation is complicated by the range of Christian confessions in the U.S.S.R. Each one has a different history, a different denominational tradition, often a different approach to church-state relations and interpretation of the Christian role in society. These factors can play a part in determining the treatment given to the various communities.

The oldest, and still the largest and most widespread Christian confession in the U.S.S.R. is the Russian Orthodox Church, shortly to celebrate its millennium. The Russian Orthodox Church today has an estimated 30–50 million adherents, although precise religious statistics are impossible to come by. There are also national Orthodox Churches in the ancient states of Armenia and Georgia.

In the seventeenth century, there was a schism in the Russian Orthodox Church which forced a considerable number of "Old Believers" out of the fellowship of the Church. The anathema pronounced at that time has recently been revoked. The Old Believers themselves suffered further internal splits, and many of the smaller groupings have disappeared. But there remains today a considerable and variegated Old Believer community in the U.S.S.R. Some parts of this are recognised by the state, others exist in an illegal condition.

Besides the Old Believers there are also a large number of indigenous Russian sects which split away from the Orthodox Church at various times. Some of these, too, have disappeared, but some persist – all without official recognition.

The Roman Catholic Church has never had a strong foothold in Russia. It was associated in Russian history with Polish imperialism and as such violently rejected. Catholicism in its Eastern-rite ("Uni-

ate") form did gain a firm footing in the Western Ukraine, and can
still be found there today, although illegal and severely persecuted.
This is an instance where the atheist establishment made use of the
"ruling" Russian Orthodox Church to put down a "foreign" Church.
Uniate believers were forced to join the Orthodox Church in the 1940's.
Those who refused either fled the country, or exposed themselves to
severe risk, including imprisonment and death.

The stronghold of Roman Catholicism in the U.S.S.R. is the Baltic
republic of Lithuania. There is also a fair-sized community in Latvia.
Roman Catholic congregations (often Polish-speaking) are also to be
found along the Western extremities of the Soviet territory. There is
also a considerable Catholic community among the Soviet Germans
scattered through parts of Siberia and Soviet Central Asia by Stalin's
deportation before the last war.

Protestantism did not take firm root in Russia until the last century.
There was a considerable influence from the west, but the movement
now has a fully indigenous character. At the same time, there are still
many Protestant communities which have retained their original na-
tional character, particularly German. An interesting example is the
Mennonite community. Originally a Dutch Protestant movement, the
Mennonites later found refuge from persecution in northern Germany.
Subsequent troubles here caused many to move further eastwards to
Russia and Eastern Europe. As a result of their long stay in north
Germany, Mennonites traditionally use low German (plattdeutsch) as
their internal community language. Because of the lingering hatred
from the last war, believers using the German language, or simply
bearing German names, are sometimes exposed to both petty and
serious discrimination from local Russian officials. Here is an extract
from an appeal from a Baptist community in Slavgorod (Siberia) dated
30 January 1974:

(A number of believers had been beaten up by hooligans, incited by the
local police. Three of them went to complain:) When sister Dyck began to
get indignant that he just stood there and laughed, and wasn't interested in
why their heads were bound up and their faces covered with bruises, instead
of answering her he asked: "What nationality are you?" We are not aware
that the first duty in such circumstances is to discover a person's nationality.
When our sister replied that she was Ukrainian, the police chief asked:
"Then why do you have a German accent? You know how much of our
property the Germans burned down." From this conversation it is clear that
they are simply seeking grounds against German citizens, as if we were guilty
for what happened during the war. Who knows how this conversation might

have ended and how the police chief would have acted if our sister had turned out to be German?[9]

The whole subject of national discrimination and persecution in the U.S.S.R. is a large one and cannot be handled here. Many Mennonites in the Soviet Union today have merged with other communities such as the Baptists, and to some extent lost their special identity. However, the Mennonite names such as Klassen, Wiebe, Dyck etc. are still easily recognisable.

Protestantism tends to be stronger in the western parts of the U.S.S.R. At the same time there is a scattered Protestant representation in many other places – this often through exile. It has been shown that the Baptists draw much of their strength from the urban working class.

The most widespread Protestant grouping is the united denomination of Evangelical Christians-Baptists. This is an amalgamation (under state pressure) of a number of Christian streams including the Evangelical Christians (similar to the Open Brethren in England), the Baptists, some Pentecostals and Mennonites. Other Pentecostal and Mennonite communities have remained outside the Union and hence in an illegal or semi-legal state. The E.C.B. denomination (usually referred to for simplicity as "Baptist") is also split in two over the issue of compromise with the atheist authorities.

There is a sizeable Lutheran community in the Baltic area, particularly Latvia and Estonia. There are also considerable numbers of Lutheran and Reformed believers among the Germans previously mentioned (who number some two million). There are also smaller numbers of other denominations such as Methodists and Adventists.

Relations between the different denominations in Russia have had a chequered history. While the Orthodox Church was the "ruling Church" under the tsars, her relations with other confessions in Russia varied from cool to viciously hostile. Even between some of the non-Orthodox denominations there could be tension or hostility. Clearly the situation today is different and Anatoli Levitin has summed it up as follows:

I can remember clearly when the Orthodox Church was much disturbed over the relative freedom acquired by sectarians after the revolution. The sects made great progress in the 1920's, and the vast majority of those converted to the sects were deserters from Orthodoxy. Orthodox propaganda responded to the sects with bitterness and anger, almost hatred. It would have seemed that there was no force that could modify this mutual antagonism. What then happened? For several decades Orthodox Christians and sectarians suffered together in Beria camps, slept side by side in prison bunks, gulped the same prison soup out of the same rusty bowls. So now the Church and the sects practically do not compete with each other.[10]

This is probably an over-simplification. However it is true that there is some ecumenical activity at official level, as well as probably a good deal of informal co-operation at local level.

After the October Revolution, there were undoubtedly cases of spontaneous violence by peasants against individual, corrupt Orthodox clergy who had suddenly lost state protection. But these manifestations only had a temporary character. Anatoli Levitin has characterised the generations since 1917 as follows:

The generation of grandfathers, those who lived in the epoch of revolution and who made the revolution, were not passive in their attitude towards religion. Its leading and most energetic representatives passionately hated the Orthodox Church, seeing in her the chief support of the Tsar's regime. This impassioned hatred of the Church soon moved on to uncontrollable anti-religious fanaticism. One of the worst recollections of my childhood is that of the chapel on Krestovsky Island in Petrograd (now Kirov Island), with icons thrown about on the floor and even the eyes poked out of their faces. A priest during these years literally did not dare show himself on the street, he would be met with hooting and insults...

The second generation of 'fathers', to which I belong, had and has a different attitude towards religion; we were brought up and lived in the era when religion was driven deeply underground, the great majority of churches closed, clergy imprisoned, and the struggle against religion conducted by purely administrative methods (this is a Soviet euphemism for persecution of a direct kind, without regard to theoretical justification – translator); it was not permitted to talk openly about religion, but with quiet steps it passed out of life... Religion in the pre-war years went out of the minds of the vast majority of Russian people, especially of the Soviet intelligentsia, and only the Patriotic War called forth a powerful wave of religious feeling in the popular masses, showing that the disappearance of religion had only been imagined, that religion continued to live underneath the surface. However, the complete absence of religious upbringing and religious teaching had done its work. The second post-revolutionary generation was the most estranged generation of any ever inhabiting the earth; it did not hate, it simply was ignorant of religion.

Modern youth holds a quite exceptional place in the matter of religion – the third post-revolutionary generation. As a rule these are persons who have no conception of religion, having received a clearly-expressed anti-religious upbringing. Although it may appear strange, this has not only a negative but also a positive side for the promotion of religion. The positive is this, that modern youth simply does not know the negative aspects of pre-revolutionary Orthodoxy, which led to so much hatred and bitterness on the part of the people... The average representative of the younger generation approaches religion with mixed feelings of incredulity and interest... Modern youth in Russia is a disturbed youth, it seethes and passionately seeks for something. A religious reaction is characteristic of quite a number of these boys and girls. It would be no exaggeration to say that in these young people the religious reaction, in intensity and strength, is no less than the feeling of fiery enthusiasm among the earliest Christians.[11]

Levitin's comments about modern Soviet youth (which might be applied to many other countries as well) bring us back to the points made by Plumpa and Dudko, quoted earlier in the essay.

IV. DISCRIMINATION AND PERSECUTION

The pattern since 1917 has been discrimination and persecution initiated from above rather than from below. This has tended to go in waves. The last great wave of anti-religious persecution was in 1959–64 under Khrushchev. The situation today is not so bad as then, but there are signs that things are worsening again. However, although the discrimination proceeds from above, it must be remembered that intensive indoctrination must produce some fruit, however mis-shapen. A good example of this is the slanderous articles often printed in the local media before a trial against believers. The intention of these articles is to whip up popular opinion against those to go on trial. This tactic was recently used against a Pentecostal believer, although he was not actually brought to trial. Here is how his friends described the incident:

On 20 February 1975 in the newspaper *Vinnitsa Truth* under the rubric "Towards militant atheism," there was an article by G. Osipov and V. Udichenko entitled "Scandalous." This article tells about some believers of Vinnitsa town and region who are supposed to have collaborated with the Germans during the war and to have killed people, despite the commandment "Thou shalt not kill"... The article devotes particular attention to Eduard Darmoros. Eduard Darmoros was born in 1935. He studied at a special school of music, at the Kiev Conservatoire – his whole life was dedicated to music. Darmoros was an able student and never got mediocre marks. During his time at the Conservatoire, Darmoros came to believe in the Lord. When this became known to the teachers and the authorities, they began to "re-educate" him. This finished by his being expelled from the

Conservatoire in his final year for "poor progress" and in May 1963 being sentenced to five years imprisonment and 5 years exile... In the article it says that during his period of study in Kiev, Darmoros incited a certain Yashin to kill a girl as a sacrifice to God. The atheists themselves do not believe this, everybody knows that there is no such heathen ritual in Christianity... The newspaper rubric "Towards militant atheism" justified its title: Darmoros began to be attacked, people consider him a murderer. He appealed to the editor, demanding that these facts be proven. They answered that there were no proofs. He asked them to print a denial. They refused, but said that they would give him a certificate in which it was stated that he had no part in incitement to murder. He could show this at work to clear his name. But how, one might ask, can Darmoros exhibit his innocence to all the readers in the Vinnitsa Region, who have accepted this article as truth? But this is the atheists' "truth", this is one of their methods for attacking believers. By such statements in the press, they stir people up to hate Christians. This leads to repercussions, demands, reprisals against believers. The atheists then try to satisfy the "demands of the workers," making appeal to the "will of the people"... Darmoros was not given the promised certificate. The brethren in Vinnitsa are now being summoned to the KGB in groups.[12]

This account underlines again the statement of the Lithuanian Catholics quoted above: "The believers are under attack, but they are not allowed to defend themselves." Similar instances have been documented in many cases.

It could also be argued that discrimination in education tends to produce intellectually deprived communities, which in turn may feed popular mistrust. It is ironical that "sociological surveys" on religious communities constantly point to the low educational level among believers. This is documented solely in terms of the number of years spent in schooling. It says nothing about intellectual talent which has been refused further training by a doctrinaire society. Thus, in these and other ways, discrimination initiated from above can engender spontaneous reactions at grass-roots level which would not otherwise take place.

V. RELIGION AND THE LAW

Discrimination and persecution against Soviet Christians have a firm basis in published Soviet law. There are also secret laws[13] and unwritten understandings – such as the ban on "bible smuggling." The unrestricted importation of bibles into the U.S.S.R. is technically quite legal. Even the published laws are often couched in terms so vague

that they leave ample room for arbitrary interpre
a saying among the political dissidents in Russia: "
a man, and they can't find a suitable law, they'll

The first, and for many, the most important Soviet
is that of 1918 on the separation of church and state.
earliest decrees of the young Bolshevik state, an
took part in its formulation, making it clear that
measure as one of primary importance. The decree

1. The Church is separate from the State.
3. Each citizen may confess any religion or no religi
   rights as the result of the confession of a religion
   religion shall be revoked.
5. The free performance of religious rites shall be granted
   not disturb the public order and infringe upon the
   of the Soviet Republic.
9. The school shall be separate from the Church. The
   is prohibited in all state, municipal or private edu
   where a general education is given. Citizens may
   ligious instruction privately.
13. All property belonging to churches and religious
    in Russia shall become public property.[14]

If Lenin's decree had been observed, even by
church in the Soviet Union might today be one
in the world. As it is, "separation" of church and
Union has come to mean that the church is cut off
social influence, while atheists retain maximum
movements.

The second provision of the 1918 decree stated
to enact on the territory of the Republic local laws
would put any restraint upon or limit freedom of
fact this is precisely what did happen. It can thus
Baptists who split away from the recognised E.C.B.
that almost all the subsequent legislation on reli
original decree and is therefore illegal!

Even provisions of the early decree which ha
been superceded are still not observed. For ex
states that: "The mention in official papers of the
is not allowed." This automatically precludes
statistical surveys of believers, questionnaires, the
affiliation in school reports, work testimonials, e

phenomena have been documented. Issue No. 6 of the "Chronicle of the Lithuanian Catholic Church" (an uncensored publication) published the text of a questionnaire used in a school in Prienai in February 1973. Children had to answer such questions as: "Does a priest visit your home?" "Who prepared you for first communion? For confirmation?" "Are your parents believers?" The same number of the Chronicle also published the text of a government instruction to agencies for the collection of material on the subject "Catholicism in Lithuania and the Present." This involved a detailed investigation of Church life. Atheists monitoring sermons were instructed to "behave politely, without participating actively in religious practices." The "Bulletin" of the Council of Prisoners' Relatives, an uncensored publication of the unregistered Baptists, in January 1974 noted that children in Dushanbe (Tadzhikistan), Simferopol (Crimea), Gorky and other towns "had to fill in questionnaires at school about adherence to religion, with specific questions." It also reported that in Shakhty, Rostov region, "in November 1973 there was a special census of Christian children at home." In January–February 1974 "Fraternal Leaflet," the bi-monthly magazine of the unregistered Baptists, spoke about the activities of the local Commissions for supervising the observance of legislation on cults. (A secret instruction governing these bodies was referred to in footnote 13.) It stated: "The illegal character of the activities of these Commissions is evident in many ways, but most of all in the fact that they instruct factories, institutions, accommodation offices, street committees, educational establishments, trade unions and other organisations to keep a systematic check on all believers, wherever they happen to be." It went on to give the text of an instruction sent in the name of one of these Commissions to factories in Kharkov, Ukraine. The instruction, dated 16 November 1973, demanded the compilation of lists of believers working in these factories. Precise details were required, including information on "violation of the legislation on cults." Lists were to be submitted by 10 December 1973. The report continues:

Thus by the beginning of 1974 there will be special lists of believers, regardless of whether they are in registered or unregistered churches, detailed information will be available and these will in future be amplified and used in the struggle against the church.[15]

The guarantees contained in the 1918 decree were incorporated in the first Soviet Constitution (July 1918) which stated that "the right to religious and anti-religious propaganda is recognised for all citizens."

However, in 1929 Stalin passed a law "On religious associations" which completely dismembered the guarantees of 1918. Step by step, it subordinated religious communities to the most thorough-going atheist supervision and interference. The 1929 law stated for example:

2. Religious associations of believers of all denominations shall be registered as religious societies or groups of believers. A citizen may be a member of only one religious association (society or group).

10. For the satisfaction of their religious needs, the believers who have formed a religious society may receive from the district or city soviet, under a contract, free of charge, special prayer buildings and objects intended exclusively for the cult... A religious society or group of believers may use only one prayer building or (complex of) premises.

12. For each general assembly of a religious society or group of believers, permission shall be obtained...

14. The registration agencies are entitled to remove individual members from the executive body of a religious society or the representative elected by a group of believers.

17. Religious associations may not: (a) create mutual credit societies, cooperative or commercial undertakings, or in general, use property at their disposal for other than religious purposes; (b) give material help to their members; (c) organise for children, young people and women special prayer or other meetings, circles, groups, departments for Biblical or literary study, sewing, working or the teaching of religion, etc., excursions, children's playgrounds libraries, reading rooms, sanatoria or medical care...

19. The activities of the clergymen, preachers, preceptors and the like shall be restricted to the area in which the members of the religious association reside and in the area where the prayer building or premises are situated...

25. Objects necessary for the rites of the cult, whether handed over under contract to the believers forming the religious association, acquired by them, or donated to them for the purpose of the cult, are nationalised and shall be under the control of the Committee for Religious Matters at the city or district soviet.

54. The members of the groups of believers and religious societies may pool money in the prayer building or premises and outside it by voluntary collections and donations, but only among the members of the given religious association and only for the purpose of covering the expenses for the maintenance of the prayer building or premises and religious property, and for the salary of the clergy and activities of executive bodies. Any kind of compulsory collection of money for the benefit of religious associations is punishable under the provisions of the Criminal Code.

64. Surveillance over the activities of religious associations, as well as over the maintenance of prayer buildings and property leased to religious associations, shall be exercised by registration agencies, and in rural areas by village soviets.[16]

... not be clearer. The new situation was reflected in ... of 1936 which altered Article 124 to read: "In ... citizens freedom of conscience, the church in the ... from the state, and the school from the church. ... worship and freedom of anti-religious propaganda ... citizens." The "freedom of religious propaganda" ... fell away, while even the guaranteed "freedom ... which remained, meant nothing in the context of ... purge against religion.

... and 1929, with their inherent contradictions, con... basic Soviet legislation on religion. There have ... other lesser decrees, but none of these alter the ... Alongside these two laws stands the Constitution, ... its equally ambiguous formulations.

... registration, mentioned in the early paragraphs of the ... to the situation of religious communities in the ... to the Soviet legislation, every religious congre... registered with the local authorities. Any group of at ... 18 years or over) may apply for registration as a ... ty' (or "group of believers" if their number is less than ... are obliged to reply to the application within one ... indicated on which a request might be refused. ... situations have tended to be processed within re... (depending also on local factors) after which fresh ... considered. The stipulation that the authorities ... month is often ignored. The establishment of new ... distinct from the registration of previously-existing ... permitted, presumably on the doctrinaire grounds that ... " Certain denominations such as Uniate, many ... groups of Old Believers, etc. are simply banned – ... by secret decree, since it has no basis in published

... is not registered, the state can label it as "illegal," ... ue. At the same time, the authorities themselves ... arbitrarily refused registration to the congregation ... it "illegal." (This is a rather similar logic to the ... Baptists and other believers are barred from ... are then labelled "uneducated.") This paradox ... in mind every time the Soviet media speak of ... manifestations.

VI. Penal Legislation

The existence of legal disabilities against Christians implies the existence of parallel penal provisions. The penal articles under which Christians are most often sentenced are 142 ("Violation of laws on separation of church and state and of church and school"), 190/1 ("Circulation of knowingly false fabrications which defame the Soviet state and social system") and 227 ("Infringement of persons and rights of citizens under appearance of performing religious ceremonies"). Article 227, which was not introduced until 1961, and which provides for the stiffest penalties, states:

Organising or directing a group, the activity of which, carried on under the appearance of preaching religious beliefs and performing religious ceremonies, is connected with causing harm to citizens' health or with inducing citizens to refuse social activity or performance of civic duties, or with drawing minors into such group, shall be punished by a deprivation of freedom for a term not exceeding five years or by exile for a similar term with or without confiscation of property...[17]

Article 142 carries a maximum sentence of one year, or three years for a second offender. Article 190/1 carries a maximum sentence of three years. Article 227 carries a maximum sentence of five years imprisonment or five years exile. By a technical variation, these may be added together in the Ukraine to give a ten-year total sentence.

Penal legislation on religion tends to affect above all those Christian communities which lay greater emphasis on the direct proclamation of the gospel, i.e. the evangelicals. However, it is known that believers of many denominations are today in detention in the U.S.S.R. – Orthodox, Catholic and Protestant. Exact numbers are not known. In some cases believers are imprisoned for "offences" connected with the struggle for human rights in the wider sense. The most precise documentation comes from the unregistered Baptists, who normally have between one and two hundred members imprisoned. The Baptist "Council of Prisoners' Relatives" produces regular prisoner lists, giving among other things precise addresses of labour camps. This has been an invaluable help to those carrying out research on such aspects of Soviet society.

When a person is arrested in the U.S.S.R., he is detained in a local prison while his case is investigated. Legally, he can be held before trial for up to nine months. In some cases of political dissidents and believers, the period has been longer. This was the case for example with Georgi Vins, secretary of the unregistered Baptist Church, who was last arrested at the end of March 1974 and not tried until the end of January 1975. Lithuanian Catholic defendants Plumpa and Petronis were held for 13 months before their trial in December 1974.

The investigation consists of a thorough examination of the whole case, including interrogation of the witnesses who are to be called to the trial, and the compilation of sometimes huge case materials. The trial is thus little more than a repetition of the results of the investigation, although the defendants are given opportunities to speak, and sometimes make brilliant use of these. It seems clear that in most cases, the verdict is settled before the trial opens. Probably many Christian defendants are aware of this, and therefore concentrate their efforts not so much on trying to secure acquittal, but rather on declaring their convictions in the most positive manner they can. Judges frequently interrupt Christian defendants during their speeches, instructing them to stop preaching.

VII. Prison Camp Conditions

Sentence is normally served in one of the many labour camps of the Soviet Union. It is estimated that there are more than a thousand of these, spread throughout the country. A first offender normally serves his sentence within his native republic. A "recidivist" may be sent to another area, which can cause difficulties of climatic adjustment, as well as making family visits more difficult. In particular, the camps in the bleak regions of the north are inaccessible to visitors through the winter months. This is the case with Georgi Vins, who is at present in Yakutia, serving the severe ten-year sentence mentioned above. Prisoners who prove particularly "stubborn" are sometimes transferred to another camp or to a severe prison such as that in Vladimir. Here the regime is even worse than in the camps, where it is already inhuman. In December 1971 some political prisoners in Mordovia wrote a letter, in which they remarked:

Those who continue to stand up for their human dignity are subjected to repressions of a yet more brutal kind. Thus in the spring of 1971 the Orthodox priest Boris Borisovich Zalivako was transferred to the Vladimir prison from camp 3/1; Father Boris won everyone's respect by his calmness and gentleness, by the shining strength of his spirit. His firmness and refusal to compromise his convictions and conscience, the inevitable moral influence which he had on those around him could not but frighten those who are accustomed to live "in conformity with baseness." He was therefore isolated in prison in yet harsher conditions.[18]

The conditions in Soviet labour camps are now fairly well known from the accounts circulating in samizdat (self-published writings) and from the details given by former prisoners now living abroad.[19] The diet is close to starvation level, and on this prisoners are expected to do hard labour. Discipline is strict and punishments are given for the slightest "offence." Despite the rules governing correspondence, there is a strict censorship which badly affects the Christian prisoners. Here is an extract from a recent appeal from the Baptist Council of Prisoners' Relatives (dated 12 July 1975):

According to article 26 of the basic laws: "Correspondence may be carried on in any language and on any subject" (see Ya. M. Tkachevsky, *Soviet Corrective Labour Law*, p. 72).

In practice this article is violated in almost all the camps where Christian prisoners are serving their sentence. Where the name of God is mentioned in letters, this is crossed out or the whole letter is disallowed. Even greetings on the occasion of annual Christian festivals such as Christmas, Easter, and Trinity Sunday are not allowed in correspondence either to or from the prisoner.

All such letters are either not delivered at all, or else are delivered with whole lines or paragraphs crossed out, or simply as strips of the original letter; if the letter is written in pencil, then lines of religious content are rubbed out. It sometimes happens that after censorship, a letter only has the first and the last line left.[19]

The same letter complained that many Christian prisoners were deprived of Bibles, without any legal justification for this.

In August 1973, ten former political prisoners addressed a letter to the Security Conference meeting in Geneva. They requested an investigation into conditions for political prisoners in European countries, and gave considerable detail on the Soviet situation. Among the signatories of the letter were Vladimir Osipov, editor of two uncensored Orthodox journals, now in detention, and Anatoli Levitin. The text includes this passage:

Receiving books is prohibited... The following are confiscated in the course of searches, and are not returned even after release from camps: the Bible, individual pages from the Scriptures and other writings of a religious nature, especially prayers, psalms and liturgies. In prisons and camps the hunt for religious literature is accompanied by the harsh persecution of believers. Breaking up prayer meetings in the yard, confinement in a punishment cell for failure to go to work on major religious holidays (Easter, Christmas), prohibiting all rites – even confession and communion for prisoners dying in the camp: such are the methods of "educational" influence by which they try to root out religious dissent. It should be added that a defendant's acknowledgment that he believes in Gold always constitutes a circumstance aggravating his "guilt."[21]

VIII. Psychiatric Detention and Arranged Accidents

Some Christians, as well as political dissidents and other sane persons, have been incarcerated in psychiatric hospitals, either normal ones, or "special" type, i.e. dealing solely with dissidents. In some cases, this may be because the person concerned could not easily be convicted in court. In other cases, there seems to be no obvious reason why this action has been taken. Here is an account of what happened to a young Pentecostal Christian not long ago:

In 1974, in the town of Dokuchayevsk, Donetsk Region, a young man by the name of Valeri Nikolayevich Andreyev came to believe in the Lord Jesus Christ. He was a ruined personality – a drug addict, a hooligan and a parasite. This is how he himself describes his life before his conversion. Nobody wanted anything more to do with him, neither the authorities, nor the people around him, not even his mother (his father is dead). Now he is a different person, a new person, full of the joy of life. His mother was happy – at long last Valeri began to help her in everything, and he got a job as an unskilled labourer. But as soon as the head of the enterprise discovered that he had become a believer, he dismissed him from work.

Valeri found another job and began to make application for it. During a medical examination, neuropathologist Anna Fyodorovna Khailo began to talk with him. She asked him whether he wasn't upset that he had been dismissed from work. He answered: No! She replied that in that case he must be ill. Valeri began to witness to her about the Lord, telling her how the Lord had healed him from a disease that 80% of all people suffer from: the disease of spite. After this conversation she opened a case on Valeri, diagnosing that he should be placed in a psychiatric hospital. This happened on 16 December 1974, despite his mother's appeal not to do it. Valeri was in this hospital from 16 december 1974 until 14 February 1975 and was given injections of triftozin and halaperidol. Now he is at home.[22]

In the persecution of the Church in the Soviet Union, there have been some documented cases of murder within recent years (we are not dealing here with the mass exterminations under Stalin). One well-known example of this was the young Baptist soldier, Ivan Moiseyev, murdered by his senior officers in the Crimea in the summer of 1972. The case is well documented, and can be followed in the book *Vanya* by Myrna Grant,[23] which re-tells the story in literary form, but also appends the relevant documentation. During persecution against the Pochayev Orthodox monastery in the early 1960's, the young monk Grigori Unka was killed in prison in 1962.[24] During the last couple of years, a good deal of material has come from Soviet Georgia concerning corruption and renewal in the Georgian Orthodox Church, and the attempts of the authorities to crush reformist groups. In this process, it suspected that the death of Fr. Victor Shalamberidze, a key witness, in a car crash in February 1974 was in fact a KGB murder.[25] There have been other cases.

Another means of repression which affects political dissidents and religious believers is violence in the form of "accidents" and poisoning, particularly in the form of injections which impair health and mental capacity. This latter unpleasant phenomenon seems to be on the increase. The Orthodox priest Dmitri Dudko, mentioned above, was involved in a car accident not long ago in which he broke both legs. It is thought to have been a KGB action. Here is part of an appeal from the family of Baptist Vasili Shcherbina:

On 14 October 1974 our father Vasili Ivanovich Shcherbina was given a conditional early discharge from intensified regime camp: Lvov region, g. Drogobych, UTsVL-315/40-5. Our father arrived home in poor health, complicated by the following circumstances: in April 1974 the whole No. 5 section, which included our father, had to give blood for some sort of analysis. After this he alone was given some kind of medicine to drink. From that moment on, his mental faculties became noticeably impaired. We were very worried about this, and so, in order to check up on his state of health, we immediately went to see him in the camp. During this interview we became convinced that he was mentally sick; our father testified that this had happened since he had given blood and taken the medicine. At a personal interview on 21 August 1974 he behaved very strangely; he was indifferent to everything and sunk in thought.

At the time of his unexpected release on 14 October 1974, he was sent to the medical unit of the labour colony for precautionary measures: two nurses gave him an injection. On the way home, father felt bad. When we got back, he was surrounded with care and quiet. On 16 November 1974 he had a paralytic stroke.[26]

Information recently reached the West about Ukrainian Baptist

Vladimir Khailo, who with his family has been subjected to intense persecution, and is seeking to emigrate. Here is part of his account of an incident in 1969; while he was working in the fire service:

One day some doctors came to our section and announced that they were going to do some kind of injection. There were three doctors; we went to them in turn. One of them, who sat at the table, apparently the senior one, asked: "Which one of you is Khailo?" The head of my team, Shevyakov, answered: "Here's my brother." "What, are you a believer too?" "No, we're brothers at the grindstone!" She looked at me and said to her assistants: "I feel sorry for him, he's only a young man." She asked how many children I had. "Eleven." She shook her head and began to whisper to the other doctors. My heart began to beat anxiously. I remembered the words of the Lord: "And if you drink any poisonous thing it shall not harm you." The senior one, the one who had questioned me, took a syringe and a filling from a different packet, and gave me the injection. All the other containers were thrown in the waste bin, but this one she put in her pocket. My work-mates also noticed this. By the evening I was feeling bad, I had a temperature and my head ached.

Khailo's condition became worse, and he was taken into hospital. During an examination of his nose, he lost consciousness. When he came to again:

The doctor was sitting on a couch; she was crying. "Where's your God, Khailo? Let him save you and then I'll believe." I felt sick again. She became very upset and said to the nurse: "I can't go on like this. I'm going to phone, let them take him and do what they want with him. I can't do any more. Look out for his wife, that she doesn't come after me." She went out and was away for half an hour. She came back, her face tear-stained. "They said: Carry on – take him to the therapist." They led me by the arm to the therapist. The therapist – I think her name was Zhidkova – was surprised to see us. Lyubov Semyonovna went away at once, but the nurse explained to her: "You remember the briefing we had – it was about him." Zhidkova became indignant: "He's a man, not a beast – why aren't you ashamed? I don't care what he believes, it's not right to treat a man like this! No, I'm not going to touch him – you started it, you can finish it." And she began to cry. "Doesn't it matter to you – he has eleven children, you're making them orphans." Zhidkova turned to the nurse. "Tell your Lyubov Semyonovna that she's an animal, not a doctor!" She turned to me. "I'm sorry, I think you understand what's going on. Tell me, do you have a next of kin here?" "My wife." She asked the nurse to call my wife. When she came, Zhidkova took from her the prescription that had been written out previously, read it and shook her head. "If he manages to survive on this, he'll be blind and deaf. There's only one thing I can do for him." She wrote out another prescription. "Is there a doctor or a nurse among the believers? Let her give him the injections every three hours. Don't trust anybody any more."[27]

After this, Khailo recovered slowly, but the persecutions against this family continued.

IX. HOOLIGANISM AS A WEAPON

Because of the contradictory situation regarding registration, communities without official registration are open to particularly severe problems. Leaders of such groups are frequently fined, also persons in whose homes meetings are held. In some cases, all those present at an unregistered meeting are subjected to a fine of 50 roubles each. Sometimes this happens repeatedly to a single congregation, which clearly causes the community severe economic pressure. It is, incidentally, illegal to give material assistance to the family of a prisoner in the U.S.S.R. Not surprisingly, this ban is not observed among Christians. The unregistered Baptists for example have a sophisticated network of relief among their congregations, and the families of Christian prisoners are cared for.

Unregistered meetings may be broken up by the police, sometimes with violence. Sometimes local hooligans are employed for this purpose and often prepared with generous allowances of vodka before they go. Here is part of an account by an unregistered Protestant community in Slavgorod (Siberia):

On the night of 31 December–1 January (1975) we were gathered for a New Year service. We finished the service peacefully and were beginning to make our way home. On the street stood two people we did not know, who set a light to matchboxes full of matches and threw these burning torches into the air. We discovered the reason for this when we had gone a short way from the house where the service had been held. A group of hooligans, about twelve of them, armed with knuckle-dusters, sticks, military belts and iron chains, using terrible, unprintable language, threw themselves like wild beasts on a group of believers, beating up old people and youngsters and throwing them off their feet. But notice this point: they only beat up men and boys, they didn't touch the women. But since this took place on the street, the hooligans did not keep up their disgraceful attack for long.

Hurling abuse at this group of believers, the young bandits headed off to chase the others. They caught up with their victims in a deserted spot outside the town, where mother Schwarzkopf was going home with her 14-year-old son. Whereas in the street the hooligans had to hurry to fulfil their "duties" for fear someone might hinder them, here outside the town any cry for help was useless and they gave their hooligan passion full rein. Of course in a letter we cannot describe the condition of the mother when they grabbed her son out of her arms and started to beat him with whatever came to hand. But notice the "mercy" of the hooligans. They held the mother and told her: "You won't get beaten up, granny." We want to draw your attention to the fact that here, too, they didn't touch a woman. When the hooligans had cut open the boy's head with an iron chain and had their fill of beating him, they issued this threat: "If we find you going to the meeting just one more time, we'll finish you off."

Sure now that no one would hinder them and that no one would come to the believers' aid, the gang of hooligans got more and more excited. So they left the boy, beaten up and covered in blood, to his mother and started back into the town looking for new victims. But before they got there they found the old man K. Dyck with his wife. This old man of 63 did not realise what was happening before he was knocked to the ground unconscious by a blow to the head. The old woman's heart-rending cry did not stop the hooligans, who had become like wild beasts. They threw themselves on their new victim, the old man lying there helpless, and began to kick him. When the old woman ventured near her husband, she was thrown to the ground with one blow. But again somebody shouted: "Don't beat the old woman."[28]

As the writers of this appeal (addressed to the United Nations) point out, the fact that the hooligans insisted upon the believers ceasing to attend meetings, and that they refrained from beating the women, demonstrates that they were sent by the authorities with precise instructions as to their behaviour.

X. DISCRIMINATION IN EDUCATION

Discrimination affecting the wider mass of believers is exercised in a number of areas. A crucial one is the field of education. This applies first on the teaching side, which is virtually closed to any believer who is not willing to keep his convictions silent. On the student side, children from religious families are subjected to discrimination both petty and serious from their earliest years. They may get lower marks from their teacher; they may be the subject of mockery in a lesson on atheism; more seriously, some teachers have actually incited other children to violence against a Christian child. Here is part of an appeal from a Baptist mother in Gorky, dated 29 November 1974:

In 1965 my eldest son Zhenya went to primary school. Because he refused to be an Octobrist and then a Pioneer, he was repressed at school. Stirred up by the teacher, the children badgered and beat him.

My other children also went to this school: Dina, Sasha, Lyudmila, Andrei and now Petya. The attitude of the headmaster and teachers has not changed: my children, each one in a different way, endure these onslaughts. When Zhenya was transferred to intermediate school No. 160 with the same class, the schoolchildren began periodically to beat him, with the same boldness and more strength, both inside and outside school. They tried to make him swear – "then we'll see what sort of believer you are" – cursing him and insulting God and believers.

Two occasions when my son Sasha (a pupil in the 7th class) has been beaten have been recorded at the police station, because passing adults have interfered. Not long ago (25 September 1974) a fellow-pupil beat up my daughter Lyuda, pupil in the 6th class of school no. 160, on the street, as a result of which she had a pain in her forehead for four days and she had a heart attack.[29]

The following account was published in Issue No. 12 of the Chronicle of the Lithuanian Catholic Church:

On 27 May 1974 Leonas Sileikis, a seventh grade pupil at Siauliai Secondary School No. 5, was summoned for an interview with the headmaster, at which his religious beliefs were to be discussed. The boy's father came to the interview, although he was not invited.

L. Sileikis was first asked whether he had read the atheist books which the school had asked him to read. The boy answered that he had read all six. "What do you think of the books you read?" "They are untrue and slanderous," the boy replied.

After a series of attacks on religion, the teacher Misiuniene twice asked Leonas: "Do you now renounce your beliefs?" "I have been a believer up to now and I shall always remain a believer."

After the schoolboy left the study, the teacher Misiuniene began to tell Leonas' father the harm religion could do to children.

"It's not true that religion is harmful," Sileikis replied. "Nowadays religion is trampled underfoot; that's why children don't respect their teachers, smoke, swear, drink, even sleep around – there you see the results of atheism."

"Nowadays only a minority go to church, so you should follow the majority," Mrs. Jakimciene explained.

"Only a corpse is carried away by the tide, a living man swims against the current."

"You will bar your children from further education because of your religion," said Mrs. Misiuniene, trying to persuade him.

"It's not I who bar them from further education, but you, the atheists. What's the use of science after all if you have to renounce the most precious thing in life – faith. But you, respected teachers, should be punished according to Soviet laws for persecuting children because of their religious beliefs."

"We will make your son an atheist in spite of you," said Mrs. Misiuniene.[30]

Considerable pressure is exerted on religious children to join the communist youth organisations (Octobrists, Pioneers, Komsomol).

Those who refuse to do so, because of the atheist bias of these groups, may be boycotted by their schoolmates as a disgrace to the class. As a child goes up the educational ladder, his chances of further education diminish if he expresses Christian convictions. He may either be barred from entry to a higher institute (even though his educational attainments are satisfactory, or even excellent), or he may be admitted and subsequently expelled. Here is an appeal from a young Baptist, Mikhail Strakhursky, dated 24 February 1975:

In the summer of 1974 I applied for entry to Lvov Polytechnical Institute. A request immediately arrived at the *sovkhoz* where my father works for a testimonial on my parents, in which it was stated that they are believers.

In the beginning I was not asked any questions at the institute, but then I was summoned to the komsomol office and to the dean's office for 5 November. Since I was in hospital and could not attend on that day, I was again summoned to the komsomol office of the machine faculty a month later. The office secretary, comrade Makar, told me to join the komsomol. I refused. Then I was summoned to a conversation with the dean, L. A. Lukoshuk. He told me that I must join the komsomol by the New Year or else leave the institute. At the same time he suggested that I give up my faith in God.

I was getting grades 3 and 4. They failed me in exams. The deputy dean, I. V. Gaivas, suggested that I come back when I had thought everything over fully. When he found that nothing had changed in my convictions about God, he said that he could not help me and that I was discharged from the institute. When I asked for a memorandum of dismissal, he refused.

Many believers have been dismissed in this way. For example, during an atheist lecture the teacher said that there had been a Baptist girl in the institute, and that "she got as far as the third year."[31]

Soviet law forbids the religious education of children under 18 in any formal manner. This clearly precludes any form of Sunday school, although this is still practised by the unregistered Baptists. A more controversial case is the catechising of children before first communion in the Catholic Church. Several priests have been harassed and even imprisoned for this "crime," although it is a normal part of Catholic church life. The basis for this accusation is the fact that, due to the numbers often involved, the priests frequently have to catechise the children in groups. This is then regarded by the authorities as organised religious instruction. Fr. Juozas Zdebskis, a Lithuanian Catholic priest sentenced for this "crime" in October 1971, admitted that children had come to him in groups of up to one hundred for catechismal examination.

According to the 1918 decree, "Citizens may give and receive religious instruction privately." Religious teaching in a special institution or course, in the words of the 1929 law: "may be given exclusively in religious courses created by citizens of the U.S.S.R. with the special permission of the Permanent Committee for Religious Matters under the Council of Ministers" (paragraph 18). This permission is the basis for a few remaining Russian Orthodox schools, a small Catholic seminary and a Baptist correspondence course – clearly these institutions could be closed at any time. The only other possibility under the law is the private instruction of children within their own home. However, even while guaranteed in theory, it was not always observed in practice. There have been a number of cases of children being removed from parents because of religious training. It happened for example to Mrs. Radygina of Perm, whose husband had already left her when she became a Christian. In the summer of 1973 a court order deprived her of her three younger children.[32] Other cases have also been documented. Sometimes this action was taken under the cover of the new law on marriage and family, passed in October, 1968, which stated that parents must rear their children in the spirit of "a builder of communism." However, the practice of removing children from Christian parents had occurred before the appearance of this law. Like some other legal provisions, it merely served as a convenient basis for action already taking place.

XI. Discrimination in Employment

Another area of discrimination is that of employment. There is manifold evidence that believers find it difficult to enter certain fields – teaching has already been mentioned. The same obviously applies to any sphere of government or public service – any area in which a believer might have influence over other people. When the Baptist Khailo, mentioned above, complained to the local authorities that his daughter had received a testimonial on finishing school which mentioned her parents' religion, so that she could not study further or get a job, they replied:

"You mean you deny that you're a Baptist?"

"No I don't. But you've no right to cite religious affiliation in documents. Believers have the same right as other citizens to study or work anywhere."

"That's rubbish. You mean you could take a job where Party members would have to obey you?"[33]

Believers who make their convictions known may find it difficult to keep a job suited to their qualifications. Here is the testimony of a Baptist woman in the Ukraine:

My name is Ulyana Sergeyevna Germanyuk and I live in Voroshilovgrad Region, Lisichansk-6, ul. Myuda No. 22. I am the mother of five children. My husband is in bonds for confessing the living God.

From my very youth I have been subject to persecutions because I wanted to serve the Lord. When I was studying at medical college, they threatened to expel me if I did not recant. Then I went to an institute; when I finished my course the same words were repeated – and I did not receive my diploma. But still despite all difficulties, a year later I got the documents stating that I had completed the institute. Then a new phase of persecution began at work, where I worked as a vet. During this time I was twice dismissed from work, even despite the fact that I have a large family.

Then I changed my place of residence, but here too "busy hands" found me again. I was only able to work for a year at the new place. After all that I have described above, I decided to forget my education and went to wash doorsteps.[34]

There have sometimes been refusals (strictly illegal) to grant adequate housing for religious believers. Houses used (sometimes with permission) for religious gatherings have been attacked, with windows smashed and doors broken down.

XII. BANS ON LITERATURE

The Soviet Constitution provides for freedom of the press. This is not observed in practice for Christians or anyone else. This is the cause of the massive shortage of Bibles in the U.S.S.R., despite occasional permission for small printings by the official Churches. Baptists, Catholics and probably others print Bibles and other spiritual literature in secret, but the need remains, despite considerable supplies entering the country from outside.

We have already mentioned that Christians may be sentenced under Article 190/1 of the Penal Code. This is usually applied against believers who have been involved in the recording or distribution of information about the life and problems of their churches, such as the Baptist "Bulletin of the Council of Prisoners' Relatives" or the "Chronicle of the Lithuanian Catholic Church." As defendants in these trials emphasise over and over again, they are not involved with "slander" of the Soviet state, but simply a recording of the truth.

XIII. Closure of Churches

During periods of intense persecution there have been mass closures of churches – this was particularly the case under Stalin, who closed all but a handful of churches until the last war forced him to alter his course with regard to religion. During the last wave of persecution in the early 1960's, it is estimated that about half of the existing 20,000 Orthodox churches were closed. Today there may be as few as 7,000 Orthodox churches still functioning. Closures still take place, although not on the same scale. A recent example was the Church of the Epiphany in Zhitomir (Ukraine), which was closed in November 1973 and demolished in August 1975, despite repeated appeals by its parishioners.[35] The excuse given for its closure was the proximity of the church to a school – although this had been the case for many years. Sometimes churches are demolished under the pretext of town reconstruction, which may not then take place.

XIV. Complicity of Clergy

Assimilation in this context can only mean the pressure exercised by the state upon believers to renounce their convictions, or at least to modify their stand. During the last great anti-religious campaign in the early 1960's, there was great publicity for the apostasy of certain leading Christian figures such as former Orthodox lecturer Osipov. It is not beyond the bounds of possibility that some of these apostates were "planted" by the authorities. It is also likely that some renunciations were made under pressure and without real conviction.

Perhaps the most significant, and unattractive fruit of assimilation in this context is the emergence over the years of church leaders who, for one reason or another, are willing to co-operate fully with the authorities. This can go so far as betraying their own members when they take a stand on certian issues. In 1966 Boris Talantov and other Orthodox believers of the Kirov Region complained that:

The complicity of the bishops in the closing of churches and in the disruption of church life became clear to believers in the Kirov region as a result of the activity of Bishop Ioann... From his first day in Kirov at the end of 1962 he became actively involved in shutting churches and destroying church life. From the end of 1963 only the malicious intent of Bishop Ioann kept the closure of the churches going. In many churches he replaced strong Christian priests by drunkards. Often in churches he himself behaved outrageously and like a hooligan... He not only closes churches, but destroys faith in the hearts of many. The Kirov believers sent a great many letters to the Moscow Patriarchate demanding that Bishop Ioann be immediately dismissed. None received an answer.[36]

It is clear that these believers had no doubt about the role being played by this "Christian" bishop. With greater ambivalence writes Orthodox Christian Felix Karelin:

Here is the bishop triumphantly celebrating the divine worship. Everything trembles before him! He is surrounded by a gleaming retinue of assistant clergy... But here is the bishop outside the church, in the world, and suddenly everything has changed... I am speaking about an inward degradation – about fear. The bishop, just now commanding the fire and thunder of the divine service, now trembles before a common official. How can the human soul bear such a terrible polarisation and not come to doubt the reality of one pole![37]

XV. EMIGRATION

One of the human rights requested by believers and others in the Soviet Union is that of emigration. In practice emigration is usually permitted from the U.S.S.R. only on the basis of family links in the country of destination. This prevents many persons who would otherwise wish to leave the Soviet Union. In particular this applies to many Soviet Germans, including believers, although increasing numbers of these have been permitted to emigrate in the last few years. This may be the reason for a number of emigration appeals from Baptists and Pentecostals, without family links abroad, which have been made recently, but which with the exception so far of the Pentecostal Yevgeni Bresenden, have been unsuccessful.

XVI. "WE CANNOT BE SILENT"

Does the Soviet establishment believe that this discrimination against the Christian Church will help it to maintain its power? Presumably it does. In human terms, this supposition might seem to be reasonable. But history has a way of vindicating spiritual truths that make no sense to the logical mind. Let us give the last word to some Baptist writers, who sum the situation up as follows:

We are sentenced for slander against Soviet reality. So why do you make that reality so disgraceful by actions like this? By not punishing anyone for these things, you yourselves are responsible that the authority of our state is being undermined in world public opinion. We cannot be silent, because we are all under the threat of being killed, poisoned, destroyed for our trust in God and faithfulness to Him.

We appeal to your conscience and your reason; stop the destruction of believers in this country; stop this genocide. Remember that the blood of righteous martyrs cries out to God, and it will give your conscience no rest for eternity.

Remember the long and ignoble list of those who have persecuted Christians, who have trampled on the principles of liberty. Do you really want to add your names to that list? May it not be so! May the Lord give you wisdom, may He open your eyes and set you on the path of righteousness and truth.[38]

NOTES

1. Schweiz. Evangelischer Pressedienst, 28 August 1973.
2. All-Russian Social-Christian Union for the Liberation of the People. See documents held at Keston College.
3. *Three Generations of Suffering*, by Georgi Vins, Hodder & Stoughton, 1976, pp. 80–1.
4. *Patriarch and Prophets*, by Michael Bourdeaux, Mowbrays, 1975, p. 270.
5. *Aida of Leningrad*, ed. Michael Bourdeaux & Xenia Howard-Johnston, Gateway Outreach, 1972, pp. 38–9.
6. *Religion in Communist Lands*, Nos. 4–5, 1975, p. 12.
7. *Keston News Service*, No. 3, 1974, p. 5.
8. *Religion in Communist Lands*, Nos. 4–5, 1974, p. 40 (quoted from *Lithuanian Catholic Chronicle*, No. 7).
9. Unpublished document held at Keston College.
10. *Church, State and Opposition in the USSR*, by Gerhard Simon, Christopher Hurst, 1974, p. 195.
11. *Ibid.*, pp. 191–2.
12. Unpublished document held at Keston College.
13. For one example of this, see *Religion in Communist Lands*, No. 1, 1973, pp. 30–3.
14. Here quoted from *Aspects of Religion in the Soviet Union 1917–67*, ed. Richard H. Marshall, University of Chicago Press, 1971, pp. 437–8.
15. Here quoted from *Religion in Communist Lands*, No. 6, 1974, pp. 14–15.
16. Here quoted from *Aspects of Religion*, pp. 438–445.
17. *Ibid.*, p. 456.
18. Here quoted from *Religion in Communist Lands*, No. 3, 1973, p. 26.
19. See for example *My Testimony*, by Anatoli Marchenko, Pall Mall Press, 1969; *One Day in the Life of Ivan Denisovich*, by Alexander Solzhenitsyn, Penguin Books, 1963; *Prisoners of Conscience in the USSR*, pub. by Amnesty International, 1975, etc.

20. Unpublished document held at Keston College.
21. *Chronicle of Human Rights in the USSR*, (New York), No. 7, pp. 48–9.
22. Unpublished document held at Keston College.
23. *Vanya* by Myrna Grant, Creation House (U.S.A.), 1974, Victory Press (U.K.), 1975.
24. See *Patriarch and Prophets, ibid.*, p. 111.
25. See *Religion in Communist Lands*, No. 6, 1975, p. 53.
26. *Bulletin of the Council of ECB Prisoners' Relatives*, No. 19, pp. 17–18.
27. *Ibid.*, No. 24, pp. 9–11.
28. Unpublished document held at Keston College.
29. *Bulletin of the Council of ECB Prisoners' Relatives*, No. 18, pp. 16–17.
30. Here quoted from *Religion in Communist Lands*, No. 6, 1975, pp. 39–40.
31. *Bulletin of the Council of ECB Prisoners' Relatives*, No. 22, 1975, p. 14.
32. See *Religion in Communist Lands*, No. 3, 1974, p. 34.
33. *Bulletin of the Council of ECB Prisoners' Relatives*, No. 24, p. 26.
34. *Ibid.*, No. 18, p. 15.
35. See *Keston News Service*, No. 17, p. 4.
36. *Patriarch and Prophets, ibid.*, p. 143.
37. *Eastern Churches Review*, Spring 1973, p. 51.
38. *Bulletin of the Council of ECB Prisoners' Relatives*, No. 19, p. 19.